Australian Horror Films, 1973–2010

ALSO BY PETER SHELLEY
AND FROM MCFARLAND

*Frances Farmer: The Life and Films
of a Troubled Star* (2011)

Jules Dassin: The Life and Films (2011)

*Grande Dame Guignol Cinema: A History of
Hag Horror from Baby Jane to Mother* (2009)

Australian Horror Films, 1973–2010

PETER SHELLEY

McFarland & Company, Inc., Publishers
Jefferson, North Carolina, and London

LIBRARY OF CONGRESS CATALOGUING-IN-PUBLICATION DATA

Shelley, Peter, 1962–
Australian horror films, 1973–2010 / Peter Shelley.
    p.   cm.
Includes bibliographical references and index.

ISBN 978-0-7864-6167-7
softcover : acid free paper ∞

1. Horror films — Australia — History and criticism.   I. Title.
PN1995.9.H6S465 2012   791.43'6164 — dc23   2012031705

BRITISH LIBRARY CATALOGUING DATA ARE AVAILABLE

© 2012 Peter Shelley. All rights reserved

*No part of this book may be reproduced or transmitted in any form
or by any means, electronic or mechanical, including photocopying
or recording, or by any information storage and retrieval system,
without permission in writing from the publisher.*

On the cover: Nathan Phillips as Ben Mitchell in *Wolf Creek*, 2005
(The Weinstein Company/Photofest, photographer: Daniel Guerra);
background © 2012 Shutterstock; front cover design by TG Design

Manufactured in the United States of America

*McFarland & Company, Inc., Publishers
Box 611, Jefferson, North Carolina 28640
www.mcfarlandpub.com*

Table of Contents

Acknowledgments vi
Preface 1
Introduction 3

THE FILMS 13

Bibliography 315
Index 319

Acknowledgments

As with my first three books, I thank Barry Lowe for his financial contribution and invaluable assistance. Additional thanks goes to Kath Perry for her financial contribution and moral support, and to Kate Avery, Bigpond Movies DVD, Alex Broun, Allyson Browne, Peter Dickson, Boze Hadleigh, Chris Lewis, Cheryl Loveridge, Annemarie Lloyd, Anne-Louise Luccarini, Kerry McDermott, Lisa Peers, Anita Plateris, Wendy Salvation, Stewart South, and Andrew Traucki.

Preface

My interest in horror movies as guilty pleasures resulted in my first book, *Grande Dame Guignol Cinema*. I subsequently wanted to find another subgenre of horror to write about. This book, then, has been written as the first literary study of Australian horror films to date to describe what is unique about them and their thematic concerns, and highlight films that may be known to horror cinephiles but neglected by the general public.

For the purposes of my study I have defined a horror title with specific criteria. By my definition a horror film features either the theme of the horror of personality, which can be demonstrated by an aggressive human or an animal behaving in a natural manner, or the malevolent supernatural being which can be also extended to an animal that has been mutated and hence behaves in an non-naturalistic manner.

Additionally, the violence expressed is employed as intentional murder rather than accidental death and the death lacking any ambiguity, e.g., when the exact reason for the death is unknown or unseen. Some may find fault with the criteria, but I chose it to differentiate the films I wanted to write about from others that may be more accurately described as examples of the mystery, science fiction or thriller format, although those I have selected may also feature elements from these related genres.

I viewed some titles that are considered by others to be horror movies: *Picnic at Hanging Rock* (1975), *Dead-End Drive-In* (1986), *Dangerous Game* (1987), *Frenchman's Farm* (1987), *Howling III: The Marsupial* (1987) where the half-human half-wolf creatures only attack in self-defense, *The Tale of Ruby Rose* (1987), *Dead Sleep* (1990), *BeDevil* (1993), *In the Winter Dark* (1998), *Reign in Darkness* (2002), *Visitors* (2003), *Sleep-Paralysis* (2004), *Gabriel* (2007), *Gone* (2007), *Lake Mungo* (2008), *The Dinner Party* (2009), and *Van Diemen's Land* (2009), which presents cannibalism out of survival necessity. However, since they lack either of the criteria, I have not included them in my coverage. I have also omitted various titles that may feature the relevant themes, but as pieces of filmmaking have no redeeming artistic merit.

Some of the titles I have chosen have foreign cast and crew but have been included as Australian horror titles since they were filmed or partly filmed on Australian locations. These include *Komodo*, *Ghost Ship*, *Queen of the Damned*, *Darkness Falls*, *Man-Thing*, *See No Evil*, *Voodoo Lagoon*, and *The Ruins*. Others have been made by Australian producers but not on location in Australia: *Dead Kids* (1981), *Demonstone* (1989), *The Mangler* (1995), *Greg Arce's Den* (2001), *Saw* (2004), and have therefore not been included.

I have also excluded titles that have yet to receive a DVD release at the time of writing and that may have fit my criteria. These include *Bad Behaviour* (2010), *Carmella Hyde* (2010) *10 Days to Die* (2010), *Uninhabited* (2010), *Come and Get Me* (2011), *Snowtown* (2011) and *Relentless* (2011).

I have viewed all of the titles to accurately describe their content and to give my critical evaluation and assessment. I make observations on the films in terms of narrative, filmmaking technique and style, and performance. I also point out the themes that are featured and how the narrative and treatment deal with the conventions of horror movies. Mention is made of any recurring motifs, including the foreigner in a strange land as an extension of international casting, the stereotype of the rural ocker, the female warrior, the presence of Aboriginal issues, and the notion of female nudity being considered as sexist exploitation.

I do not have the agenda of a slavish, biased fan, so I do not hesitate to point out elements that are disappointing or downright bad, or praise things I think are good. I present my aesthetic bias by defining the use of certain filmmaking techniques as "postmodern." These techniques include expressionist camera angles and hand-held camerawork, fast and slow motion, jump cuts and rapid editing, blackouts and whiteouts, CGI and optical effects, subjective camera and point of view.

Although I acknowledge that some of these techniques have been used in earlier films, I draw attention to them when necessary since many contemporary directors seem to rely too heavily on them for my taste.

For each film I have created a chapter with titles listed in chronological order of the year of their release, and in alphabetical order for the titles released in the same year. Each chapter has a cast and crew filmography taken from the film, supplemented by information on the Internet Movie Database to include uncredited cast and crew members. The title's name has been taken directly from the viewed film so that, for example, *Lady Stay Dead* is *Lady, Stay Dead*, and *Cthulhu* is *H.P. Lovecraft's Cthulhu*.

As many of the titles are not available commercially, I have accessed prints from auctions and collectors, and therefore not judged the quality of photography too harshly in these sometimes less than ideal copies. Additionally, some errors may have been made in the spellings of credits and cast listings owing to the poor quality copies of the films viewed, for which I apologize, although some filmmakers seem to deliberately obscure cast names in opening credits in their misguided view that the footage under the credits is more important.

In my chapter notes I also give the history of the producers and main actors and provide any known behind-the-scenes information including that disclosed in DVD audio commentaries and "making of" featurettes. I have also provided an introduction chapter with a brief history of Australian film for context and make mention of the few potential horror titles that were released prior to 1973.

I hope this study encourages readers to seek out and watch the films I am enthusiastic about, or even seek out and watch the ones I am less than enthusiastic about but which have redeeming aspects. Some believe that a horror film is successful if it can provide the jolts of shock and surprise that are the subgenre's base appeal. However, it is encouraging to see how satisfying some titles are when the filmmakers attempt more, while still contending with the narrative contrivances, silliness, graphic violence and black humor that are aligned with horror material.

Introduction

The Australian feature film, where Australian fictional storytelling was presented and made by local producers, was a development that came after baby steps were taken in the first fifteen years of cinema. Film exhibition began in about August 1894 when the theatrical entrepreneur J.C. Williamson secured the Australian rights to the American Thomas Edison 35mm film viewer, known as the kinetoscope, from which all subsequent motion picture invention was derived. The kinetoscope allowed one viewer at a time to watch a loop of film of about fifteen minutes in length. Foreign material was seen at the premiere of the instrument in Sydney on November 30, 1894. This predates what is considered the cinema's first commercial show by the Lumière brothers in Paris on December 28, 1895, although Louis Lumière admitted that his work had been preceded by Edison, whose work had appeared in Paris two years previously.

The kinetoscope traveled Australia for two years, and in September 1896, the Lumière Company cameraman Maurice Sestier came to Australia. Sestier had met Australian photographer H. Walter Barnett in Bombay where Sestier had been stationed. Dissatisfied with the films being made by the company in India, Sestier planned to make films with Barnett. At this time local audiences had an interest in seeing non-fictional documentary footage, much like the audiences in Britain and on the Continent. Announcements had been made by others that footage of the 1896 Melbourne Cup race would be made, but did not come to fruition. Then, on October 25, Sestier and Barnett filmed the short *Arrival of Ferry Brighton at Manly on a Sunday Afternoon*, claimed to be the first confirmable Australian footage shot. It was exhibited on October 27 at Sydney's "Salon Lumiere." On October 31, the pair did shoot the Flemington VRC Derby race in Melbourne, and on November 3, they also shot the Melbourne Cup in ten films.

These were exhibited at Melbourne's Princess Theatre on November 19, and over the next two months Sestier and Barnett also showed the other shorts they had filmed in Sydney.

The first totally local filmmakers were E.J. Thwaites and R.W. Harvie, who from February to March 1897 filmed in Melbourne, and their footage was screened in Tasmania. Their subsequent footage of Ballarat, Victoria, *Street Scene on Jubilee Day* and *Chinese Procession*, was screened on June 2, and their *Traffic at the Corner of Swanston and Bourke Streets* was the first Melbourne street scene to receive a theatrical exhibition on September 15.

Thwaites and Harvie would later film the Melbourne Caulfield Cup race on October 16. This was the first film to be shown on the same day it was filmed, a phenomenon they would repeat with the VRC Derby on October 30, the Melbourne Cup race on November 2, and England vs. NSW at the Sydney Cricket Ground around December 16. The pair are also said to have filmed the cricketers in Melbourne shortly afterward. The Salvation Army Limelight Department also filmed *Melbourne Street Scene* on about October 9.

Footage of events in other states also appeared the same year, with Sydneysiders Baker and Rouse shooting three local films on cameras formerly used by Maurice Sestier in May. Mark Blow shot in September the first of forty shorts he would make over the next year for his "Polytechnic" film venue, including his own coverage of the Melbourne Cup (which Baker and Rouse are also said to have filmed). Queensland footage was reportedly shot in September by G. Boivin and titled *Lunchtime Traffic in Queen Street, Brisbane*, although there is no evidence that the latter received an exhibition. On about May 11, 1899, the earliest known film was shot in South Australia of the embarkation of Salvation Army founder William Booth from Largs Bay aboard the S.S. *Arcadia*, and on July 4, 1901, the first Tasmanian footage was shot of a wood-chopping competition.

By February 1898, Joseph H. Perry had built the first Australian film studio, in the rear of the Salvation Army headquarters in Melbourne. The Army's Limelight Department shot what have been described as the first two Australian narrative fiction films there, *A Hungry Man Stealing Bread* and *Prison Gate Brigade Welcoming Released Prisoner*. The department would go on to make 300 films between 1897 and 1909. Their product was shorts which usually ran 23 minutes long; the department was the preeminent filmmaker in the country, over the next six years being responsible for 80 percent of all film shot in Australia. Although their shorts initially described the Salvation Army's social and religious work, the unit progressed to making non-religious content under contract to or commissioned by state governments and the New Zealand government, for which the films would tour.

On July 30, 1898, the first footage was made of Australian Rules Football by Thwaites and Harvie, and on September 5 and 6 the earliest movies of Australian Aborigines were produced in the Queensland Torres Strait Islands. On March 21, 1899, test films were reportedly shot by the Queensland government as the world's first government financed films; these were made by photographer Fred Wills in Sydney, although the specific subject is unknown. The first agricultural documentary films, *Wheat Harvesting on the Darling Downs* (about five minutes) and *Sugar Harvest at Nambour* (about two minutes) were filmed between August and September that year by Fred Wills and H.W. Mobsby. On October 11, 1899, film was shot of troops departing for the Boer War in Queensland and Victoria, signally the first direct Australian involvement in a military campaign since the invention of movies.

The Salvation Army Limelight Department would close in 1910, supposedly concerned over the lack of moral standards in the film industry. Their most famous product would be the biographical *Soldiers of the Cross* (1900), which some consider the first feature to be released in Australia. It predates the eleven minute western *The Great Train Robbery* (1903), said to be the first American fictional narrative title. However, the claim for *Soldiers of the Cross* is incorrect, since the film is not a continuous feature but rather a collection of shorts, slides, music and spoken word which was first screened on September 13. The Limelight Department continued to extend the running times of their shorts. *Inauguration of the Australian Commonwealth*, which included the signing of Federation documents and a review of Boer War soldiers at Centennial Park, ran for more than 35 minutes, and the coverage of the Northern Territory Aboriginal Arrente tribal ceremonies and dances from April 3 to May 11, 1901, had duration of 45 minutes.

Around December 1901, 90 minutes of footage was presented in England of the 1901 Royal Tour, and on August 10, 1902, one hundred minutes of film and slides became Australia's most elaborate film presentation up to that time. Entitled *Under Southern Skies* and tracing the history of the country from exploration to Federation, it was another Salvation Army event; these productions would tour New Zealand in 1902 and be screened in London in 1904. The Limelight Department would also produce work in Britain and continental Europe, and in October the same year in Melbourne, they screened 2½ hours of film shot during their European visit.

This time also saw Australian cinema's first problems with censorship over the mutoscope movie viewer, which made its debut in Brisbane on October 2, 1902. The mutoscope was a coin-operated peepshow whose reels worked on the flip-card principle. Cards with successive movie frames printed onto them were mounted radially on a metal drum which was rotated by a crank handle operated by the person viewing, and a metal finger in the machine flipped the successive prints past the viewer. Initially, mutoscope parlors set up in 1903 were considered prestigious venues showing films of Royal pageants, the Boer War, and Pope Leo XIII. However, the privacy inherent in the machine that was unattainable in a cinema soon allowed less inhibited patrons to watch more risqué material that ran for a minute long.

They were perhaps the earliest form of cinema exploitation and included titles like *A Peeping Tom, Who Owned the Corset? What the Butler Saw* and *The Maiden's Midnight Romp*. These mutoscopes prefigured the genre films to come and triggered outrage from clergymen (though one wonders if the cards were actually viewed by the clergy). Police confiscated the offending machines and a court case ensued, which naturally magnified publicity beyond the exhibitor's wildest dreams.

The case against Frederick G. Wilson, who ran a parlor in Melbourne, was heard on March 11, 1904. He was charged with possessing and exhibiting for profit "obscene pictures." To consider whether the films were offensive, the jury viewed *Why Marie Blew the Light Out*, *A Peeping Tom*, *Behind the Scenes*, and *The Temptation of St. Anthony*. Wilson was found guilty and the films ordered to be destroyed. While he waited for his appeal to be heard, Wilson's parlor enjoyed increased attendance. On April 27 the original decision was overturned, since there was no proof that Wilson had exhibited the reels in question, since he was not the official occupier of the parlor's premises.

The successful appeal also saved the films from destruction. The mutoscope eventually lost its novelty appeal, and by 1908 no new films expressly intended for mutoscope exhibition were produced. The future was seen to be films that were projected in public theaters. What was once considered state-of-the-art in motion picture viewing was now relegated to minor conveyor of mirth and titillation. The machines could no longer compete with theatrical film projection as a profitable means of presentation. Variations on the mutoscope continued in the 1920s with one-minute filmlets of comedies and girlie items to be seen in fairgrounds, until they disappeared from public access altogether.

The biographical crime drama *The Story of the Kelly Gang* (1906) deserves credit as the first Australian feature film, and it was released in Melbourne on December 26, 1906. This film's commercial success is a triumph over the monopoly practices of film exhibitioners who favored imported material because of the lower cost. It was also one of the first in a new subgenre of bushranger films which presented criminals as sympathetic protagonists. While it is claimed that *The Story of the Kelly Gang* was predated by *Bushranging in Northern Queensland* (1904), that title's length is about five minutes. The Salvation Army's possible second bushranging title, *Robbery of a Mail Convoy by Bandits*, aka *Robbery of a Mail Coach by Bushrangers* (1904), is said to be of only 6 minutes' duration. *The Story of the Kelly Gang* also toured the country as exhibition chains began leasing theaters and purchasing permanent cinemas for film screenings. Between 1910 and 1912 approximately 84 narrative films would be made, and the three years were later considered to be the first "golden age" of Australian filmmaking.

The bushranger film subgenre would continue, and even feature female bushrangers in *The Romantic Story of Margaret Catchpole* (1911) and *The Lady Outlaw* (1911). *Dan Morgan* (1911) reversed the trend by presenting the title character as an antagonist. The subgenre had grown troublesome because the films displeased police who sought to impose a ban on bushranger films, since they portrayed the law in an unsympathetic light, and the cycle ended in 1912 when the ban was successful. A later revival of the subgenre was seen with the release of *The Kelly Gang* (1920), *Robbery Under Arms* (1920), *The Gentleman Bushranger* (1921), and *When the Kellys Were Out* (1922), and a still later resurgence with titles like *Captain Thunderbolt* (1953), *Ned Kelly* (1970), and *Mad Dog Morgan* (1976).

Another associated subgenre was the prison or convict film, which was exemplified by *For the Term of His Natural Life* (1908) and which told of convicts transported to Australia and presented protagonists in a sympathetic light. Although convicts were equal criminals as bushrangers, it is surprising that this subgenre did not meet as much resistance as the bushranger subgenre, since there was no parallel ban imposed. Other titles that can be classified as action adventures showed miners and the gold fields beginning with *Eureka Stockade* (1907), the rural struggle to work on the land beginning with *The Squatters Daughter*, aka *The Land of the Wattle* (1910), and horse racing from the owner's point of view beginning with *A Ticket in Tatts* (1911).

By 1913 it seemed that the most prolific years of Australian cinema were now coming to an end. Production began to decline and would not recover until the heavy input of government finance in the 1970s. A myth arose that the reason for the decline was because local films were below the standard of foreign titles and Australians had less interest in seeing local product. This myth is said to have been created by distributors who realized they could make more money out of exhibiting overseas product, and this commercial factor also enabled an American expansion into the industry, contributing to the lessening number of local productions. American studios established branches in each Australian state, and though they did not venture into ownership of theaters, their presence is thought to have motivated the building of new venues. These venues included the palatial State and Capital Theaters in Sydney and the Regent Theaters in Sydney and Melbourne.

The federal government took measures to counter the fear of the American strangulation and to spur local production by imposing a tax on imported film in 1914, although it would be reduced by 1918. Between 1922 and 1923 it is said that 94 percent of all films screened in Australia had been made in the United States, the U.S. films gaining popularity during World War I. On September 17, 1935, the government finally took steps to provide a new lease on life for the industry with the N.S.W. Cinematograph Films (Australia Quota) Act. This required that at least 5 percent of all films distributed and 4 percent of films screened had to be of Australian origin, although by 1936 further legislation was passed to scale down the quotas because of the difficulty associated with enforcing them.

After the outbreak of World War I, films would initially focus on propaganda stories of the heroism of soldiers and civilians on the Allied side, and incorporated what was to be called the "chum" subgenre. This subgenre was a variation on the American buddy picture. It began with *A Long, Long Way to Tipperary* (1914), which centered on an Irish soldier, with the first Australian soldiers shown in *The Hero of the Dardanelles* (1915), and the cycle culminating in a spate of films about Gallipoli. The horrible realities of war soon changed the tone of future films so that war was now seen as a childish and pointless game. Eventually the subject disappeared altogether.

A new period emerged for comedies and escapist farces before the end of the war, in particular comedies about bucolic types considered as a predominantly working class entertainment. The first example of this was *Our Friends, the Hayseeds* (1917), said to have drawn heavily from the most popular elements of stage back-block (backwoods) farce. The disparity between the rustic Hayseeds and city sophisticates and the idea of the protagonists as pioneer battlers who fought the machinations of a greedy and unscrupulous ruling class would be explored in the following titles in the Hayseed series.

The Sentimental Bloke (1919) provided a variation on the theme by presenting an urban larrikin (rebel) with a genuine affection for his lifestyle and without regarding him as a figure of fun, or as a sociological phenomenon. The sequel *Ginger Mick* (1920) had The Bloke move to a farm to perhaps take advantage of the popularity of the *Hayseed* hillbillies and the rural concerns that would also occupy other contemporary titles like *The Breaking of the Drought* (1920) and *On Our Selection* (1920). The latter film was an adaptation of a popular stage play of the same name which featured the characters of Dad and Dave, who would become iconic in Australian culture and be seen in a series of titles. Although there would be Hayseed and Dad and Dave tiles released in the 1930s — *On Our Selection* (1932), *The Hayseeds* (1933), and *Dad and Dave Come to Town* (1938) — it is thought that by the end of the 1920s there was a move away from the subgenre and a greater focus on an amorphous city life.

Perhaps it was the grip of the Great Depression that resulted in far fewer productions being made in the early 1930s. The subject itself was not even featured in a title until 1938, in *The Broken Melody*. Or perhaps the decrease in production was due to the industry's awkward transition to sound films, although in 1929 sound technology had been demonstrated in screenings of *Movietone News* reels followed by the weekly *Cinesound Review* reels the following year.

The first Australian full-length all-talkie title released was the melodrama *Spur of the Moment* (1931), and the first Australian musical was *Showgirl's Luck* (1931), which was directed by the

American Norman Dawn, although at least the narrative was set in Australia. The plot also plays on the new sound era: its protagonist is a rural tent performer in the lead role of Australia's first talkie film.

The few local filmmakers who were working made movies that dealt with international interests, in narratives of a local context, as a way to break into the American market so that their titles could make a profit. Another approach was to cast foreigners in roles that could have been played by Australian actors to increase international interest. The case of American actress Helen Twelvetrees in the later horse-racing drama *Thoroughbread* (1936) is said to have caused dissent, although it was not the first case of an imported actor being cast in an Australian title.

The first incident appears to be the silent melodrama *Driving a Girl to Destruction* (1911). This title was based on a popular British play. British star Louise Hampton was hired to perform in both the play in Australia and then the film version. Perhaps it was the box office failure of the film that lessened any potential controversy attached to Hampton. The alleged furor attached to the casting of Twelvetrees is said to be more noteworthy since she supposedly had more of a star profile, though like the stars who were imported for Australian titles in the 1970s and 1980s, Twelvetrees' days as an important Hollywood star were behind her by the time she made the film.

American actors had been cast in *For the Term of His Natural Life* (1927) directed by Norman Dawn, and the casting was done at the insistence of the film's investors because the film had a budget and production values that were far ahead of any film produced in Australia to date. The importation of foreign crews was also presumably done with the notion that their greater expertise would guarantee commercial success, although some producers would find that the Hollywood production methods were too expensive and that ultimately these craftsmen did nothing to ease local distribution problems or attract the public. And while the film would make a substantial local profit, it ultimately lost money overseas because it had to compete with the new sound productions like *The Jazz Singer*, which was released in the same year.

The 1940s saw the government legislate a bank guarantee overdraft to companies for £15,000 for each production, but this incentive was soon abandoned with the outbreak of World War II and the effective halting of feature film production. Meanwhile, the public flocked to cinemas for news and escapist entertainment during the war, and audience ranks swelled even more by the arrival in 1942 of American servicemen in Australia. The main filmmaking being done by Australians was newsreels, although 10 feature titles were released between 1940 and 1945. As expected, much of the content was propaganda, as had occurred during World War I.

The first post-war film released was the biopic *Smithy* (1946) which, although about an Australian, was entirely funded by an American company. This would be an omen of what was to come, but in the meantime, there were still indigenous productions being made. They were mostly outback dramas with crossovers into western territory, but it is claimed that circumstances now made it difficult for Australian product to get distribution. This had come about because of the British and Americans who were said to take advantage of the need to use capital frozen in Australia by wartime restrictions on dollar exports.

After the war and for the next twenty years most of the important films were made by British and American companies. Ealing Studios is an example of a British company that set up a permanent unit in Australia and made titles like *The Overlanders* (1946), *Eureka Stockade* (1949), *Bitter Springs* (1950), *The Shiralee* (1957), and *The Siege of Pinchgut* (1960). Most of the foreign filmmakers would leave the country immediately after production had ended, and the films they made are said to reflect neither a basic commitment to Australia nor any interest in exploring the national character. The British can be less faulted than the Americans, since it is believed that their films are more curious about Australia and position the makers as sympathetic outsiders with a degree of objectivity. *The Overlanders* is said to be one example that supposedly went further in defining Australian characteristics and attitudes than local filmmakers had done.

When the Rank Organization bought the controlling interest in the Greater Union Theaters in 1947, this effectively created a monopoly for the British company to screen their films in the main venues in Australia, despite the reversed situation in Hollywood when the American government introduced law to end such theater chain monopolies. With the British product guaranteed distribution, Australian filmmakers were virtually locked out of the market, and it was only later that the Australian government would end this situation by prohibiting companies having excess capital. This edict ended the operation of the Ealing Studios unit and finally allowed local filmmakers the opportunity they had been previously been denied.

Despite the difficulties associated with distribution, the 1950s saw the emergence of some noteworthy local titles. Actor Chips Rafferty and director Lee Robinson together made *The Phantom Stockman* (1953), *King of the Coral Sea* (1954), and *Walk into Paradise* (1957), all in which Rafferty had the starring role. The first Australian color film *Jedda* (1955) was also the first to present an Aboriginal actor in a leading role, although the first Australian cinematic treatment of Aborigines had been the silent *Caloola*, aka *The Adventures of a Jackaroo* (1911). The American productions saw the importation of Hollywood units with only minor technical and acting roles available to locals. These included Lewis Milestone's adventure *Kangaroo*, aka *The Australian Story* (1952), Byron Haskin's action adventure *Long John Silver* (1954), Leslie Norman's comic drama *Summer of the Seventeenth Doll* (1959), which was based on an Australian play, Stanley Kramer's science fiction *On the Beach* (1959), based on an Australian novel, and Fred Zinnemann's adventure *The Sundowners* (1960), also based on an Australian novel. These films were made primarily for overseas audiences in spite of any Australian narrative content and shot in Australia to capitalize on Australian locations.

Australian narrative filmmaking would virtually disappear by the end of the 1950s. Only documentaries were being made. An economic recession and the introduction of television, which began broadcasting September 16, 1956, signaled the same detrimental effect in Australia that it had in the American film industry. Another factor said to have impacted the end of film productions was the perceived lack of local stars. Most actors who had achieved some degree of success moved overseas to get work. Actors simply went straight to Britain or Hollywood because they knew they had better opportunities there.

Michael Powell's comedy *They're a Weird Mob* (1966) was a box office success in Australia but not internationally, and his biographical romance *Age of Consent* (1969), Tony Richardson's actioner *Ned Kelly* (1970), Ted Kotcheff's *Wake in Fright* (1971) and Nicolas Roeg's *Walkabout* (1971) all continued the trend of foreign directors taking advantage of Australian locations. Again these narratives were from the point of view of the outsider. They provided an anthropological study of the eccentricity, idiosyncrasy and bizarre psyche of Australians as foreigners and Australia as a foreign landscape hostile to civilized Europeans. However, the late 1960s did see the release of a few local productions.

The crime drama *Clay* (1965) received a screening at the Cannes Film Festival but bad critical reception doomed it to box office failure. Another crime drama, *Pudding Thieves* (1967), was made by Melbourne film students and only received university campus screenings. Yet another crime drama was *Journey Out of Darkness* (1967), which featured a white trooper pursuing an Aboriginal murderer in the outback, although the lead role was enacted by an American. *Time in Summer* (1968) was a mood piece which was another box office failure. *You Can't See Round Corners* (1969), the film version of a television series, perhaps picked up an established audience and was a moderate success.

The trend of filming successful television series would be repeated with *The Intruders* (1969), which was based on *Skippy*; *Country Town* (1972) based on *Bellbird*; and the later *Number 96* (1974) and *The Box* (1975). The comedy *Squeeze a Flower* (1970) was a hybrid. A co-production between Australian and American television companies, it used an American television director but Australian actors, though it was a critical and box office disappointment. Another advance was the American production *Marco Polo Jnr. versus the Red Dragon* (1972) as Australia's first animated feature.

The independently financed *Two Thousand Weeks* (1969) had been burdened by advance publicity which labeled it an art film, so that expectations were raised far higher than any film could reasonably be expected to fulfill. This resulted in disappointing box office, although the film would recover a little prestige when it was screened at the Moscow Film Festival, and it received a minor release in Britain and the United States, where reviews were more positive. The sexploitation drama *The Set* (1970) controversially featured a plotline about bisexuality and female nudity. Predictably, censorship troubles beset the film and it was refused registration as an Australian quota production under the quality clause of the New South Wales state's quota act. A cut version received strong initial trading due to the publicity, but this could not be sustained and the film wasn't distributed abroad. *Jack and Jill: A Postscript* (1970) was a romance with social commentary, long in development and another box office disappointment despite its winning awards and getting critical praise.

The silence of the indigenous film industry was soon to be broken. On October 29, 1963, the Vincent Committee had been set up to recommend government aid for the industry, although the recommendations would not be implemented. It was the succeeding prime ministers of the late 1960s and early 1970s, John Gorton and Gough Whitlam, who made a commitment to the idea of an Australian film culture and approved government funding for filmmakers. On March 5, 1970, the Australian Film Development Corporation was established; it commenced operations in March the following year. Funding was also provided for the Australian Film Television School (later named the Australian Film, Television and Radio School) which would open in January 1973, after it had been recommended in 1968.

After the comedy *The Naked Bunyip* (1970) also had trouble with censors because of its use of sex and nudity, a new R rating was introduced by the minister of customs and excise, Don Chipp, in 1971. This restricted the admission of persons 2 to 18 years and allowed for more explicit presentations. More contemporary comedies like *Stork* (1971), *The Adventures of Barry McKenzie* (1972), and *Alvin Purple* (1973) became commercial hits and helped to create a form of Australian national identity, albeit satirically. It seemed that for the first time in 15 years, films made by Australians in Australia (although *The Adventures of Barry McKenzie* was made in the United Kingdom) were what Australian audiences wanted to see.

The Australian cinema's first attempt at a horror title may have been the silent *The Strangler's Grip* (1912). Although details about its narrative are elusive, it is generally thought to be more a thriller with a sequence of a furious motor drive. *The Face at the Window* (1919) seems to be a more likely choice as the first Australian horror title. Set in France rather than Australia, it presented "Le Loup," a Parisian murderer who hides his identity behind a hideous mask. A still from the film can be found in Eric Reade's book, *The Australian* Screen, and the mask prefigures the look of Freddy Krueger in *Nightmare on Elm Street*.

Guyra Ghost Mystery (1921) is the first supposed narrative with an apparent malevolent supernatural antagonist who mildly terrorized a family by throwing stones onto the roof of their house and knocking on its walls. The plot ended in ambiguity: did the ghost exist or were mortal neighborhood children playing practical jokes? Another ghost was featured in the thriller *Fisher's Ghost* (1924), but again this one was not murderous. The ghost here is more of a detective who leads a settler to find his corpse. Eventually he has the ghost's murderer arrested, tried and executed although, regrettably, the murderer's ghost then does not appear. *The Grey Glove* (1928) was a thriller about a detective chasing a murderous foreign spy who always left a grey glove at the scene of his crimes, for reasons unknown.

It would be forty years before another film would attempt to visit the genre, 1970's *Dead Easy*, and even then the treatment was more crime drama, although noteworthy for featuring a criminologist studying serial killers. *Night of Fear* (1973) is the first Australian sound horror title. It had been made for television and received a theatrical release, and its success led to *Inn of the Damned* (1975), also said to have been initially made for television. *The Cars That Ate Paris* (1974) is the first horror title made as a film release.

The small advances in genre production coincided with Australian filmmakers also exploring their past with historical titles, funded by state film corporations. The South Australia Film Corporation had been established in March 1973 and other states soon followed over the next eight years. These historical films included *Sunday Too Far Away* (1975), *Picnic at Hanging Rock* (1975), *Caddie* (1976), *The Devil's Playground* (1976), *The Chant of Jimmie Blacksmith* (1978), *Newsfront* (1978), *The Getting of Wisdom* (1978), and *My Brilliant Career* (1979). They seemed to match the country's interest in nostalgia, and achieved international success.

They were considered art cinema and more culturally acceptable, a move away from the crass titles that came to be known as Oz-exploitation that emphasized violence and sex and appealed to the drive-in crowd. (In her review of *The Getting of Wisdom* in the book collection *Taking It All In*, Pauline Kael describes some of the historical titles as essentially taxidermy.) The idea that art house titles were artistically superior and more acceptable than genre films was part of the Australian phenomenon known as the Cultural Cringe.

In March 1975 the Australian Film Development Corporation was replaced by the Australian Film Commission, and in May the first government sponsored delegation went to the Cannes Film Festival to promote Australian films. Recognizing that Australian films had to be successful in a global market, the commission opened an office in the United States. On November 28, 1978, the government changed tax laws to allow for a 100 percent tax write-off over two years rather than 15, the old norm for film investment. This move was said to have been made in view of the continued effects of inflation and the impact of color television, which pushed up the expenses of production and greatly reduced potential revenue from cinemas.

It had also become increasingly difficult for local producers to rely on the local market to recover their costs. Hence a further reliance on the government was made to provide investment capital and carry the burden of the deficit. The new tax laws therefore allowed private investors to recover their capital from a film's first earnings.

The international success of the actioner *Mad Max* (1979), which became the highest grossing film of its time, seemed to alter the government's view on funding. Some of the art and historical films had been financially successful, but the greater success of genre titles like *Mad Max* and the earlier *The Last Wave* and *Patrick* made the Australian Film Commission change its focus. In October 1979, it had decided to become a more commercial operation, aiming for self-sufficiency by recovering costs on a global market rather than funding the development of filmmakers and esoteric films. However, from June to September 1980 investment in films slowed to a trickle when the government announced it would tighten the tax laws it had previously loosened to prevent investors from using film investment as a blatant tax avoidance measure.

To counter this development, the 10BA tax shelter scheme for funding was introduced on October 1, 1980 (some sources give the date as June 24, 1981). It replaced partial funding that had been supplied by the Australian Film Commission and the state film corporations in the 1970s. The scheme provided a tax concession for financiers to initially receive a 150 percent write-off on their investment and another 50 percent on any profit up to the amount actually invested, provided that the film earned income. The resultant slew of productions that took advantage of 10BA would be criticized, since it seemed that making a profit was more important than making a good film. In his book *The Avocado Plantation*, David Stratton quotes Graham Bourke, the managing director of Village-Roadshow, who was not a fan of 10BA: "It was like someone who needed micro-surgery being attacked by a meat-axe. Talent was spread too thin and people made pictures they weren't passionate about."

Despite the government's reducing the tax concession in subsequent annual budgets—133 percent in 1983, 120 percent in 1985, and 100 percent in 1988 — foreign investment continued to be applied to films, and the fear of what had happened in Canada in the 1970s was also felt by Australian filmmakers. The English-speaking Canadian film industry had been destroyed by tax concessions and foreign investment. Foreign money demanded an Americanization of Australian product, to make films supposedly more internationally marketable and to ensure a distribution pre-sale.

The pre-sale market became particularly important to genre films, with the advent of home video around 1985, since a failed cinema release could became a successful video sale. However, some clashes between producers and the Australian Actors Equity union over what was viewed as compromised casting reflected one concern specific to the genre films made under 10BA. They were aping American films and presenting generic American material rather than attempting to present a specific national identity and to explore specific national concerns. This issue had initially come about after Actors Equity and the Film and Television Producers Association had negotiated the Film Actors Award in November 1979, which prevented filmmakers from hiring cast from overseas for local films and films that the government had sponsored.

Nonetheless, the boom in the industry would allow for unexpected benefits, which included a cross-pollination of talent. Directors Peter Weir, Fred Schepisi, George Miller, Gillian Armstrong, Bruce Beresford, and Phillip Noyce all worked in the United States, although alternatively foreign born directors like Paul Cox and Jane Campion made films in Australia. The trend was not new since American directors had been imported to make Australian films in the 1930s. The Actors Equity issue also received a turnaround when Australian actors like Judy Davis, Mel Gibson, Bryan Brown, Russell Crowe, Nicole Kidman, and Naomi Watts were cast in international titles, presumably favored over American and British actors in American and British films.

Again this trend was not new since there had been Australian actors who had sought international careers during the years of World War I, most of them now unknown to modern audiences. The only one of any lasting celebrity seems to be the swimmer Annette Kellerman, who did not make a film in Australia but became a Hollywood star, albeit briefly. The 1930s would see more actors go Hollywood, with Errol Flynn being the most famous, he who had made his film debut in a supporting role in the biographical actioner *In the Wake of the Bounty* (1933). In the 1950s it would be Peter Finch, Ron Randell, Rod Taylor, and Michael Pate who would go to Britain or Hollywood to establish international careers. Like the traveling Australian actors, other actors also came to Australia to continue their careers—Sam Neill, Bruno Lawrence, Chris Hayward, Gosia Dobrowoloska, and Debra Unger being examples. Some of these directors and actors had worked in Australian genre titles, though greater success tended to mean a move away from the films that gave them their first opportunities.

Adam Rockoff in his book *Going to Pieces: The Rise and Fall of the Slasher Film* charts the progress of the American horror genre, which can be paralleled with the years Australian horror titles were produced. The documentary gives the slasher success period as 1978 to 1986. The era begins with the release of *Halloween* in 1978, though *Friday the 13th* (1980) is said to be equally seminal in adding gore to what had mostly been suggested before. The year 1984 presented another seminal title, *Nightmare on Elm Street*. But also released that year was *Silent Night, Deadly Night*, which was met with public protests and which was said to have been responsible for the fall of the genre.

In Australia the government would eventually recognize criticism of the 10BA system, with its excessive above-the-line fees and rorts (scams) of all kinds. By the late 1980s the new funding body was more discerning in providing government money, being more concerned with commercial viability. This stand resulted in the death of the genre film by 1990. In Queensland the American company Warners and Village Roadshow would open a Movieworld studio attracting film production, although it mainly catered to foreign companies using local crews, recalling the scenario of Australian filmmaking in the 1950s and 1960s. The Fox Studios opened in Sydney in 1998 and in 2000 would be where *Star Wars: Episode II—The Attack of the Clones* was filmed.

Interest in American genre films would be revived with the Academy Award winning crime thriller about the hunt for two serial killers, *The Silence of the Lambs* (1991). While that film was not marketed as the horror title that it is, the genre resurrection would continue with the critical and financial success of *Scream* (1996). A key to the success of the latter title was in the casting of two stars of hit television shows, a formula that would also be applied to later Australian genre titles.

In Australia, though, it would take another ten years for the same resurrection to occur. Successful non-genre titles would receive critical and international acclaim: *Crocodile Dundee* (1986), *Young Einstein* (1989), *Strictly Ballroom* (1992), *The Piano* (1993) (an Australian co-production filmed in New Zealand and starring American Holly Hunter, whose performance would win her the Best Actress Academy Award), *Adventures of Priscilla, Queen of the Desert* (1994), *Muriel's Wedding* (1994), *Babe* (1995), *Shine* (1996), *The Castle* (1997), *Moulin Rouge* (2001), and *Rabbit-Proof Fence* (2002). However, it was only after the success of *Wolf Creek* (2005) that a new generation of filmmakers would be responsible for a new interest in the making of genre films that has continued to date.

The Films

Night of Fear
A Terryrod Production, 1973

CREDITS: *Director/Screenplay:* Terry Bourke; *Executive Producer:* Rod Hay; *Photography:* Peter Hendry; *Editor:* Ray Alchin; *Art Director:* Gary Hansen; *Sound:* Sid Butterworth; *Makeup:* Deryck De Niese; *Wardrobe:* Ron Williams; *Rats Supervisor:* Don Davison; *Title Design:* Albert Vos. Color, 50 minutes. Filmed in Narrabeen, New South Wales.

CAST: Norman Yemm (The Man); Carla Hoogeveen (The Girl); Briony Behets (Girl Rider); Mike Dorsey (The Lover); Peter Armstrong (The Truckie); James Moss (The Client); Curt Jansen (Garage Attendant); Pinkie (Albino Rat).

Synopsis

The Girl Rider is attacked and held prisoner by The Man, who lives in the bushlands off the highway of Silvercrest, 48 miles from Sydney. The Man shoots her horse and The Girl Rider is never seen again. The Girl's car gets stuck in a ditch after she crashes through a dead end sign to avert an accident, and she is also attacked by The Man, who seems deranged as he carries a white rat on his shoulder and does not speak. The Girl is chased at night into The Man's house and dreams that he rapes her. When she awakes the next morning, The Man releases brown rats that devour her. When police find The Girl's car in the valley, they visit The Man, who lives close by. He appears normal as he feeds his chickens. What the police do not see is that The Man has hidden human skulls in the cages where he keeps cats high in the trees. The police leave The Man, who has gotten away with murder.

Notes

Made for television but released theatrically, this standard woman in peril "B" movie perhaps created controversy because it was the first Australian title to approximate the suspense-horror style of American films. Director Terry Bourke overuses music and post-modern effects like cross-cutting, quick editing, point of view, expressionist camera angles and hand-held camerawork, extreme close-ups, slow motion, time jumps and out of focus shots. However, he compensates in the pornographic psychological torment his female protagonist endures and the lack of dialogue.

The treatment presents the horror of personality in the character of The Man, and gore is suggested rather than shown with the use of rats. Bourke features some physical objectification of women but balances it by presenting The Man equally; he doesn't stoop to exploitative nudism of his actresses' bodies when he has the opportunity. Although the narrative may suffer from a lack of context, since The Man is such an intriguing figure, the absence of a happy ending reads as pure horror. If the film has few actual shocks and its share of contrived narrative silliness, it does manage to create unease in the empathy we feel towards The Girl who, like Janet Leigh in *Psycho*, stumbles into a fatal nightmare.

The title is misleading, since nighttime occurs at the halfway point and the conclusion occurs in daytime. The film begins with a seven minute prologue featuring our view of The Girl Rider, whose blondeness will be juxtaposed with The Man's brown hair, as will that of The Girl. Our view of The Girl Rider is inter-cut with views of The Man that hide his face. The first inter-cut shot to him running a finger over the blade of a dirty scythe suggests the threat to her. This is aided by the ominous score and a seeming distortion of the soundtrack, a distortion effect that will be repeated and can be interpreted as the representation of the muteness of The Man.

He is next seen as legs walking and as the person who unties The Girl Rider's horse. The chance that The Girl Rider can catch her horse and get away is a tease. The Man takes a whip that is not used and Bourke uses fast inter-cuts of prefiguring. These shots are of the headstone in the graveyard that is in front of The Man's house, the power box that we later learn hides the release chord for the rats, and the barrel of The Man's gun in close-up.

Apart from being by a graveyard, The Man's house being in a forest where the sun is obscured by trees creates a world of darkness. This is the traditional location of horror since it is equated with night. The shot of legs running in the forest is ambiguous, but Bourke uses a tilt-up to reveal that it is The Girl Rider and not The Man. There follows a subjective camera for her point of view of a view of the forest. The strangulated sounds of the horse attract The Girl Rider, as The Man will later use sounds to make The Girl go to his house, and we see The Man loading his gun.

More quick-cutting is used with The Girl Rider's point of view, the same shot of the headstone, The Girl Rider's legs, and The Man and his gun. Bourke relieves the soundtrack by employing silence to create tension for the Girl Rider's hesitation as the camera shows her point of view pan across and back across the forest, a device he will repeat in the treatment. Bourke also has The Man's arm reach out almost comically to The Girl Rider when she begins to retreat, but misses touching her when she decides to go ahead when drawn by the neigh of her horse. Bourke resumes the use of score for The Girl Rider's advance, which reveals The Man's house and the sight of the standing horse.

The extreme close-up of The Man's eye as he watches The Girl Rider go to his house continues the reveal of his identity and his objectification as an anonymous antagonist. Bourke uses another camera pan for The Girl Rider's view of the house. We may wonder why she is investigating the house rather than releasing her horse to ride away, although that is a horror narrative contrivance of the woman in peril, and the funereal tone of the score implies that she is doomed to die. An expressionist shot of The Girl Rider knocking on a door from ground level is followed by a shot of The Man seen approaching her. When she turns around to see him, the fact that she screams rather than speaks reads as a demonstration of his character and her fear of him. It is also the non-dialogue convention that Bourke has chosen for the treatment.

The Man tears The Girl Rider's clothes when he attacks her, although Bourke spares us any reveal of her flesh. His locking her into the room behind the door on which she was knocking is ironic and the last time we see her alive. The Man's intention is shown by the act of his taking his gun and shooting the horse, which is given an extreme eye close-up before it is shot. Bourke uses a blackout for the result of the shot and the sound of the horse's pain. Then The Man is finally seen from the fallen horse's point of view as his face is revealed in a medium shot. The screen then turns to red after The Man moves to strike the horse, for the credit sequence, which inter-cuts prefiguring scenes of the forthcoming narrative.

The Girl is first seen behind the curtain of a shower but again Bourke does not exploit the actress's nudity. Her taking money from the drawer of The Client, her wearing a red dress, and the later sex she has with The Lover who is married with children all suggest that she is a prostitute. She is perhaps morally deserving of her fate. The treatment has her change into virginal white as a tennis outfit for the game she will play with The Lover before their sex, although her skirt will reveal her underwear and bottom in the tennis game sequence.

Cross-cutting is used between The Girl, The Lover and The Truckie all driving, although the relevance of The Truckie is only later revealed when he nearly crashes into The Girl's car after her tennis game. Cross-cutting is also used between the tennis game and The Man playing with his white rat to prefigure the association he will have with The Girl. The shot of The Girl's short skirt leads to the sex scenes between her and The Lover. It is an act that occurs on the ground outside, but again Bourke protects both actors from having their naked bodies exposed. The Man seen feeding bloody meat to his caged cats in their boxes is another moment that is only understood later, although the meat could be either The Girl Rider or her horse. The blood on the meat is the film's first gore.

Road workmen placing the DEAD END NO WAY THROUGH sign is shown for a later payoff when The Girl (back to wearing her red dress) drives through it. The inter-cutting between The Truckie and The Girl driving is then paid off by their near collision. The expectation of injury from The Girl's crash is not met. The Truckie leaving his truck to help The Girl is timed so that she is able to free the car from being stuck in a ditch and driving away at the moment when he sees her. The Dead End sign is used when The Truckie looks at it, so that the Dead part in is seen close-up as his point of view, with an appropriate score comment. This prefigures The Girl's destiny, since we do not see The Truckie again.

The second ditch that The Girl's car gets stuck in recalls the first, although it also reads as a trap set by The Man. Bourke uses quick blackouts in between the approach of The Man as seen by his legs. The blood on The Girl's forehead as a result of hitting her head on the dashboard is the second noteworthy presentation of blood. After the ditch site is seen from The Girl's point of view, The Man is now revealed to wear one brace boot (something not apparent in the first attack) and the sound of it is heard by The Girl. The Man walking with the white rat on his shoulder adds oddness to his disability, and The Girl runs as she senses The Man's danger. The fact of her locking herself into her car is another genre contrivance, and gets a comic payoff in the way she leaves a window half open which allows The Man to reach in. Bourke suggests a sexual act in the way The Man lunges at the car and the way The Girl reacts to it, as if riding the movement. The conveniently placed axe and spade on the ground nearby for The Man to use to break the car windshield glass is another narrative contrivance. This latter attack is given an added tension in the possibility that The Girl will be able to get the car started, although this is an expectation that is not met.

The Girl running away from her car seems a better idea to get away from The Man, but Bourke scores a laugh which is perhaps the only genuine one in the treatment. The Man stops chasing her and lets The Girl run in a circle back to him. The image of her on the ground, seen between his legs, is an iconographic one of the woman in peril. Bourke uses The Girl's objectification of her legs and exposed bra after The Man has attacked her as the cause of The Man's excitement, but again without exposing the actress's flesh. When she hides in bushes — a seemingly ridiculous place to seek refuge — Bourke adds a heartbeat to the soundtrack.

The Man is unable to locate her, which the director expresses by showing him in a long shot surrounded by bushes that don't include the one in which The Girl hides. This provides a respite for her, where Bourke uses silence and creates the expectation that she will be able to escape from this predicament. However, now that night has fallen, The Girl's next move seems even sillier. She may think that beeping her car horn will attract someone else's attention, but it is immediately obvious she has given away her location to The Man. Bourke does not make the obvious response. The Man brushes his spade against scrub to make noise to scare The Girl away from the car so that she heads towards his house.

The sign of the graveyard headstone indicates that The Man's plan has worked, and he makes more noise to draw The Girl closer. What looks like mounted animal heads in front of the house — dripping with moisture or blood, which is a nice touch — should be enough to warn The Girl away.

She is frightened by them, but she keeps approaching. The heads create the expectation of a reveal of The Girl Rider's head, which is not met. What is also a surprise is that when The Girl enters the house the treatment presents the suggestion of normalcy. A table is laid out with candles. Newspapers are ambiguously presented as either a tablecloth or reading material. The discovery of caged stuffed rats in what appears to be a bedroom is a disturbing jolt back into the macabre. On the walls are a glass case of butterflies and photographs of a bottom and breast, which all suggest The Man's fetishism.

The Girl hears a noise and closes a door to camera to make the screen go black. The newspaper clippings on the wall report of missing persons and suggest The Man has a degree of intelligence, or a sense of archival record keeping, though there is no photograph of The Girl Rider. The treatment again creates an expectation that The Girl is momentarily safe, confirmed by the shot of The Man at her car, eating what looks like bread as the white rat looks on.

An expressionist angle is used to show The Girl falling unconscious or asleep from exhaustion, and hallucinating images of rats. In what is later revealed to be her dream state she imagines The Man holding a bloody skull in front of his groin. This skull is presumably that of The Girl Rider, and another amusing effort to protect the nudity of the actor as he approaches The Girl, who is tied to a table. The dream is misleading since The Girl is unaware of The Girl Rider or that The Man has killed her. It is more likely to be that of The Man, which is confirmed later after The Girl has been killed and The Man is seen with what appears to be The Girl's skull. Her dream can be interpreted as a fear of The Man raping her.

Bourke uses fast inter-cuts to the wall photographs of the bottom and the breast, as well as the newspaper clippings. Burned out candles convey the passage of time and daylight. The Girl is presented in an extreme close-up of her ear as she hears noises, and of her eye. The turning of the door knob shows The Girl that someone is trying to enter the house. The shot of the braced leg informs us that it is The Man, though we have to wonder where he has slept the night. Bourke provides a shock moment, although expected, of a burlap curtain being pulled back to reveal The Man at the window with the white rat on his shoulder.

What sounds like a choir appears to be mixed into the score, suggesting that The Girl's death is imminent. The earlier use of the power board is explained when The Man pulls the cord that releases brown rats that enter the room where The Girl is.

The Man also inexplicably brings his caged cats to be close at hand for the event to watch with him. The Girl faints rather than attempting to fight off the rats. Bourke covers her murder by showing what passes as blood on the rats' mouths and the bloody arm of The Girl. The Man also appears to masturbate over the killing, although this is implied and not graphically shown, as suggested by his mounting grunts.

Bourke cuts to sepia-colored family photographs, toys, and a repeated shot of an angelic child. Then we see The Man cutting off the blonde hair attached to a bloody skull and him mopping up blood. This prefigures inter-cuts of a police car sign. The police are at the second ditch where The Girl's car got stuck and remains; their late arrival is a genre convention. The Man, dressed more normally, feeds his chickens as the police are seen around his house, but because no words are spoken, we do not hear him being questioned. Rather The Man acts indifferently towards them, which presents the police presence as ineffectual in the face of The Man's superior skill.

On the DVD audio commentary, producer Rod Hay says that the film was originally made as the pilot for a proposed 12 part Australian Broadcasting Corporation (ABC) television horror series entitled *Fright* that was never made. The project was envisaged to follow the lines of the American rat titles *Willard* (1971) and *Ben* (1972). Hay says the film was shot in 10 days, although in their book *Oxford Australian Films 1900–1977*, Andrew Pike and Ross Cooper claim that the shooting schedule was 12. Hay also says that The Girl's red dress was designed to recall Little Red Riding Hood. It is believed that some of the rats used in the house attack sequence, which was shot in the ABC studio, could not be retrieved and continued to live there for the next twenty years. He also advises that the conclusion of The Man not being caught for his acts was a deliberate open-ended choice, since the producer hoped to make a sequel.

Pike and Cooper also write that the film was made entirely without dialogue, and that the Australian feature release was delayed because the film was banned in November 1972 on the grounds of indecency. However a month later, with its reputation greatly boosted by the incident, the film was passed uncut on appeal and released profitably. The film was said to influence *The Texas Chain Saw Massacre* (1974), which also features a maniac who lives in a house of stuffed animals and debris. Producer, screenwriter and director Terry Bourke previously made the Hong Kong title *Sampan* (1969), and later directed the horror film *Inn of the Damned* (1975). Executive producer Roy Hay was an actor and television editor whose first producing title for the Terryrod production company was *Night of Fear*, and he later produced *Inn of the Damned*.

Release

In 1972 (date unknown) with the taglines "Hunted and Trapped Her Nightmare is Just Beginning," "A bizarre and horrific ordeal," and "A nerve-shattering experience in suspense that will leave you breathless!" The film was banned on the grounds of "indecency and obscenity," but the ban was overturned on appeal. When the film was re-released after the ban was lifted, the new tagline was, "The film they didn't want you to see!" The film was screened at the non-commercial location, the Penthouse Theater, and another season had the film on a double bill with the British horror title *Cry of the Banshee*, as advertised on the publicity material that accompanies the DVD.

Reviews

"Red, raw horror to chill the spine." — *The News Adelaide*

"An unremitting avalanche of terror." — *The Australian*

"Excellent performances, claustrophobic photography and a few 'out there' scenes make *Night of Fear* well worth watching. The moments involving the killer, a severed head, some rats and our heroine tied to a table are shocking to say the least and stronger than anything else being filmed at the time."— David Michael Brown, *Digital Retribution*, April 22, 2005

"Reasonable performances from the leads, good macabre atmosphere, and plain nasty in places. Overall a good solid harbinger of all things horror to come from Down Under in future years.... In some ways a ground breaking movie though slightly dated for modern audiences." — *ScaryMinds*

"What is striking about [it] is just how much it manages to prefigure *The Texas Chain Saw Massacre* (1974)— two years before *Texas Chain Saw* ever appeared on screens.... The film gets particularly nasty with the introduction of the rats, while the end arrived at is a much grimmer one."— Richard Scheib, *Moria: The science fiction, horror and fantasy film review site*

DVD

Umbrella Entertainment (Australia), released March 16, 2005.

The Cars That Ate Paris
Salt-Pan Films/Royce Smeal Film Productions, 1974
[aka *Cars*; *Cars That Eat People*]

CREDITS: *Director:* Peter Weir; *Producers:* Hal McElroy, Jim McElroy; *Screenplay:* Peter Weir; *Story:* Peter Weir, Keith Gow and Piers Davies; *Editor:* Wayne LeClos; *Photography:* John McLean; *Music:* Bruce Smeaton; *Art Director:* David R. Copping; *Sound:* Ken Hammond; *Wardrobe:* Ron Williams; *Makeup:* Liz Michie. Color; 91 minutes (cut to 74 minutes for dubbed U.S. release). Filmed on location at Sofala, New South Wales, from October to November 1973.

CAST: John Meillon (Mayor); Terry Camilleri (Arthur Waldo); Kevin Miles (The Doctor); Rick Skully (George Waldo); Max Gillies (Metcalf); Danny Adcock (Policeman); Bruce Spence (Charlie); Kevin Golsby (Insurance Man); Chris Haywood (Darryl); Peter Armstrong (Barman); Joe Burrow (Ganger); Deryck Barnes (Smedley); Edward Howell (Tringham); Max Phipps (the Reverend Mulray); Melissa Jaffer (Beth); Tim Robertson (Les); Herbie Nelson (Man in House); the people of Sofala and Wattle Flat.

SYNOPSIS

The residents of Paris, a small town in rural Australia, make their living by causing car accidents of passing visitors and salvaging valuables from the wrecks. George Waldo is killed when he is driven off the road entrance to Paris, but his brother Arthur survives and is brought into the community, first as an orderly at the hospital, and then as the parking inspector. On the night of the Paris Pioneers Ball, the town's youth rise up against their elders and attack the town in their cars. They are defeated, and after killing the youth leader, Darryl, Arthur overcomes his fear of driving and is able to leave Paris.

NOTES

This early film by Peter Weir presents the theme of horror of personality in the sense that the townspeople are mad in their murdering of car-driving visitors. What makes the treatment interesting is the division that exists between the older and the younger Parisians, a division that culminates in the attack that is the film's climax. While Weir's pacing is occasionally sluggish, and the score often oversells dread, there is plenty here otherwise to provide a satisfying viewing experience. Gore is provided in an initial oblique way in the wounds of the car crash victims, and the shooting murder of the Reverend Mulray. But the climax supplies deliberate sadism in the impaling of bodies and the mutual killings of the battle. The end is particularly pleasing since it is does not meet the created expectation, so that this becomes a horror movie with the triumph of innocence over evil.

The opening scene is a parody of a television commercial for cigarettes, with repeated cuts to the cigarette label as product placement during the car crash. The crash prefigures the Waldo crash, although we don't see the Parisians processing the car of the model couple as they later do for other victims. A live cow being placed in a car's trunk under the film's opening credits is the first sign of the oddness of the Paris townsfolk. The limited available

Poster for *The Cars That Ate Paris* (1974), released in the United States as *The Cars That Eat People*.

resources of the Commonwealth Rural Employment Scheme suggests the initiative Parisians have in occupying themselves. This point is later highlighted when car parts and clothes are used to barter for food. The music during the Waldos' drive into town expresses foreboding, and our initial confusion as to what has caused the crash is explained by the amusing use of follow-up models and an explanation by Metcalf to the insurance man.

The survival of Arthur will allow him to be the outsider, to create empathy for his trauma, and to let us see Paris through his objective eyes. The Frankenstein-type experimentation of the Doctor towards the accident victims isn't really paid off in a horror way, although there is a comic punchline when they are brought to the ball with their vegetated states masked by fancy dress costuming. The Doctor's photograph test of Arthur demonstrates his perversity in the way he mixes accident trauma shots with benign ones of trees and animals.

Weir uses the stoicism of rural Australians (surely an extension of British reserve), who seem to be stuck in a 1950s time warp, for comic grotesquery, and he stages posed reactions to any conflict like a western. This western theme gets its most obvious homage in the confrontation between Arthur, and Darryl and Les; the rebels' hats and long coats are complemented by the sound of a harmonica in the score. Costume therefore differentiates the older and younger Parisians, as does the multi-colored designs the youths use on their cars. The division between their ages is also paralleled by the youths' drag-racing as the elders attend church.

The night sabotages align the townsfolk with vampires; the stripped cars left in fields are equated with the human cemetery. A scene where one stripped car is set alight is evocative, although it is not explained why such an act is necessary. The Mayor's two daughters, adopted children of past sabotages, represent his own form of opportunism. Beth's disapproval of one daughter revealing the ear under her hair is a sign of the 1950s-ish repression of the Mayor's household. The murder of the Reverend Mulray, another relative newcomer to Paris, is prefigured by his driving a blood red car and his being late for the service. The narrative point of the Mayor wanting to adopt Arthur to stop him from talking to the Reverend comes after Arthur has just been evicted from the Mayor's house. This idea of adopting Arthur is only used later to rationalize the Mayor giving him the parking inspector job.

The attack of the youths in the Mayor's front yard is the first expression of their violent opposition to the apparent rule of the elders. Darryl's irreverent attitude as a hospital orderly is aligned with how the Mayor describes the town's youth as "lazy and idle." This description is actually incorrect, since the decorations of their cars show that the youths have some initiative and imagination. The Mayor's opinion is presumably based on his observation that only elders attend his meetings, and in his eyes only the elders are concerned about the future of Paris. The gum-chewing of Darryl and Les when confronted by Arthur is another expression of the youths' disrespect, as is their objection to Arthur having been given his job, since he is seen as an outsider. (The English accent of Chris Haywood as Darryl is presumably accepted, although it demonstrates that he was once a migrant.)

The shooting murder of the Reverend Mulray is committed by Charlie, who is shown to be a mentally challenged youth. This is another blow to the elders, in spite of the middle ground where the Reverend is positioned. He may be older than the youths, but his questioning of the elders, particularly in relation to Arthur, does not make him an elder either. The shooting is not shown by Weir, rather suggested by the blood on Charlie afterwards, and his wearing the Reverend's now-bloody priest's collar. The attack of the youth upon the elders' Pioneers Ball is prefigured by a gothic shot of the cars of the youths approaching the town against storm clouds, and thankfully the rainstorm does not happen. The threat of the youths is represented by one silver car with porcupine-type protrusions, which creates the expectation of impalement, which is met. Weir also uses animal growls on the soundtrack to preempt both the attacks on the Mayor's house and the climactic attack on the town. What makes the threat of the youths more resonant is that they cannot be seen inside their cars, apart from Darryl, who is identified by his voice when he attacks Arthur.

Darryl's attack on Arthur allows him to overcome the trauma of his fear of driving. Weir uses jump cuts for the repeated shots of Arthur's car ramming Darryl's. Darryl's apparent passivity in the face of Arthur's attack almost reads as an approval of Arthur's action, as if Darryl is deliberately sacrificing himself to Arthur. The withdrawal of the youths' cars gives the impression of their defeat. This is perhaps because they have an awareness of the death of their leader, although one senses that the conflict has not been permanently resolved.

The narrative returns to Arthur as the protagonist by having him attempt to leave Paris. An expectation is created that he will not be successful, because of the Mayor's warning that traps have been set for the youths. This point is actually ambiguous since the traps were meant to be set by a man that we see the youth capture (and presumably kill). We presume that the town's interest in sabotaging Arthur as a crash victim is distracted by the youth attack, and perhaps because Arthur is now considered a Parisian. Weir uses an unidentified French song on the soundtrack for Arthur's exit, as a sly reference to the town being called Paris, without irony in light of Arthur's successful liberation.

In the documentary *Not Quite Hollywood*, producer Hal McElroy claims that the film was unofficially remade by producer Roger Corman as the science fiction actioner *Death Race 2000* (1975) during the time he had been negotiating for the American release of the film. Once Corman had his own version, he was no longer interested in *The Cars That Ate Paris*. In his book *The Last New Wave*, David Stratton writes that the director of *Death Race 2000* had never seen *The Cars That Ate Paris*. Stratton also claims that the only similarity between the two films is the strange vehicles with teeth and spikes, and the cars are used as weapons against humans. Otherwise, Stratton says, *Death Race 2000* is a violent, futuristic science fiction fantasy. Stratton also writes that Donald Pleasence was originally sought for the role of Mayor in *The Cars That Ate Paris*, but budget limitations precluded his casting.

Weir had made his film directing debut with the comic-dramatic "B" movie *Homedale* (1971), and had contributed the short *Michael* to the dramatic anthology *Three to Go* (1971). He would go on to make the Australian horror title *The Last Wave*. *The Cars That Ate Paris* is the first film produced by the McElroy brothers, who would go on to produce *The Last Wave*.

Release

October 10, 1974, in Australia and June 1976 in the U.S. The taglines were "They run on blood," "In Paris, the traffic is murder," and "148 people live in the township of Paris and every one of them is murderer." The full length version was released in the U.S. in 1984.

Reviews

"Much of the pic is brilliant, although it does not always seem certain of the direction it is taking." — *Variety*

"The exercise takes only a loose grasp upon its rich potential.... A catalogue of lost opportunities.... [Weir is] an ingenue at work in a sophisticated genre." — *Cinema Papers*, July 1974

"Weir skillfully juggles a variety of themes and moods that range from science fiction and Hollywood westerns to rich Australian comedy. Terry Camilleri makes a wonderfully offbeat hero and John Meillon gives the performance of his career. Stylist and witty, the film is a genuine original, and very entertaining too." — David Stratton, *The Last New Wave*

"A surrealistic satire/allegory on Australia's car culture.... What strikes one is the coolly quiet obliqueness of Weir's approach, his insistence on viewing the entire situation as perfectly normal.... On the minus side, there is not much drama to the film and Weir's pace is slow." — Richard Schlieb, *Moria: The science fiction, horror and fantasy film review site*

"Bizarre, though poorly-produced.... This faltering though interesting film only hints at the talent Weir would demonstrate in much better films to come." — John Stanley, *Creature Features*

DVD

Released by Home Vision Entertainment on October 21, 2003.

Inn of the Damned
A Terryrod Production/Medich Productions, 1975
[aka *Death Hunter*]

CREDITS: *Director/Producer/Screenplay:* Terry Bourke; *Producer/Editor:* Rod Hay; *Associate Producers:* Peter Medich, Roy Medich; *Photography:* Brian Probyn; *Music:* Bob Young; *Production Design:* Gary Hansen; *Makeup:* Deryk De Niese; *Dame Judith Anderson's Hair:* Patricia Cunliffe; *Wardrobe:* Joan Grimmond; *Visual Effects:* Les Conley; *Sound:* Tim Lloyd, Bob Hayes. Color, 112 minutes. Filmed from November 1973 to January 1974 on location at Mongreve Mountain, Gosford, Camden, Cobbity, Bringelly, Ebor Falls and Narrabeen, New South Wales, with interiors filmed at Artransa Studios, Epping.

1975 / *Inn of the Damned*

CAST: Dame Judith Anderson (Caroline Straulle); Alex Cord (Cal Kincaid); Michael Craig (Paul Melford); Joseph Furst (Lazar Straulle); John Meillon (George Parr); John Morris (Martin Cummings); Robert Quilter (Biscayne); Diana Dangerfield (Mrs. Stephanie Millington); Carla Hoogeveen (Beverly); Don Barkham (Sergeant Malone); John Nash (Colonel Lowe); Tony Bonner (Trooper Frank Moore); Phil Avalon (Alfred); Lionel Long (Search Horseman); Jack Allan (Gypsy Jake); Colin Drake (Franz Heller); Graham Corry (Andrew Millington); Josie Mackay (Cummings' Girl); Gordon Glenwright (Squire Grimstead); Nat Levison (Undertaker); Louis Wishart (Arnold); Reg Gorman (Coach Co-Driver); Geoffrey Burton (Urchin Boy); George Pollak ("Mad Mick" Marriott); Linda Brown ("Peaches"); Anna King (Coach Passenger); Hilary Bamberger (Mrs. Bonnett); Carmel Cullen (Housekeeper); James Moss (Bristol); Graham Ware (Coach Driver); Elaine Wong (Chinese Girl Victim); Dave Proudman (Harry); Kuki Kaa (Tom); Roy Harries-Jones (Dr. Karston); Jim Clifford (Dispatch Clerk); Reg Midway (Hogg); Dave Gilard (Undertaker's Assistant); Melissa Chappel (Heidi Straulle); Terry Bourke, Jr. (Hans Straulle).

Synopsis

In 1896 in Gippsland, Australia, gold miner Martin Cummings and his girl travel by buggy to the country inn run by Austrians Caroline and Lazar Straulle. Another passenger is Biscayne, a convict, who sees the Straulles dispose of the murdered bodies of the other guests. After Biscayne and George Parr steal items from the nearby Grimstead property, Biscayne is pursued by bounty hunter Cal Kincaid and British trooper Frank Moore. When Biscayne attempts to escape from the troopers once he is caught, he is shot dead by Kincaid. Moore goes to the inn to investigate the disappearance of Cummings and is killed by the Straulles. They do not have time to dispose of his body in the lime well before more guests arrive.

The Straulles also murder their new guests, Mrs. Millington and her daughter Beverly, after killing the women's servant, Alfred, but soon Kincaid comes to the inn looking for Moore. When he sees that Lazar Straulle wears Moore's medallion, he returns as a guest of the inn. The Straulles' plan to kill Kincaid fails when he finds Moore's corpse, and seeing how the Straulles' winch device kills their victims, he tricks Caroline into thinking that it has also crushed him in bed. Kincaid overpowers Lazar and is assisted by neighbor Paul Medford in preventing Caroline from shooting them with her rifle. The men discover a locked room where the deranged Mrs. Straulle speaks to paintings of her two dead children. The police arrive and recover the corpses in the well, as the portrait painter Franz Heller tells of how the Straulle children were butchered by an escaped convict, "Mad Mick" Marriott, 14 years earlier as some kind of rationale for their murders.

Notes

This period feature, presenting the theme of the horror of personality, is a disappointment from Terry Bourke after *Night of Fear*. The subplot about an American bounty hunter chasing and capturing Biscayne does eventually join the main plot of the gothic inn run by the Straulles, but too much of Bourke's treatment comes across as bloated and unnecessarily filler scenes. However, he does come up with the occasional humorous line.

He uses utilizes post-modern techniques of slow motion, expressionist camera angles, point of view, out of focus and soft focus effects. In addition Bourke has prefiguring editing, as well as an excessive score, but he redeems himself in a fourteen minute climactic sequence of suspense. Also disappointing is the exploitative and seemingly commercial use of women's nudity, presumably following the trend of the time of ribald comedies and erotica. It reaches its nadir here in the offensive character of a sexually aggressive lesbian who makes advances on her own stepdaughter. However, kudos must be given for the restrained performance of the Australian born Judith Anderson, an actress not previously known for such subtlety, in her only Australian title and in one of her rare and her last leading film roles.

Bourke has a traveling horse-drawn buggy under the opening credits which doesn't ride directly to the Straulle inn. It does match with the closing shots of the film of a flashback of Lazar and his children in a boat, on a swing and riding a horse as presentations of movement and travel. The murder of Cummings and his girl are obscured by the darkness of night and the unlit room, so that the way in which they are killed remains unclear until later. This is a device that Bourke repeats from *Night of Fear* and the power board that held the cord that released the rats. Lazar's act of taking the woman's jewelry after she is dead is given a note of compassion when he also closes her eyes, and the girl's breasts being exposed when her body is dropped down the well is the first of the exploitative use of the actresses' bodies. There is a funny exchange between Caroline and Biscayne concerning Lazar, whom we have not heard speak up to this point:

BISCAYNE: Don't he never say nothin'?
CAROLINE: You know he has a bad throat.

The daylight robbery of the Grimstead place is a lame attempt at comedy relief, with George Parr presented as a pathetic drunken figure who is chased by a dog. The dog being friendly rather than hostile when he catches up with Parr is a surprise. The pursuit of Biscayne in the first of the extended sequences is also harmed by the performance of Alex Cord as Kincaid, who chews the scenery as if he is in an American western. The casting of Cord appears to be a commercial consideration to aid the film's international distribution. Bourke does not balance the character's obnoxiousness by making him a fatal victim of the Straulles. The first sign that Caroline is mentally ill is the scene where she talks to what appears to be a child but is revealed to be a doll, revealed in her dream as that of her deceased daughter.

Caroline's dream is introduced with a dissolve and a soft focus optical effect to suggest memory. Since it is Caroline's dream, we expect her memory to be of something she has seen or lived. Like all badly conceived film treatments of memory, she remembers something that she never saw, the kidnapping of her children. It also doesn't help that Bourke uses expressionist angles to present "Mad Mick" Marriott as a comic grotesque. The idea that what she dreams may be her imagining what might have taken place is denied by Lazar's comforting Caroline with "It was only a dream." This comment suggests that this is not the first occasion Caroline has had such a dream, which feeds into the idea of her being mentally ill.

The fight in the waterfall between Biscayne and Kincaid, and then joined by Moore, is another extended sequence that goes on too long. Moore inexplicably allows Biscayne the opportunity to get away, though presumably only to escape being drowned by Kincaid. Bourke provides a freeze frame as a button to the scene. The ease with which the hand-cuffed Biscayne is able to get Kincaid's gun soon gives way to Kincaid's control of the situation. The killing is filmed in slow motion, so that the bullethole Kincaid's gun makes in Biscayne's chest supplies gore.

The following scene, where Kincaid tells a town boy that Biscayne is dead, does not deliver on the townsfolk crowding to see the corpse. Kincaid's post-coital scene with Peaches gets two kinky elements, from the spurs on his boots and the fruit he eats off her stomach with a fork. The actress being barebreasted can be contextualized by her being a prostitute in bed with her client. However, it still reads as exploitative, although Bourke does not have Kincaid equally naked, since his groin is covered when their room is invaded.

The thunder and lightning effects which precede Moore visiting the inn are standard horror movie conventions of threat. Bourke has continuity goofs in the conversation scene between Caroline and Moore as the trooper's hair changes styles. Moore's murder is not

Trooper Frank Moore (Tony Bonner) and Cal Kincaid (Alex Cord) pursue a convict that leads them to a house of murder in *Inn of the Damned* (1975).

shown; Bourke rather saves it for his corpse to be discovered later. The attack on Alfred gets another funny conventional treatment in Lazar's arm appearing from within the barn door to grab Alfred and pull him inside. Alfred's murder is complemented by black humor, the only one to be treated as such. Lazar's difficulty in disposing of the boy is expressed by his line "Die. Die. Why don't you die?" A heartbeat is heard on the soundtrack to convey Alfred's determined existence, and the screen goes red to suggest the flow of blood (a device Bourke also used in *Night of Fear*) after Lazar hits him with an axe. The humor of Lazar's frustration is in counterpoint to the gore of Alfred's wounds and the revulsion and even remorse Lazar may have about committing the murder.

The bedroom and bathroom scenes of Mrs. Millington and Beverly are more exploitation of the actresses' nudity. The arrogance that Mrs. Millington demonstrates towards Alfred and Beverly aligns itself with the idea that it comes from anger and frustration, although the dialogue in the bath scene suggests that the two women have already been having an incestuous physical relationship. Beverly seems to allow herself to be used by her stepmother, rather than refuse, because she doesn't want to upset her father with the knowledge of her stepmother's preference. This makes Beverly a weak victim and Mrs. Millington a fortunate opportunist.

If one can put aside the insidious and pandering stereotyping of lesbians, then in horror movie terms, both women are presented as deserving of their murder. Again Bourke doesn't show the killings but uses a surprise effect. The camera sits behind one of the women upright in a chair in Caroline's locked room, and Caroline speaks, for the reveal of both women being dead. The scene also creates the false expectation that other murders will be discovered later. The arrival of Mr. Millington also creates an expectation, not met, that he will be the next victim.

Bourke uses a 360 degree pan across the interior of the inn when Caroline, Lazar, Paul Melford and his two boys await the return of Kincaid from looking upstairs. Judith Anderson gets a funny reaction shot after Lazar complains that he has not had time to dispose of corpses properly because of all the visitors. The shot is funny because the actress adopts a look of imperial disdain, a quality that Caroline has not previously displayed but something for which Anderson was renowned. Caroline also gets a speech in reply to Lazar's fear that Kincaid is suspicious and will return, where her schizophrenic nature is apparent, mixing anger with pathos: "Let him come. The fool! They are all fools! Why can't they leave us alone? But no, they come. But we know what we have to do."

Suspense is created in the scene of Kincaid's return as the Straulles wait to attack. Kincaid's awareness of being watched by Caroline through a hole behind the bookcase in his room adds to the dynamic. The spying through the wall recalls Norman Bates watching Marion Crane through a hole in the wall in *Psycho*, and the distaste for Kincaid and the perverse empathy we have towards the Straulles complicates the protagonist-antagonist horror equation. The drag marks on the floor conveniently allow Kincaid to find where Moore's corpse has been stored in a cupboard and the gore on Moore's face and hand suggests that he has been crushed under the winch. Bourke edits the four clock chimes to four images in reaction: the clock face, Lazar, Caroline, and Kincaid.

Caroline seen talking to someone is an obscure moment that will be clarified later as her talking to the paintings of her children, although it could also be interpreted as her talking to the corpses of the dead women in the dining room. Kincaid's holding a rifle aimed at the door where he awaits the entry of the Straulles creates an expectation that is teased out. The moment is also complicated by his fighting off sleep (we don't know if he has been fed the drugged wine that is part of the Straulle modis operandi), but will get an eventual payoff. This initial expectation is played with when we see Caroline enter a room that we expect is Kincaid's, but turns out to be another, since she is not confronted by his rifle.

Lazar moving the big wheel on a door to kill Kincaid finally explains how the sinister winch works. It is a panel of the wooden ceiling that holds large rocks and is lowered onto the guest's bed to crush the drugged sleeper, and we get a flashback to Moore being killed this way. Kincaid creates the illusion that he has been killed in this manner by leaving Moore's body to be seemingly crushed, and removes the body in time. Caroline's entrance into the room meets the expectation of confronting Kincaid's rifle, although Kincaid's position of strength is lessened when he is confronted by Lazar.

Kincaid will be able to overpower Lazar. The assumption that he has only knocked him unconscious is confirmed later when we see Lazar with Caroline outside the house with police. However, Kincaid will need the assistance of Melford and his boys in the ensuing gun battle after he is shot in the shoulder by Caroline and drops his weapon. This battle ends the period of suspense, since it reads as activity of lesser interest, although a close-up of the barrel of Caroline's rifle as Kincaid's point of view is noteworthy. An echo effect is utilized over Caroline's lines, "Nobody goes in that room. Don't let him catch you. Run. Run," when Kincaid and Melford decide to investigate the locked room where Kincaid has heard her talking.

Bourke features prefiguring flash-cuts of close-ups of the children shown in Caroline's dream before the men enter the room, after Kincaid shoots off the lock. The animated rocking horse we assume moves in reaction to Kincaid's gun shot. The individual paintings of the two children being the objects of Caroline's mental illness reads as a disappointing rationale, with Bourke having inset circles of images of the children and "Mad Mick" Marriott featured in the center of the paintings. We are given the backstory of the children's murder by the portrait painter, and have an obscured view of their graves.

Bourke uses point of view for Caroline's distorted belief that a girl among the gawking children at the scene is her deceased daughter, complete with the soft-focus effect from the dream. Kincaid disconnecting the wheel from the winch allows for a repeated shot of how the winch drops onto the bed. Bourke supplies slow motion romantic epilogues of Lazar and the children under the closing credits, which are strangely lacking in resonance, perhaps because Caroline is not with them to present the family as a happy unit. The film ends on a repeat of the two paintings that had been discovered in the locked room, with the haunted faces of the children the cause for mental illness and murder.

On the DVD commentary, Roy Hay says that Joan Bennett and Stuart Whitman were originally cast as Caroline and Kincaid. Bennett is said to have had concerns about the age of her character, since Hay claims she did not want to be shown as a harridan. Hay also claims that the film was the most expensive Australian film ever made up till that time, the first period Australian film ever made, and the first Australian film to get an American television sales. He says that the film experienced censorship problems, although not as severe as those suffered by *Night of Fear*.

A scene that featured Chinese girls and an Irishman as murder victims was cut for running time consideration, although Elaine Wong as the Chinese Girl Victim remains in the closing credits. In their book *Oxford Australian Films 1900–1977* Andrew Pike and Ross Copper claim that like *Night of Fear*, this film was originally a one hour script intended for Terry Bourke's projected television series *Fright*.

Since *Night of Fear*, Bourke had written and directed the action drama *Noon Sunday* (1975) and the comedy *Plugg* (1975), which was associate produced by Hay. Bourke would go on to write, direct, and produce the Australian horror title *Lady, Stay Dead* (1981). *Inn of the Damned* would be the last film from the Terryrod Production Company and Medich Productions. Hay later wrote and directed the actioner *Breaking Loose* (1988) and produced and directed *Change of Heart* (1999).

Judith Anderson had left Australia in 1918 to become a stage actress in New York. She made her film debut in a supporting role in *Blood Money* (1933). She was nominated for the Best Supporting Actress Academy Award for her performance as the mythic Mrs. Danvers in Alfred Hitchcock's romantic mystery *Rebecca* (1940). Anderson became known primarily as a supporting actress with an English accent in a series of malevolent roles that exploited her severe features and commanding presence, though she was cast against type as the Southern-accented Big Mama in the film adaptation of the Tennessee Williams stage melodrama *Cat on a Hot Tin Roof* (1958). She played the rare title role (though was not top-billed) in the crime drama *Lady Scarface* (1941) and was top-billed in the music thriller *Specter of the Rose* (1946) and *Inn of the Damned*. Anderson's greatest stage success was playing the role of Medea on Broadway in 1947, a role that she filmed for television in 1959, which gives her portrayal of the mother in *Inn of the Damned* an odd resonance.

Former rodeo rider Alex Cord made his film debut in a supporting role in the comedy romance *The Chapman Report* (1962), and continued in supporting roles and work on television. He played the lead in the Italian western *Un minuto per pregare une instante per morire*, aka *A Minute to Pray, a Second to Die* (1968), the crime drama *Stilletto* (1969), and the Italian horror film *The Etruscan Kills Again* (1972). After *Inn of the Damned* he returned to television and more supporting film roles. Cord played the title Indian but was not top-billed in the western *Grayeagle* (1977) and scored his last leading role to date in the crime drama *Roots of Evil* (1992).

Release

Australia on November 13, 1975 (U.S.A. unknown) with the taglines "Murder. Mystery. Madness," "You will never be the same after you discover the secrets of the Inn of the Damned," and "In the tradition of Hitchcock comes the classic Australian suspense thriller." The film is said to have been screened at the Cannes Film Festival but this is unconfirmed.

Reviews

"In Bourke's elephantine hands there is no mystery, no suspense, no thrills — just a few ponderously staged pretty pictures." — David Stratton, *The Last New Wave*

"This sluggish would-be tale of horror lacks overall polish and is swamped by an incongruous score. The obvious discomfort of the American, Alex Cord, and the inane gesticulation of Dame Judith, provide the only real terror." — William K. Halliwell, *The Filmgoer's Guide to Australian Films*

"This western-themed horror from Australia makes a rather incomprehensible mess of its plot and pace.... Mixing western and horror elements is an acceptable choice, but unfortunately they never mesh in any natural (or coherent) way here. The viewer is left feeling as if he's watching two entirely different storylines."— *The Terror Trap*

"Full of horse chases, action score and cigar smoking tough guys, it plays like a western; imagine Sam Peckinpah filming a Hammer film in the outback and you get the idea." — David Michael Brown, *Digital Retribution*, April 22, 2005

"Worth seeing for Dame Judith Anderson as a crazed, homicidal Australian housekeeper.... The first half moves with the agility of a wombat with two Achilles's tendons cut [but the film climaxes] in a hair-raising cat-and-mouse sequence." — John Stanley, *Creature Features*

"No more than a series of melodramatic gestures.... Judith Anderson is so resolutely strange and sinister that it is hard to feel for her supposedly tormented mind the sympathy that might have given the film a point of view. The film's best asset is cameraman Brian Probyn's splendid evocation." — Scott Murray, *The New Australian Cinema*

DVD

Released by Umbrella Entertainment (Australia) March 16, 2005.

End Play

Hexigon, 1976 [aka *Endplay*; *The Brothers*]

CREDITS: *Producer/Director/Screenplay:* Tim Burstall, based on the novel by Russell Braddon; *Associate Producers:* Alan Finney, Trevor Pope; *Photography:* Robin Copping; *Editor:* Edward McQueen-Mason; *Music:* Peter Best; *Art Director:* Bill Hutchinson. Color, 109 minutes. Filmed on location in Berwick, Melbourne, Victoria, from December 1974 to January 1975.

SONG: "End Play" (Peter Best), sung by Linda George over the opening credits; "Camptown Races" (Stephen Foster), sung by John Waters.

CAST: George Mallaby (Robert "Robbie" Stephen Gifford); John Waters (Mark James Gifford); Ken Goodlet (Detective Inspector Cheadle); Delvene Delaney (Janine Talbot); Charles "Bud" Tingwell (Dr. Fairburn); Belinda Giblin (Margaret Gifford); Robert Hewett (Detective Sergeant Robinson); Kevin Miles (Charlie Bricknal); Walter Pym (Mr. Lipton); Sheila Florence (Mrs. Lipton); Barry McQueen (TV Newscaster); Reg Gorman (TV Reporter); Adrian Wright (Andrew Gifford); Jan Friedl (Policewoman); John Lamond (Robbie as a Child); Vicki Raymond (Robbie's Mother, Mrs. Thompson); Cliff Neal (Robbie's Father, Mr. Thompson); Elspeth Ballantyne (Welfare Officer). Uncredited: Terry Gill (Ticket Collector).

Synopsis

Merchant seaman Mark Gifford is on leave and visits his elder step-brother Robbie, a paraplegic who lives in a country house in the Melbourne area of Kyneton. A serial killer of young blonde female hitchhikers, whom the media calls the Maroondah Maniac, is active, and 23-year-old Janine Talbot is his latest victim. Mark appears to be the killer and carries the girl's body into Robbie's house when Robbie is away doing archery physiotherapy at the local hospital. Mark then takes her to the Rex Cinema where the film *A Day of Horror* is screening and leaves her body in the cinema, where it is found by police. Mark takes Robbie to see the film at the cinema, which is now closed, and Robbie clashes with the police, led by Detective Cheadle.

Robbie sees that Mark has filled a drink with phenobarbital and does not swallow it. Apparently fearful for his life because he believes Mark to be the killer, Robbie writes him a letter telling how his hatred of the police means he will not give his brother up to them. Robbie's hatred is based on his childhood where the police refused to press charges against his father, who had injured Robbie's back when he had misinterpreted his parents' having sex. Robbie tries to kill Mark with his crossbow and impales Mark's leg with an arrow.

The police arrive just as Robbie is about to strike Mark with a sword from his collection of medieval weapons, and Mark confesses to being the serial killer. Cheadle realizes that Mark is lying since he gets the murder weapon wrong and is only confessing to protect Robbie, who is the real killer. Mark had disposed of Janine Talbot's body since Robbie had left her in Mark's car to frame him. When Robbie's secret is discovered, he kills himself with an arrow, in the same way he had killed his victim. Cheadle tells Mark that he will not be prosecuted as an accomplice.

Notes

This whodunit features the theme of the horror of personality, although the treatment presents only one killing from someone said to be a serial killer. Director Tim Burstall uses the postmodern techniques of point of view, blackouts, expressionist camera angles and hand-held camerawork, zooms, and out of focus effects, as well as an obtrusive score. He also uses black and white footage for flashbacks to enliven a narrative that is basically a two-hander and which has trouble not being read as a stage play, although the performances are good. The witty and clever narrative also defies audience expectations and assumptions of character by a climactic reversal of the assumed protagonist-antagonist dynamic. Though horror cinephiles may be frustrated by the lack of gore, some blood is spilled in the climax.

A prologue presents the murder of Janine Talbot, with the killer shown only by his gloved hands and her reaction to him. His touching her face with a gloved hand adds perversity to his intention. The device by which Janine is killed is also not shown; though we assume it is a knife, and there is no blood. The first encounter between Robbie and Mark includes the period usage of the word "dike" for toilet, which will be repeated in their climactic fight. When Mark brings Janine into the house he hides the dried blood of the death wound by undoing her shirt that was tied to bare her midriff.

It's hard at first to read Mark's reasoning for bringing Janine's body into the house, although we later see this is to help him get her into the wheelchair. His combing her hair may be either a humane or equally perverse touch. Given our later awareness of Robbie to be the killer, the idea of him leaving the body in Mark's car before going out for his rehabilitation creates a series of plot contrivances. At this early stage, Mark must know Robbie is the killer. Since he realizes that Robbie has put the body in Mark's car, Mark's action is only rationalized by his wanting to protect his brother. Otherwise, why wouldn't he just report the body to the police?

The information about Robbie's condition is an accumulated plot point that is sprinkled throughout the narrative. Charlie, at the hospital, reveals that Robbie's neck was broken. Dr. Fairburn tells Cheadle how Robbie slipped and fell while playing squash, which affected an existing back condition. And Robbie has a flashback, when he writes Mark a letter, showing Robbie's father pushing him in the chair as a child. Fairburn will also reveal to Cheadle Robbie's lesions that will make him a quadriplegic. Robbie claims the lesions were caused by his lifting a television. Cheadle later assumes they were the result of Robbie lifting the bodies of his victims to deliver them to the police station steps. This last act, Cheadle says, makes the police a "laughingstock." It also could be interpreted as that of someone who wants to be caught.

Mark's hippie wig and the sight of him pushing Janine's body in the wheelchair gets him some funny looks by the cinema cashier and the usher. But the fact that he gets away with the action of dumping the body in this manner is evidence of his good fortune, something which Burstall shows using point of view. The knitting woman's view appears to be that Mark is kissing Janine when he is actually removing the neck brace. And the usher's view of Mark wheeling out of the cinema looks to her as if it is Janine, since Mark wears her hat and his wig approximates Janine's hair. The whole plan is actually marvelously thought out, so it's a shame Mark is less impressive in the remainder of the narrative. Burstall also adds some humor in film being screened, known by Robbie to be entitled *A Day of Horror*, and being about a man in prison convicted of murder.

Burstall uses voiceover for the letter Robbie writes Mark and black and white footage for Robbie's memory flashback, although again the movie convention of seeing oneself in memory is evident. It's a pity that we don't learn what specifically led to Robbie being adopted by Mark's father, since the police lack of response to Robbie being hurt by his father implies that the abuse wasn't the reason. It's interesting too that Cheadle will offer a theory that Robbie's choice of young blonde victims is linked to Robbie's feeling about his mother, who is only seen in this flashback and whose fate we also don't learn.

The medieval weapons in Robbie's house get a payoff in the climactic fight after the scene where Robbie shoots at the target with arrows, and where the expectation is created that Robbie will shoot Mark. This expectation is later met when Robbie shoots Mark in the leg with an arrow, but only after the idea is raised that Mark knows that Robbie knows that he is the killer. Naturally, this idea can be dismissed in lieu of the revelation of the denouement. But at the time we don't know that Robbie wants to kill Mark, because he thinks that Mark knows that Robbie is the killer. The narrative saves the reveal of Robbie as the killer for the climax. There is no hint from Mark that he knows Robbie to be the killer beforehand, and the only reason why Robbie would want to kill Mark is one of pre-emptive self-defense after Mark puts phenobarbital into Robbie's drink.

The blood from the sword that Robbie holds against Mark's chest is the first direct act of violence and presentation of outpouring of blood, with more blood shown from the arrow wound in Mark's leg. The police entering the house just as Robbie is about to strike Mark with the sword is, of course, perfect timing to both save Mark and to make Robbie look bad. The police arrival allows for a funny exchange:

CHEADLE: Your brother tried to kill you. And you, when we came in just now, were about to kill him.
ROBBIE: We were always a close family.

For Cheadle's deconstruct of Mark's confession, Burstall again uses black and white footage, but this time repeats earlier scenes. This may be preferable to having an actor deliver a load of exposition and may help us to re-view what we have seen from the different perspective, but it still reads as a mistake. Equally, since Cheadle realizes that Robbie is the killer, we wonder why is he left in a position to be able to kill himself. Burstall adds to the moment where the dead Robbie is turned around in his chair (with its echo of Mrs. Bates in her chair in *Psycho*) by repeating the shot twice and ending the film on a close-up of Robbie's head thrown back.

The source novel was set in England although the author is Australian. The location was changed to Australia for the film, and the narrative concerning a serial killer of women in rural Australia prefigures that of the Australian horror title *Roadgames*. The film is the only Australian horror title made by director Tim Burstall, associate producers Alan Finney and Trevor Pope, and the Hexigon production company.

George Mallaby was born in England and began his Australian career in television. He made his film debut in a minor role in *Petersen* (1974), and although he played in more supporting film roles and on television, *End Play* was his only leading film role. The actor died in 2004. John Waters was also born in England and, like Mallaby, began his career in television. He made his film debut in *End Play* and later alternated between supporting and leading roles in film as well as play in television. Waters essayed the leads in the crime drama *Weekend of Shadows* (1978), *High Country* (1984), the comedy *Going Sane* (1987), *Boulevard of Broken Dreams* (1988), the thriller *Grievous Bodily Harm* (1988), the musical drama *Heaven Tonight* (1990), and the comedy *The Bouncer* (2006).

RELEASE

Australia on January 1, 1976, and straight to video in the United States in 1986. The taglines include "The loved can only hope to live…. The victim can only wait…. The dead can only be revenged," "And just when you believe there is nothing more to fear, you will begin to experience the ultimate terror of the end play," "More than just a motion picture, It's a heart-stopping experience!" "The chilling plot fits together like a jigsaw … only the last piece is missing!" and "It's a heart stopping experience in the Hitchcock tradition."

REVIEWS

"After a brilliant opening, the film develops into a rather talky, stagey affair. The running time is much too long for a film of this style and mood, and it's never really hard to decide which of the brothers is the killer. Mallaby and Waters, especially the latter, are effective."— David Stratton, *The Last New Wave*

"A painfully slow and over-long whodunit with an implausible plot. Mallaby and Waters do their best with the little they are given."— William K. Halliwell, *The Filmgoer's Guide to Australian Films*

"Emerges less as a straight whodunit than as thriller, observing the long and bizarre process of disposing of the corpse, and the tensions between the two suspects. Above all, an actor's piece."— Andrew Pike and Ross Cooper, *Oxford Australian Film 1900–1977*

"A great example of the talent we have here in Australia, both behind the lens and in front of it. From the start it may seem obvious what is happening, and who is guilty, but there is much more going on than what it seems. This film is paced brilliantly and is quality through and through." — J.R. McNamara, *Digital Retribution*, January 4, 2010

"There are revelations and red herrings along the way, though to be honest it's not that hard to work out who really is the guilty one. As a suspense thriller, [it's] quite talky and certainly too long at nearly two hours, but fortunately there are splendid performances from Mallaby and Waters." — Gary Couzens, *The Digital Fix*, January 23 2005

"An absurd mystery-thriller.... Most of the film is visually uninteresting, and the camera is almost never used to create suspense." — Scott Murray, *The New Australian Cinema*

Awards

Australian Film Institute (AFI) Best Editing award for Edward McQueen-Mason.

DVD

Roadshow Entertainment (Australia) on October 6, 2004.

The Last Wave
McElroy and McElroy Production/Last Wave Productions, 1977 [aka *Black Rain*]

CREDITS: *Director:* Peter Weir; *Producers:* Hal McElroy, James McElroy; *Screenplay:* Peter Weir, Tony Morphett, Petru Popescu; *Photography:* Russell Boyd; *Editor:* Max Lemon; *Music:* Charles Wain; *Production Design:* Goran Warff; *Sound:* Don Connolly; *Special Effects:* Monty Fieguth, Bob Hilditch; *Makeup and Hair:* Jose Perez; *Wardrobe:* Annie Bleakley; *Set Decorator:* Bill Malcolm; *Advisor on Aboriginal Matters:* Lance Bennett. Color, 106 minutes, English language and Aborigine dialect without subtitles. Filmed on location in Adelaide, The Flinders Ranges, Hammond and Mitcham, South Australia; and Avalon Beach, Bondi, Eastern Suburbs Railway, and The Rocks, New South Wales, from February 24 to April 1977.

CAST: Richard Chamberlain (David Burton); Olivia Hamnett (Annie Burton); Gulpilil (Chris Lee); Nandjiwarra Amagula (Charlie); Frederick Parslow (the Reverend Burton); Vivien Gray (Dr. Whitburn); Walter Amagula (Gerry Lee); Roy Dara (Larry); Cedrick Lalara (Lindsey); Morris Lalara (Jacko); Peter Carroll (Michael Zeadler); Athol Compton (Billy Corman); Hedley Cullen (Judge); Michael Duffield (Andrew Potter); Wallas Eaton (Morgue Doctor); Jo England (Babysitter); John Frawley (Policeman); Jennifer de Greenlaw (Zeadler's Secretary); Richard Henderson (Prosecutor); Penny Leach (Schoolteacher); Merv Lilley (Publican); John Meagher (Morgue Clerk); Guido Rametta (Guido); Malcolm Robertson (Don Fishburn); Greg Rowe (Carl); Katrina Sedgwick (Sophie Burton); Ingrid Weir (Grace Burton). Uncredited: Tony Llewellyn-Jones (Guest at Party).

Synopsis

David Burton is a corporate tax lawyer living in Sydney with his wife and children. He is asked to assist lawyer Michael Zeadler in the defense of Aboriginal men who are accused of the murder of the Aboriginal Billy Corman. David learns that the Aborigines believe that Billy was killed by the death bone of the tribal sorcerer, Charlie, for stealing a sacred stone, rather than drowning in a puddle as the police coroner believes. He urges Zeadler to follow this defense but Zeadler withdraws from the case, which pleases the Aborigines, who sense that David has the power to foresee the future.

David also believes the erratic weather, which includes hail and the phenomenon of black rain, has some connection to the Aboriginal trial. This is confirmed by the advice he receives from Dr. Whitburn, who claims that a catastrophic apocalypse is pending for the end of a tribal cycle. After he loses the case, David is told by Chris that the Aborigines are the last of the city tribe. Chris takes him to see the caves of a sacred site that is located under a sewerage plant. In the cave David finds a painting which foretells a catastrophic wave, and after being locked in the plant, he escapes to see what appears to be the wave approaching the beach.

Notes

This feature presents the Australian Aborigine as a malevolent supernatural being, but it is barely a horror title. It is more a mystery thriller, in spite of the mild shedding of blood and a murder by death bone as punishment from a tribal sorcerer. As with *The Cars That Ate Paris*, director Peter Weir continues to have trouble with pacing, and the narrative's focus on Aborigines prefigures the same *Dark Age*, *The Dreaming* and *Kadaicha*.

Weir uses the postmodern techniques of point of view, expressionist camera angles, and slow motion, and his treatment is more about mood and atmosphere than action. Although he presents several set pieces and a narrative that does not meet all expectations, the film's climax and conclusion is handicapped by ambiguity. When the narrative's protagonist is a character who has dreams and visions, it helps the audience to know when we are meant to be seeing reality, a problem that Weir doesn't overcome.

Under the opening credits, an Aborigine is seen painting under a wave-like rock, and the scene of daytime storm that hits a desert town is the film's first suspense setpiece. What sounds like thunder is heard, although the sky is devoid of clouds, and a view of the horizon shows changing light. A wind appears, followed by lighting and rain. The hailstorm specifically attacks a schoolroom — a thematic presentation of children as vulnerable victims. The blood from one child who is struck by a hail stone demonstrates the violence of the encounter. A rainbow after the storm is an image of beauty following the ugliness of the attack, although a view of Sydney's skyline shows its own rainfall.

Weir slowly tracks into a shot of the Burton family eating dinner. Their unit is in the center of the frame that is narrowed by the walls of the hallway, and he inter-cuts to water dripping inside the house and pouring down a carpeted staircase. The expectation that the water is rain is not met; it has come from an overrun bathroom, although no one admits to having left the bath running. Therefore, what cannot be attributed with a rational explanation can be interpreted as an act of supernatural malevolence, although this occurs before the connection between David and the Aborigines has been established.

David's first dream showing himself (we'll let the contrivance of someone seeing themselves in their dream pass) approaching a window and seeing a vision of an Aborigine is repeated and then paid off by the reveal of the Aborigine as Chris. Chris is at first a vision who shows David the sacred stone that Billy Corman has stolen and later is the real Chris who comes to take him to the tribal caves.

The rat in the sewage plant that has been built over the tribal caves is a florid, gruesome touch, as is the bush band that plays music as Billy is set upon by the other Aborigines in the fight in the pub. The fact that a sewage plant has been built over the Aboriginal sacred site is another slap in the face from the whites. Weir uses the sound of a didgeridoo, an Aboriginal musical wind instrument, under the scene where Billy is chased. He uses slow motion for Billy keeling over after the death bone is pointed at him. The issue of what caused Billy's death — the police coroner says he drowned from water in the

French movie card for *The Last Wave* (1977).

lungs — is another source of ambiguity dependent upon belief. The narrative offers rational and irrational explanations. David will lose the murder case using a defense of killing by death bone as punishment for tribal theft, which attests to the white man's prejudice in the trial.

Annie reading a book on Aborigines is the white European anthropological interest of foreigners for the indigenous people of the country. The book shows how alcohol consumption has ruined the Aboriginal culture. This idea is reflected in how Billy is first shown in the pub, presumably drunk. It is said the Aborigines attack him because they too are intoxicated with the white man's liquor and this is the motivation for their bad behavior. Weir uses an expressionist angled view of Chris to present him as a black-skinned, yellow-eyed demon. Charlie with his fire-stick is presented as equally malevolent. However, the Aborigine is humanized in the scene where he has dinner with David and Annie, and later Weir makes him a martyr for taking David to the caves and thereby breaking a tribal law himself.

The crying sound of frogs in the rain will be repeated for its supernatural association. The frogs we see outside David's house are both a portentous omen and a natural occurrence with heavy rainfall. David's second vision of Chris outside his window is continued when Chris appears inside the house displaying what we will later learn is the stone that Billy has stolen. The stone features a carved face and has blood on one corner — the vision's view of the stone is clarified in David's later description of it. Weir presents the vision as David's dream by having a shot of him awaken from it as he sits at a table.

The vision's view of Chris (and Charlie and Billy) as a tribal Aborigines and therefore subject to trial law and punishment will become an issue between David and Michael Zeadler and Chris himself; they deny that tribal Aborigines exist in the city. Chris' lying to David about the issue is seen as an act of self-protection, but it also presents him as a duplicitous character. Charlie is equally duplicitous when Chris says he cannot speak English and introduces him as a painter. The idea of Charlie as a painter may be an attempt to associate the Aborigine in the credit sequence as Charlie and to identify him as the person who has done the paintings that we will see in the underground caves.

Weir uses the didgeridoo on the soundtrack when Chris talks to David about the nature of dreams at their dinner — "A dream is a shadow of something real." This associates Chris' belief in the power of dreams with David's supposed gift for foreshadowing the future. When we see Charlie close his eyes, what Weir shows us is ambiguous. We initially assume that it is his vision, where a subjective camera is used to approach and enter David's house and then observe the sleeping David and Annie in their bedroom as we hear the didgeridoo. However, David shown waking up as if from a nightmare, after a shot of the painted face of Charlie, also suggests that the vision has been David's. The sacred stone with the carved face that appeared in David's vision of Chris is among Billy's personal effects held by the police, though we wonder why the Aborigines have left it on Billy's person after he has been killed, if the stone is so sacred.

David visiting the museum's Aboriginal anthropologist Dr. Whitburn allows her to identify the stone as a sacred object of the "spirit from the dream time." She speaks of the "mulkural" as one who foresees the future, which apparently is to include an apocalyptic act of natural cataclysm as the end of a tribal cycle. How Billy's theft of the stone is connected to David being a mulkural is never satisfactorily explained in the narrative, apart from the superficial connection that is made by David being the defense lawyer for the manslaughter case, and he being presented as the narrative protagonist.

Charlie is seen outside David's house and Annie is frightened by someone who knocks on the front door. She assumes that the person is Charlie and we wonder why she doesn't just talk to him since she has recently had dinner with him. This presence at the door creates the expectation, not met, that Charlie will come inside, when the person at the door is revealed to be the Babysitter. The grotesque paper hats that David and other guests wear at a party add to the treatment's exoticism. The owl that David sees outside his window when he is awake recalls Charlie being described by Chris as an owl, which is said to be the mythic symbol for impending death or catastrophe.

Weir has images of sunlight reflecting off high rise buildings and rolling black clouds to prefigure the falling of black rain (which the radio reports to be composed of oil) in the daytime as David watches Chris go to Charlie's Redfern house. When we see the smallness of the room that Charlie inhabits, it recalls the size of the cells that the Aborigines resist being locked into. Charlie dismisses the need for an interpreter when he tells David, "Sometime I speak English. Sometime I don't." The scene between the two men is perhaps the best in the film, though Weir uses unnecessary extreme close-ups for emphasis. Charlie's repeated chanting of "Who are you?" after David has asked him the same thing and his singing to communicate with David can be read as Charlie being mentally ill, although it does allow for the following exchange:

CHARLIE: Who are you? Are you a fish?
DAVID: No.
CHARLIE: Are you a snake?
DAVID: No.
CHARLIE: Are you a man?
DAVID: No.
CHARLIE: Are you mulkural?
DAVID: Yes.

David's denial of being a man is rationalized by his being in a trance from Charlie's chanting, although it does read as funny and can make David sound as mentally ill as Charlie. The scene ends with Charlie uncovering an axe to show David, which doesn't get any narrative payoff. When David is back in his car, the water leaking from his radio and the lost transmission prefigures the vision (presumably unreal) of people floating in water in the street and David's car underwater. Annie's telling David that she has sent their children away and his urging her to also leave the city is his melodramatic sense of impending doom, in view of the continued bad weather and his association with the Aborigines. (*The Chant of Jimmie Blacksmith* showed us how when Aborigines attack, their preferred white victims are women and children.)

The white wigs worn by the lawyers and the judge at the trial reinforces the difference between the colonial Europeans and the native Aborigines in the dock. However, the narrative cheats by not showing the trial judgment, when David later admits to having lost the case, although Chris' continued freedom suggests that he is not one of the Aborigines held accountable for Billy's murder. His confiding to David that he and the other Aborigines do still call themselves tribal allows for exposition about how the Aborigines' numbers diminished from thousands to only a few, presumably because of the invading white civilization, although there are still sacred sites close to the city.

Chris also tells that Billy wanted to be a tribal member but for some reason was not approved, and this is the reason he stole the sacred stone. The appearance of David's father in priest garb, after he was seen earlier in civilian clothes, adds to the narrative spiritualism. The information that David has the gift of foreseeing things is given an example in the way he supposedly foresaw the death of his mother. This foreshadowing has been seen in his visions of Chris, and will get a payoff at the film's conclusion with the titular "last wave."

Weir's next big suspense set piece is David in the house when it shakes and a tree branch falling inside. The didgeridoo is again heard with Charlie speaking in Aboriginal dialect. Water falls down the staircase again, from rain this time and not an overrun bathtub. The owl is seen and hail falls, aligning the storm with that at the film's beginning. Window glass is broken, the electric lights go out after power bursts, and the crying of the frogs is also heard. The scene climaxes in David's vision of Chris holding the stone, and leads to Chris taking David to the underground caves via the sewage plant. The fact that the moon is full on the night is surely more than coincidence, which adds to the danger that Chris puts himself in by breaking tribal law to show David the sacred site, although we don't see him punished for it.

Chris and David running through the plant, storm water drains, and climbing down to the caves are scenes of action in a treatment that features little of it. Chris leaving David to explore the caves by himself presents the limitation of Chris's generosity and the risk he is prepared to take. David must discover the interior cave that we assume Chris alone knows exists. Statues lead to David's discovery of carvings, paintings, masks, and what appear to be skeletal remains. A painting on the wall shows the black rain, hail, a wave, a second wave, and a calendar. What David sees is verbalized by him, including "mulkural." Weir then uses quick edits to the owl, the painted Charlie with a fire stick who attacks, and the dropping of the bloody sacred stone, to the sound of the didgeridoo.

David says Charlie's name but we are unsure if what David sees is real or a vision. There is a flashback to Billy's theft or Charlie's attacking now, although we presume the stone is still with the police. Perhaps we are meant to rationalize Charlie's attack with David's taking of a mask (resembling himself) which recalls Billy's theft of a sacred Aborigine item. If we are, David losing it in the pool of water outside the caves as he leaves is a pleasing narrative touch and probably saves him from the death bone. If one accepts the interpretation proffered by Pauline Kael in her review in her book *When the Lights Go Down*— that David's taking the mask is a reenactment of the white man's primal crime of colonial invasion — it seems an out of character betrayal by David. This is because he is a character whom the narrative has established as being sympathetic towards the Aborigines, though perhaps what is being revealed is that fear ultimately turns him against those he perceives will harm him.

The expectation of David's escape is not met

when he is locked inside the plant. Another expectation of him not being able to escape any other way is not met when he walks out of the water tunnel to come out on the beach in sunlight. Weir's conclusion is too ambiguous. David kneels in the sea to wash his face and we see a shadow come over him. Point of view is used for the wave — an acceptable photographic cheat in the face of staging a tsunami. But are we to believe that the wave is only a vision, or David's last moment before the real wave hits? The cave painting told of a second wave anyway, so who knows how to interpret this one. It's a frustrating end.

In his book *The Last New Wave,* David Stratton writes how the idea for the film stemmed from an experience Weir had in Tunisia in 1971 when he found a carved child's head among ruins. The film's original ending was to have shown the giant tidal wave that would envelop Sydney. However, plans to close off city streets for the scene were abandoned when the budget would not allow it to be done properly. Stratton also reports that the film went over budget because of difficulties with militant Sydney Aborigines who for a time picketed the set, and that Weir envisioned an alternate ending. This end would have the audience go into the wave, but it was again made impractical by the budget. The ending made use of stock footage for the wave that was seen from the protagonist's point of view.

The Aboriginals cast in the film are the Groote Eylandt Tribal Actors. Peter Weir would not direct another horror title but would go on to be nominated for the Best Director Academy Award for *Witness* (1986), *Dead Poet's Society* (1990), *The Truman Show* (1999), and *Master and Commander: The Far Side of the World* (2003). The film would be the only one made by Last Wave Productions, but McElroy and McElroy Productions went on to produce the Australian horror title *Razorback* (1984).

After working in television, Richard Chamberlain made his film debut in a supporting role in the crime drama *The Secret of the Purple Reef* (1960). He played the title character in the television series *Dr. Kildare,* and the film leads in *Twilight of Honor* (1963), *Joy in the Morning* (1965), and the musical biography *The Music Lovers* (1970). After *The Last Wave,* the actor focused more on television, but played occasional film leads: in the horror title *Murder by Phone* (1982), the comic action adventures *King Solomon's Mines* (1985) and *Allan Quatermain and the Lost City of Gold* (1986), and *River Made to Drown In* (1997).

RELEASE

Australia, December 15, 1977, and the United States, December 19, 1978, with the taglines "The Occult Forces. The Ritual Murder. The Sinister Storms. The Prophetic Dreams. The Last Wave," "A dream that became a nightmare. His was a premonition of doom," "From the makers of *Picnic at Hanging Rock* comes another terrifying and disturbing story," and "Hasn't the weather been strange ... could it be a warning?"

REVIEWS

"Movingly moody shock-film, composed entirely of the kind of variations on mundane behavior and events that are most scary and disorienting because they so closely parallel the normal ... an impressive work from a director new to American audiences. He's a man whose ability to find the eerie in the commonplace might please Hitchcock." — Vincent Canby, *The New York Times,* December 19, 1978

"Weir knows how create an allusive, ominous atmosphere. But the film is over-deliberate and sluggish.... It's hokum without the fun of hokum; despite all the scare-movie apparatus, this film fairly aches to be called profound." — Pauline Kael, *When the Lights Go Down*

"Strange, foreboding and brilliantly different from any other film ever made in Australia, [it] is time past, future, and present, a mingling of Aboriginal Dreamtime, Revelations, Doomsday predictions and the Deluge.... A memorable film." — Helen Frizell, *Sydney Morning Herald*

"One of the most affecting and least sensational mystery thrillers ever made." — David Stratton, *The Last New Wave*

"Intriguing if mystifying.... A film that works on several levels, and which challenges the intellect as well as pleases the eye." — John Stanley, *Creature Features*

DVD

Criterion Collection, released by Criterion on November 27, 2001.

Long Weekend
Dugong Films, 1978

CREDITS: *Producer/Director:* Colin Eggleston; *Executive Producer:* Richard Brennan; *Screenplay:* Everett de Roche; *Photography:* Vincent Monton; *Music:* Michael Carlos; *Editor:* Brian Kavanagh; *Production Design:* Larry Eastwood; *Sound:* John Phillips; *Makeup:* Deryck de Niese; *Wardrobe:* Kevin Reagan. Color, 92 minutes. Filmed in the Bownda State Reserve, Bega, New South Wales; Melbourne and Phillip Island, Victoria, from April to March 1977.

CAST: John Hargreaves (Peter); Briony Behets (Marcia); Mike McEwen (Truckie); Roy Day (Old Fisherman); Michael Aitkens (Barman); Sue Kiss von Soly (City Girl).

Synopsis

Peter and Marcia are an unhappily married couple who decide to go camping at the Moonda Beach near the Taronga abbatoir on a long weekend with their dog, Cricket. Their pleasure is hampered by the hostile environment, which includes Peter being attacked by an eagle and stalked by a dugong (similar to a manatee) when swimming and surfing. He shoots the dugong and it appears to be dead, and after Peter is bitten by a possum he agrees with Marcia to leave the site.

Before they go, Peter discovers that another group of campers whose van he had seen farther down the beach appear to be missing. He finds the van submerged in the sea. When Cricket goes missing, Marcia abandons Peter, but when she gets lost at night driving through the track that leads to the highway, she walks back to the campsite. Peter accidentally shoots her when he is spooked by noise and the continuing reappearance of the dugong. Driving away, Peter's car gets stuck in mud, and when he finds his way back to the highway, he is run over by a truck when the driver is attacked by a bird.

Notes

A triumph of atmosphere and sound design, this is the first Australian horror title to center on the theme of animals as malevolent supernatural beings, which is an extension of the foreign view of the Australian bush as a primeval danger zone. Existing as a basic two-hander, the narrative sets up expectations that are not always met or have their payoffs delayed. The couple presented as a battling marriage reads as soap opera, but the treatment's notion of them as deserving of their fate redeems the cliché. Director Colin Eggleston uses the post-modern techniques freeze frames, point of view, inter-cutting, out of focus and some arty camerawork. He also creates suspense by using silence and not relying upon score for effect.

A pre-credit prologue holds on one shot of a spider crawling up a rock ledge, and pigeons fly away from the sound of Peter's car starting as he leaves the city to go home. Eggleston inter-cuts shot of the plants in the bush with Peter driving and culminates in a cut to a plant that is in the bath being watered, with Marcia in her house. On television is a news report of a prefiguring bird attack, and Marcia drops a frozen chicken as she talks on the telephone, which prefigures the frozen chicken that she will have on the trip. A rifle point of view is used for Peter looking at Marcia with his newly purchased rifle when he gets home. Eggleston will repeat this rifle point of view later when he views the van at the beach. Although the expectation is created that he is going to shoot her with the rifle is not met, it does prefigure his shooting her with the speargun in the film's climax. Cricket the female dog is seen reacting to Peter and Marcia arguing; her refusal to eat the food left for her seems to be another omen, although she will not become as antagonistic as other animals the couple encounters.

Peter and Marcia as an unhappy couple works against the idea of them as the narrative protagonists, and although we don't learn why they are unhappy together until later; their sniping creates a karmic rationale for their fate. When Marcia tells Peter that the $200 he spent on camping equipment could have gotten them "the VIP suite at the Southern Cross," he replies, "You'd be an authority on hotel rooms." His careless throwing of a lit cigarette out the car window which lands in grassland and starts a small fire is the first of many behaviors that add to the idea of their fate as nature's payback for insensitivity.

A kangaroo on the highway creates the expectation of it being run over, an expectation that is met because Peter rubs his eyes in tiredness and does not see it in time. This act comes after we have seen him nearly collide with an oncoming car when his attention is distracted by his depositing a tape into the car's player. Marcia's moral complicity in the killing of the kangaroo can be interpreted by her being asleep when it occurs, not reacting to the impact, and not expressing any remorse when she is told about it later by Peter. The kangaroo is also run over by the van we see following Peter and Marcia's car, an act that perhaps also destines the van's occupants to their mysterious fate. The origin of the cry that we hear as the animal is run over the second time is undetermined. It may be the kangaroo, or the driver of the van, or it may come from elsewhere in the bush. The last possibility seems to be the most acceptable choice, given the animal noises we will hear in the bush.

Eggleston uses a close-up of the eyes of a man who will later be identified as the Truckie at the film's end. He watches Peter as he fills his red gas tank and Marcia in the car outside the pub near the beach. This is a moment that can be interpreted multiple ways, and the eyes dissolve to a shot of the car's headlights. The fact of the beach being close to an abattoir may add to nature's apparent hostility towards humankind, with the "Private Keep Out" sign that Peter finds discarded in the bush another omen that they are entering an unsafe locale. The red on the front of his car that Peter finds near the sign is not given a close-up, but is assumed to be the kangaroo's blood.

Thunder, lightning, and rain follow the cries in the night as horror movie conventions of foreboding when Peter stops the car to change a tire. The labyrinthine maze of the dirt track that leads to the beach creates another expectation not met that the couple will become lost. The difficulty they have in passing through it does prefigure both Marcia and Peter's attempts in the climax. It also gets a payoff when daylight reveals that where they have stopped to sleep is a mere walk away from their destination. The shot of the screaming Tasmanian devil is the first of several appearances of a creature with a state specific habitat — in the DVD audio commentary it is said that second unit animal photography was done in Tasmania. However, it does make an impressive representation of the first hostile animal in the area.

For the first day of the three that comprise the weekend, Eggleston uses a montage of animals. This ends with kangaroos hearing Peter chopping a tree that we never see fall, an act of aggressive and pointless destruction. The climax will feature a tree that creaks as if it will fall but only drops branches so the chopping is not paid off narratively. Peter's cooking bacon and later Marcia's defrosting a frozen chicken both present them as carnivores, which must certainly anger the animals around them. The couple rolling around in the sand and kissing seems to signal a change in their relationship, although their congeniality will only be temporary. Their later extended scene of kissing and attempt at having sex on the beach ceases because of Marcia's withdrawal. Her finding the eagle's egg in the sand and keeping it will be paid off — she takes it back to the campsite, where the eagle mother attacks Peter.

The underwater shots of Peter swimming create an expectation, not met, that he will be attacked. This expectation will be repeated when he goes surfing. It is the first time that we see what Marcia sees and warns Peter about — a dark shape in the water approaching him that she thinks may be a shark. He denies seeing the dark shape when we see it, but later he will acknowledge seeing it when we don't. The plot point of Marcia commenting

Poster for *Long Weekend* (1979).

that she nearly died suggests that she had survived a life-threatening condition, which may explain her mood, but also prefigures her present life-threatening locale. Her spraying insecticide around the campsite is more karmic behavior, and Eggleston has the sound of birds crying when she does it. The spear gun going off by accident and spearing a tree in front of Marcia is a shock effect, but also perhaps a psychic punishment for her insecticide use, and her death, which is another kind of spear gun accident.

The exposing of Marcia's breasts is contextualized for her having a shower, as they will later be when she sunbathes. The fact that she chooses to shower in a device from their camping set-up rather than bathe in the sea demonstrates her class discrimination. In fact, although she sunbathes, we never see Marcia swim in the sea for pleasure. She dislikes the environment and is bored and wants to leave. Her determination to leave also prefigures her abandonment of Peter, for which she is punished. Peter throws beer bottles into the sea, furthering the impression he is a careless and insensitive invader; his shooting at the second bottle is particularly arbitrary.

The naked Barbie doll he finds on the sand may represent the people in the van who followed him on the highway and who will be shown parked on the sand farther down the beach. The fact that the doll has been abandoned and has one arm missing is an omen of the violence to come. The doll's blondeness can also be equated with Marcia, and its nakedness a comparison to Marcia's lack of clothing, although Marcia's sexuality will be less available.

When Peter shoots his rifle in drunken abandon — like an old West cowboy, gangster, or a soldier with a machine gun — he is answered by birds crying and insects biting him. The scene of baby ducks and what appears to be an immobile mother duck suggests that one of Peter's shots has killed the mother; with the babies circle each other in fear and confusion. The slow camera approach to Marcia sleeping on the beach is a horror movie convention, as is the shadow that reveals the approacher to be Peter. Since Eggleston precedes the shot of Marcia with one of the van, an expectation is created that the approach may be someone from it, an expectation not met. The camera move appears to be point of view, but this is not the case. Peter's shadow appears away from the camera's eye. Marcia's sexual rejection of Peter may also be aligned to the idea that she has had a life-threatening disease and her recovery means a required re-introduction to sex, although her sexual interest will be paid off when she masturbates.

Eggleston uses cross-cutting between Peter surfing and Marcia in the camp tent reading a book. Her reading is replaced by her masturbating, where we hear her breathing and the sound of the singing of cicadas. Eggleston shoots the scene with discretion and inter-cuts between the growing intensity and Peter shown underwater. Marcia hears more animal cries that bring her to the beach; these create a second expectation, not met, that Peter will be attacked. He fires at something we have not seen in the sea, resulting in blood in the water and seagulls crying. Eggleston uses a long shot of the couple from a ground level point of view which pans as if the couple are being watched, which adds to the moment where Marcia reports that the frozen chicken has spoiled. Peter's observation that the chicken has mold on it may be another psychic phenomenon, because there has not been time for this to have happened.

The eagle attack on Peter is a shock effect, and although we see the bird pecking at Peter's body, there is no resultant blood. Marcia throws the eagle egg against the tree so that it breaks, and it's unclear whether she intentionally aims for the tree or whether it is just a lucky throw. This allows for her admission that she had an abortion, which we presume is the life-threatening trauma that was referenced before. Peter's refusal to help Marcia leave, by refusing to put back in the car the battery that is being used to power the camp's refrigerator, is presented as him being selfish more than her being unreasonable. Since he is the one who has been attacked by the eagle and nearly attacked by something in the sea, it would seem he has more reason to leave.

Eggleston uses geographic shots of dusk for the transition to night, as he will use dawn for daylight. The sequence of the possum visit to the camp is a suspense set piece where sound and silence are utilized. Although a possum may seem to be a mild antagonist, this possum will defy such an expectation when it attacks Peter. He is presented as the male version of the Woman in Peril, while Marcia's sleeping in the car protects her from attack as the conventional victim. Although Peter plays the guitar in the tent, he hears the first noise disturbance made by the possum as it walks on the table. As the creature eats grapes, we cut to Peter looking at a *Playboy* magazine and smoking dope, which adds to the moral punishment he will receive. The second noise he hears has him investigate as the Man in Peril, taking a lamp with him rather than a weapon. Eggleston shows us the possum in focus in the front of camera frame that Peter does not immediately see in the rear of the frame and out of focus, and it is with the third noise made by the creature that Peter sees it.

The expectation that the possum will attack is created when Peter teases it, offering a grape in one hand as the other moves toward it. The expectation is met when the possum ignores the offered grape and bites his free hand. Like the eagle attack, the possum bite produces no blood, but it does convince Peter to want to leave the site with Marcia in the morning. The next day they are back to arguing when Peter sees that in her packing she has spilled sugar. He tells her, "If you want to help why don't you go for a walk and let me do the packing." Eggleston uses a humorous edit after Marcia replies, "I don't want to go for a walk"; he cuts to her on the beach. This allows her to see the washed up dugong on the beach.

Peter assumes it is the dark shape in the sea that was attracted to him when he swam and surfed and which he shot. Peter also remarks that the crying they have heard has been the crying of a dugong pup in the area which sounds like a human baby crying. His attempt to cover the dugong in sand will prove to be unsuccessful. The creature uncovers itself and drags its body progressively towards the camp site. Whether the dugong is not really dead or whether it is empowered like the other animals in the area is unknown, but that doesn't really matter since it operates as a malevolent entity.

A high angle camera shot of Marcia and Peter after a shot of the eagle may appear to be the eagle point of view, but the following low angle pan cannot be the same. The couple delaying their leave so that Peter can look for the van that he saw parked down the beach will be paid off by what he discovers. Marcia driving and eventually running over a crab in the sand, with birds crying in response, is more karmic carelessness. Her argument with Peter in the stopped car reads as unnecessary soap opera. The scene begins with a funny exchange:

PETER: I realize that I can't always have everything I want. I accept that. What you don't seem to be able to accept is the reality of our situation demands that—
MARCIA: Are you being philosophical? Cause there's no point in trying to talk rationally to you when you're being philosophical.

In the argument we learn that the abortion came out of a sanctioned affair. All this nonsense can only be tolerated because it keeps the couple as antagonists to each other when they should be allied in their defense against the animals, a threat that they still underestimate at this time. Peter comments on their hostility, "How we relish the taste of human flesh" and calls them "neo-cannibals." The scene ends with Marcia's stated intention of filing for a divorce when she returns from the weekend.

Marcia's act of dropping what we assume is her wedding ring in the car is more eloquent than the dialogue that has preceded it, and her hearing the eerie cries of the pup dugong are inter-cut with Peter's looking for the van and walking in the woods off the beach. A false expectation is created that the shape Marcia sees in the sea is now the pup, which is never seen. The DVD audio commentary explains the shape is the floating roof of the van of the other vacationing couple. Eggleston inter-cuts what Marcia sees with Peter finding what we assume is the campsite of the van inhabitants: clothes, cutlery on a table, and tent with a growling dog inside, assumed to belong to the missing campers. Its hostility may also be aligned with the attitude of the other animals, except for Cricket, and Peter abandons his attempt to retrieve the dog.

We see Marcia in the car from the van roof's point of view, and her attempt to walk into the sea is odd. Perhaps she is simply investigating like a conventional Woman in Peril since we have seen how disturbed she is by the animal cries. Perhaps, thinking it is the pup, she tries to go to it because she wants to mother it. She carries something as a weapon. It's hard to see what it is, although it's not Peter's rifle, since he has it with him. But it suggests that she is not wading into the sea to suicide, and her anger at being stopped by Peter suggests an ambitious intention. Peter going in to the water is paid off, not by his finding the pup, but by the discovery of the van under water and what looks like a corpse inside. The DVD commentary claims the corpse is meant to be the child of the other couple, a child who supposedly drove the van into the sea.

The disappearance of Cricket keeps Peter from wanting to leave again, and Eggleston lets us see how the dugong has moved away from its sand covering. It will be the issue of leaving Cricket behind that enables Marcia to abandon Peter after their disagreement turns violent. He slaps and pushes her, and she knees him in the groin. Marcia does get some credit for leaving after hearing Cricket's barking at the dugong; she knows the dog is found. The DVD commentary says Briony Behets has the harder role to play in the film since Marcia is presented as such a hysterical and unlikable character, while Hargreaves' down-to-earth quality gives Peter the greater protagonistic empathy in spite of Peter's equally unlikable behavior.

Eggleston has another animal montage for the transition from dusk to night. Marcia is lit in a strange distorted way as she attempts to get through the maze of the dirt track leading away from the beach. Peter hears the car, and the splats on Marcia's windshield could be bird poop, or insects caught by the glare of her headlights. Birds fly into the car, as if trying to stop her from leaving. She inexplicably gets out of the car in the face of spider webs and a spider which is clearly on the outside of the car's windshield. When we see Peter finding the car later, the web appears strong but not strong enough to have stopped the car. His being unable to start the car immediately attests to the mechanical failure that perhaps motivated Marcia to leave it. Eggleston inter-cuts to Peter and the falling tree branch. Hearing Cricket's barking will eventually lead Peter to investigate the noise. This time he takes a branch lit by the fire he has created. His throwing of the flaming branch allows him to go after it and see the dugong again, having moved up the sand hill that leads to the camp. His shooting of it results in more animal crying heard, and the second falling tree branch is another shock effect, as is the burst of flame after Peter readjusts the fire.

Peter alone at the campfire is another suspense set piece. The sounds of wings flapping that makes him shoot his rifle are paid off when what we assume is one of Marcia's shoes is dropped to him. This sequence also lacks dialogue, naturally, since Peter has no one to talk to. The film will only feature one more piece of dialogue for the remainder of the narrative, when Peter yells for Cricket to get in the car when he burns the dugong. Peter's running out of bullets makes him load the spear gun, and our fear that he will accidentally spear Cricket is not met, though a worse one is realized. We don't see the result of his firing of the spear gun in a moment of hysterical fear in reaction to a noise. But the result will be revealed after the transition from dawn to dusk.

The pan to Peter seemingly having been awake the whole time sitting in the same position is continued to reveal the spear in Marcia's throat and her lying dead. This reveal is another shock, despite the camera panning. We wonder why she didn't call out when she was close to Peter. However, we also wonder whether the crying of the bird that motivates Peter to shoot the spear gun was the bird crying at Marcia's approach. The pan that reveals the dead Marcia also shows her bare foot to confirm that the shoe that was dropped was hers.

Peter leaving Marcia to find the car appears to be more karmic carelessness. His being unable to start it immediately creates tension and a false expectation that it will not start. His return to the camp site is a surprise, and the expectation that he will put Marcia's body in the back of the car is not met when he leaves her covered by a blanket, an act that is a mix of caring and carelessness. Cricket's growling reveals the dugong's presence again, and the gasoline tank that Peter uses to burn the creature is later featured when he becomes lost driving in the track. While his initial discarding the red gas tank appears to be more careless karma, the act is paid off when the car reappears next to a close-up of the tank. Peter has been driving in a circle. His leaving Cricket in the car that is stuck in the mud is perhaps Peter's final act of careless karma, possibly even worse than his killing Marcia, because he leaves the dog intentionally.

His running through the dirt track in an attempt to escape is another set piece, but uses more shock than suspense. The bird attack, the unlikely daytime appearance of the nocturnal possum, and shots of a lizard and a snake all seem to be nature's way of trying to stop him, as we hear the sound of birds crying. His walking into another spider web recalls the web that the car originally ran into, though this time we don't see the spider. Peter falling near the highway reveals a snake moving towards him. As he reaches the highway, we expect he is free from the animal onslaught.

The bird attacking the driver of the oncoming truck is a shock effect, as is the truck hitting Peter, and we hear the animal cry as the truck stops. Peter's body is revealed by the tire-track streaks of blood. In the DVD commentary executive producer Richard Brennan says a stronger shot was deleted that showed Peter's head being run over. In his own careless karma the driver leaves Peter on the road, though we don't see the truck driver punished for it.

The film ends in a shot that looks like the end of the spear sticking out from plants in the forest. This is odd if it is meant to be the spear in Marcia, since we saw Peter cover her with a blanket, presumably also covering the spear in her throat. Are we to presume that she, like the dugoing before her, also moves in death? In the DVD commentary Brennan claims that the shot shows how the forest's plant life has grown over Marcia. The protruding spear is said to be the one element that the plants could not decompose, since presumably the blanket that Peter had covered her with could.

The commentary also explains that despite a low budget, the story was filmed in anamorphic Panavision widescreen. This was done with resistance, because it meant the film would be subject to the period pan-and-scan system for television broadcast, to maximize potential international sales. George Mallaby, a known Australian television actor who had played the lead in the thriller feature *End Play* (1976) and had a supporting role in the British made James Bond title *The Spy Who Loved Me* (1977), was supposedly considered for the role of Peter. Briony Behets' casting as Marcia was not doubt aided by the fact of her being married to the director at the time. It is said that she was not the first choice and got the role because the first choice actress' casting fell through.

Brennan says the film was not a commercial success in Australia and theorizes that Australians did not view the bush that they lived in as threatening, as foreigners did. Brennan had been producing films in Australia since 1971, and had previously worked with John Hargreaves on the drama *The Removalists* (1975), the historical actioner *Mad Dog Morgan* (1976) and the action adventure *Deathcheaters* (1976). He worked with Behets on *The Trespassers* (1976). Brennan continued to produce features until 1999, but did not make another horror title.

After having worked in television, Colin Eggleston's previous feature as director had been the comedy *Fantasm Comes Again* (1977), although he was credited as Eric Ram. He produced and co-wrote the screenplay for *Nightmares* (1980) and produced and directed *Innocent Prey* (1984). Screenwriter Everett de Roche would go on to co-write the screenplay for the Australian horror title *Snapshot*. *Long Weekend* was the only film to be made by the Dugong Films production company, and it was remade in Australia by director Jamie Blanks as *Nature's Grave* (2008), which has its own entry in this book.

Considered the quintessential Australian man, after starting his acting career in television, John Hargreaves made his film debut in an uncredited role in *Sunday Too Far Away* (1975). He scored his first lead in *Deathcheaters*. After *Long Weekend*, Hargreaves played more supporting roles and scored more leads in the 1980s: the crime drama *Hoodwink* (1981), *My First Wife* (1984), the science fiction adventure *Sky Pirates* (1986), directed by Colin Eggleston, the romance *The Place at the Coast* (1987), and the comedy *Emerald City* (1988). The actor played his last leading role in the French *Rome Romeo* (1992) and finished his career playing supporting film roles and working in television.

Briony Behets was born in England and made her film debut in the supporting role of the Girl Rider in *Night of Fear* (1972). After working in television and supporting roles, she played the lead in *Inside Looking Out* (1977). After *Long Weekend* the actress continued in television and supporting film roles, including the Australian horror films *Nightmares* (1980) and *Cassandra* (1986).

Release

Australia and the United States on March 29, 1979, with the taglines "Their crime was against nature ... nature found them guilty," "They are trespassers. Will they survive their Long Weekend," and "A trip that becomes a nightmare." Said to have screened at Cannes in 1978, but this cannot be confirmed.

Reviews

"Eggleston creates a palpable feeling of nature under threat from humanity as the squabbling couple set out for their distant campsite.... Unfortunately the film never quite delivers the climax to which it seems to be building. Still, an intelligent thriller, with superior performances from John Hargreaves and Briony Behets."—David Stratton, *The Last New Wave*

"The film over-signals some of its thematic intentions but, in general, it works well as a tense thriller with a mounting sense of genuine menace.... Behets and Hargreaves are a convincingly disaffected pair and Eggleston's direction and Vincent Monton's camerawork intelligently create the polarizations at the heart of the film."—Brian McFarlane, *The Oxford Companion to Australian Films*

"Quite atmospheric (particularly in the final third), this one musters some fine performances from its two leads (Hargreaves especially as the well intentioned but clueless hubby). It's sluggish in spots, but more than compensates with a cool one-two power punch finish."—*The Terror Trap*

"A strikingly filmed, capably acted and intelligent horror entry from Colin Eggleston. Much of the disquieting, almost dreamlike atmosphere is provided by the locations and cinematography rather than cheap scares."—Michelle R., *Digital Retribution*, October 9, 2006

"This little seen Australian effort is one of the most impressive of the cycle of 1970s Nature's Revenge films that came out inspired by Alfred Hitchcock's *The Birds* (1963). [It] builds in with a superbly claustrophobic oppressiveness.... John Hargreaves and Briony Behets make a particularly convincing couple."—Richard Scheib, *Moria—science fiction, horror, and fantasy film review site*

DVD

Special edition released by Synapse Films on September 27, 2005. Widescreen Collectors Edition (Australia) released by Umbrella Entertainment on September 22, 2004.

Patrick

Antony I. Ginnane/Filmways Australasia, 1978 [aka *Coma*]

CREDITS: *Director/Producer:* Richard Franklin; *Producer:* Antony I. Ginnane; *Executive Producer:* William Fayman; *Screenplay:* Everett de Roche; *Photography:* Don McAlpine; *Editor:* Edward McQueen-Mason; *Music:* Brian May; *Art Director:* Leslie Binns; *Set Dresser:* Peter Kendall; *Sound:* Paul Clark; *Makeup/Hair:* Jose L. Perez; *Wardrobe:* Kevin Regan; *Special Effects:* Conrad Rothmann; *"Patrick" Logo:* Lindsay Steer. Color, 106 minutes. Filmed in 1977 on location in Melbourne at Alfred Hospital, Prahan, the basement of the Princess Theatre; Brighton; Ferrars Street; South Yarra; and Glen Waverley, Victoria.

CAST: Susan Penhaligon (Kathy Jacquard); Robert Helpmann (Doctor Roget); Rod Mullinar (Ed Jacquad); Bruce Barry (Brian Wright), Julia Blake (Matron Cassidy); Helen Hemingway (Sister Paula Williams); Robert Thompson (Patrick); Maria Mercedes (Nurse Panicale); Walter Pym (Captain Fraser); Frank Wilson (Detective Sgt. Grant); Carole-Ann Aylett (Patrick's Mother); Paul Young (Lover); Marilyn Rodgers (Day Desk Nurse); Peggy Nichols (Night Desk Nurse); Ray Chubb, Everett de Roche (S.E.C. Workers); Peter Culpan (Detective); Gillian Seemer (Nurse). Uncredited: Martin Copping (Baby in Hospital).

Synopsis

Kathy Jacquard is hired as a nurse at the Roget Clinic in Carlton, Australia, by Matron Cassidy. She is assigned to care for Patrick, a man who has been in a coma for three years after the trauma of murdering his mother and her lover. Kathy is British and separated from her husband, Ed, who also lives in Carlton. At a party given by Brian Wright—a neurosurgeon at the Southern General Hospital—that Kathy attends, Brian nearly drowns when a force pulls him under the water of his swimming pool. Patrick's room experiences strange vibrations. Kathy becomes able to communicate with Patrick, first by interpreting his spitting as yes or no, and then by typing his thoughts. When Ed comes to see Kathy at the hospital, he is trapped in a stalled elevator.

Doctor Roget brings in a cerebral functions monitor to try electric shock therapy on Patrick. Matron Cassidy terminates Kathy's employment when she encourages Brian to seek a consultation with Patrick. When Kathy tells Patrick that she has been fired, he types his fear that they are trying to kill him. Kathy breaks into the hospital at night with Brian, who tries treating Patrick with a strobe light. Matron Cassidy is electrocuted when she attempts to turn off the basement power board to kill Patrick. Roget attempts to kill Patrick with an injection of potassium chloride but is unsuccessful. When Kathy learns that Ed's car is at the hospital she goes in search of him and confronts Patrick. Knowing that his powers are diminishing, Patrick asks Kathy to inject herself with a potassium chloride syringe so that she can join him in death. She is stopped when the released Ed comes to her aid. Roget describes the presumed dead Patrick's jumping out of his bed as another motor nerve reflex. When he is put back into his bed Kathy closes Patrick's eyes, but alone, Patrick opens his eyes again.

Notes

A well-written if overlong treatment is aided by a multitude of Alfred Hitchcock imitation suspense set pieces and good performances, managing to overcome the limitations of a narrative about a man in a comatose state. The screenplay features a combination of the themes of horror of personality and the malevolent supernatural being with the title character doubling as protagonist and antagonist. Repeated expectations are created and not met, and there is some funny dialogue. Director Richard Franklin also utilizes a recurring red color motif, equal but spare male and female nudity, and silence. In addition, there is a subtle use of score, mood enhancing sound, and the occasional expressionist camera angle and slow motion effect as postmodern technique.

A prologue shows the trauma that supposedly led Patrick to his comatose state. Franklin begins the film with the sound of electric buzzing that we will later learn is the sound of the neon Emergency Entrance sign to the clinic, under a black screen. The sound of a car arriving and parking is heard, which we assume is that of Patrick's mother and her lover. Patrick's room is next to his mother's, which will allow him to hear what they intend to do. Patrick sits on his bed, already behaving in an odd fashion, which Franklin enforces by a close-up of his eye. His mother's lover describes him as a "lunatic." Patrick has a mirrored view of his mother's room from the chromium ball top of her bed head that stands against the wall that divides the rooms. That Patrick can see this view suggests that he may already have a form of ESP, since there is no other apparent way for him to do so. Franklin shows the nudity of both the mother and her lover as they have sex, but their body sizes are reduced in the ball's reflection. Equally their exposure does not read as exploitative since the nudity has context, with the distortion of their images appropriate for the ball reflection and as Patrick's revolted point of view.

The ball top hits the dividing wall and the sound thumps into the back of Patrick's head as the couple has sex, which is shown with split-screen by Franklin, with the sound of moans. Franklin stops the score for a long shot of Patrick's legs walking down a corridor holding rope, and we see the lovers reflected in another mirror as they bathe together. The camera pans to the glass door to the bathroom. Patrick opens the door only so that half of his face is shown, and a close-up of his eye reveals the bathing lovers in the reflection in his pupil. The first real shot of the lovers has them laughing in their pleasure, and Franklin cuts to the open door where a distorted movement behind the door reveals a figure that we assume to be Patrick.

This view is also assumed to be the lovers' point of view, which is confirmed by a close-up of the mother saying Patrick's name. Franklin uses a zoom in on the lovers before a heater, prefiguring the heater in Patrick's hospital room, is thrown at them and caught by the man. When he throws it to the mother her hair catches on fire; the heater is then thrown back at Patrick's legs. He throws it back into the bath, where the lovers conveniently separate to either end so that the device can fall into the water in between. A close-up of the moving bathwater dissolves to a daytime skyline and the camera pans to the window of the apartment for the opening credits.

Kathy moving into a new apartment and getting a new job after having been a housewife represents the innocent outsider entering the new but corrupt world of the hospital. Though we later learn that Patrick may have had a relationship with another of his nurses in the past, it is telling that he will communicate only with Kathy and only Kathy objects to Patrick being killed. Kathy being British

Poster for *Patrick* (1978).

also adds to her status as an outsider (actress Susan Penhaligon was born in the Philippines). Julia Blake and Rod Mullinar both also hail from the United Kingdom and have British accents. Matron Cassidy's patronizing interview with Kathy features funny lines, "We are not interested in restless housewives who'll resign at first threat of a soiled bedpan," and "We tend to attract certain types — lesbians, nymphomaniacs, enema specialists, zoophiliacs, algagliacs, necrophiliacs, pedophiliacs, scotophiliacs, exhibitionists, voyeurs." This role call of perversions will get a wonderful payoff when Matron Cassidy catches Kathy feeling Patrick's erection. The interview has a humorous end when Dr. Roget enters. Matron Cassidy tells him, "She comes to us in the wake of an unstable domestic situation," and he replies, "Hire her."

The electronic buzzing of the faulty electrical sign, where "Entrance" sometimes reads as "trance" to reference one of Patrick's powers, is heard when Kathy enters Patrick's room because it is revealed that the sign is outside his window. The issue of Patrick being "dead" is in counterpoint to his spitting at her after Kathy is shown from his point of view. Roget calls the spitting a "motor nerve reflex" and kills a frog to demonstrate to Kathy that it can move after death with electrical stimulation. He will also tell Kathy that Patrick is kept alive "to determine the exact moment of death" and to "study the gray area between life and death." When Kathy asks what Matron Cassidy thinks of his ideas, Roget replies, "She thinks they're bullshit."

It is interesting that Matron Cassidy refuses to enter Patrick's room but that she is his perhaps his strongest antagonist, and their ultimate confrontation will occur without them being face to face. An apparent subplot of Kathy having a stalker is soon changed to the stalker being identified as Ed, who has an interest in getting back with her. His red car and the use of a red payphone to call her from a pub begins the red motif of the film. This is continued with the red lighting of "Emergency" in the sign, the red floors of the hospital and the elevator emergency light, Matron Cassidy's red jacket, Ed's burn sores, red tie, the red sports car and the roses he brings to Kathy, Kathy's red handbag, and of course the red blood of Roget and the eye of the electrocuted Matron Cassidy, and the opening and closing credits.

Suspense is created when we see that Kathy's door chain is undone before she does, and the expectation of the person who breaks in raping her is not met when she recognizes Ed. We wonder whether Patrick has used some kind of power to open his windows or whether they have simply been opened by the wind. This ambiguity will extend to what happens to Brian in the swimming pool at his party. Franklin creates the expectation that something will happen by the ominous shot of Brian swimming under water. The underwater loudspeaker plays Stravinsky's "The Rite of Spring," and Franklin inter-cuts to Matron Cassidy sleeping at her desk on which a demon paper weight moves.

Matron Cassidy's walk up the staircase presents her as a Woman in Peril, the suspense heightened by the parallel action of Brian in the pool, where the underwater lights flash portentously. Matron Cassidy investigates a noise, which is the vibrating handle of the door of Patrick's room. Franklin uses a shock scare when Captain Fraser, who occupies the room next to Patrick, appears and yells at her, "What are you doing?!" Brian being pulled under the water recalls the shark's attack of the girl in the opening scene of *Jaws*. Franklin uses a subjective camera shot for an approach to Brian's legs and features the Stravinsky chords that on which John Williams based his score for the attack scenes in *Jaws*.

Brian being raised above the water is another *Jaws* touch, as is his being held under water by some kind of force. His reaching out to Kathy creates an expectation that she will be pulled into the pool by his arm, but she is not. As the scene ends Brian is saved but he doesn't tell Kathy what he thinks happened to him. Later when she talks to Paula, Kathy offers the rational explanation that Brian had a cramp from going swimming on a full stomach. We make the connection with Patrick, which he later confirms in the letter that is typed, because we had seen Paula and Kathy talk about Brian and his forthcoming party in front of Patrick. Matron Cassidy being harmed at the same time Brian nearly drowns is another expectation not met, a plot point seemingly left dangling until we see her again. When Kathy discusses with Ed why their marriage failed, she makes a comment about her past condition that prefigures that of Patrick. Also Ed's comment about being stuck in the elevator — "You should try being boxed in for 24 hours a day with nothing but four blank walls to stare at" — also draws a parallel with Patrick's condition.

When Kathy types letters on an electric typewriter in Patrick's room, suspense is created by the sound of the oxygen pump. She unintentionally types the word "Patrick," the first indication that he wants to communicate with her and that he can control electrical devices. His spitting, which Roget has previously dismissed, is now a primitive means for him to express yes or no to her, although he spits without saliva. Franklin inserts shots of Kathy from Patrick's point of view. Patrick's refusal to spit in front of Matron Cassidy is not a surprise, and validated when he types "secret." His only communicating with Kathy puts her at risk of sounding crazy to the others who don't or won't believe her, though Penhaligon reads as calmness personified in the face of the more stylized performances of Robert Helpmann and Julia Blake. The shots of Brian's swimming pool when Kathy is at his house again create an expectation that is only met by the reactive movement of the pool water. It's more of a stretch to believe that Patrick's powers have allowed him to trash Kathy's apartment; he doesn't know addresses.

The scene where Kathy tests the feeling Patrick has in his body creates the expectation that she will be curious about his groin when she learns that he has no feeling in his legs but does in his upper body. The screenplay cleverly delays Matron Cassidy's reaction when she catches Kathy encountering Patrick's erection. Kathy's punishment is to be kept on as Patrick's nurse, though with the warning, "I expect you to keep your nose clean, your mouth shut, and your hands off."

Roget's pricking Patrick with a needle to test for feeling is presumably in reaction to what Kathy has reported. It culminates in a double setup, with the addition of an electric heater that Nurse Panicale brings to the room. The expectation that Patrick causes the heater to short circuit is not a surprise, particularly as a way to stop Roget when he sticks Patrick's eyes. Ed burning his hands on the hot casserole dish reads oddly; we wonder why Ed doesn't don the oven mitts he had worn to carry the dish from the oven when Kathy warned him about the dish potentially burning the table. Perhaps in light of Patrick's seeming mind control over Kathy, we are to think that Patrick has made Ed pick up the hot dish with his bare hands. This is suggested by the lights that flash when Ed handles the dish. The idea that Ed doesn't feel the heat of the dish is only later explained when we learn about the boyfriend of another nurse who had the same numbness in his hands and whose hands caught a disease that spread and killed him.

The hospital elevator that is said to not work has its door open when Ed arrives to visit Kathy. Ed's entrapment is not shown until much later in the narrative, another plot point that is left hanging. We assume that Patrick's power has something to do with Ed becoming trapped since Franklin inter-cuts Ed entering the elevator with Kathy typing in Patrick's room amid the sound of his heart monitor pulsating. The heart monitor shows Patrick's increased heart rate as his thoughts are typed by Kathy under the guise of a letter to her mother. The lines "When he came on a bit strong I fixed him up. Ha. Ha. In his own swimming pool of all places" confirms that it was Patrick's power that held Brian under water.

The lines "Ed burned his hands but it serves the bastard wright for being such a mauler" bears out that it was Patrick's power that allowed Ed's hands to be burned. The spelling of right as "wright" is later rationalized as Patrick's request for the intervention of Dr. Wright, despite Patrick's jealousy of Brian as a love interest for Kathy. The lines "Ed's all boxed in and hung up and he'll have to stew in his own juices" refers to Ed being trapped in the elevator, although Kathy will not interpret this as such until later. The line "Patrick is waiting for his hand job" refers to Kathy's prior touching of his erection, and scores a laugh. The algebra that Patrick also types is a plot point that is never paid off. Patrick's power is also demonstrated by the flashing of lights, the closing of windows, paper that Kathy feeds into the typewriter flying out, and the knocking over of his IV drip stand.

Brian assesses Patrick's behavior as being psychokinesis (aka telekinesis), where he has the ability to make things move, though it is the electric shock therapy that Roget gives Patrick that seemingly increases Patrick's powers. In the DVD commentary Franklin comments that Robert Helpmann had observed Vivien Leigh receiving this kind of therapy when she and Laurence Olivier were touring Australia in 1948. Franklin inter-cuts between Kathy and Brian breaking into the hospital and Matron Cassidy returning after she has left. Captain Fraser is used again for a shock effect when he yells, "Look out. He's in the wall!"

The expectation of Fraser's urine being used to conduct electricity, after he has wet his pants in the hallway, is not used. This is much the same unmet expectation as Matron Cassidy's walking in bare feet so as to not to be heard as she approaches Patrick's room. Her standing at Patrick's door creates the expectation that she will catch Kathy and Brian. This is something Franklin highlights by inter-cutting between the three. However, Matron Cassidy simply walks away. In the DVD commentary Franklin also comments that the strobe itself had little effect on Patrick, and that he used his trance powers during the strobe to repel Matron Cassidy from the door. A woman at the door is repeated with Sister Panicale arriving, and a second expectation created that she will catch Kathy and Brian. Again this is not met when Matron Cassidy opens the door to find only Patrick, with Kathy and Brian emerging from the next room. They are seen leaving by Captain Fraser, but this has no plot payoff.

When we see Matron Cassidy in the basement, Franklin also shows the increased power on Patrick's monitor. When she approaches a power box, Franklin supplies another suspense set piece, inter-cutting between her and Patrick to create tension. Although we hear the sound of dripping water in the basement, Franklin only shows us the reflection of water on the floor before Matron Cassidy gets to the gate. The Danger sign on the power box is expected, though we know the real danger to Matron Cassidy is Patrick.

Franklin teases out the suspense with Matron Cassidy unlocking the gate in front of the box. He provides another close-up of Patrick's eye with Matron seen in the pupil reaching for the power lever and pulling it. The immediate blackout empowers

Patrick to use another source, in the same way that Roget will explain that the hospital has an emergency generator to provide backup power in the event of a failure. Patrick moves his head and his eyes to see Nurse Panicale, who screams in reaction, but we aren't shown what has happened to Matron Cassidy. This is another delayed plot payoff. When the police arrive the next day, we are told that a neighborhood blackout has occurred and Matron Cassidy's dead body is found lying over the box with one eye gored.

Franklin uses a hand-held camera for the scene where Kathy follows Detective Grant to his car and talks to him. Reaction shots follow of people overhearing Kathy's raised voice as she attempts to get Brian to validate them being at the hospital the previous night. The issue of Kathy being viewed as a hysterical female making a scene is ironic, given the greater moral question of Brian having consulted another doctor's patient. The Night Desk Nurse had previously questioned Matron Cassidy about a noise she heard in the basement that she thinks came from an elevator repairman, which Matron Cassidy dismissed because no one had come to fix it. Then we finally return to Brian in the elevator banging against the closed doors, which we assume is what the Nurse heard.

Kathy leaving the hospital to look for Ed is ironic given that she leaves the place where he is located. Her telephoning from Ed's house is inter-cut with Roget at the clinic and his wanting to inject Patrick with a syringe of potassium chloride. Patrick's power monitor increasing when Roget gets closer as if in fear is a phenomenon that Roget observes. This sporadic power also makes the elevator's emergency red light turn on. This relieves Ed of the darkness after he has knocked out the light accidentally. Roget's attempt to inject Patrick in the face is met by a potted plant that flies and hits Roger in the head, causing a cut on his forehead. When Roget attempts to throw a chair at Patrick it is pulled out of his hands. When Roget tries again the chair is thrown and it knocks over the drip stand and breaks the window. The fallen stand knocks out the Emergency Entrance light at the front of the building, something Kathy will notice when she returns to the hospital. Roget is thrown against the wall of the corridor and will be locked out of Patrick's room by the force that only allows Kathy back in. She returns when Grant has told her how Ed's car was found outside the hospital.

Kathy finds Roget's eating a frog in his office, which Roget explains with "He made me," presumably referring to Patrick. This prefigures the mind control that Patrick will seem to have later in making Kathy want to kill herself, to be with him when he dies. The typewriter communication between Kathy and Patrick is now different in tone, since Patrick has her type "Get stuffed slut." When she accuses him of murdering his mother for being "unfaithful" to him, the contents of the wall cabinet fly into the room. Patrick's spurts of power make the elevator move in bursts and the emergency light come on, which we see from Franklin's inter-cutting. When Patrick types "I love you," Kathy replies, "What do you know about love? Who'd love you? You're a self-centered, self-important, self-indulgent little boy who never grew up who wants his Mummy." In response a chair is thrown at her. When Kathy asks what happened to Ed, Patrick types, "Poetic justice."

He asks her, "Do you love him?" and says, "Better off without those that hurt you." Patrick quotes from Oscar Wilde's poem "Ballad of Reading Gaol": "Yet each man kills the thing he loves.... The coward does it with a kiss, the brave man with a sword." Inter-cut with Roget's attempt to axe down Patrick's door, which is met with the power's resistance, Kathy kisses Patrick on the mouth. This alludes to Wilde's "the coward does it with a kiss" although Kathy doesn't actually kill Patrick with the syringe as "sword" or any other means. Slow motion is used as Patrick's heartbeat slows down on the monitor and he types, "I'm going now. I love you." As the power decreases, Patrick types, "Come with me" as the heartbeat gets slower and the elevator doors open to release Ed.

Kathy's attempt to inject herself with the potassium chloride is presumably because she is in a trance. The act is interrupted by Ed, who is able to open Patrick's door as the heart monitor shows Patrick flat-lining and the power monitor shows no power. Now considered really dead, Patrick's flying up and crashing into a cupboard is rationalized by Roget as another motor nerve reflex. This incorrect assessment prefigures the film's end. The buzzing of the Emergency Entrance sign, which would seem to be the key to Patrick's power, follows as Patrick is put back into his bed and Kathy closes his eyes. When Patrick is alone his eyes open, suggesting that he is not dead after all. This ending foreshadowed a sequel, Franklin says, that the screenwriter de Roche objected to. Patrick's loss of power seemingly in reaction to Kathy's confrontation is a surprise, so his return to his form of life at the conclusion is more satisfying and a horror movie convention that allows for a sequel, although none was made.

In the DVD audio commentary Franklin says that the screenplay was based on a true story told by a nurse of a man whose name was Patrick who had become a paraplegic and was still able to spit and get erections. The spitting was repeated as an action done by the comatose bride in Quentin Tarantino's crime thriller *Kill Bill: Vol. 1* (2003). This Patrick had apparently caught his wife having sex with another man and had jumped out the window to commit suicide in response, an act which is reflected in this Patrick's climactic jumping out of the bed. Franklin acknowledges the references to Hitchcock in the filmmaking and the narrative, with specific camera shots and Patrick's matricidal backstory taken from *Psycho*. The clinic that was set in an abandoned private hotel was designed to echo the Bates house. The title logo broken in two by a jagged line evokes the fluctuating beep of a medical monitor and the horizontally broken line that existed in artwork for *Psycho*.

Franklin also claims "Breakdown," a 1955 episode of the *Alfred Hitchcock Presents* television series, was the "spiritual model" for his film. That episode was directed by Hitchcock himself, and starred Joseph Cotton as a paralyzed man. Franklin was also influenced by the war drama *Johnny Got His Gun* (1971). That film centered on a World War I soldier whose wounds make him a quadruple amputee. He had lost his eyes, ears and mouth but learned to communicate with his doctors. Franklin's Hitchcock connection had begun when he was a University of Southern California film student. A friendship with the director led him to being invited to observe the making of the crime thriller *Topaz* (1969), and he claims that it was *Patrick* that helped him get the directing job for *Psycho II* (1983).

Franklin claims that he was the third director offered *Patrick*, after the second (unnamed) had asked him to produce the film, which had an original running time of 140 minutes. More scenes of Patrick using the typewriter were cut after a preview, scenes that are now lost, and Franklin also participated in the cutting of more scenes for the film's American release. That release was also dubbed with American accents presumably to make it more accessible to U.S. audiences. Apparently Robert Helpmann was so offended by his dubbing that he attempted to take legal action against the American distributors. Franklin also reports that Helpmann broke his back in the scene at the film's end when Roget is required to lift Patrick into the bed. It is obvious that Helpmann's double performs the abbreviated task, as it is obvious from his hair that the double does the stunts for Helpmann when Roget is being thrown around.

An unofficial sequence was made in Italy entitled *Patrick viva encore*, aka *Patrick Still Lives* (1980), and an official sequel to be entitled "Patrick II: The Man Who Wasn't There" was written by Everett de Roche but never got beyond a storyline. The sequel would have had Patrick's corpse found by a religious cult and revived back to his comatose state, which would allow him to menace another woman.

De Roche later wrote Australian horror title *Long Weekend*. *Patrick* was Franklin's third feature, after having directed and produced the comic western *The True Story of Eskimo Nell* (1975) and the comedy *Fantasm* (1976), which was produced by Antony I. Ginnane under his Filmways Australasia production company banner. Franklin would go on to make the Australian horror title *Roadgames* (1981).

Ginnane had written and directed *Sympathy in Summer* (1971), and after producing and co-writing *Fantasm*, producing the family drama *Blue Fire Lady* (1977), and the sequel *Fantasm Comes Again* (1977), he would turn his attention to horror titles. After *Patrick*, Ginnane would go on to produce the Australian horror title *Snapshot* (1979).

Susan Penhaligon had made her film debut in a bit part in the British comedy *Say Hello to Yesterday* (1971), and played the leads in *Private Road* (1971), the Italian adventure *Miracles Still Happen* (1974), the British horror title *House of Mortal Sin* (1976), and her prior title *Leopard in the Snow* (1978). *Patrick* would be her last feature film role to date.

Portrait of Richard Franklin, the director of **Patrick** (1978) and **Roadgames** (1981).

Release

October 1, 1978, in Australia, September 7, 1979, in U.S.A. Taglines include "What Patrick does to people is Electrifying!" "Patrick has a way with people. His way. Or Else!" "He's in a coma ... yet he can kill," "Patrick lies between life and death.... Patrick loves.... Patrick kills," "There's more to him than meets the eye," and "Patrick is nearly dead ... and still he kills!" It is said to have screened at the 1978 Cannes Film Festival, but this is unconfirmed.

Reviews

"A modest but rather well-handled thriller, heavily influenced by the films of Brian De Palma, which builds to an exciting climax. There is a pleasant sense of humor about it all, the special effects are effective, and the actors serviceable." — David Stratton, *The Last New Wave*

"Patrick lives up to its reputation ... a superior suspense thriller ... gripping and brilliantly played by everyone." — *Sydney Daily Mirror*

"A film that plays impudently with the conventions of several Hollywood genres.... Franklin shows a delight in the story-telling capacity of the film, trusting his images as much as the often witty dialogue." — Brian McFarlane, *The Oxford Companion to Australian Film*

"Stylishly directed Australian offering was one of the better films to jump in on the *Carrie* bandwagon.... There are several scenes that produce calculated jolts.... On the minus side, the twist ending with its muscle motor response gag is silly." — Richard Schieb, *Moria — The science fiction, horror and fantasy film review site*

"It's obvious from watching the visuals and style of the film that Franklin learnt a lot from his time studying under his mentor Alfred Hitchcock. Scenes are viewed from some amazing angles, using reflection and color to keep the eye interested, an imperative move considering the main foe's lack of mobility. The pacing is slow but you do appreciate the slow build up." — David Michael Brown, *Digital Retribution*, May 20, 2009

Awards

Nominated for the Australian Film Institute (AFI) Best Film, Best Editing and Best Original Screenplay.

DVD

Released by Elite Entertainment on November 19, 2002. Special edition released by Synapse Films on October 28, 2008. Ultimate Ozploitation Edition released by Umbrella Entertainment (Australia) on February 2, 2009.

Snapshot

Australian International Film Corp. (AIFC)/F.G. Film Productions/Filmways Australasia, 1979 [aka *Day After Halloween*; *One More Minute*; *The Day Before Halloween*; *The Night After Halloween*]

CREDITS: *Director:* Simon Wincer; *Producer:* Antony I. Ginnane; *Executive Producer:* William Fayman; *Associate Producer:* Barbi Taylor; *Screenplay:* Chris De Roche, Everett De Roche; *Photography:* Vincent Monton; *Editor:* Philip Reid; *Music:* Brian May; *Art Direction:* Jon Dowding, Jill Eden; *Sound:* Paul Clark; *Makeup/Hairdressing:* Jose L. Perez; *Wardrobe:* Aphrodite Jansen; *Chantal Contouri and Hugh Keays Byrne dressed by Saba*; *Sigrid Thornton dressed by Vanilla*; *Special Effects:* Chris Murray. Color, 92–100 minutes. Filmed in Melbourne and Montsalvat, Eltham, Victoria.

SONGS: "Angela" (Sherbet); "Magazine Madonna" (Sherbet) (this appears in the closing credits, although I did not determine where the song is used in the film.)

CAST: Chantal Contouri (Madeline Stobar); Robert Bruning (Elmer Stobar); Sigrid Thornton (Angela Bailey); Denise Drysdale (Lily); Vincent Gil (Daryl); Jon Sidney (Mr. Pluckett); Jacqui Gordon (Becky Bailey); Julia Blake (Mrs. Bailey); Hugh Keays-Byrne (Linsey); Peter Stratford (Roger); Christine Amor (Paula); Lulu Pinkus (Wendy); Stewart Faichney (Peter); Chris Milne (Bachelor); Bob Brown (Captain Rock); Peter Felmingham (Boris). Uncredited: Steven Clark (Barman).

Synopsis

Nineteen-year-old Angela is a hairdresser who is taken by one of her clients, the beautiful model Madeline Stobar, to meet fashion and art photographer Linsey. Linsey hires Angela as the topless model for the Bermuda Cool cologne advertising campaign which features her picture printed in magazines. Thrown out of her house by her mother, Angela moves into the attic of Linsey's Paradise Pictures studio, but strange happenings suggest that she is being harassed by someone. Angela suspects her ex-boyfriend, Daryl, but she also warrants the attentions of Madeline's husband, Elmer. When Elmer tries to threaten her to pose nude for him in his office, a fire is set and Elmer is burned to death. Angela escapes with the help of Daryl, but he is killed by Madeline, who is to fly to Fiji with Angela on another assignment.

Notes

More of a thriller than a horror genre piece, this film features the theme of the horror-of-personality colored by the antagonist revealed to be a psycho-lesbian. This is similar to the sexually aggressive incestuous lesbian in a minor role of *Inn of the Damned*. The particular take on homosexuality allows some homophobic lines of dialogue and an act of misanthropy to pass, with the objectification of women demonstrated by bare breasts and a close-up of a bottom only partially contextualized. The narrative only introduces mystery in the latter stages so that it plays for a long time as a drama, but it opens and then repeats a scene of street activity at the film's climax for a pleasing cyclic effect. Director Simon Wincer does several amusing quick cuts for irony, sets up expectations that are not always met, and uses shock effect. He also employs postmodern techniques of the occasional expressionist camera angle, point of view, and freeze frames.

The film opens with a pre-credit prologue of the result of a fire that will be partially repeated later on. The first image is of two flashlight beams coming out of darkness accompanied by the sound of heavy breathing. This breathing might be interpreted as that of a stalker, but is revealed to be that of firemen entering the burned area wearing oxygen masks. Wincer inter-cuts the progress of the firemen with a scene in the street, which includes the fire trucks, police, and onlookers. The arrival of a hysterical Madeline calling out to Angela and being subdued by police is also seen, although this will later prove to be a red herring. The identity of the found charred body with its white teeth is unknown. An expectation is created that the corpse is Angela both from Madeline's behavior, and by the duplicated photographs of a bare-breasted Angela that appear on the wall in the burned area. The images suggest an obsessive interest in the subject, which will be confirmed later when Elmer entraps Angela in the room.

Wincer uses freeze frames of the fire recovery for the credit sequence, and a montage of other photographs of Angela that lead to her reveal as a living person walking in the street. No filmic device is presented for us to instantly realize that what we see is a flashback featuring the living Angela, though we still do tend to assume that the charred body we have been shown is not her. Madeline driving and parking her car recklessly indicates her sense of celebrity entitlement, though she turns the magazine that features her on the cover that she finds at the shop face down. It also suggests her danger, and an exchange between her and Mr. Pluckett shows the first of Wincer's funny edits.

When Madeline asks for the occupied Angela to do her hair, she tells him, "Why don't you take over the other client and that'll leave Angela free to do me?" After Pluckett replies "I'm afraid that's impossible," we cut to him resentfully washing the hair of Angela's client. When Pluckett threatens to fire Angela if she leaves to go with Madeline, Madeline calls him a "pathetic faggot." His response, "It takes one to know one," is only understood later when she outs herself to Angela as a lesbian.

The close-up of Lily's bottom and the low angle on her heaving breasts as she practices self-defense moves read as exploitative. This is even though Lily is clothed; there is no contextual necessity for them. Linsey's photographing a dead mouse in a mousetrap presents him as the eccentric artist, painting Madeline's fire engine red lipstick to the mouse's mouth as if it is both lipstick and blood. The Mr. Whippy ice cream truck, that Angela claims is her ex-boyfriend, Daryl, following her, is the narrative's introduction to some kind of direct antagonist for the protagonist Angela. She is presented as an innocent who naturally attracts the attention of multiple suspects. This adds to the mystery of the fire, and even the photo shoot on the beach repeats the idea of an old man who must be moved away from gawking at her exposed breasts. Wincer uses the song "Angela" for the shoot sequence and freeze frames each time a photograph is taken by

Linsey, ending in another of Linsey himself as he shoots.

Captain Rock, the lipsticked effete cabaret singer at the bar Madeline and Angela attend, is given what seems to be unnecessary screen time with no narrative payoff. His extended act presents him subsequently as a Scotsman, a pirate, and later a Mexican and a leather-wearing Elvis-type. He also presumably represents the arty world inhabited by Madeline and Linsey, with Rock's attempt at androgyny perhaps another clue to Madeline's sexual preference. When Madeline grabs the crotch of a man who comes on to Angela, the act seems overly hostile and we wonder whether Madeline's motive is protection or jealousy. The hole that is made in Madeline's car windshield is not explained, and seems to exist as another sign that Angela is being watched. The idea of Madeline later revealed to be Angela's stalker does not help to explain how she could have made the windshield hole when Wincer inter-cuts shots of Madeline watching Angela in the bar with the man when Madeline is not immediately with her. Daryl's accusation of Angela being a lesbian because she is spending time with Madeline is ignorant speculation since Daryl has no knowledge of Madeline otherwise. While Angela jokes that is it true in the light of her rejection of him, the idea allows for the later scene when Madeline makes her advance.

Wincer uses the cry of the cockatoo in Linsey's studio when Angela moves in at night as a shock effect, and the white dress she leaves hanging in her room is shredded when she returns. Angela returns to the bar so we can endure an entire song by Captain Rock, and there she is approached by Elmer. Madeline reveals him to be her husband, but he is a figure that reads to Angela as more antagonistic than Madeline describes. We must also consider the nature of the relationship, since Madeline is a lesbian married to a heterosexual man who perhaps shows no sexual interest in her because he knows it to be fruitless.

The confrontation that occurs in Angela's room when she returns to find that her mother is waiting for her is played like melodrama by Julia Blake, although Thornton's surprising line readings redeem it. We expect Mrs. Bailey to see Angela's ad in the *Cleo* magazine when she leafs through it, but Angela must show her the ad for us to get her mother's reaction. Angela's pride in the ad, despite her being half-naked in the photograph, is a defense against what she states as her mother's perception of her being "ugly, awkward and stupid." Mrs. Bailey's reaction is a disapproving banishment, not far removed from the prior banishment that had led Angela to move into the studio. The plot point of her mother stealing Angela's money is a way to get what Mrs. Bailey had come for.

Angela's nightmare features prefiguring bursts of fire. Wincer uses footage of *Patrick* on television, the moment where Nurse Panicale screams at Patrick in that film, to keep the other people in the studio from hearing Angela's waking scream. Angela's dinner with Elmer shows more of him as an antagonist, when he lies about Madeline telephoning and asks if he can take photographs of Angela to give to Paramount film studios. Wincer has his second funny edit when he cuts from Elmer's "No it's a crazy idea" to the click of Elmer loading the Instamatic camera. This attempt to get Angela topless in the flesh will fail. Her realization is handled without hysteria, in the way her arms are crossed to cover her breasts and her dressing without anger. Wincer's third funny edit is from Elmer's question to Angela, "How you going to get home?" to a shot of a train with Angela crying as an emotional release for her anger.

Wincer uses suspense for the sight of someone in Angela's bed and her reaction to it. She takes a pair of scissors; creating the expectation of a violent encounter. The expectation is also afoot since Daryl had come to the studio while Angela had been with Elmer, and the pig's head that is revealed to be in the bed is another shock surprise. Wincer presents the head from different angles and ends the scene with a close-up of the pig's eye and Angela screaming. The scene where Madeline confesses to Angela that she is a lesbian, although that word is not spoken, by kissing her is interesting in that Wincer shows the pain Madeline experiences in Angela's rejection. This makes the rejection not as severe as it might have been.

Angela sees her younger sister Becky now working at the Pluckett hairdressing shop when Angela goes to get her job back. Angela expresses a silent realization of her replacement, although we sense that she couldn't have gone back anyway. The opportune Fiji assignment has perhaps been aided by Madeline's machinations since the film's end has Madeline speaking of also going to Fiji, but more believably aided by Elmer's agenda.

Angela hears "Greensleeves" as she packs to leave the studio. This song is associated in Australian culture as indicating the proximity of a Mr. Whippy ice cream truck, and the expectation of Daryl driving it, even though neither he nor the truck is seen. Wincer shows us a photograph of Daryl in Angela's room on the left side of the frame as she is seen going down stairs from the attic on the right of the frame. The fact of her having such a photo suggests ambivalence in her feelings toward him. Daryl is only seen once for the chase sequence, which is mostly Angela running. The expectation that he will appear when she is in a telephone booth is only partly met when the truck drives past. Elmer volunteers to order a taxi to bring Angela to his house, which she declines, and it is a surprise when he is at his office to meet her. However, the office provides the reveal of the room where the charred body will be found, since it has multiple images of Angela's advertisement on the walls and floor. It is acceptable that the fire would have destroyed the ones on the floor, so that is why they aren't visible in the opening scene.

The scene confirms Elmer as a man obsessed with Angela and a dangerous antagonist. Now his desire to take her naked photograph is reinforced with a fatal threat, by his starting a fire which ironically will kill him and not Angela. She is spared the act of removing her bra and skirt by the arrival of Daryl, although being behind a bolted door makes him powerless to help her. The struggle between Angela and Daryl with the gasoline gets them equally doused. This creates an ambiguous expectation that either may be burned to become the charred body. Once Elmer catches fire the expectation is met that he will be the charred one. Angela's entrapment is easily solved by her unbolting the door once she protects her hand from touching the heated object, and Wincer repeats the prologue's street scenes from Angela and Daryl's point of view.

Daryl's character experiences ambiguities when he stops her from leaving him, and denies being the one who placed the pig's head in her bed. The Mr. Whippy truck shown being driven away from the fire gets a payoff when it runs into Daryl. Clearly he is not the driver and the crushing of his body is the only genuine bloody horror death of the film, though the gore factor matches the gruesomeness of the charred body. With Elmer and Daryl removed from the narrative, the fact that the driver is shown to be Madeline is not a surprise, since we really don't expect it to have been Pluckett or Linsey, the only other possibilities. However what is a surprise — and perhaps the most inexplicable moment in the film — is Angela's non-reaction to Madeline's reveal and Angela's willingness to go with her at the end.

Simon Wincer was a television director making his first feature with *Snapshot*; it was his only horror title. Producer Antony I. Ginnane would go on to produce the Australian horror title *Thirst* (1979), also executive produced by William Fayman. *Snapshot* was the first film made by associate producer Barbi Taylor, who would also perform the same duties on *Thirst*, and the first title by F.G. Film Productions which would also make *Thirst*. Co-screenwriter Everett de Roche wrote the screenplay for the Australian horror title *Roadgames* (1981).

Greek born actress Chantal Contouri had made her film debut in a supporting role in the comedy *Barry McKenzie Holds His Own* (1974). After appearing in more supporting roles and on television, she was top-billed in *Snapshot*, although Sigrid Thornton has the starring role. Contouri would go on to play the lead in *Thirst*. After working in television, Thornton made her film debut in a supporting role in *The F.J. Holden* (1977). After more supporting roles she scored the lead in *Snapshot* at age 19, the same age as her character. Thornton would go on to play leads in *Neil Lynne* (1985), the crime dramas *Slate, Wyn and Me* (1987) and *Whipping Boy* (1996), and the thriller *The Pact* (2002), but she would not make another horror movie.

Release

Australia June 1, 1979, with the tagline "Murder may be her only escape from terror." U.S.A., October 1980, with the tagline "They thought it was over but the real horror began ... the day after Halloween," although the film has nothing to do with Halloween.

Reviews

"A very minor effort.... Apart from Sigrid Thornton, who is very appealing, the cast is poor, with Chantal Contouri disastrously so as a lesbian. Melbourne locations are ingeniously used but Wincer is so busy stuffing red herrings into the very weak plot that he loses all suspense and sense of narrative direction."— David Stratton, *The Last New Wave*

"A patchy suspense film that suffers from predictability as well as a loose plot line. The last scene provides the only real surprise, but it's a long haul through the film for a little twist at the end."— William K. Halliwell, *The Filmgoer's Guide to Australian Films*

"This Australian thriller doesn't quite know what it wants to be when it grows up: two parts *Eyes of Laura Mars*, one part wannabe slasher. Still, [it] has some interesting vibes to recommend it, including a memorable (at times, lively) score."— *The Terror Trap*

"While the audience is intermittently titillated by Sigrid Thornton's rather gorgeous breasts, a few choice slices of bitchy dialogue and a number of nasty moments ... the actions of the players appear superficial and staged, while the 'thrilling' aspects seem contrived and formulaic."— Robert Winter, *Digital Retribution*, June 5, 2007

"[A] strange novelty."— John Stanley, *Creature Features*

AWARDS

Sigrid Thornton was nominated for the 1979 Best Actress Australian Film Institute (AFI) award.

DVD

Released by Platinum Disc on November 26, 2002.

Thirst

F.G. Film Productions, 1979

CREDITS: *Director:* Rod Hardy; *Producer:* Antony I. Ginnane; *Executive Producer:* William Fayman; *Associate Producer:* Barbi Taylor; *Screenplay:* John Pinkney; *Photography:* Vincent Monton; *Editor:* Philip Reid; *Music:* Brian May; *Art Director:* Jon Dowding; *Sound:* Paul Clark; *Makeup and Hair:* Jose L. Perez; *Wardrobe:* Aphrodite; *Special Effects:* Conrad C. Rothmann, Chris Murray. Color, 93 minutes. Filmed on location in Eltham and the Botanic Gardens, Melbourne, Victoria, from January 25 to February 1979.

CAST: Chantal Contouri (Kate Davis); Shirley Cameron (Mrs. Barker); Max Phipps (Mr. Hodge); Henry Silva (Dr. Gauss); Rod Mullinar (Derek Whitelaw); Amanda Muggleton (Martha Pearson); Robert Thompson (Sean); Rosie Sturgess (Lori); David Hemmings (Dr. Eric Fraser); Walter Pym (Ditcher); Lulu Pinkus, Yvette Rees (Nurses); Chris Milne (David); Jacqui Gordon (Leah); Val Christensen (Toni); Glenys O'Brien (Guide); Ben Nightingale (Tourist Driver); Stephan Clark (Barman); Stewart Faichney, David Vella (Security Men); Paddy Burnet (Blue Rinse Lady); Vicki Andonopoulos (The Child Kate).

SYNOPSIS

The Hyma Brotherhood believes that advertising agency executive Kate Davis is an ancestral vampire baroness and kidnaps her to keep her at their Q.A.S.T.A. dairy farm. Since Kate is repulsed by the cult, they put her through programming and indoctrination. This ultimately leads her to a ceremony where she satisfies her supposedly inherited and instinctive "thirst" by feeding from the blood of one the farm's "blood cows." She is released as the final test to see if she will feed in the outside world.

Kate does feed from Martha Pearson, the co-worker who visits her. However, she stops before feeding from her architect boyfriend, Derek. The Brotherhood recaptures Kate, with Derek, but against the wishes of the other members. Dr. Eric Fraser takes her to his retreat, where he has bled Derek and feeds from her. Kate succumbs to Eric's attack, telling him that she "is one of them." A voiceover tells us that she has married Mr. Hodge in order to protect the ancestral heritage.

NOTES

This is a well-directed tale of vampires that features a mix of the themes of the horror of personality and the malevolent supernatural being. The film is notable for a good performance by Chantal Contouri that presents her equally beautifully and unflatteringly. The narrative has its share of genre silliness, and an obtrusive score. Director Rod Hardy uses the postmodern devices of expressionist camera angles, subjective camera as point of view, freeze frames, and slow motion. However, he also elevates the treatment with ambiguity and not meeting conventional expectations. There is a nine minute sequence of suspense with an attack of an unseen threat, and some Grand Guignol effects. Since the presumption is made that once victims are bled they die, the film qualifies as a horror title, although the treatment lacks the successive victimology of other films.

Under the opening credits we are shown extreme close-ups of Kate's eyes as she awakens. Her hands are shown clutching the interior of the open coffin she is in which is surrounded by lit candles, and tears run down her face. She sits up and screams, and the image is freeze-framed for the film's title, for which the lettering changes from white to blood red.

Kate's hysteria at being locked into the tomb and her lack of fear of the sunlight that comes through

Poster for *Thirst* (1979).

though the cat will not appear again in the narrative. After she is kidnapped, the nurse that serves her a mug of warm blood begins the repeated use of the mug to get Kate to drink blood. When the voiceovers from the credit sequence are heard they accompany video surveillance footage of Kate in the tomb, although she is seen still as if paralyzed by her anxiety.

The first scene of one of the "blood cows" being bled is gruesome because of the largeness of the device that connects to Leah's neck to drain the blood. The sound of the blood dropping into jars, the sadistic smile on the face of the nurse who controls the device and Leah frothing from the mouth when she is bled add to the gruesomeness.

When blood cows are ordered into a van to be taken to the bleeding processing station, their reflection is first shown in the window pane of the van door as they advance. The cows' easy compliance is presumably based on their weakened state as research and processing victims. We don't learn where the farm has obtained the cows. Apart from Leah and her friend David, who becomes the later ceremonial bleeding victim for Kate, the other cows are presented as mindless ciphers, and they are described as zombies in the DVD commentary.

a hole in the wall suggest that she is not the vampire that the coffin implies. Voiceovers that will be heard later in a dialogue scene transition us to a flashback of the pre-prisoner Kate. A shot of a fireplace shows Kate and Derek sitting and facing each other out of focus, and they become in focus as they move toward a kiss. As with a later sex scene and a scene of Kate in the shower, the director does not use the nudity of the actors for exploitation. He also does not reveal it even when there is a context for nudity, as with the shower. On the DVD audio commentary Hardy remarks that he had wanted to include nudity when Kate and Derek have sex by the lake, and to have the blood cows on the altar to be nude.

Kate's black cat pushing a carton of milk onto the floor because it is hungry is paid off when Kate sees that the contents are blood and not milk. This is later explained by the carton being a product of the blood dairy farm. The fact of the cult being able to break into Kate's house to kidnap her also suggests that they have planted the carton in her refrigerator to start her "thirst." The cat hissing at Kate when she tastes the blood on her finger is some sort of supernatural reaction from a black cat, al-

The multiple bleedings where cows lay side by side is aided by the sound of classical music. The scream of one female cow, who pulls away from being bled, reminds us of the pain involved in what is happening to these poor people. When Kate escapes from the farm, the expectation is created that she will be caught, and the narrative teases out this expectation to eventual fruition. She gets away with ease seemingly unobserved and unpursued, but is stopped by a wire fence which she follows around to a conveniently open gate. The gate's guard seems to finally notice her, although he does not begin an immediate chase, which allows her to go to the nearby research poultry farm. The farmer is mute to her request for his help, perhaps an indication of his aged senility, although he is heard to yell when his hand is caught in the door of the truck that Kate attempts to steal. This moment is presented as an accident on her part rather than a deliberate act of careless selfishness. Kate's drive suggests that she may be able to escape, though when the truck stops it becomes a device for frustrated suspense, since pursuit is inevitable.

The narrative uses five oncoming cars to suggest

that each is a threat to her. Four are shown to be irrelevant and the fifth meets the expectation of her re-capture. Although not as long a sequence as the ones on the lake or the set piece in the room where Kate is threatened by an unseen menace, this sequence allows Hardy to toy with our expectations. It also allows the narrative to employ the conventions of suspense, which include her stalled truck, her refilling the gas tank, which still doesn't make the truck start, and her feared response to the succession of passing cars. The second car carries two black passengers which we only later realize are international guests of the forthcoming festival to be held by The Brotherhood, although they do not provide a threat to Kate. The approach of the third car is presented in a long shot so that the audience sees it in the distance before Kate does. The occupants of the fifth car are initially concealed and then revealed to be the cult leaders. Mrs. Barker gets a laugh from her comment about how nice it is for Kate to be on her way to greet their convoy, something we assume Mrs. Barker knows to be a fiction.

The opening ceremony of the festival presents a hag who feeds from a blood cow lying on an altar. The hag's eyes appearing red before she bites in to the neck of the victim is a phenomenon that will be repeated with Kate's ceremony, before Kate bites Martha, and before Dr. Fraser bites Kate. The hag feeding from a younger woman symbolizes the supposed supernatural rejuvenating powers of drinking blood, with the hag the only older vampire shown in the narrative. The farmer, Mr. Dichter, seemingly being bled as a punishment for aiding Kate's attempted getaway is a shock effect, and a surprise given that blood of his age might not be wanted. After Kate's effort to escape, her being drugged as the next step in her indoctrination allows her to be seen with a still face but heard in a panicked voice. The light distorted image of Mrs. Barker is used as Kate's point of view.

The drugged state presents the first of Kate's visions, assumed to be her memory of herself with Derek at a lake, although in a way that she hadn't originally. The idyllic picnic gets a laugh exchange when Kate says, "I've got a headache and my arm stings." This no doubt refers to the real effects of the drug injection she has been given. Derek replies, "Well I wouldn't blame an ant for having a bite of you." After Derek's face has been shown, he is then positioned with his back to the camera and this man's different hair clues us into the fact that he is not Derek. We assume that the man is Hodge, since he has previously expressed his need to marry Kate. But this reveal is delayed until after she bites into what appears to be a cooked chicken leg. Her bite results in the flesh bleeding. Hardy holds on a long close-up reaction shot of Chantal Contouri before she and we see that the man is actually Hodge.

Kate's jump into the lake utilizes slow motion, and her appearing outside the gates of her house creates the expectation that she has escaped the farm. It will later become evident this is merely more of her drugged visions, something which the apparent betrayal by her servant, Lori, suggests.

Kate's shower in blood is a grand guignol sequence, but Kate is initially unaware of the blood coming from the shower head. The flashback which reveals Kate as a five-year-old child in a boarding school is presumably more memory. Hardy transitions back and forth, perhaps too frequently, between the child and the adult Kate. Echoed voices, whispers, and the voiceover of Mrs. Barker are used with inter-cuts of the Kate's walking around the house. Hardy provides a shock effect of Lori with a bloodied face and a missing eyeball discovered by the adult Kate. A banging which Kate investigates presents her as a conventional Woman in Peril investigating a noise. The raised candlestick holder that she brandishes as a weapon and which burns her hand is an irrational phenomenon that clues us, and should tell Kate, that what she is experiencing is not real. Presumably her drugged state stops her from being rational.

Animal noises introduce the sequence that can be considered Hardy's haunted house room set piece. The unseen menace attempts to break through a door, the wall pushes in to follow Kate's movement, a chandelier shakes, and books fall from a bookcase. The room shakes and furniture moves independently, and the mug of blood appears in Kate's hand in a camera reveal. As if aware of the same intent to make her drink the blood, Kate pours it out of the mug, her act accompanied by a heavenly choir. Hardy creates a shock effect when Kate opens curtains to reveal her own mirrored reflection rather than what we presume should be a view of outside the house. A walled mirror shows Kate's distorted image; the glass shattering is another shock effect. The animal noises and the attempt to break through the door resumes until Kate backs away and finds another mug of blood. She drinks, her resistance presumably worn down by fear. Kate drinking the blood stops the door breakage, and the room is flooded with light. The screen goes white and then video surveillance footage shows Kate being observed. She pathetically licks blood off the wall she faces, a sign of the apparent victory of The Brotherhood in their reprogramming and indoctrination of her.

At the ceremony for Kate, which is attended by the festival guests, she wears a shimmery pink gown. She is given fangs and is led to the blood cow David on the altar as her feeding victim. She faints, which suggests that she is not going to be able to feed. After an incision is made into David's neck by Hodge to allow blood to spurt, Kate's eyes go red and she feeds. Mrs. Barker's voiceover tells us that Kate's release is part of her ongoing management to see if she is able to feed in the outside world.

There is the suggestion that all that Kate has experienced is merely a dream with the mug in her kitchen. However, this suggestion will be nullified when we see Kate spit out the milk from a carton and ultimately feed from Martha after Kate is shown to be wearing the fangs and after her eyes go red. The blood smear on the letter that Martha has been typing and the blood drops that fall from Martha's neck onto her legs add to the grisliness and messiness of the attack. Kate awakening screaming from an unseen nightmare is another suggestion that perhaps again she is dreaming all this, although again this idea is nullified when she bites Derek, who is in bed with her. Kate's failure to properly feed from Derek provides the comic entrance of people we assume to be from the Brotherhood to take both of them back to the farm.

Dr. Fraser's previous disagreement with the other cult leaders in their treatment of Kate creates the expectation that he will help her. The viewer knows of Dr. Fraser's plan to take Derek to his retreat but doesn't see Fraser take Derek there, a curious absence from the narrative.

The confrontation between Mrs. Barker and Dr. Fraser results in a marvelous grand guignol effect. Her fall into the vat of blood seems to occur too easily, and close-ups of Fraser suggest that he plans to help her out of it. Hardy delays the reveal of her whereabouts after Fraser no longer sees her in the vat. We don't know if she has drowned or has been able to get out, though when Fraser is informed of a blockage in the vat by a farm factory technician we fear the worst. Dr. Gauss's pursuit of Fraser and Kate in the helicopter provides for the obvious use of a body double when Gauss hangs onto the skids of the flying chopper. Gauss's fall from the skids and landing onto power lines gives him his own grand guignol electrocution. Hardy has a shot of the burned corpse after it falls through the power lines. It is after this hideous sight that Mrs. Barker's corpse is revealed via a glass window at the base of the vat. She has presumably drowned. Hodge's smile is a surprise and troubling, although it could be that he just didn't like her and is pleased by her fate.

The reveal of Fraser's retreat as a dungeon, where a rat is on a step, creates an expectation that Derek and Kate are not safe. This expectation is met by the sight of Derek being bled. We also fear that Fraser will entrap Kate, despite her demands that he release Derek from the feeder. A shot of the back of her head shown to be nuzzling Derek's neck, not the side he was being bled from, is held to present her as unaware of Fraser's intention. He is shown with his back to the camera, then turning to reveal fangs and red eyes. She does not see Fraser's advance. Derek does but he is presumably too weakened to warn her. When Kate sees Fraser, she tells him, "Let me be one of you. I am one of you." The camera pans around them to show his hesitation. His biting of her and the voiceover of dialogue between Fraser and Hodge, in a scene we don't see, repeats the line "I am one of you" and white light. The suggestion is made that Kate has not died like the other people blood fed, since she has married Hodge. There is a last shot of Derek, before the moment between Kate and Fraser, which definitely suggests that he has died. And perhaps this is the reason why Kate is prepared to give herself to Fraser, The Brotherhood, and her ancestral destiny.

The DVD commentary states that George Miller was the original director but became unavailable. Screenwriter John Pinkney had taken the idea of Kate's vampire ancestor, Elizabeth Bathory, from the film *Les levres rouges*, aka *Daughter of Darkness* (1971). Reportedly in the documentary *Not Quite Hollywood*, Henry Silva was unable to read his lines without wearing spectacles, which perhaps explains why he has so few lines in *Thirst*. The comment is made that when he does speak, he is the only be-spectled vampire in the history of cinema.

Rod Hardy made his film debut with *Thirst* and has not made another Australian horror title to date. Producer Antony I. Ginnane had previously produced the Australian horror film *Snapshot* with executive producer William Fayman. They would go on to produce and executive produce the Australian horror film *The Survivor*. Associate producer Barbi Taylor had previously associate produced *Snapshot* and would go on to co-produce the Australian horror title *Roadgames*. The film was the second for the F.G. Film Productions after *Snapshot*, and it would go on to make the Australian horror movie *Dark Age*. Chantal Contouri had played a supporting role in *Snapshot*, and after *Thirst* worked in television and played supporting film roles. She essayed the lead in the thriller *Offspring* (1996) which has been her last leading film role to date.

American Henry Silva had made his film debut

in an uncredited minor role in the western *Viva Zapata!* (1952). After appearing in more supporting film roles and on television, he essayed the lead and title character in the crime drama *Johnny Cool* (1963). After playing the title character in the mystery *The Return of Mr. Moto* (1965), Silva enjoyed leads in the Italian titles *Assassination* (1967), the war action *Probabilita zero*, aka *Heroes Never Die* (1969), and the crime drama *Quella carogna dell'ispettore Sterling*, aka *Frame Up* (1969). In the 1970s the actor played the lead in the French actioner *L'insolent*, aka *Deadly Sting* (1973), and the Italian crime dramas *Il boss*, aka *Murder Inferno* (1973), *Quelli che contano*, aka *Cry of a Prostitute* (1974), *Kidnap* (1974), *Manhunt in the City* (1975), and the Hong Kong actioner *Woo fook*, aka *Foxbat* (1977). After *Thirst*, Silva returned to lead roles in the thriller *Trapped* (1982), the Italian *The Violent Breed* (1984) and *Killer vs. Killers* (1985), followed by supporting film roles.

David Hemmings made his debut as a child in a minor role in the British film *The Rainbow Jacket* (1954) and continued in supporting and television roles until he scored the lead in the musical *Be My Guest* (1965). He made the transition to adult roles and essayed the lead in the war drama *The Long Day's Dying* (1968), a double role in the comedy *The Best House in London* (1969), and the title role in the historical drama *Alfred the Great* (1969). In the 1970s the actor was the lead in the romantic crime drama *The Walking Stick* (1970), the mystery *Fragment of Fear* (1970), the thriller *Unman, Wittering and Zigo* (1971), the horror title *Voices* (1973), the Spanish thriller *No es nada, mama, solo un juego*, aka *Beyond Erotica* (1974), and the horror title *Deep Red* (1975). With his leading man days seemingly behind him, Hemmings turned to directing with *Just a Gigolo* (1978), and he would go on to direct the Australian horror movie *The Survivor*. After *Thirst*, the actor was top-billed in the crime drama *Beyond Reasonable Doubt* (1980), but was seen in supporting film roles and on television before his death in 2003.

RELEASE

Australia on September 28, 1979, and USA September 29, 1979, with the taglines "Surrender to an unholy insatiable evil," and "This ancient evil is now a modern industry."

REVIEWS

"Chantouri is the weakest element in an otherwise rather successful — if none too ambitious — modern vampire tale. There is some baleful black humor; and several well-timed surprises, but David Hemmings seems to be slumming as the leader of the cult."— David Stratton, *The Last New Wave*

"I would recommend *Thirst* to readers who like off beat horror flicks.... There's some good concepts going down, but unfortunately they are muddied by poor script development and a movie that loses touch with what it is trying to achieve.... An okay vampire flick that takes itself way to seriously."— Jeff Ritchie, *ScaryMinds*

"A stylish and effective thriller. Don't let the fact that it's a bit predictable and deliberately paced thriller throw you off. Just let yourself go with the flow and dig in."— Lawrence P. Raffel, *Monsters at Play*

"This film takes an intelligent and refreshing approach to the contemporary vampire genre.... Contouri gives a brilliant performance in a very demanding role and is believable in every scene she does. Second billed David Hemmings is so low key it is like he is hardly there."— Mark Nichols, *Digital Retribution*, November 17, 2006

"Above average Australian vampire tale which has a compelling, perverse nature in its bite.... Henry Silva has a great death and David Hemmings is outstanding in a surprise-twist role. Well directed.... Will quench your need for a good horror movie."— John Stanley, *Creature Features*

DVD

Released by Elite Entertainment on February 4, 2003. Special Edition DVD released by Synapse Films on October 28, 2008. Umbrella Entertainment (Australia) released October 1, 2008.

Nightmares

Bioscope/John Lamond Motion Picture Enterprises Production, 1980 [aka *Stage Fright*; *Nightmare on the Street*]

CREDITS: *Director:* John Lamond; *Producers:* John Lamond, Colin Eggleston; *Associate Producer:* Michael Hirsch; *Screenplay:* Colin Eggleston, from an original idea by John Lamond and John-Michael Howson; *Photography:* Garry Wapshott; *Editor:* Colin Eggleston; *Music:* Brian May; *Sound:* John Phillips; *Art Director:* Paul Jones; *Makeup:* Margaret Archman; *Wardrobe:* Aphrodite Kondos, Jan Barkell; *Special Effects:* Conrad Rothmann. Color, 80–90 minutes. Filmed in the Princess Theatre, Palais Theatre, and the National Theatre, Melbourne.

CAST: Jenny Neumann (Helen Selleck); Gary Sweet (Terry Besanko); Nina Landis (Judy); Max Phipps (George D'alberg, aka The Director); John-Michael Howson (Bennett Collingswood, aka The Critic); Briony Behets (Angela); Maureen Edwards (Mother); Sue Jones (Fay); Jennie Lamond (Young Cathy); Adele Lewin (Sue); Edmund Pegge (Bruce); Peter Tulloch (Brian); Bryon Williams (Father); Malcolm Steed (Doctor); Denise Peterson (Bad Auditionee); Tania Uren (Nurse); John Harris (Policeman No. 1); Gary Day (Policeman No. 2); Joy Westmore (Matron); Lise Rodgers (Mousy Auditionee); Doug Bowles (Baby Sitter); Rossana Zuanetti (Girl in Lane); Gene Van Dam (Boy in Lane); Angela Menzies-Wills (Lover in Bed).

SYNOPSIS

In 1963 the child Cathy Selleck is a witness to her mother having sex with a man who is presumably not her father. She inadvertently kills her mother by dragging her over the glass of a car accident. Cathy is traumatized by the accident, and as an adult now calling herself Helen, she has nightmares and visions. She auditions for and is cast in a theater production. She begins a romantic relationship with fellow actor Terry but withholds sex from him. A local murderer slashes their victims with shards of broken glass. The members of the company also begin to fall prey, people that happen to cross Helen. After a critic and the director are killed, Helen reveals that she is responsible. A vision she has motivates Helen to slash Terry's throat after they have made love. We then see she is to audition for a new project.

NOTES

A tiresome and uninspired film featuring the theme of horror of personality, this effort by John D. Lamond overuses score and a subjective camera for point of view. The narrative boasts a few amusing lines, and some expectations are not met. The trauma of the protagonist is not aided by empathy because of the bad performance of Jenny Neumann, an American import presumably cast for the international marketing of the film. Lamond's employment of repeated blackouts and extreme long shots is particularly perplexing, with other postmodern effects like expressionist camera angles, flash cuts, and a freeze frame used. The exploitative nudity is hardly a surprise given the soft-core nature of the director's prior titles. While the treatment has more suspense than shock, the level of violence is bloody without being particularly gruesome, although an attack cut to a male victim's penis matches the cuts made to the breasts of his female companion.

The film begins with a prologue that is later revealed to be Helen's nightmare of memory, with the convention that she sees herself. A title card reads January 26, 1963, and the child Cathy sees her mother naked and having sex on a bed with a man we presume is not her father. A second title card reads February 23, 1963, and a foreshadowing storm of rain and thunder precedes the car accident that kills the mother. Cathy is blamed for the death when she drags her mother back onto the broken glass of the smashed windshield. The accident occurs because the mother is distracted by the man who slides his hand into her crotch and by turning around in response to Cathy's cry to him of "Leave my mother alone." Her use of "my mother" confirms that the man is not her father. Lamond presents the couple having sex with some restraint, although later he will be more exploitative. The blood from the mother's cut neck is the film's first gore.

Cathy is seen in close-up under the credits with blood on her face, as the lights of the presumed ambulance or police car attending the accident are reflected on her and voices are heard. While this is a low budget device, it is also an effective suggestion, with a voice telling us that the mother's death was due to being dragged back over glass rather than being killed in the car's collision. Broken glass will repeatedly feature in the narrative as the weapon of choice of Helen. Lamond provides an extreme close-up of the eyes of the child. Blackouts are used in the following hospital scene. Since Cathy has not been injured in the accident, there is no reason for her to be losing consciousness; expressionist camera angles give Cathy's point of view.

In a subsequent scene, a man we presume to be her father moves to touch her in comfort. Cathy jabs his face with a shard of broken glass, a payoff to her throwing a glass at him and then pushing him away from her. The act brings on a montage of images of a subjective camera. We see Cathy running outside, the man hitting her, breaking glass, a vision of her mother and a man embracing, and repeated flash-cuts to an extreme close-up of Cathy's eyes. These are accompanied by the sound of the siren, and an extreme close-up of an adult mouth screaming reveals Helen awakening from a nightmare.

A third title card reads February 23, The Present. The year is not given, but the fact that it is the same date as the second title card must be significant, perhaps adding to the trauma that motivates Helen's murderous rampage. No rationale is given for Helen's American accent, apart from the actress playing her being American, which is sloppy detail in an Australian movie. The device of the sound of breathing with the subjective camera is first utilized for a vision of a male and female in daylight, with the woman perhaps being Helen's mother, to justify Helen's hostility towards sexual behavior. The breathing is ambiguous since it can be interpreted as both the distress and the excitement of the stalker, as well the clichéd representation of an antagonist.

The subjective camera switches to a couple in an alley at night kissing. Although Lamond has the man and woman both unclothed, his exposure of the woman's breasts, given the context of them having sex, is given preference to exposing the man. The beer bottle the man discards is paid off when a gloved hand breaks it for a shard of glass. It is raised and cuts the woman's breast and the man's penis, with the latter cut suggested rather than shown. The naked woman flees and is chased and cut again, with the subjective camera retreating and a blackout used for time transition. If we are supposed to believe that Helen commits the murders under the guise of her antagonistic other self, Cathy, the blackouts may represent a change of mental state. This may also explain Helen's visions of the murders with no memory of them. Helen's daylight visions are shown on her date with Terry, although here they are of the couple having sex on the bed and the man's hand on the mother's leg in the car from the prologue.

Helen's next vision comes in the play's rehearsal — a play where Helen appears to have no lines based on the excerpts we see of the live performance — when The Director asks her to think of grief. We see her point of view from the hospital scene and the slashed woman in the alley, the latter suggesting that she is the killer who is yet to be identified. Helen's crying and laughing response to the visions gets a funny payoff when she is slapped by a woman whom Helen abuses and the woman comments, "She's mad." After an incident when talking to Terry, Helen again has a vision of the man's hand on her mother's leg in the car. This is perhaps in response to Terry as a sexual presence, but Lamond creates an expectation that is not met.

The breathing and subjective camera is used to suggest the killer is backstage at the theater, but there is no attack. When Helen sees Angela kiss Terry at the bar in a way we see is harmless, Helen has a vision of her mother and the man having sex on the bed. A motivation of jealousy is established to be paid off later with Angela's murder. Judy's entrance to the bar gets a laugh. She says "Hello, darling," to Helen, who walks past her to leave and ignores her. Judy responds sarcastically with what she thinks Helen should say: "Sorry, darling. Got to rush. Can't stay to talk."

Terry goes after Helen and hears what appears to be her talking to herself in her apartment. Someone passes him on the way out of her apartment whom he does not recognize. He knocks on Helen's door and gets no answer. All this creates expectation that will prove to be misleading. Helen does not live with anyone else, so the person that passed Terry has to be her, though why he doesn't recognize her is a mystery. Helen will be shown to be the killer, and her talking to herself as "Cathy" demonstrates her supposed schizophrenic mental state.

The Director's rant at Judy in rehearsal provides some humor when he describes her as 'an actress' big brown freckle," which is code for arsehole, though the nature of the play that is being performed would also seem to justify Judy's difficulties with it. The Director tells her, "The literal meaning of the words in this piece is unimportant. The beauty and drama is contained in the rhythm and the appesit nature of the juxtaposition of the words. That, and the comedy of death." The abstract nature of the play described, however, is not demonstrated in what we see performed live, which reads as a period comedy of manners.

The breathing and subjective camera are again seen in the theater, but again to no violent result. It returns before a shot of Angela and creates the expectation that she will be attacked. After a shock effect where Bruce appears wearing a mask for her to reject his romantic advance, the expectation is met after the light above her goes out. Angela going to the power box to investigate presents her as a Woman in Peril, recalling Briony Behet's same behavior in *Long Weekend* and prefiguring her torment in *Cassandra*. The subjective camera advance on her is followed by the smashing of a glass window to give Helen a shard and cues Angela to the threat.

This attack features the antagonist's laugh at Angela's attempt to open a locked door. The second attack after Angela crawls wounded and moans adds sadism to the violence. Angela's attempt to escape as she is wounded will be repeated in the attack on The Critic, with Helen running in the rain after Angela's attack to go back to her apartment being ambiguous. Are we to make the connection between the killer and Helen here, or is this Helen in an unconnected coincidence? The rain adds some resonance to the preceding violence, as if it washes away the blood that surely would have touched her. After the death of Judy we see that Helen wears a coat to protect herself from splashback and perhaps to conceal her identity.

On opening night the subjective camera is used again with no result, although a dropped painting on the set which breaks the glass of the frame gives Helen a vision of the murder of Angela. Backstage during the performance Helen's perspective of the dialogue becomes echoed voices, and light flashes lead to a vision of the child Cathy. When The Director walks onto the stage to receive applause after the performance, his pomposity is rewarded by his head being hit by the falling curtain. When the stage manager apologizes and tells him, "I've never been a stage manager before," he replies, "And you never will again." The breathing and subjective camera is again shown without result and is perhaps stopped by Terry calling for Helen, with the camera then showing an objective shot of her appearance in frame.

The walking stick of The Critic adds a vulnerability to his otherwise nasty presentation, and the physical weakness will allow him to become another victim of the killer. Why he is attacked by Helen is also ambiguous since she is the only one of the cast who gets a good review (perhaps because Helen isn't required to speak). Additionally, the issue of The Critic's sexual preference has ambiguity. This is in spite of him being repeatedly described as an "old queen" when he caresses Helen's breast at the after-party, but then touches and tries to kiss Bruce to show his willingness to have sex with him. Helen is shown dreaming after the murder of The Critic, which she has visions of, creating doubt that she is the killer. When she goes to Terry's house — to sleep with him but not have sex — the sound of breaking glass and laughing in Helen's apartment continues the idea that someone else is in there. This moment will be paid off later when Terry visits and sees the broken glass and a bloody shard.

The breathing and subjective camera is used again backstage with no result. The fact of Helen not being with the rest of the cast for The Director's tirade against Judy suggests it is Helen who watches from the point of view of the catwalk. The tirade provides more humor when he says, "Words fail me, as they failed you last night. Your most fervent admirer, had you had one, would have been disgusted."

Helen telling Terry, "I tried to get rid of her. She'll be back and I won't be able to stop her again," can be interpreted two ways — there is another person with Helen who is the killer, or Helen is schizophrenic. The shock to Fay from Bruce revealed to be hiding in the wardrobe demonstrates that he is not the killer because the breathing does not accompany his appearance. It is when the breathing occurs with the subjective camera that we know the killer is after Fay, for reasons unknown. Lamond has a sex scene between Fay and Bruce in the wardrobe room which precedes the attack where both actors are naked as equal exploitation. Fay will prove to be the more resilient of the two, and this allows Lamond to have her be chased naked in the room and then in the street. When the killer enters the room as a subjective camera, a lamp is raised to shine on the couple and to hide Helen's identity.

When Fay is slashed by the killer in the street, Lamond cuts to a shot of the audience laughing at the play. When Fay falls in the street, presumed dead, her blood washes into the rain. Blood also drips from the shard that Helen strikes into the back of The Director's seat when he is attacked during the performance. Fay returns to the wardrobe room to collapse and die, and there is a shot of hands washing blood from them. The Director's murder is given a funny line when the couple has to get past his occupied seat to get to the aisle. Thinking him asleep, the man comments, "He's dead to the world."

The breathing and subjective camera prefigure Judy finding Fay's and Bruce's bodies in the wardrobe room; it is the first time bodies are discovered by someone else. Her chase features inconsistent camerawork, mixing objective shots of Judy with the subjective. Despite being slashed, Judy's death is caused by her being pushed from the catwalk, and it is at Judy's body that Helen appears, removing her coat so that we presume she is the killer.

We assume that Helen now has sex with Terry, although Lamond doesn't show it, when we see them in bed together. It is her vision of a shard of glass that makes Helen break a mirror, take a shard from it and drive it into Terry's neck. Lamond records this in a freeze-frame and uses an echo on Terry's scream. A radio news report has Terry blamed for the killings and Helen to have claimed to have killed him in self-defense, with footage of the murders repeated. While the idea of Terry being the killer is an intriguing one, the narrative provides no rationale for him. Ultimately it is a red herring and further evidence of Helen's ability to get away with murder. The film ends with Helen at another audition, so we can presume that the cycle is about to begin again; perhaps Lamond was hoping for a sequel. One was never made.

In the documentary *Not Quite Hollywood*, Lamond says the film was shot in 24 days and that he took the idea of the subjective camera from *Halloween*. "I thought if I'm going to make a gutsy horror film, there's no point in being subtle, and I thought I'd like to slash the bare behind of some bird who'd been screwed in the makeup room. I wanted to make [the film] as gratutuitous as possible. With a film like that you think we've got to have moral justification for doing in the people because the plot's not thick. You've got to make it obvious that they've been caught in the acting of screwing."

Lamond also describes the death of Judy as the gratuitous token non-naked death because Nina Landis refused to strip for the film. He says the actress chose the part of Judy because "she doesn't get killed while screwing." Landis would say, "It's not some of my finest moments on screen and it's a far cry from content which philosophically addresses the human condition and contributes in that way." In the same documentary, John-Michael Howson comments, "I think it's a movie you have to watch when you've had one drink too many or a couple of joints because I don't think it makes sense. John may have written the script but I think he left ten pages in the printer."

The film is the only Australian horror title produced or directed by John Lamond, and made by the John Lamond Motion Picture Enterprises Production and associate producer Michael Hirsch. Producer Colin Eggleston had produced and directed the Australian horror title *Long Weekend*, and he would go on to produce and direct the Australian horror title *Innocent Prey*.

Jenny Neumann made her film debut in a supporting role in the comedy *Swim Team* (1979) and then played the lead in the adventure *Mistress of the Apes* (1979). *Nightmares* was her last leading film role, since she otherwise played supporting parts and worked on television. Gary Sweet made his film debut in *Nightmares* and would go on to appear in the Australian horror title. *The Dreaming*. Nina Landis also made her film debut here, and later appeared in a supporting role in the Australian horror title *Komodo* (1999). John-Michael Howson later appeared in the Australian horror title *Houseboat Horror*.

Release

Australia on October 30, 1980, and United States straight to video with the taglines "Many motion pictures promise you terror but this one is truly frightening" and "Screams of terror ... silenced only by the splintering of glass!"

Reviews

"A slasher-whodunit [that] holds few surprises ... combines a leering fondness of full frontal nudity with a series of particularly nasty knife killings."—David Stratton, *The Avocado Plantation*

"A result of the don't-hide approach is that there is no tension in the film. Equally one knows each potential is certainly done for; maybe Lamond felt the entertainment comes from watching numerous naked bodies get stabbed or castrated.... Most will find the murders quite disturbing, especially since most occur during sex."—Scott Murray, *Oxford Australian Film 1978–1994*

"The film doesn't help itself out by switching between genres as the mood takes it and I was left feeling pretty ambivalent towards it really.... [It] gets a recommendation due to at least some attempts being made at lifting it above the, by 1980, run of the mill horror flicks being released."—Jeff Ritchie, *ScaryMinds*

"A stylish, violent, psycho-sexual assault wrung out of a hamfisted script that really doesn't go anywhere."—Thomas Duke, *Cinema Gonzo*

"A disjointed, slightly bizarre slasher which prides itself on anonymous softcore sex, bumbling chats, and smutty, full-frontal kill scenes.... There's a failed attempt at artsy photography, a classy orchestral soundtrack, and arbitrary tangents which have no bearing on anything."—Joseph A. Ziemba, *Bleeding Skull*, March 27, 2008

DVD

VHS released by VidAmerica in 1983. DVD from Umbrella Entertainment (Australia) released September 1, 2009.

Alison's Birthday

David Hannay Production/Fontana Films, 1981

CREDITS: *Screenplay/Director:* Ian Coughlan; *Producer:* David Hannay; *Executive Producers:* Ric Kabriel, John Sturzaker; *Associate Producer:* Michael Falloon; *Photography:* Brian Bansgrove; *Editor:* Tim Street; *Music:* Brian King, Alan Oloman; *Production Design:* Bob Hilditch; *Art Director:* Lu Kanturek; *Sound:* Phil Judd; *Wardrobe:* Robert Lloyd; *Makeup:* Lesley Lamont-Fisher. Color, 99–117 minutes. Filmed on location in Sydney, New South Wales, at Fontana Films Studios, Turrella and Supreme Studios, Paddington, from January to February 1979.

SONG: "Mirne's Theme" (Ian Coughlan).

CAST: Joanne Samuel (Alison Findlay); Lou Brown (Pete Healey); Bunney Brooke (Jennifer Findlay); John Bluthal (Dean Findlay); Vincent Ball (Dr. Jeremy Lyall); Marge McCrae (Chrissie Willis); Julie Wilson (Maureen Tate); Martin Vaughan (Mr. Martin); Rosalind Speirs (Maggie Carlyle); Robyn Gibbes (Helen McGill); Ian Coughlan (Dave Ducker); Ralph Cotterill (Brian Healey); Marion Johns ("Grandmother" Thorne); George Carden (Druid Leader); Belinda Giblin (Isobel Thorne); Brian Wenzel (Police Sergeant); Bernard Lewis (Michael); Lisa Peers (Sally Brown); Sonia Peat (Hospital Clerk); Eric Oldfield (Priest); Brian Blain ("Uncle" Patrick); Adam Bowen ("Cousin" Richard); Stephen O'Rourke (Detective). Uncredited: David Hannay (Druid).

Synopsis

Alison Findlay is a 16-year-old schoolgirl. She has a Ouija board séance with her friends, Chrissie and Maureen, where the spirit of Alison's father warns her "Don't go 19 birthday." After Chrissie channels the spirit, she is killed by a falling bookcase in the room. A week before Alison's 19th birthday, she is living on the coast but is invited by her Aunt Jenny to visit their Sydney home. Alison travels with her boyfriend, Pete, and stays with the adults who raised her after she was told she became an orphan. They arrange a birthday party for her, yet Alison is frightened by the stone circle she finds in their back yard. She dreams that her relatives are part of a Druid coven, and plans to leave them before the party. Alison is drugged and hypnotized to make her stay, and the police called to arrest Pete, who attempts to help her escape.

Pete learns that Alison's parents were killed in a car crash after their baby was stolen from the hospital where it was born. His occultist friend Sally Brown tells him about the Celtic goddess Mirne who is worshiped by a Druid sect and possesses the body of a young girl every 80 years. They both believe that Alison's aunt and uncle plan to make Alison the next victim of Mirne, who occupies the body of the 103-year-old woman living in Findlay home called "Grandmother" Thorne. Pete returns to the Findlay house to save Alison. However, the demon that has now possessed Alison's body in the staged ceremony on Alison's birthday tricks Pete into discarding the consecrated crucifix he has stolen from a church. Pete is shot dead with the gun he has brought. Alison awakes in the body of "Grandmother" Thorne and sees her 19-year-old self possessed by the demon.

Notes

This is a well-written and well-directed chiller that mixes the horror of personality with the malevolent supernatural being. This tale of a young girl becoming possessed by an ancient Celtic demon also features a narrative which switches the protagonist for nearly half of the running time. While writer-director Ian Coughlan doesn't present any gore, there are two killings and the gothic change of a 19-year-old into a hag of 103. He employs the postmodern techniques of expressionist camera angles and hand-held camerawork, freeze frames, zooms, jump cuts, cross-cutting and point of view. But Coughlan's treatment manages to overcome the silliness in the narrative by providing atmosphere, a sense of impending doom and fatalism, and empathy for the girl who is the victim of evil.

A prologue introduces the first of three title cards telling Alison's age, this one being 16 years, 4 months. The expectation is created that the séance will work; it does, after the Ouija marker fails to move on the first two tries. An extreme close-up of Chrissie's mouth is used for when she speaks as the channeled father of Alison; his warning about her 19th birthday is not justified until much later in the narrative. The death of Chrissie during the storm created by the séance is ambiguous, since we don't understand what force causes the turmoil against the spirit of the father. Perhaps it is because the séance is held at the Findlay house, though the location is not confirmed, and because Chrissie is leader of the action.

The sepia shots of the stone circle and the Findlays' back yard of trees under the credits prefigure the action to take place there later. The blue coloring also prefigures the information that Sally will give Pete that blue is the signature color of the Mirne Druids. The second title card reads, "18 years 11 months 26 days," indicating one week before Alison's 19th birthday. Aunt Jenny's hand seen opening a curtain to watch Alison sitting on a swing in the back yard is a visual clue to Jenny's threat. This horror movie device will be repeated by Jenny when Alison returns to the swing after her exploration of the back yard. An expectation is created for an attack upon Alison in this exploration, which is not met, based on Jenny's warning about snakes. It does allow her to find the stone circle, which is explained by Dean as a miniature Stonehenge built by the house's first owner, said to have been an amateur astronomer.

Alison's shock view of "Grandmother" Thorne is the expectation met of the wheelchair coming into her room as she sleeps, although no attack is forthcoming. The women wearing the same pendant is paid off in the film's climax when the one worn by "Grandmother" is shown to be much larger than Alison's and which helps to differentiate them in the conclusion. Additionally the pattern on the pendant is used by Pete to help Sally define the Druid sect, and by Michael, who writes it on the note he leaves for Pete. Although it is not a shock, the reveal of Dean to be watching Alison and Pete as they talk when Pete brings her home shows that Dean is as controlling as Jenny appeared to be as she watched from the window. A comment from Dean changes him from concerned uncle to threatening antagonist: "Now listen, boy. You're meddling in something you can't begin to understand. My advice to you is to stay well away from this house and from Alison."

Alison's nightmare is presumably a result of the tonic Jenny has fed her. It is a prefiguring dream of exposition where the idea that she sees herself as a movie contrivance is used. Coughlin inter-cuts to the moon as Alison tosses and turns before presenting the Druid ceremony and the shimmery blue optical effect that we take as the appearance of Mirne. He also uses inter-cuts to fire for the possession of Isobel Thorne, who has an Irish accent, although Sally will later say the girl was from Somerset, England. Additionally there are views of "Grandmother," Jenny and Dean and one of Alison. Her echoed laughter and the fast cuts take Alison out of the dream and have her awakened in fear; another horror movie device.

Dr. Jeremy Lyle diagnoses Alison with "nervous exhaustion" for her weakened state, which we attribute to Jenny's tonics, and the expectation is created that he is a Druid, which is met by Pete's discovery that the doctor is not listed in the telephone directory. This investigation by Pete prefigures his research at the library into Alison's parents and his consulting with Sally. It also begins the forty minute part of the narrative which changes him into the protagonist, since he is at the center of the dramatic action while Alison remains in bed. He breaks into the house to take her away, creating the expectation that he will be caught. This is after Alison tells him of her nightmare where she describes "the chanting of a black magic ceremony," and he shines a flashlight on the face of the non-reacting "Grandmother." Lyle and Dean let Pete and Alison pass them after refusing to do so initially. The expectation that they will do something else to stop them is met by Lyle's applying pressure to their neck nerves, akin to what Mr. Spock could do in *Star Trek*, to make them both unconscious.

Coughlan's camera goes out of focus when Alison is drugged then hypnotized by Lyle. She delivers the false information to get Pete arrested, that she has been presumably coached with by Lyle, and Lyle gets to deliver the gothic line "She has a destiny and she must fulfill it." Out on bail, Pete in his car being followed by Michael in another car creates the expectation of Pete being attacked. This is met when he is ambushed by the "swamp zombies." Michael wears blue clothes and drives a blue car, although regrettably Pete also wears all blue. Pete's visit to Sally allows her to provide the information about the sect. Nineteen is Mirne's ritual number, and Alison is considered a special person because she was born at 7 P.M., the 17th hour, and her 19th birthday is to occur on the 19th calendar day of their year. The scene with Pete and Sally also gets a funny exchange concerning Alison being hypnotized by Lyle:

PETE: I didn't think you could hypnotize a person against their will.
SALLY: You can if you go about it the right way.

Pete's visit to the state library results in him finding the birth record for Alison, which shows that she was born to Richard and Daphne (nee Williams) Baker on March 15, 1960. There are also the headlines from newspapers" "Baby disappears from hospital" and "Parents of stolen baby killed, Freak car smash claims lives of tragic couple." The note Michael leaves on Pete's car is "Last warning (underlined). Stay away from Alison," accompanied by the drawn pendant symbol. This seems pathetic and naturally does not sway Pete's intention. The resultant car and foot chase is paid off when Pete follows Michael into a cemetery and is entrapped by the tuxedo-wearing "swamp zombies." The pitchfork that the first one holds will be paid off when it is used to attempt to stab Pete, although the expectation created that Pete will be killed is not met when the lead zombie falls for a trick that results in Pete escaping.

Pete telephoning Sally allows her to provide more information on the sect. Alison was kidnapped from the hospital and raised by members of the coven, and "Grandmother" Thorne is the last incarnation of Isobel Thorne. The scene also shows that he has obtained a gun. Her request that he take a consecrated crucifix with him as protection results in a wordless scene where Pete steals a cross from the wall of a church. He escapes being chased by a priest before he heads back to the Findlay house, where the birthday party ceremony is taking place. "Grandmother" Thorne's room, where Lyle takes the hypnotized Alison, has blue lighting, and thunder is heard for the addition of the horror movie conventional storm.

Coughlan cross-cuts between the ceremony, which has moved to the backyard stone circle, and Pete driving. There is a reprise of a scene of Alison talking about the stone circle as his memory, and the expectation is created that he will save her. The shimmery blue light appears as the spirit of Mirne from the large pendant that "Grandmother" kisses. Alison, awakening from her hypnotized trance when Pete wards off the coven with the cross, continues the expectation that she will be rescued. However, his fall and twisted ankle when they run is an obstacle, and his giving her the gun, is topped by Alison's speech that follows with shadows over the faces of Alison and Pete: "You're a fool to throw away the cross. If you hadn't I might still be Alison. But you did. And I'm not."

After the police leave the Findlays', Alison is shown to be wearing the large pendant that "Grandmother" Thorne was previously seen to have worn. The small pendant now worn by "Grandmother" Thorne suggests that Alison has been possessed. This is confirmed when "Grandmother" speaks as if she is Alison, and she sees Alison standing at her bed with Jenny, Dean and Lyle. "Grandmother" then sees her aged hand and screams, as Coughlan uses an extreme close-up of her eyes before the final title card that reads "Alison 104 years."

In the documentary *Not Quite Hollywood*, Joanne Samuel says the only budget the film had for special effects was the falling of the bookcase. Belinda Giblin, who played Isobel Thorne, says that the stones of the stone circle were actually made of polystyrene and that they kept toppling. The film was the only Australian horror title made by Ian Coughlan.

He would go on to write the screenplay for the Australian horror film *Kadaicha*, which was also produced by David Hannay, and co-write the screenplay for the Australian horror title *Hellion: The Devil's Playground*. The film was also the only Australian horror title to be made by Fontana Films, executive producers Ric Kabriel and John Sturzaker, and associate producer Michael Falloon.

After working in television, Joanne Samuel made her film debut in a supporting role in the science fiction action adventure *Mad Max* (1979). After *Alison's Birthday*, she did more television and film supporting roles but has not essayed another leading role to date. Lou Brown also began his career in television, made his film debut in a supporting role in the romance *The Irishman* (1978), and has continued in television and supporting film roles prior to and after *Alison's Birthday*.

Release

Australia on December 26, 1981; the American release date is unknown. The taglines include "Satan's only gift is death...," "She'll never forget her party ... and neither will you!" and "A young girl comes of age ... and an evil destiny awaits her."

Reviews

"Under budgeted and unevenly directed, the film has its moments (the shock opening is particularly well handled) but ultimately it's a verbose and theatrical affair with the talented Joanne Samuel manifestly too old to play the unfortunate Alison."—David Stratton, *The Last New Wave*

"Atypical of late 1970s horror-thrillers in that it concerns subtle manipulations of the soul, with only rare interest in violence or terror.... Coughlan directs in a fairly standard manner. But to his credit, the film is never silly and the dark tone is convincing."—Scott Murray, *Oxford Australian Film 1978–1994*

"Unfortunately, after a shock séance opening the pace slows to a crawl. Although the decision to not rely on blood and shock effects deserves respect, there is crippling lack of suspense in this film.... The performances, for the most part, are unremarkable."—Kyla Ward, *Tabula Rasa*

"Slightly underrated little occult piece. A likable cast performs, with an atmosphere both sleepy and effective in the right spots, this is well worth the discovery.

Kudos (and an extra half star) simply for the dark, downbeat ending." — *The Terror Trap*

"Subdued and cozy, the film's nifty PG-level thrills (a haunted forest, the cemetery showdown) are few and far between. Luckily, the likable cast, sort-of-obvious twists, and sharp direction from writer-director Ian Coughlan ceaselessly swoop in with welcomed relief. Satan never shows his face, but the almighty downbeat ending more than makes up for that." — Joseph A. Ziemba, *Bleeding Skull*, October 5, 2006

DVD

Video released on Beta in 1984 by VidAmerica and by the Uav Corporation/Saton Video on September 8, 1988.

Lady, Stay Dead
Ryntare Productions, 1981

CREDITS: *Screenplay/Producer/Director:* Terry Bourke; *Executive Producer:* Alex Hopkins; *Associate Producers:* John Hipwell, Eric Cook; *Photography:* Ray Henman; *Editor:* Ron Williams; *Music:* Bob Young; *Art Director:* Bob Hill; *Special Effects:* Reece Robinson; *Sound:* Bob Clayton; *Makeup:* Sally Gordon; *Hair:* Jan Zeigenbein; *Costumes:* Catriona Brown; *Louise Howitt dressed by:* Pierre Volz, Mark Warren. Color, 92 minutes. Filmed on location in Palm Beach, Whale Beach, and Narrabeen, New South Wales.

SONGS: "The Four Seasons" (Antonio Vivaldi); "Loving From a Distance" (Bob Young, Ted Ottley) Tina Young.

CAST: Chard Hayward (Gordon Mason); Louise Howitt (Jenny Nolan); Deborah Coulls (Marie Coleby); Roger Ward (Officer Clyde Collings); Les Foxcroft (Billy Shepherd); James Elliott (Patrolman Rex "Pop" Dunbar); Brian Hinslewood (TV Director); George Murray (Businessman/Client); Barry Donnelly, James Moss (Security Men at Crash); Allen Scholz (Chauffeur).

Synopsis

Gordon Mason is the gardener for the 24-year-old actress and singer Marie Coleby and is obsessed by her. After a shampoo commercial is filmed on the grounds of her Rocky Beach villa Gordon voices his objection to Marie's rude treatment. When he tells Marie of his feelings for her, she rejects him, and in retaliation he rapes her and drowns her in a fish tank. Gordon is caught trying to transport Marie's body by the cottage neighbor, Billy Shepherd, and his dog Cilla, and Gordon kills them both. Marie's elder sister Jenny Nolan arrives at the villa for a visit, surprised that Marie has not picked her up at the airport as planned. Believing her sister is filming on location, Jenny becomes disturbed by the behavior of Gordon, and after she finds Billy dead in the shed of his cottage, she telephones the villa's security service.

Gordon invites himself to the house for dinner but Jenny refuses him entry, which enrages him. He finally gains access to the house by cutting a hole in a door with a chainsaw, as two security guards arrive, Collings and Pop Dunbar. Gordon shoots Pop, who is also burned alive in Gordon's attempt to torch the house. It appears that Collings drowns Gordon in a fight in the pool and Collings drives to locate Jenny, whom he had ordered to run. However, Jenny sees that Collings is actually dead, and as Gordon approaches Jenny, he is run over by a passing motorbike. When he takes the gun from Collings' car he is shot by another security guard who arrives in a second car.

Notes

This inconsistent thriller features the horror of personality. It centers on a man who has previously tortured other women and who now kills the new object of his obsession and attempts to kill her sister. The initial narrative is interesting in presenting a victimized protagonist who is unlikable and a victimizing antagonist who is oddly likeable, then switches empathies during a rape and drowning murder sequence. The second half also has a fifteen minute sequence of a Woman in Peril trapped by the killer inside a house, though the remainder is standard chase fare. Director Terry Bourke uses the postmodern techniques of slow motion, expressionist camera angles and point of view, and an exploitative use of female nudity, which was also in his prior Australian horror title *Inn of the Damned*. While some performances are limited, the treatment is almost redeemed by that of Chard Haywood as the killer who adds surprising touches to his performance.

Bourke begins the treatment with a naked Marie swimming in her pool and then walking naked back into her villa, though Gordon is first seen in underwear and not naked. His obsession is presented in the multiple images of Marie he has on his walls. His act of playing a love song that Marie has recorded while he caresses a mannequin who is made up to resemble Marie suggests his sexual perversity. The idea that Marie's song is playing as he makes love to the mannequin as a Marie-substitute prefigures his later rape of her, when her song is again heard. Bourke cuts from a shot of the mannequin's face to a close-up of the real Marie. Her abusing the manicurist who attempts to apply her lipstick while she is talking on the telephone shows Marie's haughtiness.

The Polaroid photos of naked women Gordon has in his truck further suggest his sexual frustration and prefigure the footage we will see of the same women as sexual partners that he recalls during the later scene when he spies on Marie at the beach. Marie is also shown to be selfish when she pushes away the boom mike while she smokes, as her lipstick is being applied, as she prepares for the Sheena Hair glow commercial shoot.

Gordon watches Marie on the beach exercising through binoculars. His masturbation, which begins as rubbing himself against the sand as he lies on his stomach, allows for the inter-cuts to the women he has had, which we will later be told are housewives. His perversity and control of their behavior is suggested by the fact that of the women shown, two are tied and clearly being held against their will. When Marie looks at herself in a mirror before going out, we are given a close-up of her exposed breasts and the sight of her squeezing them as more exploitation.

The rape scene begins with Marie spitting in Gordon's face after promising to kiss him if he releases her from his hold. His rape, being an anal penetration, is performed under the guise of her liking it rough, and its humiliation and cruelty switches our empathy towards Marie, a character who has been previously unlikeable and lacking in empathy. Additionally, the idea that Marie does not appreciate the hunkiness of Chard Haywood's Gordon because she appears to be too class-conscious to accept the advances of a proletarian gets a turnaround when he forces himself on her, reinforcing the brutishness that she feared in the first place.

She bites his neck after the rape, which leads to Gordon hold Marie upside down to put her head in the fish tank, an activity that also has a sadistic comic element in her kicking legs next to his head. We assume that the end of movement is a sign that Marie has drowned, although the later twitches of her body when she is in the garbage bag suggests that she may not be dead after all and perhaps just unconscious. Her earrings falling off and landing in the tank will be a plot point carried forward when Jenny finds them. The stain on the carpet is presumably from when Gordon took her out of the tank, or perhaps it is the stain that Marie complains Gordon made when he entered the house wearing his boots, although there will be no direct plot payoff to these points.

Gordon carries Marie's body outside to presumably dispose of it — something he never achieves in the narrative. Bourke provides a funny cut to him being seen by Billy and the dog snarling at Gordon. He doesn't show us Gordon striking Billy, though we do see Gordon later shooting the dog. Neither does Bourke show Gordon striking Marie after he sees her body move. Rather, we see the shovel raised as if to strike her and then the shovel afterwards with what appears to be a blood stain; the treatment's first display of blood.

Jenny being naked in the shower has context and her nudity is partially protected by the opaque glass shower door. Gordon entering the bathroom with shears creates the expectation of his attack upon her à la *Psycho*. This expectation is not met; the sound of Billy's dog barking makes Gordon retreat. The barking also makes Jenny open the shower door, and her breasts are exposed. When Jenny sees Marie's earrings in the fish tank Bourke cuts from her hands in it to retrieve them to a whistling kettle in the kitchen. Billy being dead as signified by the blood on his head is only revealed after Jenny has given up trying to get his attention, since she see initially sees him through a window of his cottage assumed to be lying down.

Gordon shown via Marie's car rear view mirror, as seen by Jenny, is a shock effect. The initial difference between Jenny and Marie is presented when Jenny's asks Gordon if he wants coffee and invites him to come inside the house to drink it, something Marie never did. It's a pity that after Jenny recognizes Gordon as dangerous that her promising character deteriorates into a screaming victim, although she is given the occasional funny line and has one moment as a warrior that is unfortunately not extended further. A movie convention is employed when Jenny runs to answer a ringing telephone and gets a dial tone because she takes too long to answer. The spot on the carpet that she finds suggests a blood stain, which is not possible since no blood was seen during Marie's murder. However, Bourke uses her memory of Gordon's line "She doesn't like anyone coming in with dirty boots" for Jenny to wonder if the stain was caused by Gordon.

Jenny finding Billy hanging in the cottage shed by flashlight is another shock effect Bourke employs. The Dead End sign we see on a wall at the villa is a sly reference to Marie's murder and the future deaths of Pop and Collings on the property. Jenny being put on hold by the security service she calls conveniently gives Gordon enough time to cut the telephone wire, although Jenny gets to tell them something before the line goes dead.

The next fifteen minutes of the narrative are used as a kind of set piece for Bourke to present Jenny as a Woman in Peril and Gordon as a standard antagonist trying to get into the house to get her. His whistling adds a sly touch of amused and superior threat and a reminder of his presence. Although there are moments where the expectation is created that she will let him into the house, they are not met so that Gordon's throwing something through a kitchen window is another shock effect. Jenny begins to fill a pan with hot water, but the payoff will be delayed in the narrative. Her opening curtains to see the dead Marie in her car is undermined by Bourke having to zoom in on Marie's face from an extreme long shot; it seems unlikely that Jenny could have recognized who was in the car in the first place.

When Jenny pushes Gordon off the balcony he has attempted to scale, her comment, "Now whistle, you bastard!" is funny. After the hot water payoff Gordon is seen behind her through a windowed door. This is a horror movie conventional image, and the fact we see him but she does not is another horror convention. There is a shot of Jenny raising the fireplace poker as a weapon against Gordon that momentarily presents her as a warrior, though Jenny's use of the poker will be disappointingly obvious and brief. Gordon's arsenal of weaponry includes a rifle, and perhaps most amusingly, a chainsaw. He uses this to cut a square hole through a door while Jenny screams helplessly, although the narrative has the security guards arrive just as Gordon can get inside the hole to stop him.

The addition of Pop and Collings to the narrative makes for lesser interest and a diluted threat since Gordon will vanquish both guards, and creates the expectation that Jenny will be rescued. Bourke adds to the ambience by using the red and blue flashing lights of the security guards car as a lighting effect over the subsequent exterior scenes around the house. The expectation of Gordon's strike against Pop is met after Pop is the first to venture outside the house to find him, although Bourke delays Pop's demise.

There is black humor in Gordon's reply to Collings' question to him, "Is he all right?" referencing the blood stain on the wall from where Gordon has shot Pop. He answers, "He's kinda all over the place." The blood streak from Pop's dragged body is perhaps the treatment's biggest display of bloodletting, and Jenny gets more funny lines in her angry frustration over Collings' strategy, "All you do is talk. For Christ sake, do something, you fuckwit." He slaps her, presumably since he thinks her to be hysterical, and he replies, "We're perfectly safe here." This comment is actually accurate but is followed by his plan for Jenny to leave the safe place and run.

When Collings and Jenny go outside they retreat from a shadowed view of Gordon holding his rifle. The fire bomb that he creates gets a laugh from the way it is used, rather to roll onto Pop to burn him alive, which Bourke creates in slow motion. Collings gets a funny line in response, "I'm gonna kill you, you animal," a comment he will repeat in the swimming pool fight with Gordon.

Bourke inter-cuts between Collings now chasing Gordon and Jenny running away, although her trip down a hill is more of her as the helpless Woman in Peril. There is another laugh from Collings surprisingly turning a corner and running into Gordon, and the pool fight creates the expectation that Collings has successfully drowned Gordon. This is a seemingly ironic fate given Gordon's drowning of Marie. It also sets up the shock reveal of Collings being dead when we think he has driven his car to find Jenny and his voice heard over a loudspeaker to her, with Marie's body in the back seat another reminder of Gordon's inability to dispose of her body.

Gordon's strangling of Jenny, who again as the victim doesn't even attempt to run from him, is halted by his delusional thinking that she is Marie. This is a plot point that really comes from nowhere, and his being struck by a passing motorbike seems to finally pay off the motorbike riders that were seen earlier in the narrative. Gordon's fall into the car windshield is shown with more slow motion, and the second security car that appears pays off Collings' earlier expressed idea that someone would come after him if he had not checked in with the service in a certain amount of time. However, Gordon as the killer who seemingly cannot be killed is not able to use the rifle he finds in the car and aims at the advancing guard who shoots him multiple times.

In the documentary *Not Quite Hollywood*, Roger Ward comments that Bourke was so enthusiastic about the fish tank murder scene that he refused to call cut until he was satisfied, and that Deborah Coulls did the stunt herself and nearly drowned in the enacting of it. Bourke had previously made the Australian horror title *Inn of the Damned* and would not make another after *Lady, Stay Dead*. He died in 2002. The film was the only Australian horror title to be made by associate producers Eric Cook and John Hipwell, executive producer Alex Hopkins, and the production company Ryntare Productions.

Welsh born Chard Haywood began his career in television and made his film debut in a supporting role in the film version of his television show *Number 96* (1974). After *Lady, Stay Dead* he would go on to essay the lead in *The Killing Game* (1988) and play other supporting film roles and more television. Louise Howitt also began in television and made her film debut in a minor role in the thriller *Desolation Angels* (1982). After *Lady, Stay Dead* she had other supporting film and television Roles. Deborah Coulls too began her career in television and made her film debut in a supporting role in *It's a Living* (1983); she continued in television and supporting film roles. Roger Ward had previously appeared in the Australian horror title *Turkey Shoot*, but would not go on to make another Australian horror title.

Release

Said not to have received any wide release in Australia or the United States, although apparently it received one in Portugal in 1984. Released on video in Australia and the United States in 1984.

Reviews

"A routine exercise in suspense which is never very gripping. Though the violence is downplayed, there is a fair amount of gratuitous nudity."— David Stratton, *The Avocado Plantation*

"Surprisingly good psycho stalker pic.... This lean Aussie suspense vehicle is pretty successful, thanks to its simplistic 'trapped in the house' approach and a believable performance by lead Howitt. Maniac Hayward too does a nice job of easing into Gordon's killer psychoses and by the end helps to ratchet up the tension significantly."— *The Terror Trap*

"A frustratingly uneven mish-mash of horror and thriller clichés that, ultimately, fails to deliver on the cat 'n' mouse thrills ... tries to cram as many genres into its 90 minutes as possible and doesn't really succeed at any of them."— Justin Kerswell, *Hysteria Lives*

"The beach scenery is beautiful.... Bob Young's persistent, plonking piano score actually suits the proceedings with its mournful droning. Perhaps the overall nature of the film is a bit dubious towards women at times, but Gordon is portrayed as so utterly pathetic, and Jenny so sensible and well-balanced, that viewers — hopefully — will side with the victims."— Boris Lugosi, *Girls, Guns and Ghouls*

DVD

Not available in either format.

Roadgames: A State of Suspense
Essaness Pictures/Quest Films, 1981 [aka *Road Games*]

CREDITS: *Producer/Director:* Richard Franklin; *Co-Producer:* Barbi Taylor; *Executive Producer:* Bernard Schwartz; *Screenplay:* Everett De Roche, from an original story by Everett De Roche and Richard Franklin; *Photography:* Vincent Monton; *Editor:* Edward McQueen-Mason; *Music:* Brian May; *Art Direction/Production Design:* Jon Dowding; *Sound:* Paul Clark, Raymond Phillips; *Set Decorator:* Jill Eden; *Costumes:* Aphrodite Kondos; *Makeup:* Lois Honenfels. Color, 101 minutes. Filmed in Melbourne and Diggers Rest and the Starch Factory Studio, Victoria; Great Australian Bight, South Australia; and Eucla, Madura, Nullabor Plain, and Perth, Western Australia.

SONG: "Eine kleine Nachtmusik" (Wolfgang Amadeus Mozart), heard in Quid's truck.

CAST: Stacy Keach (Pat Quid, aka Patrick Anthony Quid); Jamie Lee Curtis (Hitch, aka Pamela Rushworth); Marion Edward (Frita Frugal, aka Madeline Day); Grant Page (Smith or Jones); Thaddeus Smith, Stephen Millchamp (Police); Alan Hopgood (Lester); John Murphy (Benny Balls); Bill Stacey (Captain Careful); Robert Thompson (Sneezy Rider); Ed Turley

(Roadhouse Proprieter); Angie La Dozzetta (Hitchhiker); Colin Yancio (Fred Frugal); Paul Harris, Rochelle Harris (Frugal Childen); Tony Bishop, Abbe Holmes (Honeymooners); Carol Ann Aylett (Cleaning Lady); Killer (Boswell, the dog).

Synopsis

Pat Quid is a 40ish American independent carrier who has been hired to haul pigs in his truck from Melbourne to Perth, where butchers are on strike. At the same time, the driver of a green van is murdering young women by strangling them with wire. Pat sees the van driver check into a motel one night and as the van is going in the same direction as him, Pat becomes intrigued by it. He picks up 20-year-old American hitchhiker heiress Pamela Rushworth, and tells her his theory that he thinks the green van driver is the reported murderer. Pamela investigates the van when Pat mistakenly thinks he has the driver trapped in a roadhouse toilet, and she is kidnapped. Pat follows the van until he is lured into an alley where the driver tries to strangle him, unsuccessfully. The police arrest the killer and rescue Pamela from the van, but are unaware that the driver has hidden the head of one of his victims in Pat's truck.

Notes

This is a huge disappointment following Richard Franklin's prior Australian horror title, *Patrick*. It is marred by a charmless lead performance, an unsubtle score, and a plodding treatment which has the occasional suspense set piece and shock effect. The narrative features the horror of personality of the serial killer van driver, who remains unheard and unseen, but also a pleasing reappearance of minor characters in the road journey and occasional humor. Franklin uses the postmodern techniques of point of view and zooms, as well as super-impositions for hallucinations and a red color motif. Casting of American stars for presumed greater international marketing does not benefit the film. A thriller with few thrills, it fails to satisfy as horror; the only killing shown on screen is presented suggestively rather than literally.

A prologue lacks score and presents Quid arriving at the Carotel motel at the same time as a female hitchhiker and the green van. In the DVD commentary Franklin speaks of how he had wanted a more ambitious original opening shot of Quid driving into the town with white lines seen on the road, which he abandoned. The narrative device of Quid talking to himself has an initial reveal where the camera pulls back to show his dog in the truck's cabin with him. Although Franklin doesn't employ dog reaction shots in a cloying way, he does cut a lot to the dog as another character with Quid. The belief that the dog is a dingo is a running gag through the narrative, paid off when the dog barks at the film's climax and thereby denies its supposed dingo breed since dingos are said not to bark.

The nudity of the Hitchhiker is not used exploitatively, given context by her presumed sex with the killer, and then her breasts covered by the guitar she holds in front of her. Franklin has an extreme close-up of the girl's eyes that prefigure the killer's guitar string placed in front of her before she is garroted, a technique which strangles and cuts the throat simultaneously, and her scream is muffled by clanging trash cans in an edit transition to daytime.

Double observers are presented with Quid watching Boswell sniffing at a trash bag and watching the killer, and the killer also watching Boswell and awaiting the trash being collected. The killer is seen by Quid as his gloves holding back the motel room curtain. Boswell's interest in the trash bag is not paid off, although a radio news report will tell us that body parts have been found around the Nullabor Plains. The reveal of what is presumably the Hitchhiker's head in the epilogue confirms that the killer decapitates his victims. Franklin cuts from the trash bag being thrown into the garbage truck to a row of hanging pig carcasses under the opening credits, and Quid's later news that he is carrying two extra bodies would suggest that these extra two are human remains. The Universal Meat rig has the motto Pleased to Meat You! on its side and the graphic of a pig brandishing a cleaver to cut meat.

The character Benny Balls, though not named in the narrative as such, is the driver of a car full of balls. Like Hitch, Madeline, Captain Careful (also unnamed in the narrative), Sneezy Rider, and The Honeymooners are minor characters that reappear in the narrative. Benny Balls gets Quid's comment, "Now there's a man with balls." His passing Captain Careful gets more visual payoffs, initially when the Captain's windshield shatters after he is passed by Quid and the green van. Franklin sets up this expectation by the sight of the Captain towing a boat, although we can't tell what makes the windshield shatter. This event also prefigures the second encounter Quid has with the Captain, where he unsuccessfully seeks revenge upon Quid. The car of the Honeymooners with the Just Married sign on the back gets another bad pun from Quid after he sees the women rise from seemingly giving the male driver a blow job, and Quid comments, "Sucker."

Quid's point of view of the heat haze and something ahead of him on the highway creates an expectation met. It is given a shock payoff when he stops the truck violently to avoid hitting the pink toilet paper that Madeline ties across the width, although one would think that paper is hardly a form of obstacle. Her criticism of him not stopping for Hitch as the white-clothed hitchhiker, for the second time in the narrative, gets his comment "that hitch's getting to Perth faster than we are." Madeline's red clothes are set off against the green bushland when she runs away from Quid, and paid off by the shock view of her running to a cliff. Franklin supplying an extreme long shot of the cliff face against the sea, a seemingly odd contrast to the highway, reads as unnecessary. Franklin supplies a slow 360 degree interior pan for the scene where Quid is on the telephone at the Yellowdine roadhouse. The music of the jukebox that makes it hard for him to be heard is conveniently stopped when he spells out his name to the operator and says "D" for "death to young girls." This creates the plot point of Quid thought to be the killer, which will be continued in an inspired way in the film's climax.

The reappearance of Captain Careful initially features ambiguity. Is he is an uncontrolled driver who cannot get out of the way of Quid's truck, with Quid chasing the killer who has apparently injured Boswell. Or is he deliberately blocking Quid from passing? As the scene continues it becomes apparent that the latter is the case. Franklin uses edits of shots of the boat's ringing bell and the uncoiled rope tied to the anchor to prefigure the trailed boat becoming detached and crashing into the truck. He also uses a circling dolly camera move for the reveal of Jamie Lee Curtis as the white-clothed hitchhiker for the third time she tries to flag down Quid, with the reveal appropriate for her successful attempt. There is a resonant image of Hitch in close-up with her face in between the red curtains of Quid's sleeping cabin when she watches the police who stop his truck. She looks at Quid's collection of magazines and one has a photograph of her namesake, Alfred Hitchcock, on the cover.

Thunder and lightning are used as the horror movie convention of foreboding, although rain does not follow, when Hitch sees the green van parked near Quid's truck at night. The expectation of a kiss between Hitch and Quid is created but not met when their moment is interrupted. It appears that the driver of the green van is in a toilet, allowing Hitch to look in the van. This is a suspense set piece, and perhaps the best sustained scene in the film.

Franklin has Hitch and Quid looking at the van, and Hitch's advance to the van is given a shock effect by Quid touching her shoulder. The alarm of the car of Benny Balls adds to the scene, as Quid thinks he has the driver trapped, with the van driver being represented by shoes seen under the toilet stall door. When the alarm stops, Hitch's attempt to look in the van driver's red lunch box is halted by her shock discovery of him sleeping on the floor. Our return to Quid in the toilet prefigures the reveal of the shoes belonging to Sneezy Rider, the only part of his outfit that is not red. Franklin uses a pan up the toilet stall door and a sneeze for the reveal. This recalls our first view of Sneezy Rider when Quid saw him sneezing as he rode his motorbike on the highway and had to wipe his nose under his helmet (thus he was named as such by Quid). When Quid leaves the toilet, he sees that the green van and Hitch are gone. Hitch's removal from the bulk of the narrative is also an interesting choice. The expectation created is that she is dead, and Quid's failed attempt to steal Sneezy Rider's bike is comical in presenting Quid as a weak avenging hero.

Franklin has the voice of the radio in Quid's truck echo to suggest the hallucinations he will later have from tiredness. The moans he hears beyond the parked green van in bushland at night make him think that the driver and Hitch are having sex. This causes him to retreat from his investigation of the noise as a Man in Peril, the masculine equivalent of the female Woman in Peril horror movie conventional figure, and to be less concerned over the fate of Hitch. Franklin pays off this assumption with a pan over bushes that reveal The Honeymooners van, from which the sex noises are presumably coming. Quid's idea that the van's lunch box contains the head of the Hitchhiker from the motel is proved wrong when we see its contents are food. The back doors of his rig being unlatched unknown to Quid suggests that the van driver has deposited corpses, including perhaps Hitch, in Quid's rig while Quid was in the bush and looking in the green van.

Quid has a hallucination of the head of a kangaroo before he stops to see a live kangaroo on the road, thankfully not run over as in *Long Weekend*. A banging of what is revealed to be a carcass hitting the wall of the rig behind Quid's cabin makes him investigate a noise, again as a Man in Peril. Quid's

Pat Quid (Stacy Keach), Boswell the dog (Killer), and Hitch (Jamie Lee Curtis) in *Roadgames*, aka *Road Games* (1981).

advance inside the rig, surrounded by carcasses, provides for another scene of suspense. The unlatched doors suggest that the killer is inside the rig. The sea of carcasses also prefigures a similar scene in the Australian horror title *Voyage into Fear*.

Quid is given interior dialogue to converse with his voiced dialogue, as the beginning of the hallucination sequence where Franklin superimposes the dividing road lines over an extreme close-up of Stacy Keach's face and red road lights on his eyes. Quid's view of the back of the driving green van has superimposed eyes and a windswept shot of Hitch's face that does not otherwise appear in the treatment.

At the state line check point, Lester observes a wire wrapped around Quid's truck axle. In the DVD commentary, Franklin explains that the wire is residue from Captain Careful's boat. This is a plot point that will be utilized in the film's climax Quid initially is unconcerned about it. Why the police car follows Quid is unknown — it is something that Franklin reports was explained in a missing scene — but it does allow for the three car action of the climax where the green van leads Quid's truck into a narrow alley where the truck gets stuck. The three car equation allows for Quid to make another bad pun, "Talk about the meat in the sandwich." However, before the truck gets stuck, Franklin provides a classic comedy moment of expectation. A man drops spectacles on the road, which are unharmed by the van and the truck but smashed by the police car.

The driver of the green van approaches Quid trapped in the alley, since he is unable to open either cabin door. Franklin has a moment where both men look at each other in wonderment, to delay the expected attack. The policeman who climbs under the truck to free the police car from it being hooked to the truck and gets caught in the wire adds another element to the scene. Franklin inter-cuts between these three scenarios: The van being stalled with Quid trying to disengage the truck from an overhead bridge; the policeman in the wire; and the other policeman trying to disengage his car from the truck. The resolution has the police car disentangled and driving back into a shed of flour, and the wired policeman unharmed when Quid's truck dives forward to land on the green van. In the DVD commentary, Franklin reports how originally the climax also included Quid destroying a new yacht that Captain Careful appears with, and a stunt shot of Sneezy Rider with Madeline as his passenger driving his bike under the truck, which was rehearsed but not filmed.

Franklin uses another shock effect for the appearance of the killer behind Quid with a wire that he tries to strangle him. Quid's brutal bashing of the killer's head against a metal drain features the treatment's only human bloodletting. The plot point of Quid tying the killer's guitar string around the killer's neck is given a superb payoff when the result is witnessed by a crowd and lights come up on Quid so it is again assumed that he is the garrote killer. Franklin reports in his DVD commentary that the planned conceit was that all the minor characters would converge for this moment. The expectation of the escape of the real killer as he backs away from the scene where Quid is apprehended is not met. The rescue of the sleeping-bag covered Hitch from the van is a surprise, a denial of the expectation of Hitch's murder, and the late return of her character to the narrative.

A shot of Quid and Hitch walking on the road and being followed by a truck doesn't get a payoff, since they seem to be unaware of being followed. Her eating a sandwich is given a comic riff in the idea that she is perhaps eating human meat via the extra carcasses in Quid's delivery. In the DVD commentary Franklin reports how this shot was to be the film's original ending, but he was told by the American distributors that a grand guignol effect was needed as a topper. The narrative's epilogue in the butcher shop of a supermarket then has a shock reveal of the presumed head of Hitchhiker falling into the bucket of the Cleaning Lady, presumably in the rig. This occurs after she pulls a wire that hangs near her head, and Franklin ends the film with a shot of the truck doors slamming shut.

With a budget of $1.8 million, the film is said to have been the most expensive title made in Australia at the time, although the production still faced financial problems. On the DVD commentary, Richard Franklin talks about how he altered the film's climax because shooting fell two days behind schedule and he was not allowed to complete the sequence as planned. He also reports that the budget wouldn't allow for the casting of Sean Connery as Quid, for whom the part was written, since the American distributor Avco Embassy had insisted on the casting of an international star.

This policy was also reflected in the casting of Jamie Lee Curtis, who replaced the Australian actress Lisa Peers, who had been cast as Hitch, a situation which brought the film bad Australian advance press. Avco apparently also insisted that an Australian could not co-star with Stacy Keach, despite Peers having had a leading romantic role in *Solo* (1978) and appearing in a minor role in the Australian horror title *Alison's Birthday*.

Franklin used his connection with John Carpenter to get to Curtis, since Franklin had known Carpenter at the University of Southern California, and Carpenter had directed Curtis in *Halloween* (1978) and *The Fog* (1980). Franklin also reports that screenwriter Everett De Roche had envisaged the film as *Rear Window* in a truck. He had observed how he kept seeing the same people passing him when he once took a road trip, which is presented by the reappearances of minor characters in the narrative.

In the documentary *Kangaroo Hitchcock: The Making of Roadgames*, Stacy Keach says that shooting on location was hampered by a plague of caterpillars. In the documentary *Not Quite Hollywood*, director Greg McLean claims that *Roadgames* influenced his later Australian horror title *Wolf Creek* in its narrative of adventure on a highway and the meeting of an evil character. Franklin later made other horror titles, including *Psycho II* (1993) and *Link* (1986), but not another Australian horror title. Co-Producer Barbi Taylor would go on to produce the Australian horror title *Subterano*, but *Roadgames* would be the only Australian horror title to be made by American executive producer Bernard Schwartz. The film is the only Australian horror title made by the production companies Quest Films and Essaness Pictures.

After working in television, Stacy Keach made his film debut in a supporting role in the crime drama *Joy Ride* (1958). After more supporting parts he scored the lead in the comedy *End of the Road* (1970), and continued as the leads in the westerns *The Travelling Executioner* (1970) and *"Doc"* (1971), the boxing drama *Fat City* (1972), the biography *Wilbur and Orville: The First to Fly* (1973), the biography *Luther* (1974), the crime comedy *The Gravy Train* (1974), and the crime dramas *The Killer Inside Me* (1976) and *The Squeeze* (1977). After this, Keach began slipping to supporting roles, although he did essay the lead in the thriller *The Ninth Configuration* (1980). After *Roadgames* the actor would work in television and more supporting film roles, although he returned to film leads in the thriller *False Identity* (1990), and the action thriller *The Sea Wolf* (1997).

Also beginning in television, Jamie Lee Curtis made her film debut in *Halloween*, and through her appearances in the horror titles *The Fog*, *Prom Night* (1980) and *Terror Train* (1980), she was tagged the "Queen of Scream." Curtis wouldn't score top-billing until after *Roadgames* with *Halloween II* (1981), and would continue as the lead in the thriller

Love Letters (1983), *Grandview, U.S.A.* (1984), the sports drama *Amazing Grace and Chuck* (1987), the crime thriller *Blue Steel* (1989), and the thriller *Mother's Boys* (1994). After working in television and playing supporting film roles the actress was top-billed for her return in a double role to the Halloween film series in *Halloween H20: 20 Years Later* (1998) and *Halloween: Resurrection* (2000), as well as leads in the horror title *Virus* (1999), and the comedy *Freaky Friday* (2003).

Release

Australia June 26, 1981, U.S.A. February 8, 1982 with the taglines "The truck driver plays games.... The hitchhiker plays games. And the killer is playing the deadliest game of all!" "One game kills time — The other kills people!" "On the world's loneliest highway it's not a game — it's murder!" and "On a 1600 mile stretch of desert highway someone is playing a deadly game of sex, violence ... and sudden death!"

Reviews

"A film to see because it is more exciting, more teasing, more amusing than any other Australian film I know. And, above all, it is a pleasure to recommend a film that takes pleasure in being a film." — Brian McFarlane, *Cinema Papers*, July–August 1981

"In many ways an ingenious thriller but the climax fails to work and it does not make for an enthralling ending. It is a thriller that does not know how to resolve itself." — David Stratton, *The Avocado Plantation*

"Franklin is unable to get this rig out of first gear as it meanders towards the resolution. Hopelessly inept comedy tries to thumb a lift, but the majority of viewers will be beyond caring." — Jeff Ritchie, *ScaryMinds*

"A stylish affair, clearly inspired by Alfred Hitchcock's original *Rear Window* (1954), as well as Steven Spielberg's TV horror *Duel* (1971). There are some nice touches of humor, a few excellent suspense setups, and several exciting chase sequences." — *The Terror Trap*

"The kind of film that makes you want to charge through the screen and throttle your way across the cinescape like Darth Vader on crack, if only to alleviate the excruciating boredom.... Franklin's attempts at stylish suspense à la Hitchcock fall flat [but] the film does occasionally have its moments." — Lauren Monaghan, *Digital Retribution*, January 24, 2007

"Well-crafted though eccentric thriller in the Hitchcock vein cleverly conceived by De Roche and intelligently directed by Franklin.... Franklin never compromises the story for shocks and shows insight into screen suspense." — John Stanley, *Creature Features*

Awards

Nominated for the Australian Film Institute (AFI) Best Cinematography, Best Editing, Best Supporting Actress (Marion Edward), and Best Score.

DVD

Released by Starz/Anchor Bay on June 10, 2003. Released by Umbrella Entertainment (Australia) on March 29, 2008.

The Survivor
Tuesday Films/Pact Productions, 1981

CREDITS: *Director:* David Hemmings; *Producer:* Antony I. Ginnane; *Executive Producer:* William Fayman; *Associate Producer:* Jane Scott; *Screenplay:* David Ambrose, based on the novel by James Herbert; *Photography:* John Seale; *Editor:* Tony Paterson; *Music:* Brian May; *Production Design:* Bernard Hides; *Wardrobe:* Terry Ryan; *Angela Punch-McGregor dressed by:* Stirling Cooper; *Makeup:* Jill Porter; *Hair:* Sash Lamey; *Sound:* Tim Lloyd; *Special Effects:* Chris Murray. Color, 77–99 minutes. Filmed on location in Adelaide, Edinburgh, Panorama, and Norwood, South Australia; and at the studios of the South Australian Film Corporation, Norwood, South Australia.

CAST: Robert Powell (Captain David Keller); Jenny Agutter (Hobbs); Angela Punch-McGregor (Beth); Peter Sumner (Harry Tewson); Lorna Lesley (Susan); Ralph Cotterill (Slater); Joseph Cotten (The Priest); Arian Wright (Goodwin); Tyler Coppin (Boy); Kirk Alexander (Dr. Martindale); Jon Nicholls (Jackson); Roger Cardwell (Flight Engineer); Jenufa Scott-Roberts (Stewardess); John Edmund (Goswell); Denzil Howson (Rogan); Edwin Hodgeman (Bain); Heather Steen (Allens); Brenton Whittle (Thornton); Geoff Pullan (Osborne); Robin Bowering (Stuart); Chrissie James (Secretary); Audine Leith (Doctor); Jacqy Phillips (Hysterical

Woman); Tim Rice (Newscaster); Maurie Saidi (First Onlooker); Henry Scott (Second Onlooker); Paul Sonkkila (Fisherman); Paul Charlish (Engineer); Don Quin (Supervising Engineer); Brigette Webster (Child).

SYNOPSIS

A TLA 747 plane crashes in a grass field after a bomb goes off inside it. The pilot, Captain David Keller, is the only survivor of the 300 crew and passengers aboard. He suffers from amnesia, perhaps because he was thrown from the plane. David observes the investigation into what caused the crash. Psychic Hobbs tells David that she believes the dead victims need to communicate with him, and together they reenact the events that led to the crash. In the meantime a photographer, his assistant, and fellow airline worker Harry Tewson are murdered. David confronts the head of the investigator, Slater, who attacks him in the hangar where the plane's parts are kept. Slater is killed, and the next day workers find the burned body of David sitting in his pilot seat in the plane's wreckage.

NOTES

This is an enigmatic title that is not altogether satisfying, perhaps due to the edits that were presumably made going from its short running time. Director David Hemmings explores the theme of the malevolent supernatural being without attributing the killings to any particular one person. He uses the postmodern techniques of slow motion, point of view, and hand-held camerawork, as well as an obtrusive score. Hemmings also has some interesting framing and composition. Of the three murders in the narrative, gore is only shown for the third, apart from the grand guignol burned corpses, and both shock and suspense are displayed in the treatment. The plane crash sequence is said to have been the largest and most complex pyrotechnics stunt staged in Australia at the time. It's a pity that parts of it are repeated as the protagonist's memory, and that the conclusion is one that denies the logic of everything that has gone before it.

Under the opening credits, children play a stylized game of hide and seek that will be repeated at the end, and which would seem to symbolize the narrative's obtuseness. The extended footage of Hobbs, who appears to be supervising the children, suggests that she will become important to the narrative. The day to night sky transition where she remains seated in the park near where the 747 will crash also suggests that she may have something to do with it. This plot point will turn out to be false, although Hobbs, as a psychic, is a witness to the accident and David's emergence from the wreck. We see in the later flashback that the bomb is in Rogan's suitcase on the plane, but his surprise upon discovering it would seem to nullify him as the one responsible for bringing it on board. We never do learn who is responsible, though it is suggested by the climax that Slater might be. The crash sequence has footage of the plane flying low over trees where the tree tops are cut off. There is a laughable shot of a girl screaming as she clings to a tree before the crash that results in the expected explosion.

A photographer (name unknown) takes pictures of the burned corpses and then takes a shot of David with his wife, Beth. This is the one scene that Angela Punch-McGregor appears in. It is fitting that it is the photographer who is the narrative's first victim. He is presented as a Man in Peril, the male equivalent of the conventional Woman in Peril, after hearing noises outside his darkroom. He sees a little girl—the girl we saw on the doomed 747 who held a doll—and he follows her. Since we have been told that David is the only survivor of the crash, we can assume that the girl is a supernatural vision and an antagonist. The sequence is shot in daylight and initially without a score, which adds to the ambience. Also effective is the camera behind the photographer's head, where the expectation of a strike against him is not met.

In the graveyard where the chase continues is a shock reveal of the girl with a half-burned face. The camera following the photographer reaching in his pants pocket for a cigarette lighter allows for a hand to touch his, and then he is shown to be holding the hand of the girl's burned doll. The photographer walking onto a train track creates the expectation of him being run over, which will be met, but only after he avoids three oncoming trains. His being hit by the fourth follows him backing away from the girl and falling backwards over the track, but Hemmings denies us a shot of the impact.

When Slater looks inside the plane wreckage he hears the muffled screams of the dead. It is only when he reappears in the narrative later that we know he is not killed in the sequence, although we see from a bandage he wears afterward he has been injured from his investigations. When David visits Hobbs, she attacks him when she is presumably channeling the dead. She tells him, "They are asking for your help" and "I am being used to reach

Belgian poster for *The Survivor* (1981).

you." We hear the screams again that now seem to emanate from the stone sculptures at her house, and a mirror cracks supposedly as evidence of the earthly powers the dead have and their threat.

The second narrative attack occurs upon the photographer's assistant (name also unknown). She develops the pictures of the burned corpses that the photographer took and then hears the whispers and screams of the dead in the darkroom. Although we don't know why, her hand is placed conveniently under the blade of the paper cutter. Inter-cut shots of Hobbs show her to be outside as the cutter repeatedly slices. The assistant's screams are heard and blood is shown pouring under what is presumably the darkroom door. Again Hemmings deprives us of the strike, although the blood is the result. Since Hobbs does not attempt to help the assistant, we assume that she is party to the attack or at least has an awareness of it. Like the death of the photographer, the death of his assistant is shown to be a supernatural act, unlike the later murder of Harry.

Hobbs and David inexplicably seek the assistance of The Priest in her plan to take David back to the plane wreckage to relive the experience. While The Priest tells them that the church does not approve of "necromancy," he does give David a bible, which is not seen again in the narrative. The memory flashback is introduced with subtlety, with Hemmings suggesting the former cockpit by lighting, even if the memory uses the movie contrivance of David seeing himself that he had not seen originally. The same plane scenes are replayed, as is the landing over the trees, but this time the bomb is revealed in the suitcase.

Harry playing with metal shavings in the airplane hangar may have some value, but plot-wise it just seems a way to place him alone and in a darkened room so that he can be the next victim. He hears a noise and investigates to present him as another Man in Peril, with the attack a shock effect. We presume that he has been struck by a human rather than a supernatural antagonist. Slater seems the most likely candidate since David will soon find him in the hangar, although that is not acknowledged. Having established that someone is in the hangar when David enters, as we see a light being turned off, suspense is created by the same threat that killed Harry.

David's advance includes him seeing the legs of the girl we assume is one the photographer followed and died because of, and the screen is almost black when David approaches to turn on a light. The light reveals the bloodied body of Harry. A hand leads David to Slater sitting in front of an engine. Why the girl would do that is unclear. Perhaps it is because Slater is thought to be responsible for the bomb and David, being really dead, is aligned with the girl.

Slater shooting David creates the expectation that he has killed him, although later we learn that David has been dead all along. The engine starts up with a promise that Slater will be thrown into it as a grand guignol opportunity unfulfilled, though it causes a fire to set Slater alight. We wonder where

David has disappeared to and presume that the dying burned figure we are shown is Slater and not him, although it's hard to tell. The cockpit discovery that a burned David is still in his seat and has been dead for days suggests that he was not the survivor we thought him to be after all. The repeat of the stylized children's game of hide and seek that we see Hobbs supervise ads to the game playing the narrative has put us through.

In David Stratton's book *The Avocado Plantation*, he writes that the film was financed by Australian and British funding bodies with tax exemptions so that both investors got a complete write-off, which made the situation a case of double-dipping. In the DVD introduction, Antony I. Ginnane reports that the film was trimmed for release and scenes with Peter Sumner and Angela Punch-McGregor were lost. Footage of wounded passengers in the plane before the explosion and a scene where a looter meets a girl ghost on a lake were also cut. Ginnane reports how Robert Powell, Jenny Agutter and Joseph Cotton were imported to aid international marketing of the film, while apparently the casting of Samantha Eggar and Susan George in the film was blocked by Australia's Actor Equity. Ginnane admits that he thinks the decision to restrain horror effects in favor of mood and a more "cerebral" approach may have been a mistake.

The Survivor is the only Australian horror title to be directed by David Hemmings and the only one made by associate producer Jane Scott. Ginnane had last produced the Australian horror film *Thirst* and would go on to produce the Australian horror title *Turkey Shoot* with executive producer William Fayman. The film is the only one to be made by the production company Crystal Films, the only Australian horror title to be made by Tuesday Films and Pact Productions, and would be remade as the American *Sole Survivor* (1983).

After starting in television, Briton Robert Powell made his film debut in a minor role in the comic actioner *The Italian Job* (1969), and after more supporting film roles scored the lead as the title character in the musical biography *Mahler* (1974). He also played the leads in the mysteries *The Thirty Nine Steps* (1978) and *Harlequin* (1980). After *The Survivor* the actor played leads in *Imperativ* (1982), the horror movie *What Waits Below* (1984), the Italian biography *D'Annunzio* (1985), the war drama *Chunuk Bair* (1992), and *The Mystery of Edwin Drood* (1993), his last leading role to date.

Briton Jenny Agutter made her film debut as a child actress in a supporting role in the adventure film *East of Sudan* (1964), and as well as working in television continued playing film supporting parts. She played the lead in the thriller *I Start Counting* (1969), the Australian-filmed adventure *Walkabout* (1971), and as the title character in the family drama *Amy* (1981). After *The Survivor*, the actress returned in a leading role in the thriller *Number One, Longing, Number Two, Regret* (2004), and otherwise has appeared in supporting film roles and on television. Australian born Angela Punch-McGregor began her career on television and made her film debut in a supporting role in the crime drama *The Chant of Jimmie Blacksmith* (1978). After *The Survivor*, the actress would score the lead role in the romantic comedy *The Best of Friends* (1982), and played the lead in the historical drama *We of the Never Never* (1982), and *Annie's Coming Out* (1984), although she has only been seen in supporting film roles and on television to date since. Making his film debut in an uncredited bit part in the comedy *They're a Weird Mob* (1966), Australian Peter Sumner continued playing supporting film roles and working on television prior to *The Survivor*, which he has continued to do since.

American born Joseph Cotten made his film debut in a supporting role in *Citizen Kane* (1941) where he was top-billed, and although he spent most of the 1940s supporting his female co-stars, he was the leading man in the romance *The Magnificent Ambersons* (1942), the war drama *Journey Into Fear* (1943), and the thriller *The Third Man* (1949). In the 1950s the actor played leading roles in the western *Two Flags West* (1950), the crime drama *Walk Softly, Stranger* (1950), the thrillers *Peking Express* (1951) and *The Man with a Cloak* (1951), the western *Untamed Frontier* (1952), the crime drama *The Steel Trap* (1952), and the mystery *A Blueprint for Murder* (1953). By the mid–1950s Cotten worked on television and in supporting roles, although he did play the occasional film lead—in the German comedy *Von Himmel gefallen*, aka *Special Delivery* (1955), the crime drama *The Killer is Loose* (1956), the western *The Halliday Brand* (1957), and the science fiction *From the Earth to the Moon* (1958). In 1965 he returned as the lead in the western *The Great Sioux Massacre*, the Italian western *I crudely*, aka *Hellbenders* (1967), the Italian thriller *Gangster '70* (1968), the Spanish western *Comanche blanco*, aka *Hour of Vengeance* (1968), and played a double role in the family adventure *Atragon II* (1969). In 1971 he was top-billed in the Italian horror titles *La figlia di Frankenstein*, aka *Lady Frankenstein*, and *Gli orrori del castello di Norimberga*, aka *The Torture Chamber of Baron Blood* (1972). *Doomsday Voyage* (1972) was to be the actor's last leading role. After this Cotten only worked on television and played supporting film roles, of which *The Survivor* was to be his last. He died in 1994.

Release

Australia on July 9, 1981, and straight to video in the United States with the taglines "A tale of death, and of an evil which transcends death," "Based on the terrifying best-selling novel by James Herbert," "A journey into the supernatural," "Tortured with Guilt.... Why Did He Survive An Impossible Crash?" and "Pilot error ... or supernatural terror? Only one man can tell!"

Reviews

"Incomprehensible. There are numerous killings, but we never find out who is doing them. There are some nice touches, [particularly] the sequence which follows the air-crash which is imaginatively staged, though they fail to redeem this totally botched film."— David Stratton, *The Avocado Plantation*

"A decidedly average guilt drama as Mr. Powell, courtesy of Mr. Hemming's concrete direction, stumbles through a wallow of self-doubt. The inclusion of a supernatural twist is just the icing on the cake for this aviation film that never got off the ground."— William K. Halliwell, *The Filmgoer's Guide to Australian Films*

"You find yourself scratching your head and trying to find something that likely wasn't there in the first place."— Josh Pasnak, *The Video Graveyard*

"Without taking a 4 by 2 to a dead equine, let's just say that Hemmings turns in a movie that tries for six each way and comes up at the arse end of the race as the final credits roll.... Hemmings threw a complete shambles my way and I couldn't pick up the pieces."— Jeff Ritchie, *ScaryMinds*

"The film flounders with an overabundance of mood-enhancing sequences, short-sharp-shocks and sentimental imagery. The pacing drags, characters react rather than act, [and] a number of plot points are left hanging by a thread.... The actors play their respective roles with intense abandon [and] some scenes also manage to raise the hairs on the back the neck."— Robert Winter, *Digital Retribution*, February 12, 2007

Awards

Nominated for Australian Film Institute (AFI) Best Cinematography, Production Design, Sound and Best Actress, Jenny Agutter.

DVD

VHS released by Warner Home Video on December 13, 1993. Umbrella Entertainment (Australia) DVD released November 1, 2008.

Next of Kin

Film House/SIS Production, 1982 [aka *Hell House*]

CREDITS: *Screenplay:* Director: Tony Williams; *Producer:* Robert Letet; *Co-Producer:* Timothy White, Michael Heath, Tony Williams; *Photography:* Gary Hansen; *Editor:* Max Lemon; *Music:* Klaus Schulze; *Makeup:* Elizabeth Fardon; *Sound:* John Phillips. Color, 86 minutes. Filmed on location in Clarkefield, Melbourne and Sydenham, Victoria; and in New Zealand.

SONG: "Love You Like a Pie" (A.P. Johnson), A.P. Johnson.

CAST: Jackie Kerin (Linda Mary Stevens); John Jarratt (Barney); Alex Scott (Dr. Barton); Gerda Nicolson (Connie); Charles McCallum (Lance Cooney); Bernadette Gibson (Rita/Mrs. Ryan); Robert Ratti (Kelvin); Vince Deltito (Nico); Tommy Dysart (Harry); Debra Lawrance (Carol); Kristina Marsh (Linda age 4); Simon Thorpe (C.F.A. Speaker); David Allshorn, Alan Rowe (Service Club Men); Matt Burns (Mr. Collins); Daphne Miller (Freda); Isobel Harley (Paula); Eunice Crimp (Cookoo); Irene Hewitt (Maid); Myrtle Woods, Vic Gordon, Peter Lord, Ernest Wilson, John Strahan, Bill Marr (Montclare Residents); John Bishop (Truckie); Mitchell Faircloth (Café Man). Uncredited: Sid Krasey; Kristine Marshall; Nora Toohey.

Synopsis

Linda Stevens is a teacher at a school for emotionally disturbed children. She has returned to the Montclare Retirement Home where she was raised and which is run by her mother, who has died. Linda has inherited the home but reading her mother's diaries discovers that patients have been dying mysteriously. She is also curious about her aunt Rita, whom apparently her mother had sent away. Mr. Collins is found drowned in a bathtub, and Linda sees that he has marks on his throat which the home's administrator, Connie, and Dr. Barton do not want to acknowledge. Linda also experiences strange occurrings; water appears in her bath and candles appear in her room.

After she finds the body of her friend Carol in the home's pond, Linda seeks the help of her boyfriend, Barney. Barney is killed when he goes into the home alone, and Linda is confronted by the new patient, Mrs. Ryan, who turns out to be her aunt Rita. Aided by Kelvin, it appears Rita has also murdered Connie and Dr. Barton, and she now wants to kill her. Linda escapes and seeks refuge at Harry's Roadside Diner. When Kelvin drives his van through the wall, Linda shoots him and drives away from town.

Notes

An obtuse narrative mars this thriller, which features the theme of the horror of personality. Director Tony Williams uses the postmodern techniques of slow motion, zooms, expressionist camera angles, hand-held camerawork, and point of view. While there is a pleasing use of silence, the climax is over the top. The treatment establishes a narrative protagonist but the reveal of who is the true antagonist is done in the abrupt climax, with plot points left unresolved. Williams favors more shock effects than suspense — given that the climax is an extended shock — though he does provide one sequence of suspense without a payoff. Cineaphiles will appreciate the climactic bloodletting and gore effects, with the suggestion of an eye being cut and the only observed murder being a head being blown off by a shotgun.

A prologue shows a bloodied Linda outside Harry's Roadside Diner, standing near a car and then getting in. This prefigures the film's end, clueing us into the fact that Linda will survive her ordeal. Voice-over is used for Linda's mother bequesting her daughter her possessions, a device that will be repeated when Linda reads her mother's diaries. A storm is used as a horror movie convention of dread. Lighting announces the appearance of Connie in the attic, which suggests she is an antagonist but is ultimately a red herring, and it is repeated for the entrance of Mr. and Mrs. Ryan to the home grounds as a tree falls in the path of their approaching van. Linda also hears a cat meowing as she goes to the attic but does not investigate the noise as a Woman in Peril until later.

Linda's dreams of herself as child of four, with the convention used of her seeing herself in her dreams. This is a device repeated in the narrative but with more visual shown each time, until the reveal of the memory of Linda finding a body in the bathtub. The echoed voice calling her name, which we assume to be part of the dream, is later shown to be the voice of Rita, since she does the same when Linda locks herself in the bathroom to get away from her. The body of Mr. Collins that Lance finds when he steps into the bath is a gruesome discovery. It is humorous in the way Lance nearly stands on him, and the mist of the hot water can be the rationale for the body not being immediately apparent. The later revelation of Mrs. Ryan being Rita can also explain Linda's vision of people, like the vision she has of someone in the distance when she is in the woods with Barney. Barney's hand on Linda's face is a shock effect, as is the cat later jumping onto her room desk as she lays her head down out of sleepiness, and the drawer which opens to reveal a doll inside when she reaches for the flashlight.

The extended sequence of Linda investigating the noise of the cat's meow is a suspense set piece, with shock used without the expected score sting when Linda's light shines on the corpse of Mr. Collins, and Mrs. Petersen. The repeat of her finding a lit candle in her room suggests that someone is toying with her. Rita's reveal in the climax making us assume it has been her and the cat's meow is again used to lead Linda to the office. Her return to her room, where she finds the second lit candle, also has her discover the running water of the sink and her bath. The closed curtain being opened by Linda creates an expectation of a shock discovery that is not met since no one is in it. The connection between Linda dreaming of her memory of finding a body in her bath may be related to the information she later discovers that this phenomenon was frequent, and presumably Rita's modis operandi given how Connie and Dr. Barton end up.

Linda's dreamed vision extends to Mr. Collins floating under water, and the tapping on her window becoming the person whose hand we see opening her window and as a shadow on her wall. The expectation that Linda's visitor is Barney is met, and their resultant sex scene is shot conventionally and protective of the actors' nudity. Williams had exposed Linda's breasts in an earlier scene where she changed clothes for the dance that she changes her mind attending; this reads as exploitative because she wears no bra.

Carol's beret found in the pond by Lance prefigures the body of Carol later found there, and Connie's reaction to Linda's claim of seeing a woman in a red coat in her room suggests that Connie is the antagonist. The idea that Connie is aware of Rita's presence seems to come later when she asks Dr. Barton to tell Linda about the deaths of the past, something Connie would not do if she was involved in the murders.

When Linda reads her mother's diaries we hear the gothic written lines, "There is something evil in this house. Something that breathes the same air." Williams has the reveal of Linda's dream of her four-year-old self discovering the drowned body of Mr. Holden by having her red ball float away to show his face. Linda's vision of the pond fountain water as blood seems to be another fantasy until she finds the body of Carol, with her throat cut. Barney seems to be disposed of quickly after he goes inside the home, with the shock reveal of his bloodied and dead body in the wheelchair. The blood on Rita's hands would suggest that she is the killer, either coming from Barney or Connie and Dr. Barton, who are shown dead in the bath. However, it is Kelvin who appears with a hammer to threaten Linda and attempt to rape her, presumably as her equally mad accomplice. It is assumed that Linda's knifing of Rita's eye kills her since Rita does not appear again in the narrative. Had she survived we would expect her to accompany Kelvin to the diner to find Linda.

Rita's eye through the bathroom keyhole sets up the shock of Linda sticking a knife through it to blind Rita, and Williams dwells too long on the ballroom dancers on television at Harry's Diner. Kelvin's van smashing through the diner wall is prefigured by the rumbling of the presumed vehicle that causes the collapse of the sugar cube mountain Linda has built, and Williams repeats the van's entrance from different angles. The loose electrical wires and the leaking gas create the expectation of an explosion that is not immediately met, with Linda's shooting off of Kelvin's head another shock effect. Williams repeats the opening footage of Linda outside the diner at the car then adds the explosion of the diner when she and Nico drive away.

In the documentary *Not Quite Hollywood*, Williams comments that he was interested in showing less gore and more fear. The ending explosion "restraint" was due to the special effects person setting it off too early before the planned camera pan could capture it. As it is, the explosion is best seen in the reflection of the sign that Linda's car passes. By the time the camera sees it, most of the explosion is over. In the documentary Quentin Tarantino compares the tone and feeling of the film to *The Shining* (1980).

Next of Kin is the only Australian horror title made by director Tony Williams, producer Robert Letet, and co-producers Timothy White and Michael Heath. It is the only one made by the SIS production company and the only Australian horror title made by The Film House production company.

Jackie Kerin began her career in television, and *Next of Kin* is the only film she has made to date. John Jarratt would go on to appear in the Australian horror title *Dark Age*.

Release

Australian and United States release dates are unknown, but the taglines used were "There is something evil in this house" and "There's no place like home, bloody home."

Reviews

"An odd film, lacking a clear vision of how to tell its slight little story. There is, however, a well-staged and rather unexpected climax at a roadside café."—David Stratton, *The Avocado Plantation*

"The plot may be a little hokey, and has more red herrings than an Agatha Christie novel, but this spooky yarn is slickly directed, intriguing and at times visually reminiscent of Stanley Kubrick's *The Shining*."—Scott Murray, *Oxford Australian Film 1978–1994*

"A likable Australian sleeper with some nice stalker undertones. Well-crafted, with decent production values and a delicately slow pace, this ghost-cum-slasher film explodes in the final third, with all the events of the past catching up with the amiable leading lady. Worth seeking out."—*The Terror Trap*

"Why the director constructs a gothic atmosphere and then discards it remains a mystery, but it certainly is effective as a plot device.... [Enjoyable] for the atmospherics and attention to detail that director Williams provides."—*ScaryMinds*

"Quite gothic at times, but just because you're going gothic doesn't mean you need to use a plot from a hundred years ago, and *Next of Kin* is essentially a re-tooling of Jane Eyre.... There are a few good, stylish moments, but none of them make [it] worth sitting through."—Devon Bertsch, *Digital Retribution*, July 9, 2007

Award

Australian Film Institute (AFI) nomination for Best Editing, Max Lemon.

DVD

VHS released by M.C.E.G./Virgin Vision on September 6, 1989. A DVD was released by Reel (Australia) but appears to be out of print.

Turkey Shoot

FGH/Hemdale/Filmco, 1982
[aka *Escape 2000*; *Blood Camp Thatcher*]

CREDITS: *Director:* Brian Trenchard-Smith; *Producers:* Antony I. Ginnane, William Fayman; *Executive Producers:* John Daly, David Hemmings; *Associate Producer:* Brian W. Cook; *Screenplay:* Jon George, Neill Hicks, based on a story by George Schenck, Robert Williams, David Lawrence; *Photography:* John McLean; *Editor:* Alan Lake; *Music:* Brian May; *Production Design:* Bernard Hides; *Art Director:* Virginia Bieneman; *Costumes:* Aphrodite Kondos; *Makeup:* Annie Pospischil; *Makeup Special Effects:* Bob McCarron; *Hair:* Maureen Wroe-Johnson; *Sound:* Paul Clark; *Special Effects:* John Stears. Color, 89–93 minutes. Filmed on location in Cairns, Queensland.

CAST: Steve Railsback (Paul Anders); Olivia Hussey (Chris Walters); Carmen Duncan (Jennifer); Noel Ferrier (Secretary Mallory); Michael Craig (Charles Thatcher); Lynda Stoner (Rita Daniels); Roger Ward (Ritter); Michael Petrovitch (Tito); Gus Mercurio (Red); John Ley (Dodge); Bill Young (Griffin); Steve Rackman (Alph, the Freak); John Godden (Andy); Oriana Panozzo (Melinda).

Synopsis

Paul Anders, Chris Walters and Rita Daniels are the latest "deviants" to be taken to the island Camp 47. It is a re-education and behavior modification location for government troublemakers ruled by Camp Master Charles Thatcher. Deviants are subject to Thatcher's special programs, which include his game where they are hunted by himself and his guests. Paul, Chris, Rita and other prisoners, Dodge and Griffin, are volunteered for the game. They are told that if they can survive the day they will have their freedom. Given a head start, the prisoners fight for their survival, hunted by Thatcher, Jennifer, Tito, Mallory, Alph, Ritter, and Red. Paul and Chris will be the only survivors; all the guests are killed as well. The couple goes back to the camp and frees the other prisoners, and a battle breaks out between them and the guards led by the returning Thatcher. He is killed before government airplanes bomb the camp believing Thatcher has lost control, and Paul and Chris have their freedom.

Notes

While perhaps questionable as a horror title, this futuristic and idiotic action thriller can be interpreted as featuring the horror of personality and has some pleasing perversity, sadism and killings. While the personality can be read as being Thatcher, the camp master, the narrative actually features multiple antagonists to match the multiple protagonists. Director Brian Trenchard-Smith employs the postmodern techniques of point of view, expressionist camera angles and hand-held camerawork, zooms, and an obtrusive score. The narrative devotes nearly its entire second half to the hunts of the title game with cross-cutting applied for the fate of the five hunted. The film uses foreign actors in leading roles to supposedly boost international market sales. Though Trenchard-Smith's climax is a mess and the narrative has delusions of grandeur as a parable about revolutionaries fighting fascism, the treatment also has humor, unintentional as it may be. Horror cineaphiles will be satisfied with the bloodletting and gore effects.

Newsreel footage of street riots is used under the opening credits to presumably provide context for the imprisonment of the three protagonists. Since a geographical location is not given for the camp, the accents of Steve Railsback and Olivia Hussey are not an issue. Flashback memories of the arrests of Paul and Chris are shown with the movie contrivance that they see themselves in their memories, although Rita only gets to tell her backstory. The sudden appearance of a man in Chris' home would seem to confirm her claim that she is not a revolutionary, although Paul's radio broadcast defines him as one. The expectation of the soldiers, whose faces are not shown, who enter his studio with guns for his arrest is met.

The camp can be paralleled with prison camps and concentration camps with a welcome sign that also says, "Your stay here will make you an asset to society." A motto is repeated by Thatcher, a name surely a reference to the British Prime Minister Margaret Thatcher. "Freedom is obedience. Obedience is work. Work is life." The motto also has a reverse variation: "Disobedience is treason. Treason is a crime. Crime will be punished." Additionally, the morality of the camp punishes promiscuity, pregnancy, homosexuality, and prostitution, although Thatcher and the guards have their own share of amorality. Prostitution is the reason given

Camp 47 guard Red (Gus Mercurio) has a hankering for "deviant" prisoner Chris Walters (Olivia Hussey) in *Turkey Shoot* (1982).

for Rita's arrest, and although she denies it, her makeup and later counseling of Chris to use her body to survive certainly seems to present her as a professional.

The perversity of the guards is shown by Red's offering Chris a drink as code for a blow job. The scene where Melinda is made to speak the language of re-education is given a sadistic touch by Ritter's tormenting of her that turns to a beating, with her wounds the treatment's first bloodletting. The beating gets a perverse laugh in the way it begins with Melinda saying the mantra that deviants are the lowest form of life while Ritter throws shadow punches at her. The nudity that is seen in the showers is shared equally between women and men, although later the breasts of Chris and Rita will be exposed, with those of Rita in particular being more exploited. The gas ball game that is played on Andy, the boy we saw hide under the van that delivered the three in the opening scene, results in his being set alight after the gas waters the ground from the guards kicking the balls that are attached to him. Tito gets a funny line in response to the guests observing this on video monitors with "Beats the hell out of network television."

The expectation of Chris getting revenge upon Red, who attacks her when she is in the shower, where her breasts are exposed, is met with her jamming his penis in the zipper of his jump suit — an action implied but not shown. The act is also a satisfying payoff to the grotesqueness of Red after the offering a drink joke, but also because of his cackling and use of a whip. The addition of Alph, the Freak, to the hunting party adds both strength to Tito, whose guest Alph is, and sadism given Alph's monstrous strength. Alph would be a comic figure with his constant growling if he wasn't so dangerous, and he also suggests a supernatural element to the antagonists. Jennifer is shown to be equally dangerous with her arrows with exploding heads. Her perversity is expressed by the two shades of eyeshadow and the wire-netted hat she wears, with her advances upon Rita and later Chris also suggesting a lesbian interest.

When Alph tears off the little toe of Dodge and eats it, this is a nice payoff to our dislike of Dodge, who has stolen the knife Griffin has hidden and who has what appears to be dyed orange-hair. The toe being torn off will get another payoff later with Dodge's line to Tito, "I can't hop all my way through the jungle." When Thatcher aims his rifle at Paul the expectation that he will fire is created. Thatcher comments, "No, too easy," but then fires at him anyway. Rita's begging Griffin to take her with him shows a moment of a character's truthful vulnerability that is otherwise missing from the performances. Alph breaks Dodge's back when Tito tells him that he is bored watching Alph beat up Dodge as are we, since the couple is so unmatched. Jennifer's shooting of Griffin with repeated arrows continues the thread of her sadistic perversity; Thatcher running Griffin over with his car is additional savagery.

Chris finding bloody skulls in the pit where she hides from Mallory and Ritter adds some horror movie color to the scene and suggests that the heads may belong to past victims. The movie convention of her hiding within proximity to her conversing pursuers is used, as is her movement away from a snake that appears and slides out of the eye socket of a skull to give away her location. Red found tied up by Griffin and hanging upside down by Mallory and Ritter gets a payoff after a rope is loosened, seemingly to free him, but which actually releases a tree that impales him. The cage that we had earlier seen Paul being tortured in is now used to house the bloody corpse of Griffin, presumably as a warning for the other prisoners in the camp. Rita's cooling off in the river also serves to wet her jumpsuit so that her breasts are more evident. Trenchard-Smith inter-cuts between Jennifer's pursuit of her with Paul fighting Alph and Tito, and Chris being pursued by Mallory and Ritter.

The expectation of Paul being cut by the oncoming tractor that Tito drives is not met when Paul stabs Alph in the eye with a tree branch, and the unstoppable tractor instead cuts Alph in half. Paul's escape then creates the expectation of him rescuing Chris, who flees the canefield that Ritter sets on fire. Mallory gets a laugh line from his "You bitch" when Chris suddenly appears in front of him, and Mallory being shot in the groin by Paul is a payoff to Mallory's intended molestation of Chris. It is interesting that Ritter does not stop pursuing Chris and Paul in order to rescue Mallory, who is entrapped and presumably now burned alive by the burning cane, and Trenchard-Smith delays showing Ritter finding the two pursued while he returns to Jennifer and Rita.

Although Rita's acquiescence to Jennifer's pursuit presents her as a victim, the narrative makes Jennifer in her apparent lesbian interest even more dastardly. Jennifer's lines, "I've been looking for you for a long long time" and "I'm going to make you feel like you've never felt before" have a definite sexual double entendre. This is aided by Jennifer touching Rita's breasts with her arrowhead and the treatment having Jennifer lunge toward Rita as if she is going to kiss her. We have to wait to see what happens with Rita while the narrative returns to Chris and Paul. His fight with Ritter in the pool doesn't result in the expected drowning of Paul, and it is topped by Chris hacking off Ritter's hands with the machete he has abandoned as he aims a gun at Paul with both hands. The result of Chris' strike is initially shown as her only cutting one hand whose fingers keep moving until the reveal of the other detached hand, and we gather that Ritter's death is due to loss of blood.

The discovery of Rita's naked and bloody body with an arrow in her mouth is seemingly made by Thatcher, going from the clothes worn by the person whose face is not shown, and before his regrouping with Jennifer as Mallory's body is piled into Thatcher's car. Rita's nudity is another sign that Jennifer has done something unspeakable and presumably sexual to her victim. Tito's pursuit of Chris is used by Paul as a distraction so that he can use Ritter's machete to strike through Tito's head. Perhaps it is Paul's discovery that the camp is located on an island, which makes escape difficult, that also drives him to go back to the camp to free the other prisoners. We could interpret this act as an expression of Paul's humanity, although we also know that he would want to get revenge upon Thatcher, which is another reason not to try to escape.

The fighter plane footage we see for the planned bombing of the camp is presumably stock footage. The philosophy that the camp must be wiped out if Thatcher has lost control recalls the idea of the Nazis in World War II attempting to destroy the evidence of their camps and killing all the inmates. Jennifer's appearance in the communication room that Chris has destroyed with gunfire allows for a struggle between the two women, and it is a surprise that Chris manages to have the power to turn Jennifer's arrow against her. The explosion that decapitates Jennifer is both comic and a fitting retribution for this creature, with Thatcher's similar decapitation attributed to the machine gun fire of Paul. With the guards seemingly subdued by the prisoners and the camp's bombing, the narrative ends with a title card quote from H.G. Wells, "Revolution begins with the misfits."

In the cast interview featurette on the DVD *Blood and Thunder Memories*, it is said that the first fifteen pages were dropped from the script. This is confirmed in the director featurette, *A Good Soldier*, where it is reported that two weeks before principal photography was to begin, $700,000 in investment money was withdrawn from the $3.2 million budget, and subsequently the shooting schedule was slashed from 44 to 30 days. Trenchard-Smith also reports that the reduced budget meant that the camp, which was designed to accommodate 500 prisoners, could now only be filled with up to 70. Additionally, there was no money to pay stuntmen, and a four page helicopter chase was dropped since it would have been too expensive. Michael Craig reports that Steve Railsback was difficult to work with because he considered himself a method actor. His technique included requesting that real weights be used in the torture scene with Thatcher, where the strain made him forget his lines because of the real pain he was in and the demand required multiple takes for the scene to be completed satisfactorily.

It is also reported that the other imported star, Olivia Hussey, was equally difficult since she seemed to be going through some personal crisis. Apparently she had heard stories about the venomous Australian animals and insects and was therefore terrified to film the exterior scenes. Roger Ward also reports that the actress was so disturbed by having to hold the machete for the scene where Chris cuts off Ritter's hands that she misinterpreted the call for "Cut" by second unit director David Hemmings and swung the blade, only missing Ward's real hands by inches. This anecdote is repeated in the documentary *Not Quite Hollywood*. *A Good Soldier* also confirms that a body double was used for the shot of Chris' breasts in the shower because Hussey refused to show her own breasts.

Australian actress Lynda Stoner is also said to have been trouble since her animal rights agenda made her refuse to gut real fish in a camp scene, so that delays occurred while fake fish were made up to placate her. Stoner also reports that she had refused to do a nude scene and that the back shot of her bare bottom in the shower sequence was the compromise she agreed upon, although clearly the scene where Rita is in the river and wet was designed to showcase her breasts in the transparent jumpsuit.

A Good Soldier has Trenchard-Smith claim that he aimed to make the film a high-camp splatter movie, with dark humor, and a satire of exploitation prison camp movies. In *Not Quite Hollywood* it is claimed that the producers were at the race course everyday gambling to try and recover the money they had lost, and presumably failed. A funny story is told about filming in the river. A local ranger had told the crew that the river was the home of a large female crocodile who had just laid eggs right behind where filming was taking place. In order to scare her away, a bomb was let off, but unfortunately the explosion occurred at the wrong end of the river, so that it caused the crocodile to go to the where the actors were submerged. Thankfully the crocodile was not seen and did not hamper filming.

Turkey Shoot was the first Australian horror title made by director Brian Trenchard-Smith, and he would go on to make another: *Out of the Body*. Producer Antony I. Ginnane had previously made the Australian horror film *The Survivor* with producer William Fayman. Ginnane would go on to make the Australian horror title *Dark Age* for the FGH production company, but Fayman would not make another Australian horror movie. This was the only Australian horror film made by executive producer John Daly and associate producer Brian W. Cook. Executive producer David Hemmings had previously made *Alison's Birthday* and directed *The Survivor*; he would not make another Australian horror film. Neither the Hemdale production company nor Filmco Limited has made another Australian horror movie to date.

American Steve Railsback made his film debut in a supporting role in the crime thriller *The Visitors* (1972). After playing more supporting roles and appearing on television, he essayed the title character but was not top-billed in the action comedy *The Stunt Man* (1980). *Turkey Shoot* was his first leading film role. Afterward he was the lead in the adventure *The Golden Seal* (1983), the horror title *Lifeforce* (1985), and the action drama *The Survivalist* (1987). In the 1990s Railsback was the lead in the Spanish *La cruz de Iberia* (1990), the actioners *The Assassin* (1990) and *Termination Man* (1998), and played supporting film roles and television. In 2000 he played Ed Gein in the biographical crime drama *In the Light of the Moon*, for which he was also the executive producer, and he played his last lead to date in the horror film *Plaguers* (2008). The actor also directed the thriller *The Flight of the Dove* (1994).

Argentinian born Olivia Hussey began her career in television and made her film debut as a teenager in a supporting role in *The Battle of the Villa Fiorita* (1965). She earned international attention as Juliet in the romance *Romeo and Juliet* (1968) and essayed her first leading role in the comedy *All the Right Noises* (1971). Hussey was also the lead in the horror title *Black Christmas* (1974), and played in supporting parts and on television. After *Turkey Shoot* the actress was the lead opposite Steve Railsback in the thriller *Distortions* (1987), the romantic thriller *Island Prey* (2001), and the horror story *Headspace* (2005), as well as other supporting film roles and television.

Carmen Duncan made her film debut in a supporting role in the New Zealand musical comedy *Don't Let It Get You* (1966), and after playing more supporting roles and on television, scored her first film lead after *Turkey Shoot* in the crime drama *Run*

Chrissie Run! (1986). She has not had another leading film role to date. Noel Ferrier made his film debut in a supporting role in the family drama *Little Jungle Boy* (1969), and was known for playing film supporting roles and television. He would not appear in another Australian horror title and died in 1997.

Michael Craig was born in India and made his film debut in an uncredited part in the British comedy *Passport to Pimlico* (1949). After playing supporting roles and on television, he essayed the lead in the British crime drama *House of Secrets* (1956), *Life in Emergency Ward 10* (1959), and the comedy *Upstairs and Downstairs* (1959). In the 1960s Craig continued as a leading man in British films like *Cone of Silence* (1960), the comedy *Doctor in Love* (1960), the crime drama *Payroll* (1961), the family adventure *Mysterious Island* (1961), the comedies *The Iron Maiden* (1962) and *A Pair of Briefs* (1962), and *Life for Ruth* (1962).

By the 1970s the actor was playing more supporting roles and television, although he was the lead in the Italian *Appuntamento col disonore*, aka *The Night of the Assassin* (1970) and the family adventure *Ride a Wild Pony* (1975). Craig played a supporting part in the Australian horror title *Inn of the Damned* and was the lead in the Italian romance *Per amore*, aka *For Love* (1976). He wrote the screenplay for and played a supporting role in *The Fourth Wish* (1976), and was the title character in the romance *The Irishman* (1978), his last leading role to date. After *Turkey Shoot* the actor has only been seen in supporting film roles and on television. Craig was also one of the screenwriters for *The Angry Silence* (1960) and the thriller *The Killing of Angel Street* (1981).

Lynda Stoner began her career in television and made her film debut in *Turkey Shoot*. To date she has not made another Australian horror movie. A former wrestler, Roger Ward made his film debut in an uncredited part in the Italian *Odissea nuda* (1961) and played supporting film roles and on television. He went on to appear in the Australian horror title *Lady, Stay Dead*. Michael Petrovitch began his career in television and made his film debut in a supporting role in the British horror film *Neither the Sea Nor the Sand* (1972). *Turkey Shoot* is his only Australian horror film to date.

Release

Australia on November 18, 1982, and the United States in October 1983 with the taglines "Hunting is the national sport ... and people are the prey," "No film for chickens," "Controversial! Violent! The film that shocked Australian critics and broke Box Office records in London!" "Experience the Year 2000.... And Hope to Hell You Can Escape!" and "The day the future had to be stopped." *A Good Soldier* has Trenchard-Smith reporting that publicists for the film sent boxes of turkey's feet with the invitation to the London critics.

Reviews

"Aside from spectacle, [it] relies almost completely on mutilation, torture and killing. The graphic nature of the violence distances the audience so that the interest is relegated to anticipation of the next atrocity."—Geoff Mayer, *Cinema Papers*, March, 1983

"Merely a catalogue of sickening horrors. It seems to be an exercise solely designed for the sadists in the community. The actors involved should have been ashamed for appearing in such trash; some apparently were. [However] the special effects are undeniably well done, and the film is certainly slick."—David Stratton, *The Avocado Plantation*

"[It] botches the hunter-versus-hunted scenario with an overemphasis on violence, appalling acting and a plot that is no more advanced than a boys' adventure comic.... So incompetent and over-indulged that one cannot be altogether sure that its creators did not have some tongue-in-cheek intentions. Unfortunately, though, the film is laughable for all the wrong reasons."—Scott Murray, *Oxford Australian Film 1978–1994*

"It is the 'car accident' factor that makes this movie appealing. You don't want to look, but you just have to. *Turkey Shoot* is a cult classic that does nothing for the reputation of the Australian film industry, but has to be seen never the less. Dumb fun!"—J.R. McNamara, *Digital Retribution*, October 17, 2005

"This futuristic splatter is clearly inspired by *Mad Max* but it's a bloody and deliciously fun mess with machetes through the head, hands/toes lopped off, death(s) by arrow piercings, bisection via heavy machinery. Poor Olivia Hussey deserves better here, but (with Railsback as support) proves a trooper. A befuddling but enjoyable outing."—*The Terror Trap*

"Unusual Australian futuristic adventure ... the bloody action is almost nonstop."—John Stanley, *Creature Features*

DVD

Released by Starz/Anchor Bay on October 21, 2003. Umbrella Entertainment (Australia) released September 10, 2003.

Innocent Prey

Premier Pictures Corporation, 1984 [aka *Voyeur*]

CREDITS: *Producer/Director:* Colin Eggleston; *Executive Producer:* David G.B. Williams; *Screenplay:* Rod McLean; *Photography:* Vincent Monton; *Editor:* Pippa Anderson; *Music:* Brian May; *Art Director:* Larry Eastwood; *Sound:* Bob Clayton; *Makeup/Hair:* Deryck De Neise; *Set Decorator:* Michael O'Sullivan; *Costumes:* Ruth Manning. Color, 87 minutes. Filmed on location in Dallas, Texas, and Sydney, New South Wales, and at the studios at Las Colinas, Dallas Communications Center.

CAST: P.J. Soles (Kathy McKae née Wills); Kit Taylor (Joe McKae); Grigor Taylor (Rick Green); John Warnock (Phillip); Susan Sternmark (Gwen); Richard Morgan (Ted); Martin Balsam (Sheriff Virgil Baker); Debi Sue Voorhees (Hooker); Karen Radcliffe (Police Officer Casey); Bill Thurman (Jim Gardner); Joe Berryman (Billy Joe); Harlan Jordan (Riley); Tyress Allen (Fletcher).

Synopsis

Kathy McRae lives in Dallas, Texas, with her oil company businessman husband, Joe. She is visited by Gwen, a friend who resides in Sydney, and after driving her to the airport, Kathy sees Joe entering the Alamo Motel Court. When she looks inside his room window she sees Joe having sex with a prostitute and then cutting her throat. At home Kathy tells Joe what she has witnessed, but when he attempts to attack her with a fire poker, the police appear to save her. Joe is committed to a state asylum but escapes and returns, killing the three police officers that have been sent to guard Kathy. Sheriff Virgil Baker saves Kathy from Joe, and buys her horse property to enable her to travel to Sydney. Kathy takes a room at the mansion where Gwen lives, but unknown to her or any of the tenants, the landlord Phillip watches their rooms on a video monitor.

Phillip becomes enamored of Kathy, but electrocutes Gwen since he finds her sexual promiscuity sinful. Another tenant, Rick Green, becomes interested in Kathy and she has sex with him. When Phillip sees this and learns of Kathy's disinterest in him, he plans revenge. He also kills Joe, who tracks Kathy down, before he can attack her. When Kathy invites Rick and Phillip to dinner, Phillip locks him in his video room and electrifies the mansion. Rick escapes and pushes Phillip into the electrified shower stall. Phillip crashes through the bathroom window and falls to his death. When Kathy goes to the hospital to discharge Rick, whose wounds have been attended to, she does not see that Rick owns the kind of razor blade that Joe used to kill the prostitute.

Notes

This title features the theme of the horror of personality in the form of two antagonists, one being a murdering husband and the other a voyeuristic landlord with romantic designs upon the protagonist. Director Colin Eggleston employs the postmodern techniques of expressionist camera angles, point of view, zooms and blackouts as well as an obtrusive score. His treatment has bloodletting, a decapitation, burning of a broken-necked victim and electrocution. The narrative's use of two antagonists to keep the protagonist victimized matches the two locations. Interest occasionally flags during the narrative's presentation of the friendship between the protagonist and the Dallas sheriff, which also lacks a payoff. However, the romantic subplot between her and a seemingly more appropriate suitor thankfully supports the main plot. Although half of the story is located in America, the casting of an actress known to American audiences in the lead role appears to be another case of a decision made to market the film to appeal to an international audience.

Under the opening credits we see Joe sharpening the same razor blade that he will presumably use on the Hooker, although his cutting his finger to produce blood seems an unnecessary proof of how sharp it is. Granted that it is a wild coincidence that Kathy should happen to pass the Alamo Motor Court just as Joe is entering it, but her decision to go and investigate is an interesting one. Eggleston provides equal nudity for Joe and the Hooker when they have sex in the bathtub, and he shows an extreme close-up of Kathy's eyes to see the sex that turns to murder from two points of view. From the window she can see the mirrored view of Joe's back to her and the reveal of him holding the razor, and the Hooker facing her so that she sees the resultant blood flow from her throat being cut. When Joe is seen having a shower in the background and the Hooker's bloodied leg is draped over the bathtub in the foreground, the swirl of blood down the shower drain recalls the same action in *Psycho*.

It is a surprise that Kathy should tell Joe that she

saw both his car at the motel and him having sex and murdering the Hooker, since we wonder what she expects Joe to do with this information. It is only after the police appear to stop Joe from striking her with the fire poker that we realize that she has told him to give the police time to get to her. When the police enter the room it does not meet the expectation of Joe's striking Kathy, whereas Joe's later return to the house to find Kathy has more conventional expectations that are met. The narrative goes to Gwen being watched by Phillip on the video monitor before Kathy's arrival at the mansion in the second half of the plot. This is perhaps to prefigure what will happen to Kathy, but also observe Gwen's swimming habit that will eventually be used by Phillip to electrocute her.

After we see Joe's escape from the prison that is later identified as an asylum, the expectation of his being at an opened door of the house that Kathy goes to is not met. There is a laugh from Kathy picking up a kitchen knife, putting it down, and then hearing a noise and picking it up again. Her walking backwards to a glass door meets the expectation of Joe's hand crashing through it. His grabbing the knife she holds, whereby he cuts his hand, demonstrates his madness and the superior physical strength in his ability to take it from her. The radio warning made to the police officers on the scene of "Don't try to be heroes" gets a payoff from their agreement not to be, and then Joe's easy stabbing of the two of them. The expectation that is created when Officer Casey leaves the frame to go to the pantry to get coffee is met when she does not answer Kathy's calls because she has been attacked by Joe. When Kathy looks for her she is the conventional Woman in Peril, and Eggleston uses her opening of the pantry door in front of the camera for a momentary blackout.

Kathy's discovery of the bloodied head of Casey on a shelf gets a laugh and then a payoff when the head falls off the shelf during the struggle between Kathy and Joe. She also does an unusual action — putting her fingers in her mouth in fear. The Sheriff's appearance is a shock effect when he puts his hand on her shoulder. We wonder why we don't see him attempting to find Joe or why Joe doesn't also attack him when the Sheriff appears to be alone though presumably isn't. This moment is also used for the transition to them at the airport, where the Sheriff sees Kathy off for her trip to Sydney, and there is the expectation that since she is leaving the country, Joe will not come after her. This expectation is not met, as we will later see.

The dinner crowd at Phillip's mansion makes us wonder just how many tenants he has, although Kathy later having to use a communal bathroom tells us that the mansion doesn't have all the modern conveniences. Phillip is presented as socially awkward in his ignorance of liquor and declining to have dinner with the tenants, and his bad haircut and nerdy clothes add to this impression. His comment to Kathy, "I'll certainly see you later," naturally plays on him as the video voyeur earlier watching Gwen. His eating frozen dinners as he watches the monitors as if they are television further suggests his social isolation, although at the climactic dinner with Kathy he will tell her how he has strict dietary demands, which may explain why he appears to eat the same thing all the time. Phillip's reactions to his watching Kathy on the monitor are telling. He smiles at her when she smiles, although she cannot hear or see him. He looks away when she removes a negligee to go to bed, thinking she will undress further, which she doesn't. Eggleston inter-cuts to Phillip looking disapprovingly at Gwen as she has sex in her bed before returning to Kathy, where he expresses concern over her nightmare presumably about Joe and sings "Hush a Bye, Baby" to her which in turn seems to calm her.

After we see Joe attack a sailor at the San Francisco docks and break his neck, the thing we see him burn is presumably the sailor, although Eggleston does not show this specifically. This is confirmed when the Sheriff rings Kathy to tell her that the body they have found is presumed to be Joe since a ring was found, which she identifies as his. Since we know that Joe has faked his own death the expectation is created that he will come after Kathy again, which will be met. When Rick takes Kathy back to her room after she is drunk, presumably celebrating her perceived freedom from Joe, he helps her into bed. He does so without even kissing her goodnight, which is a relief for the watching Phillip, but it does create the expectation that Rick will later pursue Kathy, which is met.

Phillip's second disapproval of Gwen having sex in her bed creates the expectation that he will do something to her. What he does is not shown until the climax: he leaves the video of Phillip's murder of her for Rick to watch. Gwen is said to be missing the next day and our disbelief in Phillip's story of driving her to the airport is aided by his holding a shovel; this creates what is later revealed to be the false expectation that he has buried her in his garden. The plot point of Kathy learning that she is pregnant doesn't really get a payoff apart from the idea that she is still tied to Joe even if he is dead, although she will attempt to use it as a reason for

Phillip not to kill her in the climax. Equally, the montage of Rick and Kathy's tour of Sydney with his children only seems to exist as a way to present their romance, although the fact that Rick has children also undermines the romance by suggesting that he is romantically damaged by being an abandoned husband.

When Joe appears at the mansion our wondering how he found Kathy's location is rationalized by the assumption that he knew where Gwen lived previously, and Phillip watching and recognizing creates the expectation that Phillip will do something to stop him. This is partly because of Phillip's interest in Kathy but also because of his earlier expressed knowledge and disapproval of Joe. Joe is seen by Phillip to be in Kathy's room, and Joe animalistically smells her clothes to recognize her. Kathy returning from dinner with Rick but being left by Rick creates the expectation of her being attacked by Joe, as does the shot from the open closet door of Kathy being watched. This expectation is not met when she goes to the door. Eggleston also creates a red herring from the figure that appears to be behind the glass bathroom door that Kathy goes to, only to be revealed as a hanging dressing gown. Even the shock effect of Joe falling onto Kathy from behind the staircase window curtain does not meet the created expectation of his strike, because he is shown to be dead. We never learn what has killed Joe or who has killed him, although we assume it was Phillip.

Phillip ringing Kathy's telephone to get her away from Rick, whom she has invited to her room, gets a laugh from his urging her to answer when she delays. The camera angle does not allow Phillip to see the way she rolls her eyes in reaction to the news that he is her caller. This point is followed up when she describes Phillip to Rick as a "wacko" who gives her the creeps. Naturally, hearing this upsets Phillip, and Eggleston uses a freeze frame of him after seeing Rick and Kathy having sex. Phillip is also shown to be listening but not watching the screen when they discuss inviting him to dinner. Although Kathy expresses regret in her earlier dismissal of Phillip—perhaps as a pragmatic strategy to not put her accommodation at risk—we sense that the damage to Phillip has been done.

Rick being locked in the screen room by Phillip is an interesting choice, since it reveals Phillip's secret, although we assume that the door having being electrified means that Phillip thinks Rick will be killed. This same confession relates to the tape of Phillip electrocuting Gwen that he leaves for Rick to watch. The assumption is that Phillip's screen room extends to a talent for electrifying objects and helps to explain Gwen's death and the other contrivances to come. When Rick watches Phillip and Kathy on the monitor, the expectation is created for Phillip to strike against her, as well as Rick to attempt to get out of the room and save her.

Phillip's discussion of his mother and her repentance for her sins before she died suggests that perhaps he killed her, though this is a plot point that is unresolved and not a vital one since we never saw his mother. Rick falling unconscious from the cuts he receives to his face and stomach from a shard of whatever he uses to attempt to break through the electrified door creates the expectation of his being unable to save Kathy. She now realizes Phillip's threat but, unlike with Joe, does not attempt to arm herself. The electrocution of Ted as he opens the house's front door is a cruel disposal of a minor narrative character, though it does prefigure Rick's attempt to do the same.

Phillip follows Kathy, who retreats to the bathroom. His order for her to take a shower is both an order for her to be electrocuted by the shower stall and perhaps a request to see her naked, matching the comic madness and desire of his order. Thankfully, Kathy's obvious eyeing of Rick when he is behind Phillip does not stop him from being pushed into the electrified shower stall. Phillip's crashing through the window and landing on lower steps in an upside down crucified position provides an over the top but Gothic demise.

The film's epilogue is perplexing, since the razor that we see Rick handle could easily be just the instrument for him to shave with as opposed to the suggestion that Rick is the murderer that Joe was. While it may seem to provide ambiguity and create the opportunity for the sequel that was never made, it reads rather as a cheap gag with no reality attached to it.

Director Colin Eggleston had previously made the Australian horror movie *Long Weekend*, produced the Australian horror title *Nightmares* and would go on to make the Australian horror films *Cassandra* and *Outback Vampires*. *Innocent Prey* would be the only Australian horror title made by executive producer David G.B. Williams and the production company Premiere Pictures.

German born P.J. Soles began her career in American television and made her film debut in a minor role in the horror film *Blood Bath* (1976). After appearing in more television and film supporting roles, she essayed the lead in the musical comedy *Rock 'n' Roll High School* (1979) and the romance *The Awakening of Cassie* (1982). After *Innocent Prey* the actress played leads in *Listen to the City* (1984), and more television and film supporting parts. Kit Taylor began his career as a child star and made his film debut in a supporting role in the family adventure *Return to Treasure Island* (1954). He made the transition to adult roles and appeared in television and more film supporting roles prior to and after *Innocent Prey*, including the Australian horror title *Cassandra*.

Grigor Taylor also began his career in television and made his film debut in the crime comedy *High Rolling* (1977). He continued in television and film supporting roles prior to and after *Innocent Prey*. John Warnock too began his career in television and made his movie debut in the film, which has been his last title to date. Susan Stenmark is another actor to have started in television and made her film debut here, after which she would play more supporting roles. Richard Morgan also began his career in television and made his film debut in a supporting role in *The Devil's Playground* (1976). He would continue in television and film supporting roles before and after *Innocent Prey*, including the Australian horror title *Outback Vampires*.

American Martin Balsam also began his career in American television and made his film debut in an uncredited role in the crime drama *On the Waterfront* (1954). After appearing in more television and film supporting roles, he essayed rare leads in the Italian crime drama *Il consigliore*, aka *Counselor at Crime* (1973), and *Whatever It Takes* (1986). He won the Best Supporting Actor Academy Award for his role in the romantic comedy *A Thousand Clowns* (1965). *Innocent Prey* is the only Australian horror film he made; he died in 1996.

Release

Appears to have been released straight to video in Australia and the United States with the tagline "Her husband is a serial killer out to get her.... Her landlord is out to possess her.... This is how one woman becomes their.... Innocent Prey."

Reviews

"The script is full of holes and the direction is merely functional; Eggleston even has the cheek to show blood draining down the plug-hole after a prostitute is murdered in a shower. The film is also far too long and very laboriously handled."—David Stratton, *The Avocado Plantation*

"Conventional suspense vehicle works at first (the hooker slashing in the shower is notably well done), but begins to sag under its own weight in the final third and is ultimately undone by a frazzled storyline. Still, Soles is delightful to watch throughout, and is especially a believable trooper at the climax."—*The Terror Trap*

"Not a bad movie by any means, but it's certainly a preposterous one. It works because the actors and actresses take it all seriously.... Has a good mixture of the cheesiness some of us love about films from this time and a good dose of that early '80s grittiness, too."—*Hysteria Lives!*

DVD

Not available on DVD. Video released by Intermedia Video/Sys, Inc. in 1988, exact date unavailable.

Razorback
Wonder Classics/McElroy and McElroy Production, 1984

CREDITS: *Director:* Russell Mulcahy; *Producer:* Hal McElroy; *Associate Producer:* Tim Sanders; *Photography:* Dean Semler; *Screenplay:* Everett De Roche, based on the novel by Peter Brennan; *Editor:* William Anderson; *Music:* Iva Davies; *Production Design:* Bryce Walmsley; *Art Director:* Neil Angwin; *Design and Construction:* Bob McCarron; *Sound:* Tim Lloyd; *Wardrobe:* Helen Hooper; *Makeup:* Wendy Sainsbury; *Hair:* Mara Schiavetti. Color, 95 minutes. Shot on location in Broken Hill, the Mundi Mundi Plain and Silverton, New South Wales; and Mort Bay Studios, Balmain, New South Wales.

SONGS: "Blue Eyes" (Elton John, Gary Osborne), Elton John, heard in Beth's car; "New Moon on Monday" (Duran Duran), Duran Duran; "Reckless (Don't Be So)" (James Reyne).

CAST: Gregory Harrison (Carl Winters); Arkie Whiteley (Sarah Cameron); Bill Kerr (Jake Cullen); Chris Haywood (Benny Baker); David Argue (Dicko Baker); John Howard (Danny); John Ewart (Turner); Judy Morris (Beth Winters); Don Smith (Wallace); Mervyn Drake (Andy); Redmond Phillips (Magistrate); Alan Beecher (Counsel); Peter Schwartz (Lawyer);

Beth Child (Louise Cullen); Rick Kennedy (Farmer); Chris Hession (TV Cowboy); Brian Adams (Male Newscaster); Jinx Lootens (Female Newscaster); Angus Malone (Scotty); Peter Boswell (Wagstaff); Don Lane (Himself).

Synopsis

In the outback town of Gamulla, the home of professional razorback hunter Jake Cullen is attacked by an enormous wild pig (razorback) which takes Jake's two-year-old grandson, Scotty. There is no evidence found to charge Jake with the child's death, but the township believes him guilty. Two years later, New York World Animal League reporter Beth Winters is sent on assignment to Gamulla to investigate claims of cruelty at the town's Petpack slaughterhouse. When she is caught filming at the slaughterhouse, which is run by the Baker brothers, her car is run off the road by the brothers' truck, and Dicko attempts to rape her. The Bakers are scared away by the razorback but it attacks Beth and she goes missing, thought to have fallen down a mine shaft.

Beth's husband, Carl, comes to Gamulla and visits the Bakers, who take him to the desert at night under the pretense of kangaroo shooting. Carl is left alone and seeks refuge from the wild pigs in a wind vane that sits by a waterhole that the pigs drink from. He befriends pig migration researcher Sarah Cameron, who tags the pigs for location monitoring. Jake learns that Carl thinks he saw the razorback at the lake. Jake goes after it, shoots it with Sarah's tagging gun, and finds the ring that Carl had given to Beth. Dicko breaks Jake's leg, which makes him defenseless when the razorback attacks as he hides in the pumping station. Carl goes after Benny and Dicko, dropping Benny down a mine shaft, but his attempt to shoot Dicko is stopped by the razorback who strikes Dicko at the slaughterhouse. Sarah tracks the razorback to the slaughterhouse, where Carl leads it into the machinery's blades, where it is killed.

Notes

This film features the horror of a malevolent supernatural being in the form of a diseased overgrown wild pig. Director Russell Mulcahy uses a slew of postmodern techniques — quick edits, freeze frames, zooms, jump cuts, expressionist camera angles, optical effects, and point of view. He also displays an eye for resonant imagery and cleverly utilizes the limitations placed upon him in having a treatment that centers on an obviously mechanical creation. This latter consideration also affects the minimal level of gore attached to the four killings that are presented, with shock and suggestion used as opposed to graphic literalism.

The narrative recalls that of *The Cars That Ate Paris* in presenting outback Australians as redneck grotesques, making the antagonist even more grotesque. It portrays the changing protagonists (Jake, Beth, and then Carl) as witnesses to this grotesquery. However, it also complicates matters by having two characters — Benny and Dicko — behave antagonistically towards the protagonists in a form of subplot.

The prologue shows the attack upon Jake and Scotty. We presume that the razorback takes the child so that he can be eaten, although this is not presented. The prologue is prefigured by the sound of the pig as it approaches the house during a dust storm. This is the kind of creature that screams to announce its presence and advance, and when Jake hears the noise and investigates, he is the Man in Peril, the male version of the conventional Woman in Peril.

After the razorback has struck, Mulcahy has some of the dialogue from the ensuing scene of the hearing played over shots of Jake arriving into town where the hearing is held, to show the townspeople's disbelief of him. The introduction of Beth features Judy Morris' poor attempt at an American accent. But she also gets to tell us that Gamulla is an aboriginal word for intestine, which is supposed to be appropriate because the slaughterhouse turns kangaroo meat into dog food. The Aboriginal presence in the town is fleeting — we see some Aboriginal children in the early scenes — but there are no major Aboriginal characters. This is disappointing since perhaps they could have supplied some rationale for the existence of the razorback, dream time–flavored though it may have been.

Beth's attempt to talk on the telephone in a pub as she is surrounded by locals recalls a similar scene in *Roadgames*, although here it is given a payoff. After darts are thrown at a wall near her, she deposits the darts into Dicko's beer glass. When the Baker brothers' truck taunts and eventually runs Beth off the road, it also recalls the similar scenes in *Roadgames* and prefigures the same in *Fair Game*. Dicko's intended rape of Beth creates the expectation that is met that the razorback will stop him, although we will have to wait for Dicko to get his proper comeuppance. Mulcahy uses the creature's point of view and dust rising for its advance. After

German poster for *Razorback* (1984).

While Carl is arriving in town by bus he is given a flashback which continues the plot point that was begun in his prior scene with Beth, where he gave her a ring but we did not see her reaction. Since they are already married, the ring would seem to have less significance as a life marker, although it is paid off later in the narrative when it is found to establish Beth's presumed fate. For the flashback Mulcahy uses the footage Beth has filmed as well as interviews with her cameraman, Danny, and someone else to tell him that Beth is missing. Interestingly, we get a different take for the shot where Beth is pushed out of the way by Jake's truck as he departs her interview.

Although the cave residence of the Bakers isn't used for any plot payoff, its Gothicism does add to their strange characters. Their grotesqueness is represented by Benny's half blind one eye and Dicko wearing kangaroo skin as a coat. The expectation that they will be a threat to Carl is met even before they learn that he pretends not to be Beth's husband. The bush hunting ground is presented as equally Gothic in the car that sits in a tree, and by the birds that cry after the kangaroo is shot. Carl sleeping on the dead kangaroo — which he has bludgeoned to death after it has been shot by Benny — makes for a bizarre type of pillow so that the appearance of the wild pigs and their interest in him is an expectation met. In Carl's flight, Mulcahy repeats an image of him falling into a wire fence. The expectation that Carl will be attacked by the pigs or the razorback as he climbs onto the wind vane is delayed until the next day. The pigs appearing at the bottom of the vane creates the expectation, met, that it will fall. The expectation that Carl will be attacked is not met since he falls into the water hole and apparently the pigs cannot swim. However, Mulcahy uses a shock effect for the rise of a presumably dead pig floating by Carl in the water hole.

Carl's trek through the desert is a sequence where, despite Mulcahy's fantasy moments, like Carl's imagined chase by a skeleton horse, features some

the Bakers leave, the expectation is also created that she will be attacked by the razorback. This is met, with her initial silence in reaction to seeing it being pleasing in its surprise, although it may also be a case of stillness out of crippling fear. One can also make the case for the horns of the razorback to be a phallic rape threat, with the later information given that she was six weeks pregnant, adding to her vulnerability.

The attack upon Beth recalls the first attack of the shark in *Jaws* in the way she is thrown around. The image of her hand grasping as she is seemingly pulled away by the pig is one of a resonant horror. Mulcahy goes further than the attack upon Scotty, which is not shown at all, by having Beth's attack presented. Here the only indication that she is killed is that her ring is found later at the lake, since her body is not recovered.

beautifully composed scenic long shots. After Carl is assisted by Sarah, whose house he finds, his vision of her having a pig face is presumably the last of his desert hallucinations. Sarah seen bare-breasted as she showers is Mulcahy's contextual and non-exploitative nudity for the actress. The narrative returns to another kangaroo hunter watching television at night for a comic payoff, after we have seen a trap set for the razorback that it had visited before but had not attacked. This time the creature proves to be too strong and pulls away the half of the house that includes the television the hunter had been watching.

Dicko visiting Jake so he can break his legs is as equally Gothic and cruel, as is Dicko's later running over Jake's dog, whom Jake had sent to get Sarah, although Mulcahy spares us both strikes so that we only see the resultant injuries. Mulcahy also uses the swinging door of the pumping station to ward off the approaching normal-sized pigs, although it does not stop the razorback. Again Mulcahy spares us the sight of the strike upon Jake, for which he uses jump cuts on Jake for the moments before the strike. This leaves us to see the reaction of Carl and Sarah to Jake's corpse. We presume that the animal has not eaten Jake, as we presume it had eaten Scotty and Beth, in order for Carl and Sarah to be able to recognize Jake after the attack.

Carl's chase of Benny begins with the comic notion of Carl's truck slamming into the outdoor toilet Benny was using, since he emerges with his pants down and holding a roll of toilet paper. Although we know that Benny and Dicko did not kill Beth, Carl's pursuit of them seems misguided. His scene of entrapping Benny in a mine shaft is a payoff to the story that they presumably spread that she has fallen down a mine. We assume that Benny does not die after he falls into the mine, but even though he we do not see him again, we imagine it will be hard for him to get out of it.

The town's decision to go after the razorback gets a comic moment when Turner must ride a camel to join the posse. A camel had been featured in an earlier comic moment when it had stuck its head through the door of the pub to take someone's can of drink. The posse's search is soon abandoned when the tagging of a baby pig we have seen Sarah perform earlier is used to show her finding it and not the razorback.

Lightning is used as horror movie convention of a storm for the film's climax at the cannery where Carl originally appears to pursue Dicko, although the sounds we hear before Carl arrives of the razorback clue us that it is also present. Dicko nearly pushes Carl into a blade and Carl is saved by his foot being conveniently caught on a lever. This will also get a plot payoff in the way the razorback will be killed by the blade. Dicko's truck not starting for him is another genre conventional suspense trick and the truck starting when Carl tries it a sign of narrative empathy. Carl chasing Dicko with the truck and the searchlight recalls the hunt of the kangaroo, which Dicko references by doing a kangaroo impression. Carl's hesitance in shooting Dicko is surely a sign that he has more conscience than Dicko and allows for the expectation of the razorback strike.

Like the attack upon Beth, the razorback's advance on Dicko after a chase is more explicit than those of Scotty and Jake, although still as suggestive as that of Beth. After the creature knocks down the catwalk that has kept Carl above him, Carl nearly falls into the razorback's mouth, recalling the scene where Robert Shaw

Dicko Baker (David Argue) and Benny Baker (Chris Haywood), examples of the redneck grotesques that are of one of the recurring motifs in Australian horror films, in a French lobby card for *Razorback* (1984).

slid into the mouth of the shark in *Jaws*. Mulcahy provides an extreme close-up of the razorback's eye — the only such shot of animal or human in the entire film — before the arrival of Sarah. The issue is raised whether she is killed by it. We wonder why she doesn't use the gun that we see her carry against it, and we only learn later how, somehow, she has been wrapped up and raised in chains to escape being attacked.

Mulcahy uses a shock reveal of the creature behind Carl before the delicious moment when the razorback's face is close to his and the blood from Carl's strike is spat into Carl's face. There is some ambiguity in the use of the conveyer belt that leads to the blades. We don't know if Carl is trapped or not. The idea of a creature the size of the razorback being led to the blades defies logic, although the payoff of the use of the blades is satisfying. Mulcahy also adds ambiguity to the shock reveal of Sarah, upside down and in chains, before Carl releases her and she opens her eyes to embrace him.

In the DVD making-of documentary, *Jaws on Trotters*, and in the audio commentary by Gregory Harrison, it is revealed how the actor had been raised with razorbacks in Catalina, providing an earlier connection with the film's antagonist. It is also claimed Mulcahy wanted Jeff Bridges for the role of Carl but this was vetoed by producer Hal McElroy and the distributors because he was not considered at the time a big enough international box office attraction. Apparently Arkie Whitely initially refused to be naked in Sarah's shower scene, but changed her mind when she was told that the model who had been brought in to double for her had cellulite.

In the documentary *Not Quite Hollywood*, Quentin Tarantino says he was drawn to the film because he had heard that Mulcahy was considered "the poor man's Ridley Scott." Hal McElroy comments that the film agenda was "capital C for commercial" and that "many would argue that it had little or no artistic or intellectual merit." Gregory Harrison adds that the problem was it had "style over substance, but there is a lot of style." The idea is raised that the film is considered a long music video. This is given because Mulcahy had earned attention from the music videos he had made for pop stars like Ultravox, Duran Duran, and Elton John. Judy Morris says that Mulcahy's style was seen at the time of the film's release as a minus, but it would now be seen as a plus, given the postmodern style of filmmaking that is indicative of contemporary directors. Morris also comments that the film "has stood the test of time."

Russell Mulcahy made his feature film directing debut with *Razorback* but has not made another Australian horror title. The film appears to be the only one made by the production company Wonder Classics and associate producer Tim Sanders. Producer Hal McElroy, with his McElroy and McElroy Productions, had previously made the Australian horror film *The Last Wave*, but it would not make another Australian horror movie.

American Gregory Harrison made his film debut in an uncredited part in the comedy *The Harrad*

Carl Winters (Gregory Harrison) seeks refuge from marauding wild pigs in a wind-vane in a French lobby card for *Razorback* (1984).

Experiment (1973), and after working in television played the title character in *Jim, The World's Greatest* (1976). He played film supporting roles and in more television prior to *Razorback*, and afterward returned to the same, although did score the leads in the thrillers *Body Chemistry II: Voice of a Stranger* (1992) and *Hard Evidence* (1995).

After working in television Arkie Whiteley made her film debut in a supporting role in the thriller *The Killing of Angel Street* (1981), and continued in television and film supporting roles before and after *Razorback*. The actress died in 2001 of cancer. South African born Bill Kerr made his film debut as a child actor in a minor role in the Australian comedy *Harmony Row* (1933). He transitioned into adult supporting film roles in British cinema, but came back to Australia to work in television. He also played supporting film roles before scoring the lead in the dog drama *Dusty* (1983), his prior role. After *Razorback* he was the lead in *The Settlement* (1984), but otherwise was seen in film supporting roles and on television.

A stalwart of Australian cinema, British born Chris Haywood made his film debut in a supporting role in the Australian horror title *The Cars That Ate Paris* after working in television. After playing other supporting roles and more television, he scored a lead in *The Clinic* (1982). After *Razorback* he was the lead in *Strikebound* (1984), *A Street to Die* (1985), the comedy *The Bit Part* (1987), the crime drama *Call Me Mr. Brown* (1990), *Golden Braid* (1990), and was top-billed in the thriller *Savages Crossing* (2009). The actor also appeared in supporting roles in the Australia horror film *Subterano*.

After working in television, David Argue made his film debut in a supporting role in the historical adventure *Gallipoli* (1981), co-wrote the screenplay for and played the lead in the comedy *Snow: The Movie* (1982), and was the lead in the crime drama *BMX Bandits* (1983). After *Razorback* he essayed the lead in the crime drama *Backlash* (1987), played a double role in *Pandemonium* (1988), and in the comedy *Hercules Returns* (1993). He has otherwise worked in television and played supporting film roles, including the Australia horror title *Road Train* (2010).

After beginning her career in television, Judy Morris made her film debut in the title role of "Judy" in that episode of the anthology *Three to Go* (1971). After more television and supporting roles, she was the lead in *The Trespassers* (1976), and *...Maybe This Time* (1981). After *Razorback* the actress essayed the lead in *The More Things Change...* (1986), though otherwise played supporting film roles and television. Morris also directed the comedy *Luigi's Ladies* (1989) and was one of the co-directors of the animated adventure comedy *Happy Feet* (2006).

Release

Australia on April 19, 1984, and the United States on November 16, 1984, with the taglines "It's waiting outside and it can sense your fear. No nightmare will prepare you for it," "A new breed of terror," "It has two states of being ... dangerous or dead," and "Nine Hundred Pounds of Marauding Tusk and Muscle." The DVD has deleted scenes which are actually the creature attacks on Beth, Jake, Dicko, and Carl with more graphic footage, which reportedly the distributors excised. The shots show how Beth's leg is slashed, how the creature chews Jake's face off and how he is found by Carl and Sarah with worms crawling over his face, how Dicko's leg is bitten and eaten, and more blood spurting on Carl's face.

Reviews

"The landscapes of *Razorback* have a wonderfully bizarre, almost Dali-esque character. The scenery is far more scary than the monster hog, which, according to the credits, was designed by Bob McCarron and appears to have been stuffed while still alive."—Vincent Canby, *The New York Times*, September 13, 1985

"One of the most technically accomplished and visually exciting Australian films yet made. Unfortunately, most of the images wash off very quickly as the story meanders along and viewer interest fluctuates. The elements of suspense and pace are for the most part out of sync."—Jim Schembri, *Cinema Papers*, July 1984

"A commendably inventive addition to the [man-hunting animal] genre, though it must be admitted that the mechanical pig is not always 100 percent convincing. Mulcahy delights in a bravura display of technical skill."—David Stratton, *The Avocado Plantation*

"Some surprisingly good special effects and solid direction create a well achieved sense of gritty atmosphere. When seen, the razorback is a fairly scary beast! The outcome? Razorback is truly a good little monster sleeper and worth seeking out."—*The Terror Trap*

"Mulcahy manages a dreamlike reality for his outback imagery that has the effect of putting the U.S. character in a totally alien environment, maybe reflecting overseas perceptions of the Aussie bush."—*ScaryMinds*

"A fun monster flick.... There's enough pig mayhem to make this film a worthwhile addition to the rampaging monster films catalogue. The film might've been 'better' if the pig was realised more convincingly, but the over the top silliness would've diminished, which is what gives *Razorback* most of its charm." — Devon Bertsch, *Digital Retribution*, October 31, 2005

"One of the better imitations of *Jaws*, capturing a shivery element of fear.... Mulcahy uses desert locations to great advantage, employing lights and shadows to capture an eeriness similar to the mood of *It Came from Outer Space*." — John Stanley, *Creature Features*

AWARDS

Australian Film Institute (AFI) Won Best Cinematography and Best Editing; nominated for Production Design, Sound, Score and Best Screenplay.

DVD

Released by Warner Bros. November 11, 2009. Umbrella Entertainment (Australia) on September 21, 2005.

Cassandra
Parrallel Films, 1986

CREDITS: *Director:* Colin Eggleston; *Producer:* Trevor Lucas; *Executive Producers:* Phil Gerlach, Mikael Borglund; *Associate Producer:* Steve Amezdroz; *Screenplay:* Colin Eggleston, John Ruane, Chris Fitchett; *Photography:* Garry Wapshot; *Editor:* Josephine Cook; *Music:* Trevor Lucas, Ian Mason; *Production Design:* Stewart Burnside; *Art Director:* Max Manton; *Costume Designer:* Anthony Jones; *Makeup:* Sonja Smuk; *Hairdresser:* Paul Williams; *Special Effects:* Illusion and Effects. Color, 89–94 minutes.

SONGS: "Stimulation" (Paul Gray); "Sugar Free" (Paul Gray); "Land of the Free" (Bluey and Curly); "She's a Mystery" (John Brewster, Allan Lancaster), heard at bar; "Who Killed Cock Robin" (Traditional) sung by Lee James.

CAST: Shane Briant (Stephen Roberts); Briony Behets (Helen Roberts); Kit Taylor (Detective Sergeant Harry Harrison); Lee James (Robert/Warren Roberts); Susan Barling (Libby Anderson); Tim Burns (Graham); Tessa Humphries (Cassandra Roberts, Jill Roberts); Tegan Charles (Cassandra as Child); Dylan O'Neill (Warren as Child); Natalie McCurry (Sally); Jeff Watson (Bob); Gary Traill (Mr. Stone); Jeff Truman (Detective Devlin); Kate Carruthers (Janice); John Ley (Barman).

SYNOPSIS

Cassandra is a young woman who has nightmare visions of a woman shooting herself with a shotgun and of a young boy in a farmhouse whose face burns in flames. Her mother, Helen, is concerned that she is repeating the suicidal behavior of Jill, the sister of Cassandra's father, Stephen. Stephen plans to leave Helen and marry Libby Anderson, his photographic model, because she is pregnant with his child, but she is murdered in her home. His new assistant, Graham, is the main suspect, since he is wanted by the police for rape and has been lusting after Libby.

Someone attempts to also murder Helen in her office and later in her home, but she is saved by Detective Harry Harrison. Helen confesses to Cassandra that she is not her real mother; Jill is. Cassandra and her brother Warren are the children of Stephen's incest. Helen also tells that Warren had been a violent child and had been placed in a home, although apparently he is now out. Stephen is murdered, and Robert, a man who has befriended Cassandra, reveals himself to be both Warren and the killer. Summoning Helen to the farmhouse where Robert reveals he has killed Graham, Robert plans to kill her and Cassandra. Robert stops Harrison from trying to save the two women, but is shot by his sister. Robert is then set on fire and the farmhouse burns to the ground.

NOTES

Director Colin Eggleston's second Australian horror attempt after *Long Weekend* is a more antiseptic mood piece mixing the themes of the horror of personality with the malevolent supernatural being. Overusing score and editing techniques, Eggleston also employs expressionist angles, with a subjective camera for point of view acceptable in lieu of it being the presentation of a stalking antagonist. He also has a minimal showing of blood and gore or shock effects, and a ten minute suspense set piece that defies expectations. The narrative provides multiple suspects for murder and a scenario that centers on the Gothic consequences of incest, although the plot backstory occurs two-thirds of the way into the running time and the antagonist is identified just before the climax.

The film opens with an extreme close-up of an eye and the title in flames, portending the major use of fire in the climax. The title dissolves to black and white photographs being burned in a fireplace, the photographs and Stephen Roberts being a photographer recalls *Snapshot*, as will the climactic fire. One photograph is left in a drawer, which will be later revealed to be that of Jill, but the person handling the photos is only shown by their arms. There is a later scene of Cassandra looking at black and white photographs by a fireplace, but it cannot be confirmed that the person in this first scene is her. This is particularly true since in the later scene she is surprised to find the photograph of Jill in the drawer. Eggleston dissolves from a black and white photograph of what is later shown to be Jill's farmhouse to the house location in color.

Eggleston presents what we later see is Cassandra's nightmare, beginning with a pan down to a creek below the hill on which the farmhouse stands. Water reacts to something thrown into it and a cut to a girl reveals her throwing stones. We have to accept the filmic contrivance that Cassandra is able to see something she didn't in the first place: herself, as Eggleston goes overboard in his editing. Split second cuts to an eye are used, as they will be in all the nightmare visions as Cassandra's eye, though point of view will be revealed as Warren's later vision. Singing of the song "Who Killed Cock Robin" is heard, which will also feature in the later narrative. Intercut with the creek stone dropping is a subjective camera for Cassandra in the back seat of Jill's car as she drives to a storeroom, which continues with Cassandra out of the car following her mother. What Jill gets from the storeroom is unclear, though it may be the shotgun she will use, and the drive back repeats Cassandra's subjective point of view in the back of the car.

Jill holding the rifle under her neck seems to be ordered by the little boy that we will learn is Warren. Noises on the soundtrack may be Jill's cries of distress before the shooting or Cassandra crying, they continue after Jill is shot. Eggleston doesn't show us the act; instead we see Warren's bloodied face which turns to fire with an optical effect. The suicide of Jill raises the questions. Did Warren cause it because he wanted her dead? Was he, even as a child, able to put her in a trance, as is suggested by him doing that to Cassandra later with supernatural powers? And did he want his mother dead because he knew she had committed incest and therefore deserved to die, which is his rationale for killing Stephen? Although it might seem that he is too young to under-

Poster for *Cassandra* (1986).

stand the concept of incest when we see him as a child, Warren being the result of it could make him a bad seed and explain his malevolent antagonism.

The elder Cassandra throwing rocks into the same creek near the farmhouse makes the connection with her younger self; the nightmares Helen tells us that Cassandra has been experiencing only recently suggest that the trauma has lain dormant. We wonder what has set it off, apart from being a good starting point for the film's narrative. In the farmhouse we have the same point-of-view subjective camera as Cassandra's nightmare. Eggleston intercuts to the print of a photograph of Libby with "Who Killed Cock Robin" written over it. A pigeon which flies at Cassandra, recalling the antagonistic animals of *Long Weekend*, is a shock effect and causes her to run away from the house.

Libby being bare-breasted as she emerges from swimming at the beach seems exploitative, particularly since she wears bikini pants and Stephen, who is with her, wears a bathing suit. Stephen identifies the woman in the photograph Cassandra has found as his sister, Jill, and tells her that Jill died in a car accident before Cassandra was born. This story denies the suicide that Cassandra has dreamed, although Stephen's story will prove to be a lie, which the phone call he has with Helen suggests. His "It's not your fault or mine" is misinterpreted when it is overheard by Libby, who believes that Stephen has told Helen about them, which he fails to immediately clarify. This presents Stephen as a duplicitous character, much more so than Libby, although his "It's not your fault or mine" said to Helen would seem to be a form of denial of the culpability he has for his incest.

At Stephen's photo shoot, Mr. Stone's request is expressed by Bob as if he is a pimp. Libby is asked to look windswept and wet and this reads as a man in power pornographically exploiting a woman, rather than as an aesthetic recommendation. Libby's awareness of her double exploitation perhaps informs her confrontation with Stephen. Realizing that he has not told Helen about their affair and the pregnancy, Libby's line "I don't want to see you again until you've told her" reads as soap opera. It also sets up Libby as the first victim of the killer. The music and the subjective camera watching her as she leaves the studio confirm the threat against her.

The subjective camera also being at her home is the first suspension of disbelief that the person stalking her could find her when we don't see how, although suspension of disbelief is necessary for a lot of horror stories. If we believe that Warren as the killer has supernatural powers, this allows him to travel faster than mere mortals, although the treatment has yet to identify Warren as the one who watches.

The murder of Libby is not as successful a suspense set piece as the later attack on Helen. The scene has suspense by establishing the threat against Libby, but she is not shown to have an awareness of the threatening person in the way Helen will be. Therefore Libby is not presented as empathetically as Helen, in spite of our knowledge of her being pregnant. Our seeing the same photograph of Libby in her bedroom as the one we had seen in Cassandra's nightmare makes a connection, presenting the possibility that Cassandra's visions are predictions. This will be paid off when the writing is seen on the photo after Libby's murder. Eggleston only provides one intercut to Stephen at the studio, which creates the possibility that he is the killer. This idea is continued when he shown at her home, after she is killed. However, we know that Cassandra is not the killer since Eggleston intercuts to her in bed, after a quick edit of the eye that appears in her visions.

Libby undressing and appearing naked before she goes swimming in her pool has more contexts for her nudity than her bare breasts at the beach. She covers herself with a robe to go to the pool in her back yard rather than walking naked through the house, which would have read as more exploitative. The gloved hand that we see taking a knife from her kitchen confirms the antagonist is a real person, and the raising of the knife in front of another framed photograph of Libby creates the expectation not immediately met that it will be slashed.

Libby swimming naked in the pool has more context, and as does her removing the robe to sleep naked in her bed. The subjective camera approach to her in bed and the raised knife creates the expectation of her murder, although Eggleston does not show the incision or any resultant blood. When Stephen is in the house it creates the expectation that he will find her bloody body, if we ignore the theory that he is the killer, that is, unless he is creating an alibi. When he is in the bedroom and doesn't immediately see that she is dead is another expectation not met. The idea that Stephen sneaks into bed with the dead Libby, who is faced away from him, is actually an amusing set up because we await his discovery. This occurs when he turns her around for the cut throat reveal. Stephen's scream of horror is appropriately funny because Shane Briant does it in such an over-the-top way.

When Helen tells Stephen her fear that Cassandra

is having the same sort of nightmares that Jill had before her suicide, she also responds to his desire to have left her for Libby with "I wouldn't have allowed that." This comment at first sounds like the control of a jealous wife, but only later when the incest is revealed does it take on a more concerned tone. This is in light of Helen's pretend marriage to Stephen in order to protect Cassandra and the perverse family unit they have created. This latter tone is also demonstrated by Helen's comment about Stephen: "I love him like a brother," which is also funny in hindsight, because he is her brother.

Eggleston uses a blue colored tint for Cassandra's next dream, which incorporates the eye. Superimposed are images of the camera approach to Libby, the writing on her photograph, Warren as a boy and the fire over his face, Jill holding the gun under her neck, and the approach to the farmhouse. When Cassandra tells of the dream, she also describes an image we don't see — or perhaps one that the director's quick editing makes too elusive — a man burned by fire.

When Stephen returns to his studio, he sees Graham admiring a photo of Libby from the shoot we have witnessed taking place before her death. He tells Graham that's he's not going to use them. Graham replies with, "Why not? She looks great." We don't know if Graham is aware of Libby's death — we presume he is — but Stephen responds to his comment as if it is inappropriate. He places his hand on Graham's neck and holds it in an aggressive fashion, and we wonder whether Stephen does so because he suspects Graham of being her murderer.

Robert takes Cassandra to the farmhouse on her request, and we see him waiting down the hill at a car, but when she runs to the front of the house, Robert stands in front of her. This shock moment is another that suggests that Robert as Warren has supernatural powers, because how could he have gotten to the house before Cassandra? It also makes us ponder whether Robert is the killer. We recall his earlier comment to Cassandra: "I feel like I have known you all my life." At the time he said it, it sounded like a corny romantic come-on.

Helen alone in her office begins the ten minute suspense set piece that is the highlight of the film. Seeing her alone creates the expectation of her being the next victim, although the expectation of her murder is not met either at the office or at her house, where the second act of the set piece occurs. The sound of thunder outside is the horror movie convention of a storm indicating trouble ahead. Eggleston intercuts between the killer's point of view via subjective camera, Helen, and Cassandra dreaming. Another shock effect is Helen dropping a roll of material onto a table, and the big scissors she uses to cut the material would seem to prepare her with a weapon. When the killer seems to accidentally bump into a piece of furniture that drops, Helen hears the sound and the subjective camera moves to hide among a rack of clothes. When Helen investigates the noise, she is the horror movie conventional Woman in Peril, though armed with scissors.

Eggleston errs in having Helen trying to escape before showing what has panicked her or her realization that she is in danger. However, her inability to open a door enables her to investigate further, so that her going to the clothes rack would seem like an act of bravery. Perhaps Helen's moral courage, before succumbing to the inevitable when she is in the closet, is the thing that saves her. A mirror near the clothes rack is first used to show Helen's reflection looking, and then allows Helen to see the reflection of the killer's legs in it, as he approaches her from behind. We see, as she does, his gloves. The knife recalls the same in Libby's attack, but the raised knife results in Helen fighting back. Her taking off her shoes when she runs is her realization that their sound gives away her location, and her run down a stairwell is the solution to the locked door she had tried before. The expectation is now created that Helen will escape, aided by her driving through the killer, who appears to lunge at her car but who is tossed off, and her arrival at her house.

The music that resumes tells us that the threat to Helen is not over. She finds the Cock Robin writing on a mirror, partially obscured because it is only later that Cassandra sees how this time the writing is "I Killed Cock Robin." The subjective camera outside the house presents the killer. Again a suspension of disbelief is required, with the possibility of Warren having supernatural powers in lieu of the timing. The telephone line cut when Helen calls the police for help is a standard suspense convention. Eggleston doesn't show us the line cut, and Helen does manage to talk to Detective Harrison and identify herself before she is cut off, which is paid off with his rescue of her.

Helen sees a shadow at her door and arms herself with a kitchen cleaver, as she had in the office with scissors. Eggleston uses a shock effect for the killer's arm coming through the wall behind Helen to grab her. Her hiding in a closet may seem a foolish locale, although it features a hole in the door for Helen to look through. Her dropped cleaver is used by the killer to break through the door, with resultant shafts of light appearing through the split wood. The expectation of Helen's murder is not met when the arm that reaches through the door to open it from her side is revealed to be that of Harrison. The momentary idea that Harrison may be the killer is dismissed when we see the subjective camera leave the front of Helen's house. We wonder how it is that Harrison was able to open the door when we assumed the killer was just at it.

Eggleston shows us Warren as a boy throwing stones into the farmhouse creek, and the eye which sees the boy, to suggest that he is seen by Cassandra. Cassandra's appearance allows for Helen to reveal the true backstory. Cassandra had found Jill dead; Cassandra was the child of incest with Jill and Stephen. It is all capped by Helen's line about Stephen: "He's not my husband. He's my brother." As Helen, Briony Behets delivers this information with a blank expression, as if she is horrified and ashamed of what she reveals.

Helen explains that after Jill's death, Cassandra called her mummy, perhaps because she had blocked the pain of her loss with amnesia. Warren had been an uncontrollable child, prone to violence, who had been put in a home but who she has heard has been released. The idea that the child Warren had attacked Helen with a knife is linked to the adult Warren's preference for killing with a knife. Helen's accusation to Stephen, that they have been living off the children's money, reads as odd, since Jill living in the farmhouse certainly does not suggest that she had money. Although the narrative seems to confirm that Warren is the killer, we still don't know who the adult is at this point. The focus shifts to Graham, whom Helen sees outside her house, although the fact that we see Graham rather than the subjective camera point of view suggests that he is not the killer.

Helen tells Harrison that Stephen's studio is next to the house, which would seem to rationalize Graham's proximity. His fight with Devlin results in the second detective rolling around on the ground in pain in an extended moment that reads as unnecessary filler. Graham hiding in the back of Stephen's car when Stephen drives to the beach house creates a misleading use of camerawork when we see Stephen and the car's vision from Graham's point of view. An expectation is created of an attack on Stephen as the killer's next victim. This is met when the subjective camera is used to present the killer seeing him and cutting his face. However, what differentiates Stephen's attack from that of Libby and Helen is that Stephen sees his attacker and does nothing to stop him, perhaps realizing that his attacker is the adult Warren.

The blood on Stephen's face recalls the splattered blood on the boy Warren from Jill's shotgun blast, but the difference here is that this display is more effusive. This gore and the resultant gore from Stephen being stabbed is the treatment's first real horror display; Stephen's head being cut off is the final touch of gruesomeness. When Stephen is attacked he has odd visions of the child Warren who calls him Daddy, the image disappearing and appearing in different places. Is this Stephen's memory or a guilty conscience that precipitates the ultimate price he pays for committing the incest?

The subjective camera on Graham tells us that he is not the killer. We also know it not to be Cassandra by the inter-cuts Eggleston uses to show her driving to the beach house during the attack on Stephen. Eggleston doesn't show us the killer's attack on Graham. We see Cassandra arriving and her vision of the child Warren, so that we have to wait for Graham's murder to be paid off later at the farmhouse where Cassandra goes after she finds Stephen's body. Eggleston spares us further view of the decapitation.

There is a long pan of Cassandra walking around to the farmhouse entrance from the interior of the house, which may be Warren's point of view. After she has lit a fire in the fireplace, the shadow that appears behind Cassandra is revealed to be Robert. Although she may sense that Robert is the adult Warren, Cassandra doesn't confess it, although she must realize that his story of Harrison asking him to come to the farmhouse is a lie. However, Helen believes it, which causes her to set off. Harrison seeing her leave her house, since he is parked outside, allows her to go in his car since they are convinced that trouble is forthcoming.

A burst of music accompanies Eggleston's dissolves that link Robert to the child Warren. The surprise is that he comments that he and Cassandra are twins, which may explain her visions, which seem to also be his. The idea of them as twins doesn't seem to give Cassandra the supernatural powers that Robert has, apart from the ability to have visions and foresee the future. Clearly he is the dominant and the more dangerous of the two. In fact, Cassandra reads as devoid of malevolence as the narrative's protagonist, and doesn't act suicidal the way Helen feared she would.

Playing Cassandra, Tessa Humphries supplies an oddness which doesn't stoop to the bug-eyed madness that Lee James provides for Warren in the film's climax. Warren confesses his killing of Libby because she was carrying Stephen's child, and implies that he killed Stephen and intends to kill

Helen because "they are evil and so are we." After he comments, "There's two [left]. You and Helen. Soon there'll be none," Cassandra responds with "There's you too, Warren." This causes Warren to move to strangle her, but caresses her face instead as he sings "Who Killed Cock Robin."

Cassandra's comment is funny because she realizes that he is in denial about being the product of incest. When Warren moves to kiss her on the mouth, it seems that incest is an inherited condition. Cassandra rejects his advance and runs, although we get the clichéd movie convention of her car that won't start. Her return to Warren seems to be via his psychic control over her, which allows him to tie her up. Warren's psychic intuition also observes that Helen is approaching and that she is not alone.

We then get perhaps the film's most bizarre demonstration of Warren's supernatural powers, aligned to his throwing himself at Helen's car in the office parking lot. He throws himself at the car Harrison drives as if he can fly. This is another horror shock moment. The out of control car hits a tree, which conveniently makes Harrison unconscious. A noise on the roof of the car suggests that Warren is still there, confirmed by the reveal of an axe chopping at the windshield. Again Helen arms herself, this time with Harrison's gun. This defies the expectation that she is a helpless victim without the assistance of a man, although her previous handling of the scissors and the cleaver should tell us otherwise.

During the car attack Eggleston obscures our view of Warren, even when Helen fires shots that may hit him. Her escape into the bush land recalls Briony Behets' bush ordeal in *Long Weekend*. The subjective camera is used to show Warren pursuing her. Graham's unresolved plot line is paid off when Helen sees his bloody corpse hanging upside down at the entrance to the farmhouse. Eggleston intercuts the awakening Harrison with Helen untying Cassandra at the farmhouse. Harrison will not prove to be the rescuing policeman that is expected, particularly when we know that Helen has his gun. Warren's return to the house is presented by a shot of his feet approaching, like the mirror shot in Helen's office. Eggleston pans up to reveal that the legs belong to Warren, who now holds a rifle, with his taste for using knives to murder seemingly satisfied.

The arrival of the still dazed Harrison meets the expectation of him being attacked, particularly when we do not see Warren, when Harrison sees the women inside tied up. Warren's axing of Harrison would be seem to be a deadly blow, although we will see later how Helen leads him out of the farmhouse during the fire. Cassandra finding Helen's gun and facing off with Warren and his rifle is a test of wills, one that Warren loses in his underestimating his sister's wrath. This is highlighted by her pouring gasoline over his wounded body, and perhaps Cassandra senses that shooting Warren twice is not enough to kill him.

It is ironic that Warren should become the man aflame in Cassandra's vision, although his deliberately rolling himself into the fireplace seems an inexplicable act of suicide. Eggleston uses a dissolve from Warren on fire to the vision of the boy Warren with fire on his face. To follow are transition dissolves after the farmhouse explodes and Helen, Harrison and Cassandra getting out of the burning house. The film ends with an epilogue where Cassandra sees the adult Warren in her mirror as a vision who reaches out to her, and the mirror explodes as a shock effect.

After *Cassandra*, Colin Eggleston made the Australian horror title *Outback Vampires* (1987), which was also his last film. *Cassandra* was the first film produced by Trevor Lucas and executive producer Phil Gerlach, neither of whom would produce another horror movie. It was also the first film by executive producer Mikael Borglund, who would go on to executive produce the Australian horror film *Cut* (2000) and the second and last feature for associate producer Steve Amezdroz. *Cassandra* was the first film for the Parrallel Films, aka Parallel Films, production company, which would go on to make other films, but none of them horror titles.

Tessa Humphries is the daughter of famous Australian comedian Barry Humphries, and *Cassandra* was her film debut after having worked in television. She continued in films playing supporting roles and in television but has not had another film lead to date. British born Shane Briant made his film debut in a supporting role in the Hammer title *Straight on Till Morning* (1972). He continued in films in supporting roles and worked on television, and after *Cassandra* was in the Australia horror film *Subterano* (2003).

Release

Straight to video with the taglines "Omen of Death. Cassandra has the power to see them.... But not stop them!" "Cassandra can see the future. You may not want to." and "A new look at terror."

Reviews

"A feeble combination of slasher movie and whodunit. An unanswered question [is] how come the [killing] brother was sent to a mental home at what seems to be the ripe old age of three? But, does anyone care? Certainly not the filmmakers." — David Stratton, *The Avocado Plantation*

"An unexceptional entry into the psychic link subgenre, [it] has a few merits, namely a handful of tense scenes and prowling killer's eye camerawork, but overall a disappointing effort from a talented director which lacks the offbeat, eerie atmosphere of its predecessor, *Long Weekend*." — Michelle R, *Digital Retribution*, January 19, 2007

"Muddled Australian psychological profile of a prescient child and her parents." — John Stanley, *Creature Features*

"Considered purely as a thriller, *Cassandra* is not particularly good. Some of the suspense sequences go slack and sometimes the rule-breaking backfires. But I do feel that's because it is really aiming for something else.... It uses its many atmospheric Australian locations to good effect.... Overall a quite beautiful and disturbing piece of cinema." — Kyla Ward, *Tabula Rasa*

"It's ambitious, littered with visual trickery that peaks during the stalking sequences and is let down mostly by a slack first half hour and the predictable ending. They should've tried a bit harder to conceal the killer's identity, which is made all the more glaringly evident by the limited number of characters." — Hud, *Vegan Voorhees*, January 18, 2011

DVD

VHS released by M.C.E.G./Virgin Vision on February 1, 1989. DVD released by Umbrella Entertainment (Australia) on January 23, 2006.

Dark Age
RKO Pictures/FGH Presentation, 1986
[aka *Blood Surf 2*; *Crocodile Hunter*]

CREDITS: *Director:* Arch Nicholson; *Producer:* Basil Appleby; *Executive Producer:* Antony I. Ginnane; *Screenplay:* Sonia Borg, based on the novel *Numunwari* by Grahame Webb; *Photography:* Andrew Lesnie; *Editor:* Adrian Carr; *Music:* Danny Beckerman; *Production Design:* David Copping; *Art Direction:* Ron Highfield; *Sound:* Gary Wilkins; *Wardrobe:* Ann Benjamin; *Makeup:* Sonja Smuk; *Hair:* Paul Williams; *Choreographer:* Ralph Nichols. Color, 90–108 minutes. Filmed on location in Cairns, North Queensland, and Alice Springs, Northern Territory, from April to June 1986.

CAST: John Jarratt (Steve Harris); Nikki Coghill (Cathy Pope); Max Phipps (John Besser); Burnam Burnam (Oondabund); Gulpilil (Adjaral); Ray Meagher (Rex Garret); Jeff Ashby (Mac Wilson); Paul Bertram (Jackson); Ron Blanchard (Bluey Noakes); Gerry Duggan (Joe Blunt); James Fitzgerald (Smithy); Ken Radley (Reynolds); Janet Kingsbury (Ann Wilson); Hank Mosby (Hitchens); James Mann (Kelly); Jock McCullum (King); Chris Anderson, Barry Cummings, Cameron Blackley (Thugs); Robert Anderson (Jacobs); Regan Leftwich (Boy Victim); Kaylene Leftwich (Nancy); Trudi Johnson (Receptionist); Colin MacDonald (Gerry); Elaine Mangan (TV Reporter); Adrian Barber (Press Reporter); Mark Hashfield (Weighbridge Inspector); Harry Reid (Harbour Master); Barry Graham (Skipper); John Sintome, Christopher Gay, John Schofield (Policemen); Mark Spencer (Constable); David Albert Taylor (Sergeant); Luke Cummings, William Brady (Rivermen); Geoff O'Halloran (Waiter); Lance Riley (Singing Elder); R. Wunungmurra, J. Wunnungmurra, J. Wanambi, D. Mununggurr, P. Mununggurr, F. Mununggurr (Dance Troupe); Bertie Riley, Herbert Riley, Garth Riley, Ffloyd Riley, Ernest Riley, Leslie Hobbler, Fabian Riley, Ronston Newberry (Boy Dancers).

Synopsis

A 25 foot long, 100-year-old salt water crocodile is found to be living in the Thomas River of the Aboriginal town of Malperinga, and killing people. Forestry wildlife ranger Steve Harris is brought in to investigate, but the local Aborigines refuse to help because they believe the crocodile to be sacred. The creature is scared away from Malperinga and moves into the harbor of the city and kills again. Forestry Department head Rex Garret posts a $5,000 reward for its death, and Tribal leader Oondabund agrees to help track the creature on the condition that it be released back into a Malperinga breeding pen. Steve, Oondabund and another Aborigine, Adjaral, find the crocodile and take it to the pen, but are pursued by poacher John Besser, who has lost an arm to the creature. In a confrontation, Oondabund is shot by Bluey, one of Besser's men, and Besser is killed by the crocodile, after which Adjaral feeds the creature the bones of Oondabund in an Aboriginal ceremony.

NOTES

A pedestrian treatment and political correctness mars this title that features a giant crocodile as the malevolent supernatural being. Director Arch Nicholson uses postmodern techniques of expressionist angles, zooms, and point of view and an obtrusive score. He loses audience interest with the alternate focus on the sappy love affair of the protagonist and the political infighting about killing the antagonist. The narrative has an agenda to present Aborigines as morally superior to white men for not wanting the animal killed, and poachers as opportunistic exploiters out for the reward. This may be politically correct but it detracts from the horror in an attempt to give dimension to a creature that is otherwise indiscriminate as to who it attacks. Nicholson's killings have the requisite gore and, as with the creature in *Razorback*, he uses minimalism to conceal the use of a mechanical device. However, he is more successful in providing resonant images of non-violent activity. Also as in *Razorback*, the narrative pits a second human antagonist against the protagonist, although here the main antagonist doesn't have a confrontation with the protagonist.

A pre-credit title card reads: "For more than 40,000 years Australian Aborigines have lived in harmony with their land. Many of their animals are sacred. The most dangerous and awesome of these is the giant salt water crocodile which the Arnhem Land Aborigines call 'Numunwari.'" A shock appearance of a helicopter under the credits signifies the white man's presence in what is considered Aboriginal land. The issue of the white man's invasion is applied to the problem of the crocodile, since it will be shown that only Aborigines have the knowhow to capture the creature, although the animal's eating of the Aboriginal child and its attack on Adjaral attest to its lack of assumed loyalty.

Rippling water and Aboriginal chanting signal the presence of the crocodile in the river where Aborigines and white men herd cattle. The expectation of a horse drinking being attacked is not met. Thunder and sudden rain after the creature is spotted is a horror movie convention. When Besser and his men go night hunting for crocodiles, their stalled boat after they see the giant croc is a suspense device after they have decided it is too big for them to kill. The expectation of an attack is met, although the night lighting obscures the gore of the strike against Smithy. The fact of the creature only attacking one

Poster for *Dark Age* (1986).

of the three poachers shows it has some restraint, and Reynolds being found having drowned rather than being killed by the croc the next day is a surprise. Nicholson has a bird scream when Reynolds' body is turned over by Steve, and the severed arm he also finds presumably belongs to Smithy.

The next attack occurs in daylight and the boy's crying rather than trying to get away from the advancing croc that crushes his head may be out of fear. Oondabund later rationalizes the death by saying that the boy was sickly, and to his mind deserved to die. This attack is the most effectively staged of all in the film, particularly since the victim is a child.

The light plane landing over the river that carries Mac and a passenger who reads a newspaper with the headline "Monster Crocodile Kills Man" creates the expectation of another attack that is not met. Oondabund's speech to Steve about how the creature is a "Dreaming Crocodile" allows for a polemic. Australia is owned by the Aborigines and therefore so is the crocodile, and it being old makes it smart and by implication so are the Aborigines as an old culture. However, this speech gets a camp payoff when he tells Steve he is needed to dance by the mob, and he moves to display bad dancing. In fact, the way Oondabund is presented makes him almost a comic figure, with his fractured use of the English language and his later child-like analysis of the RKO "B" western *The Renegade Ranger* (1938), which he watches on television.

Nicholson's shot of the five boats setting out into the river to search for the creature is one of the two resonant images he provides in the treatment. He uses a montage of crocodiles being shot and bullet casings falling with inter-cuts of the dance troupe so that we get the idea that the white hunters are pillaging the creatures that the Aborigines identify with. Naturally the four days of hunting does not result in finding the right crocodile. Rex Garret's entrance is in close-up as he enters the frame in front of a black and white photograph of hunters with a dead crocodile on the wall. Garret's dissatisfaction with the search also includes a disapproval of Steve's claim of how poaching is making the species of crocodiles extinct, as the second polemic raised in the screenplay.

Cathy has been established as Steve's former girlfriend, and she was witness to the death of the boy, and in fact seems to be the only one among the Aboriginal witnesses who is disturbed by it. Regrettably, she is a reactive and superfluous character. She packs to leave after the death and then doesn't leave and doesn't say why, despite the fact of her being an anthropologist who appears to work at a reserve that is featured later in the plot. The one plot point that she seems necessary for is her showing Steve the 1908 Aboriginal painting of the crocodile with human bones. Oondabund will clarify that these were bones of the deceased tribal elder who was fed to the creature and which the film's end will demonstrate.

Steve passing a drunken Joe as he leaves the city restaurant where he tried to have dinner with Cathy creates the expectation that Joe will be the next croc victim. Nicholson delays this possibility by intercutting to the sex scene between Steve and Cathy, prefigured by her calling him a "lousy fuck." Joe's chase by the three thugs into the harbor continues the expectation, as does one of the thugs holding Joe's face down in the water. After we see the croc's point of view as it advances, the surprise is that it attacks the thug and not Joe. The extended police search in the harbor creates the expectation of another attack when the croc is seen in the water, but only by us. An attempt at humor is made when Steve aims at what he thinks is the croc but what he then recognizes as a beer can.

After Garret announces the reward, he tells Steve a line that is pure genre; "I must have that head." Oondabund speaks of the dreamtime link between the Aborigines and the croc when he tells Steve how a long time ago the croc was a man, but having nothing to eat he jumped into the billabong and became a croc so he could eat. This legend makes one wonder why the man didn't look for food in the water and spare the transformation.

The inter-cuts to Besser's camp during the search by Steve, Oondabund and Adjaral create the expectation that the croc will appear near Besser. This is met when it is caught in Besser's net and the resultant struggle has Besser lose an arm to it. Since Besser survives and the croc swims away to be later caught by the search team, the expectation is also created that Besser will seek revenge.

During the croc's capture, its appearance behind the three men creates the expectation of an attack. This is met by Adjaral's fall into the river, though he gets back in unharmed. The croc must have been only playing. The aerial view of the search boat with the croc tied next to it is the film's second resonant image.

When the croc is brought to the reserve, the expectation of its attack on Cathy is met when she asks to touch it, though since its jaws are tied, it can only snap at her. Besser's appearance at the reserve after Steve, Oondabund and Adjaral have gone to take the croc to the breeding pen creates the expectation that Cathy will be harmed when she refuses to talk to Besser. The way he stands over her suggests a sexual threat, but this expectation is not met. Additionally, the scene at the Public Weighbridge gets no payoff. Steve is told, but we are not, the weight of the croc, and the weighbridge inspector only gets flicked by the croc's tail.

Besser's chase of Steve utilizes the appearance of Cathy, who adds nothing to the climax. Steve's truck stuck in dirt and then crashing within walking distance to the pen are both devices to create suspense delays. However, the climactic fight when Besser and his men arrive gets a comic touch when Oondabund has time to go offstage and paint up before he spears Bluey, who also shoots Oondabund. The fact that Steve is so easily disarmed attests to the fact that the real conflict is not between him and Besser, as an earlier halted fight suggested, but rather between Besser and the croc. The croc killing Besser after he is speared by Adjaral is the inevitable resolution of their primal conflict, after Besser uses a hatchet on the creature, which suggests that Besser will be the victor. Before he dies, Oondabund says the immortal line, "We born. We die. Spirit lives." Nicholson gives Steve an echoed yell before aerial shots of the Malperinga and the feeding of Oondabund's bones to the croc.

The conclusion is interesting for a horror story, since the antagonist is not defeated. Its behavior is forgiven because it is considered to be natural, even if the creature's existence itself is considered unnatural or supernatural, if you will. If there is a consequence it is that the creature must live in an isolated environment rather than enjoy the prior freedom it had to hunt among humans for food. It has also lost its anonymity, which is surely one of the tactics that crocodiles use to strike their victims. The implied protection by the Aborigines comes as a form of control of its threat.

The film is mentioned in the documentary *Not Quite Hollywood*, as apparently the mechanical device creature was slow in its movement, unlike real crocodiles. This had its challenges for the actors when they were meant to be pursued. The jaws stuck open in the scene where John Jarratt as Steve had to tie them shut in haste, and short-circuited when entering the billabong for the climax. Producer Antony I. Ginnane's efforts to have the film released in Australia after a spate of real life crocodile attacks was thwarted by the distribution company going bankrupt just before the planned release date. It is the only Australian horror film made by Arch Nicholson and producer Basil Appleby. Executive producer Ginnane and his FGH production company had previously made the Australian horror title *Turkey Shoot*.

John Jarratt had previously appeared in *Next of Kin*, and would go on to play the lead in the Australian horror film *Wolf Creek*. After beginning in television, Nikki Coghill made her film debut in a minor role in *Rebel* (1985), and has only played supporting film roles to date. Max Phipps played supporting roles in the Australian horror movies *The Cars That Ate Paris*, *Thirst* and *Nightmares*, but would not make another Australian horror title. Burnam Burnam made his film debut in *Dark Age* but has not made another Australian horror title to date.

Gulpilil (aka David Gulpilil) made his film debut in a supporting role in the adventure *Walkabout*, and played a supporting role in *The Last Wave*. He would not appear in another Australian horror title but would go on to play the lead in the historical drama *The Tracker* (2002). Ray Meagher also began his career in television, made his film debut in a supporting role in the crime drama *The Chant of Jimmie Blacksmith* (1978) and has continued to work in supporting film roles and on television.

Release

No Australian theatrical release, and only screened in the United States on September 18, 2008, for the Austin Fantastic Festival. The video tagline is "Death is only one bite away." In his book *The Avocado Plantation*, David Stratton writes that the reason the film has never been seen in Australia is because of the distribution deal where Embassy held all foreign rights. The planned Australian distributor CEL refused to pay more to Embassy when it had merged into another company and wished to renegotiate terms.

Reviews

"It does not have quite the impact of *Razorback* but it comes close. Nicholson directs the action scenes adroitly."—David Stratton, *The Avocado Plantation*

"Remember *Jaws*? Remember *Alligator*? Remember *Crocodile*? Well, now remember (or would you like to forget?) Australia's *Dark Age*, the tale of the legendary 25-foot salt-water croc/gator/jawbreaker.... The difference here is that the three men who set out to find the creature after he's enjoyed human hors d'oeuvres want to keep the croc alive."—John Stanley, *Creature Features*

DVD

Video released by Charter Entertainment/Embassy Home Entertainment on March 30, 1989. No DVD release.

Fair Game

Southern Films International, 1986 [aka *She Was Fair Game*; *Hunting Season*; *Death Game: The Return of Jessica*]

CREDITS: *Director:* Mario Andreacchio; *Producers:* Ron Saunders, Harley Manners; *Screenplay:* Rob George; *Photography:* Andrew Lesnie; *Editor:* A.J. Prowse; *Music:* Ashley Irwin; *Art Director:* Kimble Hilder; *Sound:* Toivo Lember; *Wardrobe:* Peter Bevan; *Makeup:* Jane Surrich; *Hair:* Beverley Freeman; *Action Coordinator:* Glenn Boswell. Color, 82 minutes. Filmed in Adelaide, Clare Valley, and Wangaratta, South Australia.

SONGS: "Seeing Things" (Ashley Irwin, Terry McCarthy), The Black Crow; "I Can Fly" (Terry McCarthy, Ashley Irwin), Keren Corby.

CAST: Cassandra Delaney (Jessica); Peter Ford (Sunny); David Sandford (Ringo Rudnick); Garry Who (Sparks); Don Barker (Frank); Carmel Young (Moira); Adrian Shirley (Victor); Wayne Anthony (Derek); Kyla, the sheepdog.

Synopsis

Artist Jessica is left alone on the desert wildlife sanctuary she manages, which has been invaded by a group of kangaroo hunters. The three men — Sunny, Ringo, and Sparks — initially run her car off the road as a "game." Stalking her as she sleeps, they leave a dead kangaroo in her car. When Jessica's car breaks down the men chase her through the desert. She melds their guns into a sculpture, and they shoot up the buildings on her property and bulldoze her house with their truck. They also humiliate her by tying her semi-naked to the truck's brush guards. Jessica traps them in a cave but her horse is shot by Ringo when she attempts to ride away, and she sets up a trap for their return. Ringo is electrocuted by a power line, and Sparks is accidentally self-impaled on an anvil in a fight with her. She finally entraps the group's leader, Sunny, when his truck is stuck in the hole in the ground she has covered. He dies when she sets the truck on fire.

Notes

This small-scale though effective film features the horror of personality of three men tormenting a woman for no apparent reason and her revenge upon them, which results in two murders and a third death that is more accidental. The narrative changes the Woman in Peril into a murderess out of revenge. The horror of personality is the protagonist, since the three antagonists don't kill anybody, although they do kill a horse and presumably injure a dog. Director Mario Andreacchio utilizes the postmodern techniques of freeze frame, point of view, expressionist camera angles, jump cuts and slow motion, as well as an obtrusive generic score. In spite of merely adequate performances, the film still manages to engender sympathy for the put-upon woman, and for one of the male antagonists.

The treatment includes a memorable tying of her semi-naked body to the brush guard of a driving truck for humiliation, though there is surprisingly little sexual threat to her. The violence includes one electrocution, impalement, and a climactic burning alive. The protagonist is also presented as a female warrior, recalling the one in *Lady, Stay Dead*, and prefiguring those in *Contagion*, *Out of the Body*, *The 13th Floor*, *Komodo*, *Ghost Ship*, *Undead*, *See No Evil*, *Black Water*, *Storm Warning*, *Slaughtered*, *Prey*, *Triangle*, *The Clinic* and *Road Train*.

The "Fair" of the red-colored titles is shown to have a horizontal break in the lettering, which perhaps prefigures the unfair treatment Jessica receives, since the rationale for her being tormented is not vocalized. As a woman she is presented as a physically weaker specimen to the men and this adds a sense of adolescent sadism to their attitude to her. They have a curious lack of sexual interest toward her. The bloodied joey (a baby kangaroo) that Jessica finds is the presumed baby of the kangaroo that we see the men kill in the prologue. Her rescue and care of it is an extension of her work at the wildlife sanctuary and the expression of the female maternal instinct, which will also be apparent in her mixed emotion at the sight of the deaths of her victims. The tusk-like metal brush guards of the hunters is both a practical instrument to aid in their hunt, and recalls the armored cars of *The Cars That Ate Paris*. The bars are also a representation of their masculine aggressiveness, which will get a payoff when Jessica is tied to them like a trophy hood ornament.

The chase that has Jessica sandwiched between Sparks' truck and the truck with Sunny and Ringo also has her brakes not working. A side window she is unable to open gets a comic payoff when it opens after she stops at the edge of a cliff. Her car's windshield that shatters is a phenomenon that she later reports to Frank as something that occurred when a stone was thrown by one of the trucks, although this is not shown at the time as a deliberate act against her. Sunny buying Jessica's painting at the store creates an expectation of his romantic interest in her, so that her rejection of him by increasing the sale price may be considered part of the reason for his leading the attack upon her. However, Jessica's clothing is a problem, since it helps to present her as a sexual creature, particularly after we learn that the shirt outfits she wears do not have underwear. This makes the idea of Ringo taking a Polaroid photograph of her under her shirt as he appears on the ground under her car when she opens the door even more salacious.

Jessica sleeping in the nude in the daytime is not used to exploit the actresses' nudity and has context from the fan that blows on her because of the outback heat. The sight is paid off when she finds a photograph of herself in that state inside her refrigerator as a testament to her being watched and her house also invaded, although the expectation of the photograph being the one Ringo shot under her shirt is not met. The sheep that she warns off getting too close to the lake is paid off when it appears to drown. This discovery is given ambiguity when Kyla finds a cigarette pack, suggesting that Sunny may have pushed the sheep in. The drowned sheep will also get a later payoff when Jessica hides behind the corpse from the pursuing men after she accidentally falls into the lake. Andreacchio uses jump cuts of the photograph found in the refrigerator and sounds of the Polaroid instamatic camera shooting, which we have seen Ringo using, for emphasis. A noise that Jessica hears in the house presents her as a conventional Woman in Peril. She arms herself with a kitchen knife, and the threat is paid off with a shock effect of a wild loose bird in her house, and not the men who are expected.

The lizards that accumulate at her door may be a natural occurrence or have been placed there—the former seems more likely given her reaction. Jessica driving to her neighbor's house is presented with an interior point of view of her at the door, her figure obscured by the thick glass. Once she is inside, feet are shown approaching her, which are revealed to be those of Sunny. Her confrontation with the men ends with her holding a rifle at Sparks and Ringo; she shoots Ringo's camera as a payback for his photographs of her. The truck that follows Jessica after her vehicle breaks down following her hitting a wombat hole is suggested by a glint through the trees where she walks. Her hiding under the rock where they stand looking for her is a movie contrivance, with a snake crawling over her added for suspense. Her managing to kill it with a stick she reaches for doesn't meet the expectation that she will be caught by the men or bitten by the snake.

Andreacchio uses Jessica's discovery of the skinned dead kangaroo as a shock effect, with her car not starting another movie suspense contrivance. At this point in the narrative, the hunters don't seem to want to kill Jessica, only scare her by firing at her property. As if aware of the questionable logic of her shirt outfits, Jessica changes into a black leotard for night Woman in Peril investigating. This would seem a wise choice after her confrontation with them over their teasing and attempting to brand her horse. The hunters being conveniently and rather unbelievably asleep in sleeping bags allows her to take their guns to make the welded sculpture. This act of hers may seem the motivation for the hunters to continue their harassment of Jessica, although it is revealed that they have other guns. The expectation of rape is not met in their tying her to the brush guard and cutting the leotard so that her breasts are exposed. Their driving her around the property may seem pointless, but dominating and humiliating Jessica would seem enough of a reason for the hunters to do it.

Even Andreacchio's later scenes of death cannot match the perversity of this treatment of his protagonist, something which Quentin Tarantino in the documentary *Not Quite Hollywood* calls a classic genre scene. It would seem plenty of motivation for her for revenge, although this is saved until later in the narrative after her horse is killed. It's not that Jessica isn't angered by what the hunters do to her—who wouldn't be? But it seems that the shooting of her horse reads as a more personal affront than being tied to the truck. Andreacchio fades to white for the transition from Jessica's ordeal to her being found on the ground outside her house, presumably after she lost consciousness.

The bird Jessica frees from her aviary seems is one that hasn't been killed by the previous gunfire attack of the hunters. Her walking into the desert with what appears to be a handbag but which turns out to be a water bag is initially inexplicable, particularly in light of what has just happened to her. Jessica finding Sparks' truck creates the expectation that she will seek some revenge upon him. Though she sets his trouser leg on fire, the narrative continues to present her as an inferior opponent to the men; she is unable to take Sparks' truck away from him. This confrontation includes the standard movie convention of the truck stalling when the expectation is created that Jessica will be able to take it. Sparks is not killed by the radio wire that she strangles him with after the truck crashes.

This attempted attack upon Sparks would seem to motivate the hunters' next onslaught against Jessica. They attempt to demolish her house by ramming it with Sunny's truck and would seem to gladly run her over in the process, as a decision is made that they will kill her. Screenwriter Rob George in the DVD audio commentary says the truck attack upon the house is in counterpoint to Jessica's idea that she is safe in her home, something which her being photographed as she slept should warn her is already not true.

Ringo on a motorbike chasing Jessica on her horse is an interesting comparison of horsepower. The expectation that Jessica will enable Ringo to fall off the edge of the cliff where he hangs is not met. Although this may present Jessica as being more humane than the hunter, it also reads as a strategic mistake in light of the further trouble Ringo causes her. Jessica leaving her horse for the hunters to find creates the expectation that they will kill it, a plot point that will be later met. Her moving a rock to start the landslide that seals the cave with the hunters inside is another surprise, given how physically weak she has been shown to be. Since the rocks do not fully cover the cave hole, the escape of the hunters is expected, and the hole also allows Ringo to shoot Jessica's horse. It appears that only the jamming of his gun stops Ringo from also shooting her—a use of a movie convention in Jessica's favor. The echo that Andreacchio puts on her scream in reaction to the death of her horse clues us into how personal the act is to her. However, one plot point that is left dangling and only partially resolved at the conclusion is the whereabouts of Kyla, since the dog disappears until the last scene.

Jessica's preparation of the covered hole in the ground is a plot point that is later paid off when Sunny's truck falls into it. The men have to dig their way out of the cave, presumably giving her time to set her traps for what she must realize is their inevitable return. Otherwise, why would she bother? The fallen wind vane may be a failure of one of Jessica's traps but it blocks the path of Sunny's truck for the tractor with the blade. Suspense is created in the truck not starting; another use of the movie convention. Even though this second trap also appears to fail, her run to make the hunters follow results in Ringo's holding onto the wires that electrocute him. Ringo's death is the narrative's first murder at eight minutes before the film's end—indirect though the killing may be. It recalls the electrocution of Henry Silva in *Thirst*. Andreacchio delays the electrocution. This allows for Sunny to realize what is about to happen and warn Ringo, whose feet are touching the ground which is wet from the petrol Jessica has left, to no avail.

Sparks chases Jessica and attacks her with a pitchfork. How's that for phallic symbolism? The scene ends with his accidental death by impalement by his jumping onto an anvil as he chases her. The narrative gives Jessica three attempts at hurtling metal spears at the oncoming Sunny in his truck. In the DVD commentary, Andreacchio describes this confrontation as like a bullfight, following the notion of the truck's bull bars (brush guard) as horns. Jessica's third attempt is prefigured by the use of extreme close-ups of the eyes of both Jessica and Sunny to show their equal determination before Sunny's truck falls into the hole trap.

Her lighting of a petrol bottle that she throws at the truck is an act of deliberation and an awareness of him being trapped. Sunny's yelling engenders sympathy for his situation because of the nature of his seemingly being burned alive, in spite of his previous aggressive behavior. The explosion of the truck would seem to signal the death of Sunny and the end of Jessica's torment, although the narrative gives us the shock effect of the reappearance of Sparks touching her. Although she decides against stabbing him with the raised wooden stake, there is some ambiguity about whether Sparks dies or is only injured. Kyla barking also signals her return to Jessica and the narrative. The dog's apparent injury was presumably inflicted by the hunters at some point off-screen. The film also ends with the song "I Can Fly" as a feminist anthem celebrating the victory of this female action warrior.

In the DVD audio commentary Rob George tells how the story was inspired partly by his experience of being taunted by another motorist during a long distance drive who tail-gated him and then passed him and came back to "play chicken." Additionally, the bush studies of Barbara Baynton, a woman living alone in the Australian outback who published a collection of short stories in 1902 about her experiences, aided George. Andreacchio advises in the commentary that he was going for a comic book style. The sequence of Jessica being tied to the truck's brush guard is something he had appropriated from the crime drama *Boxcar Bertha* (1972), where David Carradine had been tied to the front of a train. In the documentary *Not Quite Hollywood*, Quentin Tarantino also calls the film a female version of the thriller *Straw Dogs* (1971), which had a milquetoast husband of a raped woman seek revenge upon her attackers.

Mario Andreacchio made his directing debut with this film; and he later made the Australian horror title *The Dreaming*. This is the only Australian horror film made by the production company Southern Films International, and the only one made by producers Ron Saunders and Harley Manners.

Cassandra Delaney made her film debut in a supporting role in the musical comedy *One Night Stand* (1984). *Fair Game* is her only leading film role to date; after this she worked in supporting roles and on television. After working in television Peter Ford made his film debut in a minor role in the action adventure *Mad Max* (1979). He has only played supporting film roles to date, and worked in television. David Sandford made his film debut in a minor role in *I Can't Get Started* (1985) and has only worked on television since *Fair Game*. Garry Who made his film debut in a supporting role in *On the Loose* (1984) and has since played supporting film roles and worked in television.

Release

Australia on July 24, 1986, with no apparent release in the United States. The taglines were "They hunted her ... terrorized her ... and now they pay the price," and "One woman's fight for survival against man and machine."

Reviews

"An unabashed exploitation movie.... Its first half is a little slow, [many] laboriously built-up bits of suspense lead nowhere, [and] round about the mid-point, tips into outright, indigenous nastiness.... The scene where Jess is strapped to the front of the truck is loathsome, its voyeuristic intent far outweighing any dramatic justification." — Nick Roddick, *Cinema Papers*, September 1986

"Andreacchio does his best with the material but is hampered by a script lacking motivation and characterization. The film is notable only for some clever stuntwork and a general atmosphere of nastiness." — David Stratton, *The Avocado Plantation*

"A misogynistic and unartistic film, and the predictable ending gives one no feeling of justice — the damage has already been done." — Scott Murray, *Oxford Australian Film 1978–1994*

"Low-budget action thrillers are often considered watchable when they possess decent acting, an original script or just cool action sequences. This film is a miracle. It has none of those. Zip. Zilch. Zero. It's no surprise that none of the principals involved have since gone on to produce much of anything else." — Erik Childress, *Apollo Movie Guide*

"One of the more palatable offerings of the genre.... The film pretty much never slows down and it never brings in new characters to distract from the main conflict, which is something it should be lauded for.... Chief among the film's detractors is its terrible, terrible score, which reeks of all that is bad from the '80s." — *Movie Feast*, April 18, 2009

DVD

Released December 5, 2000, by Vanguard Cinema. Beyond Home Entertainment (Australia) released September 17, 2008.

Contagion
Premiere Film Marketing/Reef Films,
1987 [aka *West Coast Horror*]

CREDITS: *Director:* Karl Zwicky; *Producers:* Ken Methold, Leo Barretto; *Executive Producer:* Tom Broadbridge; *Associate Producer/Production Design:* Richard Rooker; *Screenplay:* Ken Methold; *Photography:* John Stokes; *Music:* Frank Strangio; *Editor:* Roy Mason; *Sound Design:* Tony Vaccher, John Dennison; *Sound:* Ian Grant; *Wardrobe:* Margarita Tassone; *Makeup/Hair:* April Harvie. Color, 107 minutes. Filmed in Brisbane, Queensland.

CAST: John Doyle (Mark Clifton); Nicola Bartlett (Cheryl Davies); Ray Barrett (Roderick Bael); Nathy Gaffney (Cleo); Pamela Hawkesford (Helen); Jacqueline Brennan (Trish); Chris Betts (Alec); Michael Simpson (Frank Hanes); Reginald Cameron (Henry); Michael McCaffrey (Psycho aka Tony); Tracy Nugent (Dero aka Bruce); Deirdree Wallace (Weirdo Woman); Donna Jan Newby (Hitch Hiker); Allan Harvey (Doctor); Michael Stanford (Police Sergeant);

Rosemary Traynor (Nursing Nun); Maurice Hughes (Truckie); Melody Scott (Video Shop Assistant); Greg Powell (Boy in Video Shop); James Kable (Mechanic); Craige Cronin (Priest); Penny Tobin (Receptionist); Rod Pianagonda (Policeman); Louise Ryan (Boutique Assistant); Andrew Johnson (House Purchaser Man); Pamela Norman (House Purchaser Woman); Vassy Cotsiopolous (Shopper 1); Kerrianne Carr (Shopper 2); Hazel Howson (Hospital Patient).

Synopsis

Mark Clifton is a real estate agent in a country town who goes to the aid of a female hitchhiker attacked at night by feral woods dwellers. During the struggle, Mark is raped and traumatized, and in his escape, comes across a mansion hidden away in the woods. Mark sees the inhabitants as Roderick Bael and his young female companions, Cleo and Helen. Roderick seeks Mark's help as a financial consultant. He invites him to join the household if he agrees to demonstrate his dedication by following the "Three Fold Plan" of courage, determination and ruthlessness. To this end, Mark enables the death of his co-worker, Frank Hanes. He also kills his boss, Henry, with a fire extinguisher, and threatens his girlfriend, Cheryl Davies. Cheryl realizes that Mark's view of Roderick's house is a delusion. She sees that he has murdered her boutique co-worker, Trish, and attempts to save him. Mark tries to kill her with an axe and she defends herself with a cross-bow, killing Mark instead.

Notes

This interesting but overlong film combines the themes of the horror of personality with the malevolent supernatural being, and has a narrative that presents the main character as equal protagonist and antagonist. Director Karl Zwicky uses the postmodern techniques of slow motion, point of view, and expressionist camera angles. He employs restraint in bloodletting, although the violence includes a decapitation, cross-bow arrow strikes, stabbings, finger chopping, throat cutting, axing, rape, the use of a fire extinguisher in the face, and a pitchfork. He also features what can be read as an exploitative use of female nudity, although a slim context is provided, without the equivalent male nudity. The cliché of the rural residents as feral grotesques is tempered by the locale being said to be tainted by evil. Zwicky also has ghosts performing in a style that is eccentric without being over the top before they become ultimately tedious. He fails to maintain a changing tone for the film's extended running time, although the latter part does feature a female warrior similar to those in *Lady, Stay Dead*, *Fair Game*, *Out of the Body*, *The 13th Floor*, *Komodo*, *Ghost Ship*, *Undead*, *See No Evil*, *Black Water*, *Storm Warning*, *Slaughtered*, *Prey*, *Triangle*, *The Clinic* and *Road Train*.

A prologue has the black screen divide vertically as if theatrical curtains are being parted, a device that is matched with a vertical close for the end. A narration reads, "And the traveler said: How tainted is this land? How much evil has been committed here? For evil knows no boundaries and manifests itself in many guises. I cannot live among contaminated minds lest the contagion enter my soul." It is not identified who the speaker is, although an argument can be made this becomes the philosophy of Mark once his mind is taken over by delusions.

The idea of the area being inhabited by evil is suggested late in the narrative when Cheryl is told how the mansion was owned by a family who had all been murdered by the father. We are not made aware that Mark knows of this legend, although it is possible, given that he is a real estate agent. The link between the murdering father and his family is made with Roderick and the girls, who may or may not be his daughters.

The prologue has someone unidentified, presumably one of the feral woods dwellers, tying a wire across the road; it will decapitate the oncoming motorbike rider. Zwicky uses slow motion for the resultant crash. He does not show the act in graphic detail, and the death of the rider also gets no plot payoff apart from the fact of another motorbike rider appearing to the Hitch Hiker before she is attacked by Bruce. The Hitch Hiker being picked up at the signed location of Terror Creek is an amusing touch, although the name is not mentioned again. Her sexual harassment by the Truckie is followed by the expectation of her attack when she gets out of the truck. This is aided by the subjective camera of someone watching her in the woods, though we are not shown who at the time.

There is a shock effect of a car that just misses running her down. This is a red herring, given the expectation created, as is the light of the oncoming motorbike. It is the motorbike rider's point of view from where we see Bruce coming up behind her to strangle her, and the rider driving off rather than helping her will be repeated in Mark's hesitation in helping her. This hesitation on Mark's part is naturally due to fear, but also perhaps an acknowledgment of himself as a weak hero, something the narrative will turn around in his delusional purpose.

The narrative also plays off the idea of Mark's impotence by having Tony appear behind him just when Mark decides to confront Bruce, who grunts like an animal. The exposure of the Hitch Hiker's breasts is given the context of Bruce having undressed her to fondle them presumably as a forerunner to rape. The expectation of Mark being struck by Tony is met when Tony shoots his leg with an arrow. This prefigures Cheryl's climactic murder of Mark with a cross-bow, and Tony kissing Mark's unconscious face also prefigures the assumed rape of him to come. As with the motorbike rider's decapitation, the rape is not specifically shown. Rather Tony puts on a pig mask as a perverse indication of something bad about to happen. He leans toward Mark, whom he has bent over a car hood, with the echoed sound of Tony adding to Mark's perception of trauma. After Mark frees himself from capture and axes Bruce, he is given a long close-up which is hard to read. Is it meant to be relief at his escape? Or to indicate that he has received another strike? The latter is suggested by the appearance of Cleo, although this suggestion will be proven incorrect.

Zwicky's treatment of the first thirty minutes has been tight, but he changes pacing and tone for Mark's visit to the mansion. This is perhaps to convey the idea that it is a delusion and not real. Music of the 1920s ragtime and jazz eras is heard, suggesting the eccentricity of the supposed inhabitants and perhaps the real period when they lived there. The nudity of Helen in Mark's room in the mansion can again be contextualized by her supposed sexual advance, with Zwicky exposing the actress to full nudity in the face of Mark's clothed person.

Mark challenges Frank into lifting the barbell weights more than he has been told he is capable of by his trainer. The scene plays like one of torture because of the expectation that Frank will come to harm. This expectation is met by the implied death of Frank by the weights falling on his chest, which Zwicky implies with the fall and breakage of his glasses. Again, the director does not show the graphic result of violence, and buttons the scene by having Mark throw Frank's towel onto the camera as if it is Frank's point of view. Although Mark is not directly responsible for the death of Frank because he has not touched him, it is the first demonstration of his dedication to the "three-fold plan" and his change in character.

When Mark goes home the expectation of his strike against Cheryl is not met when they have sex instead. His passionate embrace of her is presumably new to their relationship and another sign of his change. A further sign of Mark's change is his hearing the voices from the mansion as guides for his actions and answering them. The echo adds to Cheryl's comment to him, "If I were you I'd see a psychiatrist before you go away," both for emphasis and perhaps to suggest that he isn't really listening to her, because his perception has become damaged. The expectation of his pushing her over the balcony is also not met, although it is certainly confirmation for Cheryl that this is not the same man she knew before.

The orgy scene between Mark, Cleo and Helen at the mansion also features female nudity but not his nudity. Roderick watching the sex via a video monitor recalls the video voyeur of *Innocent Prey*. Zwicky also has Roderick rewinding the videotape to add to the awareness of him watching on video, with the girls looking into the camera to titillate Roderick hopefully suggesting that they are not his daughters. Cheryl in the plane flying over the location of the mansion allows for the pilot to cover the story of the family who lived there. Cheryl's observation from the air that the house is dilapidated, and seeing Mark embracing nobody, is intercut with Mark's perception of him embracing Cleo. It is a further indication of his delusion.

Mark's attack upon Henry is a surprise, and the act of releasing a fire extinguisher on someone's face, even if they are shown to be old, seems more humiliation than lethal. However, the shot of the whitened corpse of Henry — the first of violent behavior — is an impressively Gothic one. Mark appears at the airfield in an expressionist camera angle as a mirrored reflection, and the expectation of his strike against the pilot is not met, although later the plane's loss of rudder would suggest Mark's tinkering. Mark's taking of Trish as a playmate for Roderick creates the expectation of doom for her, which is ultimately but not immediately met. The attack upon her is inter-cut with the plane carrying Cheryl again falling from the sky. When Trish is taken to the mansion, we see, with her, how dilapidated it is, further confirmation of Mark's delusion. The bloodied, naked body of the woman tied to a tree in the woods that Trish sees is presumably the Hitch Hiker that Bruce had killed and whose screams Mark had heard.

Zwicky inter-cuts between the two conflicts and shows Mark wielding a knife at Trish but not the resultant strike. This is saved for a later reveal to be seen by Cheryl, and he also shows the plane diving but not its collision. Rather we see the impact, where Cheryl is bloodied but alive, and the pilot who is dead. The pilot is robbed by the Weirdo Woman whom we had seen earlier in the campsite with Bruce and Tony. Previously only an observer, here she takes a more active role, perhaps because both of her companions appear to be dead. Her cutting off the pilot's finger to get a ring is appropriately gruesome. The expectation of the Weirdo Woman attacking Cheryl is met, but Cheryl is revealed to be more resourceful when she has the Woman run into a pitchfork she holds. We can forgive not being shown where Cheryl found the pitchfork. Cheryl vomiting after the strike shows both her disgust at the gore and her remorse, and her victory over the Weirdo Woman prefigures Cheryl as a warrior who will also defeat Mark.

Zwicky again uses echoed voices at the meal between Mark, Roderick, Helen and Cleo. The suggestion that Cleo wants Mark dead and has poisoned him pre-empts his failure to kill Cheryl. The classical music and period wigs and costumes worn by the mansion inhabitants also suggest that something about their attitude toward Mark has changed. Mark's idea that his wine rather than his food has been poisoned leads him to leave and fear those he saw as allies. Given how we later learn that these figures are not real but rather figments of his deluded imagination, this also suggests Mark's further mental deterioration, since his perception of Roderick, Helen and Cleo changes to visions of Frank, Henry and Trish, whom we know all to be dead.

Cheryl at the house and investigating the sound of Mark's sobbing presents her as the conventional Woman in Peril. His crying and rocking back and forward gives way to his perception of Cheryl as the Weirdo Woman. As Mark turns on Cheryl, she becomes the narrative's protagonist, in spite of our awareness of his illness. It is when Cheryl runs from Mark's knife into the woods again that she finds the body of Trish, hanging upside down from a tree with her throat cut. This makes her return to the property perplexing and only rewarded by her being hit by Mark.

Her attempt to hold onto him is to stop him from reaching for the axe they both see in the distance. She is strong enough to stop him from cutting her throat and cuts his leg with his own knife. Her hiding in the shed allows her to see the bloodied bodies of other people, although we don't definitely know who they are. They can hardly be the corpses from the original massacre the pilot had told her had taken place twenty years prior. Considering that Cheryl will find a cross-bow to kill Mark with, it is assumed that is the same cross-bow we had seen Tony use earlier. Therefore the bodies must be those of Tony and Bruce, although we didn't see how Tony had been killed.

When Mark axes open the shed door the expectation of his strike upon Cheryl is met, but his suddenly being shot in the chest is a surprise since we cannot see yet that Cheryl has found a cross-bow. Only after he falls back and Cheryl emerges do we see her holding the cross-bow.

The film's end is troubling. Zwicky holds on a close-up of Cheryl and her expression changes to laughter. Is this to be read as relief over defeating Mark and saving her life? Or are we supposed to think that now Cheryl also has become deluded by her hearing voices? This plot point is left dangling, perhaps in anticipation of a sequel that was never made. Or perhaps the ambiguous end was deliberate.

A final narration echoes the opening one, with the following prose. "And the traveler said: And so much evil was committed here that even the innocent who passed this way soon reeked of the sickness. The contagion had entered their souls." Zwicky ends with the same aerial view he had opened with, then closes with the aforementioned vertical closing screen divide in the manner of theatrical curtains.

Contagion is the only Australian horror movie to be made by Director Karl Zwicky, producers Leo Barretto and Ken Methold, and associate producer Richard Rooker, and the only title to be made by the production company Reef Films to date. It was the first Australian horror title to be made by executive producer Tom Broadbridge and the production company Premiere Film Marketing, which would later make the Australian horror titles *Kadaicha*, *The 13th Floor* and *Out of the Body*.

John Doyle had previously made the Australian horror title *Outback Vampires* and would go on to appear in television and film supporting roles. Nicola Bartlett made her film debut in *Contagion* and continued in television. The lead in *Little Sparrows* (2010) is her only other film to date.

Ray Barrett began his career in television and made his film debut in a supporting role in *The Desperate Women* (1958). He continued in television and supporting film roles, though he played the rare lead in *Time to Remember* (1962) and *Goodbye Paradise* (1983). After *Contagion* appeared in more television and supporting film roles and essayed the lead in the comedy *Dalkeith* (2002). The actor died in 2009. Both Nathy Gaffney and Pamela Hawkesford made their film debuts in *Contagion* and have only been seen in television since.

Release

Appears to have had no cinema release and went straight to video in the United States with the tagline "There's no escape from the ... Contagion."

Reviews

"The film displays Zwicky's cinematic skills, though he is ill-served by the occasionally creaky plot development. Chilling scenes in the woods at night might not be everyone's cup of tea, but Zwicky is clearly a talent for the future."—David Stratton, *The Avocado Plantation*

DVD

Unavailable. Video released by Sony Video/Columbia-Tristar on June 30, 1989.

Outback Vampires

Cine-Funds/Somerset Film Productions, 1987 [aka *The Wicked*; *Tomorrow's News*; *Prince at the Court of Yarralumla*]

CREDITS: *Director:* Colin Eggleston; *Producers:* Jan Tyrrell, James Michael Vernon; *Executive Producers:* Peter Ramster, Robert Sanders, Grahame Jennings; *Screenplay:* David R. Young, Colin Eggleston; *Editor:* Josephine Cook; *Photography:* Gary Wapshott; *Music:* Colin Bayley, Kevin Bayley, Murray Burns; *Production Design:* Michael Ralph; *Costumes:* Helen Hooper; *Sound:* Tim Lloyd; *Art Director:* Ian Gracie; *Special Effects:* Steve Courtney; *Makeup/Hair:* Brita Kingsbury; *Choreographer:* Julie Tanner. Color, 87 minutes. Filmed in Yarralumla, Australian Capital Territory.

SONGS: "Just Begun" (Andy Clayton-Smith, Noel Davies, Perfect Strangers).

CAST: Richard Morgan (Nick); Angela Kennedy (Lucy); Brett Climo (Bronco); John Doyle (Sir Alfred Terminus); Maggie Blinco (Agatha/Frau Etzel); David Gibson (George); Antonia Murphy (Samantha); Lucky Grills (Humphrey); Ric Carter (Stinger); Andy Devine (Jock); David Whitford (Ambrose, aka Station Master); Anne Semler (Mavis); John Farndale (Herbert); Andy Clayton-Smith, Noel Davies, Marcel Kodeka, Andrew Reed, Jamie Weatherstein (the band "Perfect Strangers").

Synopsis

Steer Buster Bronco and his brother Nick are driving to a rodeo in the outback and along the way pick up knife-thrower Lucy. After their car breaks down when it hits a sword trap in the road, they walk to the town of Yarralumla. Directed to the mansion of the scientist Sir Alfred Terminus, the three learn that he and his family are vampires. Bronco seduces the daughter, Samantha. Lucy earns the attentions of the son, George, and Nick, the attention of the mother, Agatha. Samantha bites Bronco repeatedly and keeps him her prisoner, as Nick escapes with Lucy and seeks help from the town residents. Told that Alfred is "The Sla" who can only be killed with the bone of one of his victims, Nick and Lucy return to the mansion. Nick kills Agatha with a stake when she attacks him, saves Bronco by beheading Samantha, and Lucy by setting George on fire. Chased by Alfred, Lucy destroys him by throwing a bone at him and the three visitors think they are finally safe. However, while trying to fix the car they have been given to leave town, Bronco appears to turn into a vampire black bird.

Notes

This comic title features vampires for the theme of the malevolent supernatural being, with the two presented attacks not considered murder because of the regenerative nature of vampire strikes. Director Colin Eggleston uses the postmodern techniques of expressionist camera angles, point of view, an obtrusive score and a sequence where a band performs to camera as if in a music video. His treatment also supplies plenty of bloodletting. There are several vampire bites, two heads being split, one decapitation, a burning, and a gruesome vampire deconstruction prefiguring *Body Melt*. While the narrative's use of bad puns for humor is matched by the arch performances of the antagonists and some slapstick, the treatment still manages to supply empathetic stakes and horror shocks for the protagonists. This mixes genre appeal when the comedy becomes tiresome.

A black bird with a red beak seen in a tree under the opening credits watching the traveling car of the three protagonists will be shown to be a vampire itself, and later perhaps Alfred's alter ego. The title lettering changes from black to red as if to suggest bloodletting. Eggleston uses the shock of Lucy's thrown knife at Nick hitting a tree near his face as a reprise of his effect from *Long Weekend*. Lucy being a knife-thrower will get a plot payoff when she uses the skill to destroy Alfred in the climax. The bird flying after the car shows its continuing interest in the strangers. Eggleston employs another shock effect with the sword that rises from the ground from a trip wire and stops the car. Since the same device stops Alfred's car in the climax, it is presumed that the trap has been set by the residents of Yarralumla and not by the vampires. This implies that the townspeople are in cahoots with Alfred in order to supply him with victims, perhaps to spare themselves the same fate.

The bird attacking Herbert by biting him on the neck confirms that it is a vampire and explains the red on its beak being blood. Alfred's mansion is described by the camping town residents as a "slaughterhouse." The grinder that George will later attempt to kill Lucy with is a device one associates with an animal slaughterhouse, but we never see any animals killed. The mansion on the hill resembles the house on the hill in *Psycho*. In the pub scene, Ambrose repeating what Humphrey says prefigures the "You can say that again" gags the vampires will use. This also defines his character, since he will repeat words in a conversation when he is alone with Bronco, Nick and Lucy. The bicycle-powered telephone that Humphrey rides in order to speak with Alfred suggests both the primitive nature of the town and the eccentricity of its residents without resorting to the cliché of rural townspeople as inbred grotesques, as seen in some other Australian horror titles. Alfred's voice is given an echo to also suggest his threat as much as the poor means of communication. The growling dog in Frau Etzel's limousine that transports the strangers to the mansion is a red herring since it does not attack, and rather is used as a laugh in the way it sits on Nick in the back seat during the journey.

The answering machine message on the doorbell is another attempt at humor; its tape slows down after the first play. It doesn't stop the three from entering the mansion, although perhaps it is also meant to show the house's dilapidation. Bronco's knocking over a vase on a pedestal and Lucy and Nick calling him a moron gets a follow-up when Bronco knocks over the row of pedestals that hold gold vases after Lucy comments how priceless they appear to be.

Agatha's entrance with "You must be starved" begins the family's penchant for bad puns and repetition. She repeats it and then comments, "Oh, I've said that already." The sound of thunder introduces Alfred, although there is no other indication of a storm. Alfred introduces himself to the three strangers with, "You must

Poster for *Outback Vampires*, aka *The Wicked* (1987).

be Nick. You must be Lucy. You must be ... you." The latter refers to Bronco, who will be the most struck of the three guests, and Alfred continues, "I'm so glad you could make it. Usually our audiences are pretty dead." George responds with a squealing laugh that makes him sound like Dr. Frankenstein's assistant, Igor, and becomes a kind of laugh-track for us to appreciate the bad jokes to come. Lucy and Agatha have an exchange about Agatha's daughter, Samantha, which continues the same thread:

AGATHA: She's ill.
LUCY: I hope it's nothing serious.
AGATHA: Serious? No, it's terminal.

The idea of Alfred as a scientist and his family being infested by worms that attacked their intestines in the Amazonian jungle four years ago suggests it was then they became vampires, and a photograph Nick later sees of them looking normal seems to confirm this. Alfred speaks of Samantha being infested by burrowing bugs, and comments, "She lost half of her brain," to which George replies, "Oh, I don't know. She seems to smile a lot more now." To this Alfred comments, "You can say that again," and George replies, "Oh, I don't know"—before being cut off by Alfred.

Agatha floating as she exits the dining room also suggests she is a supernatural being. George's funny dancing to period music on a record player creates the impression that he is a benign fat clown, but his attempt to kill Lucy later will make this misleading. Samantha is introduced with her face down and wearing a large black hat, telling Bronco to "Rack off," which is the same phrase that Lucy employed when he and Nick approached her in the car earlier. Bronco presents himself as a sexually aggressive, speaking of how certain muscles are strengthened by his profession, and asking if Samantha wants to see one, as Eggleston has Bronco's crotch in close-up. However, the story will turn Bronco's sexuality against him in the face of Samantha as a vampire; she will seduce and devour him. The roses in the garden that scream at George and pricks his finger when he picks one are more comic effect and undercut George's attempt to be a romantic figure to Lucy. The flapping wings that Nick hears that suggest the black bird near him in the corridor gets a comic payoff in the repeated droppings it deposits on his face and shoulder.

Agatha in the shower being approached by Nick is a wink to the shower scene in *Psycho*. Here a slowly opened door and steam beckons him to enter the bathroom. The shower curtain and a floor mat are both blood red, and he opens the curtain to reveal Agatha naked except for a turban, earrings and makeup. She wraps herself in the curtain and comes on to Nick. The prospect of success is slim given that she is presented as a grande dame, with her union with Nick as unlikely as that of George's with Lucy. Samantha's seduction of Bronco is aided by the performance of the live band, accompanied by shaking skeletons. The display of Bronco's bare chest that she kisses presents him as dumb beefcake that she will soon bite into. Her supernatural powers are also evident when she suddenly disappears after being summoned by Alfred in a foreign language. Bronco comments that Alfred must be mad because he isn't speaking clearly.

Eggleston uses another shock effect for Nick pulling back a curtain to reveal a red devil painted on a wall in the room where he is locked in, and another in his fall through a hole in the floor. Nick observes Alfred and Samantha through a grated window, emerging from upright coffins and then Alfred biting her neck as Nick is annoyed by a mosquito that parallels the blood-sucking of the vampire. Samantha's collapse is misleading, suggesting her death, which does not occur. The fact that Alfred as her father feeds off her is perhaps applying mortal morality to immortal beings, and Alfred's later calling of Agatha and George also suggests that he feeds off them too. Nick is seen emerging through the broken floor of the locked room rather than using the hole through which he fell, as if empowered by his discovery by Alfred. When he tries to break down the locked door, he bounces off what is revealed to be a rubber door.

A shadow on the wall of an approaching person as seen by Nick and Lucy is revealed to be Bronco in a surprise after Nick attacks. Eggleston uses a special effect of Alfred dancing on the wall, which recalls Fred Astaire doing the wall and ceiling dance in the famous "You're All the World to Me" sequence from the musical *Royal Wedding*. This effect will be repeated later when Agatha does the same. A black bird attacks Bronco, when he, Nick and Lucy attempt to leave town on a Kalamazoo hand pump (railroad handcar). This is more of Bronco being victimized. The scene also gets a button in the rail track's abrupt end and Lucy and Nick falling to the ground, showing how the track leads nowhere.

Eggleston inter-cuts between the townspeople in the pub led by Mavis talking about rebellion against the vampires and Jock telling the long story of his grandmother's death. Both scenes go on for too long, although they both get payoffs. Jock's talking of "The Sla" is how he describes Alfred's vampire and he tells Nick and Lucy that the only way to kill him is to strike him through with the bones of one of his victims. The pub scene is paid off when Nick and Lucy arrive and an interior storm strikes, after Nick opens a can from the slaughterhouse that is said to contain human intestines and he proclaims Alfred as a vampire. This sequence also features the killings of Herbert when the No Credit sign that has been twisting in a circle lands in his head and Mavis is impaled.

Another shock effect occurs when Lucy says she dropped a crucifix on the way in and a window of the mansion suddenly closes. Her and Nick's apparent entrapment doesn't sway them from their intention of saving Bronco and killing Alfred and presumably his family. The freezer of corpses they pass through is evidence of the other human vampire victims, although Nick's being shocked by an outstretched arm of one of the frozen isn't a shock to us. The expectation of there being vampires in the coffins they find is not met. The suspense is alleviated in comic style by the first coffin housing a tape recording of the doorbell answering message. Lucy being taken by George is shown by her being grabbed from the corpse freezer and Nick being locked inside. A scream is heard that we later learn to be that of Bronco as he is bitten by Samantha; her flying is a clever effect shown without the appearance of wires, while his method of being hanged is more apparent.

When Nick gets out of the freezer and goes to the kitchen to find Agatha there, she gets to repeat in full, "Things are not always what they seem" after he tells her, "You can say that again." Her speaking of Alfred's experiments in "bio-rhythmic blue printing" where weather patterns are harnessed to change the cycles of the human body gets no plot payoff. However, Agatha's telling Nick how "The blood of centuries is on my hands" and "Our scourge must be banished from the earth forever" presents her as more serious gothic creature than she has previously been. These lines are also appropriate for being some of the last she will utter, but they also reveal her apparent human guilt over her behavior, perhaps prefiguring her forthcoming death. Agatha on the wall repeats the same effect we had seen earlier of Alfred on the wall, and Alfred's voice heard talking through Agatha seems to suggest his control over her, as does his face appearing over hers, although the actors have similar features.

Agatha is stabbed by Nick's stake when she flies at him, and her death is presented in a progressive deconstructive body melt. Blood appears on her face and throat as if it has been cut and more blood appears and steam rises until she ends as bones and steam. Agatha's blood is blacker looking than blue, and that may be due to the blue interior lighting.

Perhaps it prefigures the black blood we see Alfred release when he explodes. She gets a funny, self-referencing yet expected exit line in "You will clean up, won't you, my dear boy? I do so hate a mess in the kitchen."

Nick again hearing Bronco's scream and arming himself with a cleaver becomes the Man in Peril as the male equivalent of the conventional Woman in Peril, investigating a noise. His throwing the cleaver into Samantha's head is not a shock. Her line, "That's no way to start a meaningful relationship" follows her acknowledging his entrance into the room by axing through the wall and coming on to him. The narrative even under-cuts the horror element of her being decapitated by her talking head, which objects to how she is described but also provides a plot progression. In answer to the question of how to find Lucy, who she says has been taken by George, Samantha tells Nick to follow the bouncing ball. We then see a red ball bounce through the axed hole in the wall which leads the way. This makes no rational sense but rather is more comic invention and self-reference.

Of all the family strikes, that of George is perhaps the most disappointing, after the expectation is met that Nick and Bronco will save Lucy from the grinder. The grinder doesn't get a payoff, which is a real pity since the obvious revenge with this device out of Edgar Allan Poe would surely have been to feed the well-fed George into it. The three protagonists get out of the house, in spite of the afore-seen closed window, and Eggleston makes Bronco being run over by Alfred in a car another shock. The screenplay also pays off Nick's perception that the three are safe now being in daylight, with Bronco's comment after he is run over, "I was almost the one who couldn't live in sunlight!" The fact that Alfred should choose such a prosaic means as a car is a contrivance, and thankfully he is released from it soon enough via the sword road trap. The dynamite used creates the expectation of Alfred being trapped in the car, which is not met. He is then photographed as if he is as tall as a building to increase his threat with an obvious child-sized stunt person used when he picks up Nick. The crucifix that is proffered by Nick receives Alfred's reply, "I've always been an atheist." The assumption that all the townspeople had been in the pub for the interior story, is shown to not be true when Humphrey, Stinger and Ambrose reappear to provide the protagonists with bones to use against Alfred.

Alfred's comment "Wings don't fail me now" as he flies away suggests that he has been the black bird, since we have not seen them together, but also perhaps that he doesn't know whether he can actually fly. The issue of Lucy throwing bones at him isn't given an immediate payoff after some failures to connect. It is noteworthy that the strike that hits him apparently in the neck is the one that causes to him to be destroyed. Although his exploding is a rather disappointing method of demise for the narrative's main antagonist, the resultant black oil that lands on Stinger and Humphrey almost redeems it. Again, if this is black blood, it recalls the black blood seen on Agatha when she died.

It seems that Bronco wanting to use the siren of the ambulance the visitors have been given to leave town is the reason for the car to come to a halt, and his voice heard as he is obscured behind the hood of the car gets a payoff when we see that black bird return. This denouement also gets us past the sappy kissing between Nick and Lucy. Bronco changes from talking of "I'd kill for a beer" to "I'd kill for a handful of blood-dripped birdseed" and the bird cry we hear appears to be more in Bronco's voice. The moment is the final victimization of Bronco, as much as an eventual payoff to him being having bitten so many times by Samantha, and Eggleston ends on a freeze-frame of Nick and Lucy.

Colin Eggleston previously made the Australian horror films *Long Weekend*, *Innocent Prey*, and *Cassandra*; would be his last completed title. He died in 2002. *Outback Vampires* is the only Australian horror film made to date by producer Jan Tyrrell and James Michael Vernon, although Vernon was one of the screenwriters of the Australian horror title *Acolytes*. It is also the only Australian horror film by executive producers Grahame Jennings, Peter Ramster and Robert Sanders, and the only one by Somerset Film Productions.

Richard Morgan appeared in *Innocent Prey*; his role in *Outback Vampires* would prove to be his only lead. The actor died in 2006. Angela Kennedy also began her career in television and made her film debut in *Outback Vampires*. She would go on to appear in more television and supporting film roles.

Brett Climo also began his career in television and made his film debut in a supporting role in *High Country* (1984). He appeared in more television and film supporting roles, and after *Outback Vampires* was in the Australian horror title *Body Melt*. He would essay the leads in *The Inner Sanctuary* (1996) and *Lost and Found* (2006), as well as play in more film supporting parts and television.

John Doyle is another actor who started in television; he made his film debut in a minor role in the comedy *Bliss* (1985). After *Outback Vampires* he played the lead in the Australian horror film *Contagion*. Maggie Blinco also began in television and made her film debut in a supporting role in the comedy *The Night, The Prowler* (1978). She was in television and supporting film roles prior to and after *Outback Vampires*.

David Gibson made his film debut in *Outback Vampires*; it is his only film to date. Antonia Murphy began her career in television and made her film debut in *Outback Vampires*. She appeared in other film supporting roles and on television.

Release

Dates unknown; the taglines on the video release were "They'll invite you for dinner and make you dessert" and "Their appetite for blood is insatiable." It appears to have been released straight to video in the United States.

Reviews

"Campy little film that actually has some interesting ideas to it. The effects are very much like "Dead Alive" but the weird thing, the film is weak on actual deaths."—*Obscure Horror*, February, 2000

"The only good thing about this stupid movie is the cute vampire chick, but she never even takes her clothes off, so this piece of shit is a total waste of time."—*Mr. Satanism Video Picks for Perverts*

DVD

No DVD. American video released by Hemdale Home Video on July 8, 1992.

Zombie Brigade
Smart Egg Cinema Enterprises/CM Productions, 1987
[aka *Night Crawl*; *The Body Counters*; *Zombie Commando*]

CREDITS: *Screenplay/Producer/Director:* Carmelo Musca, Barrie Pattison; *Executive Producer:* Les Lithgow; *Photography:* Alex McPhee; *Editor:* Tang "Thien" Tai; *Music:* John Charles, Todd

Hunter; *Sound:* Hugh Cleverly; *Special Effects Makeup:* Liddy Reynolds; *Production Design:* Julieanne Mills. Color, 91 minutes. Filmed on location in Toodyay, Western Australia.

CAST: John Moore (Jimmy); Khym Lam (Yoshie); Geoff Gibbs (Mayor Harry Ransom); Leslie Wright (Constable Bill Jackson); Bob Faggetter (Alderman Wild); Adam A. Wong (Kinoshita); Michael Fuller (Uncle Charlie); Graeme Rattigan (Alderman Fowler); Brian Fitzsimmons (Alderman King); Lisle Jones (Alderman Harris); Margaret Ford (Nurse); Maggie Wilde West (Madam Rita); Andy King (Minister); Kara Barber (Cora); Dawn Maree Carter (Nora); Michelle Renay (Dora); Leigh Matthews (Workman); Alex Petersons (1969 Soldier); Joanne Bullin, Sarah Habecost, David Musca, Michael Musca (Harris Children); Dickon Oxenburgh, Daniel Luxton, Robert Patuzzi ("The Sons of Gums"); Shane Abdullah, Chris Gentle, Gary Ugle (Spirit Warriors); Gil Clark (Swagman); Keith Scudds (Stockman); Ali Roberts (Minister's Daughter); Kitty Myers (Ferguson Girl); Buddha (Killer); Maggie Musca (Mrs. Ransom); David Berman, Paul Casotti, Lance Carwardine, David Cotgreave, Chad Courtney, Brett Fischer, John Harris, Les Kane, Natalie Grinbergs, Kristof Kaczmarek, David Lithgow, Adrian Mulraney, Ray Parsons, Nick E. Richards, David Riley, Stephen Yang, Peter Van Der Gagg, Peter McGivern (Vampires), Ross Anderson, Mark Blades, Ian Cassidy, James Hagan, Robert Hansen, Graham Heritage, Rod Lipscombe, Johnnie Miller, Jon Paku, Jamie Parker, Mark Raine, Brad Williamson (Zombies); Lucien Benichou, Graham Boston, Jack Browne, George Carr, Noel Clark, Eileen Colocott, Geoff Councel, Nancy Facius, Gerry Farron, Heather Meredith, Ross Midgely, Scott Mosey, Karen Murphy, Thelma Murphy, Rose Myers, Eric Patten, Catherine Penniket, Richard Pierce, Rod Fewster, Jason Giles, John Groves, Kathryn Hall, Jack Hayne, Ray Huttestone, Richard Jeffe, Cameron Lang, Rob Lang, Kim Poke, Mavis Rowles, Trevor Rowles, Chris Tarpey, Doreen Watson, Phil Watson, Peter Webb, Bill Virgo, Paul Viskovich (Town Citizens).

SYNOPSIS

The council of the rural town Lizard Gully decides to build a Robot Man Fun Park in land where a Vietnam cemetery exists, and have investment from a Japanese businessman, Kinoshita. The Vietnam monument is blown up to make way for the development, but that night Vietnam soldiers rise from their entombment and attack as the townspeople party with Kinoshita and his assistant, Yoshie. The aboriginal Jimmy, council clerk, sees how his Uncle Charlie summons spirit warriors to fend off the attackers. The local policeman tells the concerned residents about the top secret "Operation Bodycount" which has the government plan to contain and destroy the town if the Vietnam soldiers escape their entombment. Apparently the soldiers had been infected by a Vietcong plague and were buried alive to contain the infection that has not been released. In order to save the doomed town, Jimmy suggests that Charlie summon the spirits of the dead regular soldiers to fight off the infected ones, and their graves are opened in preparation in spite of some resistance. The soldiers subdue the infected ones and bury them as the last town survivors are allowed to leave.

NOTES

This attempt at satire is a competent effort featuring the theme of the malevolent supernatural being, although it is unclear whether the infected soldiers as the antagonists are meant to be zombies or vampires. Co-directors Carmelo Musca and Barrie Pattison use the postmodern techniques of expressionist camera angles and point of view, and feature bloodletting, a body melt, and a decapitation. The violence lacks general Gothic gruesomeness and a sense of reality, which can be partly blamed on the silly narrative and partly on the production values. There is the occasional interesting touch but performances are generally poor and the film is instantly forgettable. The aboriginal element to the narrative also recalls that in *The Last Wave* and prefigures *The Dreaming* and *Kadaicha*.

A 1969 prologue shows the bloody mouth of a Vietnam soldier seen by Australian soldiers that is presumably a reference to the plague, but also implies that the Vietnamese soldier is a vampire. There is red coloring on the illustrations under the opening credits which anticipate the bloodletting of the forthcoming treatment. The credits also amusingly end with teeth biting away the last title and a blackout transitioning to the present time.

Although the treatment avoids the presentation of rural dwellers as inbred grotesques, Kinoshita's pretending to not speak English makes Mayor Ransom look silly in his fawning over him and constant bowing. There is a laugh from the staged phenomenon of the captive kangaroo that is released to jump across the road in front of Kinoshita's car, with Kinoshita's explanation of his deceit to Yoshie said to be business one-upmanship. At the party to welcome their guest, Wild comments about the destruction of the monument. "If the old diggers could see what is going on here they'd spin in their graves." There is a subsequent cut to the monument site where a hand emerges from the rubble to represent the released soldiers. Yoshie singing during the party reads as filler, and although a delay in having the antagonists strike does create suspense, the fact that she performs the entire song is a sign that the filmmakers have trouble with pace and plot point priority.

The emergence of the soldiers is noteworthy for one smoking a cigarette which he shares with another, and a third putting dirt on his face for camouflage. When the prostitute is attacked by the soldiers in the street, her being covered by them makes a sly comment on her occupational hazards. The neck bite she receives, which implies they are vampires more than zombies since convention tells us that zombies eat brains, is also the first bloodletting. Kinoshita's fate is a plot point that is left unresolved until the climax when he reappears, and when Jimmy and Yoshie visit the Ferguson house. A replaced fallen lamp reveals the body of the dead girl on the floor. The growls that are heard are presumably those of the soldiers and enough to scare away the couple, though the soldiers are only heard and not seen.

It is ironic that the car the couple drives swerves to avoid running into a soldier, perhaps before the protagonists realize that he is one of the antagonists. The swerve results in their car hitting a tree and they have to move on foot, which conveniently leads them to find Uncle Charlie, painted and chanting for his spiritual warriors. The fact that the warriors are able to handle a physical spear to strike into a soldier is a contrived mix of states, but seemingly enough to scare away the other two soldiers who accompanied the advancing one.

The directors inter-cut to the sleeping Bill Jackson being awakened by a noise and investigating it. This presents him as a Man in Peril, the male equivalent of the conventional Woman in Peril. It is interesting that the soldiers who have gathered outside the police station only advance on him when he is hostile and shoots at one of them. We aren't shown how Jackson escapes from the soldiers, who eventually break into the station, although we assume it was not easy. When we see him next he is bloodied and shows the chest bite mark that will eventually prove fatal. The return to Charlie, Jimmy and Yoshie at Charlie's campsite allows for him to have lines that are unintentionally funny. "Live fellas change the place too much. They never do what the dead fellas wanted.... Dead fellas can get real mean about that." After we see the speared soldier deconstruct via a body melt into a skeleton, Charlie then says something equally funny. "Them fellas don't last long once you put their lights out."

When the three drive back to town the next morning we get resonant visuals of abandoned cars and corpses on the road as victims of the marauding soldiers. This recalls the bird carnage seen by "Tippi" Hedren and Rod Taylor in *The Birds* after the bird attack upon the Tides Restaurant in that film. Although it is believed that the soldiers as vampires/zombies cannot circulate in daylight, the one found in the darkened hospital room scores a laugh. The Nurse is empathetic and comments, "The poor thing is trying to tell us something." When she moves her head close to him, he grabs her, and her scream is funny.

When the backstory of the soldiers is told, the Operation Bodycount strategy is also revealed to be containment and to "seal off the contagient." While the minefield where we later see Laurie Fell killed appears to be part of the containment, we are never shown the people who are in charge of the operation or see them planting the mines. Jimmy's car chase of Laurie, although it is initially assumed that the driver is the Mayor trying to flee the town, seems to exit to show the land mines which supposedly circle the area. There is a shock effect from Laurie's dead arm appearing from the fired car. Bill's idea to investigate the blown up memorial and request for assistance is met by the townsmen all afraid to go with him, positioning him as the lone brave one like Gary Copper's lawman in *High Noon*. The fact that Jimmy volunteers to go with him can be interpreted as a presentation of him having a superior moral character since he is Aborigine. This is in counterpoint to the way he feels about himself in a town as a second class citizen, and it's disappointing that the visit gets no plot payoff.

Yoshie's comment to Jimmy back in the town that she can speak five languages is ironic in view of the slipping American one the actress attempts, and Wild gets a funny comment in the face of the town's seeming entrapment. "As soon as it gets dark every man, woman and child in the district will be slaughtered. Maybe even the dogs and the sheep." We don't see the civil unrest that is spoken of over the issue of opening the graves of the soldiers to fight against the first soldiers. We only see two trucks with yelling men inside them passing the cemetery where the graves are dug up. Neither are the remains of the soldiers presented.

Nightfall creates the expectation of another attack. It begins with the comical act of soldiers ringing the doorbell of someone's house to announce their growling intention as visitors. The second soldiers are shown leaving the cemetery moving in a slow march with a bugle used on the soundtrack, although their arrival in the town and confrontation with the first soldiers is delayed. Bill's demise comes as a suicide; he has Jimmy drive a stake through him, suggesting that he is not all zombie/vampire. A hand on Jimmy's unaware shoulder by a soldier results in him being shocked though warned by Wild, and a blood spurt is provided for this stake driving. Yoshie is presented as a conventional victim when she has her head back and hair flying when being strangled but not bitten, and the unseen Jimmy is revealed behind the attacker who falls dead to rescue her.

The Mayor's poetic justice death comes from his running in the street and being chased by a group of soldiers; Yoshie stops Jimmy from helping him. The lead soldier is the nephew that the Mayor had not saved from the draft. He displays a conveniently kept newspaper clipping with the headline "Mayor's nephew loses draft lottery appeal" before the Mayor is set upon and overwhelmed by the group much in the way the prostitute was earlier. When the soldiers attempt to get to a group hiding in a room, there is a laugh from the Minister proffering his crucifix and him being grabbed. The bugle is heard to signal the final arrival of the second soldiers, which makes the attacking soldiers retreat from the room. However, Kinoshita's appearance as a vampire/zombie samurai warrior with a sword delays the confrontation of the two groups of soldiers; he decapitates one and he is overwhelmed as the prostitute and the Mayor were. This group attack adds the grisly touch of Kinoshita's being torn apart, though unseen, and body parts are flung out of the huddle.

The confrontation between the two groups of soldiers results in a fight scene that is abbreviated and cheated with a title card that reads "Later that night after their victory." It is assumed that "their" refers to the second soldiers, and as a result we are shown the two groups shaking hands, which scores a laugh. The directors add self-reference with a soldier standing in front of a video store where there are posters on display for the film, as well as *Rambo* and *Texas Chainsaw Massacre*. Since the soldiers are all nonverbal, being dead, we have to rely upon the townspeople observers describing what is being done, i.e., placing the newly dead in coffins. The burning of the town is presented as a form of revenge upon the townspeople's seeming betrayal of the first soldiers who were entombed. The next morning reveals how the second soldiers, who can seemingly operate in daylight, transport the coffins presumably back to the cemetery to give the first soldiers their proper burial, although we saw that one person who was placed in a coffin was a child. The narrative ends in hope, with the soldiers said to leave markers in the mine fields. These are to show the surviving townspeople — Jimmy, Uncle Charlie, Wild and Yoshie — a way out of the town to avoid being blown up, although this is described rather than us being shown the people following this pathway to freedom.

Zombie Brigade is the only Australian horror film made by directors Carmelo Musca and Barrie Pattison, executive producer Les Lithgow and the production companies Smart Egg Cinema Enterprises and CM Productions.

John Moore made his film debut here and later played leads in *Blackfellas* (1993), the comedy *The Life of Harry Dare* (1995), and *Cold Turkey* (2003), as well as play film supporting roles and television. Khym Lam also made her film debut in *Zombie Brigade* and later appeared in television. Geoff Gibbs began his career in television and also made his film debut here. He would go on to appear in other film supporting roles and more television; he died in 2006.

Leslie Wright also began his career in television and made his film debut in an uncredited part in the British crime drama *Five Days* (1954). He would continue in television and playing supporting film roles prior to and after *Zombie Brigade*. Bob Faggetter is another actor who began his career in television, made his film debut here, and would go on to play other supporting film roles and television parts. *Zombie Brigade* was the film debut for Adam A. Wong and his only title to date.

Release

Screened at the Cannes Film Festival in May 1988, but no apparent film release in Australia or the United States, going straight to video in Australia and straight to DVD in the United States. The DVD tagline is "The dead have awakened to seek revenge! Boy, are they ticked off!"

Reviews

"An amusing movie at times."— Peter West, *Horror Talk*, December 10, 2003

"The acting is mixed, the ethnic, political, and comic potential not realized, and the film drags. When the zombies and vampires arrive, the scenes fail to be suspenseful or funny. The few sex jokes fall flat, and the dialogue is uninspired.... A curio at best."— Nicholas Sheffo, *Fulvue Drive-In*

"Remarkably cheap, outrageous and ineffective effort.... It's played for laughs, but it isn't very funny." — Glenn Kay and Stuart Gordon, *Zombie Movies: The Ultimate Guide*

DVD

Released by Subtance/Jef Films on December 2, 2003. No apparent DVD release in Australia.

Celia

Seon Films, 1988 [aka *Celia: Child of Terror*]

CREDITS: *Director/Screenplay:* Ann Turner; *Producers:* Timothy White, Gordon Glenn; *Executive Producer:* Bryce Menzies; *Associate Producer:* Ian Pringle; *Photography:* Geoffrey Simpson; *Editor:* Ken Sallows; *Music:* Chris Neal; *Production Design:* Peta Lawson; *Sound:* Lloyd Carrick; *Wardrobe:* Rose Chong; *Makeup/Hair:* Carolyn Nott. Color, 98–103 minutes. Filmed in Melbourne, Victoria.

CAST: Rebecca Smart (Celia Carmichael); Nicholas Eadie (Ray Carmichael); Victoria Longley (Alice Tanner); Mary-Anne Fahey (Pat Carmichael); Margaret Ricketts (Granny); Alexander Hutchinson (Steve Tanner); Adrian Mitchell (Karl Tanner); Callie Gray (Meryl Tanner); Martin Sharman (Evan Tanner); Claire Couttie (Heather Goldman); Alex Menglet (Mr. Goldman); Amelia Frid (Stephanie Burke); William Zappa (Sargeant John Burke); Fion Keane (Soapy Burke); Louse Le Nay (Debbie Burke); Shannon McNamara (Slim); Luke Mathews (White Knight); Deborah-Lee Furness (Miss Greenway); Irene Inescort (Mrs. Casey); Myles Sharpe (the Reverend Mitchell); Philip Holder (the Reverend Shaw); Bruno Annetta (Hobyah); Nicholas Trinder, Kim Lardner, James Newman, Raymond Arfoui (Hobyah Pack); Peter Lindsay (Mike Mayfield); Don Kinsey (Newsreel Voiceover); Dan Webb (Radio Announcer); Ian Catchlove (Newsreel Official); Ernest Wilson (Little Old Man); Reg Evans (Jack); Robin Cumming (Doctor); John Arnold (Detective); David Burnett (Policeman); David Ashton (Pet Shop Man); Steve Payne (Government Clerk).

Synopsis

It is December 1957 and the Carmichael family lives in Melbourne, Victoria, with Celia, their only child. Granny, who lives at the back of the house, is found dead by Celia, who is about to turn nine. The Carmichaels get new next door neighbors, the Tanners. Celia befriends their three children, and they play together in the local disused quarry. Celia has vision of her dead Granny but also visions of the Hobyahs at night. The Hobyahs are blue-colored boogie men who she has learned from a school book and who are known to steal people away. Celia's father, Ray, gets her the rabbit she has wanted for her birthday but on the condition that she stay away from the Tanners, who are Communists. When Ray complains about Evan Tanner's Communist Party membership to his government employer, Evan is fired from his job as an electrical engineer. The Tanners move away to Sydney. When school resumes all pet rabbits are confiscated by the police following a government directive and held in the local zoo. When the directive is reversed, Celia finds her rabbit dead among the others. Having a daytime vision of John Burke as a Hobyah, Celia kills him with a shotgun, but is not identified or punished as the murderer.

Notes

This miniature tale features the theme of the horror of personality, although the horror is limited to one murder attributed to the fantasy life of a child. The title character has blonde pigtails and recalls the legendary Rhoda Penmark from *The Bad Seed* (1956). Director Ann Turner only uses slow motion in the epilogue and a few instances of point of view as postmodern technique. She otherwise engages the audience in the empathetic perspective of her protagonist, laying the psychological groundwork for her violent explosion. The narrative is also interesting in presenting the cruelty perpetuated by children and careless adults, the latter given the Communist-fearing 1950s as the context.

A prologue uses a shock effect for the reveal of the dead Granny that Celia finds; the loss is the first of many that she endures and perhaps the reason for her visions of the Hobyahs at night. Turner has an extreme close-up of Celia's eyes opened by the noise of the Hobyahs and a vision of a Hobyah blue hand at her bedroom window. Although Celia's mother shows her a possum in the tree of their backyard, Celia has a vision of a Hobyah sneaking through trees. Slow motion dissolves of Celia's face in close-up appear under the film's opening credits, and climax with Celia looking into the camera.

When Miss Greenway reads the story of the Hobyahs in school, Celia has visions of what she hears. The Hobyahs take an old woman, and an old man chases them when his house is on fire. Although we will later see how the Hobyahs are afraid of fire, that doesn't seem to stop them from taking the old woman, and no discernable reason is given for the fire's eruption. Celia's danger is presented when she sticks her cousin and classmate Stephanie with a tack for teasing her about not having the rabbit that Celia would like to own as a pet. The death of Granny, Celia turning nine, and the new neighbors, the Tanners, are all life changing events for the protagonist. It helps that Rebecca Smart, who plays the lonely and odd Celia, has freckles and a face that expresses her misery.

Celia's visions of Granny in the daytime are not seen by the Tanner children, who play with her in the quarry. A photograph of the Carmichaels in Granny's room shows Celia as the only one of the people photographed being in focus. Like the shot of Celia looking into the camera in the prologue, she also looks into the camera in this photograph. When Celia chases Stephanie into the forest near the quarry after Stephanie steals Granny's mask, the daytime lighting becomes blue and she hears noise of the Hobyahs. Celia performs a blood brother alliance with the Tanner children and Heather Goldman represents Celia's need for secrecy and special friends. Stephanie's payback for the theft will be the lock of hair that is found in the mask after the unseen struggle that also results in Celia's black eye.

Turner's treatment includes movie screenings of a newsreel documentary on the Australian rabbit plague and the disease myxomatosis, which has been introduced to kill them off by poison. There are also genre recreations for the detective Mike Mayfield and a South Sea Island adventure. Turner pays off the Mayfield character when he appears as Celia's black and white vision after she has shot John Burke, although the detective will fail to help Celia be identified as the shooter. The plague sets up the issue of rabbits, which is continued with Celia getting a pet rabbit and the government's ban on them. Burke must then confiscate Celia's rabbit, which leads her to seek revenge.

Ray Carmichael burning Granny's books on Marx and Lenin presents him as a fascist figure and prefigures the action he takes which leads to Evan Tanner being fired for refusing to leave the Communist Party and the Tanners moving away to Sydney. Granny having been a Communist, which had caused Ray trouble in his youth when he served in World War II, presents the idea of her as a free-thinking radical and independent woman. Granny is also a strong influence on Celia, which possibly explains why the child continues to have visions of her. Granny is also associated with Alice Tanner, who seems more of a free spirit than the corseted, inhibited Pat, which is perhaps why Celia is so drawn to Alice.

The rabbit that Ray gets Celia is white with one black ear, which marks it as being as odd as Celia, and perhaps dooms it to its fate. Although Celia refuses to accept her father's condition for the rabbit — that she not see the Tanners — he still gives her the animal. Perhaps Ray's agenda is con-

Ray Carmichael (Nicholas Eadie) and his neighbor Alice Tanner (Victoria Langley) are caught in an embrace in *Celia* (1988).

fused by his desire for Alice, who thankfully rejects his advances. The Tanners being Communists is the rationale given for the hostility between Celia and the Tanner children, and Stephanie and the other children. While their battling is perhaps the normal behavior of children before they learn the restraint of adulthood, it is also a little frightening in its brutality. Additionally, since Celia is aligned with unpopular people, it also presents her as unpopular and as a justification for her unhappiness and anger. The fear of Communists in the narrative that leads to the Tanners losing their livelihood and their home can be equated with the fear of the norm, although a fear of Celia seems justifiable in the light of her climactic act.

The noise of the Hobyahs prefigures the vision of Granny scratching at Celia's window at night. The Hobyahs throwing material at Celia is a shock moment, followed by her morning-after struggle with her bed sheet. A point of view shot of Celia in a tree watching Ray collect the box of photographs that Alice has thrown at him — photographs that Celia had shown the Tanners — creates the expectation not met of his angry reaction. Turner also uses point of view when Celia wears Granny's mask, which has eye holes. When Celia hears the Hobyahs again at night, she responds to another vision of a blue hand with a lit match and then a lit candle. She will later circle her bed with torches as a means of keeping the monsters away.

The doll effigies that the children create, particularly the one of Ray, gets a narrative payoff. Celia is whipped with a belt by her father, an act that Pat stops. Celia's scream in reaction to the idea of sticking a voodoo pin into her father's effigy occurs before the whipping, but it is interesting that she never strikes back at him for his authority over her. This is perhaps acceptable because, in the later fishing scene, we are shown that Celia still loves her father. He is presented as a man with faults rather than of only one dimension. Celia burning the doll effigy of her father reads as disposing of it rather than as an act of voodoo punishment. The fire is used by Stephanie to brand Celia's rabbit, perhaps the act of most cruelty in the story.

A newspaper headline, "Rabbit muster begins," is hidden from Celia by Alice. When the Tanners are leaving, Evan's approaching Ray after he has heard how Ray has attempted to kiss Alice creates the expectation not met that Evan will hit Ray. The loss of the Tanners, after her father has forbidden Celia to see them, is added to the death of Granny as Celia's accumulative loss. The sound of the Hobyahs precedes Celia seeing John Burke taking her rabbit at night. Her thinking he is a Hobyah prefigures the same idea that will later motivate her to kill him. The issue of Celia being allowed to have the pet rabbit goes through permutations, when it is retrieved by her parents. They let John take it again for it to be held in the local zoo because of the government directive that pet rabbits are not allowed, and then a reversal of the directive allows Celia to retrieve it.

Newspaper clippings are on the wall of the schoolroom about the rabbit problem. Celia is not the only child who owns a pet rabbit, something confirmed by the crowds who go to the zoo for rabbit retrieval, and her defacing of the face of Premier Henry Bolte in one article is funny. It is interesting that children, who are the caretakers of their pets, are not allowed into the office of the Department of Vermin and Noxious Weeds where Pat Carmichael goes to apply for a permit to keep their rabbit. Celia writes multiple letters of complaint about the confiscation of her rabbit and points out in class how the government cannot differentiate between the wild rabbits that are the plague problem and controlled and domesticated pet rabbits that are the scapegoat. Turner supplies a resonant image of the crowd of people chasing rabbits in the large pen at the zoo when they come to retrieve them. What has killed Celia's rabbit is unclear, but because it is wet when she finds it, we presume that it has drowned because of overcrowding.

Celia's move into Granny's old room would seem to be a compensation for the loss of the rabbit, another loss. Her wearing of lipstick as American Indian war paint prefigures the battle she has with John Burke. The daytime noise of the Hobyahs prefigures her vision of one in the house that she shoots that is revealed to be John. Although Turner shows blood from his wound, the sight is devoid of gore, and his death elicits no empathy, given that he had taken Celia's rabbit previously. Celia repeats a blood oath swearing with Heather over the secret of John's killing. Turner has the screen go black as Celia's point of view when she faints upon being questioned by the colored Detective, who has morphed from the black and white Mike Mayfield. Her skin rash may be as a result of Celia's contact with her rabbit. Turner gives her a rare close-up in her refusal to pray for John in school, although she does pray after Stephanie points out the refusal to the school teacher, Mrs. Casey.

The final scene can be viewed as an immoral conclusion to the narrative. It creates a gruesome expectation not met of Heather being hanged by Celia in a child game in the quarry. The white head mask that Heather wears to be hanged with slits for her eyes resembles a Ku Klux Klan headpiece. The momentary expectation of Heather being hanged is relieved by the rope falling and her being unharmed. The game demonstrates the danger of Celia and her ability to commit a crime without remorse and get away with it unpunished. This suggests that there will be more harm done by her in the future.

In the DVD interview, Ann Turner says that the film was inspired by an article she saw about the rabbit muster in Victoria in the 1950s and a friend of hers who left Melbourne because he had been blacklisted at work for being a Communist. She also advises that the film is partially autobiographical, with the games and childhood behavior coming from her own childhood. In the film she tried not to judge the behavior as cruelty since she didn't perceive it as such when it was occurring with her as a child. Turner also highlights the context of Christmas, since the time of the birth of the Christ can also be interpreted as the birth of Celia as a killer. *Celia* was Turner's film debut, and she has not made another horror title to date.

Timothy White had previously produced the horror movie *Next of Kin* (1982), but he would not go on to make another horror title. The film was the first produced by Gordon Glenn and his only horror title. Associate producer Ian Pringle would not make another horror film, but executive producer Bryce Menzies would go on to executive produce the horror movie *The Loved Ones* (2009).

After working in television, Rebecca Smart made her film debut in a supporting role in the comedy *The Coca-Cola Kid* (1985). After playing more supporting film roles, she scored her first and only lead as *Celia*, after which she returned to supporting roles and television work. After starting in television, Nicholas Eadie made his film debut in a supporting role in the comedy *Undercover* (1984) and continued in supporting roles and on television. After *Celia*, the actor continued in the same vein but played his only leading role to date in the comedy *Savage Honeymoon* (2000).

Victoria Longley made her film debut in a minor role in *I Can't Get Started* (1985) and continued in supporting film roles and on television. After *Celia* she essayed the lead in the comedy *Talk* (1994) but it would be her only lead. The actress died in 2010. Mary-Anne Fahey also began her career in television and made her film debut as the lead in the comedy *Future Schlock* (1984). This is her only film leading role to date; the actress has otherwise appeared in supporting parts and more television before and after *Celia*.

Release

Australia on May 18, 1989, and the U.S.A. on March 19, 1990, with the taglines "A tale of innocence corrupted," "The eerie, chilling tale of one child's terror," "Child of Terror," and "When fantasy becomes a dangerous game...!"

Reviews

"Celia starts out as a likeable family pic [but] it winds up as something quite different.... Smart, on-screen throughout, is effective as the ultimately scary Celia, but the film's best performance comes from Victoria Longley as the warm-hearted neighbor." — *Variety*

"A transfixing, assured, extremely lucid attempt.... Filmed in a controlled, decorous style that recalls the deceptive serenity of a *Blue Velvet*.... Miss Turner's film is as self-contained as it is self-assured.... Celia [is] played with a chilling and highly effective matter-of-factness by Rebecca Smart." — Janet Maslin, *The New York Times*, March 19, 1990

"A most impressive film debut. There are some signs that it is a first feature, an occasional lapse in the flow of the narrative and it suffers from having more than one ending, but Turner has obtained uniformly good performances from the adult actors and miraculous ones from the children." — Ina Bertrand, *Cinema Papers*, May 1989

"Until the very end, a very fine film about childhood, and Rebecca Smart is amazingly good. The film falters in the closing scenes. To succeed in this dramatic shift away from family cinema, the film needed a treatment that would have been consistently far blacker than it is." — David Stratton, *The Avocado Plantation*

"A powerful, funny and at times unsettling film about the right of all people, whether Communists, women or children, to hold and assert opinions, even in the heart of red-tiled suburbia." — Scott Murray, *Oxford Australian Film 1978–1994*

"Except for brief moments involving imaginary Aussie creatures called Hobyahs, and unexpected acts of violence during its climax, horror fans [tempted by the addition of *Child of Terror* to the title for the video release to make it look like *The Bad Seed*] will feel misled." — John Stanley, *Creature Features*

Awards

Victoria Longley, Best Supporting Actress, Australian Film Institute (AFI) Awards.

DVD

Released by Second Run DVD on March 30, 2009, and by Umbrella Entertainment (Australia) DVD on May 1, 2009.

The Dreaming

International Film Management Limited/Genesis Films, 1988

CREDITS: *Director:* Mario Andreacchio; *Producers:* Craig Lahiff, Wayne Groom: *Executive Producer:* Antony I. Ginnane; *Screenplay:* Mario Andreacchio, Rob George, Stephanie McCarthy, based on a story by Craig Lahiff and Terry Jennings; *Photography:* David Foreman; *Editor:* Suresh Ayyar; *Music:* Frank Strangio; *Production Design:* Michael Ralph; *Art Director:* Ian Gracies; *Sound:* Rob Cutcher; *Makeup/Hair:* Leanne White; *Wardrobe:* Ruth Munro. Color, 87 minutes. Filmed in Adelaide and on Kangaroo Island, South Australia.

CAST: Arthur Dignam (Professor Bernard Thornton); Penny Cook (Cathy Thornton); Gary Sweet (Geoff Douglas); Laurence Clifford (Najira); Kristina Nehm (Warindji); Patrick Frost (Dr. Graham); John Noble (Dr. Richards); Peter Merril (Archeologist); Deborah Little (Admissions Officer); Leo Taylor (Alf); Marcella Russo (Young Nurse); Kathy Fisher (Sister); Gary Goodwin (Policeman); Frank Casper (Priest); Geoff Smith (Undertaker); Brian Mulqueeny, Boris Maciburko (Hospital Aides); Ian Kakoschioe, Mike Read (Security Guards); Chris Jones, Kate Rankin (Students); Mike Norman, Peter Green (Detectives); Jack Harris (Truck Driver); Dieter Linde (Small Boy); Margaret Atkinson (Cleaner); Hedley Cullen (Drunk); Kate Roberts, Brenton Whittle (Barristers); Morris Howie (Court Ushers); Kim Hyde, Michael Evans, Geoff Ledger, Val Pylpenko, Frank Smith, Phil Swan, Ken Hopkins, Paul Cornelius, John Blocki, Jeff James, Michael Dare, Phil Van Dyck (Whalers).

Synopsis

At an island archeological dig, Professor Bernard Thornton discovers Aboriginal artifacts in a cave. They include a bracelet that appears to belong to an Aboriginal woman, Warindji, who was murdered by whalers in 1856. Nine months later, the bracelet is stolen by Aboriginal activists from a university museum. The girl who has the bracelet is caught by museum guards and beaten half to death. She dies in the hospital, and her attendant doctor is Cathy Thornton, who is the Professor's daughter. Cathy discovers marks on the girl's wrist as if she had worn the bracelet, and she has repeated visions of the whalers. After attending her mother's funeral and the death of the activist Najira, who had stolen the bracelet, she drives to the coastline off the island where her father's dig is. In the cave the Professor finds a harpoon that seems to have belonged to the head whaler who had murdered Warindji. Cathy's boyfriend Geoff follows her to the island but she finds him dead, and she is chased by her father, who is dressed as the head whaler. A battle at the top of the lighthouse has Cathy attacking the Professor with the harpoon; he falls from the lighthouse and dies.

Notes

This rather silly film features the themes of the horror of personality and the malevolent supernatural being, in the form of Aborigines. It recalls their threatening presence in *The Last Wave*, although here the threat is less overt. Director Mario Andreacchio uses point of view, expressionist camera angles, hand-held camerawork and slow motion as postmodern techniques, and overuses score. He also employs shock effects more than suspense, although he does provide two gruesome impalings. The dialogue rarely rises above competence and all created expectations are met, but the uncertainty over the mental state of the protagonist does create redeeming ambiguity. Is she a victim of the curse of the Aboriginal Dreaming or a delusional killer?

A prologue title reads: "Two hundred years ago bands of whalers roamed the oceans. In the Great Southern Land of Australia they discovered natives who cherished a mystical power they called their Dreaming. A knowledge handed down from the time their world began. The whalers were blood thirsty men and there were rapes, killings, massacres. A taint on the Dreaming. A taint that lives on into the present time and a new nightmare...."

Andreacchio uses a helicopter pan over the coastline of the island that begins the film and to which the narrative will return to in the climax. The disparity between the dark blue sea and the golden land is a striking difference, and the helicopter point of view is continued with a helicopter landing for the Professor's arrival. The surface of the cave wall where he is taken does not seem to support the excitement that the dig archeologists have. However the shock release of gas from the dug hole in the wall and the resultant explosion prefigure the danger of what is to be found inside. Among the skulls and bones is a bracelet that we presume with hindsight belongs to Warindji, the Aboriginal girl who we learn is murdered by the invading whalers. The Professor has a vision of Warindji. She looks at him, there is a wave of blood, and the whalers arrive at the Aboriginal campsite and attack. Blood is seen on a harpoon, which is the whaler's weapon of choice, and Warindji screams. The sequence ends with an extreme close-up of the Professor, and the fact that he has visions of the past prefigures Cathy's visions. It also aligns him with what may be his ancestor who is later shown to be Warindji's murderer.

Andreacchio uses shock in the breaking of the museum display case when the bracelet is stolen by Aborigines in modern dress. The girl who wears the bracelet is the one caught by security guards, and she holds a fire extinguisher as a weapon which she sprays, as expected. The mist of the sprayed foam conceals the guard's attack of retribution upon her, and this concealment of violence will be repeated in the death of Najira. Cathy's seeing a vision of the girl's moving head in the x-ray is her first vision and coincides with the death struggles of the girl. Andreacchio has a lighting effect behind Cathy as she moves away from the girl on the operating table and goes to the dig cave. Cathy also has a vision of Warindji being chased by the whalers and one whaler moving to strike Cathy with a harpoon before we cut back to Cathy at the operating table with the flat heart monitor registering that the girl is dead. The cut back to Cathy returns Cathy from her vision to reality, as will later happen when she awakes from other visions as dreams. Andreacchio cuts from the dripping of water from the operating room faucet to blood dripping onto the floor, which is revealed to be from the girl's corpse. Cathy's suspenseful advance to the table where the body is covered in a sheet gets a shock result in her seeing a wound on her that will be repeated as the harpoon cut that has killed Warindji.

An exchange between Dr. Graham and Cathy where he suggests she consult the hospital psychiatrist about her vision includes an obvious usage of qualifiers: His "If you don't mind me saying so" is met by her "I do mind you saying so." The markings on Cathy's wrist, as if she has worn the bracelet, would seem to have come to her via the girl, since Cathy has touched the bracelet that the girl had been wearing. This connection is also presumably what allows for Cathy's visions into Warinji's attack and the whalers, although the connection between the head whaler and the Professor as her father will be shown later. When Cathy goes to the library to research Aborigines, it recalls the anthropological book in *The Last Wave*. A clock is heard to tick loudly. However, the ominous ticking stops when Cathy's hand shakes, in a comical effect, to draw a map of the coastline on its own.

Andreacchio frequently uses rain in the treatment and Cathy's

Poster for *The Dreaming* (1988).

vision of the Aboriginal woman at the window of her home has the woman wet and wearing a white hospital gown. There is some ambiguity about whether this vision is Warindji or the dead girl. This is not helped by the apparent casting of the same actress as the two characters, unless we are meant to think that the girl is a reincarnation of Warindji. Cathy going to see the girl's body in hospital suggests that the vision was the girl, although the shock reveals of the whalers in the room with the corpse are shown to be Cathy's nightmare. The drawn map is shown to be the coastline off the island of the dig, although it will take a while for Cathy to go there.

Najira's theft of the bracelet and Cathy's chase of him is halted by her being paged with a telephone call from her father telling of the death of her mother. Rain is used for the funeral, although sporadically. Najira appears to tell the Professor that the dig island is known as "The Isle of the Dead," and naturally he warns the Professor to keep away. The parallel that Najira makes between the bones of his ancestors in the cave and the Professor's dead wife is apt, but his death scene after he is pursued by Cathy is perhaps presented in a far too mystical way. After she implores, "Tell me what it means," smoke obscures how exactly he has come to be impaled, although Najira walking into it creates the expectation, met, that he will die. This action is also presented as real and not one of Cathy's visions. We wonder why Najira had to die in the scheme of the narrative, other than for the shock effect of the impaling. Are we to assume that Cathy has somehow incurred his death in her attempt to understand the mystery of the bracelet? Or was it a simple case of him not looking where he was going and plain bad luck?

A zoom in on a black and white photograph of the coastline hotel with the Professor in front, which Cathy looks at, becomes color film of the location. The rain pouring for Cathy's drive at night signals more ill fate. She has a vision of driving off the highway and being chased by whalers who surround her car, with a shock reveal for her return to reality and nearly driving into an oncoming truck on the highway. Andreacchio supplies another shock with the appearance of the hotel desk clerk at her room door; he has come to deliver her a towel and water. The cries Cathy hears in the night and her looking for the source makes Cathy the conventional Woman in Peril investigating a noise, although this episode will be revealed as a nightmare.

She has a vision of the whalers in the hotel bar drinking and Warindji as the crier being tormented by them. For the first time the Professor is revealed as the head whaler. He motions for other whalers to go to Cathy; she escapes to her room but a bloody arm pushes through the door. With whalers that also appear behind her in the room, whom we have not seen enter, she awakens to confirm that the vision was a nightmare. The idea that her father is the reincarnated form of the head whaler is established, although whether it is real or Cathy's imagination will only be clarified at the film's climax. Her confused state is expressed in the following speech to the Professor, who asks her what is troubling her, which also reads as bad writing: "I don't know. Its lots of peculiar things have been going on and I don't understand them. I've been seeing things and I haven't been seeing things and I've been seeing things and I ... drawings and pictures and I don't understand and I'm scared and I don't know what to do because I don't understand what's going on."

This babble should be enough for the Professor to call in a psychiatrist, but he only responds with the banal stupidity: "It sounds to me as if you've been working too hard." The Professor gets his own obtuse form of expression when he tells Cathy why he has come back to the island dig: "I'm looking for something." To her "What?" he replies, "Don't know." And this is supposed to be the eloquence of educated people!

When Cathy hears what sounds like the cries of a seal, she investigates again as the Woman in Peril, although the daylight prefigures the fact that she suffers no harm because of it. Andreacchio intercuts between Cathy on the beach and the Professor in the cave, although he delays the Professor's discovery. The slaughtered seal on the beach appears to be related to the branch effigy that the Professor has made at the top of the hill, although this is never explained, and the seal's blood and the gutted body prefigure Geoff's murder.

The Professor discovers the harpoon in the water by sheer luck; he trips over it. Cathy washing the seal blood from her hands after she has buried the gutted seal prefigures the killings to come. She has a nightmare of Geoff boating to the island at night and his having a vision of the whalers ship among green light. The ship rams his boat, and the created expectation that he will be killed is met when he is harpooned by the head whaler. The head whaler is the Professor look-alike, so how's that for Freudian symbolism? The nightmare gets a payoff when the real Geoff in the house appears as a shock to Cathy, and he slaps her after her nonsensical repeated "You're dead" to bring her back to reality.

The Professor's fetish for the harpoon has him rubbing his face against it, and an expectation is created that he will attack Cathy and Geoff with it. Andreacchio uses a subjective camera as the Professor's point of view watching Geoff comfort Cathy, and then presents Geoff walking in the house as a Man in Peril. The sequence of Geoff's death has suspense because the audience is aware of the established threat, and the flashing of the lighthouse light adds a rhythmic darkness. The Professor is shown to set alight the branch effigy as Geoff reads a diary in the Professor's room which appears to be written by the head whaler. The burning effigy is seen by Geoff and used to attract him like the Woman in Peril investigating a noise. We aren't shown Geoff's murder. Cathy hears what we assume is his yell, although she does not immediately investigate the noise as a Woman in Peril. Rather, she too goes to the Professor's room to read the diary, with the sound of howling wind adding to the suspense.

Approaching feet are seen in the house. The harpoon is raised to show the Professor's face in the blade's reflection. Cathy's reading becomes the Professor's voice, and she has the vision of the whalers arriving at the Aboriginal campsite seen by Warindji that the Professor had when he originally entered the cave. There is a shadowed view of the whalers striking Aborigines, and then the head whaler chasing Warindji. She passes Cathy and is entrapped in the cave. Andreacchio uses music but no dialogue or cries to satisfying effect, and we see the harpoon wound to Warindji's neck that Cathy had seen as the girl's wound in the hospital operating room.

The head whaler chases Cathy outside the house in what appears to be reality, although it can be read in hindsight as more of Cathy's vision. The expectation is created that she will find Geoff, which is met when he is revealed in a shock moment as impaled and hanging off the ground. Andreacchio has bursts of music for the head whaler's chase of Cathy. Her attempt at refuge in the lighthouse reads as only partially foolhardy since she has seen how the boats have been filled with dirt to stop them from being used to leave the island. Again the rhythmic lighting provides timed blackouts, and we get a shock of the harpoon blade through the lighthouse door.

The foolhardy choice of the lighthouse is confirmed by Cathy climbing up, which is the only way to go in a lighthouse, so that the climax involves her and the whaler chasing each other around the light. The small space makes this chase even more ridiculous, although the whaler's harpoon is no joke. Cathy tripping and making herself totally vulnerable is rather painful, but the whaler smashing his glassed window reflection is odd. Presumably the action of a primitive man, it prefigures the Professor's fall from the opposite glass window. Ambiguity is created by the whaler's lines "Did you think I was going to hurt you? I wouldn't hurt you because I love you and you love me. Don't you? Don't you?!"

The ambiguity comes from whether we believe that it is the Professor as reincarnated whaler taunting Cathy, or the real Professor trying to comfort Cathy. If we believe the latter, we have to wonder why the Professor would have the harpoon with him. Cathy hits him with the harpoon which causes the Professor to crash through the window and fall out down to the ground, presumably dead. Her cry of "Dad" suggests that her pushing him has been part of her deluded vision of him as the whaler.

Andreacchio has a shot of the red sky dawn and a helicopter view of Cathy walking on the island; the fact that she is not given a full face shot denies empathy for what she has done. Rather she is a small, lost and lonely figure in a large landscape. This is reinforced by the repeat of the helicopter aerial view of the coastline that was featured in the film's opening. The screen goes black for the end.

In his book *The Avocado Plantation*, David Stratton writes that story co-writer and producer Craig Lahiff originally intended to direct but changed his mind. He was tired after directing two back to back non-horror titles, and was not happy with the way the script had changed into a "B-grade horror film." Mario Andreacchio had previously directed the Australian horror movie *Fair Game*, but after *The Dreaming* he would not go on to make another horror title. It was the first produced by Lahiff but he would not go on to produce another horror film, and it was the only horror title made by co-producer Wayne Groom. *The Dreaming* would be the last Australian horror film to date by executive producer Antony I. Ginnane. It was the first feature for Genesis Films, and the only horror title made by the production company and by International Film Management Limited.

Arthur Dignam had made his film debut in the lead role of "The Priest" segment of the erotic anthology *Libido* (1973). He played the leads in *The Devil's Playground* (1976), the comedy *Summer of Secrets* (1976), and *Night of Shadows* (1982), but otherwise appeared in supporting film roles. After *The Dreaming*, he has not had another film role to date. Penny Cook made her film debut here after working in television, and it is the only film she has made to date.

Release

It is thought to have received a screening at the 1988 Cannes Film Festival, although this is unconfirmed. The film was released in Japan on January 13, 1990, but it apparently went straight to video in Australia and the United States. Taglines include "A burial ground is unearthed, a girl dies, an ancient curse lives on," "Are they dreams or nightmares.... Nightmares or premonitions?" and "She uncovered a place where ancient mysteries survive and nightmares are real."

Reviews

"Depressingly poor. It is not very suspenseful, or well-enough acted to make the final confrontation very gripping. Nor is it visually very interesting with production design noticeably below standard."—David Stratton, *The Avocado Plantation*

"This movie looks pretty good and takes advantage of the beautiful scenery of the Australian coastline [but] the plot is a bit of a mess and seems to have trouble moving ahead. By the end of the film, I felt no more closer to a conclusion than I did after the opening narrative scroll."—*The Video Graveyard*

Awards

Suresh Ayyar nominated as Best Editor in the Australian Film Institute (AFI) Awards.

DVD

Released by Platinum Disc on November 26, 2002.

Houseboat Horror

P.M. Terror Productions, 1988

CREDITS: *Directors:* Kendal Flanagan, Ollie Martin; *Producer/Screenplay:* Ollie Martin; *Associate Producer:* Ric Lappas; *Executive Producer:* Greg Petherick; *Photography:* Bill Parnell; *Editor:* Clayton Jacobson; *Music:* Brian Mannix, Steve Harrison, Ross McLennan; *Art Director:* Brian Gunst; *Sound:* Scott Findlay; *FX Body Parts and Makeup:* Nick Dorning; *Makeup:* Vicki Freeman; *Wardrobe:* Aggie Szetey. Color, 82 minutes. Filmed in Lake Eildon, Victoria.

SONGS: "Young, Cool and Groovy" (Brian Mannix, Steve Harrison); "Suspicion" (Ross McLennan); "Acid Rap" (Steve Harrison, Ross McLennan); "My Man is Leaving Me" (Steve Harrison); "Out of Touch" (Brian Mannix, Steve Harrison); "Smack Dealer" (S. Morbid, Brian Mannix); "Overactive Imagination" (Steve Harrison).

CAST: Alan Dale (Evans); Christine Jeston (Tracy); Craig Alexander (Sam); Des "Animal" McKenna (Ziggie); Gavid Wood (Jimmy Costello); John Michael Howson ("J"); Louise Siversen (Zelia); Peppie D'or (Teresa); Steve Whittacker (Bernie); Julie Tompson (Jennie); Mark Muggeridge (Dagger); Wilkie Collins (Harold); David Blackman (Bill); Greg Latts (Con); Ian Campbell (Clap); Steve Hutchinson (Gary); Christopher Young (Norm); Don Bridges (Garage Man); Katherine Hill (Kat); Sue Hancock (Susy); Ruth Jaffe (Mertyl); Lewis Porter (Ranger); Alisa Meadows (Wendy); Jason Archer (Staked Body); Sandra "Scarlet" Wilson (Clapper Man); Ollie Martin (Ambulance Man); Zlatko Kasumovick (Luke "Acid Head").

Synopsis

A film crew travels to Lake Infinity to make a music video for a band on houseboats. However, unknown to them, there lives Luke whose face has been burned in a previous film shoot by the same production team. After killing two city backpackers and the Forest Ranger, Luke then kills off the music video crew members one by one. When it seems that Tracy has successfully burned him again and he has drowned in the lake, she is safely taken away by ambulance, traumatized by the events. A crazy lady, Zelia, tells the surviving band members about the deaths and says she will take them to her house to contact the authorities. We are told that "Peace and Tranquility returned to Lake Infinity," but as Luke's arm reaches out of his watery grave, we also read "For a Time...."

Notes

A low budget shot on video effort by co-directors, where it cannot be determined who did what, explores the theme of the horror of personality. Postmodern techniques include point of view, slow motion, freeze frames and expressionist camera angles. Women's bodies are presented in an exploitative way. The treatment also features gruesome acts of violence, with one spectacular head-splitting effect, and restrained implicit violence. Shock effects and suspense are used in a narrative that has trouble differentiating character, although there are some examples of black humor.

A prologue features the van of some of the film's crew picking up a hitchhiker; however, the expectation that she will become a victim to them is not met. Rather it is when she alights from the van that she gets into trouble. The van's crew is established as protagonists by the device of hearing them talking on the soundtrack while we see shots of the van moving. The shot of someone watching the girl as she walks through the forest is the first presumed presentation of Luke, in spite of this watcher coming from a truck which we don't later associate him with. Although he is never named as such in the narrative, Luke will be shown as a menacing stalker. This is begun with the repeated sight of his legs and feet, followed by shots of his head and body, and finally his face in the film's climax. This objectification of Luke helps to conceal his appearance as the unidentified killer as much as it conceals his disfigured face.

The girl being watched creates the expectation that she will come to harm. This is met when her point of view reveals the bloody body of the boyfriend she was due to meet. The blood pouring out of him suggests that he has only recently been attacked, which may explain why Luke is still around, and is the first gore. The unnamed boyfriend's call for his unnamed girlfriend to "Run" before he dies is comical, and the shot of her in between Luke's legs that are planted on either side of the frame as she runs is a derivate camera shot. The heartbeat on the soundtrack is equally uninspired, although there is a shock effect when the girl stands hiding behind a tree. The score is suddenly stopped and the silence creates the impression that she is no longer in danger, although true horror aficionados will know the killer is biding his time. The knife appears at her face after she turns back from turning to look around. The film's opening title adds the word "Horror" to strike the word "Houseboat" which results in a shattering effect on "Houseboat" as the sound of breaking glass is heard. Additionally the last "R" in "Horror" has a devil's arrow tail.

Gary is differentiated from the second van of crew by his reading *Sir Gawain and the Green Knight*, although his later looking for wild mushrooms to smoke and having hallucinatory drugs in a syringe indicates he can be just as rowdy as the others. The conversation of the men at the gas station after the second van leaves raises the issue of movie killings having occurred in the area "a few years back." This is a matter that will be covered in more detail by the newspaper clippings in Luke's shack and from what Zelia says. Teresa's comment to Sam that "All you're going to get into me is booze" is a mild witticism. "J" holding a book on horror in another store that the vans go to is a note of self-reference and an indication of the locals not being as benign as they seem.

The appearance of the Forest Ranger is an ambiguous one since it seems he may be the killer, a fact dismissed when he becomes Luke's next victim. However, the Ranger's disapproval of the company's careless treatment of the area — chopping a tree for no purpose, throwing beer cans into the lake, playing loud music — recalls the karmic carelessness of *Long Weekend*. The killing of the Ranger is presented by legs shown behind him, a raised axe, and blood sprayed onto a tree. We also get a shot of the Ranger's head with the axe in it, which some may find funny, but the relative restraint prefigures other killings. The bloodied hand of the killer who wears fingerless gloves is an advance on his reveal, after only his legs have been seen.

It is perhaps no coincidence that the nights the company stays at the Lake all feature full moons. The treatment uses a shock effect to defy a created expectation when two of the women play cards and are frightened by the sudden appearance of one of the men. Another created expectation, not met, follows the subjective camera and one of the women in the shower who hears a noise and is shocked by another woman. At least here the exposed breasts of the woman in the shower have an appropriate context, unlike the later examples of nudity. Luke is also shown with his bloodied gloved hands to be doing something that is not explained, unlike his later disconnecting the houseboat two-way radio and releasing one of the boats, before the transition to the next day.

Luke at his shack sharpening his blade allows us to see two newspaper clippings he has kept. The first has a headline "Four Die: Film Crew Found Guilty" and the second, "Child Burnt on Set." For the latter, Luke stabs his blade into the clipping, a shock effect, and one which makes us presume that he is the child who was burned.

The filming of the music video has problematic coverage because we only see the camera set up for one shot of the band on the houseboat, but the footage shown is obviously edited and features the band at different locations. The bloody corpse that is discovered on the exterior wall of the houseboat is presumably some kind of killed animal, but it is not referred to again and never really explained other than the act of the crazed Luke. When Gary and another unnamed crewman go walking at night looking for the wild mushrooms, the subjective camera is used to follow them as Luke's advancing point of view. However, the angle switches to the front of Gary to have his throat slit. Gary dropping the flashlight he had been holding as he falls dead is caught by Luke and paid off in the way Luke shines it into the other man's face in his advance, to conceal his identity so that the man thinks he is Gary. Luke's strike misses the man, which is a surprise and allows for a chase, and the man hiding behind a tree recalls the same act by the girl in the prologue. The man is given an extreme close-up of his eyes, which maximizes Luke's strike of the drug syringe into the man's face. This is complemented by a knife into his body, and the man gives a death gasp.

The advancing subjective camera is used for Zelia's approach to the campsite, with her reveal a surprise and not meeting the created expectation. Her wearing gumboots differentiates her from Luke's boots, although it is possible that she still could be the killer but has just changed her boots. Louise Siversen's performance as Zelia is pitched differently to the other actors. As Zelia carries what appears to be a scalp of hair, Siversen performs in a Gothic style which is appropriate and only goes over the top at the film's end with an evil smile. She supplies another clue to the backstory of the film crew fire by telling the campers that she was one of the actors in the company, although oddly, Evans does not recognize her. Her connection to Luke is suggested since after she leaves, his feet and approach via subjective camera appear to zoom in on the campsite fire.

A montage is used for what could be memory of a victim, with the contrivance of seeing oneself in a memory, or witness memory. The same shot of the burning man is repeated when Luke burns in the film's climax. This montage has flames, screams, a fire engine siren, the burning body, and a zoom out from the campsite fire to come out of the montage. When Luke walks into the crew houseboat to break the two-way radio, we get a better view of him. We see his head and body, although he is still partially concealed by the darkness of night. The next day one of the women stands naked at the edge of the lake, seen from the back by Ziggie. The pretense that she has been swimming does not pass since her hair is dry, and when she turns so that her breasts are exposed, it is exploitative because there is no context to it other than titillation.

The sequence of Bernie and another woman exploring the countryside culminates in their investigating a barn, which is a suspense set piece, set in daytime, although the barn is moderately dark. A shape is seen moving behind a wooden slatted-wall from the interior point of view, which we assume is Luke. His presence in the barn creates the expectation that he will attack the pair. The sequence is also aided by the non-use of score and the sound of insects. The attack on Bernie is prefigured by a shadow on his face, with the raised knife, his yell, the sound of the strike, and blood splatter on the wall the result. The blood spray recalls the murder of the Forest Ranger, and the treatment delays the reveal of Bernie's body for the woman's discovery. This is anticipated by blood drops on her face and her looking up to see the knife in Bernie's neck.

Luke removing a horseshoe from the barn wall is paid off when he uses it to kill the woman, after a chase in which her legs are shown as she runs. The strike is again presented abstractly, suggested by Luke's lunge of the horseshoe into the camera and the sight of the woman falling, revealing the horseshoe in her eyes as another gruesome but funny image.

Zelia at the barn door initially appears to be a red herring, with hindsight knowledge that Luke is the killer. When she says the following to Luke it reveals their backstory: "You know what all this means? We'll be hiding again. I'll have to take care of you so they don't lock you away. Is that what you want? To be taken away? What have you done? These are just innocent film people. You don't have to hate the movie people forever. Go on, get out. Go on."

The shadow that moves past her after the speech is presumably Luke, the killer that she is not afraid of. The band members at the local pub separated from the crew of the houseboats spares them from Luke's attack that night. It also allows the treatment to intercut between the attacks and the oblivious others. The nudity of another woman swimming in the lake has context. She has a flashlight shined in her face, which frightens her. Her response, "It's you," is misleading. We assume that the flashlight holder is Luke, but since he is unknown to the woman as part of the houseboat company, it cannot be. But this person is not identified as anyone else, so the moment reads as a red herring. However, the expectation is followed by the attack upon her when she is in bed.

The fact of her covering and then uncovering herself to read a book in bed when she is bare-breasted seems exploitative, and there is a narrative joke from Luke looking in a drawer for a weapon. When he first finds a spoon there is a laugh from his rejecting it, before he finds a knife. Silence is again used when the woman thinks she hears something and calls out, and the expectation of her being attacked by Luke via an advancing subjective camera is not met. Rather, a shock effect is used for his attack under the mattress of the double-bunk she lies in. The repeated strikes, the woman's jumps and the blood letting are excessive. This is perhaps to exploit the sight of her arched back and her protruding breasts as she is attacked.

Luke's gloved hand is shown at the side of the frame as he hides when Jimmy and a woman enter the houseboat, and Luke finding a spear gun creates another expectation of an attack. This expectation is only partially met. Jimmy's unwrapping a condom suggests that Luke will shoot at his penis — a Gothic strike that is not made. Rather Luke shoots him in the stomach, with blood spray on the wall repeated as a suggested device. Because we have already seen Jimmy being shot, the woman's discovery of him is less of a reveal, and a shock effect is used for her post-scream stabbing through the neck. The narrative also pays off the plot points of another crew member riding a Jet Ski in the lake, disturbing Evans and witnessed by Susy and Sam. The payoff is made by making the rider Luke's next victim, although Luke needs to use a raft to get close enough to spear him.

There only four crew members left: Evans, Tracy, Susy and Sam. Luke's burned face is revealed as he enters the lit houseboat to be seen by them. Regrettably, Luke never speaks in the narrative. He only grunts like a horror movie monster, so that we don't get his insight into the backstory. When Luke attacks Evans and strangles him, it is curious that none of the others attempt to help him, not even his supposed girlfriend, Tracy. Strangling is a rather boring weapon in horror movies but Evans' head being cut in half is good shock effect, even when the image goes a little soft presumably to conceal the mechanics of the effect.

Susy hiding in the shower seems a silly move, particularly when her shadow seen behind the curtain makes her easily found when Luke pulls it back a la *Psycho* and Sam's strike creates the expectation not met that he is killed. Tracy's run out of the houseboat may seem the most sensible action, but her leaving the others doesn't create empathy for her, which she needs when she is being stalked by Luke. Tracy finds the body of the second man in the forest, the one wearing the syringe in his face. We wonder why she doesn't take the knife from his body to use as a weapon, although later when she kicks Luke in the groin we see how perhaps she doesn't need to. Dawn falling and Tracy still running scores a laugh, and her return to the houseboat for Sam's reappearance allows for the conventional tension from the motor that won't start. When the motor does eventually start and Luke is left behind, the expectation is created that Tracy and Sam have survived, with the footage of the boat sailing adding to the expectation. However, the sudden stalling of the boat allows for Luke to reappear. How he got on the boat when it stops in the middle of the lake and he is not wet is a plot hole, unless we are supposed to think that he also has supernatural powers. Luke doesn't throw Sam overboard in their fight, which would seem the obvious choice.

Tracy threatening Luke with a lighter and then Sam throwing gas on him causes Luke to burst into flames, reliving his earlier trauma. We assume that his fall into the lake has not killed him since surely the water would douse the fire. Tracy goes to Sam, who is shown to be the burned Luke, but this is revealed as her having a nightmare. Although we see her being rescued by an ambulance we don't know what becomes of Sam.

The return of the band to the lake and them being met by Zelia allows her to convey some ambiguous information. Her little brother was killed in the fire and most of the crew is dead. We don't know whether she means that she knows how Luke has been killed in the fire by Tracy, or whether Luke was killed in the backstory, which would make him a malevolent supernatural being. Her offer to take them to her house to telephone "the authorities" is leavened by wanting to show them the barn on the way, since we assume this is code for they will be killed, too.

The end title card, "Peace and tranquility returned to Lake Infinity," is interrupted by a shock effect. Luke's arm rises out of the lake to grab a chain that ties a houseboat. Another title card reads, "For a time...." This epilogue suggests that Luke has not been burned and has not drowned. Perhaps given the time it took him to resurface, he is now reborn as a malevolent supernatural being. Since no sequel was made, it is hard to be certain.

Houseboat Horror is the only film directed by Kendal Flanagan and Ollie Martin. It is the only one made by associate producer Ric Lappas and the P.M. Terror Productions Company.

New Zealand born Alan Dale began his Australian acting career in television; *Houseboat Horror* was his film debut and his first and leading film role. Afterward he would play in supporting film roles and work in television.

Release

Dates unknown; however, the film appears to have gone straight to video in Australia via AME Video with the taglines "Something is about to happen on Lake Infinity!!" and "A new wave of blood gushing suspense."

Reviews

"A thoroughly routine slasher film closely modelled on the *Friday the 13th* series."—David Stratton, *The Avocado Plantation*

"The lasting impression that this movie will have on you is that you have seen the worst Australia has to offer, it can only get better from here ... an absolutely hideous cinematic experience that should never ever be repeated, or mentioned in polite conversation."—*ScaryMinds*

"The death scenes are actually pretty good for this kind of thing and it has a sort of goofy charm that is hard to deny. It is every bit as good as a lot of the American slasher movies from that era and better than a lot of them."—*Brain Enema Cinema Review*

"An Australian imitation of *Friday the 13th*."—John Stanley, *Creature Features*

DVD

Video Man Entertainment (release date unknown).

Kadaicha

David Hanny Productions/Medusa Communications, 1988 [aka *Kadaycha*; *Stones of Death*]

CREDITS: *Director:* James Bogle; *Producers:* David Hannay, Charles Hannah; *Executive Producer:* Tom Broadbridge; *Screenplay:* Ian Coughlan; *Photography:* Stephen F. Windon; *Editor:* Andrew Arestides; *Music:* Peter Westheimer; *Sound:* Pat Dunne; *Makeup:* Sarah Bailey; *Special Makeup:* Deryck De Niese; *Wardrobe:* Fiona Spence; *Special Effects:* Neville Maxwell. Color, 88 minutes.

CAST: Zoe Carides (Gail Sorensen); Tom Jennings (Matt Taylor); Eric Oldfield (Alex Sorensen); Kerry McKay (Shane); Fiona Gauntlett (Fizz Dryden); Natalie McCurry (Tracy Hocking); Bruce Hughes (Tony Pirello); Steve Dodd (Billinudgel); Deborah Kennedy (Mrs. Millhouse); Sean Scully (Mr. Fitzgerald); John Paramor (Detective Rose); Nicholas Ryan (Franky Boland); Rhoda Roberts (Lisa); Sara Dakin (Deb Hartley); Harry Cripps (Jeff Cross); Terry Markwell (Gloria); Nicholas Flanagan (Constable Todd); Don Chapman (Sergeant Hanley); Alan Lovell (Constable O'Bersky); Anthony Ackroyd (Constable Pritchard); Angus Banks Stewart (Security Guard); Simone Condon (Girl 1); Julieanne Evans (Girl 2); Ronald Rogers (Doctor); Mark Eady (Workman 1); Michael Green (Workman 2); Richard Talonga, Percy Jackonia, Monicka Stevens, Silvia Blanco (Aboriginal Dancers).

Synopsis

Tracy Hocking is a schoolgirl at the country town of Kangaloola. In a nightmare she sees herself confronted in a cave by an Aboriginal dancer who gives her a painted crystal. When she awakens she finds the same crystal on her pillow. Her teacher, Mrs. Millhouse, identifies it as a Kadaicha death stone given to person who is condemned to die. Tracy is killed by a wild dog that night in the park. Fellow students Franky Boland has a nightmare and awakens to find a crystal, and Gail Sorensen learns that the street where she lives is built on a sacred Aboriginal burial ground and her father had been in charge of the development. Franky is killed by the bite of a funnel web spider in the library, and student Fizz has the same nightmare as Tracy and finds a crystal on her pillow.

Gail is visited by an old Aborigine, Billinudgel, who warns her of a curse. Mrs. Millhouse explains how a tribe of Aborigines were killed by a white hunting party as revenge upon tribesmen who had attacked the white settlement after young blacks were murdered by a gang of bushrangers. When the students go swimming, Fizz is pulled under the water of the lake and her bloodied body is later found on the shore. When Gail has the same nightmare and finds a crystal on her pillow, she thinks she is to be the next victim of the curse. She seeks the help of Billinudgel, who gives her a spirit stone to ward off the demon doing the killings. The demon possesses the body of Gail's boyfriend, Matt, and he tries to kill her. Billinudgel's burning of the skeleton in the cave that the students have found behind the development's storm water drain frees Matt and seems to destroy the demon. Gail's father, Alex, agrees to relocate the residents of the street. When workers seal up the cave wall, a black snake appears suggesting the demon may not have been stopped.

Notes

This well-written and well-directed title features the theme of the malevolent supernatural being and has a narrative that includes Aboriginal concerns that also appeared in *The Last Wave*, *Dark Age*, and *The Dreaming*. Director James Bogle uses the postmodern techniques of zooms, expressionist camera angles, point of view, quick edits, and an occasionally obtrusive score. He also has trouble with the limited performance of his lead actress but succeeds in creating suspense rather than relying upon shock effects, and he presents three killings with accompanying requisite gore.

Under the opening credits we see Tracy walking in the street at night as well as inter-cuts to her sleeping to tell us that she is dreaming. She walks in the stormwater drain that will be identified later and has a vision of a group of Aboriginal dancers that beckon her into a cave. In the cave there is fire and another dancer with his back to her. When he turns around there is a shock effect of his face appearing as a skeleton, and he places a crystal in her hand. The shock awakens Tracy from the nightmare, and the crystal is explained by Mrs. Millhouse as given to someone who has broken the law and is therefore condemned to die. She explains later the motivation for the killing when she parallels the student victims with the young tribal blacks who were said to be killed by the white bushrangers. Although the students have not broken tribal law, it appears that a murdered ruthless Aborigine is killing them as revenge for their living in houses built on burial ground. We are told that Alex is about to launch a promotion for the second stage of the residence development, which may be another reason for the killings.

We see Alex Sorensen with a model, Gloria, but we don't know what happened to his wife and the mother of Gail. This doesn't have any great psychological impact on the plot other than giving her the independence of a neglected child. She isn't motivated to do something about the killings until she appears to be the next victim, although this argument could also be made for Tracy and Fizz. Tracy's death scene uses the park swings for suspense. They move with no one pushing them when Tracy enters the park. She is a variation on the conventional Woman in Peril who investigates a noise — the swings squeak as they move, yet they only get her attention when they stop squeaking.

The score uses the sound of the didgeridoo to make the connection between the killer and Aborigines, and Bogle uses an extreme close-up of a dog's eyes as his point of view watching Tracy. The swings move again when the dog strikes, which is unseen but suggested by the growling of the dog attack and Tracy's screams. Gail hears the screaming at her house, which results in Alex investigating the noise as a Man in Peril. The swings are shown to be still again before Tracy's torn throat is discovered by Alex. Tracy's body lies back over a park ride in a pose that suggests the animal was on top of her, and which also has a sexual connotation.

Franky Boland is the next victim; he also has a nightmare which features a cut to an extreme close-up of an eye. There is a prefiguring leg of the spider that will later attack him, and a shot of Franky looking directly into the camera. Since Franky is not seen in the stormwater drain and the cave like Tracy, Fizz and Gail, there is the suggestion that his death will be different. This will prove to be true; it is not as bloody as those of Tracy and Fizz.

A radio report of Tracy's attack by an animal gets a black comedy laugh because her dog, Hannibal, barks to awaken her. Fizz walking in the darkened hallway and being alone in the library creates the expectation of her attack, not met, which is not a surprise since we have yet to see her dream and receive a crystal. The close-up of the animal eyes and its point of view of her standing at the library window, to make her more easily seen, continues the expectation of her being attacked. There is the shock of the clock that chimes, and it is a surprise that Fizz is no longer in the library when Gail and Matt arrive to meet her. When Fizz reappears the expectation of her attack is a red herring, though it does help to establish that the killer is still around. It also suggests that he may have an interest in others apart from Franky, who is the latest to have received a crystal.

Franky's arrival gets a comic line from Fizz which prefigures Franky's attack: "If I was Franky and I found one of those crystals on my pillow I wouldn't be staying by myself in an empty school at night." Bogle inter-cuts to Hannibal barking to prefigure Billinudgel's appearance at Gail's house, before returning to the library. He uses a subjective camera advance at floor level to Franky's shoes and gives a close-up of his foot tapping. The expectation that his foot will be grabbed is not met. Franky putting his face close to the spider creates the expectation that it will strike him, which is met. After the movie convention of a jammed door that won't let him out of the study room, we see his hand slowly falling from the window as a more effective if conventional horror image.

Bogle saves the sight of Franky's bitten face for later when Mrs. Millhouse finds him. Instead he focuses on Fizz, who has the same dream that Tracy did and gets her own crystal on the pillow. When the narrative shifts back to Mrs. Williams entering the library, the expectation is created that she will find Franky. Bogle repeats the jammed door from her side before having Franky fall out from behind it when it is forced open, so that we can see Franky's facial disfigurement and cause of death.

Playing Mrs. Millhouse, Deborah Kennedy delivers the exposition of the curse pleasingly quickly, partly to get through it all and partly as the demonstration of her character. When Fizz, Gail, Matt and Shane go walking on the beach they are tailed by a police car. The students' exploration of the stormwater drain allows them to see that there is no cave entry as in the dreams, although Matt will later reveal it when he hammers a hole in the drain wall for Gail. Wanting to go swimming, rather than use the beach they go to a lake. This leads the scene of Fizz's death. The police car is present but the police are unable to save her. This confirms that the threat is supernatural and implies that only supernatural means will be able to defeat it. The lack of help from the police will be expressed in an exchange when Matt says to one of them, "Why don't you do something constructive?" and the policeman answers, "I'll reconstruct your face in a minute if you don't shut up."

For the swimming scene, Bogle places his camera horizontally halfway under water, even though the water is murky, so that we see the students and the waterline, which helps to suggest point of view for the threat. The lake location and the children's fun create the expectation of another strike, even though it is daytime, and the deaths of Tracy and Franky occurred at night. The narrative plays with the expectation by having Fizz laughing at something pulling at her under the water; she assumes it is either Shane or Matt, who both momentarily disappear under water. In fact, the initial disappearance of Shane suggests that he may have drowned. This expectation is not met when he emerges farther away from Fizz.

When Matt emerges next to Shane, Fizz's amused pleasure turns to frightened terror. The thing that was pulling Fizz now makes her totally submerge, and we never learn what the creature is that has taken her. It is suggested that it may be a snake or an octopus. When the police see water bubbling after they find Fizz's corpse, they comment that it could be an eel. When Fizz is found her bloody face suggests that her death has not been pleasant. Bogle uses flash-cuts to the corpses of Tracy and Franky when Fizz's covered body is wheeled into an ambulance followed by another shot of her bloodied face.

The nightmare that Gail has is a variation on that of Tracy and Fizz as she runs out of the cave. Bogle uses an effect that has been used in *The Dreaming*. Gail is brought back into the cave as she is turned away, but she seems to slide back in order to see the skeleton face effect of the dancer. There is a laugh scored from her finding the crystal on her pillow and throwing it away as recognition of its portent but also a rejection of her supposed fate. When Gail and Matt go inside the cave they find a skeleton with the horror movie convention of something crawling in one of its eye sockets. A shock effect is used when Gail screams at the flashlight of a policeman shining on her as she leaves the cave. Alex collecting Gail from the police station allows him to reveal more exposition of how his work crew had found the cave when they were excavating for the residential foundation built over it.

After Gail states her intention to find Billinudgel, Bogle provides a montage reminder of the deaths of Tracy, Fizz, and Franky after showing a sandpit and a fire. There is the conventional response of Billinudgel's relative, Lisa, who tells Gail that he is not at home and then changes her mind and takes her to him. Billinudgel tells Gail that the demon can change form and explains how his three victims appear to have been attacked by a different creature. Billinidgel gives Gail a spirit stone to take away the strength of the demon if he should attack her, but this doesn't get a plot payoff because she never uses it. We only see her put it in a drawer.

The dance at the school is only used in the narrative to show Matt's musical abilities, with his channeling by the demon meaning he doesn't get to perform at the dance, for Gail's bathroom trauma during rehearsal, and for inter-cutting during the climax where Gail is attacked. Gail's bathroom trauma is prefigured by the feedback the speakers give when Matt and Shane rehearse with the band. The expectation of a strike being made against Gail is more believable since she has been given the crystal of death rather than either of the boys being attacked. The attack can be interpreted as all Gail's imagination since her visions do her no real harm, and begins with her washing her hands and the soap turning into a crystal.

A toilet stall repeatedly slamming is followed by the exit door she tries to use being jammed. This recalls the library workroom door that was jammed. The lights flash. She has a vision of the bloodied Tracy and Fizz talking to each other. There is a respite with other schoolgirls coming into the bathroom to bring Gail back to reality, although they do not talk to her. Bogle uses a point of view under the floor drain to see Gail, and an arm comes out of it to grab her. We figure that she doesn't have the spirit stone with her to use since she runs out of the bathroom without having to grapple with the door being jammed again.

Bogle uses a long close-up of Matt as he drives his car, to suggest that he is possessed by the demon. He intercuts Matt going to visit Gail at her home with Billinidgel at the stormwater drain with Tony, although Tony will only serve as a witness to Billinudgel's action in the cave. The jammed door device is again used for Alex, who becomes a Man in Peril when he investigates noises in his garage and gets locked in. This leaves Gail alone for Matt's attack. The possessed Matt cleverly sends the police who are stationed at Gail's house to the park on a wild goose chase. The unseen Hannibal is heard barking before Gail learns that her telephone is dead and finds Hannibal dead in her pool. We assume that Matt has killed the dog, since his body is seen before Matt comes to the house's front door. Gail arms herself with a knife to answer the door, so that she is an armed Woman in Peril, and Matt's red eyes confirm that he is possessed.

For his climax, Bogle inter-cuts madly, using five different scenarios: Billinudgel in the cave, Alex in the garage, Matt chasing Gail, Gail in her room, and the band at the dance. The physical confrontation between Gail and Matt features a funny moment when his thrust knife goes into the book Gail holds up in her defense. His strangling of her soon turns to a strangling of Alex, who axes his way out of the garage. It is Billinudgel who makes the skeleton in the cave, presumably that of the bad Aborigine whose spirit has become the demon, burn by holding his own spirit stone at it. A close-up of Matt superimposed over the burning skeleton shows him being depossessed.

The discovery of severe stress fractures in the underlying sandstone of street gives is given over the radio as the reason for the residents to be relocated, after Alex has heard Billinudgel's warning that more killings will occur unless the development is abandoned. The epilogue shows two workers sealing up the cave but the black snake that appears near one of their abandoned instruments creates ambiguity. Are we to think that the demon has not been stopped and the stage is being set for a sequel? Or is this just a normal snake unrelated to the cave demon which has supposedly been defeated by Billinudgel?

Kadaicha was the directing debut of James Bogle, and it is the only Australian horror film he has made to date. David Hannay Productions had previously made the Australian horror movie *Alison's Birthday*. It went on to make the Australian horror title *The 13th Floor* with the Medusa Communications production company, producer Charles Hannah and executive producer Tom Broadbridge.

After starting in television, Zoe Carides made her film debut with *Kadaicha*, her only movie lead to date. She continued in television and supporting film roles. Tom Jennings made his film debut in a minor role in the action adventure *Mad Max Beyond Thunderdome* (1985), and after working in television scored the lead in the actioner *Watch the Shadows Dance* (1987). After *Kadaicha* he has only been seen in television. Eric Oldfield began his career in television, had played a minor role in *Alison's Birthday*, and after *Kadaicha* continued to work in television.

Release

Australian and American release dates unknown. Screening at Cannes Film Festival on May 15, 1988. Taglines include, "Who says you can't get blood out of a stone...?" and "Cast From Beyond the Grave."

Reviews

"Bogle provides a few good moments of suspense, and the film is lifted out of the routine by some of the actors, especially Sean Scully as a local headmaster."— David Stratton, *The Avocado Plantation*

"A delightful, bloody horror film that takes place in England [actually Australia], so all the characters remind you of the Spice Girls when they talk.... A more or less original concept, and proved to be an intriguing film. The acting was quite decent, as far as horror movies go. [It] is no 'Scream' but it'll do for a scare or two."—*eFilmCritic*

DVD

VHS released by Sony Video but appears to be out of print. DVD unavailable. Watched on YouTube, January 4, 2011.

Out of the Body
Premiere Film Marketing/Medusa Communications, 1988 [aka *Dream Scream*]

CREDITS: *Director:* Brian Trenchard-Smith; *Producers:* David Hannay, Charles Hannah; *Executive Producer:* Tom Broadbridge; *Screenplay:* Kenneth G. Ross; *Photography:* Kevan "Loosey" Lind; *Editor:* Alan Woodruff; *Music:* Peter Westheimer; *Production Design:* Darrell Lass; *Special Makeup:* Deryck De Niese; *Makeup:* Wendy Freeman; *Hair:* Tony Meredith; *Art Director:* Mark Ryan; *Costumes:* Catherine Martin; *Sound:* Tim Lloyd; *Special Effects:* Steve Courtney, Allan Manning. Color, 115 minutes. Filmed on location in Sydney, New South Wales.

CAST: Mark Hembrow (David Gaze); Tessa Humphries (Neva St. Clair); Shane Briant (Paul); John Clayton (Detective Sergeant Whittaker); John Ley (Senior Detective Delgarno); Linda Newton (Carla Duprey); Helen O'Connor (Barbara Sloan); Mary Regan (Mary Mason); Margi Gerard (Maggie Jarrott); Sally Hudson (Stephanie Parker); Carrie Zivetz (Dr. Lydia Langton); Tim Campbell (Security Guard); David Hannay (Henry); Trisha Treanor (Policewoman); Valerie Newstead (Neighbor); Jack Mayers (Policeman 1); Gerry Tacovsky (Policeman 2).

SYNOPSIS

David Gaze works at the University of Sydney and is a musician. He dreams of women being killed and having their eyes removed; he thinks these dreams are premonitions. His fellow worker and girlfriend, librarian Neva, theorizes that he has the power of astral travel where he "flies out of the body." David's dreams allow him to see the killings but not who the killer is. The victims are American economic consultant Maggie Jarrott and advertising executive Stephanie Parker. David sees that television newsreader Mary Mason is to be the next victim. He warns her and then tells the police, who are more suspicious of him. Mary is killed, then his ex-wife and work supervisor, Barbara Sloan, is visited by the spirit but only her cat is killed. David predicts that his psychiatrist, Lydia Langton, is the next victim. She receives a police guard who saves her when the spirit visits and kills author Carla Duprey instead. When Lydia gives David sodium pentothal in his next session, she is killed and the police find David next to her body. He is put in jail, but when visited by Neva, he warns her that she may be next. David is sedated by the prison doctor. His fear of sleeping enables the demon to attack Neva when she is escorted home by Senior Detective Delgarno. The demon kills Delgarno and two winos. Neva shoots a rifle she has found in the police car and appears to kill the demon. David is found dead in the jail as if shot by Neva's rifle, and when she is rescued by other police they do not see that she has now been possessed by the same demon that David had been.

NOTES

This title mixes the themes of the horror of personality with the malevolent supernatural being, as the antagonist is a man possessed by a demon who kills women. Director Brian Trenchard-Smith uses the postmodern techniques of slow motion, hand-held camera and subjective camera as the point of view of the killer. The narrative also presents a protagonist as morally ambiguous, given that he is also revealed to be the killer, though it has its share of red herrings. Trenchard-Smith's treatment is initially restrained, but he eventually succumbs to hysteria which goes over the line of contrivance to be presumed as unintentional comedy. There is bloodletting and gore from the victims having their eyes removed, as well as a gun fired into a mouth.

The narrative never shows why David was possessed, although his house's interior direction features primitive sculptures. He is presented as a weak person, in the form of his apparent lack of career ambition at the university, and this allows for him to be easily psychologically penetrated. The plot actually creates the expectation that the killings may have some relation to the victims all being career women who are all interviewed by Carla for her new book, although once she also becomes a victim she can obviously no longer be suspected as the killer. David's lack of interest in his unidentified work at the university is presumably due to a greater interest in his music. This gets a comic payoff since he is shown to fall asleep and dream after every time he plays his electronic organ. The narrative also later proffers the possibility that the killer is Neva, since she is said to be working on a thesis on ancient Egypt and believes in astral travel. This idea is also dismissed when she becomes a victim of the demon in the film's climax.

The first sex scene between David and Neva has the actress nude when she gets out of bed. Although it has context, it still reads as being exploitative.

The narrative's first killing, that of Maggie Jarrott, has her seeing red dust in the parking lot, which prefigures the demon as a red cloud in the climax. Falling rods behind her are used for a shock effect. Another shock is used when she is grabbed from above at her car, which also sets off her car alarm. This will continue when the security guard arrives with his dog. We don't know where Maggie has gone until the guard sees her hanging from a horizontal pole. When his dog stops barking we expect that he will also be attacked, though he is not.

Mark awakens from a nightmare and his idea that the killing is merely a dream is later dismissed by Maggie's death being reported on the television news, although it will be the police who point out that her eyes have been removed and that the dog died of a heart attack. There is a joke attached to the eye removal. Whittaker asks where Maggie's eyes are and Delgarno proposes that the killer ate them, and then he takes a bite of a sandwich he holds. The point of Maggie being an American becomes interesting in light of Stephanie Parker being apparently British and Lydia being American, although presumably their success is aligned with them being international travelers.

The killing of Stephanie is presented in a divided fashion, since her death is not immediately shown in succession. The first part features flashing lights in her house as an element that did not appear with Maggie's death, presumably because it occurred outside, but will be continued in all the subsequent interior killings. Heavy breathing accompanies the use of subjective camera approach. There is the sudden fall of a window shade as shock effect. The narrative moves away from Stephanie to Barbara being interviewed by Carla, and the information that is eventually misleading of Stephanie also being on Carla's list of women she wants to interview for her new book. It is only when we return to Stephanie's house that she is identified as such.

She is again being pursued by the subjective camera, resulting in some laughs from her producing a gun. She loads it and announces the clichéd line, "I've got a gun and I'm not afraid to use it." She then says, "I am not afraid of you," but looks clearly afraid by the repeated flashing lights. Like a conventional horror movie victim she walks backward into the camera to find the waiting killer, and is lifted above, although the director doesn't show the resultant death.

David's dream vision of Mary is followed by his television turning itself on three times, a phenomenon which aligns the demon to the control of electrical devices. David's stalking Mary after he has found her to warn her expresses his genuine desire to save her. Naturally, Mary does not appreciate the effort. This is apparent when his looking into her window interrupts her assumed sadomasochistic sex with Paul, who holds a razor blade to her bra-covered chest. The police are called and arrive in record time at Mary's house, but that does not stop the return of the demon/David to find her swimming in her backyard pool. We see a drawer opened without the aid of hands, and an electric drill in it. We expect it will be thrown into the pool for Mary to be electrocuted.

The director again delays the reveal of the murder by having David come to Mary's house. He discovers the pool water to be red and Mary's head presumably drilled, although this technique seems difficult for a spirit. Later David will have a nightmare vision of Mary's face bloodied and growling. This doesn't make any sense but can be matched by David's other vision of Neva as a similarly bloodied demon during another of their sex scenes, though this latter vision is funny when David awakens from it strangling his cat.

When Carla is interviewing Barbara again, there is an implication of Carla being a lesbian. This is from the look on her face when Barbara tells her if she rejects a man they think her a "dyke," and by Carla's comment that nowadays men are a "health hazard." When David is shown sleeping, we get a superimposition of his naked self as a double, removing himself from the sleeping body. This is the only visual presentation of David's supposed "flying" when he dreams, although later the director shows an aerial view of the city from David's point of view in the air. He tells Neva of his flying and that he visited someone. When she asks who, Trenchard-Smith cuts to a shot of Barbara yelling "Get out!" at David in her office. This tells us who, though this argument scene occurs the next day and not when David was with her after flying in.

The demon's later visit to Barbara is indicated by the still ceiling fan which turns by itself as a sign of its power over electrical objects. There is also a subjective camera that approaches the cat rather than the sleeping Barbara. It is paid off by her awakening, presented by an out-of-focus point of view, to discover the bloodied decapitated cat. The later police presence in her home can be rationalized by the police thinking the killer to be David rather than believing his story of it being something else. But the police presence creates the expectation of an attack against Barbara that is not met. We just get the lighting flashes and her blanket being pulled from her sleeping body.

David's premonition of Lydia being the next victim results in his telling her this, after she hypnotizes him, via a kaleidoscope that shines colored lights on his face. When she asks him under hypnosis if he is the killer, he says no. When she asks who the killer is, David responds with a strangulated noise. After he tells her that she is to be the next victim, David smiles in joy at the idea. The demon visits Lydia at the library after her confrontation with Neva, and it is another false suggestion that Neva could be the killer. Two books are thrown off shelves, papers are thrown at Lydia, and a skeleton moves as she passes it. We also hear growls from the stone gargoyles in the courtyard. These are all signs of the powers of the demon. The inter-cuts to Neva riding her bicycle to David's house suggest a payoff that isn't provided in the narrative, and the police protection this time at Lydia's house seems to keep the demon at bay since Carla becomes its next victim.

Carla plays with a pet lizard, showing her oddness of character and perhaps penis envy. Music stops playing to show the demon's power over electric items. After the requisite light flashes, Carla's death is only suggested by the spattering of blood on the lizard. This is a shame, since her provoking the demon with the line "Show yourself and be a man" deserves retribution.

After Lydia gives David the sodium pentothal, he is seen to become the demon with black eyes and rising up from his prone position. During the attack upon her in another room, she battles a seemingly invisible force that strangles her and makes a chair fly. Lydia's strikes at the chair with a blade result in wounds on David's face and arm. This prefigures the gunshot wound by Neva at the climax, and as if the black eyes weren't enough of a clue, certainly makes it apparent that David is possessed by the demon rather than simply being its observer.

Trenchard-Smith spares us the impact of Lydia being forced to strike her own forehead with a knife, as he will later avoid showing the impact of the gun in Delgarno's mouth. Rather we see the police find Lydia's bloodied and eyeless corpse laying back over a table and David inexplicably sitting next to her. When Neva visits David in jail, the hysteria of the playing of the resultant scene gets a much needed laugh. The police mock David's idea of him being a medium with "The devil made me do it — the same old story." When Delgarno takes Neva home, she senses the presence of the demon before we are shown evidence of it, which suggests that Neva has paranormal powers. Delgarno being lifted by the demon recalls the same action that happened to Maggie and Stephanie, and his shooting himself recalls Lydia's implied stabbing herself. The director will inter-cut the climax with shots of the writhing and screaming David; this propels the treatment over the top into comedy territory, which may have been avoided without these inter-cuts.

When Neva is in the police car it is apparent that David is controlling her driving. The subjective camera returns after she gets out, and finds a rifle in the trunk. An armed Neva joins the ranks of other female warriors in Australian horror titles, including *Lady, Stay Dead, Fair Game, Contagion, The 13th Floor, Komodo, Ghost Ship, Undead, See No Evil, Black Water, Storm Warning, Slaughtered, Triangle, The Clinic* and *Road Train*. The demon is suggested by red smoke that she fires at and turns to white smoke; it is aligned to David shown shot in his cell. This seems like an incredibly easy defeat of the spirit, but now Neva has the black eyes that David had when he was possessed, implying that the demon has only moved to a new host. A sequel is suggested but none has been made to date.

Director Brian Trenchard-Smith previously made the Australian horror title *Turkey Shoot*, but would not make another. Producers David Hannay and company, David Hannay Productions, had previously made the Australian horror title *The 13th Floor* with producer Charles Hannah and executive producer Tom Broadbridge and the production companies Medusa Communications and Premiere Film Marketing. They would go on to make the Australian horror movie *Hellion: The Devil's Playground* without the others.

Mark Hembrow began his career in television and made his film debut in a supporting role in the war drama *The Highest Honor* (1982). He played in more supporting film roles and television prior to and after *Out of the Body*, which has been his only lead to date. He also co-wrote and directed the comedy *The Argues: The Movie* (2010). Tessa Humphries had previously played the title role in the Australian horror title *Cassandra* (1986) and went on to more film supporting roles and television.

Shane Briant previously appeared in *Cassandra* and went on to the Australian horror film *Subterano*. John Clayton also began his career in television and made his film debut in a supporting role in *Sidecar Racers* (1975). He had television and film supporting roles before and after *Out of the Body*, including *Subterano*, although he played a rare lead in the comedy *Unfinished Business* (1985). The actor died in 2003. John Ley made his film debut in a supporting role in the thriller *Solo Flight* (1975) and continued in more film supporting roles, including *Turkey Shoot* and *Cassandra* and in television. Linda Newton also began her career in television and made her film debut in a supporting role in *Cathy's Child* (1979). She would continue in more television and film supporting roles. Helen O'Connor is another actor to have started her career in television and made her film debut in a minor role in *The Everlasting Secret Family* (1988). She would continue to be seen in supporting film roles and television.

Mary Regan made her film debut in a supporting role in the New Zealand drama *Strata* (1983) and continued in film supporting roles and on television. Margi Gerard made her film debut in *Out of the Body* and would only be seen in one more supporting film role. Carrie Zivetz also made her film debut here; it is her only credit to date.

RELEASE

Screened at the Cannes Film Festival in May 1988 and apparently released straight to video in the United States and Australia with the tagline "A demonic force lurks...."

REVIEWS

"There are some amusing red herrings and a neat final twist. There are also some engaging performances, especially John Clayton and John Ley as policeman and Mary Regan as one of the victims. Nor does the director wallow in gore, since the violence takes place mostly off-screen."— David Stratton, *The Avocado Plantation*

DVD

Not available. Video released by SVS/Sony Columbia Tristar on June 28, 1989.

The 13th Floor

Premiere Film Marketing/Medusa Communications, 1989 [aka *Electrocutor 1*]

CREDITS: *Screenplay/Director:* Chris Roache; *Producers:* David Hannay, Charles Hannay; *Executive Producer:* Tom Broadbridge; *Photography:* Stephen Prime; *Editors:* Adrian Carr, Peter McBain; *Music:* Garry Hardman; *Special Makeup:* Deryck De Niese; *Production Design:* Darrell Lass; *Sound:* David Glasser; *Art Director:* Peter Davies; *Wardrobe:* Rosalea Hood; *Makeup:* Sue Matak; *Hair:* Tony Meredith. Color, 103 minutes. Filmed on location in Hyde Park, Sydney, New South Wales.

CAST: Lisa Hensley (Heather M. Thompson, age 20); Tim McKenzie (John Burke); Miranda Otto (Rebecca); Tony Blackett (Robert Thompson); Jeff Truman (Bert, the Caretaker); Vic Rooney (Brenner); Paul Hunt (Nick, the Cleaner); Michael Caton (Dr. Fletcher); Kylie Clare (Heather Thompson, age 8); Allen Long (Brian Chung); Matthew Nicholls (Boy); Nicholas Forster (Tom Poulson); Georgie Parker (Maid); Adam Cook (Allistair); Cathren Michalak (Tea Lady); Andrew Ferguson (Young Boy).

SYNOPSIS

As an eight-year-old child, Heather Thompson saw her father murder the son of Nicholas Forster on the thirteenth floor of a high rise building. Twelve years later she moves into the same location to live with her friend Rebecca and is aided by the building's cleaner, Nick. She also captures the interest of John Burke, a worker for the Department of Social Security, which has an office on the twelfth floor. Heather has stolen a file of incriminating documents from her father and hidden them in an electrical power box on the floor. Her father, Premier Robert Thompson, hires the private investigator, Brenner, to find her and retrieve the documents.

Brenner finds Heather but is killed after he falls down an empty elevator shaft. Rebecca becomes jealous when Heather has sex with John and overdoses in the bathroom. Thompson's men come to the building to follow Brenner. They beat John to death, stab Bert the caretaker, and drown Nick. Heather is taken to a sanitarium where she is injected with heroine and watched over by Dr. Fletcher. She escapes and goes back to the building's thirteenth floor, where she meets the ghost of the murdered boy who asks her to help him. She invites her father to the location and, empowered by electricity, shocks him until he also falls into an empty elevator shaft. Heather awakens to find herself on a harbor side dock, seemingly free of her trauma, although alone.

Notes

This story features the theme of the malevolent supernatural being in the ghost of a murdered boy who is now empowered by electricity and seeks revenge. Director Chris Roache uses the postmodern techniques of expressionist camera angles and blackouts and an obtrusive score. The narrative spaces out killings over long periods of waiting time and presents alternative antagonists for the protagonist and her allies. There is some resultant bloodletting with beatings, stabbings, burns, drownings, and two falls into an empty elevator shaft, and a seemingly forced lethal injection of drugs. The main protagonist also appears to become possessed by the electrified spirit of the ghost and to become a warrior that recalls those in *Lady, Stay Dead*, *Fair Game*, *Contagion*, *Out of the Body*, *Komodo*, *Ghost Ship*, *Undead*, *See No Evil*, *Black Water*, *Storm Warning*, *Slaughtered*, *Prey*, *Triangle*, *The Clinic* and *Road Train*.

A prologue presents Heather at age eight witnessing her father's murder of Tom Poulson's son. Robert Thompson taking his eight-year-old with him is as irresponsible as leaving her alone in the car while he goes to the thirteenth floor of the building, though her not staying in the car as he told her to do also makes her complicit in her own trauma. Tom is tied to a pole and a knife is held at his throat, creating the expectation of it being cut, which presumably eventually happens, although we do not see. The electrification of the unnamed boy is a surprise. Roache repeats the scene in Heather's later nightmare to give more detail as to how the boy is pushed into a power box and his spirit is seemingly entrapped in another box in the ensuing narrative.

A title card reads "12 years later," and the now twenty-year-old Heather is missing. She has stolen a file of documents which incriminate her father and which he has hired the private detective Brenner to find. Thompson is more interested in finding the file than his daughter. This callousness will be demonstrated when, after she is found, he has her committed to a sanitarium and made a drug addict, presumably to keep her quiet and controlled. Why Heather has decided to live on the abandoned thirteenth floor of the building, the same location of the murder she witnessed as a child, is not made clear. It seems it is only the boy's request for her to help him that motivates her to invite her father to visit. Her friendship with Nick, who tells Brenner that he used a share a house with Heather and presumably also Rebecca, would seem to account for the choice of location. The fact that the floor is uninhabited also implies that it is cursed by the murder. A flickering white light and a voice heard by Heather suggest the ghost's presence. She is seen to follow these phenomenona as a conventional Woman in Peril investigating a noise, but she is shown to be more focused on hiding the document files behind the power box, since no payoff is immediately provided for her awareness of the devices.

A shock effect is used for Heather's vision of a skeleton head when she submerges her face into the bathroom sink full of water. The bathroom will again be used as a location for supernatural appearances when later Rebecca has a vision of the electrified boy. The flickering light of the power box serves to distract Brenner's attack upon Heather and the electric strikes upon him create bloody gore as burns. His leaning back against the elevator doors creates the expectation, which is met, of them opening and him falling back into the empty shaft. This implies that the ghost has control over the building's electrical machinery. The boy's laughter heard after Brenner's fall also confirms that the action was implemented by him, and Roache uses another conventional shock effect with the hand on Heather's back that is revealed to belong to Rebecca.

The issue of Rebecca's lesbianism is first confused by what appears to be Heather's observation of a romance between Rebecca and Nick, although it is presented as coming more from Nick's interest. While the word lesbian is never said in the screenplay, Rebecca's later apparent jealousy over Heather's romance with John certainly implies it, as does Heather's confession to Dr. Fletcher. Roache supplies suspense when John attempts to create a new Social Security account for Heather. He cross-cuts to the return of Allistair, who has forgotten his umbrella, Bert patrolling the floor, and Heather hiding. The sequence gets a laugh from John telling Allistair the truth about him falsifying records to defraud the governor and Allistair not believing him. The expectation of Allistair seeing the fraud John has attempted is not met.

When Heather seduces John, the scene begins with her as the sexual aggressor, which prefigures the supernatural warrior she becomes in the climax. Roache spares the actors from nude exposure by having their eventual sex clothed, although afterwards they are shown to be undressed but under sheets. There is a laugh from John's line, "I enjoy meeting your friends," after Rebecca's tirade against what Heather has done, which mixes her apparent jealousy and her concern over making John aware of the group living on the floor. Rebecca's death is presented with ambiguity following her earlier demonstration of being a drug addict. Are we to think that she has deliberately overdosed out of depression from her perceived rejection by Heather? Or does her vision of the electrified boy in the bath mirror suggest that he has made her commit suicide?

After her death we see the boy now in the bathroom with her. His electrification is suggested by the blue halo around his body, and his voice calling for Heather is equally ambiguous. Is he calling her to save Rebecca? Or to show her what he has done? And if he has killed her, has he done so to punish Heather? The narrative also delays the discovery of Rebecca's body by Heather and Nick, so that makes her seem more disposable. Roache makes a big deal over them dumping her body in the street and presenting her as beautifully windswept and peaceful and Heather as windswept and emotional over the death.

One interesting touch to Heather finding Rebecca's body is that she is not on the floor where we had last seen her. Rather she is found in a toilet stall, and we don't know how she has been moved. At least, however, Rebecca's body is found. The same cannot be said for Brenner, whom it seems no one cares enough about to follow up on — not even his employer, Thompson.

Nick removes one page from the file to speak of illegal acts performed by Thompson that will cost him his position, later said to show how he fixed the results. This page being separated will become an important plot point when it seems the rest of the file is retrieved by Thompson's three thugs. The attack upon John by the thugs and their pursuit of Heather and Nick presents them as alternate narrative antagonists. We have to wait until Heather makes her way back to the building for the ghost boy to become the major antagonist again, although then his seeming possession of Heather makes him a protagonist. We assume that is the thugs that have killed Bert, whose location on the top floor is not made apparent in the earlier scene when he had rescued her from Brenner and tried to seduce her. His bloodied body is even bloodier after John's beating and murder.

Roache also doesn't show us the thugs drowning Nick, only his resultant drowned body in the pool. The expectation of Heather being drowned by Brian Chung is not met even though Roache's blackout could imply her death. We see her waking in a hospital bed, which could imply that she has been saved, although this is an expectation not met when we learn how Heather is being kept in the sanitarium under the guise of a cure for her being a heroin addict. Perhaps her friendship with Rebecca as a drug addict means we are to assume Heather was a drug user in the past, but here it seems a cruel parallel with Rebecca, whose murder is under the guise of an overdose.

Heather dreams of herself at eight, seeing the murder of the boy, with the contrived convention of memory for Heather being able to see herself. Roache uses the same footage from the opening scene but adds more detail for us to see how he was pushed into the power box. Her waking up screaming is the conventional response to a nightmare. Heather pretends to cry to Dr. Fletcher. This is in order to get his keys, although we have to consider him even more of a fool since we imagine he must use his keys quite often.

Heather goes back to the building, although she knows all her friends to be dead, because presumably that is still her home. The electrified boy appears to her as a vision with his request, "Help me," and he has the separated page from the file. The narrative doesn't have the boy offer any further information. When Thompson arrives, alone, to the floor, he sees Heather with big hair and white eyes apparently having become possessed by the ghost. She leads him to find the document in the box. The expectation of him being electrocuted is met. Roache presents the various wounds from burns that Thompson endures from Heather's strikes. The rising elevator is inter-cut with Thompson backing up to the doors. The repeat of Brenner's fall down the empty shaft is an expectation that is met after we see the elevator doors open. We are left unsure what to make of Heather's collapse and her awakening on the dock the next day. We assume that her fall is due to her being exorcised of the ghost, though we don't know how she got to the dock. Her walk down them suggests her triumph, although it is an odd one, given that she is alone and has killed her own father.

This is the only film made to date by Director Chris Roache. Producers David and Charles Hannay had previously produced the Australian horror title *Kadaicha*. He would go on to produce the Australian horror movie *Out of the Body* for David Hannay Productions with executive producer Tom Broadbridge and the production companies Premiere Film Marketing and Medusa Communications.

Lisa Hensley made her film debut in a supporting role in *The Umbrella Woman* (1987), and after appearing in television and *The 13th Floor*, she went on to television and film supporting roles and the lead in the war romance *15 Amore* (1998). Tim McKenzie made his film debut in a supporting role in historical adventure *Gallipoli* (1981), and played in television and more film supporting roles before and after *The 13th Floor*.

Miranda Otto made her film debut as the title character but not top-billed in *Emma's War* (1986). She appeared in television and supporting film roles. After *The 13th Floor* she played the leads in *The Girl Who Came Late* (1992), the comedy *Love Serenade* (1996), the romantic comedy *Dead Letter Office* (1998), *Kin* (2000), the romance *Julie Walking Home* (2002), the Italian *La volpe a tre zampe*, aka *The Three-Legged Fox* (2005), and the romance *South Solitary* (2010).

Tony Blackett began his career in television and made his film debut in a minor role in *Freedom* (1982). He would continue to appear in television and film supporting roles prior to and after *The 13th Floor*. Jeff Truman also began his career in television and made his film debut in a supporting role in *The Wild Duck* (1984). He appeared in more television and film supporting roles prior to and after *The 13th Floor*, including the Australian horror title *Cassandra*. He also co-wrote the screenplay for the thriller *Envy* (1999). Kylie Clare made her film debut in *The 13th Floor*, her only title to date.

Release

Screened at the Cannes Film Festival in May 1988, this film appeared to go straight to video in Australia and the United States with the taglines "Pray you don't reach," "Where terror reaches new heights," and "Even office buildings can be haunted."

Reviews

"Unconvincing. Roache makes heavy weather of the nonsense." — David Stratton, *The Avocado Plantation*

"The movie is not the type of haunting film we would imagine. There is no teleportation, no telekinesis and only one or two apparitions. The revelation is pretty foreseeable. The story remains interesting but does not deliver the potential that it inspires." — Steve, *Shade*, March 20, 2002

"This is a marvelous film right up until its inappropriate ending leaves you feeling betrayed." — Roger Ebert, *Chicago Sun-Times*

DVD

Not available. Video released by Prism Entertainment/Warner Home Video on May 23, 1995.

Bloodmoon

Michael Fisher Productions, 1990 [aka *Blood Moon*]

CREDITS: *Director:* Alec Mills; *Producer:* Stanley O'Toole; *Executive Producers:* Graham Burke, Gregory Coote; *Associate Producer:* David Munro; *Screenplay:* Robert Brennan; *Photography:* John Stokes; *Editor:* David Halliday; *Music:* Brian May; *Art Director:* Philip Warner; *Sound:* Ian Grant; *Wardrobe:* Helen Mains, Phillip Eagles; *Makeup:* April Harvie. Color, 97 minutes. Filmed on location at the Marist College, Ashgrove, Brisbane; Suttons Beach, Redcliffe; the Gold Coast; and the Warners-Roadshow Studios in Queensland.

SONGS: "Bloodmoon" (Brian May, Hunt Downs), Vice; "Keep Holding On" (James, Peters, Roberts and Warner), Vice; "Standing in the Line of Fire" (Joan Beauvoir), Vice.

CAST: Leon Lissek (Myles Sheffield); Christine Amor (Virginia Sheffield); Ian Williams (Kevin Lynch); Helen Thomson (Mary Huston); Craige Cronin (Sergeant Matt Desmond); Hazel Howson (Sister Mary-Ellen); Suzie MacKenzie (Michelle); Anya Molina (Jennifer); Brian Moll (Mr. Gordian); Stephen Bergin (Mark); Christophe Broadway (Scott); Samantha Rittson (Gretchen); Tess Pike (Kylie); Jo Munro (Jackie); Michelle Doake (Linda Chandler); Chris Uhlmann (Chip); Justin Ratcliffe (Zits); Damien Lutz (Tom); Warwick Brown (Billy); Gregory Pamment (Rich, aka Richard Hampton); Sueyan Cox (Sandy Desmond); Narelle Arcidiacono (Mrs. Bacon); Michael Adams (Mr. Owens); Sue Lawson (Mrs. Owens); Jonathan Hardy (Mayor); Elizabeth Williams, David Clendinning, Jane Dormaier, Helen Strobe (Teachers); Les Evans (Kevin's Father); Ray Turner, Shawn Kristofer (Policemen); Kate Riley (Daughter

Desmond); Sean Anderson (Baby Desmond); Kasha Loy, Lisa Hamilton (Two Girls); Matthew Smith (Murphy); Karen Miers (Susan); Lindy-Jo Free (Choirmistress); Stuartholme Choir (Choir).

Synopsis

Virginia Sheffield is the headmistress and her husband Myles the biology teacher at St. Elizabeth, a Catholic boarding school for girls in the beach town of Cooper's Bay. The girls have romances with the boys from the local Winchester School for Young Men. Jackie plans to elope with Rich but finds his murdered body in the Lovers' Lane of the woods near St. Elizabeth, and she is strangled by an assailant with a circle of barbed wire. At the Winchester dance, local Kevin Lynch becomes interested in schoolgirl Mary Huston, an American exchange student. Gretchen and a Winchester boy are the next victims of the killer, and Myles shows an odd interest in Mary. When Michelle and Jennifer break into Myles' office to get the upcoming exam questions, they discover that Myles has the barbed wire and a jar of eyes. Myles finds the girls and kills them both.

Sergeant Matt Desmond is investigating the killings and is suspicious of Myles. He learns that the Sheffields are wanted by the American police after children were found dead in their previous school in California. Myles arranges for Mary and Kevin to meet in the woods so he can kill them, but is found by Matt. Myles stabs Matt, who shoots Myles. Sister Mary-Ellen appears to save the children by throwing acid in Myles's face. Myles gets a gun and we hear him fire two shots in the house where Virginia awaits.

Notes

This dull story features the theme of the horror of personality but has a narrative which delays the killings in favor of boring teenage romances. When the killer is revealed halfway through the narrative, the treatment improves with the addition of suspense. Even though director Alec Mills presents the antagonist in classic horror movie conventional poses, the material still defeats him. Mills uses postmodern techniques like point of view, zooms, and blackouts, and has an obtrusive score. There is also an exploitative use of female nudity, although the killings provide satisfying bloodletting and gore.

A pan over the lovers' lane in the woods at night under the opening credits reveals the crucifix from rosary beads that drips blood, which is a red herring since the murderer will use a circular piece of barbed wire. Mills cuts from the crucifix to a cross in the church where the choir sings. The treatment's use of female nudity begins with the schoolgirls in the shower block, although that can be contextualized. Jackie discovers Rich's body with his throat slit and eyes removed; this is the first gore. The plot point about the removed eyes is never explained, although it is suggested that Myles feeds them to his cats.

A whispery voice is heard calling for Jackie, and her backing up creates the expectation of her attack, which is met. This is followed by the inevitable shot of dirt being thrown at the camera when her and Rich's bodies are buried.

When Sister Mary-Ellen prays for her sins to be forgiven, her anger suggests that she may be the killer. This idea matches the shot of the bloodied rosary, although it will be prove to be another red herring. Rather, the Sister practically disappears from the narrative until she reappears to confront Myles after taking his barbed wire and then as deus ex machina to throw the acid on him.

Susan being bare-breasted at the beach is partially contextualized. The fight between the Winchester boys and the three locals presents a class rivalry that has no bearing on the horror plot. Equally, apart from the whispering voice calling to Mary once at the dance, the hosing of the Winchester boys in the parking lot is just as irrelevant because it offers no plot payoff. Additionally, while Scott is presented as the instigator of the boys' rivalry and is shown to be having an affair with Virginia, he isn't used to further the horror narrative. He also gets no payoff, apart from adding to Myles' sexual frustration and jealousy, which can be seen as the motivation for his behavior.

The dance sequence works to allow more of the boys and girls to hook up in the Lovers' Lane. Susan's breasts are again exposed for her sex with Zits. The expectation of their attack is not met when they are scared away by another couple. The arrival of the new couple creates the expectation of *their* attack, which is met. There is some filler with Mary on the telephone with her mother and then with Kevin, and Gretchen's breasts are exposed in her sex with an unidentified boy. She is seen to run when the killer attacks the boy, as opposed to how Mary will stay to attack Myles when he attacks Kevin. Mills cuts from Gretchen's scream to a girl in the choir singing.

When it is shown that Virginia is having an affair with Scott, the scene reveals both the actresses' turn at nudity — contextualized by their sex — and Virginia's perversity for having sex with a minor. The fact of Myles being cuckolded by a boy rather than another man surely adds to his humiliation. It's a shame we don't learn what has turned Virginia off him, though Myles later seen in the shower perhaps gives us a clue, as does the performance of Leon Lissek, which recalls Peter Lorre. This humiliation also creates the expectation that Myles is the killer, since his victims are associated with sex, although his fascination with Mary seems more than just sexual.

Michelle and Jennifer in Myles' office is a set piece, given how Mills uses suspense in the cross-cuts to the approaching Myles. There is some wit in Michelle saying, "If I don't do well in that test my father won't just kill me, he'll do worse. He'll take away my car." Michelle finds the barbed wire and jar of eyes, and what looks like fingers, which confirms Myles as the killer. His violent bashing of Michelle's head against a desk provides more bloodletting. Myles having his hand cut by the blade of the knife that Jennifer reaches first is a surprise. Her leaving the room creates the expectation of her escape, although we have seen Myles lock the front door. Jennifer tripping down the stairs disables her so that she continues in a crawl, as the shadow of Myles holding the knife is used as to present him as a conventional horror threat. The locked front door proves to be the problem we expected. Mills uses the sound of music from a girl outside passing who holds a boom box to cover Jennifer's screams. Jennifer's death is shown by her outstretched hand with fingers that stop moving, another conventional device.

Myles' vision of Mary and Scott kissing in the shower imagined when Myles is in the shower presents his imagination and obsession. When he pretends to telephone Virginia for Matt, his authoritarian attitude clues us in to the fact of the deception.

The film's climax is prefaced by a storm as another conventional narrative device. Linda's emotional voice when she telephones Kevin to meet Mary prefigures the fact of Myles forcing her to make the call before killing her. Myles revealing himself with bloody clothes to Virginia is an interesting moment. Her response, "You've done it again," her slapping him and saying, "I'm not helping," is disappointing and portrays Virginia as an ungenerous woman when she has the opportunity to be kind. The barbed wire missing from Myles' room provides a surprise when Sister Mary-Ellen appears with it, although his ability to get it back from her is not. The film's climax utilizes cross-cutting with Myles' pursuing Mary, the approaching Matt, Kevin arriving, the choir rehearsing, and Virginia packing. The hand on the turned door knob and the hand that reaches in to turn off the light is revealed as a surprise to be that of Scott. Virginia is hardly glad to see him as her lover; she is afraid, as expressed in her following awful speech in heightened language that is not otherwise used in the narrative: "This is nightmare night. The end of the fucking world night. All the bugs and the bats and the goblins are coming out tonight and no one can stop them."

The expectation for the appearance of Matt in the Lane when Myles attacks Kevin and fights off Mary for Matt to rescue the children is not met. This is even though Matt shoots Myles, when Myles stabs Matt. Sister Mary-Ellen's appearance is a surprise that stops Myles. His disfigured face from the acid attack is more gore and enough of a shock to the groundskeeper to not try and stop Myles from getting his rifle.

Thunder and lighting are used again for Myles' approach to the house where Virginia awaits, after we have seen her plan to escape stopped by Matt's earlier appearance where he shot at her. Mills uses an extreme close-up of her before cutting to the exterior of the house for the sound of the two gunshots. We presume that Myles has shot Virginia and himself to end their antagonism, although Mills stays on the exterior shot with a slow panning back before the end credits. Since we do not see who has been shot or who fired a gun, it is possible that Virginia has shot Myles or that he has only shot her twice and not himself, alternatives that lay the ground for a sequel that has not been made to date.

This is the only Australian horror film to be made by Alec Mills, producer Stanley O'Toole, executive producers Graham Burke and Gregory Coote, associate producer David Munro, and the Michael Fisher production company.

Leon Lissek made his film debut in a minor role in the musical drama *Marat/Sade* (1967), and after a career playing supporting film roles and on television essayed his first and only leading role to date in *Bloodmoon*. Christine Amor began her career in television and made her film debut in a supporting role in the comedy *Alvin Purple* (1973). She was seen in *Snapshot* and other supporting film roles and on television, but has not essayed a leading role to date.

Release

Australia on March 22, 1990, and straight to video in the United States with the tagline "The last full moon you'll ever see." The film included a William Castle–like "Fright Break," a short intermission which gave audiences a chance to walk a yellow line to the cinema's exit if the film was too frightening for them, giving those who took the so-called "Chicken Walk" to the exits their money back. This "Fright Break" sequence was included on the Australian Roadshow Home Video release. The documentary *Not Quite Hollywood* says the "Fright Break" had more to do with those who asked for their money back because they hated the film than were frightened.

REVIEWS

"A truly memorable cinematic experience — for all the wrong reasons. It is an unspeakably funny film, but in the saddest possible way. It is a film promoted as a horror fillm, and it is for anyone with any faith left in the Australian mainstream film." — Jim Schembri, *Cinema Papers*, May 1990

"A truly memorable experience, an unspeakably funny film in the saddest possible way. Bereft of originality or even the ability to copy with style.... A major problem is that it lacks a convincing killer who looks motivated enough to scare you. It also lacks convincing victims who look scared enough to scare you." — Scott Murray, *Oxford Australian Film 1978–1994*

"This was one of those movies that was entertaining in its absurdity.... Between the cheeseball music, barbed wire killing tool, and a variety of slightly off-kilter characters thrown together in a plot that could only exist in the '80s, there was rarely a dull moment." — Josh Pasnak, *The Video Graveyard*, October 31, 2005

"There's plenty of problems with the film beyond its out of place soapy elements. It's adequately if unremarkably shot, [and] the performances are mostly mediocre.... The scripting is also largely uninspired. The film just doesn't work on a suspense level, and that's its real downfall." — James Gillett, *Digital Retribution*, November 9, 2010

"The first half of this Australian psychothriller is deadly dull [but] the second half builds to a suspenseful climax.... Leon Lissek is memorable as an impotent biology teacher-serial killer protected by his wife." — John Stanley, *Creature Features*

DVD

Lionsgate on April 20, 2004. Roadshow Entertainment (Australia) on January 13, 2010.

Body Melt
Dumb Films, 1993

CREDITS: *Director:* Philip Brophy; *Producers:* Rod Bishop, Daniel Scharf; *Associate Producer:* Lars Michalak; *Screenplay:* Philip Brophy, Rod Bishop, based on four short stories by Philip Brophy; *Photography:* Ray Argall; *Editor:* Bill Murphy; *Music:* Philip Brophy; *Production Design:* Maria Kozic; *Art Direction:* Peta Lawson; *Special Effects:* Bob McCarron; *Costumes:* Anna Borghesi; *Makeup and Hair:* Christine Miller; *Sound:* Craig Carter, Philip Brophy. Color, 80 minutes. Filmed on location in Melbourne, Victoria.

SONGS: "Highway Star," Deep Purple; "Masterpieces" (Maria Kozic, Philip Brophy), Maria Kozic and the MK-Sound; "Body Melt" (Maria Kozic, Philip Brophy), Maria Kozic and the MK-Sound.

CAST: Gerard Kennedy (Detective Sergeant Sam Phillips); Andrew Daddo (Detective Johnno); Ian Smith (Dr. Carrera); Regina Gaigalas (Shaan); Vince Gill (Pud); Neil Foley (Bub); Anythea Davis (Slub); Matt Newton (Bronto); Lesley Baker (Muck); Amy Grove-Rogers (Old Woman); Adrian Wright (Thompson Noble); Jillian Murphy (Angelica Noble); Ben Geurens (Brandon Noble); Amanda Douge (Elouise Noble); Brett Climo (Brian Rund); Lisa McCune (Cheryl Rund); Nick Polites (Sal Ciccono); Maurie Annese (Gino Argento); William McInnes (Paul Matthews); Suzi Dougherty (Kate); Bill Young (Willie); Tommny Dysart (Sergeant); Stig Wemyss (Jordan); Matthew Green (Forensic Cop); Phillip Green (Station Cop); Russell Alan (Patrol Cop 1); Lance Anderson (Patrol Cop 2); Robert Simper (Ryan Brennan); Parthena (Dimitra); Matt McLean (Beauvillo); Barry Whitnell (Boughman); Roberto Micale (Attendant); Lucinda Cowden (Andrea); Graham Dow (Doctor); Tiffany Lamb (Secretary); Gaby Porras (Punk); Chris Whitmore (Punk's Boyfriend); Greg Tingate (Accountant); Rosemary Margan (Bag Lady).

SYNOPSIS

Dr. Carrera uses the Vimuvilla health resort to test a new designer drug, as well as market sachets labeled as vitamins which have been delivered to residents of the Pebble Court Homesville housing estate in Melbourne. The resort's administrator, Shaan, injects her lover, Ryan, with a lethal dose of drugs to stop him from exposing the resort's practice. The police are brought in when Ryan's car crashes in front of the house of Sam and Gino at the estate, and the police are witness to Ryan's hideously deformed body. Sam and Gino stop at a rural garage to have their car's windshield replaced but are attacked by the family of Pud, a former chemist for Carrera. Other residents of the estate have hallucinations and alien viral growths from the vitamins, including Paul Matthews and Brian and Cheryl Rund, who is heavily pregnant. When Cheryl is found dead, Brian is arrested for her murder, although we see that she has been killed by the vitamins.

The Nobles, who are also residents, go to the resort. After eating the food there they become sick from the vitamins, as do Shaan and her bodybuilder attendants. Dr. Carrera visits Pud, who gives him the additive that has been missing from the drug, but is met by the police at the resort. The doctor shoots himself, and the investigating detectives return to their station to find Brian spewing green slime before he dies. Thinking the threat over, the police do not notice that more vitamins are stocked in the local Road Pantry, waiting to start a new wave of horror for those who consume them.

Notes

This story can be interpreted to feature the theme of the horror of personality via the drug testing of Dr. Carrera at the Homesville housing estate and the Vimuvilla health farm, but the fact that he doesn't deliberately set out to kill people makes him a lesser antagonist. The gross-out killings definitely qualify the treatment as horror, more than, say, science fiction. Director Philip Brophy has trouble with pacing, and the narrative focus on the farm of Pud where he and his family are presented as deformed and grotesque experiments gone wrong reads as superfluous. Thankfully, Brophy's sense of the ridiculous carries his treatment to a satisfying conclusion. Performances are over the top but perhaps necessarily so in order to match the special effects which supply gore and goo aplenty to please horror cinephiles. Brophy also uses the postmodern techniques of blackouts, slow motion, point of view, expressionist camera angles, fast cutting and time-lapse tracking shots, and optical effects.

A prologue avoids female exploitation by showing equal male and female nudity in the context of Shaan and Ryan having sex, with Ryan's penis also visible in his autopsy scene. The burning of Ryan's identification card where the photograph of his face melts prefigures Ryan's later real face melting, and the cuts on his neck is the first suggestion that something is waiting to burst out of him. His drinking detergent at the Road Pantry is a nice touch, although it doesn't stop the inevitable onslaught of the poison. The tentacles we see coming out of his ripped open stomach suggest an alien presence. For this and the subsequent attacks, Brophy inter-cuts to shots of the bloodied internal organs as if the point of view of the attacking virus.

We assume that Pud's family is deformed from his later admission to Dr. Carrera that he had self-experimented with the drugs they were working on together. But their ocker (redneck) grostequery recalls the same type of behavior in *Razorback* as the mark of rural Australians. The killing of a kangaroo by the family after it has been mesmerized by noise results in Gino seeing how the animal is torn apart so that its adrenal gland can be eaten. The attack upon Sam by Pud's daughter follows Sam's sexual interest in her, despite her obvious deformity. Her apparent eating of him adds cannibalism to the perversity. Pud gets a black comedy laugh when he becomes aware of the attack by yelling, "How many times have I told you to keep it in the family."

Ambiguity is attached to Paul's interaction with Kate, whom he meets at the airport and changes from a deformed vision to normal, but then she removes a bloody rib from him. We don't know if she is only a hallucination and whether the rib removal is just a nightmare. Cheryl's placenta appears to drop from her prematurely and it is shown on the floor pulsating. It then disappears from the place where she had seen it, although a blood smear attests to its initial presence. Cheryl looking for it is funny, as is it jumping onto Brian's face as he sees Cheryl about to stab herself in order to stop her labor. The steam that rises from Cheryl's belly attests to the labor being extraordinary, and although we see how something has been torn out of her, we don't see if it is the baby or another alien.

The snot that appears from Thompson's nose at the meal gets a laugh from the other Nobles and is a phenomenon that builds until Thompson is eventually covered by slime. Elouise's comment to Brandon, "Hope you break your neck" when he tells of his intention to go skateboarding, turns out to be prophetic, as expected. Paul's corpse being found with an ear on his hand is another sign of the deforming side effects of the vitamins. The exploding erection of the bodybuilder who watches porn is both shock and a payoff to the porn that we saw the matriarch of Pud's family watching. The obviously dubbed high pitched voice of the bodybuilder

Beau is a nod to the side effects of steroids. We don't get a payoff to him stealing vitamins from Shaan's office, but Dimitra's accidental strangling by another bodybuilder during their sex shows another fatal result. It's a pity that the fingernail cuts on her back that she makes during their sex isn't shown to have an alien burst through them, as a kind of retribution to his unintentional murder.

Shaan taking the vitamin pills is unbelievable, since she knows about the side effects. But her head sinking into her body after her face has been gooed is a satisfying payoff to her complicity with Carrera, even when the image is shot from behind her to no doubt aid the visual effect. Angelica's tongue enlarging to strangle her is another camp killing. We are spared the sight of Carrera shooting himself under the neck after he has shot his own hand since Brophy cuts from the intention to a shot of the yellow and green vitamin pills dropping from a dispenser. Willie scores a laugh from his line about how the multicolored gore of Brian's bloodied head copies Willie's tie-dye shirt design. There is another laugh from the policeman who faints at the sight of Brian's death — although the expected head explosion does not occur. The narrative epilogue is appropriately fatalistic and a continued expression of the police's general incompetence in the narrative. It also paves the way for the sequel that was not made.

In the "Behind the Scenes" featurette on the DVD, actors Ian Smith and Vince Gill give more information about their characters. Smith says Carrera is a scientist who uses the chemical experiments in the hope of creating a perfect human being, and Gill gives the backstory of the two chemists' relationship. He claims that Pud and Carrera were in the army together working on germ warfare and discovered that their chemicals could both destroy and enhance. They aimed to achieve super beings, but Carrera resisted experimenting on human, whereas Pud was willing to do so on himself. However, when Pud saw the mutant side effects of the experiments, he left Carrera and retreated to the desert, where he raised his mutant family. The film is the only feature and the only Australian horror title Philip Brophy has made to date, which is also true for producers Rod Bishop and Daniel Scharf, and associate producer Lars Michalak. It is also the only Australian horror movie to be made by the Dumb Films production company.

Gerard Kennedy started his career in television and made his film debut in a supporting role in the adventure *Eliza Fraser* (1976). He essayed the leads in the western *Raw Deal* (1977) and *The Last of the Knucklemen* (1979), but otherwise played supporting film roles and television. *Body Melt* is the last leading role for the actor to date. Andrew Daddo made his film debut in a supporting role in the comedy *A Kink in the Picasso* (1990), and has played other supporting film roles and worked in television since. After working in television, Ian Smith made his film debut in *Body Melt*, and worked in television afterwards.

Regina Gaigalas also began in television and made her film debut in a supporting role in the historical romance *For Love Alone* (1986). After *Body Melt* she was in other supporting film roles and on television. Vince Gill had appeared in a supporting role in the Australian horror title *Snapshot*. After *Body Melt* the actor played a supporting role in the Australian horror movies *Voyage into Fear* and *Razor Eaters*, as well as other supporting film roles and on television.

William McInnes began in television and made his film debut in a supporting role in the romance *Wendy Cracked a Walnut* (1990), and played other supporting film roles. After *Body Melt* he took the lead in the romance *Unfinished Sky* (2007), and played the title character in *The Hopes and Dreams of Gazza Snell* (2010). Brett Climo had previously appeared in a supporting role in the Australian horror title *The Wicked* and after *Body Melt* essayed the lead in *The Inner Sanctuary* (1996) and *Lost and Found* (2006), but was otherwise seen in supporting film roles and on television. Lisa McClune also made her film debut in *Body Melt* and later appeared in other film supporting roles and on television.

Release

Australia on October 28, 1994. United States release date unknown. Tagline was, "The first phase is hallucinogenic.... The second phase is glandular.... And the third phase is...."

Reviews

"A schlocky, tongue-in-cheek gore pic ... a moderately enjoyable item for fans of the genre ... full of gruesome deaths but is also cluttered with too many characters and needs a surer touch to sock over this brand of cheerfully sick humor.... Special effects makeup is revolting enough to please the fans."— David Stratton, *Variety*, December 2, 1993

"Pure cinema, visually and aurally exploding and imploding the limits of possibility. It is cerebral and visceral — fast, funny, clever and vile; an experience with a dialogue."— Scott Murray, *Oxford Australian Film 1978–1994*

"[It] can get a little loopy. Fortunately, though, the craziness is all part of the movie's quirky appeal. Though at times the movie suffers from its all-over-the-shop plot, it's the visuals of the film that really make it worth a watch. They're all side-splitting and eye-popping. Literally." — Laura Monaghan, *Digital Retribution*, December 26, 2006

"Gruesome gore stuff, from Australia.... Plenty of graphic carnage earmarks this film." — John Stanley, *Creature Features*

"Not a film for those who prefer to take their horror seriously, but if you like gore and grotesquerie with a great sense of humour, it's a real treat. A hilarious tribute to the best-loved cliches of the exploitation genre." — Jennie Kermode, *Eye for Film*

DVD

Released by Vanguard Cinema on November 25, 2003. Umbrella Entertainment (Australia) released on August 7, 2006.

Voyage into Fear

A Coventry/Winfalz Production, 1993 [aka *Encounters*]

CREDITS: *Director/Producer/Screenplay:* Murray Fahey; *Photography:* Peter Borosh; *Editor:* Brian Kavanagh; *Music:* Frank Strangio; *Production Design:* Robin Monkhouse; *Art Director:* Tor Larsen; *Sound:* David Olasser; *Special Effects:* Tim Adlide; *Wardrobe:* Kirsten Smallbone; *Hair:* Joe Maclean; *Makeup:* Jennifer Eady. Color, 88 minutes.

CAST: Kate Raison (Madaline Carr née Manning); Martin Sacks (Martin Carr); Martin Vaughan (Harris); Maggie Kirkpatrick (Aunt Helen Manning); Tiana Fahey-Leigh (Young Madaline Manning); Arlan Fahey-Leigh (Thomas Manning); Vince Gill (Keith Evans); John Krummel (Miles); Peter Carmody (Detective); James Hoss (Doctor); Anne Fahey (Lady With Dog); Brett Wood (Attendant); Alita Fahey (Mrs. Manning); Stephen Leigh (Mr. Manning); Malcolm Knoledew (Policeman 1); Phil Blackmore (Policeman 2); Chris Gillette (Miss Renshaw); Meredith Johnston (Policewoman); Yanis Garrett (Patient in Robe); Matthew Ferguson, Victoria Santos (Visitors); Elaine Arnold (Lady in Chair); Rob Lockhart (Researcher); Craig Carlton (Businessman); Monique Dykstra (Librarian); Angela Pinson (Reader 1); Leonie Pinson (Reader 2); Marcus Santos (Student 1); Kylie Pearce (Student 2).

Synopsis

Twenty-nine-year-old Madaline Carr experiences dreams and fractured memories. They are about the death of her parents and her younger brother, Thomas, when he was age four and she age six. Her husband, businessman Martin Carr, suggests they drive to the country Oberon mansion of Madaline's now deceased Aunt Helen. There Madaline has waking visions of Thomas. Martin leaves Madaline in their car when it gets stuck in the dirt so he can see help, and farmer Keith Evans comes to tow her out. Looking for Martin, Madaline goes to the farmhouse of Harris. When she finds a bloody shirt in his bathroom she fears that Harris has harmed Martin. Harris locks Madaline into a closet but she escapes. Seeing blood dripping from the ceiling, she finds a collection of dead skinned foxes. Martin appears but Madaline stabs him in fright. A police detective tells her how Martin had drugged her with a hallucinogenic so that she would be declared incompetent and he could inherit her money.

Notes

A conventional thriller that features the horror of personality and some mild violence, this treatment from director Murray Fahey includes slow motion, point of view and expressionist camera angles as postmodern techniques. The narrative improves with a twenty minute set piece in the later stages. Here silence and performance create a quiet atmosphere that is superior to the shock effects and feigned hysteria that are otherwise evident. The treatment also suffers for the most part from a lack of narrative inspiration and a studied performance by the protagonist which distances us from her trauma. However, Fahey succeeds with a gruesome horror scene where she is surrounded by hanging skinned animal carcasses. Additionally, the narrative reveals the protagonist as a victim of another character who can be considered an antagonist, but it still does not dismiss the protagonist's culpability in performing the acts of violence in the film.

Fahey is perhaps overly fond of a tracking camera when it does not present as subjective point of view, although this is not as unacceptable as other postmodern camera techniques. Voices are heard as we are shown framed photographs of what we will later realize are Thomas and Madaline in a dream that is a flashback to her as a child, with the movie convention of a person seeing themselves in memory. Echoed voices are used as evidence that it is memory. The child Madaline is afraid of the dark and is locked into her bedroom at night, as a sign of the cruelty of her aunt. Madaline appears to have visions of Thomas. Fahey cuts from Thomas hitting Madaline's bed with a pillow because he wants to play to the lights of the oncoming logging truck that will collide with the car of Madaline's parents. We hear the sound of the crash and see a face half in shadow smoking; this will later be recognizable as Harris. Harris being a witness to the accident doesn't really get a narrative payoff. That is apart from the fact of him having been a servant of the Mannings, hunting foxes illegally, and later keeping the adult Madaline in captivity.

The narrative sets a pattern where Fahey shows images that are later explained. An example of this is the dropped doll whose porcelain head smashes, which is presented as a shock. Madaline had a breakdown when her parents and Thomas died, although we only learn later that Thomas died in the car with his parents. This informs the adult Madaline's mental condition and why she is having the dreams. They are presented as a recurring trauma, although at the end we learn they are the result of the hallucinogenic given to her by Martin. Madaline's nightmares become waking dreams and they are aided by Martin's idea of her talking about her memories into a tape recorder. The shock of broken glass is a vase hit by a ball thrown by Thomas. Aunt Helen scolds Madaline because she thinks the girl is avoiding blame by putting it onto her dead brother. The tape recording scene gets a laugh in Madaline's line to Martin, "You are playing with my mind. Of course, I'm defensive." When she drives a fork into his hand in anger because Martin is "pushing her" about her memories, this act of violence is revealed to be another dream. The fork into Martin also prefigures the knife she will stab him with in the film's climax. Aunt Helen's cruelty is said to be based on her being engaged to a man who was killed in the war. Her being a woman who never married and was lumbered with child of her dead sister is the cliché of the virgin spinster.

The narrative objective of driving to the Manning country mansion is never met, which seems a cheat although we don't know who would be living there. Madaline's comment on Mark wearing a "country" style shirt will be paid off in her believing she finds his shirt bloodied in Harris' bathroom, although Harris and Keith Evans also wear the same blue plaid shirt. Martin racing Madaline in the forest transitions to the child Madaline racing Thomas. This gets a shock result in Madaline running into a man that is not identified, but could be either Harris or Keith. The car passing the logging truck is paid off when Madaline has a vision of Thomas, who beckons her, and she is so transfixed that she walks to him and doesn't see the oncoming truck. The moment of Martin saving Madaline from the truck is spoiled by what appears to be the use of rear projection for the medium shot of the actors. The idea that the Manning car wreck is still in the forest after twenty-three years is dubious, although at least the expectation that it will be found by Madaline and Martin is not met with the reveal of the wreck as they walk away.

Madaline's dream in the traveling car has Fahey superimpose the tracking shot of Martin's point of view of the scenery to the side of Madaline. Their discovery of the dead skinned fox in the forest prefigures the attic where Madaline will be surrounded by them, though this individual dead fox doesn't appear as gruesome as the bunch of them later.

The adult Madaline's vision of her younger self sitting on a tree stump disappears when Martin appears near her. Fahey uses a multitude of Thomas' visions for Madaline's faint and a black screen, although her loss of consciousness still allows for a montage of memory and dream images with the scenery superimposition. A laugh is scored from Madaline's question to Martin, "You think I'm crazy, don't you?" when her feeling for Thomas changes from "I've got to find him" to "He's after me" and later "Keep away from me, Thomas."

Fahey draws out the suspense of Madaline alone in the car at night; the rain helps to entrench the car and is a horror movie convention sign of dread. A noise of hail on the car roof is revealed as a shock effect. The expectation of her being locked out of the car after she attempts to wave down a passing one is not met, although her returning to the locked door to the one she got out of creates a momentary expectation. The legs that approach the car recall the figure that Madaline had run into in her race with Thomas, although they could also conceivably belong to Martin. The animal being dropped on her windshield is another shock effect. Perhaps it is done by the man revealed to be Keith as an act of careless pragmatism rather than deliberate fright. Keith is presented as a potential threat in another moment when he tells Madaline, "Your husband offered me money ... but on a cold night like this I'd rather have a kiss." This idea is dismissed by her fearless eye roll of rejection and his laugh.

Martin is taken out of the narrative, creating the expectation that he has been harmed, perhaps by Keith, who is the last person we have seen him with. Later we will learn that Martin is simply waiting for the right moment to go back to Madaline, although his timing will be fatally lousy. Madaline needing to wait for Martin is also altered by her having the car pulled out of the bog and being able to drive again. Why she stops at Harris' farmhouse is not explained. Presumably it is the first house she finds, and the set piece is only momentarily interrupted by Madaline's vision of Thomas outside a window.

The long scene is full of tension and ambiguity, and Kate Raison's performance improves in her playing off Martin Vaughan. It also helps that the scene is devoid of score. There is humor from Harris holding her arm a moment too long when he offers to dry her jacket. She withdraws her arm and he tells her, "Your hands are like ice." There is another laugh from Harris, "You should get under a hot shower."

The expectation that he will take money from the wallet in her car is not met. Surprisingly, she does take a shower before he returns with the suitcase from her car. We presume that her having a suitcase is because she had planned a long visit to the mansion. Madaline finding the bloody country shirt has Fahey provide blood on her hands from it, and a red pool of blood in which a droplet falls prefigures the later blood drop in the glass of milk.

When Madaline goes outside her walking into a fox trap is a shock effect that makes Fahey show the blood pool again. There is another laugh from the unseen act of Harris changing the unconscious Madaline into dry clothes, to which she comments, "How dare you!" Her aiming Harris' rifle at him is disempowered by it not being loaded, and even her later loading of the rifle does not result in her firing it. We can only think that Madaline is not good with guns.

Hysteria and score return for Madaline's physical struggle with Harris when he locks her in the closet. This recalls the same act by Aunt Helen, although why Harris does it seems less clear. She easily breaks out and her locking him out of the house is irony, although he just as easily gets in. There is a shock effect for his arm breaking through a window to strangle her. The shock of Harris grabbing in the darkened house is met by her spraying his eyes with an aerosol can. There are blood drops in a glass of milk — the milk being part of the dinner Harris has prepared. This is a disturbing sight, though not as disturbing as the attic of skinned animals to come. There is also blood on Harris's forehead from Madaline's strike at him with a fire poker. The anguish of her mental condition rationalizes her fury at a man that we will learn means her no harm.

The scene with the skinned animals allows for the memory of blood on the child Madaline's hands. This can only be later explained as Thomas' blood from the door accident, and Fahey again repeats the blood pool shot. We assume that Madaline retrieves the knife which she stabs the hanging and swinging cadavers she has been found in the attic, and it allows her to cut Harris when he grabs her again as she descends. The man that appears behind Madaline is pretty clearly Martin. Her stabbing him when she turns around from his touching her on the shoulder and saying her name is a shock defensive reaction.

The sight of the dead Martin allows Madaline to finish the dream/memory of Thomas. We see the shot of the lights of the oncoming truck, the child Madaline pushing open a door into Thomas and the key from the lock presumably cutting his face, which explains the earlier shot of Thomas and blood. Though it is not stated, it is assumed that the Mannings are taking Thomas to hospital or a doctor when they collide with the truck, although the reason for the collision is also unclear.

The voice of the detectives' exposition to Madaline of Martin's rationale and the reason for her dreams goes soft, as she has memories of her and Martin together and then finally of her stabbing him. Then Madaline is shown sitting on a bench alone but free of anxiety. It is assumed that Martin's nasty agenda saves Madaline from a murder or manslaughter rap, and that nice Mr. Harris isn't going to have her charged with assault.

Voyage into Fear was Murray Fahey's second feature as a director and first horror title. He went on to direct the Australian horror title *Hellion: The Devil's Playground*. *Voyage into Fear* is the only film made by the Coventry (aka Conventry) Films production company.

Kate Raison made her film debut in a minor role in the historical romance *For Love Alone* (1986), and *Voyage into Fear* is her only leading film role to date. After working in television, Martin Sacks made his film debut in the comedy *Emoh Ruo* (1985), and had previously played one of the title characters (but was not top-billed) in the crime drama *Slate, Wyn and Me* (1987). After *Voyage into Fear*, he would go on to play other supporting film roles and work in television.

Martin Vaughan was in a supporting role in the Australian horror movie *Alison's Birthday* (1981), but has not played a leading film role to date. He has continued to work in supporting film roles and in television.

RELEASE

Unknown; it appears the film was released straight to video. The DVD tagline is "An intense thriller where dreams become reality."

REVIEWS

"One of those movies that you wish would end pretty much as soon as the opening credits have rolled.... Director Murray Fahey has given us a talky, uninspired mess of a movie that doesn't seem to have any idea of what it wants to be [and] it all just feels like a big waste of time." — *The Video Graveyard*

DVD

Released by Platinum Disc on November 26, 2002.

Komodo

Scanbox Asia Pacific, 1999 [aka *Komodo: The Living Terror*]

CREDITS: *Director:* Michael Lantieri; *Producers:* Alan Riche, Tony Ludwig; *Co-Producer:* Chris Brown; *Executive Producers:* Devesh Chetty, Cammie Morgan, Richard Vane, Chris Davis; *Screenplay:* Hans Bauer, Craig Mitchell; *Photography:* David Burr; *Editor:* Michael Fallavollita; *Music:* John Debney; *Production Design:* George Liddle; *Art Director:* Ian Allen; *Set Decorator:* Michael Tolerton; *Costumes:* Helen Maggs; *Makeup:* Sally Gordon; *Hair:* Michelle Ritchi. Color, 89 minutes. Filmed on location in Wynnum, Brisbane, and at the Warners Roadshow Movie World Studios, Gold Coast, Queensland.

SONG: "Sultans of Swing" (Mark Knopfler), Dire Straits.

CAST: Jill Hennessy (Dr. Victoria Juno); Billy Burke (Oates); Kevin Zegers (Patrick Connally); Paul Gleeson (Denby); Nina Landis (Annie); Simon Westaway (Bracken); Michael Edward Stevens (Martin "Gris"); Bruce Hughes (Mr. Connally); Jane Conroy (Mrs. Connally); Melisa Jaffer (Grandmother); Brian McDermott (Sheriff Gordon); Nique Needles (Hippie).

SYNOPSIS

Teenager Patrick Connally and his parents visit Emerald Isle, North Carolina. Nineteen summers before, imported Komodo dragon eggs were dumped by a trader. The now adult Komodos living in the swamps have had their food supply cut off because Pontiff Petroleum has poisoned the land. Patrick finds a baby Komodo in the swamp reeds and accidentally kills it. Returning to his house, his dog and his parents are attacked by an adult Komodo. Suffering from post traumatic stress disorder, Patrick is brought back to the isle by his psychiatrist, Victoria, who believes that facing his past will cure him.

Patrick's Aunt Annie is attacked and then taken by a Komodo. Victoria and Patrick flee but their car crashes into the truck of Oates and Denby. The men have been hired by the head of Pontiff Petroleum, Bracken, to exterminate the Komodos. Patrick runs away from the others and the men travel back to the Pontiff worksite with wounded ferry operator Martin. Martin dies and Denby is attacked in the laundry room and dies. Oates takes Victoria to the oil filler station where he believes Patrick is hiding. Victoria finds the boy and he saves her from an attacking Komodo, but Oates is wounded in the swamp. He arrives in time to kill a second Komodo that threatens Victoria, and steals the helicopter that Bracken arrives on the isle with. Oates then rescues Victoria and Patrick from another Komodo and the three find safety back on the mainland, with Patrick's condition seemingly cured.

NOTES

This story features the theme of the horror of personality of fifteen foot long Komodo dragons, a large species of lizard. These fish-out-of-water antagonists cannot be considered malevolent supernatural beings since they are behaving naturally and merely killing for food. Director Michael Lantieri employs the postmodern techniques of animatronics and CGI, blackouts and whiteouts, point of view, slow motion, and hand-held camerawork, and an obtrusive score. He also manages to invest a lot of humor in the treatment. As is sometimes expected in this kind of sub-genre, the creatures are the most impressive thing about the film. Lantieri often deprives us of seeing their strikes, and he appears to be better at action scenes than emotional ones. In the DVD director's audio commentary he reveals that the low budget and juvenile rating he wanted for the film demanded a restraint in the presentation of violence. The narrative also presents the female protagonist as a warrior, but Lantieri regrettably doesn't supply empathy for the antagonist creatures that perhaps deserve it.

A prologue shows how the Komodo eggs were left in the alien swampland. The smell experiences by the Hippie who throws them away from his consignment either suggests that he is unfamiliar with the odor of the eggs or that they are broken and therefore of no saleable use. The fact that the eggs manage to produce live Komodos under such conditions is perhaps a contrivance. The title card that reads "19 Summers Later..." is aligned with Oates telling Victoria that the Komodos were dumped twenty years ago.

The swampland location of Pontiff Petroleum suggests that the oil will have a mutating effect on the Komodos, but that is not confirmed. The DVD director's commentary and making-of featurette states that the creatures are meant to be unusually big at fifteen feet long, with the oil refinery prefiguring the same locale of *Man-Thing*.

When Patrick is in the grass field, the expectation is created of a strike against him, which is met. This occurs after it appears that he has killed the baby Komodo he has lassoed, although when he returns to the house there is no evidence that he has been physically wounded. His dog being attacked by an unseen Komodo through the dog hole is a shock effect, and the killing of his parents is unseen and only suggested by their screams as heard by Patrick.

Another shock effect is Annie falling through the floor of the house, which prefigures her later being pulled through a hole in the floor by the Komodo. Her seeing a light outside which she investigates presents her as a conventional Woman in Peril. The expectation of a strike against her is met, although it is unseen, and her bloody is wound only revealed when she re-enters the house to be seen by Victoria. Victoria's hears a sound, presumably the sound of Annie's attack, and investigates. This also presents her as a Woman in Peril, although Victoria will prove to be more of a warrior than Annie. Annie's rosary beads, which we had seen her earlier kissing, may suggest that her faith gives her strength, but they get an amusing payoff as she holds them when she is dragged under by the Komodo.

Poster for *Komodo* (1999).

The sight of the Komodo in the living room is quite impressive. Victoria and Patrick running from it and leaving Annie prefigure the creature taking Annie after it has been pushed back by Victoria. Victoria as an armed warrior recalls the female warriors in other Australian horror titles *Lady, Stay Dead, Fair Game, Contagion, Out of the Body, The 13th Floor, Ghost Ship, Undead, See No Evil, Black Water, Storm Warning, Slaughtered, Prey, Triangle, The Clinic* and *Road Train*.

Another shock and funny moment comes with the baby Komodo in the grocery bag in the car that Victoria and Patrick get in. After the reveal of the big Komodos behind the car in the rear view mirror, there is another funny shot of the Komodo sticking out of the back of the car that Victoria drives, even if the head being unable to bite either occupant is a contrivance.

A bloodied Martin appearing at the car's window is another shock and a payoff to his earlier decision to come back to the isle to help Patrick. The car's near collision with the hunter's truck results in a surprising alliance between the two groups. When Victoria chases after Patrick in the grass field, the expectation of a strike against her is created but not met. Rather we get another shock effect when she is grabbed by Oates. Patrick having cut out the heart of the Komodo that was presumably killed in the collision is never given a plot payoff, although it supposedly enables him to leave Victoria and set up camp at the oil filler station.

Patrick's temporary removal from the narrative makes Victoria the main protagonist, although this is seen coming after the prologue. Even Patrick's return does not restore his character as the main protagonist. When the group gets to the worksite quarters, Victoria and Denby have an amusing exchange after they assume that the Komodos have been inside:

VICTORIA: Is there anything these things don't eat?
DENBY: Yeah. Anything faster than them. And raisins. They don't eat raisins.

When Martin dies there is more relief attached to the scene than empathy, since he has been holding the group back. Victoria eavesdropping over the telephone conversation between Oates and Bracken creates the expectation of his betraying her. This is not met in spite of his suggestion that she and Patrick, and Annie and Martin, can be considered food for the Komodos. Patrick being still alive is implied by the small and faceless person we see taking an orange and rope from the worksite. The rope is later paid off with the rope trap he sets for a Komodo. Victoria reading the faxed newspaper sheet with the headline "Biologist Suspected of Wife's Murder" suggests that Oates will be a more antagonistic character than he turns out to be. His later explanation of his presumed dead wife as a presumed victim of the Komodos is told to Victoria after the death of Denby.

The issue of Bracken hiring the hunters to eliminate the Komodos is told as a change of policy, since Oates first says that the company was aware of the creatures but was afraid to kill them because of the bad publicity they feared over harming an endangered species. It would seem that the only person associated with the company who has been killed by them to date was Oates' wife, but we do not know what has changed Bracken's policy now that he wants them dead. However, given that Oates was hired to perform the task in exchange for him to flee a trial over the murder charge, we can assume that the company is killing the creatures on the sly.

Denby's strike by a Komodo is another attack not shown. His bloodied neck is the result, although what he was doing to be bitten in the neck is hard to fathom. The expectation of the Komodos being clever enough to catch the same elevator that Victoria and Oates do to take Denby's body and talk more about Oates' backstory is not met. Oates' alliance with Victoria is confirmed by his taking her to the oil filler station where he thinks Patrick has gone. The rain, thunder and lightning are used as a conventional horror movie portent, although one wonders how Oates is able to light his cigar in the rain.

Another shock comes when Victoria goes into a tunnel as the Woman in Peril, thinking she has found Patrick, and a Komodo appears. Patrick's real reappearance occurs behind the rope trap the creature walks into. Patrick as a junior male warrior is indicated by the spikes he drives into the Komodo. It is a surprise later when a second Komodo approaches Victoria and Patrick does not attempt to help her.

Lantieri inter-cuts to Oates in the swamp and his own shock attack by a Komodo, although this comes with the contrivance of the creature not biting his head or dropping the deadly saliva that had injured Martin. This is presumably aligned to the equal contrivance of Oates being strong enough to hold off the head of this enormous creature who straddles him. The conventional suspense of his rifle being just out of reach is followed by Oates seeming to find a metal poker to strike the Komodo with. When we return to Victoria there is another funny image presented. She clings to the hanged corpse of the Komodo that had been caught in Patrick's rope trap as the second Komodo prowls the ground underneath her. The presumed dead Komodo opens an eye so that we can see it is not really dead, and she says, "This is not happening." Her fall results in her convenient landing under a grated cover that protects her from the ground Komodo. Oates soon appears in another shock moment to shoot it.

When Victoria climbs up to go to Patrick in a nest, Oates stays behind to re-load his gun. This creates the expectation of him being attacked again, with his arm also shown to have suffered a wound presumably from the Komodo that had been on top of him before. Oates uses the blood from his wound to divert the attention of the inevitably appearing Komodo in order to save the others. The Komodo that appears wearing a spike is said by Lantieri in his DVD audio commentary to be the one that Victoria had struck in the house and that had taken Annie. The creature is led to Oates after it had been head-butting the nest tower where Victoria and Patrick are.

Oates lighting a cigar also seems to be a final gesture before his death. It is a surprise when he throws the light into the oiled swamp so that the Komodo and presumably he are immolated. This assumption that Oates is dead is later be shown to be false when he reappears to steal Bracken's helicopter. The Komodo appears to have survived the fire since it again approaches Victoria, who has come down to the ground to voice a "No!" in her assumption that Oates is committing suicide. Her repeatedly striking it with a rock is Victoria as a female warrior. In the DVD audio commentary Lantieri also adds that her repeated blows are to drive the stake further into the creature's eye.

Bracken coming to the isle with two other men and they and the pilot leaving the helicopter allows for Oates to steal it, although when they see him doing it they make no attempt to stop him. The idea of Braken being stuck on the isle and soon to be a victim of the Komodos, however, is a plot point not taken advantage of. Rather we see Oates rescue Victoria and Patrick from a cliff top with an obvious CGI sea below, and his flare gun dispatches the Komodo that follows them. It's a pity Lantieri doesn't repeat the funny idea from the earlier car scene of a Komodo half in the helicopter. An epilogue shows the three safely returned to the mainland. Sitting on the pavement as observed by the sheriff, Oates doesn't seem in a hurry to have his wound attended to. The fact that the Komodos are not seen again is disappointing. Given that both hunters are no longer able to kill them on the isle, we assume that if there are any left, they would be striking Bracken and his men.

The film is the debut of director Michael Lantieri and the only Australian horror movie he has made to date. It is also the only Australian horror title made to date by producers Tony Ludwig and Alan Riche, executive producers Devesh Chetty and Chris Davis and Cammie Morgan and Richard Vane, and the production companies Komodo Film Productions and Scanbox Asia Pacific, to date. Co-producer Chris Brown went on to produce the Australian horror title *Hellion: The Devil's Playground*.

Canadian Jill Hennessy made her film debut in a supporting role in the thriller *Dead Ringers* (1988) and appeared in television and other supporting film roles. *Komodo* is her only lead film role to date; after it she was in more television and film supporting roles. She also co-wrote, produced and co-directed the comedy *The Acting Class* (2000).

American born Billy Burke made his film debut in a minor role in the musical comedy *Daredreamer* (1990) and appeared in film supporting roles and on television, and played the title character in the comedy *Dill Scallion* (1999). After *Komodo* appeared in more television and film supporting roles. He also assayed the lead in the thrillers *Forfeit* (2007) and *Removal* (2010), and co-wrote the horror title *Dead and Breakfast* (2004).

Fellow Canadian Kevin Zegers began his career in television and made his film debut in a supporting role in the family comedy *Life with Mikey* (1993). He continued in television and film supporting roles prior to and after *Komodo*. He played the lead in the horror film *Fear of the Dark* (2003), the thriller *The Narrows* (2008), the musical *The Perfect Age of Rock'n'Roll* (2009), and the horror title *Vampire* (2011).

Paul Gleeson also began his career in television and made his film debut in a supporting role in the actioner *Watch the Shadows Dance* (1987). He would continue in television and in film supporting roles prior to and after *Komodo*. Nina Landis made her film debut in the Australian horror title *Nightmares*; she appeared in more film supporting roles and television. She played the title role but was not top-billed in the comedy *Ricky and Pete* (1988).

American Michael Edward Stevens began his career in television and made his film debut in a supporting role in the romantic comedy *Lucky Break*

(1994). He continued in television and film supporting roles; *Komodo* is his last title to date.

Release

Straight to video in the United States with the taglines "On Emerald Island, you are at the bottom of the food chain," "The Living Terror," "Welcome to the bottom of the food chain," and "They exist. You are history." Release information in Australia is unknown.

Reviews

"Low-key thriller. Michael Lantieri takes his time to establish a creepy mood; the dragons don't make their first appearance until halfway through the film. For the impatient, the slow buildup may be an annoyance, but it pays off, to a degree, in terms of suspense.... The dragons themselves are impressively created."— David Stratton, *Variety*, August 29, 1999

"Very boring and totally unbelievable, but at least the komodo effects are actually kinda good. The plot is the worst thing and the actors are stale and as bored as me. This one would have worked in the 1950s but the cliché is just work out."— Jareprime, *Horrorwatch*

"If only as much effort had been put into the script and acting as it had in the special effects then *Komodo* would have been a lot better. But as it stands, you're better off watching the Discovery Channel and seeing some real life komodo dragons fighting each other."— *Popcorn Pictures*

"A bad movie, but not the worst I've ever seen. The special effects in this film really are top notch, and in a way, out class the acting in this movie. If you enjoy watching bad actors get eaten alive, then Komodo is your film ... but really it's not."— Patrick, *Bad Movie Knight*, May 10, 2006

"Clearly desirous of jumping aboard the CGI monster movie bandwagon that had been created by Jurassic Park.... The main problem with Komodo is that while Michael Lantieri conducts an impressive build-up and revelation of the monsters, he fails to allow this to pay off, and the final showdown is tame and disappointingly brief."— Richard Scheib, *Moria — the science fiction, horror, and fantasy film review site*

DVD

Released in the United States by Sterling Home Entertainment Millennium Series/Lions Gate on August 8, 2000. Not available in Australia to date.

Cut

MBP/Mushroom Pictures/Beyond Films, 2000 [aka *The Curse*]

CREDITS: *Director:* Kimble Rendall; *Producers:* Martin Fabinyi, Bill Bennett, Jennifer Bennett; *Co-Producer:* Julia Overton; *Executive Producers:* Mikael Borglund, Michael Gudinski, Gary Hamilton, Rainer Mockert; *Screenplay:* Dave Warner; *Photography:* David Foreman; *Editor:* Henry Dangar; *Music:* Guy Gross; *Production Design:* Steven Jones-Evans; *Sound Design:* Andrew Plain; *Art Director:* Richard Hobbs; *Special Effects Makeup:* Makeup Effects Group Studio, Paul Katts, Nick Nicolaou; *Costumes:* Katie Graham; *Makeup/Hair:* Jen Lampher. Color, 83–98 minutes. Filmed at Raywood House Bridgewater and on location in South Australia from April 6 to May 27, 1999.

SONGS: "Time to Do Some Killing" (Lamar Lowder), Lamar Lowder; "I Got You" (Neil Finn), Split Enz; "Brighter Sound" (L. Finn), betchadupa; "Venus" (J. Reid), The Feelers; "Tamarama Doorslammer" (A. Wilson, C. Sue), Killers on the Loose; "I Wish I Was a Man" (Fiona McDonald), Fiona McDonald; "Jesus Saves" (Lamar Lowder), Jerk; "I Can't Sleep at Night" (Lamar Lowder, J. Thomas), Josh Stanley; "Here Comes Another One" (S. Crichton, S. Lewicki), Groove Terminator featuring Basshoppa; "Electricity" (P. Dempsey, C. Hyndman, S. Ashworth), Something for Kate; "Stop the Rock" (Noko, I. Hosley, T. Gray, H. Gray), Apollo Four Forty; "Scissorman" (P. Annison, J. Love), Pound System; "Paranoia (B. Clarke, S. Chapman, T. Buchen), On; "The Cut" (C. Sue, A. Wilson), Killers on the Loose.

CAST: Molly Ringwald (Chloe/Vanessa Turnbill); Jessica Napier (Raffy Carruthers, Director); Simon Bossell (Bobby); Sarah Kants (Hester Ryan, Producer); Kylie Minogue (Hilary Jacobs); Frank Roberts (Brad/Scarman); Geoff Revell (Lossman); Stephen Curry (Rick Stephens, Sound); Matt Russell (Paulie Morrelli, Boom); Erika Walters (Cassie Woolf, Wardrobe); Cathy Adamer (Julie Bardot, Makeup); Steve Greig (Jim Pilonski, Electrics); Sam Lewis (Damian

Ogle, Cinematographer); Paul Blackwell (Vanessa's Manager); Scott Heysen (Original Director); Don Barker (Original Producer); Phyllis Burford (Martha); Dominic Pedlar, Holly Myers, Patrick Frost (TV Reporters); Edwin Hodgeman (Mr. Drivett); Peter Green (Senior Detective Ian Hollander); Caroline Mignone (Detective Lucy Carter); Bronwyn James (Forensic Supervisor); Huong Nguyen (Cleaner); Pamela Shaw (Lecturer); Tiriel Mora (Archives Projectionist).

Synopsis

Hilary Jacobs is the director of a slasher film called *Hot Blooded*. She is murdered by the actor who plays the film's antagonist, Scarman, who also unsuccessfully tries to kill actress Vanessa Turnbill. The film is left unfinished, and when a student, Angelo Zabriki, screens it he is found dead. Twelve years later the students of film teacher Lossman, who worked on the original film, decide to finish the film because the new director, Raffy Carruthers, is the daughter of Hilary. The team recasts Vanessa in the film and travel to the original location, a mansion in the country. However, one by one they become the victims of murder. It is revealed that Scarman is not human but rather a being that has been reborn in the film, and only by destroying the film can they destroy him. This is eventually accomplished by Raffy, with Vanessa and Lossman being the only other survivors. However, when a copy is screened at another film class, Scarman reappears.

Notes

This slasher movie features the theme of the malevolent supernatural being and has a narrative with humor and genre self-reference. Director Kimble Rendall employs the postmodern techniques of slow motion, expressionist camera angles, point of view and freeze frames. His presentation of violence is relatively restrained. Molly Ringwald is an American whose career as a leading actress was declining at the time. The stunt casting of Kylie Minogue in a minor role also recalls that of Drew Barrymore in *Scream* (1996), existing as a prologue to the narrative.

Rendall lights the scene being filmed for *Hot Blooded* in a golden glow. He inter-cuts to the boiling food in a saucepan to add tension and the anticipation of the violence to come. The only payoff the heated meal gets is Scarman turning off the hotplate, perhaps to stop her from using it as a weapon against him. His wearing gloves is a clue to his threat, and Chloe finding her cat dead prefigures the attack upon her. We wonder why Scarman telephones her to say "Now you're dead" when we assume he is already in her house and he has already written it on her shower-steamed mirror. Rendall does not exploit Molly Ringwald's nudity in the shower in the same way he doesn't exploit Jessica Napier's nudity when Raffy later has her shower.

Scarman's use of shears as a weapon is an indication of his taste for excess violence, and he later explains they are garden shears he has personalized. The action of his cutting Chloe's throat is followed by Hillary's yell of "Cut" because she is unhappy with the take, but this is also ironic counterpoint. Rendall then has the lettering of the film's title on screen being cut away and a resultant blood effect.

Hilary's public humiliation of Brad, the actor who plays Scarman, prefigures her as a victim. Brad puts on the Scarman mask to attack Hilary. We don't learn what becomes of him after the narrative moves twelve year later. But the connection that is made between him and the later figure of Scarman — who is presented as not a human — is misleading. This is although Vanessa'a later comment, "I killed him once," would suggest that she has killed Brad. Hilary sees him brandishing the shears and tells Brad, "Take one step closer and I'll scream." He replies, "It's hard to scream without a tongue." This comment is paid off with the shot of the tongue on the table, after Rendall deprives us of the sight of Brad's strike. Rather there is a long shot of the house and we hear Hilary's scream. When Brad as Scarman comes after Vanessa as the actress playing Chloe, an electrical effect is used when she stabs him with scissors. This is an effect that is later shown on the electrocuted editor, on Scarman's unmasked face and at the film's conclusion connecting the projector and the film being screened.

Rendall presents the flashback to the screening of the film for Angelo Zabriki in an overexposed film stock. This is a style he will also use for the video image of Vanessa at the press conference and the electrocution of the film's producer who had attempted to finish the film in the editing room. It is interesting that Lossman should tell his students about the film in spite of his considering it "trash," and refusing to include slasher film in his class. The idea of horror films or at least the slasher subgenre of slasher films as "trash" is the first of the many examples of the narrative's self-references.

Rendall uses a montage to present Raffy and Hester searching the Internet to research the film, and Hester asks the assembled group at a cafe table, "Who wants to make a mainstream slasher movie bigger than *Halloween*, creepier than *Friday the 13th*, more blood and guts than *The Texas Chainsaw Massacre*?" Freeze frames are used for each of the individuals who agree with hands raised to be the crew, each named and their crew position given.

Vanessa as a failed movie actress plays off the casting of Molly Ringwald, although Vanessa still has plenty of ego, which Ringwald makes funny rather being seen by the others as a diva. When asked at the press conference what she thinks of the idea of the film being cursed, she replies, "There's a special clause in my contract. If I die I get paid extra." The way Vanessa delivers the lines without irony perhaps suggests that she is not supposed to be too bright. Bobby introduces himself to Vanessa at the film screening as the actor who is to play Scarman. When he describes the character as the "psycho killer guy," Vanessa replies "Good casting."

A funny speech is given by the projectionist, who describes Hilary as a "bit of a hack, she was, or should I say she was hacked." The screened scene that we see being filmed has retained a lot of what Hilary had shot. The footage also has intercuts to Scarman outside Chloe's house and additional closer shots of her. The sticky substance under Raffy's feet we presume is blood and the person we see entering the screening behind her prefigures the gag to come. Hester's apparent throat being cut can be bought as real, but the fact that everyone else has their throats cut as well reads as too much and impractical, so that Bobby's reveal as Scarman being the person behind Raffy is not a surprise. However, the film's image of Scarman looking at the camera in the footage as if he is looking at the crew leaving is an effective button to the scene.

When Vanessa tells Lossman of her disappointment with the motel and the bed she is given for the location filming, she comments, "If I spend one night in this thing I'm going to need a masseuse." He tells her, "I did a course in Reiki," and she replies, "Reiki. No shit,"

Poster for *Cut* (2000).

lounging back on the bed in a seductive smirk. Rick explains the labyrinthine love complications of the crew to Paulie. Hester has an amusing exchange with the owner of the mansion, Mr. Drivett, about his concerns about young people's use of it:

> HESTER: I'll make sure they treat it like it was my own house.
> MR. DRIVETT: It's no comfort to me, young lady. You look like you'd live in a dump.

Raffy gives the crew, Vanessa — although surely she already knows — and us the backstory of Scarman. Charlie was the brother of Chloe, and together they had been left alone in their house by their parents. It caught fire, reason unstated. Charlie was horribly burned but Chloe was unscathed, which made the boy hate his sister and his parents. In the shot film, he had killed his father and some other people. Hilary had not completed the scene where he killed Chloe or the climax, where the mother was to be killed — the part that is to be played by Vanessa. Hester does not speak about finishing the scene of Chloe's death, although presumably she thinks she can salvage it in editing since Vanessa is now twelve years older and couldn't pass as the same girl.

The subjective camera approach to Vanessa's back as she looks in the mansion's refrigerator creates the expectation, not met, that she will be attacked, since the person is revealed to be Bobby. After he holds a knife to her throat and asks, "Scare you?" she knees him in the groin and replies "Hurt you?" This scene demonstrates, as had the earlier one where she had defeated Scarman, that Vanessa is not a conventional horror movie victim and can defend herself. Her courage will be presented in the film's climax when she chooses to pursue Scarman rather than be pursued by him.

Another movie self-reference moment occurs. Hester tells Lossman how she thinks horror movies have a social value because their narratives about the high stakes of life and death put life's small fears into perspective. The killing of the projectionist is the act that gets the police involved with the film crew, since it is said he was killed soon after they had their screening. This makes sense if we are to believe that the screening has brought Scarman to life. The murder is introduced by blood on a stairway that leads to a reveal of the dead projectionist, said to have been disemboweled.

The sex between Paulie and Cassie occurs as if its immorality leads them to be Scarman's next victims. Additionally it makes them physically vulnerable to the attack, since only she sees him and Cassie is under the weight of Paulie. Like the projectionist's disembowelment, Paulie's beheading is equally gruesome but Rendall doesn't dwell sadistically on it. Rather it is a shock effect that he quickly moves on from. The heavy breathing of Scarman may seem like a corny horror movie convention for an antagonist. But it can be rationalized by him wearing a mask to protect his burned face, although since he is a supernatural being we wonder whether this should apply. Additionally, the issue of difficulty breathing under a mask is demonstrated by the heavy breathing that Bobby also does, although he may only be repeating Scarman's behavior when he is playing him.

Rendall uses slow motion for Scarman's throwing of the knife that kills Cassie. Her prior cries of "What do you want?" — a seemingly silly question to ask a serial killer — recall the same question that Vanessa asked and that she answered with "Sex?" After the knife to Cassie, Rendall cuts to Raffy's "Cut" to Vanessa in the car scene being filmed, more irony.

The expectation is created for an attack upon Raffy when she is in the shower and someone is seen to open her room door. When the lights go out, her investigation presents her as a Woman in Peril. There is the shock reveal of the person in her room being Damian on her bed and who turns a light on. Raffy tells him that she has personal and unstated reason to want to finish the film, which Lossman will later reveal is the fact of her being Hilary's daughter. It is interesting that the corpses of Paulie and Cassie are never recovered by the others, although one of them may be the corpse that later drops onto Hester, or that may be Jim.

Another movie moment of self-reference is the scene where Hester tells Raffy: "This isn't life imitating art. I don't believe there's some cracked killer out there stalking us like we're in the plot from Bride of Chuckie 7. Life doesn't work like that."

Regrettably, Hester is wrong, although the life she speaks of has to be contextualized as life in a horror movie. Julie's reports that the wardrobe and mask doubles for Bobby are missing. This seems a red herring since we wonder why the real Scarman would need them. Rendall has Scarman seen by Jim in the rear view mirror of the bus before his death.

The appearance of Scarman on the set for the filming of his attack of Vanessa creates ambiguity as to whether it is Bobby or the real Scarman, although the scene of his murder of Hester soon after suggests that it is Bobby. This ambiguity will be teased out in a later scene, after Bobby has been killed, when Scarman steps in to shoot the scene.

A blood drop on Hester's cell phone when she is outside trying to get a signal prefigures the dropping of the corpse in the tree onto her, and her running into Scarman is a shock effect.

In the scene of Hester's murder, Rendall uses the quiet and darkness of the shack Hester seeks refuge in for suspense, although the expectation is created that she will die. Scarman's shock reveal in the shack is perhaps his first act of super-naturalism, since we don't see him come into the shack. The inter-cuts of the buzz saw–like device with the knife attached is paid off when Hester is wounded and laid down so as to be in the device's path. Rendall doesn't show the time of impact. Rather the camera is outside a window as we hear Hester's cry and see blood splatter.

A label from the Film Audiovisual Radio and Television School (FARTS) is given a joke from the first letter of the words being highlighted and the words being written horizontally. Lossman's hand on Raffy's shoulder when she goes looking for Jim is a shock reveal. His question "Why this move?" leads to her admission of what he knows — that she is the daughter of Hilary.

The tires of the car having been slashed is paid off later in the immobility of the car that Rick and Julie are trapped in. The scene of the death of Bobby begins similarly as the death of Jim — by Scarman being seen in a mirror. Bobby putting the mask back on when he thinks Scarman is Rick still seems an odd choice, although the potential for ambiguity in a struggle is not taken advantage of in the narrative in light of the quick strike upon Bobby. However, the following scene, where Scarman is thought to be Bobby for the delayed filmed scene of Vanessa's attack, is perhaps the most intriguing in the film.

Scarman is given trick shears so as not to hurt Vanessa but he, unseen, switches it with his shears, which have been taken by Hester. The expectation is created that Vanessa will be hurt by the real shears. The horn of the approaching car of Martha, which affects the scene's sound recording, stops the scene being filmed. This momentarily saves Vanessa from harm. The idea that perhaps Lossman is Scarman, before we realize that Scarman is a supernatural being, is dismissed when Lossman volunteers to go and investigate the horn honking. Since the horn stops once the car does, the expectation is again created that the scene can be filmed and Vanessa hurt. Martha's speech is melodramatic yet acceptable given that this narrative is about a supernatural being. Being aware of the filming, she tells Lossman: "You must stop. The evil is back. There is a force at work here. It is not human and unspeakably evil. You must destroy the film at once or you will all die."

Meanwhile the scene is halted when Vanessa has a concern about a loose false eyelash she doesn't want seen in her close-up. The second take is stopped by Raffy's "Cut" and Lossman yelling "That's not Bobby." How he knows Scarman is not Bobby is not explained but he is believed, possibly because Scarman is too quick to give himself away. While the others flee, Damian keeps filming, creating the expectation that he will be attacked, and he is. Scarman goes to the camera and waves at it, meaning at Damian, before he attacks. The wave is a sly and funny touch of an expectation that he won't kill, which we know won't be met.

Vanessa's comment, "I killed him once and I can do it again," is the voice of courage, even though it will be revealed as bravado since she does not kill him. The separation of Rick and Julie who go to the car from Vanessa and Raffy presents the former as victims, an expectation that is met when Scarman appears at the car. His being locked out of the car would appear to protect them from his shears, but the gasoline he uses is a new weapon. Fire is utilized further into the narrative as an echo of the fact that he has been burned. Scarman's pouring of gasoline onto the car is an act that gets a later payoff, since Julie decides it is better to get out of the car and she becomes Scarman's new point of focus. He pours gasoline onto her, as he will do to Vanessa later. Rendall repeats the use of slow motion for the lit match to reach Julie.

Rick's hand sliding down the car window as the car is set alight is a resonant horror image. His cry is muffled from behind glass before the car explodes. Vanessa and Raffy getting knives from the kitchen presents them as armed Women in Peril. There is a shock effect of Lossman appearing from Mr. Drivett's room. He is found hanged presumably killed by Scarman, and his dog licks the blood on the floor. Poor Martha — who Lossman says had found Drivett and had a stroke — now reaches for Raffy, in another shock moment in a death grasp. Lossman says that Martha had believed that the film had created Scarman and that the only way to destroy him is to destroy the film, which is kept in Drivett's room.

Lossman adds, "He's not human. He's the sum total of all the creative energy that's gone into the film." Vanessa replies with a funny line, "Believe me, there was no creative energy that went into that piece of shit."

The expectation of Lossman's death when Scarman stabs him in the neck will be unmet since Lossman returns later in the narrative to save Raffy. Vanessa's courage is further highlighted when she makes herself a decoy for Raffy to burn the film in the conveniently burning car that Rick is in. When the detectives arrive, the expectation is created that Vanessa can be rescued, although sometimes police in horror movies don't seem to be as effective as in other genres.

Scarman yells when a frame of him in a medium shot of the film burns as he is about to strike Vanessa. This creates the expectation that he will now be stopped. He will prove to be harder to destroy than first thought, since it will take the whole film being destroyed to put an end to him, at least until he reappears in the film's epilogue. Rendall uses a melting effect for Scarman's face as he burns, and when he removes what is revealed to be a mask again, we see the electric effect on his face.

His apparently leaving Vanessa to come downstairs creates the expectation that she is dead, or are we to think that he has left her unharmed because he wants to stop Raffy from burning the film? Detective Carter stopping Raffy from finishing burning the film also stops Scarman's burning. We see that Raffy is not locked in the police car and she only stays in it because Carter tells her to. Scarman's jump down the stairs to meet Detective Hollander in the house is another supernatural move, and the expectation is met that the detective's gunshots will not stop Scarman is met.

It is odd hearing Scarman speak because it makes him sound human, particularly as he speaks in colloquial language, unlike the Gothic formality of Martha's language. Although he doesn't say anything to create empathy, it does add a dimension to him as a horror movie monster. After the gunshots are shown to be ineffective, Rendall has a pause for the faceoff between Scarman and Hollander. It is a welcome anticipation of the inevitable strike, but we do wonder why Hollander doesn't run when he has the opportunity. Rendall also presents Hollander's beheading as a shadow effect from outside the house, again restraining the gore display, as with the strike upon Hester.

Carter going into the house creates the expectation that she will meet the same fate as Hollander. She is the Woman in Peril armed with what she doesn't realize is an ineffective weapon. However there is humor in Scarman saying "I'm something special, huh?" after Carter sees how her gunshots don't hurt him.

Rendall uses slow motion for Scarman throwing the shears after the running Carter, and her falling onto an outside faucet adds an additional impaling to her cut. Why Scarman runs water over her is unclear, although perhaps it is to clean off the blood from the shears that he will use again. Raffy is shown to defy Carter's orders and resume burning the film.

A closeup of Vanessa's eyes shows how she has survived Scarman leaving her before, so that the previous expectation of her death is not met. However, another expectation is created when she backs away from the returned Scarman and falls out of a window, since we think the impact may have killed her. This expectation is also not met, although the fall seems to have injured her, naturally. Scarman pouring gasoline on her recalls his murder of Julie and Rick.

Raffy continuing to burn the film does not stop Scarman from continuing his attack upon Vanessa. However, Rendall does not show Vanessa on fire. This is perhaps to spare us the sight since later we learn that she has been burned, but also to create ambiguity and the possibility of an expectation not met. Lossman reappears to help save Raffy from Scarman's attack, inexplicably pulling the knife out of his throat to enable him to burn the rest of the film. The cries of the dying and melting Scarman finally create sympathy for him, although we know we shouldn't have any for such a demon. Rendall tweaks the sympathy by dripping Scarman's melting face over Raffy.

Rendall provides another montage of Internet or newspaper headlines showing how Vanessa has been burned but had survived. Lossman has survived his neck wound, and he visits Vanessa in hospital. Her commenting about now that Scarman is dead she can sleep again sets up the film's epilogue.

We wonder how another copy of *Hot Blooded* has been found in order to be screened at another film class, particularly if the original had been successfully destroyed in order for Scarman to have been destroyed. The expectation now that he will be reborn is met. The electric effect is shown to travel from the film in the projection room to the screen. Rendall uses a freeze frame for the film's last shot of Scarman sitting behind the female lecturer, so as to present a strike and paving the way for a potential sequel.

Cut was the film debut of Kimble Rendall and his only horror film to date. It was the first Australian horror title for producer Martin Fabinyi, who later was executive producer of the Australian horror title *Wolf Creek*, working with executive producer Michal Gudinski. *Cut* is the only Australian horror movie made by producer Jennifer Bennett, co-producer Julia Overton, and executive producer Rainer Mockert under his MBP production company. Mikael Borglund was the executive producer on *Cassandra*, and he later was executive producer of the Australian horror title *Hellion: The Devil's Playground* with executive producer Gary Hamilton. *Cut* was the first feature made by Mushroom Pictures, which later made *Wolf Creek*; it is the only horror film made to date by Beyond Films.

After working in television Molly Ringwald, made her film debut as a child actress in a supporting role in the comic fantasy *Tempest* (1982). She secured fame as the lead in the romantic comedy *Sixteen Candles* (1984), and continued as the lead in the romantic comedy *Pretty in Pink* (1986), was the title character but not top-billed in *P.K. and the Kid* (1987), the romantic comedies *The Pick-up Artist* (1987) and *For Keeps?* (1988), and *Fresh Horses* (1988). By the 1990s Ringwald essayed fewer leads as she made the transition to adult roles. These include the comedy *Face the Music* (1993), the thriller *Malicious* (1995), where Ringwald attempted to broaden her range by playing a mentally disturbed stalker, and as a drug dealer in the crime thriller *Baja* (1996), and the thriller *Requiem for Murder* (1999). *Cut* was the actress's last lead role to date; since then she has been seen in supporting film roles and on television.

Release

Australia on March 2, 2000, with the taglines "They just have to finish the film ... before it finishes them," "It's hard to scream without a tongue," "Audience Warning — Important Cinema Safety Notice — Caution: Movies Can Kill," "Finishing the Movie Could Be the Death of Them," and "Warning: Movies can kill." The film appears to have gone straight to DVD in the U.S.

Reviews

"A knowing post–*Scream* schlocker with its tongue more or less firmly in its cheek and a screenplay with insider references to spare, *Cut* is a no-nonsense commercial package that should hit the spot."—David Stratton, *Variety*, March 5, 2000

"Satisfying and highly watchable slasher import.... With one cool mask on the killer, competent acting and lots of above average death scenes, this is a surprisingly enjoyable and fun time. The fact that this continually jabs the industry in the ribs and brings up past horror films makes this perfect viewing for the genre fan."—*The Video Graveyard*

"Combining the spoof aspect of *Scream* and the documentary style of *The Blair Witch Project*, this movie emerges as a decrepit and uninteresting mess. Amateurish all the way, this takes the horror genre to a new low."—Ryan Cracknell, *Apollo Movie Guide*

"Sub-sitcom-level wisecracks alternate with lazily orchestrated bloodshed as the killer works his way through cast and crew, but *Cut* never works, either as a slasher movie or as a film-savvy behind-the-scenes comedy. Casting teen-movie icon Molly Ringwald as a temperamental American star was an inspired move, but that's where the inspiration ends."—Nathan Rabin, *The A.V. Club*, March 29, 2002

"There's no emotion involvement, hence I didn't give a rat's about what happened to the characters, and with no attempt to bring anything new to the table *Cut* is simply bland."—Jeff Ritchie, *ScaryMinds*

DVD

Released by Lions Gate on May 8, 2001.

H.P. Lovecraft's Cthulhu
Onara Productions, 2000

CREDITS: *Producer/Director:* Damian Heffernan; *Executive Producers:* Kevin Dunn, Tracy Cook; *Associate Producer:* Michelle Ryan; *Screenplay:* Damian Heffernan, based on "The Call of Cthulhu" by H.P. Lovecraft; *Photography:* Carl Looper; *Editors:* Andy Marriot, Sophia Platty; *Music:* Jason Sims; *Art Director:* Mayer Samuel; *Prosthetic Makeup Effects:* Nik Dorning; *Costumes:* Kelly Smith; *Makeup:* Kent Vaughan; Color, 73 minutes. Filmed in Canberra, Australian Capital Territory.

SONG: "Too Close for Comfort" (Jerry Bock, George David Weiss, Larry Holofcener), heard as muzak in Galaxia Bookstore.

CAST: Paul Willamson (Inspector Legrasse); James Payne (Edward Derby); Adam Somes (Dan Upton); Malcolm Miller (Professor Armitage); Melissa Georgiou (Asenath Waite); Margaret Forster (Doctor Reeves); Chris Georgiou (Ephraim Waite); Bianca Nogrady (Sonia);

Adam Tonge (Bookstore Geek); Mikel Simic (Dingo); Kylie Chapman (Warden); Martin Toman, Casey Tonge (Guards); Sharon Tonge (Nancy); Steve Poskitt (Cthulhu Victim); Kelly Somes (Running Girl); Tracy Cook (Receptionist); Kent Vaughan, Michael Monaghan (Orderlies); Grant Akersten, Keiran Morrow, John McGrath, Travis Kirk (Police Officers); Matthew Heffernan, Cath and Peter, Sunil Bhandari, Rajesh Bhandari (Fake Shemps); Jane Rawson (Nudist Gardner).

Synopsis

Miskatonic University student Dan Upton visits his friend, Edward Derby, in the Arkham asylum and shoots him dead. Sentenced to life imprisonment in the Arkham Penitentiary, Dan is found hanged in his cell after six months, an apparent suicide. A manuscript written by him is left to tell the story of why he killed his best friend. Dan's interest in the occult has him purchase rare books that require his translation. Edward becomes involved with Asenath Waite, the daughter of the leader of a cult that performs human sacrifices and drinks blood. Edwards tells Dan how Asenath has the power to take his body as he sleeps and go to places for rituals, leaving her in his body.

Meanwhile the Dunwich police department, led by Inspector Legrasse, investigates a series of killings they have traced back to the Waite cult in Innsmouth. They kill the cult leader and arrest members, but also arrest Edward, who is found naked and rambling insanely on the road. Legrasse calls in Dan for Edward. Their mutual interest leads them to the university's Professor Armitage, who tells them about the mythic Cthulhu. It is believed it has been awakened by the cult to use his powers to take over the earth. With Armitage, Legrasse attempts to send the spirit back to wherever he came from, but they are both killed in the process. Thinking that Edward is possessed by the spirit of the son of Cthulhu known as Yog Sogof, Dan goes to the asylum where Edward is being held and kills him.

Notes

This low, low budget title mixes the themes of the horror of personality with the malevolent supernatural. This is represented by occult cultists who have raised the spirit of Cthulhu, a mythic high priest who seems to be invisible and can kill with lighting effect. Director Damian Heffernan employs the postmodern techniques of point of view, expressionist camera angles and hand-held camera, jump cuts and forward cuts and slow motion, optical effects and CGI, and blackouts. He also uses grainy film stock as well as black and white and sepia tones. Heffernan's low budget may explain his lack of coverage in scenes since shot variation is rare. Close-ups are not provided at all which makes scenes static, and sound makes the dialogue seem post-synchronized. Performances are reasonable, with only one really disappointing one, and there is some bloodletting. However, the treatment confuses rather than clarifies the narrative. It uses a flashback memory structure where the protagonist is established at the beginning as being already dead, and narration is used from a manuscript he wrote of his story.

The treatment's first bloodletting is Dan shooting Edward in the head in the opening scene, although the device of narration is only spasmodically used. Why Dan's death is shown via black and white footage is perhaps an aesthetic choice rather than a logical one. It reverses the trend of showing flashback, which is what the bulk of the narrative is, as a different toned memory. We see Dan via the manuscript memory and it is perhaps a more acceptable device than direct memory, although we do not know who it is that reads the manuscript of his story to allow for the memory.

The first death presumably via the Culthulu cultists is presented in a humorous way — the standard chalk outline used by police shows one leg having been amputated and the leg receiving its own chalk outline. When a woman is attacked by Cthulhu as she walks in a park in the daytime, the expectation of a strike is created by the use of an approaching subjective camera. Her death is shown in long shot, with the passing of the lighting through her, and there is a momentary vision of a green creature. The idea that the woman is thought to be Asenath is dismissed by her being seen alive later, although Asenath is soon removed from the narrative.

Other victims of the cultists are found by police and they are headless and bloodless, although not shown to us and only spoken of. Cthulhu's strike against Dingo is suggested by a blood splatter on a wall behind him. Edward telling of the death of Asenath's father is shot in sepia, as if it is her memory with the convention of her seeing herself. Given the supposed power she has over Edward and her involvement with the cult, her subsequent removal from the narrative is questionable.

Edward tells Dan of Asenath's power over him. Heffernan presents the scene of the police battle with the cult as if it is Edward's dream, with whiteouts, although neither Edward nor Asenath are in the scene. After the lead cultist is shot, Heffernan inexplicably repeats dialogue from the car scene between Edward and Dan over the footage of the cultists being shot or arrested. A subsequent scene of Dan being chased by men gets no plot payoff. Dan sees Edward driving a car, and he has a funny line to Legrasse: "Ed just drove out of here and considering he can't drive that's pretty fucking funny." Dan and Legrasse respond to two yells in the street to find two more presumed victims of Cthulhu. A man is seen with his intestines on the ground, and a woman who is chased has the lighting effect go through her and ends up bloodied, sitting against a tree.

Heffernan uses jump forwards in the scene where Edward sets the car he had been driving alight as well as slow motion for Edward walking away from the fire. Dan and Legrasse going to see Professor Armitage provides for the longed for exposition of Cthulhu and the murderous lighting effect. Although the mythology is not identified as being of Aboriginal origin, the name suggests a link. However, the exposition becomes confusing as to who is the real narrative antagonist. Is it Cthulhu or his born human son, Yog Sogof, who is needed to awaken the creature? The lighting effect murders would seem to make it clear that the creature is already awake. We never see Yog Sogof, even in the climactic battle scene. Additionally, the victims of Cthulhu seem arbitrarily chosen. For a creature that is said to have the power to take over the earth, its efforts appear rather mild.

When Edward is in the asylum, the expectation of the narrative return to the scene of his death is created, although a corpse seen rising from the ground is another unexplained plot point. The chanted spell needed to send Yog Sogof back to his "pit" isn't used by Armitage, Dan or Legrasse in the climax. The Inspector's use of a gun reads as comical to attack the lighting effect.

Heffernan features a crowd of locals to observe the climax, where optical effects present rolling fast clouds, although they don't join the three in the battle. Dan appears to be injured with Legrasse and Armitage by a Cthulhu lighting effect, though we assume he recovers because he seen going to the asylum in a repeat of the opening scene. Heffernan also repeats the shots of Dan being found hanged in his cell. The funeral shown is presumably for him, although there is no plot end demonstration that Cthulhu or Yog Sogof is still around.

The narrative is credited as being based on the short story "The Call of Cthulhu." However the plot is much more closely related to Lovecraft's "The Thing on the Doorstep" and incorporates elements from his other stories, "The Dunwich Horror" and "The Shadow over Innsmouth." The film is the only Australian horror title made by director Damian Heffernan to date, producer Kevin Dunn, and the production company Onara Films.

Paul Willamson aka Paul Douglas had made his film debut in a supporting role in the action adventure *Twister* (1996). His lead in *H.P. Lovecraft's Cthulhu* has been his last to date. Melissa Georgiou, Malcolm Miller, James Payne and Adam Somes all made their film debuts here, and it has also been their last to date.

Release

Screened in Australia on July 23, 2000, at the Melbourne Underground Film Festival and in the United States on October 7, 2006, at the H.P. Lovecraft Film Festival. It did not appear to get a wide release in either country and went straight to DVD in the United States, with no tagline known.

Reviews

"The entire production is less than amateurish. This just looks and feels like what all the actors who weren't good enough for summer stock productions did with their time. The effects are laughable, the cinematography is uninspired, and the acting is atrocious." — Talyseon, *Epinions.com*

DVD

Released by Video Disc DVD/Onara Films on October 7, 2009, in the United States. No release in Australia to date.

Ghost Ship
Warner Bros. Pictures/Village Roadshow/NPV Entertainment/Dark Castle Entertainment, 2002

CREDITS: *Director:* Steve Beck; *Producers:* Joel Silver, Robert Zemeckis, Gilbert Adler; *Co-Producers:* Richard Mirisch, Susan Levin; *Executive Producers:* Bruce Berman, Steve Richards;

Screenplay: Mark Hanlon, John Pogue, based on a story by Mark Hanlon; *Photography:* Gale Tattersall; *Editor:* Roger Barton; *Music:* John Frizzell; *Production Design:* Graham "Grace" Walker; *Costumes:* Margot Wilson; *Art Director:* Richard Hobbs; *Set Decoration:* Beverley Dunn; *Sound:* Paul Brincat; *Makeup:* Anita Morgan, Nadine Wilkie. Color, 88–90 minutes. Filmed on the Gold Coast and Warner Bros. Movieworld in Oxenford, Queensland, and Vancouver, Canada, from January 24 to April 24, 2002.

SONGS: "Senza Fine" (Gino Paoli), Monica Mancini; "Superhoney" (Edwin, Thomas Salter, Jeff Dalziel, Memphis, Meher Steinberg), Edwin and the Pressure; "Not Falling" (M. McDonough, G. Tribbett, R. Martinie, Chad Gray), Mudvayne; "Love Boat Theme" (Charlie Fox, Paul Williams); "Caliente" (Coti Sorokin, Pablo Luis Duchovny), Natalie Oreiro; "Slippin' Into Darkness" (Sylvester Allen, Harold Brown, Morris D. Dickerson, Leroy Jordan, Lee Oskar, Charles Miller, Howard Scott); "My Little Box" (John Frizzell, Gabriel Rutman, Micha Liberman), Gabriel Mann.

CAST: Julianna Margulies (Maureen Epps); Ron Eldard (Dodge); Desmond Harrington (Jack Ferriman); Isaiah Washington (Greer); Alex Dimitriades (Santos); Karl Urban (Munder); Emily Browning (Katie Harwood); Gabriel Byrne (Captain Sean Murphy); Francesca Rettondini (Francesca); Boris Brkic (Chief Steward); Robert Ruggiero (Captain); Iain Gardiner (Purser); Adam Bieshaar (First Officer); Cameron Watt (Second Officer); Jamie Giddens (Friendly Officer). Uncredited: Matthew Wollaston (Steward 3).

Synopsis

In 1962 the Italian ocean liner *Antonia Graza* has its passengers garroted by a seemingly random loosened cable and is reported missing. Forty years later, the civilian salvage tugboat *The Arctic Warrior* is on its way back to Alaska. Jack Ferriman shows Murphy, the captain of the tugboat, photographs of a ship. Jack thinks it is the *Antonia Graza*, adrift in the Bering Sea. The tugboat finds the ship and its cargo of gold. The ghost of a little girl, Katie Hardwood, warns the tugboat's officer Epps not to take the gold with them. The tugboat is sunk as a result of a gas fire and engineer Santos is killed.

The crew decides to fix the holes in the hull of the sinking ocean liner and pump out the water so that they can transport the gold. The members are killed off one by one until it is revealed that Jack is responsible for the murder of the passengers. A supernatural salvager who collects souls, Jack has brought the tugboat's crew to the ship to fill his quota for management. Epps blows up the ship to ruin Jack's quota and swims to safety. She is rescued by another ocean liner and taken ashore. Epps sees the recovered cargo of gold being deposited onto the ocean liner and Jack follows it onboard.

Notes

A forgettable mystery actioner with shock effects and gore used for horror, this title features the theme of the malevolent supernatural being that we only see kill in flashback. Director Steve Beck employs the postmodern techniques of slow motion, subjective camera as point of view, expressionist camera angles, quick edits and cross-cutting. He also has an obtrusive score, and a four minute flashback scene of exposition to identify the killer, but fails to create atmospheric suspense from the abandoned ocean liner locale.

The narrative is interesting in the way it delays the present day killings and delays payoffs to plot points. It is also noteworthy for presenting a female protagonist as both a maternal and feminist figure. She recalls the female warriors of *Lady, Stay Dead, Fair Game, Contagion, Out of the Body, The 13th Floor, Komodo, Undead, See No Evil, Black Water, Storm Warning, Slaughtered, Prey, Triangle, The Clinic* and *Road Train*. Horror cinephiles may object to the absence of back to back killings. Additionally, none of the subsequent ones top the opening sequence of group garroting, which recalls the garroting killer of *Roadgames* as grand guignol. However, the film's end is satisfyingly bleak in its presentation of the victorious power of evil.

The opening sequence recalls *The Poseidon Adventure* (1972) in showing an ocean liner party with that film's tidal wave here paralleled by the group garroting. The later exploration of the abandoned ghost ship recalls the earlier title's attempted escape out of the upside down ocean liner. *The Poseidon Adventure* had recalled the tale of the doomed ocean liner RMS *Titanic*, as does this narrative, although the design of the *Antonia Grava* is said to have been copied from the Italian ship the *Andrea Doria*. Although we are never shown who specifically instigates the opening act of violence, the pause of the victims before their bodies fall in pieces is effective grand guignol. The scream of Katie is used as a time transition as the camera goes underwater.

Although the narrative doesn't give the 1962 time of this prologue, we get a title of "Present Day" for the transition. Epps' ignoring Murphy's order to abandon the vessel she is attempting to salvage prefigures her later heroics. It presents her rather than Murphy as the tugboat's captain, as the narrative protagonist. Unlike the heroine of other horror titles, however, Epps is not a victim. Even the visits she has from Katie's ghost assist her rather than torment her. Additionally, since Katie only shows herself to Epps, this sets up Epps as the sole crew survivor.

Jack's presentation as an outsider to the crew of the tugboat will be paid off in the reveal of him as the antagonist. His apparent naivety and innocence will become ironic in the face of his manipulation and his description of the job given to him "after a lifetime of sin." Beck's use of shock after the garroting continues with the chime of the clock on the ocean liner. The twist of the letter game we had seen Katie earlier playing with that said "I am so bored" now changes to "Welcome Abored." This is presumably done by Katie and not Jack. The narrative will repeat the device of supernatural effects that are un-witnessed, presumably to enable Beck to create ambience. The interference of the crew's walkie talkies prefigures those in *Wolf Creek*.

Munder's near fall through the floor into a lower level is another shock effect. Epps' attempt to rescue him is sidetracked by her vision of Katie, who initially appears to be a threatening presence. The scene has a rather lame joke after Munder is rescued and comments, "I think I just shot my pants." Dodge replies, "No, you always smell that way." Epps' later memory of Munder's accident will have her remember the vision of Katie, although Epps also sees things in her memory that she did not originally see — the movie contrivance of memory.

Beck has another shock effect for the crew: divers emerging from the sea to startle Jack, although we get both points of view, which dilutes the shock. Epps being shocked by Katie as Epps climbs up the ladder of the swimming pool allows her to fall back into the empty pool. There is a blood droplet, which is presumably Epps', shown to fall into a drain and then reappear from a bullet hole in the pool's wall. Epps has seen the empty bullet casings on the pool's floor. However, the explanation of how they and the holes in the pool's wall got there will only be given later in the flashback sequence. Before that happens, Beck also has more blood drops coming from the pool walls and then the pool filling with blood and corpses as more un-witnessed phenomena.

Beck's intercutting of Epps in the pool with Murphy's vision of the Italian Captain in the reflection of his cabin's mirror will be later paid off when

Poster for *Ghost Ship* (2002).

the Captain talks to Murphy. The singing and music heard on the walkie talkies that stop the crew from communicating with each other will also get a later pay off. This occurs with the reappearance of Francesca, who had been seen singing in the opening 1962 scene. The water that bursts from the flooded ventilation shaft is another shock. This is predicted by Epps, though she doesn't predict the corpses that also flood in. These corpses are said to be recent. Like the plot point of the digital watch that Dodge finds, it suggests that others have recently been on board the ocean liner and have been killed. Francesca being unseen by Greer as he exits the ballroom is more un-witnessed phenomena and will also be paid off in her later scene with him.

Something moving in the cargo hold gets one shock reveal of rats, but since they appear scurrying over the gold bars, the moment has another payoff. Epps looking in the galley and being scared by Dodge and Munder, who hide to scare her, is an attempt at comedy. Her advance into the room after Jack tells her "Don't go in there" has initial suspense because of the expectation which is not met. We can forgive the contrivance of how the men knew she would look in the galley in order to set up their gag on her.

The reappearance of Katie to Epps as a warning to not take the gold is presented ambiguously, since at this time we do not know if Katie is a threat. Her warning is paid off by the death of Santos that occurs as a result of the tugboat trying to leave with the gold. The turning on of the propane gas that leads to the explosion and the death of Santos is done in a supernatural way, presumably by Jack, although we may think at the time that is due to Katie. However, it is interesting that Santos is the first of the crew to be a victim, and that this death does not occur until halfway into the narrative.

When Epps looks for Katie, Beck uses a shock effect of doors slamming in a row and the creaking, slowly opening door of Katie's room as a horror movie convention. The hanging skeleton that Epps finds is another shock effect, suggesting that Katie has committed suicide, a plot point that will be explained in the later flashback. Dodge and Munder eat what they think are canned beans but which are revealed to be maggots, another shock. It is also confusing because we wonder what power is creating the vision, though presumably it is Jack, and how maggots could have been hatched in a sealed can. Equally inexplicable is Greer's vision of the furniture in the ballroom that returns to its original state, the crowd that applauds Greer and the sight of Francesca. Since all these visions eventually lead to Greer's death, they are more believably the act of Jack. The crowd applauding Greer is initially perplexing until Francesca appears to kiss Greer rather than dance with him, as is expected. Beck inter-cuts between Greer, Epps with Katie, and Murphy, who is visited again by the ship's captain, although Murphy's drinking may also be the reason for his vision.

When Epps talks to Katie, the pendant Epps removes from Katie's skeleton drops onto the vision of Katie's hand and goes right through it, which confirms that Katie is a ghost. The scene between Murphy and the Captain features its own reveal of a photograph of the sole survivor of the ship *Lorelei*. "Die Lorelei" is a German poem about a siren-type woman who lures boats to ruin and sailors to their deaths. The photograph is seen by Murphy but not shown to us. This latter plot point is told by the Captain about how the adrift *Lorelei* had been rescued by the *Antonia Graza*.

Francesca's breasts are shown in the one sexually exploitative moment in the film in the context of enticing Greer to follow her, with the payoff delayed. Katie's conversation with Epps also has her speak of herself as one of the trapped souls among the shipmates, who are being counted for a "quota." Katie's urging for Epps and the crew to leave the ship then confirms that Katie is the victim of the malevolent supernatural force of Jack.

The ghost of Santos returns — presumably as another trapped soul — with a shock confrontation for Murphy. This is complete with Santos' face being burned. Santos is confirmed as a ghost since he moves distances in a supernatural way. Beck intercuts to the naked Francesca, leading Greer to fall down a shaft, although the reveal of his fate is delayed with another shock effect of Francesca turning into an aged hag after Greer's fall. Murphy's view of Epps has her change to Santos, and the flashlight she carries appears to be a knife. This causes him to attack her, and her rescue by Jack is only later acknowledged in that Jack needs Epps to fix the ship for his mission. Epps begins this work, including pumping water out of the sinking vessel. Beck reveals Greer's grand guignol death by impaling, which is only the second murder of the crew, two-thirds of the way into the narrative.

Katie touching Epps allows for the four minute flashback, although it is aided by the fact that both of them are witnesses in the scenes of exposition provided. The material presented offers a multitude of betrayals, with the poisoning of the soup served presumably to kill off the passengers who eat it and a repeat of the opening scene's garroting. The sequence also shows passengers shot by the swimming pool to explain the bullet holes in the walls and the casings on the floor. We also see how it is suggested that Katie is hanged by sailors, and Francesca being struck and hanged by a hook by Jack is the reveal of him as the antagonist. The one responsible for Murphy being drowned in the aquarium, where he had been imprisoned after his attack upon Epps, is not identified, though also presumed to be Jack. His holding the photograph that the Captain had shown him gives the reveal of Jack as the sole survivor of the *Lorelei*.

The death of Munder as crew death number four appears to be accidental — he is caught in gears. When Jack appears to Epps as Dodge, there is the suggestion that Jack was responsible. Dodge's presumed death occurs off screen after his confrontation with Jack. Jack's supernatural powers are shown when Dodge's shooting of him does not kill him, as revealed by his opening his eyes after he is presumed dead from the gunshot. It has been established that Jack cannot be killed easily, although this is not witnessed by Epps. It makes her decision to shoot the explosives control rather than him not a surprise. Katie leading Epps to safety under water is a reversal of Francesca's leading Greer to his death.

Beck has images of multiple souls swimming around Epps as she swims to the surface, in an obvious use of CGI. The vertical sinking of the ocean liner recalls the way the ocean liner *Titanic* sank. Multiple edits of Epps at sea are used to create an expectation that she is as adrift as the other ocean liners were before. This expectation is not met; a ship rescues her. Her being tied to an ambulance stretcher as she witnesses the gold and then Jack boarding the same ship allows for her disempowered scream for the narrative's horror movie conclusion, where evil cannot be defeated, although she appears to be safe.

Gabriel Byrne is said to have replaced Brian Cox, who was originally cast as Murphy. The opening floor deck sequence where passengers are severed by the cable was originally envisaged to have the victims decapitated. Jack Ferriman's character is named for Charon the Ferryman, the Greek mythological spirit who collected souls from one side of the river Styx and ferried them across to Hades. Also, the painting at the end of the Grand Hall is inspired in Michelangelo's painting *The Ferry Man of the Styx*. Although it shows Poseidon instead of Charon, position and painting arrangements are the same.

Steve Beck was a visual effects art director who made his film directing debut with the horror title *Thir13en Ghosts* (2001). *Ghost Ship* is his second and last film to date. It is the only Australian horror title to be produced by producers Joel Silver, Robert Zemeckis, Gilbert Adler, co-producers Richard Mirisch and Susan Levin, and executive producers Bruce Berman and Steve Richards. *Ghost Ship* is the only film to be made by the Village Roadshow Pictures production company and the only Australian horror title made by the production companies NPV Entertainment, Dark Castle Entertainment and Ghost Ship Films.

Julianna Margulies made her film debut in a minor role in the crime thriller *Out for Justice* (1991) and, after working in television and playing supporting film roles, scored her first and only prior lead in the comedy *The Big Day* (2001). After *Ghost Ship* she has not essayed another film lead to date, rather working in more television and film supporting roles.

Irish born Gabriel Byrne made his film debut in a minor role in the British-made *On a Paving Stone Mounted* (1978), and after playing in television and in film supporting roles scored the lead in the romance *Reflections* (1984). The actor was the lead in the thriller *Defence of the Realm* (1985), the biographical horror *Gothic* (1986), the war romance *A Soldier's Tale* (1988), and the thriller *Diamond Skulls* (1989). In the 1990s he continued as the lead in the crime drama *Miller's Crossing* (1990), the family adventure *Into the West* (1992), the adventure *Prince of Jutland* (1994), and *Somebody Is Waiting* (1996). Although now more cast as a supporting player, his interest turned to screenwriting and producing. Byrne also directed *The Lark in the Clear Air* in 1996. In 2002 the actor returned as the lead in the family drama *Virginia's Run*, and after *Ghost Ship* he was top-billed in *Wah-Wah* (2005) and *Emotional Arithmetic* (2007).

American Ron Eldard made his film debut in a supporting role in the comedy *True Love* (1989), and after playing in television and more supporting roles scored the lead in the comic thriller *Delivered* (1999) and the crime drama *The Runner* (1999). After *Ghost Ship* he was the lead in the crime thriller *Already Dead* (2007) but otherwise played supporting film roles. Fellow American Desmond Harrington made his film debut in a minor role in the biographical drama *Joan of Arc* (1999) and after more supporting roles essayed the lead in the comedy *Massholes* (2000). After *Ghost Ship* he played the leads in the horror title *Love Object* (2003), the thrillers *Taphephobia* (2006) and *Exit Speed* (2008), and the romance *Not Since You* (2009), as well as playing supporting roles in other films and working in television.

American Isaiah Washington made his film debut in a minor role in *The Color of Love* (1991) and continued in supporting film roles and working on television before and after making *Ghost Ship*. The actor would play his only leading film role to date in the mystery *The Least of These* (2008). New Zealand born Karl Urban began his career in television and made his film debut in a minor role in the New Zealand made war drama *Chunuk Bair* (1992). The actor scored the lead role in the New Zealand horror title *The Irrefutable Truth About Demons* (2000) and after *Ghost Ship* essayed the leads in the crime drama *Out of the Blue* (2006), was top-billed in the action adventure *Pathfinder* (2007), the crime drama *Black Water Transit* (2009), as well as playing film supporting roles and working in television.

Australian Emily Browning began her acting career in television and made her film debut in a supporting role in the comedy *The Man Who Sued God* (2001). After more television and *Ghost Ship*, she played a supporting role in the Australian horror title *Darkness Falls* and would essay the lead in the mystery *The Uninvited* (2009).

Release

Australia on December 5, 2002, and United States on October 25, 2002, with the taglines "Sea Evil" and "You will not only see evil but you will feel it crawl all over your body as the ultimate terror hits the high seas."

Reviews

"An incoherent supernatural thriller that would like to think of itself as a Halloween-ready horror fusion of *The Perfect Storm* and *Titanic*.... If the movie sustains an eerie visual mood, its screenplay is frustratingly sketchy. And with the exception of Ms. Margulies's sensible first mate, the acting is at best functional."— Stephen Holden, *The New York Times*, October 25, 2002

"It breaks no new ground as horror movies go, but it does introduce an intriguing location, and it's well made technically. It's better than you expect but not as good as you hope."— Roger Ebert, *Chicago Sun-Times*, October 25, 2002

"An entertaining ride for horror fans with stylish direction, decent mood and some really neat effects sequences. Throw in a competent cast of mostly unknowns, a well-staged flashback sequence that explains why the ship is haunted and a generally interesting script and you have a movie that's better than expected."— *Video Graveyard*

"Grows less interesting as you find out more of what happened to those passengers, and the whole 'collecting souls' thing is superfluous, but for a little slick, mindless entertainment, you could do worse. But you could do better, too."— Graeme Clark, *The Spinning Image*

"A pretty decent ghost story. Not necessarily the usual bitter, ruthless disquiet ghost (although there are a few), the ultimate reason for this haunting is a satisfying change from the norm.... The only problems are that it is never quite creepy enough, and the ending is a little too Twilight Zone like."— J.R. McNamara, *Digital Retribution*, August 9, 2005

DVD

Released by Warner Home Video on March 28, 2003.

Hellion: The Devil's Playground

Cubbyhouse Production/Pictures in Paradise/David Hannay Productions, 2002 [aka *Cubbyhouse*; *The Cubby House*; *The Third Circle*]

CREDITS: *Director:* Murray Fahey; *Producers:* Chris Brown, David Hannay; *Co-Producer:* Murray Fahey; *Executive Producers:* Mikael Borglund, Gary Hamilton; *Screenplay:* Ian Coughlan, Murray Fahey; *Photography:* Philip M. Cross; *Editors:* Marcus D'Arcy, Antonio Mestres; *Music:* Peter Dasent; *Production Design:* Sean Callinan; *Sound:* Phil Judd; *Art Director:* Adam Head; *Makeup/Hair:* Lynne O'Brien; *Wardrobe:* Ken Bushby. Color, 88 minutes. Filmed on the Gold Coast, Queensland.

SONGS: "Sunshine" (B. Nash), 78 Saab; "Be Sure" (Hogg/Hasman/Peters/Watson/Milligan), Pumpkinhead.

CAST: Joshua Leonard (Danny); Belinda McClory (Lynn Graham); Jerome Ehlers (Harrison/Harlow); Craig McLachlan (Bill); Lauren Hewett (Bronwyn McChristie); Amy Reti

(Natalie Graham); Joshua Tainsh-Biagi (Ivan Graham); Chris Brown (Newsreader); Belinda Ann Gavin (Julie); Chris Roughan (Chris); Stefan Kluka (Surf Reporter); Carita Farrer (Sandra Hickey); Peter Callan (Don); Ingrid Mason (Ailsa McChristie); Brian Hinselwood (Joel McChristie); Craig Marriott (Kirby Hickey); Murray Fahey (Gary the Pest Man); Jonas Morrisy (Byron); Madison Dohnt (Hope); Steve Harman (Nurse); Shaun Wainwright (Child).

Synopsis

American divorcee Lynn Graham brings her three children, Danny, Ivan and Natalie, to live in a house in Rainbow Bay, Woodland, on the Gold Coast of Queensland. It was the former residence of a family whose two children, Byron and Hope, were murdered in a Satanic ritual. In the house's back yard is a cubby house (playhouse) where the children had been killed. Ivan and Natalie are drawn to play in it as they hear the voices of the dead. The cubby house's evil is represented by serpentine moving vines that attempt to drag away Kirby, the son of Lynn's sister who is a neighbor. The children use their possessed powers to have cockroaches attack him. Danny becomes interested in Bronwyn, the daughter of his other neighbors. She introduces him to Harlow, whose twin brother, Harrison, is imprisoned at the Criminal Psychiatric unit of the Woodland Institute for killing Harlow's two children.

When Ivan and Natalie become possessed by the dead children, they perform a ritual which also affects Harrison. Danny breaks into Harlow's house and steals a book about the occult. He escapes from Harlow, who is dragged by the vines under a water drain and killed. After a second ritual attempt by the children, Harrison breaks out of the institute. Bill, the real estate agent who sold Lynn the house, is taken by the vines when he comes to date her. Harrison tries to exorcise Satan from the cubby house with Harlow's book but is killed by a flying stake after being wounded by the possessed Graham dog. Danny takes over the exorcism and succeeds, and the children are released from their possession. The Grahams decide to move out of the house and pass another family arriving to move in with a child. The cubby house is seen reconstructed.

Notes

This title features the theme of the malevolent supernatural being as Satan who has taken the spirits of two children and possessed a cubby house. Director Murray Fahey employs the postmodern techniques of point of view, subjective tracking camera, slow motion, expressionist camera angles, and CGI and optical effects. There is an obtrusive score and a treatment which has some shock effects and its share of ridiculousness. The film has plenty of bloodletting and some resonant horror strikes, including an attack by cockroaches and a body dragged under a water grate. However, the family of protagonists as transplanted Americans reads as a choice to make the film appeal to the international market without providing any narrative payoff. This additionally allows for the casting of an actor who indulges in annoying method mannerisms.

A prologue has Fahey expose the naked breasts of Julie as seen by Harlow as he arrives home to find Harrison performing a satanic ritual. Her partial nudity suggests some context since it is implied that she is implicit in the activity. Although a later scene of Bronwyn undressing creates the expectation that she will be equally exposed, it is not met. This helps the argument that Julie's exposure is not intentionally exploitative.

The blood on the floor of the cubby house and the blood on Harrison's axe are used to suggest the killing of Harlow's children, since Fahey thankfully spares us the sight of the axe's strikes. A title card reads "30 Years Later" for the transition to Lynn's arrival at the house under the film's opening credits. The aged house surrounded by modern houses adds to its Gothicism. The tracking cameras used for the moving vines that prefigure the same in *The Ruins* do not get an immediate payoff until the later party. The deep bushes in the back yard and that cover the cubby house suggest that the house is located at the back of an estate.

The Graham dog being afraid to go into the bushes suggests the satanic danger, even in daylight when the vines attack Kirby and Ivan. It is interesting that the vines retreat when faced with the entrance of Danny, which prefigures his climactic ability to exorcise the demon. There is a joke after the vine attack when Ivan accuses Kirby of being scared and he replies, "I'm scared of nothing." At this a ball is thrown out of the bushes and both boys run and cry for their mothers.

The tracking camera is again used for the appearance of Gary, with the expectation of his attack met, although the plot point of his disappearance is not followed up on. When Lynn argues with Danny in the cubby house she is oblivious to the echoed cries of Natalie who observes the wind blowing in the backyard and a whirlwind of leaves circling her. Lynn is equally oblivious to the eyes of the doll on the floor of the cubby house that turn red. The circling leaves get no payoff, nor do we

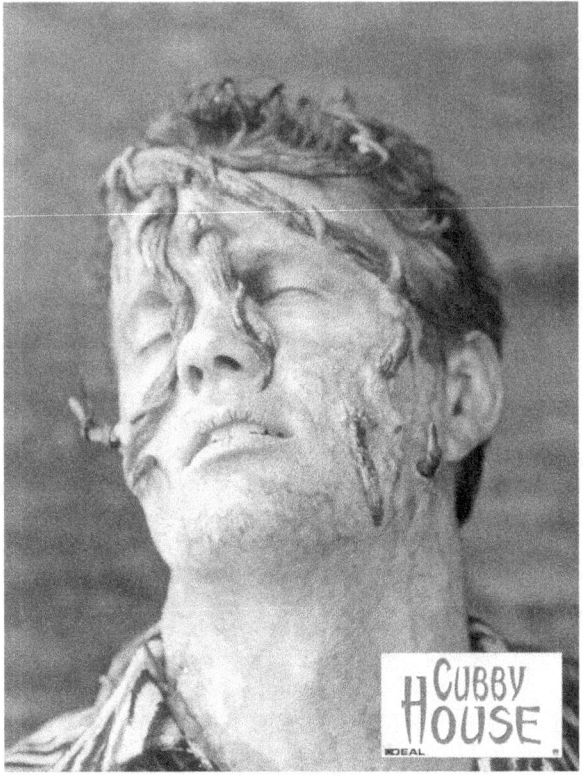

Bill (Craig McLachlan) is attacked by serpentine moving vines in a French lobby card for *Hellion: The Devil's Playground*, aka *Cubbyhouse* (2001).

What follows is later assumed to be another nightmare of Danny's, since we see him awaken from it at the end. A golden light from the cubby house introduces a vision of Byron and Hope to entice Ivan and Natalie. The voices of the children calling the names of the Grahams change to laughter to suggest their evil intentions. Toys are seen floating in the cubby house before the vortex appears in the wall. Fahey inter-cuts between the action in the cubby house and Harrison in his cell tossing in his sleep, before we learn his identity and location. Since both Harlow and Harrison are played by the same actor it is only Harlow's hair being shorter than suggests that this is not Harlow. If it is meant to be Harrison we do wonder why he hasn't aged in thirty years, as Harlow has seemed to. Harlow's opened eyes recall the cubby house doll's red eyes. Ivan chanting prefigures him holding a knife that he has found in the cubby house and cutting Natalie's willing arm, as we see that Harlow has bloody arms, though not how they were cut. The idea that what we have seen is just Danny's nightmare is violated by Lynn's discovery of Natalie wearing a bandage for the cut we saw Ivan make. Lynn accepts Ivan's implication that it covers nothing with his explanation that they were playing doctor.

see how Natalie gets away from then to appear in the cubby house. The expectation of Lynn slapping Danny for telling her that she is divorced because she couldn't keep her husband is met.

The voices heard by Ivan and Natalie in the cubby house suggest the dead children. The vines that seemingly cut the power to the computer that Lynn uses also allows for vines, symbols and writing to appear on the screen. Fahey uses a shock effect for the release of pages from the printer of the writing. He uses another for the first of three of Danny's nightmares about the vines, which here bleed when he cuts one. The blood drop from Natalie's cut finger absorbed by the floor is later changed when she shows her mother how she cannot get a blood stain off the floor. The wall that appears to be rubber that Ivan reaches his hand in and is grabbed is a weak special effect, although it does prefigure the vortex later seen. Danny's second bloody vine nightmare also features the vision of Harrison raising an axe to him, presumably after he has been freaked by meeting Harlow and researching the deaths of his children.

The romance between Danny and Bronwyn comes with its own heavy metal theme music to presumably appeal to teenagers. The subplot is intermingled with the cubby house narrative. The scene where Harlow visits Harrison presents one split screen moment between the actor playing twin brothers. Kirby steps on a cockroach as he enters the cubby house. The ability of Ivan and Natalie to bring on a plague of roaches to attack him follows Kirby calling himself the "King of Cockroach City." Some shots of the attack make the optical effect obvious. Others convey the appearance of real bugs on Kirby for disgusting realism, with added slow motion.

The killing of Harlow after his tiresome fight with Danny in the street is successfully presented by beginning with a vine that drags him down the water drain. Blood splashes on the camera lens and there is a funny touch of his glasses left behind and then taken by the vine. The vine emerging from another drain that comes out into the Graham house backyard is perhaps too convenient, but at least we get a button with the vine seen to be still holding Harlow's glasses.

The nails pushed out of boards covering up the entrance to the cubby house attest to the powers of the demon. Fahey has the last shot of *Alison's Birthday* watched on television by Danny. The view of Bronwyn's bedroom from Danny's room is another convenience. The expectation of her exposing her breasts is not met, as previously noted, when she turns off a light after removing her bra. The assumption that she was being unconsciously spied upon is proven to be false when Bronwyn tells Danny after he asked her what happened, "Show's over. Leave 'em wanting more." The couple kissing in the cubby house gets added interest from the fact of the expectation of an attack created but not met. This is represented by the sight of approaching vines, Natalie seen watching them and Bronwyn telling Danny that her behavior was altered as if she was possessed. This latter point is particularly important, as it presents Bronwyn to have more dimension than that of the female horny teenager. It also reveals that as a presumed virgin, she is not so different from the reactionary parents she criticized earlier.

Ivan and Natalie chanting for the second time is again inter-cut with Harrison in his cell, where we see blood on his hands. Fahey also inter-cuts quick repeat shots from the prologue of Harrison's axe strike. Blood seen on his cell wall by a nurse and then legs hanging suggests that he has cut and hanged himself. The legs grabbing the nurse, and then Harrison striking her, show that this is a ruse to enable him to escape.

Danny's third nightmare about the vines also features a shot of Harrison's axe before his vision of the strike, although our knowledge that Harrison is presumably at large informs Danny's vision. Fahey uses another shock effect for the grabbing of Bronwyn by Danny in her garden, with the relief that it is not a vine. Lynn's disappearance from the narrative after we see her prepare for the date with Bill is perplexing, seemingly a plot contrivance to allow him to be killed. It also hurts that the idea of Lynn finally agreeing to the date had the narrative potential to add depth to what is otherwise a conventional and thankless role, although Bill's manner of murder is the best use of the vines as antagonist.

His crotch is grabbed as a sly comment on his agenda with Lynn, indicated by his animal print shirt. A vine enters his mouth to drag him into the cubby house, and later a vision of Bill will be used to represent the demon. Bill's murder is also represented by the red glow inside the cubby house after he is taken. The shock of Harrison grabbing Danny when he is on the telephone with Bronwyn also gets a laugh as much as it pays off our seeing Harrison outside the house earlier. Equally funny is how Bronwyn enters the room to walk into Harrison's throat hold of her, and the explanation for his appearance is tempered by Danny fighting him simultaneously.

Harrison's pronouncement that he has come to save Ivan and Natalie puts a different spin on the prologue's presumed idea of him murdering Harlow's children. Rather he claims that he was attempting to save them then from exorcism, as he wants to do for Graham children now, but had erred in using the wrong name for Satan. This also partly alters our view of Ivan and Natalie, although we are aware they are possessed antagonists, to being protagonists needing saving. The furniture moved in the room to stop Bronwyn leaving to call the police is presumably empowered by the demon, who has also restored the cubby house to its original new state after reconstructing what we had seen Bill deconstruct. These powers will also be demonstrated later in the stakes that fly into the ground around the cubby house to form a fence and the stake that will kill Harrison.

Harrison advises that it is the third ritual that releases Satan's power for ever. Ivan and Natalie chant for the third time and Natalie cuts Ivan's arm instead of vice versa. The children's awareness of Harrison's efforts but lack of action to stop him is as contrived as their possessed facial expressions and attitudes. Fahey compensates somewhat with the shock of their dog attacking him and biting his neck, although it is an antagonist easily called off by Danny. Harrison is disposed of and Danny takes it upon himself to fight the demon. The wall where the vortex had been now becomes a screen for optical effects. There is a vision of Bill with the chainsaw we saw him use to deconstruct the cubby house, and Danny throwing a knife into the screen is a seemingly impotent act.

The climax now gives Ivan and Natalie the red eyes seen on Harrison and the doll and uses the screen as the vortex again. Satan is presented by a reptilian head, and Danny's victory seems far too easy over such an omnipotent supernatural being. The last gasp of the demon is setting the doll alight, which enables the whole cubby house to catch on fire, with a convenient gap in the staked fence allowing the protagonists to get out. After the main house door is shut in front of them, the garage door opens to allow tools fly and chase, another narrative contrivance. It is partially redeemed by the blade that slices the neck of the policeman who stands with the returning Lynn.

The epilogue sees a car containing the new family passing the Graham car as it drives away from the house. Fahey cleverly denies us the faces of the parents of the new family by only showing their feet getting out of the car and only revealing the child. He ends with another tracking shot that leads to the cubby house reconstructed once again.

Murray Fahey had previously made *Voyage into Fear* but has not made another to date. Producer Chris Brown had previously made *Komodo* and would go on to make the Australian horror titles *Triangle* and *Daybreakers* with the production company Pictures in Paradise. Producer David Hannay had previously made *Alison's Birthday*, *Kadaicha*, *The 13th Floor*, and *Out of the Body* but not another Australian horror title after *Hellion: The Devil's Playground*. Executive producer Mikael Borglund's prior efforts were *Cassandra* and *Cut*. Executive producer Gary Hamilton made *Cut* and would go on to make the Australian horror movies *Wolf Creek*, *Storm Warning*, *Acolytes* and *Nature's Grave*. *Hellion: The Devil's Playground* is the only Australian horror film to be made by the production company Cubbyhouse Productions to date.

American born Joshua Leonard made his film debut in the lead role in *The Blur of Insanity* (1999). Besides supporting film roles and television, he also essayed the lead in the romantic comedy *In the Weeds* (2000). After *Hellion: The Devil's Playground*, he played more film supporting parts and television, and the leads in the comedy *Larceny* (2004), the thriller *Madhouse* (2004), and the romantic comedy *Expecting Love* (2008), and directed *The Lie* (2011). Belinda McClory began her career in television and made her film debut in a supporting role in *Life* (1996). After appearing in more television and supporting film roles she essayed the lead in the thriller *Redball* (1999). After *Hellion: The Devil's Playground*, she appeared in the Australian horror title *Acolytes*. Lauren Hewett also began her career in television and made her film debut in a supporting role in the romantic comedy *Strictly Ballroom* (1992). Although appearing in more television and film shorts, she has not made another feature title since *Hellion: The Devil's Playground*.

Jerome Ehlers began his career in television and made his film debut in a supporting role in the western adventure *Quigley* (1990). He played the lead in the crime drama *Deadly* (1991), but prior to and after *Hellion: The Devil's Playground*, he has otherwise been seen in television and film supporting roles. However he did write the screenplay for the thriller *After the Rain* (2000). Craig McLachlan is another actor to have begun his career in television and made his film debut in a supporting role in *Mad Bomber in Love* (1992). He would essay the lead in the war romance *Absent Without Leave* (1992), but has otherwise played more television and film supporting roles prior to and after *Hellion: The Devil's Playground*. Joshua Tainish-Biagi also began his career in television and made his film debut here, after which he has been seen in more television. Amy Reti also made her film debut here and has not made another title to date.

Release

Screened at the Cannes Film Festival on May 18, 2001. Australian release date unknown. In the United States, released straight to video. The taglines were "A portal to unspeakable evil" and "Playtime will never be the same."

Reviews

"Fails to come up with anything very original or genuinely exciting.... Fahey seems constrained by the commercial demands to provide another thrill every few minutes. [The] thrills and spills are underwhelming and only the most tolerant fans of the genre will go for this minor-league shocker." — David Stratton, *Variety*, May 18, 2001

"Fun; probably more fun than it has any right to be." — Jared Roberts, *The Lair of the Boyg*, November 3, 2009

DVD

Released by Key DVD/20th Century–Fox on September 2, 2003. Released in Australia by Imagine Entertainment on November 10, 2006.

Queen of the Damned
Village Roadshow Pictures/NPV Entertainment/Material Productions, 2002 [aka *Interview with the Vampire II*; *The Queen of the Vampire*]

CREDITS: *Director:* Michael Rymer; *Producers:* Jorge Saralegui, Andrew Mason; *Co-Producer:* Channing Dungey; *Executive Producers:* Su Armstrong, Bill Gerber, Bruce Berman; *Screenplay:*

Scott Abbott, Michael Petroni, based on the novel *The Vampire Chronicles* by Anne Rice; *Photography:* Ian Baker; *Editor:* Dany Cooper; *Music:* Richard Gibbs, Jonathan Davis; *Production Design:* Graham "Grace" Walker; *Art Director:* Tom Nursey; *Set Designers:* Michael Bell, Fiona Donovan; *Sound Design:* Tim Walston; *Special Makeup Effects:* Bob McCarron; *Makeup and Hair:* Nikki Gooley; *Costumes:* Angus Strathie. Color, 98 minutes. Filmed on location in Melbourne, Eltham, Portsea, Ripponlea, Sorrento, St. Albans, and Werribee, Victoria; and Griffith Park Observatory, Los Angeles, from October 2, 2000 (end date unknown).

SONGS: "Forsaken" (Jonathan Davis, Richard Gibbs), Jonathan Davis, David Dralman; "Redeemer" (Jonathan Davis, Richard Gibbs), Jonathan Davis; "System" (Jonathan Davis, Richard Gibbs), Jonathan Davis; "Slept so Long" (Jonathan Davis, Richard Gibbs), Jonathan Davis; "Not Meant for Me" (Jonathan Davis, Richard Gibbs), Jonathan Davis, Wayne Static; "Body Crumbles" (Jeff Gutt, Judd Gruenbaum, Brandon Brown, Dan Hartwell, Jeff Blue), Dry Cell; "Cold" (Wayne Wells, Antonio Campos, Kenneth Lacey), Static-X; "Dead Cell" (Papa Roach), Papa Roach; "Stay Down" (Sunny Phillips, Christian), Candyhateful; "Excess" (Adrian Thaws), Tricky; "Invitation" (Robin Casinader), Robin Casinader; "After" (Tristan Hervo, Silvere Marcel), Wide Open Cage; "Temptation" (Frank Fitzgerald, Diana Williamson, Nikolai Rimsky-Korsakov), Sasha Lazard featuring E-Day; "Headstrong" (William Martin, Scott Kohler, Gary Couturier, Todd Wyatt), Earshot; "Penetrate" (Jason Miller, Ullrich Hepperlin), Godhead; "Down with the Sickness" (Mike Wengreen, Dan Donegan, Dave Dralman, Steve Kmak), Disturbed; "Change (In the House of Flies)" (Camillo Moreno, Chi Cheng, Abe Cunningham, Stephan Carpenter), Deftones; "Before I'm Dead" (Free Dominguez, Bruce M. Somers), Kidneythieves.

CAST: Stuart Townsend (Lestat de Lioncourt); Aaliyah (Queen Akasha), Marguerite Moreau (Jesse Reeves); Paul McGann (David Talbot); Vincent Perez (Marius de Romanus); Lena Olin (Maharet); Christian Manon (Mael); Claudia Black (Pandora); Bruce Spence (Khayman); Matthew Newton (Armand); Tiriel Mora (Roger); Megan Dorman (Maudy); Johnathan Devoy (James); Robert Farnham (Alex); Conrad Standish (T.C.); Richael Tanner (Young Jesse); Christopher Kirby, Miguel Ayesa, Joe Manning (New York Vampires); Pip Mushin (Guy Being Sucked); Kat Rhodes (Vampire Girl); Christopher Connelly (Mortal Yuppie); Renee de Bondt, Renee Quast (Vampire Girls Sucking); Dan Zizys (Vampire Doorman); Taylor Kane, Imogen Annesley, Daniel Schlusser (Club Vampires); Rowland S. Howard (Vampir Guitarist); Hugo Race (Vampire Bass Player); Robin Casinader (Vampire Pianist); Aimee Nash (Vampire Singer); Nicole Pantl, Alyssa McClelland (London Groupies); Marnie Reece-Wilmore (L.A. Groupie); Andrew L. Urban (Himself); Jo Buckley (French Journalist); Dino Marnika (Music Journalist); Kirsty Meares (Lifestyle Journalist); Bruce Myles, Marg Downey, John Dicks (Talamascans); Fouad Harraka (Greek Father); Mandie Vieira (Young Violin Player); Bobby Bright, Darren Wilson (Sound Engineers); Russell Kiefel (Fire Marshall); Nandila Gaskell, Nalshebo Gaskell (West Indian Girls); Tamasin Ramsay (Woman Victim); Michael Azria (VW Driver); Arrowyn Lloyd (VW Passenger); Antonios Greige (Camel Driver); Nicola Paull (Flight Attendant—Scene Deleted); Peter Olsen (Enkill); Franklyn Ajaye (French Dealer); Matthew Hassall (Lestat's Violinist Double); Duncan Myers, Mark O'Halloran (Rent Boys—Scene Deleted); Twapa Kapote (Prostitute); Ron Bingham (Businessman); Strawberry Fields (Girl with Businessman); Bob Halsall (Businessman with Girl); Antony Neate, Karoline Hohlweg, Rochelle Ward, Anni Finsterer, Alistair Reid (Euro Trash Vampires—Scene Deleted); Suzi Dougherty (Pale Faced Vampire); Humphrey Bower (Nigel); Pia Miranda (Jesse's Roommate—Scene Deleted); Simon Wilton (Vampire in the Park); Enrico Mammerella (Greek Fisherman); Serena Altschul (Herself); Nick Gill, Becky Thomas (Band Members). Uncredited: Felicity Andersen (Flight Attendant); Tracy Downs; Daniel Gardner (Lestat's Fan); Shayne Greenman (Band Member); Rashad Houghton (Queen Akasha's Voice); David Lorensene (Vampire); Anita Marelic (Goth Girl); Jet Tsui (Asian Vampire); Richard Wiggan (Plantation Worker).

Synopsis

In Glastbury, West England, the vampire Lestat is awoken from his tomb by the sound of music. He decides to become front man for the New Orleans death rock band "The Vampire Lestat." Since he admits to the world press that he is a vampire, he violates the rule that vampires must "remain in the shadows." Jesse is an apprentice for the London Talamasca Center for Paranormal Studies. She has been raised by vampires led by her aunt Maharet, and she steals Lestat's journal. From the journal she learns how Lestat was an 18th century French nobleman made a vampire in 1788 by the Mediterranean vampire Marius. During Marius' training, Lestat finds the tomb of Akasha and drinks her blood to revive her spirit. Lestat and his band go to Los Angeles for a concert in Death Valley.

Marius appears to warn Lestat that other vampires have conspired to kill him in his first public appearance.

During the performance, Lestat is attacked by Akasha. She flies him away to her island since she wants Lestat as her king for eternity. Wanting to settle the score she has with Maharet, Akasha flies Lestat to the Mojave Desert camp. She orders Lestat to kill Jesse, whom he has previously declined to make a vampire. Lestat bites Jesse and then feeds off Akasha. The ancient vampires allied to Maharet attack Akasha when she is vulnerable. Maharet takes Akasha's last drop and turns into a sleeping statue as the new queen after Akasha dies, and Lestat revives Jesse. The couple return Lestat's journal to David Talbot, the head of the Talamascans, and then walk into the night to spend eternity together.

NOTES

This film received notoriety because of the death of the actress Aaliyah during post-production and before its release. The film is dedicated to her, even though as the title character, she only has a secondary role. Director Michael Rymer uses the postmodern techniques of point of view, slow motion, blackouts, expressionist camera angles, time lapse photography and other optical effects. However, the result is mostly dull, conventional and lacking in suspense. As a vampire tale it features the theme of the malevolent supernatural being. It has a narrative that uses a fifteen minute flashback sequence for backstory, alternates victims as mortals and other vampires, and presents a protagonist with moral ambiguity. The screenplay offers some amusing lines and situations, and Rymer provides a variation on the standard vampire strikes with an impressive visual effect at the climax. One encounter shows gore as a shock effect, a beheading, and plenty of bloodletting as a requisite for a vampire story.

Under the opening credits are shots of Akasha's statue, although we won't return to her for another third of the narrative. The film's protagonist is presented as Lestat, whose long-fingernailed hand we see opening the lid of the crypt coffins where he rests. The idea that he has been awakened by the Goth band's music is a funny one. Equally funny is the idea of him wanting to be the group's lead singer, particularly as his voice is awful. The treatment uses narration as a device peppered throughout the screenplay, which may be done as a respect for the source novel's prose but reads as unnecessary.

Rymer uses the back and white music video footage of the band for the remainder of the credit sequence. In the DVD commentary Rymer comments that the music videos use imagery from *Nosferatu* (1922), *The Cabinet of Dr. Caligari* (1920), and *Dracula* (1932).

When Roger brings two groupies to Lestat, the expectation of his violent strike upon them is met. This is after seductive play which seems to suggest only sex, although sex and death seems to be the same thing for a vampire. This idea is reinforced in the scene where Marius turns Lestat into a vampire because of the homo-eroticism of Lestat sucking Marius' wrist to drink his blood after Marius has bitten Lestat's neck. Lestat's hunger, which exceeds Marius' offer, will be repeated in the film's climax when Lestat feeds off Akasha and thereby makes her vulnerable to attack. Lestat only discovers the secret passage to Akasha's tomb by accident. His violin playing awakens her, prefiguring the music that will later awaken him and linking these vampires to music appreciation. The idea that Marius calls Akasha his mother adds the perversity of incest to Lestat's attraction to her, although perhaps vampires are perverse enough already.

Jesse visits the Admiral Arms hotel, which she knows operates as a coven for vampires. Lestat is presented as a protagonist in the way he rescues her from the three vampires on the street outside and then as antagonist when he pricks her thumb on a jagged wall stone in order to taste her blood. However, Lestat's rejection of her with his line, "Your kind never satisfies my thirst," does not meet the expectation of his strike upon her. In the DVD commentary Rymer states that Lestat's prejudice against Jesse is due to his knowledge that she is a Talamascan. Another idea is taken from the Anne Rice source is that vampires only strike evil-doers, which Jesse is not.

When Marius visits Lestat in Los Angeles, Lestat makes a funny remark. "It's a little late to start to come over all paternal now, Marius. Two hundred years and not a word from you." There is another laugh from how they sit in a scaffold to view Los Angeles in front of the crotch of Lestat's billboard. Akasha has a funny entrance at the Admiral Arms hotel in the disparity of her period Egyptian goddess costume among the contemporary Goths. Her blackness among the all white coven makes her all the more exotic. In this scene Aaliyah has trouble with her dialogue and creates the expectation of a bad performance, something her later scenes disprove. Her grabbing the heart of a vampire to eat is the film's only gore effect apart from the blood

Poster for *Queen of the Damned* (2002).

drinking. The camera angle creates the expectation that she has actually grabbed his genitals, which would have been funny considering the seductive behavior of the victim. This scene also shows that Akasha has additional supernatural powers, rightly as a queen, in her ability to turn immolate vampires. Rymer makes her exit from the hotel a resonant image in the combination of her emergence from fire, her sashaying movement in slow motion, and score.

The voiceover narration supplies another funny line in Lestat's "Not only had the concert sold out among the living, it seemed the undead were coming too." Jesse as a band groupie willing to offer herself to Lestat is a repeat of her earlier intention from the encounter in the street. They have a witty exchange when he tells her, "I don't have time for this," and she replies, "All a vampire has is time." Rymer gives them a romantic moment when they hold each other to imply Lestat flying her as he inter-cuts aerial views of the city. Jesse scratches her breast to offer herself to Lestat and again he rejects her, his hesitance perhaps because he has feelings for her that he denies. His showing how he feeds, when he strikes a woman in the park, is perhaps his attempt to scare her away by showing that he is not a romantic creature.

At the concert, we see still vampires among the dancing mortals. The attack of the vampires upon Lestat on the stage results in one impressive effect. He decapitates one victim by cutting his throat and then pushing him so that the head is knocked off. An impaling of another vampire with a microphone stand is less gruesome. The fight sequence has humor from the fact the audience thinks it is part of Lestat's show. The vampires being burned suggests the arrival of Akasha, who enters amusingly bursting through the stage. Rymer adds an echo to Akasha's voice in the conversation she has with Lestat after she has shown him how drinking her blood allows him to be in daylight.

Aayilah sells the purplish prose, and the corpses we see strewn around the pool and beach are evidence of their presumed feeding. When Akasha and Lestat have sex by blood transfusion Rymer uses a montage of impressionistic images which he calls "blood flashbacks" in the DVD commentary. We don't know why Akasha feels she has a score to settle with Maharet. Rymer says in the DVD commentary that it is explained in Anne Rice's book but was too complicated to include in the narrative. But the climactic confrontation may be due to Akasha's intuition about Lestat's attraction to Jesse.

Lestat biting Jesse as per Akasha's order creates the expectation of her victory. The fact that he strikes Jesse's breast, where she had scratched herself earlier for him and not her neck, may be a clue. The attack of the Ancient vampires upon Akasha is presented as horrible, with our empathy going towards the sabotaged queen. Her ability to push away some of the attackers and immolate them suggests that she may be able to do so to all of them. This expectation is not met and Rymer tops the horror of the attack with the effect of her turning back into a statue and then to dust.

David reads the headline, "Lestat Concert. Drugs in the water?" in another touch of humor. The heavy breathing that David hears and that he investigates presents him as a Man in Peril. The expectation of David's attack by Lestat and Jesse is not met for the epilogue. The final moment of Marius passing Lestat and going into David's house suggests that Marius will strike David, which Rymer advises in the DVD commentary occurs in a later Anne Rice book where David becomes Marius' vampire partner. The final image of Lestat and Jesse walking away from the camera and into the night as time lapse photography shows time accelerating around them suggests their partnership and isolation from mortals as a romantic and yet still bleak future.

In the DVD commentary Rymer rationalizes his changes from the two Anne Rice adapted books, *Vampire Chronicles: The Vampire Lestat* and *Queen of the Damned*. This includes how Akasha was written by Rice as Caucasian and that the concert was held in San Francisco and not Los Angeles. It is said that Tom Cruise declined to repeat the role of Lestat that he had played in the fantasy *Interview with the Vampire: The Vampire Chronicles* (1994) and that Wes Bentley had been cast as Lestat but then dropped out of the film. The singing voice of Lestat was supplied by Jonathan Davies of the heavy metal band Korn.

The film is the only Australian horror title made to date by Michael Rymer, producers Jorge Saralegui and Andrew Mason, co-producer Channing Dungey, and executive producers Su Armstrong and Bill Gerber. Executive producer Bruce Berman would go on to executive produce *Ghost Ship*. Village Roadshow Pictures had previously produced *Bloodmoon* and would go on to produce the Australian horror title *Darkness Falls*. The film is the only Australian horror title to be produced by the companies NPV Entertainment, Material Productions, and WV Films.

Irishman Stuart Townsend made his film debut in a supporting role in the crime drama *Trojan Eddie* (1996), and continued to play supporting film roles. After his lead in *Queen of the Damned* he essayed the lead in the romantic comedy *The Best Man* (2005) but has otherwise appeared in supporting roles and on television. He also wrote and directed the actioner *Battle in Seattle* (2007). American born Aaliyah made her film debut in a supporting role in the crime drama *Romeo Must Die* (2000), and died in a plane crash on August 25, 2001, at age 22 before *Queen of the Damned* was released.

Fellow American Marguerite Moreau began her career in television and made her film debut in a supporting role in the action comedy *Champions* (1992) and continued in supporting roles and on television. After *Queen of the Damned* the actress essayed the lead in the romantic comedy *Easy* (2003), the surfing comedy *Off the Lip* (2004), and the horror title *The Uninvited* (2008), and continued in television and other supporting film roles.

British born Paul McGann also began his career in television and made his film debut in a supporting role in the comedy *Withnail and I* (1987). After more supporting roles and television, he played the lead in *Dealers* (1989), the thriller *Paper Mask* (1990), the horror title *The Monk* (1990), and the thriller *Downtime* (1997), his last leading role to date. After his supporting role in *Queen of the Damned*, the actor continued in supporting film roles and on television.

Swiss Vincent Perez also began in television and made his film debut in a supporting role in the comedy *Gardien de la nuit*, aka *Guardian of the Night* (1986). He played the lead in the comedy *Il viaggio di Captain Fracassa*, aka *Captain Fracassa's Journey* (1990), *La neige et le feu*, aka *Snow and Fire* (1991), *Line of Life* (1996), the title character in the action fantasy *The Crow: City of Angels* (1996), and the comedy *The Libertine* (2000).

After *Queen of the Damned* the actor would go on to essay the lead in the horror title *The Pharmacist* (2003), the title character in the romantic comedy *Fanfan la tulipe* (2003), the comedy *Bienvenue en Suisse* (2004), and *Demain des l'aube*, aka *Tomorrow at Dawn* (2009), as well appearing in supporting film roles and on television. Perez has also directed two features: the music romance *Once Upon an Angel* (2002), which he co-wrote, and the horror title *The Secret* (2007).

Swedish-born Lena Olin made her film debut in a minor role in *Ansike mot ansikte*, aka *Face to Face* (1976), and after playing supporting film roles and on television essayed the lead in *Pa iv och dod*, aka *As a Matter of Life and Death* (1986). The actress also played the lead in *S/Y Gladjen*, aka *S/Y Joy* (1989), but only appeared in supporting parts and on television prior to *Queen of the Damned*. However, Olin enjoyed a return to leads in the mystery *Devil You Know* (2009).

Release

In the United States on February 22, 2002, and Australia on March 13, 2002, with the taglines "The Mother of all Vampires," "All she wants is hell on earth," and "This time there are no interviews." The DVD features scenes that were trimmed or deleted. Deleted scenes include shots for the original opening that showed time lapse photography for the passage of time on the exterior of Lestat's tomb; Jesse's dream of herself as a child with Maharet, Euro Trash vampires and with her London roommate; a longer scene of Lestat talking with Marius on the beach that had moments deleted; a scene of Jesse walking in the street that leads to the Admiral's Arms; performance of the band at the Admiral's Arms; Lestat finding a clove of garlic in Roger's pocket in the scene where he brings him the groupies; Jesse on the plane to Los Angeles dreaming of being attacked by Akasha and the band watching their music video; the ancient vampires rising and them talking with Marius at the Hollywood sign; the end of the scene when Akasha leaves the Admiral's Arms and calls for Lestat, saying "Come out, come out. Wherever you are"; moments from the Los Angeles mansion with Lestat and Jesse talking before he takes her flying; scenes of Jesse writing Maharet a farewell note before she hitches a ride to the concert; and a scene of the band backstage before the concert.

Reviews

"Handsomely mounted, this direly conventional bit of vampire business is enlivened by flashes of humor and game performances. It isn't great entertainment or camp, but pic sets its ambitions so low, it can't help partially delivering on them."— Scott Foundas, *Variety*, February 11 2002

"Directed with meaningless fashion-victim chill by Michael Rymer, *Queen of the Damned* is itself a casualty of an awful trend, the corporatization of horror movies ... big-budget spectaculars with so much at stake, like Anne Rice's good will, that the studios can't afford any eccentricity, the kinds of idiosyncratic gestures that used to make horror movies memorable."— Elvis Mitchell, *The New York Times*, February 22, 2002

"[It] may not please everyone with its music video approach, but there's a feast of visuals to lap up with its spectacular production design and vampish escapism costumes of black leather. It's a dizzy ride of distinctive debauchery and a fun bloody feast of vampire diversion."— Louise Keller, *Urban Cinephile*, October 10, 2002

"Filled with MTV-style direction, many attempts to make a 'alternative' vision of a vampire movie and lots of dopey narration and at times muddled plotting; this is one awful movie.... The special effects are weak with too much CGI work and the whole movie just stinks."— Chris Hartley, *The Video Graveyard*

"This is as bad as a big budget movie can get. Bad writing, bad accents, bad voiceover, bad acting, bad everything ... even the FX often leave much to be desired.... The slight boost the film might've gotten by having a gothic nu-metal score involving many popular artists is lost completely."— Devon Bertsch, *Digital Retribution*, December 1, 2010

DVD

Released by Warner Home Video on August 27, 2002. Roadshow Entertainment (Australia) on October 16, 2002.

Darkness Falls
Distant Corners/Blue Star Pictures, 2003 [aka *The Tooth Fairy*; *Don't Peek*; *Fear of the Dark*; *The Tooth Fairy: The Ghost of Matilda Dixon*; *The Tooth Fairy: Every Legend Has its Dark Side*]

CREDITS: *Director:* Jonathan Liebesman; *Producers:* John Hegeman, John Fasano, William Sherak, Jason Shuman; *Executive Producers:* Derek Dauchy, Lou Arkoff; *Screenplay:* John Fasano, James Vanderbilt, Joe Harris, based on a story by Joe Harris; *Photography:* Dan Laustsen; *Editors:* Steve Mirkovich, Tim Alverson; *Music:* Brian Tyler; *Vocal Effects:* Gary Hecker; *Production Design:* George Liddle; *Creature Design:* Stan Winston Studios; *End Credit Design:* Maurice Binder; *Costumes:* Anna Borghesi; *Art Director:* Tom Nursey; *Set Decorator:* Rebecca Cohen; *Makeup and Hair:* Viv Mepham; *Sound Design:* Randy Thom. Color, 86 minutes. Filmed on location in Melbourne and Yarraville, Victoria; Sydney, New South Wales, the Gold Coast, Queensland; and Maine, USA.

SONGS: "Look out Below" (Brian Howes), Closure; "Hand of Emptiness" (Brian Tichy), Brian Tichy; "Gunboat" (Jamie Blake, Paul Andrews), Vixtrola.

CAST: Chaney Kley (Kyle Walsh); Emma Caulfield (Caitlin Greene); Lee Cormie (Michael Greene); Grant Piro (Larry Fleishman); Sullivan Stapleton (Matt McKelsky); Steve Mouzakis (Dr. Murphy); Peter Curtin (Dr. Travis); Kestie Morassi (Nurse Lauren); Jenny Lovell (Nurse Alex); John Stanton (Captain Henry McKelsky); Angus Murray Lincoln Simpson (Ray); Charlotte Rees (Ray's Wife); Joshua Anderson (Young Kyle); Emily Browning (Young Caitlin); Rebecca McCauley (Kyle's Mom); Daniel Daperis (Young Larry); Andrew Bayly (Officer Andy Batten); Aaron Gazzola (Little Boy); Cecelia Specht (Little Boy's Mother); Matt Robertson (Little Boy's Father); Mark Blackmore (Bartender); Joshua Parnell (Store Clerk); Rayne Guest (Spilled Beer Girl); Andrew T. Dauchy (Drinking Buddy); Bruce Hughes (Medical Examiner); Roy Edmonds, Phil Reilley, Mark Wickham, Marnie Statkus (Police Officers). Uncredited: Antony Burrows (Matilda Dixon); Gerard Cogley (Security Guard); Christopher T. Warren (Onlooker).

Synopsis

In the town of Darkness Falls ten-year-old Kyle Walsh pulls out his last baby tooth and leaves it for the tooth fairy. The fairy is the ghost of Matilda Dixon. One hundred and fifty years previously she had been unjustly hanged for the perceived killing of two children, who were later found alive. Matilda's curse is quoted as "What I took before in kindness I will take forever in revenge." She vows to kill anyone who sees her, and her ghost as a demon spirit wears a porcelain mask to hide her fire-scarred face. Kyle sees the demon's face but hides from her, although his mother is killed and he is thought to have murdered her. Twelve years later Michael, the nine-year-old brother of Kyle's childhood friend Caitlin, also suffers from night terrors and is haunted by the demon as he stays in Saint Francis Hospital. Caitlin tracks Kyle down in Las Vegas where he now works in a casino, and Kyle comes back to Darkness Falls.

Caitlin is now involved with the attorney Larry Fleishman, and when he takes Kyle to a bar for drinks, Kyle is taunted by Ray. Kyle walks away from the fight but Ray follows him outside to the porch and they fight in the woods. When Ray is killed by the demon, Kyle is accused of killing him and held in jail. Meanwhile Michael's doctors decide to put him in a sensory deprivation chamber to help him overcome his condition. Larry posts Kyle's bail and drives him out of town. After the demon kills Larry, Kyle goes back to the hospital. He convinces Caitlin not to let Michael be put in the dark chamber since he believes it will allow the demon to get him. When Kyle is taken back to the jail the police officers are attacked by the demon, and Kyle goes back to the hospital to rescue Caitlin and Michael. The demon kills the nurses and doctor who have seen her. The surviving policeman, Matt, drives his car into the hospital foyer to collect the survivors. They go to the town's lighthouse and Kyle finally manages to kill the demon when her face is exposed to the light and he burns her with the flame of a kerosene lamp.

Notes

A title that features the theme of the malevolent supernatural being has director Jonathan Liebesman overwhelm an interesting narrative antagonist with postmodern technique and fails to provide empathetic protagonists. He uses a seemingly constant moving camera, slow motion, point of view, expressionist camera angles, and quick edits for montage, and an obtrusive score. Liebesman also relies upon shock effects more than suspense and ultimately delivers a conventional product. Horror cinephiles will be frustrated by the minimal blood and gore in the treatment. Additionally the beauty of the tooth fairy demon is wasted, as she is presented with windblown black clothes and a porcelain mask to hide her burned face.

The prologue uses narration and a montage of sepia-colored photographs to provide the exposition of the legend of Matilda Dixon, with accompanying sound effects. In the filmmakers' DVD commentary it is told how the original epilogue had a child telling the legend of Matilda Dixon to a class. The blood from Kyle's pulled tooth is the first shown in the film. The commentary also advises that originally Kyle had stabbed a boy with a compass for reasons unknown and Kyle's Mom's dialogue to him was redubbed to remove the lines concerning this plot point. Caitlin's appearance at his window is the first shock effect. It sounds as if Caitlin's voice has been dubbed since it is worldlier than that of a ten-year-old girl, a character trait that is not carried over into the adult Caitlin.

Murmurs and growls signal the presence of the demon, noises that the commentary says are meant to be the gurgling of an old woman. A shock effect is used when her face is seen by the boy Kyle. Kyle's Mom is presented as a Woman in Peril when she investigates the noise of Kyle's scream. Another shock effect is used when Kyle from the bathroom grabs her arm. The expectation of an attack is created when she goes into Kyle's room and she sees the reflection of the demon in a mirror.

The narrative uses the convention of Kyle's Mom telling him that there is no one there before her attack, a device that will be repeated for more comic effect later. Kyle hiding in the bathroom rather than going to help his mother can be partially accepted by the fact of his being a child. The bathroom door opening is another shock effect, though thankfully, we are spared the cliché of the doorknob moving.

Liebesman provides two resonant images: Kyle half concealed by the shower curtain as he sits in the bathtub, and the windswept demon on the wall above the door seen from the aisle since the demon cannot enter the brightly lit bathroom. Liebesman uses the conventional dissolve of Caitlin from age ten to twenty-two for the change of actress. The information that Michael has lost his last baby tooth would seem to explain why he has gained the attention of the demon. Presumably him having seen her because he peeked after the tooth was left for her is the same scenario as Kyle's, although he is one year younger.

Liebesman uses fast edits for Kyle taking antipsychotics and a reveal for his wall drawings of the masked face of the demon. Larry gets a funny joke when he gives Kyle a beer, with "I figured you'd like this one. It's a light." This is considering how Kyle, and Michael, favor the light to keep the demon away. Kyle having visions of the demon and distorted sounds in the pub would seem to be paranoia based on the dark interior since the narrative does not have the demon attack inside the pub. Ray's antagonism towards Kyle in the bar is explained in the filmmakers' commentary by Ray being the boy that the Young Kyle had stabbed in school.

Ray's attack on Kyle on the bar porch is another shock effect. The expectation of the strike against Ray by the demon is met after he sees her face. Although there is the suggestion that the demon also attacks Ray because he has attacked Kyle, the attack by Ray seems enough justification for him to be punished.

Matt and the police officers search the woods after they hear a noise, which is presumably Ray's yell. This presents them as People in Peril (they are men and a woman). The device of a comic set-up to a shock is used when Ray's body falls onto Larry after he has repeated, "You're a grown man. Completely safe." This device will be repeated with Caitlin in her car: "I can handle this" before the shock of a black cat jumps onto the hood. Kyle being questioned by Captain Henry over the death of Ray allows more information about his past to be revealed. This includes how he spent nine years in an asylum presumably because he was thought to have killed his mother and told how the real killer was a demon tooth fairy, and how in that time he attempted suicide. The latter is a plot point that will be repeated with Michael's self-inflicted wounds.

Liebesman again uses quick edits for Kyle's purchases of flashlights at Barney's Goods and Hardware Store. We presume that he is stocking up, though later we realize that he has also bought flares, since he uses them in the hospital battle. Larry's car smashing into the tree in the woods is another shock effect, caused by his not watching where he is going as he argues with Kyle. It is also caused by the shock appearance of the demon in front of them; Larry being killed by the demon is an expectation met.

Given that the demon is supernatural, we can accept her ability to travel distances in order to harass Kyle and Michael separately, although her stamina and determination in tracking Kyle for twelve years has to be admired. Also to be admired is her cleverness in later taking out the lights on the police station and the hospital as a battle strategy. Kyle entering the room just as Michael enters the sensory deprivation chamber is conventionally perfect timing. The storm we see over the lighthouse aerial view is also a horror movie convention of dread and a prefiguring of the climax location.

Matt investigating a noise at the police station is him again as a Man in Peril, although the expectation of his attack is not met. The device of his flashlight losing its power is a moment of conventional suspense. Liebesman holds the dark screen for fifteen seconds, although using sound to suggest the demon's presence. The expectation of the shadow he sees and fires at being the demon is not met when he says that he shot Andy Batten's dog instead. However, the expectation of an attack upon Batten, left alone to watch Kyle and making fun of his fear of the demon, is one that is met. One might question the strategy of shooting at a supernatural being, but since she is later shown to have a gunshot wound in her mask, it doesn't read as silly as it initially seems.

The demon's attack at the hospital includes the shock effect of Kyle grabbing Caitlin to move her and Michael into the elevator, with it being stalled another conventional suspense device. The elevator doors being opened by Dr. Murphy is another shock. More suspense is used for Kyle, Caitlin and Michael climbing through the reduced space of the doors before the elevator cable snaps. The appearance of the two nurses and the decision for all of them to go through the darkened piped hallway to the foyer establishes a new team of protagonists. Although the order of the members being picked off by the demon is not a surprise, the lack of empathy created for the new team is disheartening. The deleted scene of the "hallway of lights" featured on the DVD creates some empathy when Caitlin and Nurse Lauren get separated from the others. Caitlin gets a laugh line at the sight of the darkened hallway when she comments, "This just keeps getting better and better."

Matt's police car smashing into the glass doors of the foyer is another shock effect, in spite of the horn blaring as a warning. Kyle's request for Matt to get gas cans to take to the lighthouse reads as a request unstated. Dr. Murphy's "We're safe in the car" is an ironic prelude to the shock of his being grabbed by the demon.

Matt also gets a funny line at the lighthouse with his "All this over a fucking tooth." Matt and Kyle needing to fix the generator creates the expectation of a demon attack, which is met, although the expectation of a fire being caused by all the leaked gas is not. When Michael is asked to pull the lever for the light of the lighthouse, suspense is added by the possibility of the flame going out and the advancing shadow of the demon. The expectation that the demon has been permanently repelled by the light is not met when she returns and grabs Kyle. Although her striking Kyle's eye has no seem-

Poster for *Darkness Falls* (2003).

ing effect, his knocking off her mask allows her real face to be exposed and her burning.

Liebesman errs in using the quick edits for the struggle so that we don't know what is happening. However, he succeeds in making the demon's destruction empathetic, much in the manner of the Queen of the Damned in that film. We miss the demon when she does not appear in the narrative epilogue, which creates the expectation of her return, which is not met. Rather we see what is the norm. Billy's mother is revealed, in a shock effect, to be the giver of the money as the tooth fairy even after he peeks when his father warns him not to.

The DVD featurette *The Legend of Matilda Dixon* says that the film was inspired by real life events in the small fishing town of Port Fairy, South Australia.

In 1840 Matilda's face was burned in a house fire after which she wore the porcelain mask and would only go out at night to deliver her tooth fairy gifts. On September 3, 1841, apparently two children went to visit Matilda and could not be found. She was accused of killing them and hanged. After the hanging the two children reappeared, but Matilda was already dead. In 1861 the cemetery where she was buried was moved to a new location for the original land to be used in another way. In the hubbub, Matilda's body was lost. A memorial that was created for her was desecrated in 1951 by teenagers who subsequently went missing, although it is thought that they probably just left town on their own. A new plaque was made in 1953, and there has no been no more trouble with children since.

DVD commentary also states that another original idea was to have delayed the sight of the demon until it took Larry. This was to suggest that Kyle was madder than he claimed to be and that perhaps he was the killer. The original creature was a winged and toothy Angel of Death played by actor Doug Jones, who was taken out of the film. The design by Steve Wang bears no resemblance to the final creature created by the Stan Winston Studios.

The writers' commentary reveals that the film was based on a five minute short film written and directed by Joe Harris entitled *Tooth Fairy* (2001), and that earlier drafts of the screenplay included many ideas that were subsequently dropped: the demon lived in another dimension in a castle made of baby teeth, which her porcelain mask is also made of. Kyle, Caitlin, Larry and Matt had deliberately pulled their baby teeth and held a séance to await the Tooth Fairy, but fell asleep before she came. Young Kyle's annoying older sister was killed first rather than his mom. The narrative moved to twenty years later rather than twelve. Michael was Caitlin's son and not her brother, and it was explained what had become of Caitlin's parents when Michael was her brother.

Kyle worked in a Las Vegas strip club. Larry was Kyle's cousin. The bar that Larry takes Kyle to was a strip club. A character called Old Moe was a vagrant and seen in the jail where Kyle is held as someone who had seen the demon and spent all his subsequent life waiting for her to kill him. Michael was given a brain scan rather than put into the sensory deprivation chamber. Larry's car crash was under water and he pulled himself out of the water by holding onto the arm of the demon, unknown to him. Matt looked at a box of pictures of child murders in the police station backroom. Caitlin was visiting Kyle in jail when the power went out and the demon attacked. Kyle was blinded by the lighthouse bulb that burned the demon, and the demon appeared to Billy in the epilogue without harming him because he had not peeked a look at her.

Darkness Falls is the only Australian horror title made by director Jonathan Liebesman, producers John Hegeman, John Fasano, William Sherak and Jason Shuman, executive producers Derek Dauchy and Lou Arkoff. It is the only Australian horror movie made by the production companies Distant Corners and Blue Star Pictures.

American Chaney Kley began his career in television and made his film debut in a supporting role in the comedy *Legally Blonde* (2001). He essayed the lead in the mystery *The Skin Horse* (2003) and after *Darkness Falls* would go on to play the lead in *Mr. Blue Sky* (2007) as well as appear in supporting film roles and on television. Fellow American Emma Caulfield also began her career in television and made her film debut in *Darkness Falls*. She played the lead in *Bandwagon* (2004), the comedy *TiMer* (2009), and the thriller *Confined* (2010), as well supporting film roles and on television.

Lee Cormie also began in television and made his film debut in *Darkness Falls*. He has gone on to otherwise appear in more supporting film roles and television. Another television beginner, Sullivan Stapleton made his film debut in a supporting role in the romance *River Street* (1996) and after playing more supporting parts essayed the lead in *City Loop* (2000), but after *Darkness Falls* he has not played another leading film role to date. Steve Mouzakis also made his film debut here after starting in television, and he has continued supporting roles.

Release

The United States on January 24, 2003, and Australia on August 28, 2003, with the taglines "Stay in the light!" "Every Legend Has Its Dark Side," Evil rises," and "An eye for an eye. Your life for a tooth."

The DVD has deleted scenes. These are the Young Caitlin giving the Young Kyle a sun charm necklace, telling him, "I believe you"; Dr. Murphy's advice to Catlin that she get the opinion of someone experienced, which leads her to ring Kyle; Caitlin hanging up on Kyle and him looking at the necklace she gave him to make him decide to help her; Dr. Murphy explaining to Caitlin how he has brought in a specialist, Dr. Travis; Dr. Murphy initially refusing to join the others in the darkened corridor but changing his mind when frightened by a light that goes out in the direction he is headed in; a "hallway of lights" a demon coming face to face with Kyle, a moment kept in the film for later; Kyle throwing the necklace he received from Caitlin to break a window and let light in; Caitlin and Nurse Lauren separated from the others and advancing with their eyes closed following Kyle's voice; Nurse Lauren reciting "Hail Mary" but seeing the reflection of the demon when she opens her eyes prematurely and being taken by the demon, while Caitlin does not open her eyes and reaches Kyle for a hug; and the final confrontation which includes some minor and unnoteworthy additions.

REVIEWS

"Film lovers beware! The evil spirits of boredom will befall should you enter a darkened cinema and endure *Darkness Falls*.... An abhorrently loud, brash and boorish creature feature starring a CGI ghost that fails to scare, Darkness Falls ... quite literally ... flat on its face." — Shannon J. Harvey, *Urban Cinefile*

"An efficient little horror movie [which is] about as scary as a ride on a minor roller coaster." — Stephen Holden, *The New York Times*, January 24, 2003

"An entertaining, if mindless, horror flick that has some logic lapses and is sort of predictable but is quickly paced, has good effects and is fairly fun. It's not bad but it's not spectacular; however it is steadily directed." — *Video Graveyard*

"The movie is okay, I guess, if only because it finally introduces a situation where flashlights do make a logical weapon choice. A lacklustre monster, a boring story, and overlong at 85 minutes (which includes 11 minutes of end credits), Darkness Falls is one to skip." — Devon Bertsch, *Digital Retribution*, July 4, 2006

"Liebesman opens his movie in quite the tension laced fashion, unfortunately he blows his load in doing so. Liebseman is unable to capture the glory of his opening gambit as *Darkness Falls* swerves off the road and into the swamp of mediocrity." — Jeff Ritchie, *ScaryMinds*

"The great, eerie beginning gives way to tepid one-liners and an almost video game-like plot, with the characters having to overcome objective after objective. Truly disappointing, because the creature design was quite good, giving the Tooth Fairy some genuine menace, looking ethereal yet all too real." — Carl Lyon, *Monsters at Play*

DVD

Special edition released by Sony Pictures on September 2, 2003.

Lost Things
ISM Films/Agenda Films, 2003

CREDITS: *Director:* Martin Murphy; *Producer:* Ian Iveson; *Screenplay:* Stephen Sewell; *Photography:* Justine Kerrigan; *Editors:* Karen Johnson, Benita Carey; *Music:* Carlo Giacco; *Production Design:* Karla Urizar; *Costumes:* Theresa Jackson; *Sound:* Andrew Belletty. Color, 80 minutes. Filmed on location at Tuggerah Beach, New South Wales.

CAST: Leon Ford (Gary); Charlie Garber (Brad); Lenka Kripac (Emily); Steve La Marquand (Zippo); Alex Vaughan (Tracey); Vanessa Downing (Brad's Mum); Annie Byron (Emily's Mum); George Whaley (Emily's Dad).

SYNOPSIS

Four eighteen-year-old school friends — Gary, his cousin Brad, and their girlfriends Emily and Tracey — go on a weekend surfing trip to a secluded beach. A surfer forager, Zippo, finds the teenagers' camp and warns them to leave because he says three people were killed there and another went missing. The teenagers decide to stay, but become concerned when Emily goes missing. After she returns, Zippo arrives and Brad stabs him, fearing he has a knife. They teenagers bury the dead Zippo and decide to flee the site leaving behind Emily, who claims that their leaving is pointless. The van is attacked by what appears to be Zippo on the track back, and they return to their camp. Emily helps the others to remember that they were the three people who were killed at the site a year ago, and their spirits appear to be trapped in a limbo.

NOTES

With a narrative that plays with time and reality and finally becomes too ambiguously clever for itself, this title features the horror of personality. Director Martin Murphy uses the postmodern techniques of optical effects under the opening credits, point of view, slow motion, out of focus effects, expressionist camera angles and hand-held camerawork, memory flashbacks with quick edits, flash-forwards and time lapse photography. A good score deteriorates at the climax into an obtrusive one. Killings are performed with a knife and no accompanying gore. Murphy goes in for more shock than suspense, although an eerie mood of foreboding is presented. The screenplay provides some humor in regards to teenage angst and stupidity, and there is one scene repeated and extended to suggest the complicity of Emily in the murder of her friends.

A prologue has Tracey on a telephone call with Emily as we see Emily meeting with a man we will later recognize as Zippo from his wearing army fatigues. Given what we know of the fate of the teenagers, this opening can be interpreted as Emily's original meeting with Zippo as the devil "charmer." This is in order to lure the other three to their deaths, although the trip is presented as the return of them to the site a year later. The mannequin arm buried in the sand of the beach and the later sight of the buried mannequin's body with its eyes removed would seem to be omens perhaps made by Zippo. They also prefigure the buried bodies of Gary, Brad and Tracey.

There is a funny exchange when Brad tells Emily that he thinks he has been in the area before, when the van is thought to be lost. This is before they find the beach; Brad is looking into the sun in a moment that will be later repeated:

EMILY: Brad feels like he's been here before.
GARY: Great. Get him in here and he can navigate.

The isolated beach and the track to it surrounded by bushland recalls the same in *Long Weekend* and its remake *Nature's Grave*. The bare breasts of Tracey and Emily read as exploitative, given the context of Tracey sunning herself and Emily baring her breasts to compete with Tracey. Zippo is seen on the bushland around the beach in a shot of his legs before his face is shown when he appears to warn the teenagers. The warning seems odd if he realizes that they are ghosts and not able to leave anyway. His explaining his bandaged arm was due to a fishing accident might have been a better payoff if we had seen him being injured by one of the teenagers in their fight for life.

The DVD audio commentary says Steve Le Marquand had injured his arm in a motorbike accident prior to filming and his arm is bandaged because of an operation. Emily's idea of leaving the site after Zippo's warning seems to be disconnected to her awareness of Zippo's identity. As with Tracey's later desire to leave after the snake incident, the idea is soon dropped by the person who raises it.

The visions that the teenagers have of each other are peppered throughout the narrative until their realization of their condition. The dead bunch of flowers that Tracey finds, like her ring that Emily finds, will both get payoffs later. This is when the flowers are seen left by Brad's Mum and Emily's ring is pulled off when her dead body is dragged by Zippo. The red belly snake that Zippo kills to save Tracey from is a red herring. Although Zippo tells of the death adders that lay under the sand waiting to strike, none ever does in the narrative, though Emily describes herself as a death adder in her diary that Tracey reads. Tracey's scream and the impression that Brad and Gary have that she been attacked by Zippo when he is seen with his bandaged arm around her neck creates a certain expectation of Zippo's threat. This is misleading for the moment. The blood from the stuck snake is the treatment's first show of blood.

The issue of Emily having gone missing is a plot point whose payoff is muffled by the time jumping. There is ambiguity attached to Brad's seeing her having sex with Zippo since this could be another flash-forward, though witnessed by someone who is meant to be dead. What he sees is lessened because there is no consequence since he doesn't try to intervene, and he doesn't tell the others, including Emily, what he saw. The DVD commentary also points out how Brad's view changes the human legs that are presumably Emily's to mannequin legs, which may be the reason he does not mention the vision.

When Gary finds Zippo's site in the search for Emily there is another funny exchange between them:

GARY: All I want to know is, where is Emily?
ZIPPO: Ask her.
GARY: Don't try and fuck with my mind, man.

Zippo telling the teenagers that he is "a thousand years old" and "old as sin" confirms the idea of him as the devil. He may also be joking to the eighteen-year-olds who consider him old when he only looks to be in his thirties. Brad's stabbing of Zippo is in reaction to Brad's vision of Zippo stabbing Gary as an event we later see. The "mimby" spirit in the bushlands seems to exist only as a shock effect since it has no later plot payoff unless we are to consider that Zippo has some relation to it. The blood we see pour from Zippo's grave may be an indication that he is not really dead. The hand bone in Zippo's lair that the teenagers find cannot be identified as belonging to anyone in the narrative. It may suggest that Zippo has killed others before the three teenagers, as does the container of eyes they also find, which also recalls the eyeless mannequin seen earlier. The DVD commentary states that Zippo has a severed penis in a jar, to which one of the teenagers responded, "He's got a dick in a jar." The line was deleted. The Polaroid photograph they also find of themselves, presumably taken by Zippo, prefigures those appearing in the Australian horror title *Wolf Creek* and is the sign of people being stalked.

The image of Zippo attacking the van when Gary, Brad and Tracey try to drive away via the track is hard to read. They have just apparently buried Zippo, who we thought had been stabbed dead by Brad. This is on top of the idea that the three are already dead from having been stabbed by Zippo. However, if we are to read Brad stabbing Zippo as Brad's ghostly imagination, then we can think the same of the Zippo's attack of the van. After this Murphy uses time lapse photography as if it is a rewind of the van's driving to show that perhaps it never occurred, although he will repeat the footage of Zippo's van attack after Emily comments, "It's already happened." Murphy uses Emily's request for Tracey and Brad to look at the moon as a transition for a memory flashback to daytime where Gary is killed, so that the return to nighttime explains why Gary is not with Tracey and Brad.

Murphy jumps back in time for Gary's argument with Tracey and Brad after they find Zippo's body is no longer buried. His decision to abandon them can be read as a fateful horror movie conventional error of the person who isolates themselves, creating the opportunity for them to be killed, although we have seen how Gary is killed in front of the others. Gary's vision of his own buried self suggests that the teenagers' memories of their own deaths are returning. The argument scene between Brad and Emily is repeated, but this time extended to show how her telling him that she is not the "nice girl" he believes her to be implies her relationship with Zippo and her complicity in the deaths.

It also ends with Brad being more aggressive with her than he had previously told Gary, in the face of her rejection. He holds her down rather than simply grabbing her hand, as he had earlier claimed. Emily has Brad and Tracey look at the full moon as it dissolves to the sun, showing how the nighttime events may be their imagined fiction; all of Zippo's stabbings occur in daylight on the beach. His attack upon Tracey is the most duplicitous since it begins with his seemingly comforting her before he strikes. Her blood drops on the sand show how alien human blood looks on the white pure sand.

Additionally, Brad stabs Zippo after he has seen him having anal sex with Emily, and there is the suggestion that Zippo's knifing will be more sadistic than it turns out to be.

Murphy has the teenagers seen observing themselves, and Brad's Mum leaving the flowers, in visions to show that the dead are not resting in peace. We don't learn what happened to Emily, who is the person we presume is now missing but not dead. Perhaps it is only known that the three are dead because their bodies have been found, which is suggested by the police tape we see at one point, and Emily's has not.

Murphy ends the film on Brad deep in thought back at the side of the road where the teens had stopped to check the map. This adds the suggestion that perhaps all we have seen was his imagination and nothing had really happened. The DVD commentary also states that the film's ending had been changed after they filmmakers saw *Donnie Darko* and realized that their proposed ending was the same. They do not give details about their original ending other than it paid off Gary's earlier mention of his hat having gone missing.

Interviewed in a DVD featurette, Murphy says that the film was inspired by a Frederick Neitsche story of the eternal return, where people are fated to relive events of their life over and over again. He also repeats an anecdote heard in the audio commentary where a parks and wildlife ranger had visited the location during filming on Halloween night. The company was told how some children were murdered and buried at the same site ten years previously. *Lost Things* is the feature directing debut for Martin Murphy, who has not made another film to date. It is the only Australian horror movie made by producer Ian Iveson to date and the only Australian horror title to be made by the production companies ISM Films and Agenda Films.

Leon Ford began his career in television and made his film debut in *Lost Things*, after which he has only been seen in supporting film roles and more television. Charlie Garber also made his film debut here, and after it has played in other supporting roles and on television. Lenka Kripac also began in television and made her film debut in a supporting role in the comedy *The Dish* (2000). She continued in more supporting film roles and television. Steve La Marquand also began his career in television and made his film debut in a supporting role in *In the Winter Dark* (1998). He has continued in supporting film roles and on television. Alex Vaughan also made her film debut in *Lost Things* and has otherwise worked in television to date.

Release

In Australia on November 11, 2004, with the tagline "A weekend to remember." No American feature release.

Reviews

"An understated cerebral film that burns slowly into your mind ... one of those psychotically gentle movies that at times seems obvious ... almost too obvious, but still keeps you guessing until the very last frame." — J. R. McNamara, *Digital Retribution*, August 15, 2006

"Fresh and unpredictable, with top performances and an intelligent script.... Murphy's direction is assured and keeps us involved, off balance and entertained." — Andrew L. Urban, *Urban Cinefile*

"[It] owes something to the classic British ghost movie, *Dead of Night*, but don't expect too much in the way of horror action. This is a slow-burning movie, a character study set against a creepy packaging, and, within its modest, unpretentious packaging, it's pretty effective." — David Stratton, *At the Movies*, November 11, 2004

"A sparse, atmospheric film that applies considerable sophistry to the telling of a simple story.... It looks beautiful and it never resorts to the crass or the cheap." — Kyla Ward, *Tabula Rasa*

"It employs a basic Twilight Zone structure. The very observant will figure out what lies behind the veils, and the rest will have to think about it, but eventually realize that the film does make some sense.... Not a bad little film which succeeds remarkably in making a sunny, inviting beach in broad daylight seem frightening." — Tuna, *Movie House*

"I'd be tempted to say that figuring [it] out is half the fun, but it turns out it's actually no fun at all. I'm sure director Martin Murphy had more in mind than giving us a massive brain cramp, but if you can figure it out be sure to let me know." — Christopher Null, *Filmcritic.com*, August 11, 2006

DVD

An American DVD was released by the Maverick Entertainment Group in 2004 but is out of print. Released by Accent Film Entertainment (Australia) on June 4, 2005.

Razor Eaters
Hybrid Films, 2003

CREDITS: *Screenplay/Director:* Shannon Young; *Producers:* Nick Levy, Paul Moder; *Executive Producer:* Ranald Maclurkin; *Photography:* Karl Siemon; *Editor:* R.J. Maclurkin; *Music:* Jim Shnookel, R.J. Maclurkin; *Sound Design:* Steve Burgess; *Special Makeup and Effects:* Mary Cleary; *Sound:* Rob Hornbuckle, Simon Wright, Simon Endberger. Color, 99 minutes. Filmed in Melbourne, Victoria.

CAST: Paul Moder (Detective Inspector Danny Berdan); Richard Cawthorne (Zach, aka Peter James Vessi); Teague Rock (Orf, aka Orville Hurstleigh); Fletcher Humphrys (Roger Rocatenski); Campbell Usher (Anthony); Matt Robertson (Chris); Julie Eckersley (Jenny Berdan); Angus Sampson (Syksey, aka Andrew Lloyd Sykes); David Bradshaw (Hersch); Vince Gil (Lonnie Evans); Shannon Young (Rob); Peter Hoskins (Mr. Hurstleigh); Craig Madden (Garth); David Serafin (Parking Inspector); Chris Mclean (Dean); Nathan Bosckay (Jason); Jeanette Cheah (Jenny Chen); Simon Gowling (Tony Stapedo); Stuart Orr (Tailgater); Cameron Knight (Peter); Ben Dixon (Stevo); Drew Basford (Darren McKellar); Michael King (Paul McKellar); David Tulk (News cameraman); Jacinta O'Dowd (Forensic Officer); Leigh Whannell (Nick D, scene deleted); Julieanne Tait (Reporter); John McConnell (Defense Minister Brian Worthy, aka Politician); Ian Young (Water Wally); Gawain McLachlan (Cop); Shaheer Akbam (Impound Manager); Sadie Kohl (Mickey Briggs); Paul Khoury (Dealer 1); David Ewing (Dealer 2); Danny Esber (Adam Starr, aka Bouncer); Denis Rebic (Kevin, aka Pitbull Trainer); Georgina Hallam (Tina Labass, aka Advertising Executive); Caroline Witchell (Casino Manager, scene deleted); Ayla Audelle, James Tinney, Isaul D'Sousa (Paramedics); Margie Bainbridge, Adam Vorherr, Bryan Duke, Ayla Claudelle, Lisa Baldwin, Ashley Bear, Mickey Nguyen (Press); Justin Fowler, John Lowry, Anthony Fricka, Anthony Woodcock, Chris Longheed, James Romeril, Nick Baker, Tony Edney, Marc Wilson (Police); Leisha Young, David Lorensene, Gerry Raffaut, Judy Poll, Mark O'Donovan, Jack Lambeth, Bob Laidlaw, Brett Lambeth, Shara Huren (Razor Fans). Uncredited: Chris Lougheed, John K. Lowry (Policemen); Steve Syson (Detective); Nathan Hill (Policeman).

Synopsis

Detective Inspector Daniel Berdan goes to the house where the gang The Razor Eaters has been located and leaves it after the house explodes in fire. Reviewing the video footage that the gang had filmed of their exploits, Berdan follows the progression of their crimes in country Victoria. These are done as revenge against drug dealers and people they see to be social undesirables. He also recalls the police's inability to track the gang even when the Razor Eaters send the police clues, realizing that they must be caught to achieve the infamy they desire. The gang moves to Melbourne and attack the lair of Darren McKellar. His younger brother Paul tells Berdan of their location at the home of Garth, unaware that the gang has planned it, so that the police will arrive to find a bomb ambush.

When Berdan goes to the house alone, he hears the gang members arguing since Anthony is against the police trap. Before Berdan enters the kitchen where the gang is, Anthony shoots at the others and is killed. Berdan shoots the still-living Zach, who is thought to be the leader, and gets out before the bomb goes off. Orf has survived Anthony's shooting, and he appears at Berdan's home. He has Berdan's wife, Jenny, tied to a wheelchair bomb. Orf boasts to being the gang's real leader and allows Berdan to untie Jenny if Berdan lets Orf escape. However, once outside, Orf triggers the bomb and the Berdan house explodes.

Notes

This crime thriller features the horror of personality in the form of gang members who kill people in their crime spree upon drug dealers and other people they dislike. Director Shannon Young employs the postmodern techniques of slow motion, expressionist camera angles, jump cuts and especially point of view. The latter is a device of one of the gang, ironically played by Young, which records their activities with a video camera. This adds immediacy and a kinetic energy to the treatment, although the video footage presented under the guise of being reviewed by the narrative protagonist has clearly been edited, and the narrative also includes the plot of the police tracking the antagonists. The treatment provides bloodletting, torture and some gore, as well as several explosions. It also presents the antagonists as eloquent and witty to create empathy and moral ambiguity.

Under the opening credits we see Berdan's arrival at Garth's house and entering the property, although we aren't shown what he finds inside until the climactic memory. The time and memory structure that the narrative uses is the usual movie convention of seeing oneself in a memory that one did not see originally. It presents the video footage of the gang members who are all, apart from Orf, now dead, although this fact is not realized until the end. Berdan therefore entering the house with his rifle and then shown leaving suggests that he has used it to kill the gang and somehow enabled the house to be set on fire, an assumption that will be disproved in the climax. Young uses echoed voices heard by Berdan when he is at his home and before he plays the video to suggest aural memory and flash-cuts for visual memory. We wonder how he got the video footage if the house presumably containing them is burned and the evidence destroyed.

A title card reads "One week earlier" to begin the chronology of the gang's crimes. The video footage shown starts with them in a house they have broken into. We don't see the owners return before the convenience store holdup is shown. The gang's name is never explained and we don't see them performing the title literally. The gang not killing Jason, the convenience store clerk, is a relief, although they will not be as sparing of the Tailgater. Zach's funny tirade against the Tailgater recalls that of Robert Loggia's Mr. Eddy in the mystery *Lost Highway* (1997). This preempts the gang's attack of other non-drug dealer figures in the "Dungeon of Arseholes" and the Tailgater being shot is shown to be done by Roger as arbitrary fate after he fires at him in the dark of night.

Garth being a wheelchair-bound drug dealer is an interesting touch of ambiguity. The motivation given for the gang's anti-drug stance is said to be a brother of Zach's who became a drug addict. Later we hear the tale of Roger's younger brother who was killed in a home robbery by a drug addict. This motivation will also prove to be ironic, given that when Orf tells Berdan that he is the real gang leader it is implied that he was a drug dealing rival to McKellan.

In the electronic store robbery Roger jokes, "The prices are crazy. We're practically giving them away" to parody advertising for sales as he steals appliances. He also scores a laugh when seen choosing what CDs to take with "I just don't listen to anything, you know." The gang members read their press coverage, show clippings to the camera and post them on the walls of Garth's house. This is their appreciation of their fame. Young uses aural news reports for the same effect: to present the world view of the gang and update the number of dead victims. We aren't shown the Tailgater's shot body as it appears covered when the police talk over it, but the treatment's first presentation of murder occurs with the gang invading the house of Lonnie Evans. Orf will explain in the climax to Berdan how Lonnie was targeted as one of the McKellar gang. The fact that Lonnie is an arms dealer and has explosives will up the level of violence of the gang's actions. When Lonnie is shot in the back by Zach, Young has blood splatter on the video camera lens, the only time he uses this gruesome effect. Anthony's shooting of one of Lonnie's men is viewed as his initiation into the gang which makes Anthony's final turning against the others to be read as either a betrayal or an expression of his greater morality.

The t-shirts that Syksey has made up for the gang reads on the back, "Organise. Traumatise. Immortal." A message to the public has Zach say, "To those on our side, if you can't join 'em, beat 'em" as a reversal of the proverb "If you can't beat 'em, join 'em." Roger shooting garden gnomes can be read as an action against bad taste similar to his punching Water Wally wasting water hosing his driveway and Roger hosing his face. The police interview with Syksey breaks the flow of the video coverage. The police at the Orchid Thai restaurant, where it is reported but not seen that the gang has struck, continues this focus on the police as protagonists, which lessens the treatment's pace. The gang at the Tow Away Pound resumes the video footage, although the expectation of an attack upon the bureaucratic impound manager is not met when we later see he has survived the bomb attack. Equally, the expectation of a strike against the news cameraman is not met, since the gang uses him to pass on video footage to the media.

The scene of the gang watching the television screening of the footage has multiple use of point of view. The gang is on the watched footage wearing masks, watching the footage, Rob films the gang watching them watching the footage, and Young presents the scene of Rob filming and Berdan watching what Rob has filmed. Berdan tells Jenny to leave town because he fears for her safety. This initially reads as soap opera, although her suspicion that he is going to perform an act of vigilantism to capture the gang partly justifies his request. This warning is later seen to be warranted in light of the gang's attack upon her and her eventual entrapment by Orf. The narrative never makes the plot point of Berdan's vigilantism in a previous case clear, something which Berdan discusses with Jenny in a deleted scene, with the gang also being aware of it.

Young's use of the video used by Rob to interview Orf and later Roger includes inter-cuts to edited footage of the subjects. The jump cuts we see in other scenes make it apparent that the video footage has been edited. In a deleted scene Rob says that the equipment taken from the electronic store now enables him to edit footage and add music. These inter-cuts get past the contrivance of technique by showing Orf making a bomb and Roger handling his rifle as expressions of the behavior of the two characters. Orf's interview also supplies the back-story information that the five gang members all met in juvenile detention, which explains their bond. This is particularly important for Zach and Anthony, since Zach's feeling towards Anthony as a replacement younger brother makes his seeming betrayal all the worse.

The gang at Parliament House in the daytime begins their collection of undesirables who become the "Dungeon of Arseholes." We aren't shown the politician being taken, but we do see the parking officer being attacked. The expectation of his strike is met, after the video camera described as the television station WFOS is explained to stand for We're Full of Shit. The football player Tony Stapedo refusing to sign an autograph for Anthony is, like the politician, another victim we don't see attacked. The carjacking of the car of Chapel Street Boys Peter and Stevo is funny in Zach's mental torture of them by having them repeat insults while guns are held to their heads.

The advertising executive and the dog trainer, like the politician, are not shown to have done anything specific against the gang. At least the bouncer is seen to spit at Roger. The expectation of the dog trainer being attacked by a dog is met when we see the police discovery of the resultant strikes against the dungeon victims the next day. The bloody dog revenge recalls Roger's interview comment about how he prizes dogs above humans. Young uses photographic freezes for images of the victims with cards around their necks describing their crimes. The discovery of the dead drug dealer in a pool of blood after having been shot in the head follows him having needles in his chest in the dungeon, with Tony Stapedo's bloodied broken knees perhaps the worst for the surviving victims.

The video sent to the police is shown to be of the gang's idolatry, a kind of rock concert, although they don't play music, they sign autographs and finally fire guns over the heads of their fans. This fandom is followed with fans at the site, where another drug dealer's house is rammed with a car by the gang, and Rob is seen as one of the cameramen filming Berdan talking to the press. This shot of Rob is one of the few times we see him out from behind the camera, and it gets a sly turnaround in

Anthony's turning the camera onto him. This scene shows Anthony's discouragement with the gang and Rob's humiliation in being filmed against his will. This perhaps motivates him to want to kill Anthony, independent of Zach's later idea of finding Anthony a "liability." It is presumed that Anthony is not taken for the McKellar strike and Rob's attempt to shoot Anthony is an act that is interrupted by the other members returning from that scene.

The scene of the police finding the slaughter at the house of Darren McKellar allows Young to present perhaps the most blood and gore in the treatment; McKellar's head is apparently hammered in. The voiceover of Paul is used to lead Berdan to Garth's house after burning the tape he had left by the gang when they visited his house. This visit, where we see Zach holding a photograph of Jenny, is used as a threat to Berdan. It is only later that the rest of the tape viewed by him will show how at the time the gang had found Jenny, who we had thought had gone away. The fact that we don't know exactly what has happened to Jenny in between the invasion of the house by the gang and Orf's appearance doesn't seem to matter, since she has remained relatively unharmed.

Roger having been injured in the massacre is perhaps a further sign of the gang's downfall, after Zach's rejection of Anthony. Young spares us the sight of the iron Zach uses to cauterize Roger's wound. Young also repeats the film's opening shots of Berdan approaching the house but this time inter-cuts to Berdan later watching the videotape of the gang and them in real time arguing. When Anthony aims a gun at Zach it creates the expectation of him being stopped, with the additional expectation of Berdan entering the room. This makes Anthony shooting Zach and the others, and being shot by Roger before Berdan enters, all surprises.

Berdan's entry is presented first in a mirrored reflection. Zach is shown to be wounded but still alive, and it creates the expectation, which is met, of Berdan shooting him as well as finishing off Roger. Young also has Berdan see the filming video camera on a tripod with only forty-five seconds left on the bomb timer. Again we wonder how he had time to retrieve the video collection before the resultant explosion. Another contrivance is the fact of the additional footage seen by Berdan of Jenny's attack in the house being after a filmic pause, although Young covers it by having Berdan watching static.

Once we get past the further contrivance of Orf in Berdan's house with the tied up Jenny and the bomb in the wheelchair, the narrative creates two more expectations. They are that Berdan will kill Orf and that Jenny will be blown up. The fact that Orf is willing to let Berdan untie Jenny is because presumably in exchange he will let Orf escape. However, since Orf hesitates once he gets outside, the expectation of him setting off the bomb is created and met. The resultant coverage of the explosion and fire doesn't reveal if Berdan and Jenny survive.

Young films their attempt to flee in slow motion. Since he doesn't show them surviving, the assumption is that they do not, aligned to the idea of Orf escaping victoriously from the scene. This downbeat ending sees the protagonist presumably defeated and one of the antagonists surviving. The edited video footage under the closing credits is equally ambiguous, being either celebrating or denigrating the gang and their crime spree.

The film is dedicated to the memory of Professor Wayne Levy, teacher and filmmaker. Shannon Young made his film directing debut with *Razor Eaters* and has not made another title to date. He also made his acting debut in a minor role in *A Bullet in the Arse* (2003); *Razor Eaters* is also is his last acting title to date. The film is the only Australian horror movie to be made by producers Nick Levy and Paul Moder and the production company Hybrid Films to date. Moder had made his film debut in a supporting role in the horror actioner *Bloodlust* (1992). After playing in more supporting film roles and television, he essayed the lead in *A Bullet in the Arse*, which the actor also produced, co-wrote and co-directed. After *Razor Eaters* he played more supporting film roles and television.

Richard Cawthorne was born in Hong Kong and began his career in shorts and television. He made his feature film debut in *Razor Eaters* and later appeared in more film supporting roles and television. Teague Rock began his career in television and made his film debut in a supporting role in *Pozieres* (2000). He continued to play supporting film roles and in television prior to and after *Razor Eaters*. Fletcher Humphrys made his film debut in a minor role in *The Heartbreak Kid* (1993) and continued in film supporting roles and television before and after *Razor Eaters*. Campbell Usher made his film debut in a minor role in the comedy *Prisoner Queen* (2003), and after working in television made *Razor Eaters* as his last role to date.

Release

Screened on July 13, 2003, at the Melbourne Underground Film Festival and received a wide release in Australia on July 10, 2006. Release in the United States was in 2007, though date unknown. The taglines are "The film that launched a police investigation" and "Organise. Traumatise. Immortalise."

The DVD has deleted and extended scenes. The extended scenes are Berdan at home, Berdan and Chris at the shooting gallery, Berdan interviewing Jason, a reference to Roger as Lee Harvey Oswald, the gang preparing for the attack upon Lonnie, playing with the guns in Lonnie's house, Anthony's video interview, the gang reading the newspaper articles about themselves, the police discussion of Ken Bone, who was a 1980s bank robber, Berdan talking to Hersch, the gang's torture of the Peter and Stevo, the police finding the body of the shot drug dealer seen in the "Dungeon of Arseholes," and Nick D. interviewing Berdan outside the drug dealer house where the car had been driven inside and the reporter interviewing fans. The deleted scenes are video footage of the gang introducing themselves, Zach warning the gang not to masturbate in the same scene where Orf and Anthony are also shown to be filming, Rob commenting that the equipment from the electronic store raid can now enable him to edit footage and add music, Berdan and Jenny having sex but being interrupted by a telephone ringing that he answers, Zach discovering that Roger has masturbated, Orf using a grenade to blow up a garden gnome, Berdan cooking dinner for Jenny, the gang stealing the car they will use for the pound bombing, Garth in his wheelchair on the floor of the house being ignored by the gang, Berdan's confession to Jenny that he set up a criminal to get him convicted, the gang parked in the street to observe Berdan after he talks to Syksey in his store, Orf making a bomb to plant under Berdan's car and Beran finding it, Berdan's vision of the ghosts of Zach and Roger with Jenny in his house, more "Arseholes" for the dungeon — Craig Bromley, a debt collector, and Adriana, a casino manager, Zach telling the gang about Operation "Makin' Bacon" where Berdan will be blown up in Garth's house, and Zach telling of the plan to have Paul McKellar leak the location of the gang to set up the police for the bomb ambush since the police are said to be the gang's greatest enemies.

REVIEWS

"A mixed bag of thriller, quasi-documentary and vague social commentary ... has energy, but is never particularly convincing. Recalling the likes of *Romper Stomper* and *Man Bites Dog* in a more imitative than flattering way. Adequately handled effort aims for shock value, but in the end, seems familiar and rather conventional." — Dennis Harvey, *Variety*, May 25, 2004

"The story isn't very interesting and has been done to death by many other movies. The acting is mediocre. But I have to give these guys some props for pulling off some cool scenes and explosions. There were also parts of the movie that were sort of fun, but overall I just found this movie to be a drag." — John "El Juan" Shatzer, *Bloodtype Online*

"The best Australian film ever made. Classy, intrepid and totally refined.... Young's directorial stamp is made up of such strong wax that no one could even try to do it better. Destined to be the next great cult film and deserves to find a great deal of success all over the world." — Daniel Bernardi, *Film Threat*, August 7, 2005

"This is truly a piece of cinematic terror that projects a raw and real portrayal of youth on a brutal rampage.... Young's overall direction is seamless and is surely the roadmap for many things to come." — Steve Genier, *Cinema Nocturna*

"Has the kind of intelligence, energy and filmmaking ingenuity that American independent cinema once had in abundance but seems to be too rarely displaying these days. It's a little ragged round the edges, but in these days of over-polished, CG-driven mainstream pap this only serves to increase the film's outsider appeal." — Slarek, *DVD Outsider*

"In spite of its confrontational approach and an unreserved violent tone, Razor Eaters proves to be a lackluster affair.... [It] offers nothing new and lacks anything to make it worthy of a recommendation. As heavy-handed and self-important as the gang it portrays, Razor Eaters is a total misfire." — Paul Pritchard, *DVD Verdict*, June 6 2008

DVD

Echo Bridge Home Entertainment on June 10, 2008. Released in Australia by Fox on October 17, 2007.

Subterano

Becker Films/Showtime Australia, 2003

CREDITS: *Director:* Mort S. Seben; *Producers:* Richard Becker, Barbi Taylor; *Executive Producers:* Richard Becker, Michael Bischoff; *Screenplay:* Esben Storm; *Photography:* Graeme

Wood; *Editor:* Simon Martin; *Music:* Chris Weller, Curl Cross; *Production Design:* Chris Kennedy; *Art Director:* Scott Bird; *Sound:* John Patterson, Penn Robinson; *Costumes:* Tess Schofield; *Makeup and Hair:* Jennifer Lamphee; *Visual Effects:* Phenomona at AAV. Filmed in Sydney, New South Wales, in 2000.

SONG: "I Am" (Chris Welter, Curl Cross, Sven Schumacher).

CAST: Alex Dimitriades (Conrad); Tasma Walton (Grace Stone); Alison Whyte (Sheriff, aka J.D.); Chris Haywood (Ian Cleary); Kate Sherman (Angie); Jason Stojanovski (Slick); Scott Swatwell (Max); Veronica Segura (Monkey); Nikolai Nikoloaff (Todd); Shane Briant (Cunningham); David No (Colonel); Morgan O'Neill (Chauffeur); Annette Shun Wah (Presenter); Cristina Pettenon (Newsreader); Troy Planet (Cashier, aka Attendant); Christian Marchington (Jake); Larry D'Ercole (Emboman); Miguel Ayesa (Puppeteer); Nicholas Gregory-Roberts (Squish); Michael Saunders (Bickle); Morgan Evans (Homeless Guy); Nina Therapou (Molly); Michael Anderson (Voice of the Messenger); Keith Scott (Voice of the Puppeteer). Uncredited: John Clayton (Bruce); Anne Tenney (Elaine); Alyssa-Jane Cook (Mary); Janet Edwards (Laura); James Judge (Military Police); Barry Quinn; Sascha Raeburn (Video Game Girl).

Synopsis

Some time in a future world, Conrad is an assassin for the group "Orphans for the Revolution." He escapes from the vehicle that was transporting him to his execution. He finds his former girlfriend, Grace Stone, who drives him to the Embo Industries car park (parking garage), "Safe Park." The car park is closed for the night and Conrad, Grace, and a group of feral children are locked inside with Sheriff. They are challenged to play a game with Emboman. People are killed one by one by Emboman's toys. His virtual reality figure is defeated by Conrad, who discovers that he has a son by Grace, named Jake. Conrad, Jake, and Grace exit the car park through the sewers and head to the mountains. Emboman is revealed to be Todd, the son of Cunningham, the president of Embo Industries.

Notes

Based on comic book stories, this ridiculous science fiction story features the theme of the horror of personality in the succession of murders that occur under the guise of a virtual reality game held in a building parking garage. Director Mort S. Seben overdoes the postmodern techniques of slow motion, point of view and expressionist camera angles, jump cuts and a roving camera. He also pitches performances at an arch level. Given the established threat, there is some suspense, with a few shock effects, and two gory deaths. The film is unsatisfying as both horror and drama. It fails to rise above the comic book mentality of the material, and the screenplay is lumbered by lame puns and soap opera.

The film begins with a black screen and the sound of a helicopter. There is a news report about the hijacking of Conrad's vehicle, although the footage we see occurs before his driver can report what has happened. There is an element of homoerotisim in Conrad having stripped the driver down to his underwear to have taken his suit. The expectation that Conrad will shoot the driver is not met, which would seem to nullify Conrad as the murderous assassin he is meant to be. Cunningham's scene in his limousine provides a proposed trailer for the new Emboman game, which he calls "shit." Cunningham dismiss Ian Cleary with "You're just a shape on my screen," a line Todd will repeat to Conrad in the film's climax. Cunningham also not having time to speak to Todd would seem to give Todd the motivation to create his own version of the game, although ultimately he doesn't win.

The Safe Park car park has a sign that reads "Trespassers Xecuted." This prefigures the deaths that will occur for the trespassers, although the Cashier and Sheriff being employees don't qualify as such. The Cashier talking about sex on the telephone to what we presume is a prospective date is given an erectile light on his desk. His murder includes the payoff of him having a chain of condoms around his neck when he is found. His death is prefigured by the Messenger watching him, in a treatment where the action is seen via security cameras as Emboman's point of view. Although it is unseen, his yells are heard by Conrad in the car park.

It would seem that Grace taking Conrad to the car park is foolhardy, although we presume that she is not to have known how it will trap the both of them inside. Sheriff's comment to Conrad that "I don't think I like your attitude" is met by his "I don't like your perfume." This is highlighted by how close she stands to face off to him. When Sheriff asks the multi-colored haired ferals for identification, Max turns around and farts at her in response. Sheriff's resultant head-butting Max pays off her earlier use of the line to Conrad in a funny way. Sheriff is established in the narrative as a dividing presence among the group that are the protagonists to the Emboman's antagonist. She will ultimately consider taking Conrad in for his reward more important than defeating Emboman.

The attack of Monkey as she sits on the toilet makes her doubly vulnerable. High angle shots and jump cuts are used before the Messenger appears with the expectation created for the attack. Like the Cashier, the attack on her is suggested by her scream, and it will only later be shown when Slick puts his head in the orb. The Messsenger's claim that he has taken her would seem to deny her death, although this claim is later confirmed as a lie. When the Messenger deconstructs to slip down a drain hole, its body turns into ball bearings. This is something that also occurs with the other toys, although describing them as toys gives a false impression of their threat. The "Flatten" car which growls recalls the battling vehicles in *The Cars That Ate Paris*. When Conrad's reckless driving causes the inhabitants to get thrown around inside, Grace's excitement about being physically close to her former boyfriend is a camp-ish touch. After the group's car crashes, the image is repeated from two different angles in the security monitors. This is a device that demonstrates that the monitors are recording events and will be paid off when Emboman rewinds for a "flashback" in order to read Grace's address from her papers displayed to Sheriff in an early scene.

Each floor of the car park has a different color lighting scheme, and the ceiling neon lights flicker on and off for ambience. A circling camera is added for the killing of Ian Cleary, which ironically makes Chris Haywood's performance unbearable to watch when Ian begs not to die. The expectation that he will be killed is created and met with two effectively gruesome attacks. His feet are cut off by a wire, and then the Sluggo toy stabs him in the eye. Given that the Cashier also seemed to lose an eye, Sluggo may have performed the same action for him.

After the murder, Emboman comments, "What an eyeful," and the Messenger tells Conrad, "My friend Sluggo and Mr. Cleary didn't exactly see eye to eye." When Conrad replies, "You're a sick fuck," the Messenger says, "I know. I've been a bad toy."

When Angie is attacked by multiple spears and lifted into the air, her electrocution is introduced by Emboman saying, "Welcome to my Web site. You'll really get a charge out of this one." The fact that the expectation of Angie's death is not met is perhaps influenced by the group who free her from the spears having her repeat the mantra of "I'm going to the mountains." This is something which it seems she ultimately will achieve, although her vision of white light and the mountains can also be interpreted as her immediate death before she is seen to survive the ordeal. Whether Angie has survived the attack, however, is not immediately apparent. Conrad carrying her body is ambiguous, since we only learn later that she has been unconscious and not dead.

The expectation of Slick's death is met when he puts his head into the orb to see the fate of Monkey and Max, who turn out to have been murdered and not taken as the Messenger had said. Slick's beheading is commented on by Emboman as "That's what I call a head job." When Emboman says "Time to pump up the volume," a mirror ball appears, the lighting becomes red and fractured, and dance music is heard.

Sheriff aiming her gun at Angie and using her as a means to force Conrad to find a way out of the car park is an odd narrative choice. It establishes her as the dividing force in the group, which will be paid off when she is attacked by Conrad and killed by Grace and not one of Emboman's toys. The idea that she wants to get out of the car park would seem to be the same as the others, since it was perhaps only Slick who was more interested in playing the game. As the car park's employee, it would seem that she would know a way out better than Conrad, although it is presented as if she is reliant upon him to find one.

When the group goes behind the car park wall to find a water-filled backroom, they are out of range of Emboman. This is presumably because the room is not covered by the security cameras. Conrad finding a plug to release the water and that leads to the sewers is a plot contrivance. The drain itself is a bit of red herring. We see how both Angie and Grace will go down it and return to the car park when needed, and at the film's end the three survivors travel back through the drain to escape.

When Conrad returns to the car park, Emboman says, "No more Mr. Nice Toy." Sheriff's shooting the mirror ball with "I hate disco" is the narrative's one funny line. The blood from her mouth when she is shot by Grace is the death in the film that is presented with graphic bloodletting. This is saved for an unlikable character.

The plot point of Molly's appearance is truly bizarre. It pays off Emboman's flashback. However, the idea that a nanny would bring a child to a locked car park in the middle of the night, even if asked to by her mother, is totally unbelievable. Perhaps what looks like a billiard ball in her dead mouth is the payment for her act of silliness. Additionally, bringing Jake to the scenario adds the element of soap opera to the narrative — "I have a son" — even if it does raise the dramatic states for Conrad. At least Emboman's comment "It's a family affair" makes fun of the situation.

Grace provides the rationale for her having informed on Conrad because Jake's life was being threatened. It was an act of maternal protection. This changes our former perception of her as a duplicitous femme fatale. Regrettably, having Grace as a mother also prefigures her survival, even after her battle with Emboman creates the expectation that she has been killed.

Prior to what is initially presumed to be Grace's death scene, after an attack by the "Fat Boy" toy, she teases Emboman by offering her body to him. This moment, although obviously a ploy by her, only makes sense in retrospect when we realize that Todd is Emboman and can be seduced by a woman. The scene's erotic potential is also different in tone to the rest of the film, although it does recall the homoeroticism of the opening scene. Emboman's silence as a consideration of Grace's offer is a welcome relief to the cartoon action.

Before we see that Jake is real, we hear his voice calling out. In spite of our view of the dead Molly, the idea that he is not really there and his voice being a creation of Emboman is a plot point not taken advantage of. However, while the narrative shows the child in a toy car as vulnerable, he is never shown to be in danger from Emboman. This is presumably because Emboman is more interested in Conrad. The ball bearings that form Emboman's surrogate to face Conrad get two resultant lines. Conrad comments, "Gotta lotta balls, I'll give you that," and Emboman replies, "I'll show you my balls."

The narrative uses a horror convention and a shock effect. Conrad hides behind a pillar, looks twice around him and is then confronted by the threat at the third look. Despite the surrogate being seen to be on wheels, Seben has it move in supernatural ways, and the strikes against Conrad are shock effects. Conrad's defeat of the surrogate is inexplicable. The destruction of the creature, despite it being presented as an antagonist, provides some pathos in its vulnerability of being cut in half and burning.

Todd is generous enough to unlock the car park once he has lost the game to Conrad, though Conrad leaves via the sewer. There is no narrative payoff to Todd being revealed as Emboman when he goes to bed upon hearing that his father has come home, although his telling Squish about the game suggests that he is lining up his next player.

Seben ends the film with a freeze frame of the survivors jumping out of the sewer with the view of the mountains that Angie had seen. There is an ironic news report on the black screen which tells of the bodies found in the car park and spins the deaths as the work of the Orphans of the Revolution.

Mort S. Seben is a pseudonym for Esben Storm. The film is the only Australian horror title he has made to date. It is the only one by producer Richard Becker and his Becker Films Production Company, and executive producer Michael Bischoff. Producer Barbi Taylor had previously co-produced *Roadgames*.

Alex Dimitriades made his film debut in the title role but not top-billed in *The Heartbreak Kid* (1993). After working in television he played the lead in *Head On* (1998) and supporting film roles, including *Ghost Ship*. Since *Subterano*, the actor played the lead in the comedy *Bang-Bang Wedding!* (2008), and has played more film supporting roles but has not made another horror title to date.

Tasma Walton made her film debut in a supporting role in the thriller *Fistful of Flies* (1996) after working in television. After *Subterano* she had a supporting role in the Australian horror title *Safety in Numbers*, as well as other supporting film roles and more television.

Release

Apparently the film was shelved for three years and then released straight to DVD in the United States and Australia with the taglines "Evil on every level," "Evil lurks on every level," and "The next level in terror."

Reviews

"An average and familiar movie with few rewards. The last scene left an odor of cheese in my living room so strong that I am still trying to get rid of it." — Michael Mackey, *Monsters at Play*

"What starts out as a claustrophobically tense tale of lurking dread à la Cube quickly degenerates into convoluted, conspiratorial mumbo jumbo and some sketchy sub-plot about a holy mountain where men live freely?! ... Although the production was obviously made on the cheap, the cinematography is perhaps the film's biggest asset." — Robert Winter, *Digital Retribution*, November 28, 2007

"If you can ignore the pseudo-futuristic technology and clothing, *Subterano* is a good, violent romp. Although it needs to be said that the movie constantly shows more ambition by way of irrelevant storyline than it does concentrating on its bloodletting." — *BeyondHollywood.com*

"From the plastic-pants costuming to the ultra low-grade effects to the lack of any discernable acting talent, *Subterano* is nowhere near worthy of its pretty cool title and bloody-hand-reaching-up DVD cover.... The script is plodding, and the direction is simplistic. *Subterano* just isn't scary, interesting, or close to watchable." — Christopher Null, *Filmcritic.com*, January 28, 2003

DVD

Released by REP Films on January 28, 2003, and Magna Pacific (Australia) on November 26, 2003.

Undead

Spierig Films, 2003

CREDITS: *Screenplay/Editor/Producers/Directors:* The Spierig Brothers; *Photography:* Andrew Strahorn; *Music:* Cliff Bradley; *Production Design:* Matthew Putland; *Special Makeup Effects:* Steven Boyle; *Costumes:* Chintamani Aked; *Sound:* Peter Spierig; *Art Director:* Jane Cuiverhouse; *Set Decorator:* Maxine Dennett. Color, 104 minutes. Filmed in Woodford, Queensland, from August 6 to September 2001.

SONG: "Little Green Men" (Cliff Bradley, Damien Taylor), Buttkrak, heard when crowd welcomes the aliens.

CAST: Felicity Mason (Rene Chaplin); Mungo McKay (Marion); Rob Jenkins (Wayne); Lisa Cunningham (Sallyanne); Dirk Hunter (Sergeant Harrison Ringwald); Emma Randall (Constable Molly Ford); Steve Greig (Agent); Gaynor Wensley (Aggie); Noel Sheridan (Marvin "Chip" Chipperson); Eleanor Stillman (Ruth); Robyn Moore (Constable Wendy Moore, Officer in Locker Room); Robert Johnovic (Man in Office); Peter Mensiorin (Fred, the Cricket Batsman); Jacob Andriolo (Young Cricketer); Michele Still (Screamer); William John King (Angry Father); Tom Dickinson (Fisherman 1); Brad Sheriff (Fisherman 2); Georgia Potter-Cowie (Young Zombie Girl); Francesca Arakemian (General Store Owner); Kyan Marie Salter (Baby in Crib); David Whitcomb (Newsreader); Paul Guthrie (Disco Zombie); Rob Doran (Bullet Wound Victim); Kristiana Maric (Marion's Ex-Wife); Ann Ricketts, Saive Norris, Cyril Ungyari, Matthew Boyle, Urani Buchanan, Stephen Woodward, Lisa Puddicombe, Troy Linster, Anne Taylor, Scott Hamilton, Paul Nash, Peter Norton, Jenni Lynch, Kathleen McGowan, Paul Guthrie, Chintamani Aked, Marc T. Brailak, Craig Woodward, Sharon Reeves, Dinez Kassif, Adam Kilnan, Nadia Isippi, Claire Hallam, Alan Gibbs, Renie Dignam, Michael D. Dimarikis, James Brough, Megan Bennetts, Christopher Armstrong, Troy Perry, Romina Castano, Brendan Rook, Julie Lee Rae, Osman Asian, Jason King, Justin Palazzo-Orr, Jo Wintzer, Tanya Batorsky (Zombies).

SYNOPSIS

In the country town of Berkeley, Rene Chaplin has been named the 2002 Catch of the Day Queen. After inheriting her grandmother's debt-ridden farm, she decides to leave town with an agent. Meteorites strike and start turning those they hit into zombies. On the road Rene and the agent are confronted by zombies and he is killed. Fleeing during an acid rain outpour, she seeks help at the farm of Marion of Marion's World of Weapons. Marion and Rene are joined by the pregnant Sallyanne, her husband Wayne, and police officers Harrison and Molly, who also flee the zombies. When the zombies attack the house, the six hide in Marion's bomb shelter, but Sallyanne's labor makes then re-emerge. Fighting off the zombies, they drive away but discover that there is a spiked wall blocking the path out of town.

Harrison climbs the wall and discovers electrified clouds at the top. He falls and dies when the acid rain returns, as the rain burns the clothes of the others. Marion assumes that the plague is now airborne since Molly gets infected, but the acid rain returns her to being a human before she is abducted into the sky by a beam of light. The others drive to the General Store to get new clothes and supplies before heading to the airfield. The zombies attack again and Marion is abducted by the aliens. At the airfield the zombies begin to be transformed back into humans and then abducted. Sallyanne is also abducted and an alien reveals itself to Rene. It comments how the rain cures the plague before also abducting her.

Wayne flies a plane and sees the abducted humans suspended in the sky, crashing into some, including Molly. He flies over the wall and parachutes to the ground, where he finds a crowd of people who have come to welcome the aliens, and armed forces. The abductees are lowered by the aliens, the spiked wall is lifted, and the alien aircraft flies away. Sallyanne has her baby in hospital, but when Wayne meets Marion there he bites him. The plague has returned, and Rene keeps guard on her farm against the zombies that are held in a cage.

Notes

An overlong narrative mars the otherwise quirky and funny treatment the Spierig Brothers give to this tale of zombies and aliens that features the theme of the malevolent supernatural being. The Spierigs use the postmodern techniques of expressionist cameras angles, quick edits, point of view, slow motion, and an obtrusive score. They also create suspense in spite of using shock effects, and provide plenty of gore for horror enthusiasts. The narrative makes an interesting climactic choice in revealing how the aliens we thought to be antagonistic are actually benign friends who help to cure the plague the meteors have introduced, although a second plague follows after the aliens have left, for a downbeat ending.

The Spierigs present the men of the town of Berkeley as ocker (redneck) grotesques, including Chip, the bank manager with the combover. The plot point of Rene inheriting her grandmother's farm isn't given a payoff until the end. The first meteor hits Ruth, who is zapped behind the two drunken Fishermen, who in the foreground add humor. The idea that she has been killed is expected but not met when she revives with a hole in her chest. Her knocking the head off one of the drunks makes the screen go red from the blood spatter for the opening credits. These feature the white billowing clouds that will signify the appearance of the aliens and monsters eyes and the growls that will signify the zombies.

When Rene's agent stops at the sight of the car pileup, the expectation of an attack is created and suspense introduced when he goes to investigate as a Man in Peril. Inter-cuts are used between the agent who finds a girl in one of the stopped cars and who is shown with her back to him, and Rene who sees meteorites in the sky. The girl's strike upon the agent is not shown, although her growl is heard. It is a surprise when the agent appears back at Rene's car with a cough for a shock effect, and his attack is another shock effect, the attacker unseen.

Clouds appear behind the zombie that Rene cuts in half to change the color palate to blue. Another shock effect is used for the agent turning into a zombie and him being shot by Marion, whose face is not revealed until the scene in his house with Rene. The agent being cut in half so that his bottom remains standing with his spinal cord gets a laugh, and the Spierigs like it so much that they repeat it later.

The car pile up is again used for the arrival of Wayne, Sallyanne and Aggie Whipple for Aggie to be the Woman in Peril investigating the crash. The scene allows for the reveal of Sallyanne's pregnancy, which will become a plot point. A shock effect is used for the girl zombie's fist through Aggie's head. The girl eating Aggie's brain is the other presentation of this behavior, although Marion will speak of it as what zombies do. Wayne's running from the scene and momentarily leaving Sallyanne creates the impression of his carelessness which will be repeated when he leaves her in the climax.

Before Rene goes into Marion's house, she sees a grasshopper hit with a beam of light and abducted by the aliens. This prefigures both the later abductions, including Marion's flashback, and the cow seen hanging in the sky with the humans in the film's climax. Marion's laconic speech reads as both macho funny and that of someone who is considered by the town as a "loon" for lunatic, for claiming to have seen aliens before. Wayne will comment on this with, "Can I get a cup of tea with this fruit cake?" The DVD commentary states that Mungo McKay had done all his lines as Additional Dialogue Recording (ADR) for the somber subdued effect desired.

The Spierigs provide a laugh when Marion advances on the frightened and wet-haired Rene only to tell her, "Dry your hair," giving her a towel. Sergeant Harrison also scores a laugh from his entrance to Marion's house with his lines, "When I was a kid we fuckin' respected our parents. We didn't fuckin' eat 'em." Although we haven't seen Harrison and Molly facing zombies as we have Rene, Wayne and Sallyanne, we accept that the police officers have also experienced the same. The Spierigs will play Harrison's constant swearing and aggression off Marion's laconisms for male one-upmanship, although neither man will be seen to survive as human by film's end. Marion's dexterity with his guns is demonstrated when shooting the zombies with action moves. These include throwing two revolvers in the air, grabbing a police rifle to fire, and then catching the two falling revolvers to fire them again.

When five of the six hide in the house's basement, the expectation that Marion will follow is met by him falling down the stairs as he is pushed and pursued by zombies. The group going down another level to the bomb shelter is another surprise. A shot of the zombies outside has the back of one's head shown to be missing a section. Back inside the shelter, Sallyanne tells Rene, "You know, roping two pigs together isn't a talent fit for winning Miss Catch of the Day Queen! No bloody way!" The comment reveals Sallyanne's jealousy of Rene having been chosen over her, since she was the usurped reigning queen. Rene's roping ability will be paid off later when she ropes a zombie to rescue Sallyanne at the airfield. In the DVD commentary it is noted that for the competition Sallyanne had sung "Like a Virgin" as she had in the previous years, but this year it didn't win her the prize because she sang it being seven months pregnant.

Tobacco-amber light is used in the same way it was for the film's opening scenes and will be for the prologue. This is different from the blue light used for Marion's flashback, with additional soft focus to indicate that it is a flashback. The sequence shows a meteor hitting his fishing boat and the fish turned into zombies that attack him. It also shows the cloud and rain that cures the cuts he sustains from the attack and the beam of light that we know is used for abduction. Marion's fish lure is presumably a kind of lucky token that we will see broken in the epilogue to explain his fate. This flashback will be returned to later, but for now Marion is awoken out of it by Sallyanne's screams of labor.

Her pregnancy is a plot conflict device to move the group out of the bomb shelter, since she needs to go to hospital. Her contractions stop once they leave the room and aren't used again as a plot point until much later. When the group climbs back to the next level the expectation of zombies waiting for them is not met. This is also the initial case when they return to the shop floor, although the expectation is met when an arm grabs Harrison through the wall.

The second attack of the zombies is an extended sequence that perhaps goes on for too long, suffering from repetition. Sallyanne later comments on this at the wall with "I can't take this anymore. It's just one monster after another." However, the Spierigs find some variations. Two zombies are shot by Marion and fall back in the kitchen and two knives fall into their heads, and Marion hangs upside down connected by his boot spurs to shoot with more revealed revolvers. Marion suggests the group goes upstairs to the bathroom. He sees how shooting a zombie in the brain will stop it for good, though he doesn't voice this observation until later. The hole that he shoots in the bathroom floor is situated above the garage where an escape van awaits. Harrison's chest-pounding about his being in charge results in the rather obvious gag of having him order Molly to go down to the garage first to investigate. The expectation of there being zombies is not immediately met, though there is a bluff fright.

Before they descend, Rene gets to shoot three zombies in a line at once. The garage door stalling when it is half-open and then opening all the way to allow the van to drive out is a standard suspense device as the zombies begin their attack. The group's escape is introduced by zombies being run over. Their blood soaks the van's windshield, and it is wiped away before they drive on. The cars that the van finds suggest a repeat of the previous car pile-up before the alien spiked wall is revealed. Marion's second return to the flashback continues with the beam on him to show that he was abducted. Molly's transformation into a zombie as seen by Rene is initially inexplicable. This is particularly when the expectation of her attack of Marion, who approaches her, is not met. It is explained by Marion, after Molly is abducted, by the idea that the plague is now airborne and that the rain cures it. The vision of the alien at the wall will not be explained, as is the alien who confronts Marion and who is shot by Wayne at the General Store, until the film's climax.

At the store Marion tells Rene how he was abducted. Because he was thrown back to Earth he believes he has a "gift," a "power" to fight the aliens, although this belief is based on the wrong assumption that the aliens are malevolent. Marion's idea that only the strongest survive is aligned to his having a faith in Rene, which prefigures her as the lone narrative warrior. The zombie that grabs Wayne in the store is another shock effect, and the zombie attack includes some more invention. Marion puts a can of "Head Crush" soda into the mouth of one zombie. He slides back on the floor in the milk that has been spilled. He takes a pen that has fallen from the counter where he has landed and throws it at the can which explodes in the mouth of the zombie.

The return of Chip from the opening scene as a zombie has Rene paying him back for the patronizing way he spoke to her by her hitting him with a spade, which digs into his head. The spade hits a wall twice before being pushed back the third time and pulling Chip's face off. Rene grabs a broom as a weapon. The end of it gets caught on a blade and allows her to slice off heads. The Spierigs use a sequence of shots of blood spray to represent the zombies being struck and sliced. When all the zombies around Rene have been defeated, an Australian flag falls behind her. The store scene ends surprisingly when another alien throws liquid from its hand on Marion and he is abducted.

Wayne drops the box of groceries Rene has given him to take from the van to the plane, and he collects them behind an umbrella. When he picks up the umbrella, zombies are revealed. The zombie becomes human. It holds onto Wayne and Wayne is abducted; his fall is not a surprise. Equally unsurprising is the van that Rene drives crashes; this allows the attempted abduction of Sallyanne to be completed, although the fact that the van roof stops the abduction beam of light seems farfetched. The crash occurs at the same car pile-up site on the road that leads out of Berkelely where the agent and Aggy were killed.

The Spiergis inter-cut between Wayne flying the plane and Rene left alone after Sallyanne is abducted. The alien reveal to Rene is another surprise, showing their faces underneath the hooded cloaks they have worn. Them being benign is further surprise. The goat's head that had been in Marion's house that Wayne sees among the sea of suspended abducted humans scores a laugh, although Molly crashing into the plane and presumably killed is less funny.

The aliens speaking to Rene is shown in subtitles, although it is said in third person from one alien to another. "It is the last to be cured by the rain. It is beginning to understand. It will join the rest of the cured." The conversation includes a funny exchange. The second alien says, "Put your clothes back on," and the naked first alien replies, "I'm comfortable with who I am." The abductees — including Marion, Rene and Sallyanne — are lowered. The white cloud disperses and a full moon is visible when the alien wall is lifted and flown away.

Sallyanne back in labor is plot payoff. After a television news report of how Berkeley has been quarantined by the army, we see her in the hospital telling Rene that she has given birth to a boy. The tobacco-amber light has returned, and as Marion sits with Rene this repeats the idea that she is the strongest of the group and he is not as powerful as he thought. Wayne running into Marion causing his fishing lure to be pushed into Marion's chest perhaps suggests the end of Marion's good luck. Wayne's appearance at the hospital coughing prefigures his zombie biting of Marion, another shock effect.

The film ends with a voice-

Poster for *Undead* (2003).

over by Rene: "The outbreak moved faster this time. It spread so quickly it couldn't be stopped. It spread beyond Berkelely and across the country. Those that I could save from the medical center are here now, safe. At least, for the time being. The last couple of months have been nothing but clear skies. The aliens haven't come back. Maybe someday they will. Until then, I must contain the infection. Sallyanne said that my first duty as Catch of the Day winner is to preserve the best interests of the town. So that is what I'll do."

Rene is presented as a warrior recalling the female warriors of *Lady, Stay Dead, Fair Game, Contagion, Out of the Body, The 13th Floor, Komodo, Ghost Ship, See No Evil, Black Water, Storm Warning, Slaughtered, Prey, Triangle, The Clinic* and *Road Train*. She wears boots with spurs and a gas mask, and holds Marion's three-barreled shotgun guarding over a cage of zombies that include Wayne, Sallyanne and Marion.

In the DVD commentary it is revealed that the film was originally planned to be less comic and more serious. Rene was to come to the town to have an abortion, a place that was to be known as "Death Town" because they had legalized abortions. Michael Spierig can be seen as Marion in the long shots of his flashback sequence because they were filmed before the actor had been cast for the inserted closer shots. Mungo McKay says Michael Spierig appears in the long shots because he was late for the day's shooting and that's why Michael filled in.

The film is said to be based on three shorts that the Spierig Brothers had previously made that starred Paul Guthrie. He has a cameo in the airfield scene as Disco Zombie, the reason for his name presumably given in the shorts. The making-of documentary on the DVD advises the shorts were all made in 1994, and entitled *Attack of the Undead, Rampage of the Undead*, and *Massacre of the Undead*. The character of Harrison had been originally cast with an older actor who was forced to withdraw due to illness, and Dirk Hunter was cast after he became known to the producers after having auditioned for Marion.

The film was the first and last feature to date for the Spierig Films production company. The Spierig Brothers went on to make Australian horror title *Daybreakers*.

After working in television, Felicity Mason made her film debut in a supporting role in the comic musical *Hollywood* (2003), and has worked in television to date since *Undead*. Mungo McKay also began his career in television, and after *Undead* appeared in supporting film roles, including a minor one in *Daybreakers*. *Undead* was the film debut of Rob Jenkins, whose later work was in television and short films.

Lisa Cunningham also made her film debut in *Undead* and played a minor role in *Daybreakers*. Dirk Hunter began his career in television and after *Undead* played more film supporting roles. Emma Randall also made her film debut in *Undead*, after which she played more supporting film roles, including one in *Daybreakers*, and worked in television.

Release

Australia on September 4, 2003, and the United States July 1, 2005, with the taglines "Prepare yourself," and "Crazy has come to town for a visit." The DVD has extended and deleted scenes. The extended scenes are Rene in the bank with Chip, the agent on his cell phone, the cricket scene, the group in the bomb shelter (where some of the actors are laughing in the take), and an alternate title sequence where skeleton imagery is used.

The deleted scenes are the group in the basement going into the bomb shelter as Marion shoots more zombies; in the bomb shelter where Sallyanne uses the toilet behind a sheet, Marion writing on his wrist the time of the rain he hears, Wayne telling Harrison of Aggy's death and how he can fly a plane and Harrison tazering Marion; action moments where Marion rolls a table over a zombie to get his three-barreled gun and Rene shooting zombies; Wayne talking outside the van in front of the General Store; and Wayne in the store trying the telephone and taking money from the cash register.

Reviews

"A stale, derivative mess that borrows heavily from every zombie and alien movie worthy of imitation, to only ho-hum effect.... The film's visual effects, though impressive in number for a low-budget production, are mostly amateurish (the same goes for the acting), but there are a few inventive, comic moments scattered throughout and effective tongue-in-cheek snippets of dialogue."—Laura Kern, *The New York Times*, July 1, 2005

"The Spierig brothers have done an admirable job. They've done the entire thing with goofy vigor and have captured the film's comic book presentation look perfectly using over-exaggerated action, [and] a cartoony score ... but that feeling of 'emptiness' just kept worming its way into my brain, thus making *Undead* what could best be termed as an 'interesting failure.'"—Chris Hartley, *The Video Graveyard*, April 5, 2006

"A huge achievement for a low budget film. A few things are admittedly hampered by the budget, but directors Peter and Michael Spierig do a good job covering their limitations…. The gore is often just silly, but this fits with the film's overall cartoony style." — Devon Bertsch, *Digital Retribution*, February 21, 2010

"An all out, style packed zombie movie with major science fiction elements to set it well apart. The newcomer brothers Spierig exploit the power of the cinematic frame and its attendant soundscape possibilities to breathe blood-spurting life into this genre, of which Australia's cupboard is almost totally bare." — Andrew L. Urban, *Urban Cinefile*

"The kind of movie that would be so bad it's good, except it's not bad enough to be good enough…. *Undead* will launch the careers of the Spierigs, who are obviously talented and will be heard from again." — Roger Ebert, *Chicago Sun-Times*, July 8, 2005

"Quite belying the guerrilla filmmaking tactics, *Undead* comes together on the screen with a considerable slickness and professionalism [but] it feels like two films, one a gore-drenched zombie movie with tongue considerably planted in cheek, and the other a puzzle film about alien abductions, which takes itself seriously." — Richard Scheib, *Moria — science fiction, horror, and fantasy film review site*

DVD

Lionsgate Home Entertainment on October 11, 2005.

Man-Thing

Lions Gate Films/Marcel Enterprises/Fierce Entertainment/Screenland Movieworld, 2005 [aka *Man Thing*; *Marvel's Man-Thing*]

CREDITS: *Director:* Brett Leonard; *Producers:* Avi Arad, Christopher Petzel, Scott Karol, Gimel Everett; *Executive Producers:* Stan Lee, Kevin Feige, Ari Arad, Rudolf G. Wiesmeier, Christopher Mapp; *Associate Producers:* Hans Rodionoff, Brendan Fletcher, James Coyne; *Screenplay:* Hans Rodionoff; *Photography:* Steve Arnold; *Editor:* Martin Connor; *Music:* Roger Mason; *Production Design:* Peter Pound, Tim Ferrier; *Costumes:* Cappi Ireland; *Visual Effects:* the LaB Sydney, Rising Sun Pictures; *Prosthetics and Special Makeup Effects:* Paul Katte, Nick Nicolaou; *Art Director:* Charlie Kevai; *Set Decorator:* Faith Robinson; *Set Designer:* Brian Nickless; *Sound:* Mark Cornish; *Hair and Makeup:* Tina Gordon. Color, 93 minutes. Filmed in Sydney, New South Wales, from August 25, 2003, to October 23, 2003.

SONGS: "Tainted Love" (Ed Cobb), Imogen Riley; "Dead Man Walking"; "How You Let Me"; "Crazy Turn"; "Moonlight on the Bayou"; "2 Dollar Bottle of Wine"; "Tonight on My Mind"; "Take U Down," Tim L.; "Manthing."

CAST: Matthew Le Nevez (Sheriff Kyle Williams); Rachael Taylor (Teri Elizabeth Richards); Rawiri Paratene (Pete Horn); Steve Bastoni (Rene LaRoque); Robert Mammone (Mike Ploog); Alex O'Loughlin (Deputy Sheriff Eric Fraser); Jack Thompson (Frederic Schist); Pat Thompson (Jake Schist); William Zappa (Steve Gerber); John Batchelor (Wayne Thibadeaux); Ian Bliss (Rodney Thibadeaux); Brett Leonard (Val Mayerick, the Coroner); Imogen Bailey (Sarah); James Coyne (Billy James); Cheryl Craig (Michele); Gary Waddell (Cajun Pilot); Xoqui Pesce (Nurse); Mark Stevens (Man-Thing); Shannon Leonard (School Boy).

Synopsis

Kyle Williams arrives in the Louisiana town of Bywater to be the new sheriff. This is after the disappearance of their previous one, Jim Corely, and just in time to attempt to solve several other missing persons cases. There has also been an attack upon Billy James in the swampland, which is thought to have been done by an alligator but which was actually a swamp creature. When the sheriff is called to the worksite of the Schist petroleum company to handle a protest, he meets the leader, Teri. She believes that Frederic Schist has stolen sacred ancestral land from the Indians. Schist security guard Steve Gerber is found murdered. The former sheriff's body is discovered by Kyle when he enters the swamp at night.

Locals Wayne and Rodney Thibadeaux are attacked by the creature. Schist believes that the culprit is the Indian activist, Rene LaRoque, who is in hiding in the swamp. Kyle sees his deputy, Fraser, killed by the creature. When Teri learns that Corely was shot in the back, she goes after Kyle who she believes is in danger from Schist. Schist catches

Rene attempting to blow up the company's main rig in the swamps "Dark Water" area. Kyle and Teri arrive to stop Schist from killing Rene. However the creature appears and kills Schist. Rene sets off the explosive and the creature burns, although he is killed. Kyle and Teri watch the creature sink into the waters of the swamp.

Notes

This forgettable title features the theme of the malevolent supernatural. It is in the form of a tree come to life that is said to be the guardian of a southern American swamp. It seeks vengeance on the people using the land for oil refinement. Director Brett Leonard employs the postmodern techniques of point of view, blackouts, fast edits, jump cuts and fast motion, hand-held camerawork, expressionist camera angles, and an obtrusive score. While he has the ability to present suspense, he relies too much on shock effects. The screenplay with its multiple characters and alternate antagonists demands that he use heavy cross-cutting for the battle scenes in the swamp which compose the bulk of the narrative.

The narrative also parallels the cliché of the Australian rural ocker with the American Southern redneck and additionally can be read to parallel exploitation of the American Indian with the Australian Aborigines. Thankfully the latter's piety is resolved by making the Indian elder one of the victims of the Marvel comic book creature, whose specific look is left unexplained. Supporting performances are generally on the level of the comic book base with the leads disappointingly bland. The treatment has plenty of bloodletting since the creature enjoys impaling its victims and carries out decapitations, shootings, and a climactic feeding of oil into the oil baron.

An opening narration sounds like the voice of the Indian elder Pete Horn and reads: "There is a sacred place in the deep swamp where the mangrove trees grow close together and the rays of the sun are never seen. My people call this The Dark Water. It is here that the spirit of the swamp lives. This place was always filled with life and beauty but evil man has changed that with their drills, their pipes, greed and murder. Now the swamp cries out a warning — a time of retribution is here."

This speech is accompanied by a full moon, thunder and lightning. Fast cuts are used for the emergence of the swamp creature from the water. Leonard is smart enough to suggest rather than reveal what is eventually shown, after seventy minutes of the narrative, to be a pretty silly looking antagonist.

The first strike appears to show the creature's arbitrary agenda since the victim can only be accused

Spanish poster for *Man-Thing*, aka *Man Thing* (2005).

of having sex in a boat in the swamp at night, with no connection to the Schist oil drilling operation. Leonard shows the exposed breasts of Sarah as exploitation even though there is context of her sex with Billy. It is the only time he does so with an actress, although this is also partly due to the minor role Teri will play in the proceedings. The expectation of the attack is created with point of view and a subjective camera. Blood is seen to be from Billy being impaled from behind and landing on Sarah, although she is not attacked since Billy is taken by the creature. Sarah will be seen later in an asylum; she has not spoken since the night of the attack, although she will lunge at Kyle when he questions her.

The plot point of the missing Indian Ted Sallas that the former sheriff was said to be investigating is never resolved. It is assumed that he has been killed by Schist in order to take the land. The protest at Schist's worksite allows for Kyle to meet with Teri, who kicks him and he falls in mud. The idea of the town having protestors creates ambiguity towards the later perceived vandalism of rigs attacked at the site, in light of how close the swamp is shown to be to the site.

When Kyle enters the swamp at night it has a green lighting. Leonard uses shock effects for someone running in front of his car and then behind him to suggest the creature. This is revealed to be Rene, since the final reveal of the creature will show it not to be man-size, although clearly played by a man in a fright suit. Jake investigating a noise and a shadow in the swamp as he guards the site presents him as a Man in Peril, although he has a rifle and is not helpless.

With both Kyle and Jake in the swamp around the site the expectation is created of them meeting, though they don't. Rather the man who approaches Kyle and is unafraid of his armed threat is Rene, who is dressed in a hooded trench coat. The further expectation of Rene's strike against Kyle is not met with Rene's warning to Kyle. This presumably suggests an awareness of the existence of the creature, who regrettably never attacks him.

The fate of Jake in the swamp is a plot point that is left dangling, and the narrative turns to make fellow security guard, Steve, the Man in Peril. When he retreats to the office, the expectation of a strike against him is created with the lights going out. Leonard uses another shock effect for the door of the office blown in, presumably by the creature. He uses another shock effect for the corpse of Corely thrown on Kyle's car windshield, although presumably not done by the creature, since it would seem to be with Steve. The discovery of Steve's body the next day shows gore — a tree branch is in his throat — although the coroner makes the observation that it is coming out rather than having been put in. This point will be elaborated on in the murders of the Tibido brothers later when we see that the creature has moving vines that impale; these recall the vines in *Hellion: The Devil's Playground* and *The Ruins*.

Jake is later shown to be alive and seen with the Thibodaux brothers. Leonard provides perhaps his one beautiful shot of the film — the boat containing Kyle and Fraser cutting through the river at night. When the boat breaks down, the expectation is created of a strike against them, which is not met. The moment allows for an exchange between the two men. When Kyle comments, "There's too many things alive out here," Fraser replies, "Yeah, I'd like to remain one of them." The Thibadeaux brothers also being in the swamp creates the expectation of them being attacked. The narrative misses the obvious but still golden opportunity to have Rodney attacked when he goes to the toilet in the swamp.

When the brothers are separated later in their boats, a yell heard by Wayne creates the expectation that Rodney has been attacked, which will prove to be false. Someone seen to approach Wayne, which is presumably Rene, provides a decoy for his attack from the creature. This is prefigured by vines moving through the water before they impale him and one going into Wayne's mouth.

Kyle leaving Fraser alone at the house of Mike Ploog also creates the expectation of an attack upon Fraser, which is not met. Rodney is seen alive, confirming that the scream we had assumed to be his earlier was not. This makes him finding the impaled corpse of Wayne ironic. Rodney's expected attack makes the impaling vines this time appear to be more like tentacles. Fraser leaving the Ploog house to go into the swamp again creates the expectation of his attack, as does Kyle being caught in a trap and being hung upside down. Although Renee's appearance again does not meet the expectation of him attacking Kyle, this time it appears that it is the only case because Kyle unties himself before Rene can attack. Rene knocking Kyle unconscious does stop him from being able to help Fraser when he is finally attacked. Fraser's attack by what looks like a tree shows the developing exposure of the creature, and it being a tree also demonstrates its camouflage ability so that it can attack as a shock effect.

When Kyle awakens he finds Mike taking flash photographs of Fraser's amputated arm, and we never learn what happens to the rest of Fraser. When Kyle visits Teri at her schoolyard, Leonard focuses on a shot of a schoolboy hitting the ground with a branch, perhaps because he is played by a relative. The idea of Teri's schoolchildren being threatened by the creature or Teri as a schoolteacher doesn't get a plot payoff. Since Kyle asks her to stay behind when he tells her of his intention to go back into the swamp at night, Teri seems to be a passive subsidiary character, although her eventually joining him redeems her somewhat. The night swamp scene then is complicated with three agendas — Frederic and Jake Schist look for Rene, Pete Horn looks for the creature, and Kyle looks for both.

It is the creature's confrontation with Pete that finally gives us a good look at it, as a tree with vine tentacles and red eyes. Thankfully it is not stopped by Pete's chanting, although the posthumous chanting heard in the climax after Pete has been impaled suggests that perhaps the chanting has a delayed result. Mike Ploog in the swamp becomes an additional protagonist but quickly disposed of when he is shot by Frederic for allegedly taking his photograph without his permission. Jake is also disposed of by Rene in a shock attack. It is the coincidental appearance of Kyle and Teri at the place where Frederic has caught Rene that allows for Rene's rescue. The "Dark Water" location is disappointingly ordinary after the buildup created by Teri whereby she and Kyle are forced to travel through a dark area. Perhaps Kyle can rationalize not trying to help Frederic when he is attacked by the creature, since he has shot Kyle and Rene before the strike.

The expectation of Frederic being attacked is met since he stands facing the others, but with his back to where the creature enters. The creature using one tentacle to take in oil and then another to feed it into Frederic also results in oil spraying out of Frederic's mouth. Naturally the oil being fed to the oil baron is poetic justice, but Rene shown to be still alive so he can finish blowing up the rig is a conventional disappointment.

Kyle finally shooting at the creature shows how it regenerates, and Rene distracting it to allow Kyle and Teri to get away from it does not result in the creature attacking him. The resultant explosion sets the creature on fire — the oil it had channeled for Frederic's attack must have helped — and presumably finally kills Rene. The creature then appears to regenerate again, so its sudden sinking into the swamp defeated is inexplicable even when it provides a happy ending for Kyle as the protagonist.

The film is the only Australian horror title to be made to date by American director Brett Leonard, producers Avi Arad, Scott Karol and Christopher Petzel, co-producer Gimel Everett, associate producers James Coyne, Brendan Fletcher and Hans Rodionoff, and executive producers Kevin Feige, Stan Lee and Rudolf G. Weismeier. It is the only Australian horror movie made to date by the production companies Lions Gate Films, Artisan Entertainment, Marvel Enterprises, Fierce Entertainment, Screenland Movieworld GmbH, and Samurai Films.

Matthew Le Nevez began his career in television and made his film debut in a supporting role in the musical comedy *Garage Days* (2002). He was seen in more television and film supporting roles before and after *Man-Thing*, which has been his only leading film role to date. Rachael Taylor also began her career in television and made her film debut here. She later worked in more television and film supporting roles, including the Australian horror title *See No Evil*.

New Zealand born Rawiri Paratene began his career in New Zealand television and made his film debut in a supporting role in the romance *Arriving Tuesday* (1986). He was seen in more television and film supporting roles prior to and after *Man-Thing*. Steve Bastoni was born in Italy and is another actor to have started his career in television. He made his film debut in the comedy *Melvin, Son of Alvin* (1984), and appeared in more television and film supporting roles prior to and after *Man-Thing*. He also essayed the leads in *Natural Justice: Heat* (1996) and the action comedy *Wanted* (1997).

Robert Mammone also began his career in television and made his film debut in a supporting role in the romance *The Crossing* (1990). He continued in television and supporting film roles, and was later in the Australian horror movie *Storage*. Alex O'Loughlin began his career in television and made his film debut in the lead role in the romantic comedy *Oyster Farm* (2004). After *Man-Thing* he played the lead in the crime thriller *Feed* (2005), which was based on his idea and which he co-produced. He appeared in more television and film supporting roles.

Jack Thompson is another actor who started his career in television and made his film debut in a supporting role, his in *Personnel, or People* (1969). He continued in television and film supporting roles prior to and after *Man-Thing*. He essayed the title character in *Petersen* (1974), and the leads in *Sunday Too Far Away* (1975), the mystery *Scobie Malone* (1975), the comedy *The Journalist* (1975), the sports comedy *The Club* (1980), the thriller *Bad Blood* (1982), the adventure *Burke and Wills* (1985), the comedy *The Sum of Us* (1994), and *Under the Lighthouse Dancing* (1997).

Pat Thompson is the son of Jack Thompson and made his feature film debut in a supporting part in *Kokoda Crescent* (1989). He has appeared in television and more supporting film roles before and after *Man-Thing*. William Zappa was previously seen in the Australian horror movie *Celia*. Imogen Bailey went on to appear in the Australian horror title *The 7th Hunt*.

Release

No apparent wide release in the United States, rather it went straight to DVD. Australian wide release information unknown. The taglines include "The nature of fear," "Your fear is your deadliest weapon," and "When nature fights back!"

Reviews

"Not to be taken seriously, but with a sense of fun, *Man-Thing* is a big pot of extra-spicy gumbo, full of good ol' southern hospitality. Stupid cheap thrills and a great way to waste 92 minutes, this is a B grade monster movie at its best."—J.R. McNamara, *Digital Retribution*, September 16, 2005

"Leonard does a decent top of capturing the feel of our backwater town location and he keeps things moving for the first half, *Man-Thing* soon loses momentum before closing with a junky finale. Script is loaded with underdeveloped Native American mumbo jumbo, weak scenes of characters walking aimlessly through swamps, pointless sub-plots, and not enough Man-Thing action."—Chris Hartley, *The Video Graveyard*, December 11, 2005

"Leonard shoots in a sickly green light and cruises his camera through midnight-lit swamps. Alas, the script is generic and there is nothing in *Man-Thing* that does not come by cliché. We also see surprisingly little of the title character—although when we do, [it] is an impressive creation."—Richard Scheib, *Moria—science fiction, horror and fantasy film review site*

"[Unless] you're really into watching people walk around doing nothing and being unbelievably bored, you'll probably want to take a nap until Man-Thing finally shows up at the end, then you'll want to throw this crappy movie away and watch something good."—*The World of Mr. Satanism—Video Pick for Perverts*

"I can recommend the film as a rental to fans of the comic or those who enjoy bayou-bound movies. But, despite the fact that the film is fairly well-made and contains a cool monster, it also shies away from the horror side and is dull at times."—Mike Long, *DVD Crypt*

"Succeeds as a middle-of-the-road B-Grade creature feature, one [with] a great-looking creature and some decent acting from its cast of virtual unknowns.... Leonard's decision to keep the monster hidden from view until the last thirty minutes or so may be the reason so many people dislike this movie. I, however, think it's a brilliant technique."—T. Rigney, *Filmfiend*, 24 May 2006

DVD

Released by Lions Gate on June 14, 2005. Released in Australia by Force Entertainment on August 26, 2005.

Safety in Numbers
Multivision 235/Down Under Films, 2005

CREDITS: *Screenplay/Director:* David Douglas; *Producers:* David Douglas, Kelvin Crumplin; *Executive Producers:* Michael Douglas, Alan Douglas, Bruce Morrison, Frank Runge, Don Spencer; *Associate Producers:* Lawrence Brotherton, Louis Melville, Bob Morris; *Photography:* Mark Bliss; *Editor:* David Stiven; *Music:* Carlo Giacco; *Production Design:* Ian Allan; *Costumes:* Robyn "Doll" Smith; *Makeup:* Sue Kelly-Tait; *Sound:* Rob Schreider. Color, 85 minutes. Filmed on location in Sydney, New South Wales.

CAST: Jessica Napier (Jennifer Kelly); Ben Tari (Joe); Tasma Walton (Caroline Childs); Henry Nixon (Nigel Harper); Teo Gebert (Matt); Karen Pang (Lisa); Peter Rasmussen (Wesley); Christian Marcel (Roger); Gabriella Masselli (Maddi); Tory Mussett (Sarah); Alan Lock (Alan Carter); Leslie Bell, Dichen Lachman (Reporters); Barbi Brown, Rachael Luff (Cheque Girls); Therese Pientka (Extra Repoter).

Synopsis

Briton Nigel is the one million dollar winner of the American *Castaway Island* game show. He sails the yacht he has also won, *Serenade*, with the losing contestants to an island for a cast reunion show. The show's host, Roger, is not to be found. "You Will *All* Die" is seen written on the wall of the beachhouse, and the cast suspect Wesley is responsible. He was the cast member they had evicted and who had gone wild on location with a machete. Dead rats appear in the water tank and the next day the beachhouse is blown up as the group discovers that the yacht has disappeared. As video cameras are spotted around the island, the group is killed off one by one, until only Jen remains. She sees that the killer is Wesley and, finding the yacht offshore, seeks refuge in it.

She finds Maddi, Matt's wife, onboard. Maddi tells her how she and Wesley had planned a revenge on the group because of their perceived humiliation, but that Maddi had not wanted to kill anybody. When Jen sees Joe is alive on the beach she sails back, and he saves her from Wesley, who tries to drown her. Joe and Jen sail away, although Maddi is killed onboard by a spear gun. Two days later the yacht is found by the *Cruising Cats* yacht with Jen's sister Sarah on board. However, the *Serenade* has no passengers and a dismembered arm found on board suggests Jen and Joe have met foul play.

Notes

A simple tale of revenge with an ambiguous denouement features the theme of the horror of personality. Director David Douglas uses the postmodern techniques of blackouts, expressionist camera angles and hand-held camerawork, slow motion, point of view, and out of focus effects, as well as an occasionally obtrusive score. Killings are performed in daylight rather than the night of conventional horror movies, and there is plenty of bloodletting and an epilogue dismemberment. Douglas favors shock effects, although there is one effective scene of suspense with empathy created for the antagonists via a tender bonding of two characters.

A prologue shows Jen running, which turns out to be a nightmare since we see her wake up from it. This also prefigures her later being chased by Wesley. The first in Douglas' shock effects is a spade appearing in front of Lisa, which Matt is using to bury the dead rats. The idea that the rats have been poisoned rather than just drowning in the water tank seems to be the next act of antagonism after the writing on the beach house wall. A storm at night is used as a conventional horror device and prefaces the noise of the unsecured water tank that the group investigates. The bird that flies past Matt and Joe's flashlight is a shock effect, as is the house being blown up, as heard by the girls on the beach.

The blood on Joe's head from his fall off the rocks is the first bloodletting. Joe is the character who will be most bloodied in the attacks he endures. Caroline investigating the yells of Nigel being caught in the spike trap presents her as a conventional Woman in Peril. Although Douglas shows blood pouring from Nigel's mouth to suggest his death, the later video cam montage will have another shot of him definitely dead. Caroline's fate is not revealed immediately. She is heard to scream once she goes off-camera to investigate another noise, which may not be Nigel. This may suggest that she has found Nigel or that she has received the strike that we will later see looks like an arrow or spear.

Douglas uses another shock effect for Lisa running into Joe and Jen. Their finding the trap pit gets a payoff from Joe being pushed into it from a flying weight and having one leg impaled. Lisa abandoning Joe while Jen helps him out of the pit can be read as a way of sealing her fate. Her hearing Matt's "Lisa. I'm here" is shown to be footage taken from Matt's earlier conversation with her when she told him that she is pregnant. The log that hits her is another shock effect. It is also the last we see of her until Jen later falls into the pit to find Lisa dead, with Matt, Roger and another unidentified man.

When Jen and Joe hide from someone that we later learn is Wesley, he is only shown via his legs. He wears army camouflage pants and carries a machete. After Jen leaves Joe to get help, the spider we see crawl near is not shown to strike him after Jen returns.

Jen finds the video cam that is marked "Play Me," which allows her to watch a montage of Nigel, Jen and Caroline voting Wesley off the *Castaway* show. This confirms that the camera recorder is Wesley. After the "You Will *All* Die" sign, we see video surveillance of the group, Matt shown to be hit and bloodied and unconscious, and the bloodied Nigel. The last shot is the same one seen earlier in the film of blood pouring out of his mouth. This reads as a questionable choice, though the video follows the shot with a new one of the dead Nigel.

A close-up of the vomit that Jen produces is for gross-out effect; the shot is repeated when Wesley follows her. She initially only appears to be walking away from the video cam, but it becomes apparent that Jen is aware of herself being chased before she returns to Joe and identifies the killer as Wesley. Joe and Jen have a moment of tender bonding that initially appears to be his comforting her before he dies. The scene of them hearing Wesley approaching them is perhaps the best in the film in its suspense.

She holds a knife but doesn't use it to kill the snake that appears and crawls over her. The snake is a conventional test to stop the hunted from making a noise in reaction that would give their location away. This is a device also used in *Turkey Shoot* and *Fair Game*. The couple being quiet also would allow for the element of surprise if they are to attack Wesley if he appears. This is an expectation that is not met, after he sees the same snake passing him and kills it.

Jen walking is revealed to be her dream, where she also sees the dead Nigel's eyes open. This suggests that perhaps he could be faking, although her awakening from a nightmare and the later narrative shows that this is fiction. The spear that Joe gives her is used after he decides they must go on the offensive by Joe pretending to call for Jen to give away his position. A close-up of Wesley is shown, and it is the first in the treatment. He shoots an arrow at Joe before Jen gets to spear him. Given how Wesley's antagonism makes him hard to kill, the spear is not fatal. It allows him to chase her, the footage recalling Jen running in the prologue. After she falls in the pit to find the other bodies, her reaching the beach creates the expectation of her escape. Continuing the idea that Wesley is unstoppable, his being caught in a trap and hanging upside down is overcome by his ability to cut himself down. Douglas creates more tension with cross-cuts between Jen's swim to the yacht and Wesley in the motorized raft chasing her.

Jen gets to the yacht, meeting the expectation of her escape, then Wesley climbs aboard. Even though she spears him and he falls overboard, we still expect him to return. The narrative delays that, as Jen sails away. The noise she hears onboard creates the expectation that it is Wesley. Her holding a knife also suggests that she may stab someone else and that it may be as an act of counter-production. Jen's calling out "Who are you?" may seem conventionally silly, but it also may stop her from harming someone she will regret.

The reveal of the tied up Maddi explains why she cannot identify herself, and our question of why she is there is answered by the expected explanation that Maddi is in on the plan with Wesley. This assumption is based on the apparent sighting of Maddi in the jungle earlier. She tells Jen that the plan was to only scare the group but that Wesley had gone too far in deciding to kill. This explains why Maddi is tied up, presumably by him, because of her disagreement with him, with the expectation that he would return to the yacht once he had killed the group. We aren't told how Wesley and Maddi got to the island, or whether they were there before the others. Maddi as an accomplice is also not a surprise. This is given who else has been presented in the narrative as prospective antagonists, with Maddi seen on camera denouncing Matt for having left her for Lisa.

Jen seeing Joe on the beach alive makes her come back to the island. His apparent death before she can get to him will prove to be a red herring. Wesley's reappearance on the beach is his expected return. Joe revives to remove the arrow from his body and stab Wesley with it in order to save Jen. This is a deus ex machina, given the expectation of Jen being drowned. Wesley floating in the sea may create the expectation that he is finally dead, an expectation not met when he is later seen on the beach alive again. Neither are Joe and Jen now safe, given that Maddi is still on the yacht.

When the focus returns to Maddi she is inexplicably shown in the same pose she was left in, inexplicable given the battle we have seen Jen endure in the meantime. Maddi's death by a spear gun that fires from an open door is also ambiguous. We can't tell whether it was set up as a trap to whoever opened the door, or if it is handled by a present person, the latter perhaps explaining the epilogue.

Douglas freeze-frames on a close-up of Jen after Wesley is seen on the beach, and after the title that reads "2 days later." The *Serenade* is boarded by a man with Jen's sister, Sarah. We aren't shown how the other yacht has come to be near the yacht, and the fact of Sarah being onboard the other yacht seems a remarkable coincidence. The apparent disappearance of Jen and Joe is left unexplained. The dismembered arm we see presumably is one of theirs, but perhaps it's not. While this prologue may add mystery to the fate of the protagonists, it is dramatically frustrating. It is also a cheat, although at least the treatment ends on gore with the shot of the arm.

In the making-of documentary featured on the DVD, it is told how the actors lived together on the island to create a group bond, and that they also undertook a commando course in survival training. Footage from the training appears to be deleted scenes, with the small excerpts we see from the original show having the cast wearing red t-shirts. The film is the only one to date by director and producer David Douglas. It is the only Australian horror movie made by producers Kelvin Crumplin, executive producers Michael and Alan Douglas, Bruce Morrison, Frank Runge, and Don Spencer, and associate producers Lawrence Brotherton, Louis Melville, and Bob Morris. It is also the only one made by Down Under Films production company.

Jessica Napier was born in New Zealand and

began her career in television. Her film debut was in a supporting role in the comic crime drama *Love Serenade* (1996), and supporting roles included one in *Cut* and in television. *Safety in Numbers* is her only leading film role to date. Ben Tari was born in Hungary and began his career in television. *Safety in Numbers* is his only film role to date. Tasma Walton previously appeared in a supporting role in *Subterano*, and after *Safety in Numbers* continued supporting film work and television. Henry Nixon began his career in television and made his film debut in a supporting role in the romance *Somersault* (2004). After *Safety in Numbers* he played a supporting role in the Australian horror title *Triangle*.

Teo Gebert is another actor to have started his career in television and made his film debut in a supporting role in the thriller *Fatal Bond* (1992). He followed more supporting parts and television with the lead in *Square One* (1997) and *A Cold Summer* (2003), for which he co-wrote the screenplay. Since *Safety in Numbers* the actor has essayed the lead in the crime comedy *Crooked Business* (2008) as well as playing other supporting film roles and television. Karen Pang also started in television, made her film debut in a supporting role in *Low Fat Elephants* (2001) and has continued working in supporting film roles and television. Peter Rasmussen made his film debut in *Safety in Numbers* after working in television and has not made another film to date. Gabriella Masselli is an actor to have begun in television; her only leading role to date is *Hostage to Fate* (2001). Otherwise she has been seen in supporting film roles and on television.

RELEASE

Cannes Film Festival screening, May 2005. Australian release date unknown. Straight to DVD in the United States with the taglines "It was only a game show" and "Reality was their worst nightmare"

REVIEWS

None available.

DVD

Released by Image Entertainment on September 12, 2006. Sony Pictures Home Entertainment (Australia) on April 11, 2009.

Wolf Creek

Mushroom Pictures/403 Productions/True Crime Channel, 2005

CREDITS: *Producer/Screenplay/Director:* Greg McLean; *Producer:* David Lightfoot; *Co-Producer/Executive Producer:* Matt Hearn; *Executive Producers:* Gary Hamilton, Simon Hewitt, Martin Fabinyi, George Adams, Michael Gudinski; *Photography:* Will Gibson; *Editor:* Jason Ballantine; *Music:* Francois Tetaz; *Production Design:* Robert Webb; *Costumes:* Nicola Dunn; *Makeup and Hair:* Jen Lamphee; *Sound:* Les Kenneally. Color, 94–101 minutes. Filmed on location in Adelaide, Barossa Valley, Flinders Ranges, Glenelg, Hawker, Port Germein, Sandy Creek, and Semaphore, South Australia; and Wolfe Creek Meteriote Crater, Western Australia from May 24 to June 16, 2004.

CAST: John Jarratt (Mick Taylor); Cassandra Magrath (Liz Hunter); Kestie Morassi (Kristy Earl); Nathan Phillips (Ben Mitchell); Gordon Poole (Old Man); Guy O'Donnell (Car Salesman); Phil Stevenson (Mechanic); Geoff Revell (Gas Attendant); Andy McPhee (Bazza); Aaron Sterns (Bazza's Mate); Michael Moody (Bazza's Old Mate); Andrew Reiner (Flashback Dad); Vicki Reiner (Flashback Mum); Isabella Reiner (Flashback Girl); David Rock (Irish Backpacker); Jenny Starvall, Guy Petersen (Swedish Backpackers); Paul Curran, Christian McMillan, Sean Gannon, Aaron March, Eddie White, Geoffrey Yu, Amy Schapel, Teresa Palmer, Bow Vayne, Renee Chomel, Simone Luntone, John Henry Luscan, Chloe Gardner, Greg Sara, Renee Luna, Michael Soung, Neisha de Jong, Leesa Milhouse, Alex de Roga (Pool Party People); Darren Humphries (Detective); Peter Alchin (Police Officer); Rory Walker, Jon Blaike (Roadhouse Guys). Uncredited: Greg McLean (Old Man's Body/Police Officer).

SONGS: "Sunshine" (Ben Nash), 78 Saab; "Eagle Rock" (Ross Wilson), Daddy Cool, heard over opening credits; "Double the Bass" ("Rx8" (Justin Astbury, Rob Biancetti), SystemBot; "You're No Good to Me" ("Devil's Ride" (Col Finley),

Synopsis

In 1999, Australian Ben Mitchell plans to drive from Broome, Western Australia, to Darwin and Cairns via the Wolf Creek crater. With him are two English backpackers, Liz Hunter and Kristy Earl. Their car breaks down at the crater site. Outback shooter Mick Taylor tows it to the abandoned Navithalim Mining company campsite, where he keeps the three tourists prisoners. Liz rescues Kristy from Mick's torture of her and drives Mick's truck over a cliff. When Liz goes back to get another car, she is caught by Mick, who severs her spine. Kristy finds her way back to the highway and is aided by another driver, whom Mick shoots dead. Mick chases Kristy in his car, causing her to crash, and he kills her by shooting her and burning the car. Ben escapes from his entrapment and is found by two Swedish tourists. He lives to tell the story to the police, who we are told are unable to locate Mick or recover the bodies of Kristy and Liz.

Notes

This simple tale from director Greg McLean uses suspense and a few shocks for its exploration of the theme of the horror of personality. The film is said to have been entirely shot with the postmodern technique of handheld camerawork in high definition digital, also using jump cuts, zooms, slow motion and point of view. The treatment manages to invest empathy with the protagonists, despite their lacking in individual personality. The narrative defies created expectations and succeeds as a Gothic warning to international tourists about the dangers of Australia, despite the scenic beauty of the landscape. The antagonist is likened to an exterminator of vermin who also has a perverse sexual agenda. McLean adds sadism to his horror, with plenty of bloodletting. By sparing one of the three protagonists from death, he supplies hope to a dark narrative.

An opening title tells us that the narrative is based on actual events. Thirty thousand people are reported missing in Australia every year, apparently, and while 90 percent are found within a month, some are never seen again. Given that someone needs to survive to report the story, this creates an expectation that is met by the film's conclusion, although McLean manages to maintain ambiguous suspense for Ben's fate as the witness.

A prologue presents the three protagonists as wild party animals, which is a moralizing that can be used to make them deserve their fate. A confrontation at Emu Creek is interesting in the way the men at the café are presented as drunken misogynistic grotesques and how Ben backs down from accepting a fight to defend the two girls who are jokingly threatened with rape.

The Wolf Creek crater is perhaps not as spectacular as it might have been shown, given that it is said to be the result of a meteorite strike. The rain that seems to spoil the walking trail prefigures the less than ideal adventures to come. The romance that buds between Ben and Liz is pleasingly adolescent, with the two of them laughing as they kiss and not shown to have sex. This form of innocence will help to establish empathy for characters which the screenplay fails to give depth. The watches that stop and the later video camera reveal of Mick having been at Emu Creek would suggest the possibility that he has tampered with the car while the three are on the trail. Alternatively, the car may not work because of the same mechanical problem their watches experience, or because it is a cheap dysfunctional car. Or perhaps it stops because of the protagonists' plain bad luck?

The lights of Mick's approaching truck is used as a horror threat, particularly after Ben has been telling the girls about UFO sightings. It is also a foreshadowing of the real threat that Mick is. The long wait for the tow is perhaps a clue that Mick has another agenda. Although he presents as a jovial larrikin, Mick's disturbed mental state is revealed in the long look he gives Ben at the campfire of the mining town, when Ben comments that Mick must enjoy the freedom his lifestyle gives him. On the DVD commentary McLean reports that Mick's look is based on anger at Ben's presumption that he knows anything about Mick's life. John Jarratt as Mick perhaps overplays Mick's forced larrikinism so that his later antipathy does not come as a surprise. McLean uses blackouts when the three fall asleep. The fact that their rain water has been drugged, which is confirmed in the DVD commentary, to allow Mick to tie them up reads as a contrivance. This is particularly in light of the way Ben is crucified.

An extreme close-up of Liz's face is used before the reveal that she is tied up and not in the location where she fell asleep. She is a Woman in Peril investigating a noise when her apparent decision to leave the site is stopped by her hearing the scream of Kristy. Mick's treatment of Kristy is undetermined, although the blood on her suggests torture. Her screaming and beseeching is almost unbearable to witness, with the corpse shown hanging near her suggesting a previous victim. Liz using a fire to distract Mick and free Kristy is plot point that shows

Liz's resourcefulness. The narrative will continue to present Liz as a heroic figure but then later alter that view when she is defeated by Mick. Kristy then takes on her own form of heroics, albeit brief and unsuccessful. Liz's holding the gun on Mick is revealed by the click of it being loaded, and his being shot in the neck creates the question of whether he has been killed. Her having to retrieve the car keys from the pocket of his prone body also sets up the expectation that he will regain consciousness and stop her. This expectation is not immediately met, but later we will know he is up when the truck starts.

The expectation that the truck will hit Mick is not met. Another expectation of the girls escaping successfully is created when they leave the site, although the fact that they haven't tried to look for Ben creates moral ambiguity. Their unfamiliarity with the area is paid off when they stop at a cliff top. Liz's decision to push the truck over it to make Mick think that they have perished is an interesting strategy. The lights of Mick's following car creates an awareness that he is tracking them. The moment where the girls hide over the cliff's edge as Mick looks with a flashlight also creates the expectation that he will discover them, but he doesn't. Actually this moment has ambiguity. Kristy's movement and Mick's hearing it suggests that he does see them, although he does not come down after them, which suggests otherwise.

Since they have Mick's keys, Liz figures that they can get another car, although the return to the mining site is loaded with fear. Kristy's dread about Liz leaving her alone is later shown to be justified, although not for the expected reason. Kristy being left alone as Liz looks for a car creates the expectation that Mick will find Kristy. This expectation is not met, at least not in the mining site. McLean supplies a shot of Ben unseen by the girls in the mine cave, although we can't tell if he is alive. It prefigures Ben's escape much later. This shot is perhaps to remind us of his own plight. It is also perhaps the subconscious concern of the girls, who we gather aren't really selfish enough to want to abandon him as their previous escape attempt suggested.

Liz finds memorabilia of other tourists who we presume have been Mick's victims. The clothes, photographs, foreign money, tickets, and passports

A bloodied Kristy Earl (Kestie Morassi) is on a highway in this French lobby card for *Wolf Creek* (2005).

Tourists Ben Mitchell (Nathan Phillips), Kristy Earl (Kestie Morassi), and Liz Hunter (Cassandra Magrath) are in their car before the horror begins in a French lobby card for *Wolf Creek* (2005).

add to the idea that he is a serial killer exterminator. Liz finds video cameras and watches footage from the point of view of a family as they interact with Mick at the crater site. We question the time Liz takes in watching this footage. She could be using it instead to find a car, and we are aware that she is keeping Kristy waiting. However the sequence does provide a payoff of shock reveal of how Mick's car was at the Emu Creek site as seen behind Ben in his video footage. This suggests that Mick has been stalking the three, and would seem to confirm the idea that he has made their car break down. It also aligns Mick with the antagonistic and grotesque men we saw in the Emu Creek cafe, who had an equally disturbed sense of humor.

McLean uses suspense for Liz's trial of various keys in a car's ignition, but her moment of success is spoiled by the shock appearance of Mick in the car's backseat. This is perhaps the worst contrivance of the narrative: how did he know she would choose this car? He is revealed by the sound of his laugh and then the reflection of his face in the car's windshield before he stabs her. His cutting off the fingers of her raised hand is a grand guignol moment lacking immediate bloodletting. Liz's cowardly cries recall that of Kristy when she was being attacked, and her threatening him with a small penknife is pathetic. But Mick's act of severing her spine tops the prior grand guignol since it reduces her to what he calls a "head on a stick," resembling a puppet. This is the last we see of Liz. Her disabling is a shock, because she was previously presented as heroic. McLean supplies a transitional edit from Mick's line "Let's talk about your little mate, Kristy" and the cut to Kristy, establishing her as the narrative's new protagonist.

Kristy's former behavior — her whining in reaction to Mick's torture — makes her seem less heroic than Liz. Liz has told her to leave if she has not returned in a specific time, but we still judge Kristy for seemingly abandoning her friend. She earns some respect from being able to find the highway through the bushland, although some might consider that sheer luck. The sight of an approaching car creates the expectation that it is Mick. This expectation is not met; the driver is an old man, and a new expectation is created that Kristy will be rescued. She is not; we see bullet holes in the thermos on the car's roof.

The shot thermos prefigures the shooting of the man — for which McLean uses blood splatter on the car's rear windshield. Kristy is seen in the eye of the rifle viewfinder as the shooter's point of view. We assume that the shooter is Mick, although McLean delays the reveal after showing the driver of an approaching car wearing a hat that makes him resemble Mick. After the clichéd moment of Kristy being unable to start the old man's car, the chase that ensues reads as predetermined by the fact of how slowly Kristy's car travels, perhaps appropriate for an old driver.

Mick is revealed as the driver, as seen in her rear view mirror as he perversely waves at her and wags his tongue at her as he drives parallel to her car. His car suddenly going off the road is a surprise and creates the expectation that Kristy will get away from him. It doesn't help her case that she laughs at him when she sees how he loses control of his car. His shooting out one of her tires is not a surprise, although the double roll her car does is, as well as being a stunt marvel.

Kristy crawling out of the wreck is a pathetic defense. It is interesting that Mick shoots her to kill her in daylight on the highway, although there appears to be no one else in sight, rather than take her back to the mining site. McLean films Kristy's shooting in a long shot, which McLean describes in the DVD commentary as an attempt to top the spine severing of Liz. The moment he gives Mick in close-up after the killing is meant to make us wonder what Mick could be thinking after he has committed such an act. Putting Kristy in the trunk of the wrecked car and then setting it alight would seem to finalize his opinion of how he has no more use for her. It also will ensure that she is never found, as we are told in the film's closing titles.

When the narrative finally returns to Ben and his grand guignol crucifixion, it is aided by a caged snarling dog, and a corpse hanging next to him. Although he makes the monumental effort of pulling his wrists out of the crucifying nails, he doesn't look for the girls when he doesn't have our knowledge of their fates. His escape into bushland creates the expectation that he will be found by Mick, whom McLean shows in cross-cuts driving back to the site. We are uncomfortable with Ben yelling in the bushland; we assume he thinks someone may hear him and help, but it could give away his location to Mick. The solar eclipse that is shown adds a yin-yang element to the treatment. The shadow over Ben and a dark profile of the Swedish backpacker wearing a Mick-type hat creates the expectation of Mick finding him. We know how Mick feels about tourists, so the expectation that Ben, and the Backpackers, will be stopped by Mick remains. This is even when we see them arriving at Kalbarri, which appears to be another version of Emu Creek.

The Flying Doctors plane that we see Ben put into finally defies the expectation that Ben will not escape. As the last survivor he has to be the reporting witness for the story. McLean uses slow motion for a shot of Ben with police, which suggests as the titles confirm that he was considered a suspect. The titles read as follows: "Despite several major police searches no trace of Liz Hunter or Kristy Earl has ever been found. Early investigations into the case were disorganized, hampered by confusion over the location of the crimes, a lack of physical evidence and the alleged unreliability of the only witness. After 4 months in police custody Ben Mitchell was later cleared of all suspicion. He currently lives in South Australia."

A silhouette of the outback serial killer Mick Taylor (John Jarratt) in a French lobby card for *Wolf Creek* (2005).

McLean ends with a shot of Mick walking away from the camera at sunset in bushland with his rifle. This image dissolves to his disappearing from view, making him seem a supernatural Gothic threat awaiting new tourists and a film sequel which to date has not been made.

On the DVD making-of documentary, Greg McLean says that the weather rained on location for the first time in ten years for twenty-one out of the twenty-five days of shooting and that he adapted the narrative to incorporate this weather. The film is said to have originated as a standard slasher narrative set in the Australian outback which Mclean wrote it in 1997 but never liked. When the Ivan Milat backpacker murder case came to light, it inspired McLean to rewrite the script and introduce the concept of the nice guy who seems to be there to help you but in reality is a murderer.

The name of the mining company, "Navithalim," is the name of Ivan Milat spelled backwards. The director of public prosecutions in the Northern Territory asked the film distributor to delay screening until after the trial of Bradley John Murdoch, accused of murdering British backpacker Peter Falconio. Although Murdoch's trial commenced 17 October 2005, it did not finish until December 13, after the film was released in Australia. Murdoch was found guilty of murder and sentenced to life imprisonment.

Advertising for the film claims it was based on true events, but this is not entirely accurate. *Wolf Creek* was influenced by the Ivan Milat and Bradley John Murdoch cases, but it was not based specifically on any one event, and the four principal characters are all entirely fictitious. At the end of the movie Ben is rescued by a young couple in an orange and white Volkswagen microbus, which pays homage to the real-life Peter Falconio and Joanne Lees, on whom the story is partly based. Peter had obtained an orange and white van for the couple's planned trip through Northern Territories, but he has never been found after Joanne claimed they were assaulted in their van by a mysterious outback traveler.

Wolf Creek is referenced in the documentary *Going to Pieces: The Rise and Fall of the Slasher Film* (2006). It is the only Australian horror title mentioned, as an example of the resurrection of the slasher genre which was now flavored by torture porn. Mushroom Pictures had previously made *Cut*, and *Wolf Creek* is the last such movie made by the production company to date. It is the only film to have been made by 403 Productions and the True Crime Channel production company.

Wolf Creek was the film debut of Greg McLean, who would go on to make the Australian horror title *Rogue* with producer David Lightfoot and co-producer/executive producer Matt Hearn. Gary Hamilton had previously executive produced *Cut* and *Hellion: The Devil's Playground* and afterward the Australian horror title *Storm Warning*. *Wolf Creek* is the only film to date made by executive producer Simon Hewitt. Executive producers Martin Fabinyi and Michael Gudinski had also produced *Cut*, and *Wolf Creek* is their last Australian horror title to date. Executive producer George Adams also worked on the Australian horror film *Prey*.

John Jarratt's film debut was as the title character in the sports comedy *The Great MacArthy* (1975). He scored the lead in the thriller *Summer City* (1977), was the title character in *Fluteman* (1982), played a supporting role in *Next of Kin* and the lead in *Dark Age*. After playing the lead in *Wolf Creek*, the actor returned to supporting parts in Greg McLean's *Rogue* and other films.

Beginning in television, Australian actress Cassandra Magrath made her film debut in a supporting role in the romantic comedy *Hotel de Love* (2006), which was her only film role prior to *Wolf Creek*. After it, the actress narrated the animated feature *Ink* (2009), and played a supporting role (with Nathan Phillips) in the romance *Summer Coda* (2010).

After beginning in television, Kestie Morassi made her film debut in *The Merchant of Fairness* (2002) and played a supporting role in *Darkness Falls*, as well as other supporting film roles. After *Wolf Creek* she worked in more supporting roles, then scored the lead in *Birthday* (2010).

Also beginning in television, Nathan Phillips made his film debut in a supporting role in the fantasy *Warriors of Virtue: Return to Tao* (2002). He scored the lead in the sports drama *Australian Rules* (2002), and after supporting film roles played the lead in his prior title, the comic thriller *Under the Radar* (2004). After *Wolf Creek* the actor played the lead in the actioner *Redline* (2007) and the Australian horror movie *Dying Breed* (2008).

RELEASE

Australia on November 3, 2005, and United States on December 25, 2005, with the taglines "How can you be found when no one knows you're missing" and "The Thrill is in the Hunt." Two new scenes were added to the American DVD unrated version that had been deleted: Kristy wakes up next to Ben (Nathan Phillips) after the party, and Liz goes down into a well in Mick's yard and discovers decaying bodies. In the DVD commentary Greg McLean also talks about a deleted subplot that had Ben and Kristy having sex at the Broome party which informed her antagonism toward him and jealousy of his feelings for Liz, and another deleted scene shown on the DVD has Ben buying a road map.

REVIEWS

"The vogue for retro-horror, particularly the stripped-down shivers of 1970s slasher flicks, continues apace in this nasty little piece of work from Australia.... Using a mixture of old-school hokum and new-school hucksterism, McLean keeps his storytelling tight and the plot admirably pared down.... Alas, [his] commitment to contemporary genre expectations turns out to be unwavering and what follows these imaginative night tremors is just the usual butchery."— Manohla Dargis, *The New York Times*, December 23, 2005

"More like the guy at the carnival sideshow who bites off chicken heads. No fun for us, no fun for the guy, no fun for the chicken. In the case of this film, it's fun for the guy.... [A] sadistic celebration of pain and cruelty." — Roger Ebert, *Chicago Sun-Times*, December 23, 2005

"You can tell a movie is doing its job well and effectively when it manages to get under your skin in such a way." — Chris Hartley, *The Video Graveyard*, February 3, 2006

"Recommended to [those] who don't mind their horror on the more brutal side of the knife.... I can't say I enjoyed the movie, it's certainly an unpleasant feeling sitting through it, but I can see the merit of the movie and the craftsmanship put into it." — Jeff Ritchie, *Scary Minds*

"[It's] continually playing on the viewer's expectations.... I was genuinely disturbed by the brutality and ruthlessness in which the latter sections of the film played out.... [It creates] a very raw and incredibly intense experience through realism and minimalism." — Trist Jones, *Digital Retribution*, February 17, 2006

"There is no doubting the talent of McLean. He manages to ratchet up the tension in the second half of the film to almost unbearable proportions. The violence is nasty and sadistic, made much more effective by the convincing naturalism that precedes it ... and the performances are fantastic." — Margaret Pomeranz, *At the Movies*, November 2, 2005

Awards

Nominated for Australian Film Institute (AFI) Best Direction, Best Screenplay, Best Cinematography, Best Editing, Best Score, Best Sound, and Best Supporting Actress — Kestie Morassi.

DVD

Released by Weinstein Company's Dimension/Genius Products on November, 4, 2006.

Like Minds

Bluewater/Gunpowder Films/Lumina Films/Tempo Productions, 2006 [aka *Murderous Intent*]

CREDITS: *Screenplay/Director:* Gregory J. Read; *Producers:* Jonathan Shteinman, Piers Tempest, Carol Hughes; *Co-Producer:* Richard Johns; *Executive Producers:* Cyril Megret, Damita Nikapota, Robert Bevan, Toni Collette, Hugo Heppell; *Associate Producer:* Sarah Giles; *Photography:* Nigel Bluck; *Editor:* Mark Warner; *Music:* Carlo Giacco; *Production Design:* Steven Jones-Evans; *Art Director:* Lucinda Thomson; *Set Decorators:* Nicki Gardiner, Sara Mathers; *Costumes:* Odile Dicks-Mireaux; *Sound:* Toivo Lember, Keith Silva; *Makeup/Hair:* Wizzy Molineaux, Scott Beswick. Color, 104–110 minutes. Filmed in Adelaide, South Australia; Cessnock, New South Wales; and Yorkshire, United Kingdom, from December 1, 2004, to March 29, 2005.

CAST: Eddie Redmayne (Alex Forbes); Tom Sturridge (Nigel Colbie); Toni Collette (Sally Rowe); Richard Roxburgh (Detective Martin McKenzie); Patrick Malahide (Headmaster, aka Dr. Forbes); David Threlfall (John Colbie); Cathryn Bradshaw (Helen Colbie); Jonathan Overton (Josh Campbell); Amit Shan (Raj); Kate Maberly (Susan Mueller); Hugh Sachs (the Reverend Donaldson); Liam McKenna (Mr. Fergus); Bryan Robson (Mr. Evans); Paul Sonkkila (Police Bureaucrat); Craig Crosbie (Coroner); Paul Blackwell (Geoff Burns); John Cooney (Police Guard); Jordan Prosser (Boy on Train); Henry Hereford (Tom). Uncredited: David Lampard, Ben Szoradi (Matthew Mills).

Synopsis

Alex Forbes is a seventeen-year-old private school boy who has been charged with the shooting murder of his seventeen-year-old school roommate, Nigel Corbie. As he explains his story to the forensic psychologist, Sally Rowe, it appears that Alex is the submissive Gestalt partner to the dominant and disturbed Nigel who believes he is a direct descendant of the medieval Knights Templar bloodline. Alex and his friend Josh find Nigel's diary writings about them, and Alex decides to teach the boy a lesson on a train ride to frighten Nigel.

Josh is accidentally killed when Nigel fails to save him from falling. The school rehearses a stage production of Lord Tennyson's play *Becket*. A schoolgirl, Susan Mueller, is killed on the night that Alex has asked her on a date. Sally finds the knife that Alex claims Nigel used to kill Susan and the bodies of Nigel's parents in a room under Nigel's house. Sally believes Alex's claim that Nigel pulled the trigger of the shotgun that killed him. Alex is acquitted of the murder charge. Sally discovers that Alex may have lied to her when the body of Susan is discovered to be missing its head, something the Templars did as an act of personal empowerment.

Notes

With a narrative that features the horror of personality, this effort by director Gregory J. Read is rather slow-paced. His treatment deprives us of on-screen killings, although it does provide the resultant gore. Read initially employs the postmodern techniques of zooms, expressionist camera angles and hand-held camerawork, slow motion, point of view, and out of focus effects. However, the majority of the treatment is devoid of such apparent tricks. His screenplay presents a large amount of flashback since the present day story is reliant upon discovering the truth of past events. He also borrows from the Alfred Hitchcock crime mystery *Strangers on a Train* (1951), another tale of two males who conspire to kill, although Read's narrative adds British historical references to the motivation.

The film opens with Alex, Josh and Raj on a train at night, with Josh taking explosive caps that will be let off later. The train stops once they alight but not because of what they have done. A shot of Alex holding the dead Nigel on the tracks in the rain is an image which will not be explained until the film's climax. It recalls the Pieta of Mary holding the dead Christ, and Nigel is considered to be a sacrifice to God. Alex's claim that Nigel "got what he wanted — eternity" is something that Read will repeat for the conclusion. The idea that Nigel wanted to "experience God first-hand" alludes to the delusions of grandeur of a psychopath and the religious-political connection of the Templar Brotherhood.

The preserved animals that Alex finds in Nigel's suitcase when Nigel is moved into Alex's room at school suggest that Nigel may be a potential serial killer, as does his fascination with dissecting the human body. This idea will be reinforced when Nigel shows Alex the room under his house where he has animal body parts and surgical instruments. Nigel's perversity extends to the moment where he doesn't save Josh from falling from the train, in spite of the fact that Nigel is on the train because Josh and Alex have taken him there to punish him. The disembodied hand that Nigel appears to have sent Alex, that is assumed to belong to Josh, is a continuation and an advance on Nigel's fascination with dead things. Its state prefigures the foot that Sally comes across under the Corbie house that presumably belongs to either John or Helen Corbie.

In a treatment that is elegantly photographed, Read provides a beautiful, resonant long shot of Alex walking in the snowfield. Susan's offer for Alex to go with her to see *Strangers on a Train* is a direct reference to what is otherwise only suggested.

Poster for *Like Minds* (2006).

Read's film has the same homoeroticism as Hitchcock's, with the beauty of the boys adding to this idea. The way Nigel looks at Alex also alludes to the idea that he may be homosexual. In the DVD commentary Read acknowledges the sexual tension between the boys but denies that either is meant to be homosexual; rather Nigel is considered to be asexual and Alex heterosexual. The Hitchcock narrative is also reflected in Nigel's notion that the two boys are fated to be united and that their union is a way to "fulfill our full potential."

Susan's blood on the knife that Nigel leaves in Alex's room is the treatment's first sign of the narrative violence. It prefigures the discovery of her disemboweled body in the glasshouse, with the killer having strung her intestines around the roof adding to his perversity.

When Sally goes to look at the room under the Corbie house, Read has her investigating a noise twice to present her as a Woman in Peril. The first time occurs before she enters the room when she sees that the noise is rats. The second is when she is in the room and after she has discovered the Polaroids of Helen and the knife. The room also has a lamp made from skin that we see but that Sally does not. The second time uses a shock effect, revealed to be a growl from the neighbor's black dog we had earlier seen in a flashback acting aggressively toward Alex.

Sally attempts to use the knife as weapon, thereby adding her fingerprints to Susan's murder weapon. When she drops it the expectation is created that her discovery will come to naught. This is not met, given the plot point of her falling back to accidentally discover the foot in the soil, from which the police learn that Nigel's missing parents are buried under the house. Their deaths being stated as shotgun deaths align them with the shotgun shooting of Nigel. Additionally, Sally being careless with the knife is a continuation of a character trait. Already she has nearly run over policemen when parking, dropped file papers in the street and dropped her purse at home. The trait is paid off in the idea that she has been careless in her assessment of Alex.

The school performing *Becket* is connected to the Templars since they are associated with Becket and became ex-communicated heretics. Alex looking in Nigel's "bible" shows Nigel's research into the Templars family tree to prove his contention that he is directly descended from the Templar bloodline. Nigel equates the Templar symbol of a looped spike with the playing card the Jack of Spades.

Alex tells Sally of Maraclea after Sally has seen the word written as "My Beloved Maraclea" on the back of the playing card that she finds in Nigel's "bible" in the room under the house. The fable tells of the lost love of a 13th century woman who died before she could wed the knight, and how the Templar opened her grave to make love to her and behead her corpse to use her head as a sign of power. Considering Susan to be Alex's Maraclea, Nigel breaks into the morgue to show Susan on the slab. We don't immediately see anything happen. Later Nigel will comment that he left Alex alone with Susan's corpse, which will be revealed to be headless. The card Sally is given saying "My Beloved Susan" recalls the earlier "My Beloved Maraclea" and implies that Alex has beheaded her.

John Colbie confronting Helen and Nigel suggests that mother and son have slept together. John telling them how he has found the Polaroids of Helen is considered by Alex to be a setup by Nigel so that he can make Helen his own Maraclea, after John shoots her. Alex shooting John is shown to be an accident when John grabs the gun that Alex has aimed at Nigel, but John being killed fits the flashback information that both parents' corpses have been found under the house thanks to Sally's visit.

Nigel seen to dispose of his father's internal organs also continues his interest in taxidermy and surgery after the earlier animal body parts and surgical instruments we saw. Read shows the resultant blood spray from John shooting Helen but not the act since it is presented by a gunshot that Alex hears. John's shooting also deprives us of the sight of the resultant blood.

Nigel's pursuit of Alex with the shotgun on the train tracks in the rain presents Nigel as a direct antagonist for the first time. The rain is added for atmosphere, and an oncoming track is added to raise the stakes. However, Nigel saving Alex from being hit by the train nullifies Nigel's apparent antagonism, and allows Alex to get the gun which he aims at Nigel. Why Nigel should reach to pull the trigger is an act that seems inexplicable, because we don't know why Nigel would want to kill himself. It perhaps suggests that this version of Nigel's death is only Alex's fictional version.

A title tells us that nine months have passed as we see Alex using Nigel's "bible" as a scrapbook, pasting in a news clipping with the headline "Boy Frames Own Death." In the DVD commentary Read states that the box that Alex carries when he leaves the room, and when he is on the train, is meant to contain Susan's head.

Sally' lecture clearly references her experience with Alex. This explains the film's title when she talks of a "dominant and submissive partnership producing a subjective Gestalt of similar thoughts, fantasies and other interlocking elements which conspires to form a greater and more volatile whole; the merging of like minds." The scene shows how Sally has earned fame from her work on the case and the lecture she gives is presumably from her published paper. Alex leaving her the card is a way for him to undercut her success.

The card which leads Sally to see the headless corpse of Susan, and the epilogue where Alex approaches a handsome boy on a train who is reading a history book and asks him "Do you like history?" perhaps suggests two ideas: either Alex has been lying to Sally, and us, and he was the dominant partner. Or that what we have seen has been true but that now with Nigel dead, Alex now wants to assume the position of the dominant party in a new partnership. In the DVD commentary Read claims that we are meant to believe that Alex's flashbacks are all true, but this still doesn't explain why Nigel has deliberately killed himself.

Read states on the DVD commentary that the film was originally planned as a documentary about a sociopath, but instead he became interested in partners in crime who behaved as in Gestalt psychology with one dominant and the other submissive. Read considers the tale of Alex and Nigel to be a Frankenstein story, where the monster that they create together is psychological. He also considers that Nigel as the dominant psychopath trains Alex in becoming a killer.

Nigel is envisaged as a young Ted Bundy type, who perhaps would not have gone on to become a serial killer if he had not met a sociopath to train. Equally, Read thinks that Alex would not go on to be a killer, as the films epilogue implies, if he had not been trained by Nigel. Read also states that the production deal required that the film be half made in Australia and half made in England. To this end he shot interiors in Australia and exteriors in England. He decided against casting Australian actors in the leading roles to accommodate the artistic team provision so they could be played by English actors.

Gregory J. Read made his directing debut with the film and he has not made another to date. The film is the only horror title made by producer Jonathan Shteinman, who would go on to executive produce the documentary *Not Quite Hollywood*. Piers Tempest later produced the Australian horror title *Coffin Rock*. Carol Hughes would not produce another Australian horror title after *Like Minds*. Co-producer Richard Johns would not make another Australian horror title, and neither would executive producers Cyril Megret, Damita Nikapota, Robert Bevan, Toni Collette, Hugo Heppell, and Associate Producer Sarah Giles. The film is the only Australian horror title made by Bluewater Pictures, Gunpowder Films, Lumina Films, and Tempo Productions.

Eddie Redmayne began his career in television and made his film debut in *Like Minds*. He has not had another leading role to date, having worked in more television and supporting film parts. Tom Sturridge also began in television and made his film debut in a supporting role in the family fantasy *Fairy Tale: A True Story* (1997). He continued to play supporting film roles before and after *Like Minds* and worked again on television.

Toni Collette started in television and made her film debut in a supporting role in the crime drama *Spotswood* (1992). She essayed the title character though was not top-billed in the romantic comedy *Muriel's Wedding* (1994). As well as playing supporting roles, she was the lead in the comedy *Clockwatchers* (1997), the romantic comedy *Diana and Me* (1997), the comedy *Hotel Splendide* (2000), and the romance *Japanese Story* (2003). After *Like Minds*, the actress played the lead in the mystery *The Dead Girl* (2006), and continued in supporting film roles and in television. Collette was nominated for the Best Supporting Actress Academy Award for her performance in the mystery *The Sixth Sense* (1999).

Richard Roxburgh is another actor who began his career in television; his film debut was a supporting role in the actioner *Dead to the World* (1991). He essayed more supporting roles and worked in short films and television before playing the lead in the biographical musical *Passion* (1999) prior to *Like Minds*. He was the lead in the actioners *Ice* (2010) and *Sanctum* (2010), played supporting film roles and worked in television.

Release

Australia on November 9, 2006, and a screening on June 8, 2007, at the Seattle International Film Festival, but no general release in the United States until the DVD. The taglines include "Fear and evil make deadly companions," "Two evil geniuses. Too brilliant to be caught. Except by each other," and "A thousand year old secret leads to murder."

Reviews

"Structured in a mix of linear and flashback storytelling which is sometimes confusing; it is also burdened by some extraneous material that adds to this confusion [but] it tackles material not usually the domain of Australian filmmakers.... Eddie Redmayne and Tom Sturridge deliver chillingly effective performances, every bit the match of the two Australians playing central roles."—Andrew L. Urban, *Urban Cinefile*

"The story does get a bit extravagant, but Read is a skillful enough juggler to keep us watching all the way. While not hugely original, [the film] still makes for a decent diversion."—Walter Addego, *San Francisco Chronicle*, September 23, 2007

"What starts out as an intriguing psychological drama becomes, in the end, just another murder movie.... The wintry English settings cast a pall over the grim proceedings, and Read takes himself far too seriously to allow the audience to have much fun with an increasingly bizarre storyline."—Margaret Pomeranz, *At the Movies*, November 8, 2006

"With its wild plot elements and constantly lurking sense of the dark and perverse, [it] is never an uninteresting film but the plot never seems to quite grapple with the ideas it introduces.... Collette impresses with the cool professionalism of her performance and Redmayne and Sturridge give strong and intelligent performances of considerably shaded nuance."—Richard Scheib, *Moria—the science fiction, horror and fantasy film review site*

"Psychotic thriller includes a great mix of twists, flashbacks, investigative details and touches of the occult topped off with a totally unanticipated ending.... From script to score, acting to set design this Australian/British creation is a fine piece of film art."—*VideoHound's Movie Retriever*

"Read fails to build suspense around the carnage.... Redmayne holds his own opposite Collette, but neither actor has any standout moments. If great minds think alike, they'll be giving this one a miss."—Stella Papamichael, *BBC Movies*, May 6, 2007

DVD

Released by the Weinstein Company on August 14, 2007. Magna Pacific (Australia) on August 8, 2007.

See No Evil

Lionsgate/WWE Films, 2006 [aka *Eye Scream Man*; *Goodnight*; *The Goodnight Man*; *see no evil*]

CREDITS: *Director:* Gregory Dark; *Screenplay:* Dan Madigan; *Producer:* Joel Simon; *Co-Producers:* Jason Constantine, John Sacchi; *Executive Producers:* Vince McMahon, Peter Block, Matt Carroll, Jed Blaugrund; *Associate Producer:* Sharlotte Blake; *Photography:* Ben Nott; *Editor:* Scott Richter; *Music:* Tyler Bates; *Production Design:* Michael Rumpf; *Costumes:* Phil Eagles; *Art Director:* Adam Head; *Set Decorator:* Gillian Butler; *Sound:* Guntis Sics; *Makeup and Hair:* Lynne O'Brien. Color, 80 minutes. Filmed at Warners Roadshow Studios, Gold Coast, Queensland.

SONGS: "Jesus Loves the Little Children" (Clare Herbert Woolston), heard in Jacob's house and the Blackwell Hotel; "X-Ed" (Featuring Kamikaze) (David Banner, Kamikaze), David Banner; "Gone" (James Root), James Root; "Army of One" (Bob Mair, Don Reynolds, Joel Wachbrit), Donzelli; "Back to Boston" (Jeff Cohen, Aria Pullman), Aria Pullman; "My Deliverance" (Michael Sokolis, Joel Wachbrit), Burning Mary.

CAST: Kane (Jacob Goodnight); Christina Vidal (Christine Zarate); Michael J. Pagan (Tye, aka Tyson Simms); Samantha Noble (Kira Vanning); Steven Vidler (Sergeant Frank Williams); Luke Pegler (Michael Montross); Cecily Polson (Margaret Gaine); Rachael Taylor (Zoe Warner); Penny McNamee (Melissa Beudroux); Craig Horner (Richie Bernson); Mikhael Wilder (Russell Wolf); Tiffany Lamb (Hannah Anders); Sam Cotton (Young Jacob); Cory Robinson (Blaine); Zoe Ventoura (Eyeless Woman); Annaliese Woods (Young Girl); Tim McDonald (Officer 1); Trent Huen (Officer 2); Matthew Okine (Officer 3); Jason Chong (News Reporter); Greg Skipper (Bus Driver).

Synopsis

Sergeant Frank Williams is called to a Los Angeles house where a noise complaint has been made about loud music. He discovers a woman inside who is alive but her eyes are missing. Frank is attacked by a man with an axe that cuts off one hand, but he manages to shoot the attacker in the head. Four years pass. He is now a prison officer in charge of a co-ed program for eight offenders who are cleaning the Blackwell Hotel, which had been damaged by a fire thirty years ago and has been used as a shelter for the homeless. Unknown to the group the hotel's manager, Margaret Gaine, is the mother of Jacob and a religious zealot. Jacob has been killing the hotel's occupants and keeping their removed eyes in glass bottles in his room.

Margaret had kept Jacob caged as a child. When he brought home a woman, Margaret tore out the sinner's eyes. During the night, Jacob kills the women's prison officer, Hannah Anders, as well as Frank, Tye, Zoe, Richie, and Russell. He also enables Melissa to be eaten by wild dogs. Jacob, however, does not kill Kira, as he is attracted to her religious tattoos. Christine and Michael manage to rescue Kira and overpower Jacob, after he kills Margaret when she demands that he kill Kira. The three survivors leave the hotel.

Notes

This title features the theme of the horror of personality in two characters: a religious and abusive mother, and her son who kills people as God's work, to punish sinners and remove their eyes, which are considered the windows to the soul. Director Gregory Dark over-employs the postmodern techniques of expressionist camera angles, blackouts and whiteouts, fast edits and jump cuts, slow and fast motion, point of view, zooms, CGI and optical effects. His treatment includes plenty of bloodletting and gore, including eye gouging, hooked body parts and death by an inserted cell phone. But there isn't much here that's original. The screenplay's dialogue is functional at best. The attempt to create a killer of moral ambiguity doesn't work, although the treatment does present one female character as a climactic warrior. Dark uses shock effects but also creates some expectations that are not met. Flashbacks are used to present some of the motivation for the killer's actions but plot holes still remain, though the killer gets a comeuppance of poetic justice and the narrative concludes with an upbeat ending.

The idea that the playing of the song "Jesus Loves the Little Children" is a cause of noise disturbance is a funny one in the prologue. Equally funny, although in a more black fashion, is William's hand that is severed and yet seen to still hold a flashlight and move as if in pain. When Williams and the other police officer hear the scream of the Eyeless Woman, they investigate the noise as the male equivalent of the conventional Woman in Peril, even if they being police officers makes the investigation standard procedure.

Jacob is only represented as an abstract madman with an axe, but the idea that he will seemingly survive a bullet to the head is a contrivance, although the narrative has its share of them. Presumably the bullet to the head is enough to send Jacob away so as not to finish off Williams, and Dark ends the scene with the camera entering the eye socket of the Eyeless Woman. The narrative doesn't explain the connection between Margaret and the Blackwell Hotel and how she ends up there. Neither does it bridge the gap between the young skinny Jacob, whom she keeps in a cage, and the adult, beefy and independent Jacob.

By showing Williams in the prologue, the narrative presents him as the protagonist. Later it will alter this assumption when he is killed halfway through. This initial presentation adds moral ambiguity to the prison offenders who are identified with freeze frames looking into the camera and their rap sheet, since they will become the new narrative protagonists. The issue of Christine having a lesbian interest in Kira is introduced but never paid off. It can perhaps be a misreading of Christine, since her history of assault is said to come from protecting her sister by attacking an abusive stepfather.

The crimes of the others are later paid off in the following ways. Richie is a computer fraudster and has the layout to the hotel. Zoe is a shoplifter who steals Hannah's cell phone that will end up choking her. Michael is guilty of assault and battery, which aids him in fighting Jacob. Tye's breaking and entering helps him to unlock doors, but it also eventuates in his being crushed and killed by the safe that he seeks. Melissa's charges for breaking into a pet store will also be used in her attempted kindness to the stray dog, although her being killed by the pack of dogs is a perverse irony. Additionally, Michael being a drug dealer that employed Kira initially creates the expectation of him wanting to abuse her again, although this plot point is dropped.

The ideas that prisoners are given the task to clean the hotel is another plot contrivance, given its serious dilapidation where rats and cockroaches reside, although the aligned idea that it has been left as it was after a fire is equally unbelievable. Dark's use of misleading shock is when Christine is pulled into a room by Kira. The expectation of them being criticized by Williams when caught smoking is not met when he simply takes one of their cigarettes to smoke. Kira being watched as she showers creates the expectation of her being attacked, given that she is being watched, although again this expectation is not met, with the reveal of Michael watching her. Dark does not exploit the actress's nudity for Kira's shower, as a genre convention, at least by not exposing her breasts. Her being watched by Jacob is an important plot point in his interest in her tattoos.

Another shock effect is when Tye and Richie find the body of an apparent homeless lodger man whose death it seems is recent. The plot point of the two of them leaving the others to search for the hotel's safe is paid off in the climax when Tye finds money stuck on the walls of Jacob's room. Margaret has said that all the homeless have been evicted from the hotel, but the bodies we see as the victims of Jacob confirm that she is a liar and that she has the agenda of revenge upon Williams.

When Jacob appears behind Richie unseen by him and holding a chained hook, the expectation of a strike is created and met. Richie's running from Tye when he had found the dead man is followed by Tye not helping Richie when he is being dragged into the elevator by Jacob. The narrative will repeat this behavior, where the prisoners fail to aid each other. It is only Christine who attempts to aid anybody, which perhaps ensures her survival by moral superiority. Jacob's presence will be repeatedly signaled by the prior appearance of flies, and this point will be paid off when he is struck in the skull and we see maggots in his scalp. In the DVD audio commentary it is also suggested that the flies are around Jacob because he has poor personal hygiene.

When Hannah enters the elevator the expectation is created and met of her attack. This is another shock moment when she is grabbed by the throat, although the idea that her arm and then head will be crushed by the closing doors is not met. The use of the dumb waiter by Jacob to capture Kira is a variation on his use of the elevator, although the hook on her neck and his taking her do not meet the expectation of her death as we will later see.

Christine and Tye are separated from the others when they go to the penthouse floor to party. It is a plot point that has the couple disappear from the narrative for a good fifteen minutes, but this occurs only after the death of Williams. The blood dripping onto Christine in the elevator is presumably that of Hannah. This is not paid off since we only see that the blood is coming from what appears to be part of her scalp on the elevator ceiling, and Hannah will be seen later as dead in Jacob's room. Thudding heard by Tye that is assumed to be Jacob is revealed to be Christine and Williams. His flashback of the prologue connects Jacob as the attacker when Tye comments that the attacker has a hole in his head.

The narrative focus on Russell, Michael, Zoe and Melissa in the penthouse is given suspense by Jacob seen watching them through what is later said to be two-way mirrors, and the expectation of a strike is created by his proximity. Dark delays the scene of Russell and Melissa having sex in the maids' quarters by showing how Kira is being kept alive by Jacob in a cage. This recalls the cage in which he was kept by his mother. Then Richie becomes conscious only to have Jacob rip out his eyes. Jacob's flashback shows how a woman holds the Young Jacob in the shower, saying "Open your eyes and wash the sins out," although only later will the flashback reveal this woman to be Margaret. When we see Russell and Melissa start to have sex, a wire under the bed rings a bell as a sign for Jacob, and Melissa's odd feeling about the mirror in the quarters leads to Jacob's breaking through it.

Russell's attempt to lower Melissa down the building with her tied to a fire hose meets the created expectation of Russell being caught by Jacob and Melissa being lifted back up. She tries to free herself before she gets back to Jacob but gets her foot caught and she hangs upside down, and the expectation of Jacob dropping her is met. However, the surprise is that Melissa lands on the floor then bounces back a little, since the fire hose stops short. When the same stray dog that she attempted to feed before appears, the expectation is created that it will help her, although how is a good question. When it licks her blood that has dropped onto the ground and then barks to call other dogs, the attack upon her by the pack is perversely ironic.

When Jacob pursues Michael and Zoe, Michael's unwillingness to help Zoe may be based on her rejection of his sexual advance. The cell phone she has stolen rings to give away her hiding place. This is remarkably bad timing, and Jacob choking the cell down Zoe's throat is perhaps the story's cruelest method of killing.

Dark again uses the expectation of an approach not met when Michael appears to be near Tyson and Christine, and a tripwire that they walk into serves as the same warning to Jacob as the wire under the maid's bed. Another false expectation is created when the elevator doors open but only flies appear, and Dark adds a shock reveal of Jacob crashing through the wall instead. When Tye takes the reluctant Christine and leaves Michael to fight Jacob alone, this perhaps seals Tyson's later fate. Tye and Christine in the stalled elevator as Jacob axes through it has Christine pulled up out of the top by Tye in the nick of time as a conventional suspense moment.

Tye zapping Jacob is the delayed use of the taser

he had been given by Williams, although the climax will have Jacob using the taser back on Tye. When Christine calls her, Kira, who answers her, is the conventional Woman in Peril since we know Kira to be encaged. The eyes that Jacob collects in glass bottles in his room like trophies is the gruesome payoff to his removing them from his victims, although it is ironic that he would seem to place more importance on them than the money Tye sees on the surrounding walls.

An odd moment occurs when Kira's cage is found but Christine decides against unlocking it with the keys that are handy when Tye tells her that Jacob is heard approaching. Dark provides a resonant image of conventional horror with the elevator doors opening to reveal Jacob. Christine promises to come back for Kira, which she does, after she has already put herself at risk to find her. But this momentary thinking of herself over Kira is troubling. However, if Christine had freed Kira we would have been deprived of the funny moment when Jacob masturbates as he looks at her, funny because of Kira's disgust at him.

Jacob unlocks Kira's cage but the sound of Tye smashing the eyeball bottles distracts Jacob and allows for Christine's promised return. Dark intercuts between Christine trying to open the cage lock with a knife, since Jacob now has the key, and Tye hiding from Jacob, with both Christine and Tye shown to be unsuccessful. The shot of the turning door knob is a conventional horror device. The expectation that it is Jacob after having killed Tye is not met when the person is revealed to be Margaret. By now we have assumed that she is Jacob's mother, since otherwise how would she have gotten past him? This seems to vanquish the prospect of Kira and Christine being able to escape. Margaret's comment to Jacob, "I'd like you to tell me, why is that whore still alive," aligns her to the flashback mother.

Margaret refers to Jacob's killings as "the hand of God." She tells the girls that she had arranged the cleaning operation to only get Williams, and that "You were a bonus." Her answer to the question of "why here" is given as "The hotel caters to deviants, sinners, and the ones that hear voices." This is a judgment of homeless people as worthless and disposable rather than people who need empathy and social assistance, and her comment to Jacob that God has told him what to do is also an indication of her madness.

Given the torment the flashbacks have shown that Jacob received from his mother, it is not a surprise when he turns against her, stopping her from shooting Kira and eventually throwing her against the wall where she is impaled on a conveniently protruding spike. The flashback that precedes this last action shows Margaret removing the eye of a girl tied to a bed as witnessed by Jacob, although like all his flashbacks, we have to contend with the conventional contrivance that he can see himself in his own memory. Therefore it appears that Jacob's act of removing eyes is copying his mother, and is telling that he gets his only line when he says "I see it" before he throws her.

Again Christine behaves oddly by hesitating when she lets Jacob take Kira out of the cage before reaching for the gun. Perhaps this can also be read as waiting for the right moment. When Christine is armed and searching the corridors she is the Australian horror movie female warrior that is also seen in *Lady, Stay Dead*, *Fair Game*, *Contagion*, *Out of the Body*, *The 13th Floor*, *Komodo*, *Ghost Ship*, *Undead*, *Black Water*, *Storm Warning*, *Slaughtered*, *Prey*, *Triangle*, *The Clinic* and *Road Train*.

The song "Jesus Loves the Little Children" is heard again, and Christine being drawn to it is again the Woman in Peril. Jacob is in what is apparently a trance as he holds Kira. This is perhaps because of the awareness of having killed his mother. This is followed by Christine holding the gun to his forehead, but with the inevitable conventional device of it being empty. His awakening and strangling the two girls simultaneously attests to his physical strength. Michael enters to strike after we had thought him dead, just as Jacob tries to pull out one of Christine's eyes.

Even Michael using the axe on Jacob does not permanently stop him, although Michael's failure to help Zoe is redeemed by his telling the girls to run to save them. Their running upstairs and not downstairs to the hotel's entrance, no matter how many floors up they are, seems like a stupid horror movie convention. The action, however, is redeemed when we see how we need them to be high to allow for Jacob's fall. In the DVD commentary it is advised that Jacob stops the people from going down by locking the access so that they can only go up.

The three pushing Jacob out the window is still not an easy victory when his hand is revealed in a shock moment to be holding onto the ledge. Christine driving a stake into his eye is the comeuppance for all his eye surgery. Jacob's fall, despite the apparent use of CGI, is still spectacular. The interior view of his heart being stabbed by the rib cage as he lands is perhaps unnecessary, and Dark provides an equally unnecessary but comic epilogue where the stray dog urinates into the dead Jacob's eye.

The audio commentary also notes that the neo–

art deco design for the Blackwell Hotel was based on the Los Angeles Ambassador Hotel where Robert J. Kennedy was assassinated in 1968 and which was demolished in 2005. It is also noted that Jacob's surname was only mentioned in dialogue that was cut. In the making-of documentary, *Do You See the Sin*, Dark advises that he based the film's aesthetic on 1980s horror titles like *Friday the 13th*.

See No Evil is the only Australian horror title made to date by the American director Gregory Dark, who had previously made music videos and adult movies for video. It is also the only Australian horror title to be made to date by producer Joel Simon, co-producer John Sacchi, associate producer Sharlotte Blake, and executive producers Jed Blaugrund, Matt Carroll and Vince McMahon. Co-producer Jason Constantine would go on to executive produce the Australian horror title *Daybreakers* with Peter Block.

Spanish born Glenn Jacobs, aka Kane, began his career in television and made his debut in the film, which is his only leading role to date. Known as a wrestler, he appeared in more wrestling television and made one supporting film role to date. American Christina Vidal made her film debut in a supporting role in the family comedy *Life with Mikey* (1993) and appeared in more supporting film roles and on television prior to and after *See No Evil*. Fellow American Michael J. Pagan also began his career in television and made his film debut in a supporting role in the crime drama *Fallen* (1998). He continued in television and film supporting roles prior to and after *See No Evil*, and produced the thrillers *House of Fears* (2007) and *Chain Letter* (2010), which he also co-wrote.

Samantha Noble made her film debut in a supporting role in the thriller *Court of Lonely Royals* (2006) and after *See No Evil* appeared in television and other supporting roles, including the Australian horror film *The Gates of Hell*. Steven Vidler is another actor to have started his career in television and film supporting roles. He assayed the lead in the science fiction thriller *Encounter at Raven's Gate* (1988) and *Dogwatch* (1999), and directed the thriller *Blackrock* (1997).

Luke Pegler began in television and made his film debut in the comedy *Getting Square* (2003). He would continue in television and film supporting roles before and after *See No Evil*. Rachael Taylor had previously appeared in *Man-Thing* and went go on to essay the leads in the crime drama *Cedar Boys* (2009) and the romance *Summer Coda* (2010), and was seen in television and film supporting roles.

Penny McNamee began her career in shorts and on television, making her film debut in *See No Evil*. She went on to more television and film shorts. Craig Horner also began his career in television, made his film debut in a supporting role in the comedy *Blurred* (2002), and has continued in television and film supporting roles. Mikhael Wilder also began in television and debuted in a supporting role in the horror film *Voodoo Lagoon* (2006). After *See No Evil* he worked in television.

Tiffany Lamb is another actor to have begun her career in television. She made her film debut in a supporting role in the comic adventure *Breakaway* (1990) and would play in more television and film supporting roles, including the Australian horror titles *Body Melt* and *Daybreakers*.

Release

Screened at the Cannes Film Festival on May 18, 2006, and opened in the United States on May 19, 2006. Taglines include "Eight Teens, One Weekend, One Serial Killer," "This Summer, someone is raising Kane," "You Don't Know Evil: Unless You See It," and "This Summer, Evil Gets Raw." No known cinema release in Australia, where it apparently went straight to DVD.

Reviews

"Shooting everything with an inebriated camera that bounces off walls, crawls over cockroaches and, at one point, roots around in an empty eye socket, the appropriately named Mr. Dark has no use for actors as anything other than body-bag fillers. He does, however, provide us with one of the most inventive cinematic examples of death by cellphone."—Jeannette Catsoulis, *The New York Times*, May 20, 2006

"The extreme levels of gratuitous gore make the picture difficult to recommend. Consenting adults who know what they're getting into will have a better-than-average time at *See No Evil*. People who don't might end up spending $20,000 on therapy in hopes of making the nightmares go away."—Peter Hartlaub, *San Francisco Chronicle*, May 22, 2006

"A bottom-rung slasher movie [with] sub-par acting. I will admit to liking a few scattered moments (the opening and our killer's quite impressive send-off in the finale), but it's not nearly enough to dig this one out of the tremendous hole writer Madigan puts it in."—Chris Hartley, *The Video Graveyard*, May 24, 2006

"Flashy visuals, a relentless pace, a huge psychopath and dumb teens getting slaughtered like cows on their way to McDonalds Value Meal Land. But if you're craving characterization, a fleshed out plot or a pinch of originality, look somewhere else, you won't find them here." — John Fallon, *Arrow in the Head*

"Not an original film, but a formula played to its strengths and not caring about its weaknesses. It entertains, but no more nor less than any other average slasher film. A treat if you want a great setting, but otherwise, a title best left to the wrestling fans for whom this film was made." — Timothy J. Rush, *Classic-Horror.com*, June 19, 2007

"A generic slasher film that offers nothing new to the genre ... oddly devoid of any charm or fun." — Mike Long, *DVD Crypt*

DVD

Released in the United States by Lions Gate on November 28, 2006, and in Australia by Sony on May 28, 2008.

Voodoo Lagoon

Matador Pictures/Taylor Brown Corporation/Shoreline Entertainment/Legaba Productions/Regent Capital, 2006 [aka *Hunt*]

CREDITS: *Screenplay/Director:* Nicholas Cohen; *Producers:* Nigel Thomas, Taylor Brown, David Cohen; *Executive Producers:* Maurice Ruskin, Lauri Apelian, Matthew Mitchell; *Photography:* Ian Thorburn; *Editor:* Peter Davies; *Music:* Peter Dasent; *Production Design:* Eugene Intas; *Sound:* John Schiefelbein; *Set Decorator:* Lenny Holmdahl; *Costumes:* Megan Hyde; *Makeup and Hair:* Jules Korshoonoff; Color, 80 minutes. Filmed at Warner Roadshow Movie World Studios, Gold Coast and on location in Queensland, and in London, England.

CAST: Ashley Hamilton (Tom); John Noble (Ben); Lara Cox (Carolina); Lincoln Lewis (Aaron); Erika Heynatz (Penny); Natalie Blair (Kate); Kristian Schmid (Kevin); Beau Brady (Lee); Kelly Atkinson (Jessica); James Stewart (Craig); Jared Robinsen (Ash); Gabriella Dilabio (Kevin's Mother); Deborah Schmid (Laura); Chris Hillier (Gary); Mikhael Wilder (Jason); Lauren Orrell (Lucy); Paul Shedlowich (Nelson); Kenneth Ransom (David).

Synopsis

Seven American tourists visit a tropical island for a holiday. The island is ruled by Ben. The visitors are unaware he is a serial killer who takes pleasure from torturing and murdering his victims with what is their greatest fear. Jessica is attacked by spiders. Kevin is attacked by rats. Lee is castrated by nails and attacked by worms. Kate is buried alive under sand, and Tom driven mad by the memory of his dead father who had committed suicide. Ben's initiate, Penny, shows an interest in Aaron.

Penny's apparent seducing of Aaron makes him no longer the virginal sacrifice Ben needs him to be. Ben attempts to kill Aaron, and the sixteen-year-old is aided by the spirit of David, the original owner of the island who had initiated Ben into the voodoo, and Ben's henchmen. Aaron kills Ben. He inherits his father's taste for killing, but decides not to murder Carolina since he states that his management will be different from that of Ben, whose heart we see Aaron pull out of the body.

Notes

This completely underwhelming movie features the theme of the horror of personality. This takes the form of a psychopath, who under the pretense of being a voodoo spirit leader takes a group of American tourists to his tropical island to torture and kill them. Director Nicholas Cohen employs the postmodern techniques of flash cuts, point of view, expressionist camera angles and hand-held camerawork, fast and slow motion, CGI effects, and an obtrusive score. He also uses torture that reads as torture porn and which results in plenty of bloodletting and gore.

While the treatment supplies gruesome violence, the use of torture porn is the basest form of suspense and practically unwatchable. This is in ironic contrast to the performances of the victims which are forgettable and lacking in protagonistic empathy. Cohen supplies some female nudity which can be read as exploitative, and a homoerotic fascination with naked male chests. The American accent of the characters, where no geographic location is given for context, is presumably an attempt to market the material to an international audience.

A prologue shows a male tourist being tortured and killed by Ben, who wears a black voodoo mask with hair to perform his murder. He reveals himself after the victim is dead. This narrative choice therefore identifies Ben as the threat when he is introduced to the new tourists, rather than leaving the killer unknown. Even more troubling is that the man that we see killed is never mentioned again other than appearing in the climax among the ghosts of Ben's victims. This provides no connection between the prologue and the ensuing narrative, apart from the idea of Ben being a killer and visitors to his island being his prey. The nature of the death of the man, whose eyes are both burned with a fired metal stake, is satisfyingly Gothic.

The narrative offers one attempt at comedy in the slapstick fall of Kevin into the sea due to his fear of seeing a shark, which is revealed to only be a prank. Later there will be an unintentional laugh when Carolina spits into Ben's face. The potential power of Aaron is prefigured by his vision of first Penny and then Ben killing David in the reflection of a mirror, although this latter scene is only explained in the climax. Additionally, Penny's interest in Aaron reads as partly sexual as much as she is thought to somehow need him for her own initiation. This isn't given any plot payoff, although it does interrupt the countdown of Ben's progressive murders.

The idea that Aaron has been brought to the island on his forthcoming sixteenth birthday and as a virgin is later revealed to be a deliberate act by Carolina seeking Ben's favor. The other tourists as victims are presumably collateral damage, although Carolina will claim that she was unaware of Ben's propensity to murder. Her presentation as a duplicitous character gets its best expression in the death of Tom, when she hands him the cigarette lighter she had earlier taken off him to prevent him from suicide. This is as if she wants him to die, which makes Aaron's decision not to kill Carolina in the climax disappointing.

When the seven tourists sit by a campfire at night, three of them reveal their fears after we presume that Kevin as the fourth has already revealed his as sharks. This information sets up the modes by which Jessica, Kate, and Tom will be killed. Tom is a different case since Ben appears to use telepathy and psychic power to make Tom see his dead father. Kate's demise is also different from that of Jessica and Kevin, since she is entrapped by Ben's henchmen rather than personally entrapped by Ben. Kevin's capture is aided by Ben's telepathy being overheard by Lee and Kate and Lee punishing him by tying him to a pier pole. The expectation of Kevin being attacked by a conveniently appearing shark is created but not met when Ben learns that Kevin's real fear is rats.

The deaths of Jessica and Kevin will feature attacks by spiders and rats, separately, with the creatures' biting showing bloody torture before expiration. One may be disappointed that Ben does not directly kill these two, although neither does he directly kill Lee and Kate. However, his creating the environment for the deaths would seem to make him just as culpable.

In the skinny-dipping scene Kate's breasts are shown as she disrobes. The sight is not made as much of as that of Penny in her sex scene with Aaron, where her breasts are shot in close-up. Both incidents of exposure read as unnecessary exploitation. Cohen is more prudish when it comes to the sex scene between Jessica and Craig; she is not exposed. Craig's sudden disappearance and her looking for him is a variation on the convention of the Woman in Peril since Jessica does not investigate a noise. Cohen also delays showing the attack upon Jessica after the expectation is created for it, a device he will repeat with the attacks on Kevin and Lee.

A scene where a flock of birds fly at the tourists on the beach at night, after the birds have flown at Kevin in the woods, is a shock effect. Another is Penny's arrow killing the unidentified resort worker who is helping the tourists. Ben's use of telepathy, which we have seen with Kevin, will be repeated more successfully with Tom, although Ben's early attempts fail. Tom will seem to turn against the others in the way he kidnaps Aaron. This is rationalized as self-defense when the others easily believe Ben's henchmen's lies about Tom being dangerous and a threat, although there is more irony when Tom takes Aaron to Ben.

There is an interesting moment with the possibility of Lee saving Kate from suffocation, when he frees himself from the nail trap. This will be shown to be false hope, but Lee will again rise to aid the later escape of Tom, Aaron and Carolina. More hope of escape is created when the three make it to the ship that brought them to the island, although again this is vanquished in light of Tom's suicide and Carolina's apparent betrayal. Cohen's use of CGI is apparent in the back and forth morphing of Aaron into David in the climax. Regrettably the ghosts of the dead don't get to avenge themselves upon Ben, and the denouement denies us the sight of Carolina when we get a shot of Aaron looking ominously into the camera. This is perhaps because Cohen wants to end with ambiguity and the hope of a sequel that has not been made to date.

The film is the only Australian horror title to be made to date by British born director Nicholas Cohen, producers Taylor Brown, David Cohen and

Nigel Thomas, co-producer Sharon Miller, associate producer Charlotte Walls, executive producers Lauri Apelian and Matthew Mitchell, and Morris Ruskin. It is also the only Australian horror movie to date by the production companies Matador Pictures, Taylor Brown Corporation, Legaba Productions, Regent Capital, and Shoreline Entertainment.

American born Ashley Hamilton made his film debut in a supporting role in the family comedy *Beethoven's 2nd* (1993). He would continue in other supporting roles and on television prior to and after *Voodoo Lagoon*, which is his only film lead to date. John Noble made his movie debut in a supporting role in *The Dreaming* and worked in supporting film roles and on television before and after *Voodoo Lagoon*. Lara Cox began her career in television and made her film debut in a supporting role in the comedy *Angst* (2000). She would appear in more film supporting roles and television prior to and after *Voodoo Lagoon* and was the lead in the thriller *The Dinner Party* (2009).

Lincoln Lewis began his career in television and made his film debut in *Voodoo Lagoon*. He would go on to appear in more television and film supporting roles. Erika Heynatz too began in television and made her film debut here, going on to appear in more film supporting roles. Natalie Blair is another actor to have started in television; she also made her film debut here. She continued in film supporting roles and television.

Beau Brady also began in television and made his debut in this film, after which he would be seen in more television. Kelly Atkinson made her film debut in a minor role in the romantic comedy *Love in the First Degree* (2004) and after *Voodoo Lagoon* appeared in television and a supporting role in the crime drama *Crooked Business* (2008), her last title to date. Kristian Schmid is another actor to have started in television and made his film debut in a supporting role in the family comedy *Scooby-Doo* (2002). He would be seen in other film supporting roles and more television prior to and after *Voodoo Lagoon*.

Release

No apparent cinema release in the United States or Australia, but the DVD tagline is "Paradise can be hell."

Reviews

"Only when it comes to the torture scenes, the film begins. These are quite aesthetically pleasing, but not excessively bloody presented. Used are spiders, rats and worms.... The film is certainly not everyone's cup of tea." — Marcus Littwin, *Slasherpool*

DVD

Released by Metrodome Distribution in the United Kingdom on April 11, 2011, but not available in the United States or Australia.

Watch Me
Scopofile, 2006

CREDITS: *Director:* Melanie Ansley; *Producer/Editor:* Sam Voutas; *Screenplay:* Melanie Ansley, Sam Voutas; *Photography:* Xue Feng; *Music/Sound Design:* Jericho, Preuss and Huf; *Set Design:* Moli Maeoa; *Costumes:* Oscar Pang; *Sound:* Buzz Burkawitz. Color, 78 minutes. Filmed on location in Melbourne, Victoria, and Beijing, China.

CAST: Frances Marrington (Tess Hooper); Sam Voutas (Taku, aka Freakboy); Tanya McHenry (Redhead, aka Sadie Borden); Glen Hancox (Detective Sanders); Katrina J. Kiely (Jill Walters); Dave Peterson (Jared); Steve Van Spall (Lars); Celeste Barry (Detective Rigby); Thomas Lim (JoJo Lim); Sharn Treloar (Cop 1); Riley Shefford (Jason); George Ivanoff (Voice of University Lecturer); Melanie Ansley (News Reporter, aka Barbara Hending/Cop 2); Edwina Fraser (Voice of Mrs. Hooper).

Synopsis

In China, Jojo Lim finds his friend Gary Wang dead as if he has fallen from his high-rise apartment. In Australia, Lars opens an e-mail attachment forwarded by Gary entitled "Watch Me." He is visited by a red headed girl who kills him and sews his eyes shut. Cinema studies student Jill Walters visits film collector Taku to rent three foreign cult titles for her thesis. She receives the e-mail, opens it and is found dead with her eyes sewn shut by her friend, Tess Hooper. Detectives Rigby and Sanders question Tess about the e-mail but disappear when they watch it at Tess' apartment. Her flat mate, Jared, is also killed by the girl when he watches the video. Tess visits Taku to see if he knows about the video.

Apparently the "Watch Me" video is a rare and original snuff film that shows the killing of the girl and kills the viewer. As someone who has survived watching the video, Taku tricks Tess into watching to see if she will be killed. She is not, and together they plan to find out why. They go to the home of Detective Sanders as the person Rigby has forwarded the e-mail to, where the girl is. Taku stops the e-mail being forwarded to anyone else via Sanders's computer. The girl kills Sanders while Taku and Tess escape after seeing that in Sanders's darkroom are photographs of the girl. The couple listens to an audio tape of the cinema studies class, where the girl is interviewed and identified as Sadie Borden. They theorize that they have been spared because neither of them enjoyed the snuff video. When Tess' brother Jason visits and watches it, the girl appears again.

Notes

This is a surprising and little known gem shot on digital camera. It features the theme of the malevolent supernatural being in the form of the ghost of a murdered girl who appears when the video attachment to a spam e-mail is opened by its receiver. Director Melanie Ansley employs the postmodern techniques of expressionist camera angles, jump cuts and fast motion, point of view, and blackouts. Her treatment uses of the convention of the Woman and Man in Peril investigating noises heard. She has lesser success in her dialogue scenes, but Ansley has a real talent for creating suspense in silent action, with a score that is more complimentary and less obtrusive than most genre titles. There is bloodletting when eyes are sewn closed and gore in the form of an amputated hand, and a few shock effects. The narrative also recalls the fatal videotape in the horror movie *The Ring*; the alabaster-skinned specter in that film was named Sadako. The counterpart in this film is named Sadie, and the facial contortions that the victims had in the former film are perhaps not as Gothic as the eye sewing here.

A prologue shows the deaths of Gary Wang and Lars. The opening scene has the anguished face of the girl on Gary's laptop screen shown briefly, although not noticed by JoJo, who enters the apartment. JoJo is the Man in Peril, the equivalent of the conventional Woman in Peril, when he goes into the bathroom after hearing a noise and sees red hair in the sink. Although he does not receive the expected strike, the head that rises out of the sink suggests the ghost's presence. Since Gary is said to be disfigured from his fall, it is hard to tell whether the disfigurement he has came from the eye sewing that we will see the girl do to her later victims.

The attack upon Lars is more explicit. The girl crawling also recalls the crawling demon of *The Ring*, and her placing fingers in Lars' mouth is not immediately understood. She is seen with her back to the camera, blocking our view of the girl sewing his mouth, with her singing "Mary Had a Little Lamb," something she will do repeatedly.

When Jill visits Taku, his nickname of "Freakboy" can be partially attributed to his being a salesman of pornography, and perhaps due to his having a monobrow. There is a laugh from Jill's repulsed reaction to the newspapers that cover his walls with her sarcastic line, "I like what you've done with the place." Ansley cross-cuts between Jill opening the spam e-mail video attachment and Tess in the kitchen. Tess drops something red on the floor and the girl's legs are seen behind her but unseen by Tess. The expectation is created of a strike in the kitchen but is not met. This is repeated when Tess changes a light bulb in a closet and the girl is seen for a flash when the new light bulb comes on.

Ansley delays the evidence of the attack upon Jill and prefigures our view of Jill's bloodied body with the blood drops Tess sees and follows. Tess hearing cries and then investigating them positions Tess as a Woman in Peril with her separated from the apparent source by a curtain over a doorway. There is a shock effect of red hair seen and retreated from under the curtain before Tess finds Jill's body in a closet with her eyes bloodied and sewn up.

A car conversation between Tess and Detective Sanders reads oddly in retrospective. This is because they talk about Tess's hit and run, which she later tells Taku happened some time ago. Thankfully, Ansley has the girl appear on the front of the car but unseen by either Tess or Sanders. Detective Rigby opens it, and not the girl, as expected. When the detectives are at Tess's apartment a telephone call received by her seemingly stops them from watching a copy of the video that Rigby has on CD. Tess takes her call outside the room and the detectives are missing when she returns. We are presumably to think that the detectives went ahead and watched the video. Sanders' comment that he has already seen it later is linked to the idea that he is the snuff filmmaker since he has the photos of the girl in his house. The expectation is also created that after the apparent watching of the video, the girl is now at Tess's door. This is an expectation not met when the person is revealed to be Jared.

Ansley cross-cuts between Jared, who has been forwarded the spam e-mail and watches the attachment video, and Tess in the bath with a cloth over her face. This is so that she is not aware of the girl with her in the bath. The expectation of a strike against Tess is again not met; the girl walks backwards to leave the bathroom. The expectation is created of her attack upon on Jared, and it is teased with a shot of the girl seen behind him but unseen by him.

There is a funny moment where he removes his glasses, then goes to pick them up from where he left them and they are gone. Jared's poor eyesight is used for his out-of-focus point of view, and he is then a Man in Peril when he investigates a noise. Although we don't see when Tess has left the bathroom or where she has gone to, Jared in the bathroom putting in contact lenses returns the point of view to a normal vision. His finding a red strand of hair in the bath drain is followed by the shock effect of the girl's hand that grabs him to pull him into the bathtub. Ansley then returns to Tess for the discovery of Jared bloodied and his eyes sewn closed.

Tess goes to see Taku and their power struggle is over the fact that she has the video and he wants it. This antagonism is aided by the exchange where she asks him if he has a computer, and he replies sarcastically, "No, I use a typewriter." When Taku knocks Tess unconscious it is a surprise, and his tying her to a chair and taping her eyes open so she can watch the video reads as torture. She is not killed by the girl. It is only after the expectation is created that she will be that we learn he has done this to see if she is like him — to see if she is able to watch the video and not be killed, unlike all the others. Ansley also inter-cuts in between Tess and Taku, and gets a laugh from him finding a long strand of red hair in the noodles he eats. The resultant expectation of a strike against him is also not met, and we get the camera's point of view of watching Tess in black and white stock and the girl's red hair reading as blonde. Ansley also offers the expectation of a strike when the girl sits between Tess's legs, which the blackout also suggests, so it is another surprise when we see that Tess is unharmed afterward.

Thankfully, Tess makes Taku explain his comment to her, "Welcome to the club." We get the reversal of their previous positions where he is now tied up and she tortures him by dropping tapes from his collection into a bath of gasoline to get him to talk. They watch the film of Tess watching the video to try and understand why she was not attacked by the girl. The antagonists become allies in their quest to stop the girl and to stop the "infection" from spreading. They learn that the e-mail has been forwarded from Rigby to Sanders, although we had thought earlier that Sanders had already seen the attachment video. Tess and Taku's visit to his house has the reveal of the girl behind Sanders's door when he opens it further to speak to them.

The electric hum of a kettle that Tess turns off is shown to be a red herring, although her investigating it is her again as a Woman in Peril. The phenomenon does get a payoff in the red hair that she pours out of it. Ansley cross-cuts between the three scenarios of Sanders trapped in his bedroom, Taku in the office, and Tess with a knife. When the girl is shown to be with Taku the expectation of a strike against him is not met. Then again perhaps this is not a real expectation, given the girl's seeming lack of interest in killing Taku or Tess. When Tess holds Sanders's hand to lead him out of the house, it is inexplicably severed. The cause is unknown, although it is presumably attributed to the girl. The sight of the detached arm is perhaps the treatment's most explicit use of gore. Equally inexplicable is the unwillingness of Tess or Taku to stop the girl from attacking Sanders further and sewing his mouth up.

The photographs of the girl discovered in Sanders's darkroom create more questions than they answer. Why Tess and Taku go to the beach to listen to the audio tape that identifies the girl as Sadie Borden is equally unexplained. This is even though the audio tape pays off the early scene where we had seen how Jill and Tess listen to recorded lectures rather than attending them. The idea that what has saved Tess and Taku from the girl's wrath is the spurious idea that they did not enjoy watching the video. This is presumably unlike how Gary Wang, Lars, Jill, Rigby, Jared and Sanders reacted. The girl's sewing up their eyes is assumed to be her revenge upon their seeing her being snuffed. This idea seems spurious since there would seem to be a difference between enjoying the video and simply watching it out of curiosity, the latter apparently the case for Jill, Rigby, and Jared.

The epilogue where Jason watches the video and is visited upon by the girl is a conventional device to show that the infection has not been stopped. Again he is simply an observer rather than an enjoyer of pornography. The girl appearing behind him unseen by him is a shock effect and only suggests an intention to harm him. The idea that Tess would leave a copy of the disc in her laptop seems careless for her, particularly when she is aware of how dangerous it is. Perhaps ultimately the epilogue exists as a commercial device for a potential sequel, which has not been made to date. In the DVD featurette, "Dissecting Watch Me," Ansley comments that if a sequel was to be made it would include more information about Redhead.

This was the film debut of director Melanie Ansley and her only Australian horror title to date. It is the only Australian horror movie to date by producer Sam Voutas and the production company Scopofile.

Frances Marrington made her movie debut here and would go on to appear in other supporting film roles. Sam Voutas made his film debut in the science fiction thriller *Crash Test* (2004), which he also wrote and directed, and after *Watch Me* he would go on to appear in film supporting roles as well as direct the comedy *Red Light Revolution* (2010). Tanya McHenry made her film debut in *Watch Me*, her only movie to date.

Glen Hancox began his career making film shorts and doing television. He made his film debut in a supporting role in the science fiction title *Parallels* (2005). After *Watch Me* he worked in shorts, film supporting roles and television. Katrina J. Kiely made her film debut in a supporting role in *Crash Test*, and aside from making a film short, *Watch Me* is her last title to date. Dave Peterson and Steve Van Spall both made their film debuts in supporting roles in *Crash Test*; *Watch Me* is the last film for both of them to date. Celeste Barry began her career in television and made her film debut with *Watch Me*, also her last movie to date.

Release

Screened in the United States in October 2006 at the Atlanta Horror Festival, October 14, 2006, at the Freak Show Horror Film Festival, December 29, 2006, at the Phoenix Fear Film Festival, October 2007 at the Thriller! Chiller! Film Festival, and on October 28, 2007, at the It Came From Lake Michigan Film Festival. Screened in Australia in September 2007 at the Melbourne Underground Film Festival. The film was then released straight to DVD in the United States with the tagline "It's death at first sight!" The DVD features an alternate opening part of the prologue where we see JoJo walk up more steps to get to Gary's apartment. Toilet paper rolls on the floor to beckon him into the bathroom. The toilet is seen stained by something that is perhaps blood, and a cat is seen licking something on a table which could be a body part.

Reviews

"Competently shot (on digital video), well-edited, and featuring some effective sound design, this film is weighed down by a script full of truly awful expositional dialogue and frequently stupid character behaviour. Worse still, the script's central horror conceit is bodily lifted from *The Ring* series.... The majority of the performances are painfully amateurish."— Paul Ryan, *Digital Retribution,* January 10, 2008

"A highly exciting and at times gripping thriller, expertly shot to provide a sense of claustrophobia throughout.... The acting is of a reassuringly high standard.... The main problem of the film, however, is its screaming similarities to *The Ring* and its American re-make.... Drawbacks aside, this is a gripping piece of cinema which shows real promise and direction."— David Stephenson, *Rogue Cinema*, October 31, 2006

"Works up its own atmosphere of dread, mainly thanks to the cramped camera style that makes for a claustrophobic air — there are hardly any establishing shots, for example.... The filmmakers know their genre, and have crafted professionalism with little money. Horror fans will find a lot to enjoy here."— Graeme Clark, *The Spinning Image*

"A clever and genuinely creepy pastiche of Asian horror plot devices and storylines forming its own wickedly entertaining horror film with a well paced plot, strong acting, and wonderful direction. I had fun." — Felix Vasquez, Jr., *Cinema Crazed*, December 7 2006

"Shot with a human touch when necessary and a distorted sense during the murders. Ansley's use of agonizingly slow motions and gels creates a feeling of tension enhanced by the light piano work or high-pitched electronics of the soundtrack. Viewers are constantly looking over the character's shoulders, into mirrors, and behind opened doors for the inevitable shock."— Catwalk, *Horrorview*

"The actors are relative unknowns. But their acting abilities were so strong that I found myself becoming emotionally involved in their quest.... The scenes were simple and believable. There is no orchestrated music but the background "sounds" are creepy and memorable.... For a short-length movie this movie packs a lot of punch. [It] will not disappoint."— *Wickedly Scary*

DVD

Released by Midnight Releasing/Scopofile on September 2, 2008. No release in Australia to date.

Black Water

Black Water Films, 2007 [aka *Predator*]

CREDITS: *Screenplay/Producers/Directors:* Andrew Traucki, David Werlich; *Producer:* Michael Robertson; *Co-Producers:* Paul Cowan, Chris Wheeldon; *Executive Producers:* Gary Rogers, Michelle Harrison, Germaine McCormack-Kos; *Photography:* John Biggins; *Editor:* Rodrigo Balart; *Music:* Rafael May; *Production Design:* Aaron Crothers; *Makeup, Hair and Special Effects Design:* Sheldon Wade; *Costumes:* Justine Seymour; *Sound:* David Glasser. Color, 89 minutes. Filmed on location at Gungah Bay, Oatley, Lime Kiln Bay, South Hurstville, Kurnell, Woolooware, and the Australian Reptile Park, Sommersby, New South Wales; and Darwin Crocodile Park, Crocodylus Park and Territorial Park, Northern Territory.

SONG: "Don't Walk Alone" (Kevin Mitchell), Bob Evans.

CAST: Diana Glenn (Grace); Maeve Dermody (Lee); Andy Rodoreda (Adam); Ben Oxenbould (Jim); Fiona Press (Pat).

Synopsis

Twenty-two-year-old Lee, her older sister Grace and Grace's boyfriend, Adam, are on holiday from Sydney. They leave their mother's home and travel to the Ainsley Crocodile Adventure Park. Wanting more crocodile experience, they go to Backwater Barry's Alternative River Tour and they are taken fishing by Jim. Their boat is struck by a crocodile in a mangrove swamp and capsizes. Jim is killed by a crocodile. Adam and Grace hide in a tree but Lee is trapped on the boat. She eventually swims to the tree to join the others, and the three try to plan a strategy to escape the lurking creature. When Adam goes to the boat and turns it back up, he is taken by the crocodile.

The girls try for the boat. Grace is attacked, although she manages to escape. Lee leaves her wounded sister and tries for the boat. She gets in it to find the outboard motor is dead. When the crocodile jumps into the boat Lee runs into the river and she is attacked. She awakens to find herself on a small island with the body of Jim. She takes the gun she had seen him bring along for the trip. The crocodile appears but the gun does not fire. After the creature attacks her, the gun eventually goes off and kills the beast. Lee goes back to Grace, who she finds has died. Placing her in the boat, she paddles them out of the swamp.

Notes

A small-scale triumph. This title is said to be inspired by real events and features the theme of horror of personality as a saltwater crocodile who terrorizes three tourists in the Northern Territory waters. Directors Andrew Traucki and David Werlich employ the postmodern techniques of blackouts, expressionist camera angles and hand-held camerawork, jump cuts, optical effects and point of view. They turn the limitations of the narrative into a frightening and empathetic experience full of suspense and tension. The treatment also presents a female character as an armed warrior, although her mythic status is humanized by reality. There is a pleasing use of silence to convey the passage of time and the isolated predicament of the protagonists.

An opening title reads "The Saltwater Crocodile population in the Northern Territory is expanding. So is the human population." This is misleading since it implies that the conflict to come will involve encroachment rather than a random encounter. A storm with thunder, lightning and rain is shown before the tourists go to Adventure Park. The phenomenon will not operate as the conventional horror movie premonition here as it will be later in the narrative.

The plot point of Grace learning she is pregnant doesn't really get a payoff aside from the point that she doesn't tell Adam before he is killed. Thankfully, her being so doesn't allow her to be a moral survivor. The expectation of the fishing boat being hit on the tour is first teased with an oil drum hitting the boat as a false scare. The expectation is met when the crocodile strikes. Water is shown on the lens during the capsizing of the boat as the filmmakers' only self-conscious touch. Jim's death is suggested by his body floating in the water rather than the viewer seeing him being attacked. His body also not taken by the crocodile is a plot point later paid off when it disappears, and paid off again when Lee later awakens next to the remains on the island.

When Adam travels in the water to the tree, the expectation is created but not met of a strike against him. The same expectation is also created for Lee as she travels from under the boat to lying on top of it. It is only when she is on top that the crocodile returns to menace her by knocking the boat. One wonders why the crocodile doesn't knock her off easily if it could capsize the boat and attack Jim so easily before. Another expectation not met is Lee being attacked as she leaves the boat and wading through the water to get to the tree to join Adam and Grace.

The idea that the crocodile is hunting in waist deep water is aligned to the seeming vulnerability of the three in the tree. This tree and none of the others get broken branches during the narrative, which makes the trees seem to be sturdier than anticipated. The tourists being in the tree gets a laugh because of mosquitoes that plague them. Adam comments, "We'll die from malaria while we're waiting."

Grace's idea of climbing over the trees to escape provides a comparison of the three's perceived weaknesses — Adam without his spectacles, Lee with a foot injury she has presumably sustained in the boat's capsizing, and Grace being pregnant, which Lee refers to but does not verbalize.

Grace climbing the trees then creates expectations: of a branch breaking or her falling into the river, or as later shown, of the crocodile jumping up to bite her. None of these expectations are met, even if the tree climbing is shown not to result in a viable escape route. The payoff to the tree climbing is the shock effect of Grace finding an amputated ear in the water. This presumably belongs to Jim. The expectation is that what she sees initially bubbling is the crocodile — although we don't see why she would be poking the crocodile with a stick.

When Adam goes into the water to get to the boat, his apparent tripping halfway is initially thought to be a sign of a strike by the crocodile and another false scare. The boat not being easy to turn over necessitates his going under water, where a subjective camera implies the approach of the creature. The boat rocking is initially ambiguous. The idea that Adam has been attacked is a possibility also aligned to the boat turning over but him not being seen. The expectation of a strike is momentarily avoided when he appears out of the water, but then quickly met in a shock effect of his being pulled under water. The crocodile emerging with Adam's body is almost a perverse display for the girls. The treatment will repeat this idea of the crocodile's sense of humor and its apparent arrogance. This is an awareness of a superior physical strength and cunning, although ultimately it will be defeated by a man-made weapon.

The creature jumping up to the tree to try and get Grace as she reaches for a branch to catch the boat rope with is another shock effect. It is also the treatment's first coverage of the full length of the antagonist. The transition to night features the second storm, although it has thunder and lightning without rain, perhaps because Lee asks for rain to

Poster for *Black Water* (2007).

drink. The intermittent lighting is used for screen blackouts with the storm as premonition, perhaps prefiguring the reappearance of the crocodile and the sound of it crunching and eating Adam, as heard by the girls.

Before they try to climb the trees to get to the boat, the girls chant "Go away, croc" for good luck. This is as opposed to the "Three Cheeky Monkeys" song that Adam and Grace had sung earlier that may have brought them bad luck. When they come face to face with the emerged crocodile in the water there is an interesting momentary standoff before the girls flee. It is a surprise that Grace is able to escape from the creature when neither Jim nor Adam could, although her wounds will eventually kill her. The blood we see from her wounds represents the first bloodletting in the treatment, given the lack of it in the crocodile's attacks upon the men.

The boat that approaches is used as an expectation of hope that is dashed when it does not get close enough to hear Lee's screams for help. The expectation that the dripping blood from Grace's wound will cause the crocodile to jump up to her is also not met. Another created expectation not met is Lee being struck when she goes back into the water to get into the boat. The creature's jumping into the boat is a shock effect, and the expectation of it killing her as it pursues her in the water is created when a blackout is used after her strike. However, Lee awakening on the island, injured but still alive, is the expectation of her murder not met. Apart from her apparent dislocated finger, the blood on Lee's forehead and on her waist where it appears she was bitten by the crocodile are more mild bloodletting. Lee taking Jim's gun is a payoff to the earlier plot point of him bringing it on the trip.

The gun not working because it appears to be blocked with mud is a conventional stalling device that also attempts to hamper the expectation of Lee being able to use the gun to kill the crocodile. There is a black comic moment as Lee apologizes to the headless and legless torso of Jim for taking one of his arms to use as bait to lure the crocodile. Lee as an armed female protagonist recalls the other female warriors in Australian horror titles like *Lady, Stay Dead, Fair Game, Contagion, Out of the Body, The 13th Floor, Komodo, Ghost Ship, Undead, See No Evil, Storm Warning, Slaughtered, Prey, Triangle, The Clinic* and *Road Train*.

Another shock effect is used when the crocodile appears behind Lee, unseen by her, after it has not taken Jim's arm as bait. The gun not firing then creates the expectation of Lee's defeat, particularly after the creature grabs her again when she runs in the water. This expectation is not met when the gun finally discharges. The crocodile's blood is sprayed on Lee's face in a moment of irony, with the creature's submergence signifying its death.

The final expectation is created of Lee's return to Grace to tell her of her success. However, Lee's victory is partially dashed in a cruel twist of fate by her discovery that Grace appears to have died. The denouement's triumph over the antagonist is mixed with pathos with the assumption that Lee has survived but is alone. Though we see her having Grace's body with her in the boat, we aren't shown how she managed to carry Grace out of the tree and get her into the boat. Also, Lee is only shown leaving that part of the river and not arriving back at land, though these are minor quibbles.

The making-of featurette on the DVD says footage of real crocodiles was used and composited into the footage with the actors to create the illusion of the crocodile in the mangrove swamp. Green screen was used rather than the animatronics and CGI used for the crocodile in the Australian horror movie *Rogue*. The film was the directing debut of David Nerlich and his only one to date, and the debut of Andrew Trauki, who went on to direct and produce the Australian horror title *The Reef*. Producer Michael Robertson went on to make, with the production company Prodigy Films, the Australian horror films *The Reef* and *Road Train*. *Black Water* is the only Australian horror film made by co-producers Paul Cowan and Chris Wheeldon, and executive producers Michelle Harrison and Germaine McCormack-Kos and Gary Rogers.

Diana Glenn began her career in television and made her film debut in a supporting role in *Lennie Cahill Shoots Through* (2003). She continued in television and film supporting roles; *Black Water* was her only lead film role to date. Maeve Dermody made her debut in a supporting role in *Breathing Under Water* (1993), and has appeared in more film supporting roles and television before and after *Black Water*.

Andy Rodoreda also began his career in television and made his debut in the film, followed by more television and more film supporting roles. Ben Oxenbould made his film debut as a child star playing the title role in the family comedy *Fatty Finn* (1980) and was seen in more film supporting roles and on television prior to and after *Black Water* as he made the transition to adult roles. He went on to assay the lead in the thriller *Caught Inside* (2010).

Release

Screened at the Cannes Film Festival on May 21, 2007, released straight to DVD in the United States, but released theatrically in Australia on April 24, 2008. The taglines include "Are you ready to die? "What would you do?" "Black Water: Based on true events," "You are dead meat," "What you can't see can hurt you," and "Take your last breath."

The DVD features three deleted scenes. These show the tourists arriving in the seaside town, with Adam on the beach and the girls at a shop where Grace buys the pregnancy test, Lee showering at the motel and Adam walking in on her as she finishes, and Lee getting off the overturned boat and into the swamp water to untangle the boat rope which is stuck on a submerged branch, then going back to the boat before attempting to travel to the tree.

Reviews

"A lack of incisive action takes the teeth out of croc pic. Pitched squarely at the creature-feature market, but offering too few scares and insufficient tension for audiences to take the bait.... Performances are competent, but actors are stranded by flat dialogue and narrative inertia." — Russell Edwards, *Variety*

"It's a tension-filled thriller, made more effective by the realism of its characters and the almost non-sensational style in which it's been directed. Performances from the tiny cast are tops. Andrew Traucki and David Nerlich have made an impressive debut with this one. I had my knees up under my chin watching it." — Margaret Pomeranz, *At the Movies*, April 23, 2008

"This sort of film really does get you on the edge of your seat. There's no doubt about that ... they keep the overt horror to an absolute minimum, so the suspense is well created ... it's a good Australian film and it definitely deserves to be seen." — David Stratton, *At the Movies*, April 23, 2008

"Splendid in its economy, [it] gets a grip on our senses and never lets go, rather like a crocodile with its victims.... Among the highlights of the film are the many instances of restraint, making the audience do the dirty work of imagining the terror lurking and stalking our human characters." — Andrew L. Urban, *Urban Cinephile*

"The film's not perfect, but remains an impressive debut feature. The makers of *Black Water* used ingenuity and talent and have produced the best movie about three people stuck up a tree you're ever likely to see. And there's a crocodile." — Devon Bertsch, *Digital Retribution*, April 29, 2008

"An instant classic of the dark genre Down Under.... The directors follow a Speilberg truisim by not showing their croc for the vast majority of the movie, hence when you do get to see [it], it's always an impactful moment.... Warning, you may need a change of undies during certain scenes." — *ScaryMinds*

Awards

Nominated for Australia Film Institute Best Editing and Best Supporting Actress for Maeve Dermody.

DVD

Released by Sony Pictures on February 19, 2008. Released in Australia on November 21, 2008 (distributor unknown).

Rogue

Dimension Films/Village Roadshow Pictures/Emu Creek Pictures, 2007 [aka *Rogue Crocodile*; *Territory*; *Solitaire*]

CREDITS: *Screenplay/Producer/Director:* Greg McLean; *Producers:* Matt Hearn, David Lightfoot; *Executive Producers:* Tony Cavanagh, Gary Hamilton, Robert Kirby, Joel Pearlman, Bob Weinstein, Harvey Weinstein; *Photography:* Will Gibson; *Editor:* Jason Ballantine; *Music:* Francois Tetaz; *Production Design:* Robert Webb; *Costumes:* Nicola Dunn; *Hair and Makeup:* Jena Lamphee; *Sound Design:* Craig Carter; *Art Director:* Lucinda Thompson; *Set Decorator:* Lisa Thompson. Color, 99 minutes. Filmed on location at the Nitmiluk National Park and the Kakadu National Park in the Northern Territory, the Yarra Valley in Victoria, and at a studio in Maidstone in Melbourne, Victoria, from November 14, 2005, to February 17, 2006.

SONGS: "Take a Long Time" (John Brewster, Rick Brewster, Doc Neeson), The Angels; "Never Smile at a Crocodile" (Frank Churchill, Jack Lawrence), The Paulette Sisters; "(We're Gonna) Rock Around the Clock" (Max Freedman, Jimmy De Knight), Bill Haley and His Comets; "Stranger's Song", "Mother I'm Coming," "Good-bye Song" (Bobby Bunnungurr), Malibirr Tribe, Gannalbingu Language Group, North-East Arnhem Land, Northern Territory.

CAST: Radha Mitchell (Kate Ryan); Michael Vartan (Pete McKell); Sam Worthington (Neil Kelly); Caroline Brazier (Mary Ellen); Stephen Curry (Simon); Celia Ireland (Gwen); John Jarratt (Russell); Heather Mitchell (Elizabeth); Geoff Morrell (Allen); Damian Richardson (Collin); Robert Taylor (Everett); Mia Wasikowska (Sherry); Barry Otto (Merv); Shaun Longiliam (Barfly).

Synopsis

Chicago travel writer Pete McKell is one of many tourists who join the Ryan's Wildlife River Cruise. Twenty-eight-year-old Kate Ryan takes guests in her boat, *The Suzanne*, to view saltwater crocodiles in the Kingston Gorge of the Northern Territory of Australia. One group spots what they think to be a distress flare and travels into the sacred Arnhem Land waters. They find a sunken boat. Their boat is hit by a crocodile and sinks, stranding the group on a small tidal island. Locals Neil and Collin ride by but their boat is also hit by the crocodile. Neil joins the stranded group.

American Everett is taken by the lurking crocodile. Neil swims to the opposing land and ties a rope in between so the group can climb on it. However, the rope gives way when three members of the party weigh it down. Neil is taken by the crocodile. The ducks that Neil had caught are used as bait with a hook to entrap the creature while the group swims to the other side, although Kate is taken when it gets free. Pete is the last to reach the other side. Searching for the others, he comes across the crocodile's lair where he finds the bodies of Neil and Kate. Finding her still alive, Pete battles the crocodile and kills it. He carries Kate to where help has arrived.

Notes

This title features the theme of the horror of personality in the form of another large saltwater crocodile that becomes hostile when its territory is perceived to be invaded by humans. Director Greg McLean employs the postmodern techniques of point of view, expressionist camera angles, handheld camerawork, animatronics and CGI, and an obtrusive score. Like other Australian genre horror titles that feature a creature as antagonist, here again the creature is perhaps the best component of the film. McLean presents plenty of suspense and some shock moments, but his treatment is a little disappointing. There are perhaps too many aerial views of the landscape and its wildlife, and the only memorable encounter is the climactic fight between the creature and the protagonist. The casting of the American actor Michael Vartan may be viewed as a marketing choice to enhance international sales, although his character has the context of being a tourist.

A prologue shows how lightning fast a crocodile takes a buffalo which drinks in a river. Pete's arrival in the country town has him study the wall of newspaper articles about crocodiles, which will get a payoff at the end when he joins the wall with the headline "Tourist Defeats Killer Croc." The newspaper headline we see outside the pub which reads "Fishing Boat 3 Still Missing" may allude to the occupants of the boat that is found sunken. There is a laugh from Merv placing a dead fly in Pete's coffee after Merv has heard Pete tells someone on his cell phone that the service at the bar "sucks."

Characters are introduced when they board the boat. This introduction is like a forties movie bomber crew, although the character of the cancer survivor Elizabeth isn't paid off as an obvious victim. Antipathy is created between Neil and Kate when we first meet the speedboaters Neil and Collin. This comes from her making him fall into the river when he refuses to get off her boat. It also preempts the hesitation the men will later have about rescuing the group on the island.

The distress flare that is seen by Everett is presumably that of the occupants of the boat we see sunken when the group goes into the inlet. The shock of the strike against Suzanne creates narrative conflict after thirty minutes of setup. Everett being taken by the crocodile is suggested rather than shown. This is aligned with the way the creature had struck the buffalo in the prologue as evidence of how quick it is. The strike against the boat of Neil and Collin is another shock moment; Collin's disappearance also credited to the crocodile.

Suspense is created with Neil going into the water to swim to the other side and prepare the rope. The expectation of his being attacked is not met. The idea that the creature will be able to jump up to snatch the climbers is carried on from the earlier shot of a crocodile jumping in the air to take food offered from another tourist boat. The expectation that the crocodile will do this is not met, although the expectation itself sustains the suspense. The night's full moon adds to the convention of dread. Dread is also attached to Mary Ellen, who stops halfway along the rope, although she will not receive moral retribution for her apparent weakness.

The rising tide which makes the island a location that must be abandoned is of more import.

Allen's addition to the rope will ultimately ensure the failure of the plan. His lingering on the water's edge also prefigures his being the next crocodile victim. The suspense established by the expectation of the failure of the rope is aided by shots of the rope straining. The tree on the other side that holds the rope ultimately being uplifted signals the collapse of the strategy.

Mary Ellen, Sherry, and Allen all being in the water also creates the expectation of a strike that is only met after they have left the water and Allen is taken. McLean plays with the expectation by having the surprise and shock of Neil being attacked on the other side before the rope drops and the three fall. Neil's taking is perhaps moral retribution for his earlier behavior at the boat, and as with Collin, his initial refusal to assist the stranded group. The blood sprayed on his flashlight is the treatment's first bloodletting after having two previous takings where no blood was apparent, although the next strike against Kate will present more blood.

More suspense and another strike expectation is created but not met when Pete goes to collect the first aid kit from the half-sunken *Suzanne* for Elizabeth. The idea of Kate's dog to be used as bait for the trap is an interesting narrative moment, given that it is only Kate who objects to it. The ducks are a plot payoff for Collin having shown them to Kate earlier. There is more suspense in the group waiting for the crocodile to take the bait and to be entrapped to allow them to cross. The expectation created for Kate to be taken is met in light of her waiting until all the others except Pete make it across safely and by the crocodile seen approaching her. Like the taking of Allen, there is some moral retribution to her being taken in lieu of the predicament being her fault. She will return and presumably survive, although regrettably she is never presented as a warrior.

Pete slides down the interior of a tree hole and fortuitously finds the crocodile's lair. He follows Kate's barking dog to find her. The return of the crocodile is suggested by the sounds of it killing the dog. More suspense is then created by Pete hiding himself and Kate in a tree as the creature passes him. Pete seeing where the crocodile has stopped to attempt an escape gets a cheap scare device in his turning around to see the creature is not where it had just been.

Poster for *Black Water* (2007).

There is a shock effect when it jumps to bite him, and the long sequence that follows is perhaps the best in the film.

The creature's attempts to get Pete and Kate separately are repeatedly thwarted by it being unable to reach them. Pete does score a cut hand from one of the bite attempts. When Pete finally waits with a stake for the crocodile as if he is committing suicide, the expectation that it will run into it is met with the additional expectation that Pete will also be struck in the process. When the creature is impaled by the stake, its squealing creates empathy for it, since the animal is only behaving in a natural hunting manner. The expectation that Pete has been eaten is not met; we see how he has barely avoided its jaws. His sitting against it after the struggle may seem foolhardy, but thankfully McLean does not have the creature reborn to strike again. The helicopter Pete sees as he carries Kate out of the lair suggests their rescue. The fate of the others is resolved when we see them all alive with the rescue team. Kate gets a laugh line when she regains consciousness and before she is whisked away. She asks Pete, "What did you think of the tour?"

Director Greg McLean previously made *Wolf Creek* with the Emu Creek production company but has not made another Australian horror title to date. Matt Hearn co-produced *Wolf Creek* but has not made another Australian horror movie to date. David Lightfoot also produced *Wolf Creek* and would go on to executive produce the Australian horror title *Storage* and produce the Australian horror movie *Coffin Rock*. *Rogue* is the only Australian horror film to be executive produced by Bob and Harvey Weinstein.

Radha Mitchell began her career in television and made her film debut in a supporting role in the romantic comedy *Love and Other Catastrophes* (1996). She continued in television and film supporting roles and played the leads in the romance *High Art* (1998), *Everything Put Together* (2000), which she also associate produced, the mystery *The Shearer's Breakfast* (2001), *Ten Tiny Love Stories* (2002), the mystery *Visitors* (2003), played the double lead but was not top-billed in the comedy *Melinda and Melinda* (2004), and the horror adventure *Silent Hill* (2006). After *Rogue* the actress worked in more film supporting roles and television, played the lead in and executive produce the romance *The Waiting City* (2009), and wrote and directed *Four Reasons* (2002).

French born Michael Vartan began his career in television and made his film debut in a supporting role in the French *Un homme et deux femmes*, aka *A Man and Two Women* (1991). He followed this with more film supporting roles and television and played the lead in *Sand* (2000). *Rogue* is the actor's last leading film role to date, after which he appeared in more television and film supporting roles.

Briton Sam Worthington started in television and made his feature film debut in a supporting role in *Bootmen* (2000), a romantic comedy. He continued in television and film supporting roles. He assayed the lead in the comic crime thriller *Getting Square* (2003), was in the actioner *Fink!* (2005), and portrayed the title character in the thriller *Macbeth* (2006). After *Rogue* the actor took on more film supporting roles and played leads in the action fantasies *Avatar* (2009) and *Clash of the Titans* (2010), and the thriller *The Debt* (2010).

Caroline Brazier is another actor to have started her career in television and made her film debut in *Rogue*, after which she has worked in television. Stephen Curry also began his career in television and made his film debut in a supporting role in the comedy *The Castle* (1997). He continued in television and film supporting roles, including *Cut*, before and after *Rogue*.

John Jarratt played the lead in *Wolf Creek*. After *Rogue* he was in more film supporting roles and television and the lead in the thriller *Bad Behavior* (2010). He executive produced and co-wrote the thriller *Savages Crossing* (2009) and appeared in a supporting role in the Australian horror title *Needle*. Geoff Morrell went on to appear in the Australian horror film *Coffin Rock*. Robert Taylor was previously in the Australian horror title *Storm Warning* and followed up with Australian horror titles *Nature's Grave* and *Coffin Rock*.

Release

Australia on November 8, 2007, and in the United States on April 25, 2008, with the taglines "Welcome to the Territory," and "How fast can you swim?"

Reviews

"Greg McLean's follow-up to Wolf Creek achieves precisely what it sets out to do, which is to scare the pants off the audience. It's not exactly original — we've seen plenty of films in the past about uncomfortably large predators that terrorise a gradually diminishing cast of characters — but McLean handles it with style." — David Stratton, *At the Movies*, November 7, 2007

"I think if Greg McLean wants to really mature as a filmmaker he needs to put more work into his characters because really this is just situational stuff of a fairly ordinary sort.... But even so it's a fun ride. It's effective for what it is."—Margaret Pomeranz, *At the Movies*, November 7, 2007

"A ripper of a thriller ... a cohesive piece of writing and direction that finds exactly the right mix of commercial and creative balance to bring in a movie that can charm and scare us by turns, that offers credible characters and an unmistakable Australian ethos."—Andrew L. Urban, *Urban Cinephile*

"A disappointing movie. It's okay, but isn't fun enough to justify its characters' stupidity.... If some effort had been made with the script, *Rogue* could've been a hugely entertaining movie, but the film is really dragged down by the lazy plot contrivances."—Devon Bertsch, *Digital Retribution*, November 12, 2007

"For two thirds of the movie Mclean has the audience eating out of his hands, he then totally blows it with a huge change of direction that does nothing for his reputation in horror circles.... The post production shenanigans have pretty much destroyed what could have been a great movie."—*ScaryMinds*

"McLean has skill blending muted moments with horror and has a good knack for making the most of his locations and actors. It offered up enough satisfying moments but, it's stumble into by-the-book territory in the finale felt more like treading water than taking a chunk out of the audience."—Chris Hartley, *The Video Graveyard*, August 16, 2008

DVD

Released in the United States by Genius Products/Weinstein Company on August 5, 2008, and in Australia by Roadshow Australia on March 3, 2011.

Storm Warning

Darclight Films/Resolution Independents, 2007 [aka *Unsane*]

CREDITS: *Director/Music:* Jamie Blanks; *Producers:* Gary Hamilton, "Pete!" Ford; *Co-Producer:* Ann Darrouzet; *Executive Producers:* Michael Gudinski, Martin Fabinyi, Greg Sitch, Mark Pennell; *Associate Producer:* Ian Gibbins; *Screenplay:* Everett DeRoche; *Photography:* Karl Von Moller; *Editor:* Jamie Blanks, Geoff Hitchins; *Special Makeup Effects:* Justin Dix, Gab Facchinei; *Visual Effects:* Scott Zero; *Production Design:* Robby Perkins; *Costumes:* Michael Chisholm; *Makeup and Hair:* Heather Ross; *Sound:* Ben Banks; *Art Director:* Justin Dix. Color, 83 minutes. Filmed on location in Melbourne and in Central City Studios, Melbourne, Victoria.

CAST: Nadia Fares (Pia); Robert Taylor (Rob Brewer); David Lyons (Jimmy); Mathew Wilkinson (Brett); John Brumpton (Poppy); Jonathan Oldham (Red Tracksuit Guy); Puss (Honky, the dog).

Synopsis

Barrister Rob Brewer takes his French artist wife, Pia, on a fishing trip on an island, but their boat gets stuck in a mangrove. That night they find a farmhouse, but when the residents — Poppy and his sons, Jimmy and Brett — return the couple is kept hostage. Jimmy has Pia kill a baby wallaby he has brought home to eat and Brett breaks the leg of Rob. Poppy stops the boys from attempting to rape Pia in their barn, and Pia uses fishing wire to set a trap for Brett, who comes back to shoot Rob. Poppy has Jimmy collect Pia but Poppy's attempted rape of her is stopped by a spiked vaginal device she has made in the barn to protect herself. She and Rob try to escape in the family truck. Poppy's pursuit of them is halted by his dog, Honky, who attacks him since he has a taste for human blood. Jimmy also attempts to stop the escaping couple by driving a hovercraft. When Pia sees how it gets caught in the barn, she drives him back into the blades. Pia and Rob then drive away free from their ordeal.

Notes

High definition digital movie features the theme of the horror of personality. It prefigures the clichéd convention of the lowlifes in the Australian horror title *Dying Breed*, although here a sub-plot about the antagonists being marijuana growers may also explain their perverse behavior. The simple narrative presents a fish-out-of-water scenario adding class, nationality and gender differences to a treatment of psychological torture. It is redeemed two-thirds of the way in when the female protagonist becomes an opportunistic warrior that recalls the heroines of *Lady, Stay Dead*, *Fair Game*, *Contagion*,

Out of the Body, *The 13th Floor*, *Komodo*, *Ghost Ship*, *Undead*, *See No Evil*, *Black Water*, *Slaughtered*, *Prey*, *Triangle*, *The Clinic* and *Road Train*.

Director Jamie Blanks uses the postmodern techniques of expressionist camera angles and hand-held camera, blackouts, point of view, one superimposed dissolve and CGI effects, as well as over-editing and an obtrusive score. In addition his shock effects are unnecessarily highlighted with music cues. The narrative's idea of the antagonists as Neanderthals unfortunately also allows for one performance to indulge in counterproductive method mannerism. There is also some suspense, and the treatment has plenty of bloodletting and gore.

Blanks presents storm clouds in the opening credits and during the fishing trip, using them as the horror movie convention of foreboding that the protagonists do not heed. Rain will feature doing the treatment, as will thunder and lighting at pivotal moments to heighten atmosphere. The idea of Pia being French adds exoticism to her character and a European sensibility, in contrast to the ockerism of Rob. This is shown when she catches a fish and Rob reels it in. The following exchange occurs after he beats the fish to death with a wine bottle:

PIA: That's disgusting.
ROB: That's fishing, baby.

Rob takes Pia's fishing rod because she is not strong enough to reel in the fish, presenting the idea of her being a physically weaker character. The narrative will reverse this later when he is immobilized and she becomes the main protagonist. Pia's complaining about Rob's boat getting stuck in the mangrove low tide gets a funny payoff in her sarcasm. Rob tells her, "I'm gonna go scout around. Are you coming or you're gonna wait here?" She replies, "No, I'd like to wait here, Rob. With the crabs and mosquitoes."

The attack of the Red Tracksuit Guy by Poppy, Jimmy and Brett is presented via a shock effect of the Guy's victimization and his blood. We do not know where the Guy came from and who he is; only later do we see how he has been killed. The abandoned cars the couple passes and the farmhouse gate with the bull's head skull on it are more indications of the redneck mentality. The cars recall the junkyards of *The Cars That Ate Paris* and are a sign of how isolated the farmhouse location is.

Pia's hesitance in entering the farmhouse is voiced as a moral concern to Rob. "Are you sure we should be breaking into somebody's house?" His reply, "We're not breaking in. There's no one there," reads as feeble. The idea that the couple has violated the privacy of the residents is a point raised by Jimmy. Rob's apparently inadvertent turning on of the sprinklers, which makes the marijuana crop moldy and worthless, adds to the idea that the invading couple deserve the hostility heaped upon them.

The presentation of the residents as lowlifes continues with the interior shown to be a pig sty and the blowup sex doll and pornographic pictures of naked women evidence of sexual frustration and perversity. Blanks inter-cuts between Rob and Pia in the house and the return of the residents in their truck to create suspense. The expectation of the couple being caught is created, and the bright lights of the truck recall the hunting lights of trucks in *Razorback* and *Wolf Creek*. Jimmy's reveal of the baby wallaby that he has found suggests that perhaps he and the others have killed the mother.

The idea of the residents as lowlifes is continued with Jimmy and Brett shown to be dirty, drinking, swearing and having bad teeth, with Jimmy in particular also spitting as the apparent head dog. The narrative decision to initially present Poppy as a barely seen drunk and not have him involved in Jimmy and Brett's torment of the couple delays the real threat of the character, although Jimmy's fear of awakening Poppy hints at Poppy as the one in control. It's not a surprise and rather funny that Pia should describe the men as "cavemen." She and Rob are heard talking by the eavesdropping residents. They hear how Rob has found the marijuana shed, and Pia and Rob think that this discovery is unknown. The fact of their clothes being taken suggests otherwise.

Pia's killing of the baby wallaby is an interesting moment, given that she does it to protect Rob from being castrated. The blood spurt we see makes some attempt to cover what has looked to be a fake creature from the first time it was seen, perhaps because it is furless. The issue of the dog guarding the barn where Pia and Rob are taken remains a threat spoken of but unseen, though it will not stop the couple's attempt to escape. The expectation of them being caught is eventually met when they stop to find the corpse of the Red Tracksuit Guy and Jimmy arrives in the truck. Blanks uses the shock of the dog barking at the couple. Its licking the blood of the Guy seems to confirm the theory that the dog has a taste for blood.

It is appropriate that Rob, being a barrister, is the one to point out that Jimmy is keeping the couple in "unlawful incarceration." The fact that residents grow and sell marijuana seems to imply that they don't have much concern for the law. However, this plot point will get a later payoff in Poppy's reaction to the incarceration, since he says he cannot be found to be committing another crime after a prior conviction. This suggests that Pia and Rob must be killed to rid them of the problem.

The fact that Pia is two months pregnant doesn't get a payoff, since we assume that Rob knows and that it won't stop Brett or Jimmy from raping her. The entrance of Poppy is a grand narrative one since it is our first proper look at the character who has been spoken of, and because it stops the rape. However the expectation that Poppy's entrance also means that Pia and Rob can escape is not met, since he is revealed to be even more psychopathic than Jimmy. Although Pia is saved from the rape by Poppy's arrival, this is misleading, since his scene with his sons in the house displays his own abuse and sadism. The turnaround on the boys does not inspire empathy because they have been so horrible previously.

Pia's resourcefulness is displayed by her work in the barn, in the face of Rob's broken legged impotence. She sets his leg in a splint and creates the vaginal and barn traps. The vaginal "surprise" is particularly disturbing, but logical given the former near-rape and her fear that Poppy will eventually want the same. The narrative is clever in delaying Pia's use of this trap until later. Blanks also spares us and the actress the sight of her inserting the device. This is in a treatment where the only other physical exposure is contextual, when Brett asks her to show her bottom and she does. Pia rationalizes her activity to Rob by telling him, "My father said to me once, to catch a mad dog you must think like a mad dog ... only madder." Pia as the warrior energizes the treatment without becoming a superwoman with supernatural powers.

The horse porn that we see Poppy and Brett watching is another example of their sexual perversity. Thankfully Blanks spares us the graphic illustration of a girl having sex with a horse, and the sight of the men masturbating to it. It's actually a little funny that the men seem to have no reaction at all to the video, as if they have either seen it one too many times or they are so sick as to be indifferent to it. When Brett investigates the dog barking he is the conventional Man in Peril because of the context of our knowledge of the traps in the barn having been set by Pia. Unlike other conventional investigators, he lacks empathy because we want this one to be attacked.

Pia has an interesting conversation with Brett where she tells him, "When I look deep in your eyes I can see that you're not like your brother," which allows him to reveal that he is the son of a different mother who has left the family. It also has Brett tell her, "Poppy says women are only good for getting fucked. Then they eventually try to fuck you." This misogyny will be explored later in the tale Poppy tells Pia of how he murdered and mulched his black wife, who is presumably Brett's mother, for fertilizer and dog food. Pia's attempt to spare Brett does not stop his agenda of wanting to kill Rob.

His being caught in the wire trap pays off her earlier scene work, and the blood seems to show Brett's face being torn off, and later it appears that he has been scalped. While the wires suspend Brett they are not enough to kill him. Pia manages this after using his gun, which fails to fire in a moment of conventional frustration, and her repeated eleven hammer strikes of him display both the resultant gore of the head wound and her release of hysterical anger. Rob encourages Pia to kill Brett and does the same later when she is in the truck facing down Jimmy.

Jimmy looking for Brett doesn't result in the expected secondary Man in Peril, as Jimmy does not continue looking. The dog at the barn door creates the expectation of it being Pia's next victim, although one imagines defeating the animal will be a harder task. However, the expectation of the dog getting under the door is not met and we will have to wait until it later attacks Poppy to get a payoff of its reputation for having a taste for human blood. When Jimmy arrives in the barn to get Pia for Poppy, the doors being open do not allow the dog to enter, as is expected, upon the helpless Rob. It is a surprise that Pia goes with Jimmy.

Even though we know she has created the vaginal surprise, the expectation that Jimmy will be another victim of her barn traps is not met, as if she has only made one and that was used upon Brett. The expectation of her attack upon Jimmy is also created but not met by the shot of her standing behind him when he talks to Rob. Blanks confesses in the audio commentary that this is a directorial error. Jimmy seeing what we assume is the covered body of Brett is not followed up on, since he leaves with Pia after she runs to presumably get him away from it.

Jimmy putting lipstick on Pia for her to meet Poppy is another perverse touch. Blanks features thunder and lightning for her scene with Poppy, where the expectation of his being entrapped by her vaginal surprise is met. Blanks again spares us the specific result. Presumably Poppy's penis is caught in the jar, though he supplies blood. Pia returning to the barn to Rob when chased by Jimmy shows her moral loyalty to her husband. The expectation of them being shot by Jimmy, who fires at the cupboard where we believe they hide, is not met. A shock effect is used for the reveal of Brett's bloody body falling out of the cupboard onto Jimmy when he opens the door. The facial blood and the wires that Jimmy appears to be caught in imply otherwise, but it is not known whether Jimmy thinks that he has killed Brett as opposed to knowing it was done by the couple. Since he appears to be momentarily trapped under Brett's body, the expectation is created but not met that the dog will enter to strike Jimmy.

It is not a surprise that the keys are not in the truck ignition when Pia and Rob get inside. It is rather a conventional plot point, necessitating her going back inside the house to search for them or perhaps going back to Jimmy. Blanks inter-cuts between Pia searching the house, Poppy's screaming in pain and Jimmy trying to get out of the barn. It is Poppy who gets to Pia first in a shock appearance with a knife just as she finds the keys. Her smashing his head with a bottle seems a little too easy. His reappearance outside as she tries to find the right key for the truck creates suspense, and Poppy's inability to stop the dog strike against his bleeding groin is another surprise, given Jimmy's later ability to scare the dog away. Blanks scores a black laugh from Pia, presumably unintentional, driving into Poppy's body in her attempt to drive away, with the body only halting the truck momentarily. Jimmy's escape from the barn to discover the disemboweled Poppy supplies more gore.

Jimmy reappears in the hovercraft from the barn to try to stop the couple from escaping, but wires around Brett's body are entangled with the vehicle, so that the dragged body eventually halts its progress. Pia's decision to ram Jimmy with the truck because she sees him entrapped is not immediately paid off by Jimmy being caught in the blades, although this expectation will be eventually met. Rather his bravado in having her strike him seems a choice made from ego, as opposed to him logically getting out of the way of the oncoming truck. Therefore Jimmy being run into the blades, since we see the fan turn around to expose the blades as Jimmy is on the truck's windshield, allows for the shocking effect of Jimmy's explosive deconstruction.

Blanks ends by returning to the black and white photograph of Poppy, Jimmy and Brett we had seen earlier when Pia and Rob had first entered the house. This is perhaps to remind us of who we have lost and to add some slight pathos to the fate of the narrative antagonists. However, it denies us celebratory coverage of the couple's escape, even though we see the truck drive away from the farmhouse.

On the DVD audio commentary screenwriter Everett DeRoche advises the script was based on the fairytale story of Goldilocks and the Three Bears and had been written thirty years prior. He says he had trouble selling it because it was considered "too gamey," including the idea that Pia and Rob would be naked after their shower sequence for the remainder of the narrative, although covered in horse blankets and hessian sacks. The climate became easier after the success of *Wolf Creek* and Blanks says that Brian Trenchard-Smith was originally attached as director. Once he came on board Blanks originally wished to cast an Asian actress as Pia.

Blanks also mentions a cut scene of Pia in her art studio making metal sculptures which showed the skills she would use later in making the barn trap. In the scene where Poppy meets Pia there was a cut shot where he twisted her nipple when telling her about Honky's taste for human blood. The vaginal device is described alternatively as a "Shanghai Surprise," a "Singapore Surprise," and "A Penis Fly Trap." It is said to be a jar with the metal of the lid serrated. The horse in the horse porn was named Mr. Velvet.

Blanks also says he wanted the truck to run over the dog when it ran over Poppy's body because he felt Honky also needed to be punished. However, he couldn't do the effect because he had too much trouble with the dogs used. Jimmy's original demise was to have seen him decapitated from a trip wire in the barn, as a second Pia trap, and his torso was to collapse into the hovercraft blades and explode.

Storm Warning was the first Australian horror movie made by Jamie Blanks, who later made the Australian horror films *Nature's Grave* and *Crush*. Producer Gary Hamilton was an executive producer of *Wolf Creek* and would go on to produce the Australian horror title *Acolytes*. Pete Ford later produced the Australian horror title *Prey* with executive producer Mark Pennell. The film would be the only Australian horror title by co-producer Ann Darrouzet and made by the production company Resolution Independents.

Moroccan born Nadia Fares began her career in French television and made her film debut in a supporting role in the comedy *Les amies de ma femme*, aka *My Wife's Girlfriends* (1992). She worked in supporting film roles and on television before and after her lead role in *Storm Warning*. Robert Taylor began his career in television and made his film debut in a supporting role in the science fiction adventure *The Matrix* (1999). He continued to be seen in supporting film roles and on television, and after *Storm Warning* played a supporting part in *Rogue* and the lead in the Australian horror title *Coffin Rock*.

After working in a short film and on television, David Lyons made his film debut in *Storm Warning*, after which he went on to more supporting film roles and television. Mathew Wilkinson made his film debut in a supporting role in the crime thriller *Two Hands* (1999), and has only played supporting film roles to date.

John Brumpton also began his career in television and made his film debut in a supporting role in *The Man in the Blue and White Holden* (1990). As well as playing more film supporting roles and television, he essayed the leads in *Life* (1996), which he also co-wrote, and *Dance Me to My Song* (1998). After *Storm Warning*, the actor played a supporting role in the Australian horror movie *The Loved Ones*.

Release

Screened on May 17, 2007, at the Cannes Film Festival, October 19, 2007, at the ScreamFest Film Festival, and released straight to DVD in the United States. Australian wide release date unknown. The tagline is "Survival can be murder."

Reviews

"Blanks delivers a tension laced excursion into psychoville without apology.... If you don't like your movie fare with plenty of sauce then give this one a miss. Worth a visit but be careful what you might hook on this horror fishing trip." — *ScaryMinds*

"For the first two-thirds it just feels like we're going through the motions. But then the last half-hour kicks in and our asses get thoroughly kicked. [It] ramps things up to such an extreme and brutal level you can't help but sit up and take notice." — Chris Hartley, *The Video Graveyard*, February 4, 2008.

"A Backwoods Brutality film by the numbers.... Blanks only serves up serial brutality, there is no sense that the film is attempting to dig any deeper than this. There is only the sense that the brutalities are part of a series of novelty gore effects being put on like gleeful shock exhibits." — Richard Scheib, *Moria — science fiction, horror and fantasy film review site*

"The opening of the film comes off as somewhat silly but once the couple reaches the house, all bets are off. *Storm Warning* isn't very original, and it isn't fancy, but it is effective and fans of brutal 70s horror will get a kick out of this one." — Mike Long, *DVD Sleuth*, February 3, 2008

"For its first hour, been there done that and dumber than the norm kept ringing in my ear [but it] managed to always be entertaining, looked uber slick, had a solid cast and it sucker punched me hardcore with its no holds barred, gore to the wall final act." — John Fallon, *Arrow in the Head*

"An intense, violent thriller featuring some of the most inventive graphic blood-letting ever captured on celluloid.... [It] manages to orchestrate the mayhem in a way that is gruesome, funny, and completely satisfying to anyone who cares about story and characterization." — Steve Biodrowski, *Cinefantastique*, February 13 2008

DVD

Released by the Weinstein Company on February 5, 2008. Released by Reel DVD (Australia) on May 6, 2008.

Acolytes
Darclight Films/Palace Films/Stewart and Wall Entertainment, 2008

CREDITS: *Director:* Jon Hewitt; *Producers:* Penny Wall, Richard Stewart; *Executive Producers:* Grant Bradley, Gary Hamilton, Ian Gibbons; *Associate Producers:* Pam Collis, Antony Accosta; *Screenplay:* S.P. Krause, Shane Armstrong, Jon Hewitt, based on an original screenplay by S.P. Krause and Shane Armstrong; *Photography:* Mark Pugh; *Editor:* Simon Martin; *Music:* David Franzke; *Production Design:* Michelle Sotheren; *Art Director:* Chris Cox; *Set Designer:* David Hansford; *Costumes:* Vanessa Loh; *Makeup:* Veronique Keys; *Hair:* Bronwyn Fitzgerald; *Sound:* Mitchell Walter Berther. Color, 87 minutes. Filmed on location in the Glasshouse Mountains, Queensland, from April to May 2007.

SONGS: "Alone Again," Teenager; "Lonely Hands," Hot Little Hands; "Menace," Lady Red; "Candy Cut," I Heart Hiroshima; "Sweetheart," Nick Littlemore/Died Pretty; "Kingdom," Wolf and Cub; "Atlas," Battles; "Take the Plunge," Darker Half; "March of Clouds," Wolf and Cub; "Rocquefort," Karnipool; "Scorpius," Midnight Juggernauts; "Ending of an Era," Midnight Juggernauts; "Nosssiene No. 1" (Erik Satie), Hummed by Belinda McClory as Kay's lullaby.

CAST: Joel Edgerton (Ian Wright); Michael Dorman (Gary Parker); Sebastian Gregory (Mark Vincent); Hanna Mangan-Lawrence (Chasely Keys); Joshua Payne (James); Belinda McClory (Kay Wright); Holly Baldwin (Tanya Lee); Anthony Phelan (Tanya Lee's Dad); Betta Heathcote (Petra); Sue Dwyer (Ma Parker); Todd Levi (Detective 1); Danny Baldwin (Detective 2); Harley Bennick (Young James); Ryan Sheldrake (Young Mark); Leigh Grewecki (Kay and Ian's Baby); Jessie Hazell (Kay and Ian's Baby Photo); Rocco Joyce (School Bully); Veronica Gregory (Girl in Street); Kransky (Dog in Street); Joey (Gary Parker's Dog). Uncredited: Samuel Nolan (High School Student).

Synopsis

Fifteen-year-old schoolgirl Tanya Lee is hit by a car in the woods of Redcliffe. Her buried body is found by three of her schoolmates — Mark, James and Chasely. Since Mark says he saw Ian Wright bury the body, they blackmail him into killing Gary Parker, a man who had raped Mark and James when they were younger. Ian does not kill Gary, who finds the three and hunts them in the woods with a crossbow. Mark is injured but manages to kill Gary with a large stone. Ian finds and kills James. Ian also kidnaps Chasely and takes her to his house, where he has her chained in the basement. Ian has Mark confess to Chasely that he had chased Tanya Lee before she was accidentally hit by Gary's car. Ian kills Mark. Before he dies Mark stabs Ian. Chasely escapes from her chains to freedom.

Notes

This title features the theme of the horror of personality in the character of a serial killer. The treatment by director Jon Hewitt adds nothing memorable to the genre. The film is overwhelmed with his use of postmodern techniques of jump cuts and repeating of some shots, superimpositions and dissolves, expressionist camera angles and hand-held camerawork, zooms, blackouts and strobe, quick edits, point of view, and shock effects. Hewitt occasionally uses silence pleasingly and has an eye for composition. However, he fails to make the narrative protagonists empathetic, although cinephiles will be satisfied by the bloodletting. There is also ambiguity and confusion over the title of the film. The person described as an acolyte is not shown to have behaved in an acolyte way, although the serial killer is presented as a man of intelligence and perverse integrity in not wishing to be blamed for kills he has not made.

The scene of Tanya Lee's death under the opening credits uses a shock effect in her being hit by the car. The assumption is made that the driver is the one from whom she runs, but we find later this assumption is incorrect. A flashback is used to present the Young Mark and James in a stormwater tunnel hiding from Parker where an aerial view of the playground spinner dissolves to the circular entrance to the tunnel. At this time Parker is not identified; the suggestion is that the man we see is Ian, whom Mark has seen in the woods. The issue of what has become of Tanya Lee's body is also unresolved and initially has some ambiguity. It is presumed that the body the three teenagers find is a Canadian backpacker, because of the Canadian flag they find and leave on Ian's car windshield. The idea of a Canadian backpacker is furthered with the character of Petra, the Norwegian backpacker who is with Ian when he picks up Mark to take him to Chasely. This is because the backpacker is shown to be Ian's preferred victim, described by Ian as a person who "won't be missed." This is a philosophy recalling that of the killer in *Wolf Creek*.

Hewitt provides a slow zoom in on Chasely while Mark and James dig up the body in the woods, and one gets the feeling that the director is more interested in showing off the songs Chasely listens to. There is another shock cut to Tanya Lee running as Chasely's imagined memory when the teens see a poster about her disappearance on a street utility pole. The sequence where the three bash up Chasely's mother's car to give the impression that it has been stolen reads like a celebration of nihilism. The narrative positions Gary as the antagonist to the three when he will turn out to be the lesser one in comparison with Ian. Hewitt also provides a slow zoom in on Ian sitting on his bed with what sounds to be aural memory of his victim's screams. The exposure of Kay's breasts has the context of her being naked in the bath with her baby. Ian stalking Gary in order to comply with the blackmail by Mark and James is presented via intercuts with Chasely having clothed sex with James, and Mark masturbating as he stands in front of a mirror, presumably at a different location.

When Ian follows Gary, it appears that Gary is in a gay cruising zone, and that the men who beat him up are homophobes. This might be consistent with his being said to have raped the boys. Gary's awareness of his pursuit by Ian can be read as a form of sexual attraction, with the pistol Ian holds in Gary's ear a phallic symbol of penile insertion. The DVD commentary confirms that the men who beat him up are the detectives seen at his house in an earlier scene, and that Gary has been in a bar, presumably heterosexual. The expectation of Ian not killing Gary just because the boys have demanded he do so is not met. This is not a surprise, given that Ian needs Gary to identify the teenagers, although Gary's chase of the teenagers in the woods with a crossbow is.

The weapon recalls the hunting of *Turkey Shoot*. It is somewhat satisfying when Ian shoots Gary's barking dog, which has been used to track the teenagers. Hewitt uses shock appearances of Mark and James to strike Gary. Mark's repeated striking of Gary with the rock is both an exorcism of the rage he has from the past rape and prefigures Chasely's repeated stabbing of Ian in the film's climax.

When Chasely removes the arrow from Mark's arm, his screams of pain provide the first feeling of empathy for his character. This is apart from the minor stakes of him being a third wheel to the romantic relationship that seems to exist between Chasely and James. James' attack and presumed murder by Ian is only suggested. His bloodless body later found by Mark shows no sign of the ordeal. Mark also appears to have a dream of Chasely buried in the woods, which may be an omen of her capture by Ian. When Petra realizes the danger of Ian and pleads to be let out of his car, empathy is created for her immediately.

Ian releasing her is a surprise, although the held shot of her watching his car drive into the horizon has tension in that we don't know if he will change his mind and return for her. When Ian tells Mark that Gary only accidentally hit Tanya Lee with his car, we wonder how he knows that, and consider that perhaps he is the one for whom the point of view watching is for. This assumption is later invalidated when we are shown that the person having witnessed Gary's accident was Mark, and worse, because he had been chasing Tanya Lee himself.

The idea of Tanya Lee being brain damaged from a prior car accident and being a teenager with the mind of a ten-year-old makes her pursuit by Mark and death by Gary more poignant. Additionally it aligns her with the deaf wife of Ian, who is later revealed to be his accomplice by stabbing Mark in the basement, as another person who is not what she appears to be. Chasely being kept alive by Ian would seem to be a plot contrivance so that she can hear how Mark is the supposed acolyte, rather than being immediately killed in the way James appears to have been. Thankfully her being chained does not allow us to be witness to her being tortured.

Hewitt uses dim lights for the basement scenes, which allows for the shock reveal and stabbing by Kay. Ian removing her hearing aids provides an inspired touch since she no longer has to hear Chasely's cries or Mark's gasping. This will be also be used for Chasely's escape, where Kay's humming as she bottle-feeds her baby stops her from hearing Chasely. The blood dripping from Mark's mouth is perhaps the film's most unappetizing display of bloodletting, but his stabbing of Ian presumably with the knife used to stab *him* is a contrived surprise, as is Chasely's later stabbing of Ian.

When Chasely finds the keys to unchain herself the expectation is created that her escape will be thwarted by Kay being in the house. We initially think Chasely foolish to return to the basement after she finds the upstairs door locked, before we think that she has to go back to get the keys. Her return is met with the expectation of Ian's next attack. Again we wonder where she has obtained the knife she uses to stab him. Presumably the knife that Mark has stabbed into Ian is still in him for Chasely to remove and use.

Chasely's seeming escape is followed by an extreme long shot of her walking on the road, in the rain, where she is met by the lights of an oncoming car. The expectation of her being struck is not met so that we get a form of happy ending. In the DVD commentary Chasely is described as the horror movie convention of the lone girl, the survivor of the narrative.

Jon Hewitt in the audio commentary claims that he made the film for a teenage audience, which presumably rationalizes his "aesthetic" choices. The style is said to be influenced by the horror fantasy *Suspiria* (1977) and Larry Clark's adult tale of bored teenagers, *Ken Park* (2002). He also states that Ian and Kay Wright as a serial killer couple were inspired by the Perth couple, David and Catherine Birnie, who in the 1980s murdered and buried many female teenagers. *Acolytes* is the only Australian horror movie Hewitt has made to date. It is also the only Australian horror title to have been made by producers Penny Wall and Richard Stewart, executive producers Grant Bradley, associate producer Pam Collis, and the production company Stewart and Wall Entertainment. Executive producer Gary Hamilton had previously worked on *Storm Warning* and went on to the Australian horror title *Nature's Grave* with executive producer Ian Gibbons.

Joel Edgerton began his career in television and

made his film debut in a minor role in the comedy *Race the Sun* (1996). After playing in supporting film roles and more television, he essayed the lead in the comedy *Kinky Boots* (2005), and in *Open Window* (2006). After *Acolytes* the actor had the lead in the romantic comedy *Separation City* (2009), and worked in supporting film roles and television.

Michael Dorman was born in New Zealand and made his film debut in a supporting role in the Australian comedy *Spudmonkey* (2001). After playing more supporting film roles and working in television, he played the lead in the comedy *Prime Mover* (2009) and supporting parts in the Australian horror titles *Triangle* and *Daybreakers*, and the lead in *Needle*.

Sebastian Gregory also began his career in television and made his film debut in *Acolytes*, after which he played other supporting film roles. Hanna Mangan-Lawrence also made her film debut in *Acolytes* and continued in supporting film roles and on television. Joshua Payne and Holly Baldwin also made their film debuts with *Acolytes*, their only film roles to date. Belinda McClory previously appeared in *Hellion: The Devil's Playground* and essayed the lead in *Darklovestory* (2006), also directed by Jon Hewitt, her husband.

Release

Screenings in Australia at the Melbourne International Film Festival, August 1, 2008, and the United States at the Austin Fantastic Festival on September 20, 2008. Australian wide release April 30, 2009, with the tagline "Nothing stays buried forever." It apparently went straight to DVD in the United States.

The DVD features deleted scenes and an alternative ending. The deleted scenes are moments before used scenes that were trimmed: Gary in the carwash in an extended title sequence, James and Mark smashing bottles at the drive-in, Mr. Lee dragging the lake for Tanya's body, Mr. Lee outside his house where there is a mannequin wearing Tanya's clothes, Gary hunting the swan in the woods lake, the three teens following Ian's car, James and Chasely finding Mark after he had been attacked by Gary, James telling Mark how as a boy he was chased after school by Gary's dog, James and Mark at the bus stop across the road from Ian's house in a stakeout before James sneaks inside their garage, Ian getting off the train to go to his car, Ian sitting on his bed out of focus with superimposed dissolves in a shot described as "Francis Bacon"; Gary driving his car fast in a freak-out when the teens are back-seat passengers; and Kay speaking to her baby before feeding it the bottle and humming.

The alternative ending has Mark dying and not stabbing Ian, and Ian closing the sliding basement door in front of the camera as our point of view. He is then seen opening it after a few days have passed, according to the audio commentary, Ian cutting off Chasely's clothes, wrapping her in plastic, driving her to the woods, and rolling her alive into a shallow grave to make the screen go black.

Reviews

"Smart and tight teenage fright'ner. Well placed mini-shocks keep us unsettled and increasingly sensitive to the building tension. Hewitt teases with finesse, and works the well observed script into a crafty and insightful piece of cinema, with defined and tangibly real characters, thanks to his perfectly picked cast."—Andrew L. Urban, *Urban Cinefile*

"While the story has some nicely grim elements and some very bleak things to say about human nature, it's ultimately told in such a dreary fashion that no one will give a fuck.... A few nice moments, but the other 87 minutes aren't worth slogging through to get to them."—Devon Bertsch, *Digital Retribution*, January 18, 2010

"Hewitt delivers on expectations and turns in one of the finest thrillers released thus far this year. I was enthralled by both the movie making craft on display and the above average script thrown my way."—*ScaryMinds*

"Jon Hewitt's very well-made film rings a few changes on the familiar teenagers-in-peril genre. Also admirable is the use of locations [but] unfortunately, after a strong first half, the film degenerates into some messily unconvincing blood-letting which might attract devotees of the genre but which is disappointingly conventional given what's come before."—David Stratton, *At the Movies*, April 15, 2009

"Something happens midway, where a lot of the good ingredients just sort of seem to be lost somehow. It doesn't come together as strongly as you would have liked it to because it's taking you into strange territory.... I was really into this film for most of it."—Margaret Pomeranz, *At the Movies*, April 15, 2009

"Saddled with an almost maddeningly uneven sensibility, *Acolytes* ultimately possesses the feel of a sporadically engaging yet entirely underwhelming horror effort that admittedly benefits from a thrilling third act.... *Acolytes* primarily comes off as an endeavor that probably would've been better off as a short."—David Nusair, *Reel Films*

DVD

Released by Starz/Anchor Bay on July 28, 2009. Released in Australia by Madman/Palace Films on May 20, 2009.

Dying Breed
Ambience Entertainment/Omnilabmedia, 2008

CREDITS: *Director:* Jody Dwyer; *Producers:* Michael Boughen, Rod Morris; *Executive Producers:* Christopher Mapp, Matthew Street, David Whealy; *Screenplay:* Michael Boughen, Rod Morris, Jody Dwyer; *Photography:* Geoffrey Hall; *Editor:* Mark Perry; *Music:* Nerida Tyson-Chew; *Production Design:* David McKay; *Sound Design:* Emma Bortignon; *Sound:* Mark Cornish, Paul Clark; *Costumes:* Katie Graham; *Hair and Makeup:* Zelika Stanin; *Special Makeup:* Paul Pattison; *Art Director:* Jamie Parker; *Set Decorator:* Jeremy Fuller. Color, 88 minutes. Filmed on location in Tullan, Tasmania, and Coal Creek Heritage Village, South Gippsland, the University of Melbourne, Gilwell Park, Footscray, and the Dandenong Ranges National Park and St. Helliers, Victoria.

SONGS: "Where You Been" (J. Tovey, T. Cooper), The Cheats heard in Troopers Arms; "Burn It Up" (J. Tovey, T. Cooper), The Cheats; heard in Troopers Arms; "Let's Pretend" (J. Blanchard, M Morgan), Jack Blanchard and Misty Morgan, heard in policemen's car.

CAST: Nathan Phillips (Jack); Leigh Whannell (Matt); Billie Brown (Harvey/Rowan); Mirrah Foulkes (Nina); Melanie Vallejo (Rebecca); Ken Radley (Liam); Elaine Hudson (Ethel); Sheridan Harvey (Katie); Peter Docker (Alexander Pearce); Boris Brkic (Sgt. Symons); Phillip McInnes (Guard 1); Paddy McIvor (Guard 2); James Fortanier (Guard 3); Sally McDonald (Nina's Sister); Peter Finlay (Hunter 1); Christopher Stevenson (Hunter 2); Ian Scott (University Professor); Des Fleming (Colleague 1); Michelle Jones (Colleague 2); Steven Haar (Mechanic); Pamela Acheson Harding (Woman in Window); Brendan Donoghue (Gareth); Reg Evans (Alfred); Dylan Lloyd (Trooper Drinker 1); Tim Harris (Trooper Drinker 2); Andy Poulter (Trooper Drinker 3); Greg Parker (Older Policeman); Tim Stitz (Younger Policeman).

Synopsis

In 1824 in Tasmania Irish convict Alexander Pearce escapes from the penal colony and eludes capture. He cannibalistically attacks the pursuing British Sgt. Symons. In modern times (the year is not given) Irish zoological student Nina comes to Tasmania to search for the elusive Tasmanian tiger. This is something her twenty-year-old sister had also done eight years prior, only to be found drowned in the Pieman River. Nina is accompanied by her boyfriend Matt, his friend Jack and Jack's girlfriend Rebecca. The group travels in Jack's car to the Pieman Foundry. This is a backwoods area where inbred lowlifes reside, although there are few adult women to be seen. Jack knifes the tire of the car of Gareth, who he thinks nearly collided with Nina when she was driving. Jack finds his car has been deliberately scratched. He thinks Gareth was spying on him and Rebecca having sex in the Troopers Arms hotel bathroom, and Jack beats up Gareth. The next day the group ventures into the woods and takes refuge in a cave when it rains. Nina spots a tiger at night and the four look for it. Rebecca is attacked and killed by someone after Katie, a little girl from the foundry, appears to her.

The others search for Rebecca and Jack separates from Matt and Nina. When Ethel, Katie's mother, sees the child is missing, she sends her husband, Liam, to find her. Liam finds Matt and Nina and leads them through a miner's tunnel. On the other side of the tunnel the couple finds Jack, who has discovered Rebecca's bloody coat and cell phone. Jack is surprised by Harvey from the foundry. His cross-bow accidentally shoots Harvey in the head and Nina helps free the wounded Harvey. Matt joins Jack to investigate the hut of Ethel and Liam, which is filled with bloody bones and body parts. In the woods outside Jack finds Rebecca's body hanging in a tree; he gets caught in a double hunter trap and dies. Harvey and Nina are joined by Rowan, who is presumably Rebecca's killer. Nina escapes from them when they threaten her. Matt goes under the hut to follow another tunnel that leads to a precipice. He sees Nina on a bridge being threatened again by the two men. Nina jumps from the bridge to escape, and Ethel arrives to kill Rowan with an axe. When Matt gets to the bridge Ethel cuts her own throat. Matt appears to be safe with police at the foundry, but after they leave, he falls unconscious since the tea Harvey has given him is apparently drugged. Matt awakens to see that Nina has been captured and hears her being molested. Katie bites Matt as if she is another of the cannibals.

Notes

This tale of cannibals in the wilderness features the theme of the horror of personality. Director Jody Dwyer supplies plenty of gore and bloodletting, but he also relies too much upon shock effects. He utilizes the postmodern techniques of quick edits, slow motion, expressionist camera angles, blackouts and point of view. Dwyer's treatment lacks excitement and originality, in spite of the gruesomeness of the violence. The film's main assets are the brooding wilderness locations, with misty mountains and black trees that recall the swamplands of *Acolytes*. The fatalism of the narrative is pleasing but the Tasmanian tiger, which is occasionally seen, doesn't get a plot payoff. The notion of inbred country lowlifes is a cinematic cliché. Their also being cannibals is hardly a refreshing addition, though the view of the protagonists as expendable tourists recalls the same feature in *Wolf Creek* and *Acolytes*.

The film opens with sepia-toned footage of what is presumably the now thought extinct Tasmanian tiger in captivity. This is confirmed by the DVD audio commentary; the tiger is thought to have been made extinct 100 years ago. A title gives the following information: "Between 1788 and 1868 Australia served as a penal colony for the British empire. Van Diemen's Land, now known as Tasmania, was the most feared. Survival was hard. Few convicts escaped. Alexander Pearce 'The Pieman' found a way." Under the credits blood droplets are used to show the progression of a bloodline. This will apply to the cannibals as the descendants of Alexander Pearce, since they work to maintain the purity of their bloodline.

The prologue's chase of Pearce by the Troopers has Dwyer going overboard with fast cuts and slow motion effects. He adds gruesomeness in the tracker dog's biting of Pearce, the dog being disemboweled presumably by him as the first hint of his cannibalistic tendencies, and Pearce biting the neck of Sgt. Symons, who confronts him. Symons' gun stalling is a suspense device used to delay Pearce's expected killing, and of course allows him to take advantage of Symons by attacking him, as a second suggestion of his taste for cannibalism. The appearance of the tiger creates the expectation of its attack upon Pearce, which is not met with Pearce throwing what he has bitten out of Symons to the tiger to take and presumably eat.

Nina's sister's body being found drowned is presented as Nina's vision as she looks at a photograph of her sister at the same Piemans River location. Clearly the vision cannot be her memory. The eel sliding out of the corpse's mouth is an additional touch of perversity as well as a realistic phenomenon, considering the girl has been in the water. When Rebecca goes to urinate in the outback woods in the daylight, the expectation is created, but not met, that she could be attacked. The point of view shots presented indicate that she is being watched. The bloodied cloth that Nina sees through a window gives her another vision of her sister, as a shock effect, when the sister's teeth are removed. The idea of removed teeth will be evident from the set Katie plays with. The foundry residents wear dental plates to hide their filed down teeth that are used as fangs. The residents' supposedly being inbred lowlifes also seems to extend to them being unhygienic, given the disgusting state of the Troopers Arms bathroom. Dwyer supplies another shock effect in Alfred removing his dental plate to show the group.

The nudity of Rebecca has context when she has a bath. Dwyer protects the actress from exposing her breasts, although he will not do this later when Rebecca's corpse is found. The theory of the Pieman's Curse is introduced via the newspapers that Nina shows Matt. This presumably parallels Pearce's cannibalism as payback for being penalized, although it seems unlikely that Pearce himself would have come across any hikers in his appetite for human flesh. We are told that he survived in the woods but not how long he lived, and the idea that Rowan is supposed to be Pearce doesn't make sense. The DVD commentary states that Rowan is Harvey's wayward sibling, although the treatment suggests that he is some kind of ultra-inbred werewolf who is also able to hunt in the day.

The tattooed lamp we see in Nina's room when she talks with Matt and which we get a better look at when Nina is with Rebecca has the suggestion of being made of skin, alluding to the human sacrifices the locals make. The expectation of the sex scene between Jack and Rebecca being witnessed by someone is created. Although Gareth is assumed by Jack to be the one watching, based on circumstantial evidence, Jack's reaction is consistent with his obnoxious personality. This isn't necessarily a bad thing. In fact, it's good in creating conflict within the primary group and suggests that he has an attraction toward Nina. It also sets up Jack to be an eventual victim as moral payback. After Jack's savage beating of Gareth, the barbed wire he uses to hold him in place allows for the prospect of Gareth to become a victim of the tiger, but this expectation is not met. When Gareth yells, "It's me, you idiot" after freeing himself from the wire, that implies that the creature near him is Rowan and not a tiger.

When Nina sees a rabbit in the woods the next day, the expectation of its attack is met, but by

Jack's cross-bow and not by the tiger, which makes sense, since the tiger seems to be nocturnal. Nina's third vision of her sister being chased in the woods is brought about by her looking at the dead rabbit and is intercut with a scene of a woman giving birth. We don't make the connection that the sister has been impregnated and given birth to Katie until later in the narrative, when the child looks at Nina's photo of her sister and says "Mamma." Nina's sister will end up at the same ravine that Pearce did, although he did not jump the way she does. The vision of Nina's sister's fall makes Liam awaken, as if it has also been his memory, which is possible given that the faces of the men around the girl are not shown.

Dwyer supplies some suspense when the group looks for the tiger at night, since at this point in the narrative the tiger seems to be the antagonist. Katie's appearance to Rebecca is another shock effect. The appearance is introduced after Rebecca's cell phone photograph of Katie is revealed, although the narrative will conclude with the phone also having a photograph of the elusive Tiger. The person that cuts Rebecca's hand is not shown, although there is some assumption that it may be Liam after we have seen Ethel tell him to go find Katie. The attack upon Rebecca as she is held against a tree appears to be a rape. It seems that she is killed from having her neck broken, and her tongue being eaten recalls Pearce's strike against Sgt. Symons in the prologue. Dwyer again uses a shock effect for the appearance of Katie in the cave to Matt and Nina, with Katie's identifying Nina's sister in a photograph as her mother, confirming the earlier vision of the childbirth. The sight of a mouth eating Rebecca's bloody amputated leg is comic. The leg is confirmed to be Rebecca's when we see that her corpse has one missing. The mouth cannot belong to Liam or Harvey since they are shown to also be in the cave with Matt and Nina.

When Liam shows Matt and Nina the Troopers trap at the opening to the miner's tunnel, the expectation is created that they will come across another inside. This expectation is not met, although the traps will later be seen around the cabin to capture and kill Jack. Although Liam's behavior before and after Matt and Nina have entered the tunnel suggest that he is sending them into danger, his calling for Rowan is the first suggestion that Rowan is the killer.

Liam's comment — "We don't have to do this. We don't have to live by the rules" — suggests his regret and results in the shock of an axe into Liam's head. Dwyer intercuts in between Matt following blood spots on the ground, which are presumably those of Liam, to finding a body part and Jack also finding bloody gore in the greenery that a Tasmanian devil is eating from. Jack firing an arrow into Harvey's mouth and pinning his head to a tree is another shock effect. We initially wonder why Jack doesn't go to help Harvey as Matt and Nina observe, but Jack's reveal of Rebecca's bloody coat and cell phone explains his hesitation.

Rebecca's body hanging from a tree behind the hut is shown via a reverse zoom and revealed with the horror conventional use of the blood drop onto Jack's face. Jack's revengeful bravado gets paid off by the shock of him being caught in a double trap. The trap actually has some ambiguity to it. We don't know whether it has been set by Ethel and Liam deliberately or whether it is the same Trooper holdover as the one in the entrance to the tunnel. Equally there is ambiguity in the contents of the hut since the bones and body parts on display could be animal rather than human. Dwyer actually plays with the expectation of them being human, with the reveal of the contents of the boiling pot being only a sock.

Matt leaves Nina alone so that he can go to the car they see parked in the distance, which allows for the convention of him not being able to start it and for Nina to be entrapped by Harvey and Rowan. There is a perverse laugh line provided when Nina is held by Rowan and Harvey says, "I can feel the family resemblance" after smelling his hand that has presumably touched her vagina. The crossed necklace that Nina wears is paid off when she uses it to slash Harvey's throat, although Harvey is shown to be repeatedly and incredibly resilient to attack.

Nina running from Matt rather than going to him when he calls her may set her up for her moral fate, as much as his earlier leaving her to go to the car. It also allows her to be alone for the scene on the bridge. The expectation of another miner's trap in the tunnel Matt follows under the cabin is not met. The precipice he finds at the end doesn't really get a payoff since he is able to climb over it to eventually get to the bridge. It's probably a better choice that his view of Nina on the bridge from the precipice is not clear, since this isolates her further and denies the opportunity for her to be immediately rescued. The person who finds Nina on the bridge is the first reveal of Rowan, with Harvey to follow. Her pathetic attempts to back away from them are another horror movie convention of the female victim.

Thankfully Nina's choice to jump into the river

redeems her. This is after Dwyer supplies flash cuts of her sister's experience as reminders, including the sister doing the same jump to escape the residents who have held her captive and presumably raped her for breeding. Ethel's appearance on the bridge is a surprise, as is her shock stabbing of Rowan with an axe in his chest. Her comment, "Should have been done when you were a pup," recalls her earlier observed bloodied slaughter of incestuous puppies. Matt's appearance on the bridge to confront Ethel starts with her brandishing another knife and then her shock suicide after telling him, "I'm sorry." This suggests her own form of regret over the fate of the tourists.

The policemen eating the pies of the Troopers Arms suggests that they are made from human flesh. The police presence creates the expectation of Matt's escape. This makes his labored breathing after the police have left when he starts Jack's car a surprise, and Dwyer supplies flashbacks of Matt's drinking to imply that he has been drugged.

Matt seen tied up and still partly paralyzed shows that the expectation of his escape is not to be met, as does the reveal of Nina tied up behind a door. The expectation of Harvey hurting him with the tinsnips is also not met, since only Matt's shirt is opened. However the expectation of Katie biting him is met after she repeats the Simple Simon rhyme and removes the dental plate to display her filed down teeth. End titles recall those of *Wolf Creek* and state: "Over 250 people have disappeared in the Tasmanian wilderness. No remains have ever been found. Sightings of the Tasmanian tiger continue to be reported in the same area."

In the making-of documentary on the DVD, entitled *Recipe for a Horror Film*, Dwyer says the film was influenced by the adventure thriller *Deliverance* (1972) and *The Hills Have Eyes* (1977). He also says the filming was hampered by unseasonal heavy rain on location, the most rain in ten years. This recalls the location problems endured by the production team of *Wolf Creek*. The DVD audio commentary also mentions that one plot point that was not included in the shooting script was the idea that Liam and Ethel are brother and sister, although since Katie is said to be the child of Nina's sister, the siblings don't appear to have bred. Since Ethel is the only adult female among the cannibals, it would seem that she may be sterile or perhaps just no longer able to bear a child. The film also prefigures *Van Diemen's Land* (2009), which also tells the story of Alexander Pearce and how his cannibalism came out of desperate hunger rather than as the murderous expression of a psychotic.

The film was the feature debut of Jody Dwyer and the only film he has made to date. Producer Michael Boughen would go on to produce the Australian horror title *The Loved Ones* with executive producers Christopher Mapp, Matthew Street and David Whealy.

Dying Breed is the only Australian horror film made to date by producer Rod Morris and the production company Ambience Entertainment.

Nathan Phillips appeared in *Wolf Creek* and went on to other supporting film roles. Leigh Whannell began his career in television and made his film debut in a supporting role in the science fiction adventure *The Matrix Reloaded* (2003). He appeared in *Razor Eaters*. and played the lead in the American horror title *Saw* (2004), which he also co-wrote, and that was based on an Australian short that he wrote and starred in, in 2003. The actor appeared in other supporting film roles, and after *Dying Breed*, was in other supporting roles. He executive produced the five *Saw* sequels and wrote two other screenplays.

Billie Brown made his film debut in a supporting role in the comedy *Fierce Creatures* (1997), and has worked in supporting film roles and on television before and after *Dying Breed*. Mirrah Foulkes began in television and made her film debut in a supporting role in *Long Road to Heaven* (2007). After *Dying Breed* she appeared in more supporting film roles and on television. Melanie Vallejo also began in television and made her film debut in *Dying Breed*, and followed this work with film supporting roles and more television.

Ken Radley is another actor to have begun his career in television and, seen in *Dark Age*, he has appeared in other supporting film roles and television. Elaine Hudson made her film debut in a minor role in *Third Person Plural* (1978) and has held supporting film and television roles. Sheridan Harvey made her film debut in *Dying Breed* and it is her only role to date.

Release

Australia on November 6, 2008; screened in the United States on April 26, 2008, at the Tribeca Film Festival and on January 9, 2009, at the After Dark Horrrofest before being released straight to DVD. The taglines were "Every body has different tastes" and "Some species are better off dead." The DVD has one deleted scene which comes after Nina's Dublin University funding proposal presentation is made, where she meets Matt afterwards to tell him that she didn't get the grant.

REVIEWS

"This poor man's *Texas Chainsaw Massacre* fails on just about every level. It tries hard to be horrific and gruesome, even introducing a bit of fashionable torture near the end, but only the most credulous will find it genuinely scary. I enjoy a really good horror film, but *Dying Breed* is an exceedingly feeble addition to the genre." — David Stratton, *At the Movies*, November 12, 2008

"It's not my cup of tea, this appetite for mass sadism experience, this sort of like nastiness where there's this ruthlessness as far as all the characters are concerned. It's this appetite for sadistic horror that I'm actually reacting a little bit against. I know people like it more than I do." — Margaret Pomeranz, *At the Movies*, November 12, 2008

"Grisly as it needs to be, *Dying Breed* is nevertheless quite a sophisticated horror film, layered with elements and peopled with leading characters who are more than stereotypes, thanks also to top performances ... direction is taut, disciplined and cinematically astute." — Andrew L. Urban, *Urban Cinefile*

"A decent horror exercise. It's not particularly scary, nor does it have that insidious, keeps-you-thinking quality that elevates 'good' horror films to 'great,' but it's heaps of fun, and quite technically remarkable to boot. Overcome the scripting difficulties, and there's an excellent movie there." — Julian, *Digital Retribution*, November 20, 2008

"Dwyer introduces nothing you haven't yet seen in other movies, and offers nothing new for audience members hoping to stay awake. [It] doesn't provide the cinematic morsel one might expect, toss it back and get something with more meat on the bone." — *ScaryMinds*

"One for genre devotees who just can't get enough of the City Kids Fall Victim to Mountain Crazies subgenre, though even they should be prepared to be just a little short-changed by the visceral elements." — Slarek, *DVD Outsider*

DVD

Released by Lions Gate on March 31, 2009, as part of *After Dark Horrorfest* III. Ambience Entertainment (Australia) released April 8, 2009.

The Gates of Hell
Cascade Films/Rapid Fire Productions, 2008

CREDITS: *Screenplay/Director:* Kelly Dolen; *Producer:* David Parker; *Co-Producer:* David W. Allen; *Photography:* Mark Windon; *Editor:* James Cole; *Music:* Keith Moore; *Production Design:* Justin Dix; *Costumes:* Michael Chisholm; *Hair and Makeup:* Helen Magelaki; *Sound:* Lloyd Carrick; *Art Director:* Dante Sapienza; *Set Dresser:* Harvey Mawson. Color, 82 minutes. Filmed in Victoria.

SONGS: "Comfortable," "A Device," "Drifting," Miniatures of Massive; "Rock a Bye Baby," Maddi Moore; "Deepest Fear," C.E.E.D.

CAST: Michael Piccirilli (Kyle Walker); Samantha Noble (Leah Rhodes); Christian Clark (Dylan McCourt); Amy Beckwith (Maddy Hayes); Bradley Tomlinson (Adam Richards); Steve Carroll (Mandible); Dawn Klinberg (Petra Von Diebitsch); Kelly Dolen (Tom Gaf); John Higgins (Sheriff Dieter Von Diebitsch); Steve Simmons (Mayor John Berringer); Klara Lisy (Elizabeth Berringer); Pedro Lopez (Baby Jeffrey Berringer); Lois Collinder (Haggis); Dave Dawkins (Jeffrey Berringer); Jenna Golusin (Stumpy); David Hankin (Testi Eyes); Rodney Appleyard (Two Heads); Robbie Bull (Rainer Von Diebitsch); Zac Swies (Baby Dieter Von Diebitsch); Stefan Dennis (Old John Berringer, Voice); Tyler Coppin (Sheriff Dieter Von Diebitsch, Voice). Uncredited: David Dawkins (Brother); Emma Lung (Anna).

SYNOPSIS

An American film crew comes to the apparently abandoned Von Diebitsch manor to make a horror film. They are director Kyle, photographer Adam, makeup artist Leah, and actors Dylan and Maddy. A cassette tape they find in the house recorded by John Berringer tells us he persuaded his wife Elizabeth to leave their infant Jeffrey with Petra Von Diebitsch, unaware that the woman was an insane torturer of retarded children left in her care. Maddy is taken by Tom when she has sex with Dylan. In a plan organized by Kyle, however, Tom is killed by one of Petra's grown-up mutants. It appears that the others are being chased by another mutant, Mandible. In fact Mandible is trying to save them from the rampaging killer, the grown up Jeffrey Berringer.

Berringer will also murder Dylan, Adam and Leah. Maddy is killed in the house when she trips and falls into the antlers of a stuffed deer's head. Kyle attacks Mandible, believing the mutant has hurt Leah, then finds the mutant burrow and Leah's decapitated head. Kyle is attacked by the other mutants but escapes to get the main gate of the manor. The sheriff arrives at the manor then walks away rather than helping Kyle, since the sheriff wears the name tag of Dieter Von Diebitsch, the son of Petra.

NOTES

This title feature the theme of the horror of personality. This is shown in the form of carnivorous in-bred mutated beings who attack a film crew who decided to shoot their online horror movie on the grounds of the mutant's home without permission. Director Kelly Dolen employs the postmodern techniques of point of view, expressionist camera angles, flash cuts for memory, hand-held camerawork and a camera that repeatedly zooms in and out, and an obtrusive score. It doesn't help that his narrative is obtuse, although it does have an interesting apparent late antagonist switch. Dolen provides some effective gruesomeness — with the lock of a gate pulled through the disemboweled body of a victim — being the highlight, even though this fails to redeem the generally unimpressive treatment. The American accents used by the characters are presumably an attempt to make the film more marketable internationally, although location reads as irrelevant to the narrative.

A prologue dated 1949 shows the Berringers handing over their baby to Petra. Rain, thunder and lightning are used for the conventional representation of a storm as foreboding, and the period is also suggested by a yellow tint in the lighting. Elizabeth's regret over giving her baby up is shown as another prefiguring of the supposed harm that will come to it and anyone else who comes to the manor. Dolen will use shock effects for both real and false alarms. The group's investigation of the manor house has curtains being pulled and doors being opened as false alarms. The attempt to open the chained trap door is initially a failure but will later be successful when they are being apparently pursued by Mandible. The playing of the cassette tape with the narrative exposition to explain the prologue features flash cuts to it, and introduces the idea that Petra's manor was a house of torture rather than the haven the child sought. In his DVD audio commentary Dolen explains that the Berringer baby grows up to be the killer, with the suggestion that it was handed over because it was deformed at birth and that the adult Jeffrey's harelip is a result of his torture by Petra.

The full moon shown is, like the opening storm, more conventional prefiguring of doom. The night that the narrative encompasses for the bulk of its running time will be one of murder and bloodshed. The taking of Maddy as she has sex with Dylan is like the conventional punishment of teenagers for being sexually active. It is ambiguous as to whether the culprit is Tom acting as Kyle's accomplice wearing a horror mask that we see him take off or Jeffrey. However the game turns deadly when Tom is axed and decapitated. Dolen suggests rather than shows the strike, although later it will be made more explicit in the montage of attacks presented as the memory of Mandible. Unlike other genre filmmakers who use female nudity for exploitation, Dolen spares the actress such exposure despite the fact of Maddy being taken when she is naked.

Dylan's leaving the group sets up his death from isolation. Dolen uses another conventional device when Kyle, Leah and Adam run into the house and the hand of Adam as the last to be safe is caught by Mandible before he can get inside. The expectation that this means an immediate strike against Adam is not when Adam frees himself from Mandible's grip. Maddy's death is another shock effect, doubly so because it comes from an accident rather than her being attacked. Another expectation for a conventional scare is met when Leah looks through a hole in the wall to see Mandible and then he looks back at her through the hole on his side, after having momentarily disappeared from her view.

Mandible as a mutant that wears the headpiece from an electric chair and a straitjacket suggests that he is the victim of another. This idea is confirmed in the climax when he is shown to be of lesser power than Jeffrey in the burrows mutant community. Mandible's apparent pursuit of the group continues when they go into the cellar, revealed to be a torture chamber, although they seem to get out easily enough via a hole in the wall that leads to outside the house. Dolen does not let Mandible into the cellar after them — one of them not making it out through the hole is another conventional moment not used.

When Adam inexplicably decides to chat online in his tent when Kyle and Leah search for the car keys, Dolen has the online chatter message Adam, "Dude behind you," when Mandible appears behind him as seen in the camera point of view. The easy escape of the three from him is perhaps only later rationalized by the idea that he does not want to harm them since Adam's hooking the baby skeleton away from Mandible makes him pursue it rather than them. Dylan found crucified on the gate also shows him to have been blinded and disemboweled. Adam pulling the gate lock through Dylan's stomach is the perhaps the treatment's most effective use of gore, although it isn't paid off by having the lock undone.

Adam being struck in the head with an axe is another shock effect. The car driving back to run over Mandible also assumes that he had axed Adam, which we will later learn is not true. Dolen uses another conventional moment when the car stalls and we see Mandible's hand moving to show his gaining consciousness. The car's attempt to smash through the gate proves unsuccessful, which doesn't meet a created expectation, although the idea that the car will need to also run through Dylan makes the expectation less likely.

When we see Mandible digging graves to place Maddy and Dylan in rather than chasing Kyle and Leah, this supports the idea we get of him later as unantagonistic toward them. The expectation of Kyle being able to climb over the wall is created and not met with the observation of there being spikes and barbed wire on top. The idea to burn the manor from the inside, after rain has spoiled the idea of burning logs, is also not followed up on after Leah falls into one of the graves and breaks a leg.

There is a cut to Mandible pretending that the dead Adam is talking with his baby skeleton as a sign of his innocent playfulness rather than insanity. Leah not being in the grave when Kyle retrieves rope which he had used to try and scale the wall with is a contrivance, given that she is later said to have been taken by the killer mutants. Kyle finding Mandible's hut under a fallen tree and entering it seems another contrivance, given the perception that Mandible is the antagonist, although perhaps we are to think that Kyle goes in looking for Leah.

The expectation that the dogs that are also in the car quarry with Mandible will attack Kyle is not met. They attack Mandible, with the cars presumably belonging to previous manor invaders. Kyle going back to Mandible's hut is even more contrivance, though his lying on the ground perhaps gives Mandible time to get back to the hut first so that Kyle can again pursue him. At first it looks like Kyle's hesitance in attacking Mandible with the knife he finds in the hut when he has the chance is a missed opportunity, although he will stab Mandible after being pushed away from him. Kyle's ability to run after he pops back the knee that has come out of its socket is more contrivance.

Kyle's chase of Mandible leads him to a hole in the ground to find the mutants' burrow, and to find Leah's decapitated head in a pot. The memory flashes we see of the reveals of the killer being Jeffrey are neither the memory of either Kyle or Mandible, so it seems their telepathy allows for Kyle to learn that Mandible is not the antagonist. This reveal is particularly interesting because it is a surprise in the way Dolen usurps the created expectation of who the narrative's antagonist has been, although it is not used to save the protagonist from the real antagonist and his allies.

Dolen uses a blackout after Kyle is attacked by Haggis, with his throat presumably cut, but his bloodied appearance at the gate reveals how he has survived. Dolen in his DVD audio commentary also explains that the sheriff's refusal to help Kyle is because, as the son of Petra, he must keep the secret of the manor. Although we don't see Kyle attacked again, his being left behind the gate provides a downbeat ending to the narrative for the character who is the surviving protagonist.

The Gates of Hell is the first and only Australian horror movie to be made to date by director Kelly Dolen, co-producer David W. Allen, and Rapid Fire Productions. Dolen made his film acting debut in the actioner *Reign in Darkness*, and *The Gates of Hell* is his last acting title to date. This the only Australian horror title to be made by Producer David Parker and his production company Cascade Films to date.

Michael Piccirilli began his career in television and made his film debut in a supporting role in *Floodhouse* (2004). He continued in television, film shorts and feature film supporting roles, and after *The Gates of Hell* played the lead in *Obselidia* (2010). Samantha Noble previously appeared in *See No Evil* and in television and other film supporting roles; *The Gates of Hell* was her last title to date. Christian Clark began his career in television and appeared in film supporting roles in the Australian horror movies *Crush* and *Prey*.

Amy Beckwith made her film debut in *The Gates of Hell* and later worked in television. Bradley Tomlinson debuted in a supporting role in the romantic comedy *Battle Therapy* (2007) and worked in television, more film supporting roles and shorts prior to and after *The Gates of Hell*. Steve Carroll made his film debut in a minor role in the romantic comedy *The Extra* (2005) and afterward appeared in television. Dawn Klinberg followed with roles in Australian horror titles *Prey* and *Damned by Dawn*.

Release

Screened at the Cannes Film Festival on May 14, 2008, and released in the United States in October

2008 with the tagline "Evil breeds beyond...." No cinema release in Australia to date.

Reviews

"A classic of Australian dark cinema in the process.... The movie delivers on all fronts and shows a director with a strong nose for the horror genre.... The cast, full of relatively unknowns, is pretty professional and nail their individual requirements to the delight of all."— Jeff Ritchie, *ScaryMinds*

DVD

Released by Rapid Fire Distribution on October 31, 2010.

I Know How Many Runs You Scored Last Summer
Media 42, 2008

CREDITS: *Screenplay/Producer/Photography/Editor/Director:* Stacey Edmonds, Doug Turner; *Makeup and Special Effects:* Kym Grima, Aline Joyce, Cat Sherwin; *Wardrobe:* Janine Thompson; *Music:* Dallas Johnson. Color, 78 minutes. Shot in location at Joadja and Sydney, New South Wales, on weekends from December 2005 to June 2006.

SONGS: "Settle the Score" (L.A. Edwards), L.A. Edwards; "Out of the Darkness" (Mortal Sin), Mortal Sin; "Broke Down" (Hell City Glamours), Hell City Glamours; "White Trash, Hot Love" (Hell City Glamours), Hell City Glamours; "My Heart's a Breakin'" (Hell City Glamours), Hell City Glamours; "Chorus of Approval" (Vox Mortis), Vox Mortis; "Say Your Prayers" (Mortal Sin), Mortal Sin; "Dead Man Walking" (Mortal Sin), Mortal Sin; "Pretty Far from Perfect" (Hell City Glamours), Hell City Glamours.

CAST: Jai Koutrae (Gary Chance); Stacey Edmonds (Detective Inspector Kim Reynolds/Phillips); Az Jackson (Detective Senior Constable Shane Scott, aka Gregory Scott Taylor); David Gambin (David Yeo); Ben Paul Owens (Terry O'Sullivan); Aaron Scully (Craig Stedman); Alex Sideratos (Jonathan Wiley); James Winter (Matthew King); Doug Turner (Phil Phillips); Arianna Starr (Stacey Edmonds' Body Double); Otto Heutling (Doug Turner's Body Double); Brendan Arlington (Gavin Peacock); Jeff Bye (Opposition Captain); Eithne Freeney (Julie Wheeler); Sarah Linton (Belinda Berry); Ben McLaine (Ian Ryder); Robin Royce Queree (Harry Farquhar); Robert Ramka (Danny Danger); Lisa Scope (Detective Thomas); Brett Grebert, Neil Rainey, Janine Thompson (Detectives); Kym Grima (Girl in Police Station); Dexter Edmonds Turner (Jonathan's Baby); Mette Hay (Terry's Wife); Luke McKean (Terry's Son); Carla Weatherer (Police Officer); Simon Weatherer (Police Photographer); Lisa Hockton, Melinda McCallum (Matthew's Customers); Joshua Wheeler (Real Tied-Up Hugh Trenchard); Justin Hooper, Shaun Scott, Christopher Beacroft, Shaun Cooper, Jordan Hagivassiles, Jordan Brocking, Tomas Avins, Jared Ball, Dale McIntyre, Grant Cooper, Ian Cooper (Young Cricket Team); Michael Stinson, Jonathan Prescott, Rod Grosvenor, Mark Wallace, Frank Spee, Ashley Johnston, Iris Bell, Niall Owens, Keith Langley, Luke Whitington, Dave Cooper, Ken Hungself, Martin Grosvenor, Rob Puffet, Tom Neilson, Ted Bye, Greg Bye, Andrew Whitington (Cricket Team).

Synopsis

Cricketer Gavin Peacock is killed by a man dressed in cricket whites who forces a stump down his throat. The killing is identified by police as another in a spate of similar killings of cricket players. The investigation is led by Detective Inspector Gary Chance and assisted by Detective Senior Constable Shane Scott. At the scene of the killing of another player, Ian Ryder, Gary is introduced to Detective Inspector Kim Reynolds from Scotland Yard. She has been assigned the case because it is said to have begun in England. The main suspect is Phil Phillips, who it is said was bullied by his fellow under 12s school cricket team as a boy twenty years ago and is killing the team members.

Five members of the team who reside in Australia are collected and housed at the Joadja house under police protection. However, the killer finds them and picks them off one by one. Killed are Terry O'Sullivan and his visiting girlfriend Belinda, Matthew King, David Yeo, Craig Stedman, and

Jonathan Wylie. Gary is attacked by the killer but avoids being killed when he hides in his car trunk. Kim kills Shane, who she learns is actually Gregory Scott Taylor, another member of the team who has changed his name. Shane has discovered that Kim is the twin of Phil and has apparently aided him in killing the team members by bringing them all to Joadja. When Gary reappears he seems to kill Phil in self-defense. He goes to the aid of Kim, who he does not know has been the killer's ally. It seems that Kim will also kill Gary, with a last shot showing Phil blinking to suggest that he is still alive.

NOTES

This title features the theme of the horror of personality in the revenge of an Englishman upon the men who bullied him as a boy at school. Co-directors Stacey Edmonds and Doug Turner employ the postmodern techniques of jump cuts and flash cuts, point of view and subjective camera, slow motion, multiple split screen and freeze frames, and an obtrusive score. There is plenty of bloodletting and gore, and the treatment uses some humor in the cricket motif that the killer uses, with his homemade knifed glove an obvious homage to *Nightmare on Elm Street*'s Freddy Krueger. The narrative reads as a by-the-numbers picking off of victims with the only surprise being the late reveal of the complicity of a policewoman thought to be protecting potential victims. The killer's motivation is expressed in a point of view flashback that is repeated during some of the attacks, but he is otherwise a loser whose depravity is implied by an apparent incestuous relationship with his sister. The treatment is also notable for the exploitative use of a body double in a shower sequence that recalls other genre filmmakers exploiting the nudity of their actresses.

A prologue where Gavin Peacock is killed shows how the killer dresses in cricket whites but does not show his face. A cricket ball spiked with nails is used as the weapon that will ironically defeat the killer in the film's climax. Phil also has radio coverage of a cricket match playing as he strikes Gavin with a cricket bat to drive the stump down his throat. A title card shows us that the body is found "One week later" in a garage, although we don't know how. There is a funny edit from Gavin's bloody wound being looked at to a girl at the police station eating in extreme close-up.

Gary is presented as sexist, a reluctant police officer, which informs the idea of the case being taken over by Kim, and an obnoxious anti-hero and protagonist. The narrative will play on this latter idea by having Gary being the one to defeat Phil, although the ambiguous denouement suggests that he may then be defeated by Kim. Unlike Shane, Gary's not being one of the bullying team may have spared him from moral retribution.

A shock effect is used for the murder of the next

British poster for *I Know How Many Runs You Scored Last Summer* (2008).

victim when he appears at the cricketer's car, although the police do not give his identity when his body is found. The DVD audio commentary identifies him as being Ian Ryder. The focus is more on the introduction of Kim as the new case leader. Her not removing the blood sprayed on her face when she removes the stake from the victim's groin is odd. This perhaps alludes to her pleasure in finding the man dead, and the later real of her duplicity. Additionally, the flashback that we see could as easily be from her point of view in lieu of the argument that the twins share a psychic telepathy. This is despite the fact the device of point of view has not accompanied either murder. The flashback also shows blood on the hands of the victim after he is hit with a towel, and later we will be told that the injury wounded his penis, so that it can be viewed as a form of emasculation.

Freeze-frames are used for the identification of the five team members to be protected. Split screen is also used to show their work habits and lifestyles that will have some later payoffs. Hairdresser Matthew is killed when he is cutting David's hair. Born again Christian Craig will be crucified. Cross-dressing Terry will be caught during a sadomasochistic session with his girlfriend. Macho television show renovator David will be emasculated with a nailed athletic cup.

The apparent incompetence of Joadja's security officer Hugh Trenchard is presented to the men and paid off in how easily Phil is able to enter the property. The DVD audio commentary explains this further by stating that this Hugh is actually Phil in disguise, which makes sense of the alignment Hugh being English has with Kim. It is interesting that when the real Hugh is shown, he is tied up but not killed by either antagonist.

When Belinda visits Terry, the expectation of a strike against her is created but not immediately met when a shock effect is used for Terry appearing to her. The subjective camera approaching the room of the couple also creates the expectation of a strike. Terry's mouth being gagged as part of the sadomasochistic play stops him from warning Belinda of Phil being behind her. Phil whipping Terry is a funny payoff to Terry's sadomasochistic play, since we assume that the whipping he receives here is much harsher than what Terry is accustomed to. His escape and pursuit by Phil is capped by the contrivance of Phil throwing a nailed cricket ball that lands in Terry's mouth, although Phil will use a stake to kill Terry.

The inter-cuts to Kim in the shower during the attack upon Terry and Belinda are the director's exploitative use of female nudity. Although Kim being naked in the shower has context, the lingering close-ups on her breasts, bottom and groin attest to another agenda. The obvious use of a body double, which is confirmed by the film's credits, spare the original actress personal exploitation. The scene is somewhat redeemed by the appearance of the subjective camera. The expectation of an attack upon Kim is not met when the curtain is opened; she reacts as if she knows the person who we later assume to be Phil. The facts that she should not be disturbed by his appearance and his willingness to go to her when she is in the shower are also suggestions of an incestuous relationship.

The subjective camera at the window to the room where Matthew has taken David to cut his hair also creates the expectation of an attack by Phil. The idea that the two men having been exiled to the room because the others do not want to see the activity also sets the two of them up to be isolated victims. Phil first appears behind Matthew in the reflection of the hand mirror that David holds, although he disappears when Matthew sees him and turns around. This suggestion that what Matthew sees is only a vision is dismissed when Phil reappears in the mirror. Matthew's attack and disembowelment is perhaps the treatment's most gruesome strike. Matthew's murder is the first to feature the accompanying flashback footage superimposed, a device that will be repeated with the killings of David, Craig and Jonathan.

The earphones that David wears as he listens to music stop him from being aware of Matthew's attack. The expectation of David escaping when he opens a door is thwarted when we see that it is a closet. David entering a second closet creates the expectation of Phil being in it, and he is. David's willingness to put on the nailed athletic cup shows David's thinking is wrong, and his stabbing in the back with stumps features the resultant blood spraying onto the camera as the treatment's only self-conscious touch.

When Craig goes to the outside toilet, the expectation of his attack is also met, particularly as he wanders on the grounds rather than returning right away to the room where the others are. His picking up a chainsaw in the shed and then putting it down is a missed opportunity, in light of the appearance of Phil. This is although the killer is first shown to be with the tied-up Hugh and injured presumably by the scissors Matthew had stabbed him with. However, Phil makes record time in appearing in the shed.

A stand-off between Craig and Phil shows

Craig's unwillingness to run, although this will prove to be misguided. Phil pouring petrol over Craig creates the expectation of Craig being burned alive. This is an expectation that is not met when Phil throws away the lit match and cuts Craig's throat with a sharpened stake. The DVD audio commentary explains that Craig is not burned because that would not be a cricket-related death. The "Howzat" sign behind the crucified Craig that Gary sees is another cricket reference to a run achieved, although Craig's is the only death that features such a reference. The audio commentary also states that Phil had one-liners to match this in the scenes of the other killings that were dropped in editing.

Phil chasing Gary creates the expectation of Gary being the next victim. Even though we know that Gary goes to his car to collect the gun we saw earlier that he keeps in his trunk, the idea that Gary as a police officer does not have any self-defense skills is a surprise. When Phil uses a stake to create a hole in the trunk where Gary hides, there is a laugh from Phil looking into the hole and Gary poking his eye. Phil's surprise retreat from Gary in what we might think is a vulnerable position is followed by his attack upon Jonathan, whom Kim has conveniently left alone. Jonathan's playing chicken in stabbing a knife around his extended palm gets a payoff in Phil's stabbing a stake into his hand. The idea of Jonathan as a trained army reserver and his bravura over it gets the expected payoff in Phil's ease in dispatching him.

Shane's discovery that Kim is the twin sister of Phil, information that has been presumably squashed by Kim prior, results in her attempt to kill him. The reveal of her duplicity matches his own concealed identity. Shane is able to injure Kim before Phil arrives to defeat him. The timing of Gary's reappearance doesn't allow him to know about Kim's duplicity, which flavors his fate in the denouement. Gary's ludicrous cricket helmet that is initially struck by one of Phil's nailed cricket balls actually works to help him defeat Phil. This is after the expectation that Gary will be defeated without Kim being able to help her brother. The film ends on a freeze frame for ambiguity over whether Kim will be able to strike Gary with the stake she is seen reaching for. Additionally, a shot in the middle of the credits has Phil blink to suggest that he is not dead, as a horror movie conventional shot to suggest a possible sequel.

The DVD audio commentary explains how the two credited directors shared the workload. Stacey Edmonds directed the acting scenes and Doug Turner directed the fight scenes; Turner also used a body double. A different actor had been cast as Gary but was let go, as he didn't work, and Jai Coutrae had been originally cast as Terry. This the only Australian horror movie to be made to date by Edmonds and Turner, and the production company Media 42. Edmonds and Turner also made their film debuts here; it has been their only movie to date.

Jai Koutrae began his career in television and made his film debut in *Rooms for Rent* (2001). He followed this with supporting film roles and played the lead in the mystery *Watermark* (2003). After *I Know How Many Runs You Scored Last Summer*, the actor would appear in more television and film supporting roles and assay the lead in the science fiction thriller *Dark Island* (2010). He was also associate producer for *Broken Sun* (2010). Az Jackson made his film debut in a supporting role in the thriller *Gene-X* (2006) and continued in more supporting parts prior to *I Know How Many Runs You Scored Last Summer*, his last title to date.

David Gambin also began his career in television and made his film debut in a supporting role in the crime thriller *Instant Karma* (2001). He would appear in more film supporting roles and television prior to and after *I Know How Many Runs You Scored Last Summer*. Ben Paul Owens made his feature film debut here and has made shorts to date.

Aaron Scully also began his career in film shorts and as well as appearing in television made his feature film debut as the lead in *Souvenir* (2006). He also played the lead in *Virtuous* (2007) and film supporting roles, and after *I Know How Many Runs You Scored Last Summer* played the lead in the romance *Monkeyshine* (2008). Alex Sideratos started in television and made his feature film debut in *I Know How Many Runs You Scored Last Summer*, his last title to date. James Winter also debuted here, and it is also his last title to date.

Release

Screened in the United States on October 17, 2008, at the Freak Show Horror Film Festival, and in Australia on March 26, 2009, at A Night of Horror International Film Festival. No apparent wide theatrical release in either countries and went straight to DVD with the taglines "Mass murder.... It's just not cricket" and "This time, they'll get to keep the Ashes."

Reviews

"There's a slight feeling that the directors are pandering to the lowest common denominator here, but overshadowing this is a return to the slasher movie without the Hollywood polish that has ruined recent yank efforts. Slashers should be raw and ruggard in my opinion, and Turner and Edmonds have hit that requirement for six." —*ScaryMinds*

"Full of cheap blood and boobs tactics to appeal to the horror crowd but the lifeless script, dull characters and idea that cricket can be entertaining just bowls this one out for a duck!"— Andrew Smith, *Popcorn Pictures*

"It sounds like a can't-miss horror-comedy premise, but sadly, the filmmakers don't get as much gory fun out of the situation as they should have.... The entertainment value is minuscule. It's a little like watching a test match between Bangladesh and Zimbabwe ... women's teams ... with lots of rain delays ... and with the Chappell brothers on commentary."— Ryan McDonald, *Horror Asylum*, January 19 2011

"When it comes to dealing with the comedy aspects, that is where the film trips up especially [and] when it comes to the slasher aspects of the film [it] is frustratingly uneven.... A mishmash of underdeveloped ideas resulting in an unfocused film."— Brandon Sites, *Big Daddy Horror Reviews*

"A patchy but likeably slapdash indie combination of '80s slasher parody, broad Australian-British culture clash and slapstick crudity, this movie is engagingly performed but suffers from the fact that its one joke is contained within its title: it's the world's first cricket-based slasher movie."— Steven West, *The Horror Review*

"Amiable enough, and though largely ineffectual is largely inoffensive. Only likely to be a hit with the most undiscriminating of genre fans, it flounders both in terms of laughs and scares, and as such is a lesser effort, even in the not exactly overburdened with quality field of horror comedies."— James Mudge, *BeyondHollywood.com*, May 30, 2009

DVD

Released in the United States by Celebrity Video Distributors on June 30, 2009, and in Australia by Anchor Bay Entertainment on October 19, 2009.

Nature's Grave

Darclight Films, 2008 [aka *Long Weekend*]

CREDITS: *Director/Editor/Music:* Jamie Blanks; *Producers:* Gary Hamilton, Nigel Odell; *Executive Producers:* Jamie Blanks, Ian Gibbins, Victor Syrmis; *Screenplay:* Everett De Roche; *Photography:* Karl Von Moller; *Production Design:* Robert Perkins; *Costumes:* Michael Chisholm; *Set Decorater:* Lance Whitehouse; *Sound:* John Wikinson; *Hair/Makeup:* Heather Ross. Color, 88 minutes. Filmed in Wilson's Promontory National Park, Victoria, from November 19 to December 21, 2007.

SONGS: "The Legend of Cajun Beau" (Everett De Roche, Lily Kechyas), in closing credits but unknown when it appears in film, "For the Good Times" (Kris Kristofferson), sung by Jim Caviezel.

CAST: Jim Caviezel (Peter); Claudia Karvan (Carla); Star (Cricket); Robert Taylor (Bartender); John Brumpton; Mark Ward; Lara Robinson (Little Girl); Garry McMillian (Pool Player); Everett De Roche (Barfly); Christopher Brown.

Synopsis

A married couple go on holiday in a secluded forest on Moondog beach for a long weekend. They plan to meet another couple to camp with, but they never arrive. When Peter is swimming in the ocean, Carla sees a dark shape in the water. This is revealed to be a dugong looking for its pup, which has washed up dead on the beach. After an eagle attacks Peter at the campsite and he is attacked by a snake, the couple agree to leave. Peter insists on talking to the inhabitants of a camper van he has seen parked farther down the beach, but finds their van submerged in a lake and dead bodies at their campsite. Frightened and wanting to end her marriage, Carla drives off without Peter. When she returns to the campsite after getting lost at night, she is accidentally killed by Peter firing his spear gun. Peter makes his way back to the highway but is run over by a truck, when the driver is attacked by a bird.

Notes

An unnecessary remake of *Long Weekend* with an American actor cast to presumably aid an international market sale. This title lacks the original's atmosphere and Colin Eggleston's suspense set pieces. Updates have been made in technology (cell phones, GPS tracking), and other changes are made to the original narrative, also written by the original screenwriter Everett De Roche to explore the theme of nature as a malevolent supernatural being. The most successful change results in a switch in audience empathy towards the female character, since Claudia Karvan is a much more likeable and a less mannered performer than Jim Caviezel.

Perhaps a viewer who had not seen *Long Weekend* may appreciate the work of director Jamie Blanks more. He uses constant score (although it is not intrusive), occasional expressionist camera angles and point of view, blackouts within a scene, and black and white flashbacks. The treatment ultimately reads as bland and disappointing, with corpses provided for the lowest form of horror movie schlock shock effect. However, it does manage to make the problematic argument scene in the car on the beach play better here.

Blanks follows the basic framework of De Roche's original screenplay, and even repeats some of Eggleston's shots, though there are noticeable changes. The opening aerial views of the forest appear to be enhanced with CGI. Blanks shows us the passengers of the camper van when the protagonists' SUV passes it on the highway, which will be partially paid off when their corpses are later discovered by Peter. In response to Carla's "Get fucked," Peter responds with the mildly amusing "There's not much chance of that this weekend." Their swearing will be repeated in the car scene on the beach where they exchange "Fuck yous." The issue of bringing the female dog, Cricket, with the couple on their trip is given earlier coverage, when Carla hears it making noise before Peter finds her, as in the original. We assume that Carla is the one who has chosen to bring her, although later she will say to Peter, "You're the one who let her come."

At their first stop a sign reads, "Last Fuel Before Tathra," although we don't see Peter fueling his car. The idea that Peter and Carla are to be joined by another couple is new. It appears that the couple are named Luke and Skybug so Carla can riff on the name Skybug. Peter will later rationalize wanting to talk to the camper van people to see if they have seen Luke. A kangaroo warning appears on the highway before it is hit, which appears to be new, and the pub where Peter stops is called the Eggleston Hotel, a nod to the original director. Peter stops to find the discarded Keep Out sign at the beginning of the dirt track, and we see, but he does not, the blood on the front of his car from the kangaroo he has hit. The white plastic bag he carelessly throws into the bush, which had wrapped the bottle of alcohol he drinks, will get a later narrative payoff in the blue plastic bag that the pup dugong is wrapped in on the beach.

Peter and Carla argue about sleeping in the car because they are lost. This does not appear in the original, and includes her pointing out the irony of their not taking advantage of the expensive camping gear he has purchased. A dead seagull shown in the sea also does not appear in the original, noteworthy because it is one creature that has not died because of the influence of the invaders. When Peter goes swimming, Blanks repeatedly shows water spray on the camera lens as a postmodern self-consciousness. Cricket barking at the dugong shape in the water occurs before Carla calls out to Peter to get out of the water, and Blanks has a shot of a piece of glass broken by Peter's shooting fall to the ocean seabed. Peter also shoots at flying ducks here, as opposed to the random shooting that seemingly results in the death of the mother duck in the original.

When Peter comes across the doll on the beach it is not the Barbie of the original, although this brunette matches better with Carla, and here he throws it into the sea. On the beach his sexual advance to her is rejected before any kissing, as he reaches between Carla's legs, and his handling of the rifle has phallic symbolism. The eagle egg is found by Cricket at the campsite, not by Carla on the beach, and we are shown how it must have fallen from the tree above. When the dugong cries draw Carla to the beach where Peter has been surfing, she is panicked by seeing his surf board washed up by itself and the shape of the dugong again in the water.

A dead baby seal is not featured in the original, and here provides the dugong a reason to be crying. However, the reason for the mother to be drawn toward the campsite when we don't know that Peter has killed the pup is unclear, apart from it being the phenomenon of the malevolent supernatural being. In counterpoint to Peter's earlier sexual advance towards Carla, she makes one to him to convince him to leave, which is not featured in the original screenplay. The mold on the frozen chicken is shown to be green growths and the chicken having been kept in a cooler.

Shots of the eagle flying and then on a branch prefigure its attack upon Peter, and this eagle is a brown one and not white. These images may create suspense with our knowledge of the egg found being the eagle's egg, but only if we also know that it will attack rather than having the action a shock effect. When the eagle flies toward Peter Blanks provides a subjective camera point of view shot,

Poster for *Nature's Grave*, aka *Long Weekend* (2008).

and the lighting obscures the reason for Peter's fall. He may just trip in fright. We will see that he has a bite mark or scratches on his neck, but we don't know for sure that is a snake bite since he is more concerned with a head pain. His getting into the car with Carla to tell her that they will leave the site in the morning is also different.

When the dugong is found on the beach it is shown as a complete animal, unlike the obscured image of the original, and it is left uncovered rather than covered in sand by Peter. When Peter tells Carla that he wants to talk to the camper van people about Luke, he has a line that echoes the film's tagline, "Not everybody's afraid of Mother Nature." The scene in the car on the beach is superior to the original, but it is only after Peter's lines: "I'm not sure how I'm scoring on nature's little snap exam but I don't reckon the old earth mother's too pleased with you. It must be a female thing. Right? Different chemicals. You know, the truth here is I can see the world with more clarity than you can. Must be a male thing."

Peter finds the camper van in a lake here rather than Carla seeing it in the sea, and here Carla's throwing of the egg that hits the tree seems a deliberate target, whereas the original had some doubt. Carla barricading herself into the car after the attack and Peter's refusal to switch the power back so she can drive away is also new, as is Peter's singing of "For the Good Times" as he plays the guitar at night, with the song's lyrics a comment on his marriage.

The original film's possum attack sequence here is shortened, and although we see a possum eating grapes on the campsite table, a black snake is used instead as the threat. A shock effect is used for the reveal of the snake under something on the table, the roof is not as obscured or ambiguous as in the original film. Peter opens the van and swims inside to find a female body behind a curtain as a shock effect. Blanks uses a white lighting flash on her face and then ups the horror aspect by having the corpse float next to Peter in the van. He then finds items strewn in the mud and the camper van people's campsite, with more shock reveals of the corpse in a tent and a man hanged from a tree. Peter's analysis of the scene as a murder-suicide and the sight of the parents isn't an improvement over the missing parents of the original and the idea that the child has driven the van into the sea.

When Cricket goes missing Peter tells Carla to look for him on the beach. Carla's story that the dog is dead and that she buried her in the bushes is exposed as a lie by the sound of the dog barking at the dugong on the beach. Blanks provides a striking image — perhaps his treatment's most successful — in a group of standing kangaroos at night that reads as odd and menacing. Carla abandons the SUV after one bird hits the windshield rather than the multiple bird hits of the original and the spider web and spider. Peter's ordeal at the campsite is also shorter than the originals, and the plot point of the dropped shoe is practically thrown away by it being shown in a long shot. Blanks also does not repeat Eggleston's wonderful reveal of Carla's death with the idea that Peter has been awake all night as the transition to day. Rather he begins the day with Cricket's growling at what is revealed to be the dugong at the campsite. This image is funny because the dugong appears to be so close to where Peter has slept, and the reveal of the fate of Carla is delayed.

Frightened by the dugong, Peter runs and Cricket follows. The sound of the car radio attracts Peter to find the abandoned SUV, with the radio a payoff to Carla playing it in her night drive. Peter tells the dog to find Carla as Peter follows. Blanks uses blackouts in between shots of Peter following the dog, presumably as ominous signs. Peter crying over the dead Carla is new to this screenplay, with a long shot provided for the echo of his cry in the forest, and he doesn't cover her with the blanket the way Peter did in the original. Instead of being stuck in the mud, here the SUV hits a tree to stop. Peter's run out of the forest is embroidered with Carla's voice of past statements and black and white flashbacks of the car scene, the corpse in the submerged camper van, and the eagle attack.

These flashbacks are shown as images that are objective, and not as Peter's memory as point of view, which can pass as movie contrivance, although why they are black and white is a mystery. These "memories" are topped by a black and white shot of Carla with the spear gun in her neck opening her eyes, used as a horror movie shock effect. Blanks ends with home movies of Peter and Carla's wedding, after we have seen him killed and the Eggleston shot of the spear protruding from vegetation. This is presumably to remind us of what we have lost. Blanks also writes "In memory of Colin Eggleston," in the closing credits; Eggleston died in 2002.

Blanks had previously made *Storm Warning* (2007). *Nature's Grave* is his last film to date. Producer Gary Hamilton produced *Acolytes*, also executive produced by Ian Gibbins as his last Australian horror title, but he has not made another Australian horror title to date. *Nature's Grave* is the only Australian horror title produced by Producer Nigel Odell, executive producer Victor Syrmis, and Darclight Films to date.

American born Jim Caviezel had made his film debut in a minor role in the romance *My Own Private Idaho* (1991), and after playing more supporting roles scored the lead in the sport drama *Madison* (2001). He played the leads in the adventure *The Count of Monte Cristo* (2002), the crime thriller *Highwaymen* (2004), the title roles in the historical drama *The Passion of the Christ* (2004) and the sports biography *Bobby Jones: Stroke of Genius* (2004), the crime drama *Unknown* (2006), and the science fiction action adventure *Outlander* (2008). *Nature's Grave* is his last film role to date.

Claudia Karvan had made her film debut as a child actress in a minor role in *Going Down* (1983), and played the lead in *Molly* the same year. She made a successful transition to adult roles, scoring leads in the thriller *Redheads* (1992), *The Heartbreak Kid* (1993), the comic romances *Dating the Enemy* (1996), *Paperback Hero* (1999) and *Strange Planet* (1999), as well as appearing in supporting film roles and on television. After *Nature's Grave*, Karvan would be seen in a supporting role in the Australian horror title *Daybreakers* (2009).

RELEASE

Although the film was screened at film festivals in Spain, France, the U.K. and Finland, it appeared to go straight to DVD in Australia and the United States. The taglines were "Don't mess with Mother Nature" and "Mother Nature has a dark side."

REVIEWS

"Pretentious and not all that interesting for those of us who have seen the far superior original. Put the movie on at your own risk, it's going to seem like a bloody long weekend before the end credits come up."—Jeff Ritchie, *ScaryMinds*

"Terrible.... The plot is all over the place, no coherent structure or story development, cliches galore from all the wrong types of film, and no attempt made to try and make it scary or to develop anything from the characters upwards, never mind any attempt to try and explain anything in the film."—*Filmstalker*

"It all sounds preposterous, and it is. The scenery is perfect, the two leads carry the movie with ease but it leaves an overwhelming sense of 'What?' and 'Why?'

Even though the closing scenes are very graphic and powerful, there's just too much left unexplained." — DJ Benz, *HorrorTalk*, February 7, 2010

"The actors and the filmmakers seem to be going through the motions. Blanks delivers a slicker but bland image than the atmospheric original but the pacing and buildup of what should be odd occurrences is haphazard. It's bad but not in the sacrilegious way of many remakes, it's just unnecessary." — Eric Cotenas, *DVDBeaver*

"This new version of *Long Weekend* feels a near clone of the first film that somehow loses the essence of what made its predecessor so creepily effective. If you've not seen Eggleston's original then you'll probably have less to gripe about, but I'd seriously suggest you hunt it out." — Slarek, *DVD Outsider*

"A thriller that thrilled, a cautionary tale that prompted 'some' thought and an overall gnarly ride that came through as to entertaining me hardcore and whooping me silly with its finale. Overall I had a blast with this one!" — John Fallon, *Arrow in the Head*

DVD

Released August 4, 2009, by Screen Media Films.

The Ruins

Spyglass Entertainment/Red Hour Films, 2008 [aka *Ruins*]

CREDITS: *Director:* Carter Smith; *Producers:* Stuart Cornfield, Jeremy Kramer, Chris Bender; *Executive Producers:* Ben Stiller, Trish Hofmann, Gary Barber, Roger Birnbaum; *Screenplay:* Scott B. Smith, based on the book by Scott Smith; *Photography:* Darius Khondji; *Editor:* Jeff Betancourt; *Music:* Graeme Revell; *Production Design:* Grant Major; *Costumes:* Lizzy Gardiner; *Art Directors:* Michelle McGahey, J.D. Wingrove; *Set Dressers:* Gillian Butler, Laura Elkington; *Hair and Makeup:* Shane Thomas; Vine Vocal (Karen Strassman). Color, 87 minutes. Filmed at Warner Roadshow Movie World Studios, Gold Coast, and on location at Mount Tamborine, Queensland, from March to April 2007.

SONGS: "Solta O Frango" (Pedro D'Eyrot, Rodrigo Gorky, Thomas Pentz, Marina Vello), Bonde Do Role; "Mexico Mi Amor" (Marc Ferrari, Matt Hirt, Julisa Kruydenhof), David Gomez; "Phenomena" (Brian Chase, Karen Orzolek, Nick Zinner), Yeah Yeah Yeahs.

CAST: Jonathan Tucker (Jeff, aka Jeff Dean MacIntyre); Jena Malone (Amy); Shawn Ashmore (Eric); Laura Ramsey (Stacy); Joe Anderson (Mathias); Sergio Calderon (Lead Mayan); Jesse Ramirez (Mayan Bowman); Balder Moreno (Mayan Horseman); Dimitri Baveas (Dimitri); Patricio Almeida Rodriguez (Taxi Driver); Mario Jurado (Mayan Archer); Luis Ramos, Walter Quispe (Mayan Riflemen); Pauline Whyman (Wailing Woman); Nathan Vega (Mayan Boy); Tanisha Marquez-Munduate (Mayan Girl); Chris Argirousis, Alexander Gregory (Greeks); Michelle Atkinson, Bar Paly (Archeologists); Jordan Patrick Smith (Heinrich); Jovina Riveros Padilla, Lucia Caballero (Mayan Women); Rufino Hernandez, Carlos Enrique Delgado, Mario Freire Rivera, Elmer Alaya, Jesus Tugumbango (Mayan Guards). Uncredited: Andy Meritakis (Mayan Boy 2); Vivica Mitra (Lady at Pool); Robert Munns (Groundskeeper — scene deleted).

Synopsis

A group of four American twentysomething college students and friends are vacationing in Mexico. They are Jeff, Amy, Eric and Stacy. They are invited by a German backpacker, Mathias, to see a secret Mayan site dig that his archeologist brother Heinrich is working on. The Americans agree to go and at the site find a stepped pyramid. Mayan natives appear and threaten the tourists by killing their Greek companion, Dimitri. The group climbs the pyramid and at the top finds the abandoned tents of the archeologists. The Mayans set up camp at the base of the pyramid to stop the tourists from leaving. It appears they are to be a form of sacrifice to whatever is inside the pyramid. Hearing a ringing cell phone, the tourists lower Mathias into a deep pit. The rope of the windlass crank breaks and Mathias breaks his back in the fall. Stacy volunteers to be lowered to rescue him but cuts her knee when she jumps to the ground. When Amy joins her, they place Mathias on a backboard they have created. All three are brought back up.

Overnight it seems indigenous vines attach themselves onto the wounds of Mathias and Stacy. When she and Amy return to the pit they learn that the sound of the ringing cell phone is being made by the vibrating flowers of the vines which chase the girls. Because Mathias' legs are infected by septicemia, a decision is made to amputate them. He is killed by vines that now encroach upon the campsite and enter his mouth and strangle him. Some of the vines that had attached themselves to Stacy seem to be under her skin. Jeff cuts into her leg and back to remove them. When she thinks that she has another in her head she cuts herself in an attempt to remove it. The others see what she is doing and try to stop her. Stacy unintentionally stabs Eric, who dies. Stacy asks Amy to kill her to stop the pain, and it appears that this is done for her. Jeff helps Amy to escape the pyramid, acting as a decoy for her to run after making the Mayans believe that she is dead. The Mayans kill Jeff. Amy finds the Jeep of the archeologists and drives away, as the Greek friends of Dimitri arrive at the pyramid in search of him.

Notes

This title mixes the themes of the horror of personality with the malevolent supernatural being to create an effective thriller with suspense and gruesomeness. Director Carter Smith uses the postmodern techniques of point of view, expressionist camera angles, hand-held camerawork, CGI and blackouts. He provides eventual empathy in his treatment of seemingly bland and hedonistic twentysomethings who are the narrative protagonists. The narrative's use of flesh-eating moving vines may seem totally ridiculous, aided by the human Mayans as the horror of personality. However, the behavior of the plants is unsettling and bizarre enough to make them successful antagonists. Carter also supplies plenty of bloodletting, shock effects and gore.

A prologue presents a girl in a darkened pit that resembles Amy calling for help and then snatched away, presumably by the vines. This girl could be one of the female unidentified archeologists since the number of tents makes it obvious that Heinrich is not camping alone. The DVD audio commentary says that this girl is not Amy, but rather the same one that Stacy and Amy find in the pit with the cell phone.

Mathias looking at the Americans initially suggests that he may be an antagonist, although this is revealed in the narrative not to be the case since he becomes the first protagonistic victim. Carter shows Stacy's breasts and nudity in the context of her dressing in her hotel room. However he does not provide equal opportunity nudity for Jeff when we see him in the shower and then also dressing for the trip to the site. Carter also supplies a funny edit from Eric about to get a blowjob from Stacy to Amy vomiting into her toilet because she is hung over. The barking dog in the back of the taxi truck is used as a shock effect.

There is a funny exchange over the idea of the track supposedly leading to the site being covered:

JEFF: Maybe the archeologists don't want people to find their site.
AMY: Great. They're gonna be thrilled to see us then.

Carter holds on the shot of the taxi truck carrying the tourist driving into the horizon a moment longer than necessary to perhaps suggest their disappearance. The attack upon Dimitri by the Mayans also uses shock effects for the arrow that strikes his arm and the gun shot that hits his scalp. Only later is the narrative point made that the Mayans want the tourists to go up the pyramid rather than leave the site altogether. Although Eric will hypothesize that they are being used as a sacrifice, this idea is never clarified. This is perhaps because the Mayan language is not understood by any of the tourists. However, given that the Mayans shoot the boy who is touched by the vine that Amy throws and later lay salt at the bottom of the pyramid, they are aware of the threat of the vines. The DVD audio commentary points out the Mayans only become hostile towards the tourists when Amy steps back into the vines and that Dimitri is killed because he too steps into the vines and then approaches them. The idea is proposed that the Mayans quarantine the tourists to keep the vine contained, with the twentysomethings presumably collateral damage.

The ringing of the cell phone that leads Mathias to go into the pit is the conventional noise that is investigated, and he is the conventional Man in Peril. When Stacy and then Amy are lowered into the pit to assist Mathias, they are Women in Peril. They are used as weaker potential victims because of the idea that Jeff and Eric as men are needed for their strength in managing the windlass crank. Before the sound of a cell phone is revealed to be mimicking by the vibrating flowers of the vine, there is the possibility that it is the Mayans who are ringing the telephone of Heinrich with Mathias' phone that they took. This could be a way to lure the tourists into the cave, although this requires the assumption that the isolated jungle Mayans know how to operate a modern cell phone.

When Stacy is in the pit with Mathias, Carter creates suspense from the possibility that there is something in the lower level to be feared, later shown to be the vines that also appear around the tunnel. Stacy's cut knee when she lands in the pit is also paid off in the narrative by her being, like Mathias, wounded and her flesh open to invasion by the vines. Because the girls move Mathias with his broken back, they are responsible for making his condition worse, rather than having the boys invent a longer rope to handle Mathias more appropriately.

Stacy and Amy get Mathias onto the backboard to allow him to be lifted up to the surface, and Carter jumps to the sight of the three of them on top, not bothering to show the effort it took to do so. The vines shown to be on Stacy's leg after she awakens first appear to be spiders, since movement was seen on the tunnel walls when she was first lowered. The fact that vines are on her leg in this way suggests their supernatural powers. Because they also appear on Mathias' legs, it is apparent that these vines definitely have an agenda. Since the vines on Stacy in particular have invaded her wound, this is a particularly unsettling phenomenon, and will be paid off after it is thought that they have been removed from her when they are first discovered.

The reveal of the vibrating flowers of the vines as mimics comes with the shock of a vine grabbing Amy, who gets close to a flower to see it vibrating. The mimicking is also later used in an almost comic fashion to mimic Stacy's screams of "You're not listening to me" and "I wanna cut it." Jeff being a medical student allows for the plot point of him suggesting that Mathias' infected legs be amputated. The operation scene includes both the horror of the patient's pain and the gore of the amputation, with an operation scenario to be repeated later when Stacy is cut to remove the vines apparent under her skin. The gruesomeness of the operation is also demonstrated by Stacy and Amy in the tent covering their ears to block out the sound of Mathias' screams. This represents exactly how the audience feels in reaction to the scene.

Stacy argues with the others, thinking she has heard Amy and Eric having sex presumably because of sounds made by the vines. Her seeming paranoia is said to be because she has the vines in her, but her point of view can be considered the truth. This is considering how Amy was kissing Mathias in the opening scenes as witnessed by Stacy and Eric but not by Jeff. The conflict also stops the arguers from seeing the vines that attack Mathias and go into his mouth. Eric's line after they find Mathias dead, "Well thank God we cut his legs off," is black comedy. It is also a swipe at Jeff's idea about the amputation, which in hindsight was unnecessary.

The moving vines under Stacy's skin are more gruesomeness, as is the gore of Jeff cutting into her leg and lower back to remove them. Her idea that there is also one in her forehead, seen by the others, creates the expectation which is later met that she will want to keep cutting herself. This is first presented as a sign of her growing madness, which will allow her to slash Jeff's hand and stab Eric. But Stacy's pain turns empathetic when she begs Amy to kill her. Carter presents the presumed moment of Stacy's death by showing the Mayans standing at the base of the pyramid no longer hearing Stacy's cries, and since Stacy does not appear again, we assume that this death occurred.

Jeff's plan for Amy's escape by using himself as a decoy and that may involve his own death is presumably not something he considers, given his remark to her that he will wait for her return, unless he is only saying this to help her escape. A deleted scene where Jeff goes over the escape plan with Amy makes it more apparent that he has planned to sacrifice himself because he knows he will die since he has been infected. Given the Mayans' reaction to him and his deliberate provoking of them, his being struck by arrows is not a surprise although her being chased and avoiding arrows is.

Amy getting to the Jeep defies the expectation of her being caught, although the momentary stalling of the Jeep is a conventional cliché. Carter uses two blackouts, the first after Amy is seen driving away. The second is after the appearance of the other Greek boys in the jungle and at the base of the pyramid who have come for Dimitri. We assume that the Greeks will also be killed by the Mayans or the vines. However, the fact that they have come is an ironic payoff to what Jeff claimed and no one else believed — that someone would come to help them.

In the DVD audio commentary Smith states the look of the vines is based on Tiarella Jeepers Creepers and pumpkin vines, neither of which are flesh-eating plants. He said he also sourced the films *Cannibal Holocaust* (1980), *The Brood* (1979), and *Rabid* (1977) for references. It is also stated that the sourcebook does not feature the plot point of the Mayans killing their child and that it was Eric and not Stacy in the book that has the vine. The scene where Stacy and Amy search in the pit with flashlights for the ringing cell phone was originally placed before Mathias' amputation scene. It was moved since it was thought that the girls would not step into vines in the pit once they had seen how they moved and caused Mathias to lose his legs. A fact pointed out in the narrative is that the vines only actually kill Mathias. Dimitri and Jeff are killed by the Mayans. Eric is killed by Stacy, and Stacy is presumably killed by Jeff. Although this may read to make the vines less antagonistic, their threat is still the reason for the others to seemingly turn against each other.

Carter Smith made his feature film debut with *The Ruins* and has not made another to date. This the only Australian horror movie to be made by producers Stuart Cornfield, Jeremy Kramer, and Chris Bender, and executive producers Ben Stiller, Trish Hofmann, Gary Barber, and Roger Birnbaum. It is also the only Australian horror title to be made by the production companies Spyglass Entertainment, Red Hour Films, and Internationale Filmproduktion Prometheus.

American Jonathan Tucker made his film debut as a child actor in a supporting role in the Italian western *Botte di Natale*, aka Troublemakers (1994), and after more supporting roles and work on television, essayed the lead in the romantic comedy *100 Girls* (2000). He was also the lead in the comedy *Ball in the House* (2001), and transitioned into adult roles with the lead in the comedy *Love Comes to the Executioner* (2006). After *The Ruins*, the actor had supporting roles and acted in television.

American Jena Malone was also a child actor and began her career in television. She made her film debut in a supporting role in *Bastard Out of Carolina* (1996). After playing more supporting roles and appearing on television, the actress essayed the lead in the crime drama *American Girl* (2002), which she also co-produced, and the comedy *Saved!* (2004). Malone transitioned to adult roles with the lead in the thriller *Corn* (2004) and played more supporting film roles. After *The Ruins* the actress continued in television and supporting film parts.

Like Jena Malone, Canadian born Shawn Ashmore was also a child actor who began his career in television. He made his film debut in a minor role in the comedy *Married to It* (1991), and after more television and supporting film parts transitioned to adult roles. He has yet to essay a lead in films to date, continuing with supporting parts and television after *The Ruins*. American Laura Ramsey began her career in television and made her film debut in a supporting part in the sports biography *Lords of Dogtown* (2005). She continued in supporting roles, essaying the title character but not top-billed in *Whatever Lola Wants* (2007), and after *The Ruins* continued in television and film supporting roles. British born Joe Anderson made his film debut in a minor role in the mystery *Creep* (2004), and after appearing in television and in supporting film roles he would go on after *The Ruins* to essay the leads in *The 27 Club* (2008), *Flutter* (2010), and the action comedy *Rogues Gallery* (2010), as well as playing other supporting film roles.

Release

In the United States on April 4, 2008, and Australian release straight to DVD with the tagline "Terror has evolved." The DVD includes deleted scenes and an alternative ending. The deleted scenes are Jeff and Eric covering the pyramid top campsite with a plastic sheet to capture a possible rain; the group eating oranges in their tent, and then going outside when it does rain to fill containers and to wash themselves; after the rain the four Americans drinking shots of Tequila in celebration and Jeff dancing with Amy; Stacey shown to be stabbed presumably by Jeff and his arm showing a line that means the vine has infected him from the cut he received from Stacy; Jeff going over the escape plan with Amy knowing that he is going to die but not telling her and her speaking of her hope for them to go on a future road trip by themselves; and Amy and Jeff kissing.

The alternative ending begins with Amy driving the Jeep away from the site and showing she has a vine under the skin of her face, then a groundskeeper going to her tombstone in a cemetery because he hears the cell phone ringing noise. He finds the vine flowers growing on it and touches them. The flowers then seem to be whistling the tune he was whistling.

Reviews

"More disgusting than scary, [the film] could have been the most politically provocative horror film since *Bug* was released last year. It settles for gore and pain instead."—Matt Zoller Seitz, *The New York Times*, April 5, 2008

"This is one solid little flick that works better than expected thanks to being different than expected. It doesn't rely much on special effects to do its job and it gets decent performances across the board."—*The Video Graveyard*

"Modest and above average.... Smith does a good job of drawing the tension out and plays it with far more conviction and seriousness than such a premise might indicate. The CGI plant effects are generally convincing, [though] there are times the film staggers a fine line between inherent risibility and conviction."—Richard Scheib, *Moria—science fiction, horror, and fantasy film review site*

"It belongs to a shrinking sub-category of the genre: adult films more concerned with generating tension and promoting viewer unease than reveling in an orgy of unrelenting violence. *The Ruins* is bleak and edgy and delivers the goods." — James Berardinelli, *ReelViews*

"A surprisingly effective little horror nightmare. I jumped legitimately at least twice, covered my eyes during most of the amateur on-site surgeries and felt the pit of my stomach tighten up." — Wesley Morris, *San Francisco Chronicle*, April 7 2008

"It doesn't achieve squat as a horror movie. It's an OK survival story though, since the stars, playing inevitable victims that you'll semi-care about, possess something that's become less and less integral to the genre: acting ability." — Matt Pais, *Chicago Tribune*, April 3 2008

DVD

Released by Paramount/Dreamworks Video on July 8, 2008. Released in Australia by Paramount/DreamWorks Home Entertainment on December 4, 2008.

Coffin Rock

Screen Australia/Head Gear Films/Metrol Technology/Bankside Films/Ultrafilms, 2009 [aka *Seed*]

CREDITS: *Screenplay/Director:* Rupert Glasson; *Producers:* David Lightfoot, Ayisha Davies; *Executive Producers:* Piers Tempest, Phil Hunt, Compton Ross; *Photography:* David Foreman; *Editor:* Adrian Rostirolla; *Music:* John Gray; *Production Design:* Tony Cronin; *Sound Design:* Craig Carter; *Sound:* Rob Stankovich; *Set Dresser:* Gareth Wilkes; *Costumes:* Theo Denton; *Hair and Makeup:* Jodie Lenaine-Smith. Color, 88 minutes. Filmed on location in Adelaide, Thompson's Beach and Café Jaffa, South Australia, and at the South Australia Film Corporation studio in Hendon, Adelaide.

CAST: Robert Taylor (Robert Townsend); Lisa Chappell (Jessica Wills); Sam Parsonson (Evan); Terry Camilleri (Tony); Geoff Morrell (George); Jodie Dry (Megan); Joseph Del Re (Benny); Guy O'Donnell (Spud); Peter Green (Dr. Bass); Sally Davis (Dr. Davis); Sasha Carruozzo (Female Doctor); Bernie Ledger (Da, aka Evan's Father); Rani Chaleyer (Mother); Milla Glasson (Toddler); Deborah Landua (Bar Maid); Elizabeth Van Dort (Tony's Wife); Dawn Wakelin, Finn Wakelin (Clinic Woman and Child); Darryl Hyland, Chris Daniels, Mark Braithwaite, Mark Reidy, Peter Hales, Brett Wiley, Patrick Rayner, Daniel "Crack" Quarrel (Cray Workers); Michael Moody, Barry Barrett, Frank Sebastyan (Men in Pub); Anthony Candish, Joe Russo, Mick Juliano (Kytes of Omar Band); Zoe Behan, Casey Cummings, Mick Curtis, Levi Whitworth (British Robots Band).

Synopsis

In a rural fishing town husband and wife Rob and Jess are trying to have a baby without success. At the Lucanae IVF Clinic they are noticed by the receptionist, Irish traveler Evan. He follows them back from the city and gets a job at the local Crayfish Factory. Evan makes contact with Jess by showing her a bird's nest he has found. Rob receives a letter from the clinic with their latest results but is too afraid to open it. In anger Jess gets drunk at the local pub. Spurning the advance of Rob's coworker, she is shown a baby kangaroo that Evan has found and they make love. Taking a home test, Jess learns that she is pregnant. Rob assumes that the baby is his. She refuses to go away with Evan, who becomes obsessed by Jess and in his rage kills the baby kangaroo. When her friend Megan catches Evan in Jess' house talking on a disconnected telephone to his Da, Evan attacks her and hides her in his caravan.

Rob and Jess plan a holiday. She is disturbed to learn that Rob has hired Evan to look after their fishing supply store. Rob and Jess have a fight and he goes fishing on his boat with Tony and Evan. Rob is disturbed by Evan's behavior when Tony assumes that Evan is gay and fires him from the shop. Barney goes to see Evan at the caravan, and he is attacked and burned by Evan. Rescued by Rob, Barney tells how he saw Evan and Jess having sex. Rob confronts Jess, and Evan appears and attacks Rob. Jess agrees to go away with Evan to stop him from hurting Rob more, and sees that Evan has Barney in the car with him. Jess tries to run away. Evan kills Barney with a stick, and tears off the "Rob" tattoo Jess has on her shoulder before the car stops at a clifftop. When Evan is asleep, Jess releases the brake and gets out before the car falls over the cliff. Rob finds Jess and drives toward her. Seeing Evan coming at her with a rock, Rob runs down Evan. After the town holds a funeral for Barney, Rob finally opens the clinic letter.

NOTES

A relationship thriller shot in high definition digital, this title features the horror of personality. It centers on the obsessive love of a madman backpacker for a married woman whom he has impregnated. Director Rupert Glasson uses the postmodern techniques of blackouts, expressionist camera angles, hand-held camerawork, jump cuts, zooms, and point of view. His camerawork is often self-consciously obscuring of the action. The antagonist only successfully kills one person, but the treatment features plenty of bloodletting, a fire burn, and one murder presented effectively by sound. It is aided by the serio-comic performance of Sam Parsonson and the grounding empathetic one of Lisa Chappell.

It is unknown why the film is entitled *Coffin Rock*. It opens with a Super 8 home movie of a child that is unidentified. The film will also end with more of the same footage, so presumably it represents the child that Rob and Jess do not have. Rob seen fishing on the beach recalls Robert Taylor doing the same in *Storm Warning*, and that characters' emasculation also prefigures Rob, who it appears is unable to impregnate Jess. The shadow of Evan on the wall as seen by Jess is a conventional horror representation of the antagonist, with Evan not revealed to be the owner of the shadow and denying that it was him. The crayfish races at the pub are an eccentricity of the locals, but perhaps not the clichéd inbred rural lowlifes of *Storm Warning* and *Dying Breed*. The expectation of Rob hitting Barney when Barney makes an advance to Jess is not met.

Evan's appearance to Jess is a surprise given that we see Barney following her, although it is only a partial surprise given we know Evan to be interested in her. Barney's arrival conveniently allows him to witness Jess and Evan's sex. Evan killing the baby kangaroo after Jess rejects him is a sign of Evan's madness, with Glasson sparing us any gore and only using sound for the creature's demise. This is the way he will also later present the death of Barney. Evan's obsession with Jess can also be equated with her obsession as an older woman about becoming pregnant.

Glasson supplies a cut from Evan turning on the television he has placed outside the caravan to the television at the house of Rob and Jess. He also cuts from Rob promising Jess he will not tell anyone about her pregnancy to Rob being hugged by George and Tony, presumably because he has told them. The idea that Evan would place his furniture outside the caravan also alludes to his madness. Glasson uses flash-cuts to Evan elsewhere when we see him on a public telephone talking to his Da. Glasson will feature more of these flash-cuts as memory later when Evan is on the telephone at Rob and Jess' house. Here the idea that Evan is not really talking to anyone is another sign of his madness, and is suggested by the camerawork which moves around the telephone box exterior.

When Evan goes to Jess' house his appearance is presented as a shock at a window, and his breathing on the glass is then explained by him drawing a heart in the moisture. When Jess goes outside to confront him, Evan is oddly missing. This either suggests that he is a quick retreater, he has supernatural powers which the narrative does not otherwise suggest, or she has imagined his presence. Evan having killed the baby kangaroo is paid off when he leaves it in Jess' baby cot as a created expectation met. Glasson provides a surprise when Evan is revealed to be still in the nursery after Rob closes the door to comfort the hysterical Jess. Rob hitting Benny is the punch he failed to deliver in the pub earlier, although here his idea that Benny left the kangaroo in the cot is wrong. This is perhaps what leads Benny to go to Evan's caravan later since Benny thinks it was Evan who left the kangaroo.

Evan talking to his Da on the disconnected telephone at Jess' house is confirmation of his madness. Here Glasson provides the extended flash-cuts of Evan to perhaps reveal that he killed his wheelchair bound Da. Evan hitting Megan with the detached telephone receiver is not a surprise. His second strike of her suggests that she is dead, as does his dragging her body away, but later we will she is alive. Glasson also presents a split frame where Jess leaves a telephone message on Megan's answering machine on the right of the frame as her blood spray on a wall from Evan's strike is shown on the left.

When Evan joins Rob and Tony onboard the fishing boat, Tony's idea that Evan is gay infuriates him enough to push Tony overboard. After Rob rescues Tony, Evan's putting a fish in his mouth as if it is a penis and sucking it is both funny and bizarre enough to have Rob and Tony stare at him in disbelief. Naturally Evan ends this comic display by biting off the fish's head, and Glasson supplies a funny cut to Rob in his car telling Evan, "It's not going to work out at the shop."

Evan's setting Benny alight at the caravan is a shock. We don't what he uses for the fire, although the making-of featurette tells us that an oil lantern was used to attack Benny. Like the early scene where Benny follows Jess and then Evan appears first, this time we expect Rob to appear and we get Benny instead. After Jess agrees to go with Evan after he has attacked Rob, Glasson does not immediately show us that Evan has Benny in the back seat of the car, which is what she screams at because of his burned state. This is also a surprise, given that we saw Rob rescue Benny from burning. Presumably Evan has come back to collect Benny after Rob had left to confront Jess with his knowledge that she had slept with Evan.

Evan's strike of Rob during this confrontation is also a surprise, and Rob's going back to Evan's caravan does not have him find Evan and Jess there, which is not a surprise. Rob's trashing the caravan is also expected, but at least it is paid off with his discovery of Megan. Her being alive is only revealed after she is carried by Rob and George outside the caravan, like Evan's furniture.

The assumption of Benny being dead is not met when he speaks to Jess after her expected escape attempt from Evan's car. Her not finding the keys in the ignition is a conventional plot device. Benny still being alive, however, makes sense since we would wonder why Evan would transport Benny's dead body with him, and he seems to be there to be able to tell Jess to look for the car keys in the glove box. Evan's appearance at the window is another shock effect after Jess looks back up from the glove box. It also gets a laugh from Jess' resultant scream. Evan's finishing off of Benny, since we assume that his burns have already harmed him, is presented by Glasson with the sounds of the stick squishing into Benny's eye and without Glasson's visual accompaniment. He also does not show Evan disposing of Benny's body during the forthcoming scenes with Evan and Jess.

After Evan sees the "Rob" tattoo on her shoulder his biting it off is both a shock effect and expected. The car stopping at the cliff top after being out of control seems to be a plot point to allow for it be to later pushed over. When Jess releases the car brake so that it rolls to the edge, Evan's awakening is expected. Even when Evan does go over with the car and Jess manages to get out beforehand, the expectation is created that the fall has not killed Evan since any good horror movie antagonist never dies easily.

Rob's advance to Jess with his car suggests that he is going to run her down because of her infidelity, despite the fact that he has presumably followed her to rescue her from Evan. Glasson inter-cuts between Jess standing on the road waiting for Rob, Rob advancing, and then Evan appearing with a rock to strike Jess. Evan appears to be unaware of the advancing Rob. The idea that he would want to kill Jess is unbelievable, given that he thinks she is carrying his child, and Rob running down Evan rather than Jess is both a surprise and expected.

At Benny's funeral, Jess communicates her remorse silently with Megan and Rob. Jess' burning of what appears to be the baby cot represents the idea that she is not going to have what she thinks Evan's baby. However, Rob finally opening the clinic letter as he stands on the wharf suggests that perhaps the baby is his, after all, although this is not clarified. Glasson's repeat use of the home movie of a child from the beginning of the film is now ambiguous. Is this the child the couple had or lost? Since the movie does not also show either Rob or Jess with the child either idea cannot be confirmed. But a third idea is also possible. This is Evan as a child, an innocent with potential that will be wasted.

In the DVD featurette, "The Making of *Coffin Rock*," it is told that the film was originally envisaged as a supernatural slasher but that the infertility issue was introduced to make the narrative more realistic. The part of Rob was written for Robert Taylor. It is said that a great white shark had been spotted in the waters that were used for the boating scene where Tony goes overboard, although it did not come near the crew when filming took place.

Rupert Glasson made his feature directing debut with the film and has not made another since. David Lightfoot was the executive producer of the Australian horror title *Storage*, but has not made another Australian horror movie to date. *Coffin Rock* is the only Australian horror film to be made by producer Ayisha Davies, executive producers Phil Hunt and Compton Ross, and the production companies Head Gear Films and Ultrafilms. Executive Producer Piers Tempest had previously produced *Like Minds*, but has not made another Australian horror title to date.

Robert Taylor previously appeared in a supporting role in *Rogue*, and after *Coffin Rock* has only been seen in television to date. New Zealand born Lisa Chappell began her career in television and made her film debut in a supporting role in the New Zealand comedy *Desperate Remedies* (1993). She continued in supporting film roles and on television prior to and after *Coffin Rock*. Sam Parsonson also began his career in television and made his film debut in *Coffin Rock*, and has since appeared in television. Terry Camilleri played a supporting role in *The Cars That Ate Paris*. Geoff Morrell appeared in *Rogue*. *Coffin Rock* is the only feature film made by Joseph Del Re to date.

Release

Australia on October 22, 2009, and screened on October 16, 2009, at the Chicago International Film Festival with the tagline "Be careful what you wish for...." The film apparently went straight to DVD in the United States.

Reviews

"A tightly made genre film that boasts outstanding performances and dynamic direction ... edgy and engrossing entertainment, the kind of movie that knows its audience — and delivers to them." — Andrew L. Urban, *Urban Cinefile*

"The movie wears its Hitchcock influences with pride and Director Glasson goes one step beyond the requirements for a solid thriller. Get ready to rock, if you don't like this one then you are probably ready for a coffin." — Jeff Ritchie, *Scary Minds*

"[It] can't quite decide whether to be a relationships drama or a slasher thriller; it's more successful as the former than it is as the latter, because Robert Taylor and Lisa Chappell both give good performances as the couple [but] Sam Parsonson's Evan is a stock character, and the madder he gets the sillier the film becomes." — David Stratton, *At the Movies*, October 21, 2009

"I think it's a shame that you establish two interesting characters, an interesting situation, and then instead of exploring that you go off on this madman rampage that becomes full of improbabilities and so there's a disconnect. And, it's sort of like a waste." — Margaret Pomeranz, *At the Movies*, October 21, 2009

"It isn't a particularly bad movie, but the story just happens in front of your eyes. You'll never feel particularly invested or shocked at what goes on during the runtime, and things are severely marred by a slow but almost devoid of the intended tension last 15 minutes." — Gareth Jones, *DreadCentral*

"It looks amazing, the music score fits perfectly and the acting is first rate. On the downside, it is predictable and almost falls into several genre clichés, however because it relies on execution rather than concept, it remains a winner. It is beautifully crafted and keeps the tension well." — Samantha Knowles, *Stalk'n'Slash*

DVD

Released by MPI Home Video on October 12, 2010, and by AOI Entertainment in Australia on the same date.

Crush
Nexus 6 Films, 2009

CREDITS: *Directors:* John V. Soto, Jeff Gerritsen; *Producer:* Deidre Kitcher; *Executive Producers:* Ray Meadowcroll, Andrew Morgan, Michael Favelle; *Associate Producers:* Linda Brnjich, Maria Brnjich, Mark Scholmann, Donato Iacovantuono; *Screenplay:* John V. Soto; *Photography:* Richard Malins; *Editor:* James Ballantine; *Music:* Jamie Blanks; *Production Design:* Nigel Devenport; *Costumes:* Susi Rigg; *Sound:* Glenn Dillon; *Makeup/Hair:* Liddy Reynolds, Karen Sims. Color, 76 minutes. Filmed on location at Perry Lakes Basketball Stadium, Floreat, and the University of Western Australia, Crawley, in Perth, Western Australia.

SONGS: "Waiting All Day" (Johns/Hamilton), Silverchair; "Animal," Ravior; "Ordinary Life," Kristen Barry; "Bodies," Little Birdies; "Vampire Racecourse" (Luke Steel), The Sleepy Jackson; "Crazy," Cordrazine; "Cigarettes and Suitcases," Something For Kate; "Everything," Shihad; "Last Resort," Papa Roach; "I'm Carrying," Ravior.

CAST: Chris Egan (Julian); Brooke Harman (Clare Johnson); Emma Lung (Anna); Christian Clark (Wesley); Kane Manera (Phil); Jenna Lind (Logan); Ian Toyne (Harry Loomis); Helen Searle (Kelly Loomis); Alicia Place (Bella Loomis); Samantha Collins (Andrea Loomis); Luke Hewitt (Ralph); Kerry Ella McAullay (Samantha); Elwyn Edwards (Professor Poulson); Eddie Stowers (The Coach); Steve Burridge (Referee); Gemma Pranita (Nurse); Fabian Peters (Damian); Ben See (Taekwondo Opponent 1); Adam Swayer (Taekwondo Opponent 2); Glenn Studdens (Chauffeur); Brooke Kammann, Ellie Matthews (Anna look-alikes at University); Braden Izydorski, Jeremy Yap, Andy Hong, Helen King Ross, Jade Gillespie, Gerald Hayes (Taekwondo Competitors); Brendan Coniglio, Archie Shaw, Sally Mather, Kathrine Hale, Christine Hale, Wendy Hale, Angie Radford, Jasmine Shurlock, Benjamin Shurlock, Gerald Hayes, Jodie Castlehow, Ben Lacey, Rhys Mota (Taekwondo Extras); Stuart Ross, Helen Ross (Taekwondo Judges).

Synopsis

Julian is an American visa student studying architecture in Perth. He has also qualified for the Australian Taekwondo finals. He takes a job as a house sitter at the mansion of Harry Loomis, who is going on vacation, and meets a girl whom he assumes to be Harry's niece, Anna. Attracted to the seductive girl, Julian has sex with her even though he has a girlfriend, Clare. Clare visits the house and is scared away after being locked in the toilet. An e-mail is sent to Clare with Julian's confession of his relationship with Anna. Julian breaks his training and drinks before having sex again with Anna. His weakened state helps him to lose the fight final. Clare breaks up with him over the e-mail she has received. Julian learns from Loomis' neighbor and from Internet research how Anna is the deceased daughter of Harry, who had died after falling down the staircase of the house in an attempted robbery. Anna tells Julian he must kill himself to be with her forever, but Julian refuses. In a struggle she pushes him down the same staircase and he dies. Anna has succeeded in having Julian.

Notes

A simple story of obsession featuring the theme of the malevolent supernatural being, with only one killing. This film with two directors is marred by an overuse of postmodern technique and a method-mannered lead performance. John V. Soto and Jeff Gerritsen use flash and jump cuts, black outs, point of view, expressionist angles, hand-held camerawork, optical effects, montage, prefiguring edits, aural memory flashbacks, and an obtrusive score. Horror cinephiles will also be frustrated by the lack of gore in the one killing, although the antagonist gets to wear demon makeup.

The opening scene of Taekwondo competition presents the importance of the sport for Julian and the "focus" that his coach reminds him he needs to win the upcoming finals. This focus will include not drinking, and beer is stocked in the Loomis house refrigerator as a temptation. The information that Julian has a drinking problem is not revealed until after he loses the finals fight. The coach says that he was warned because of Julian's previous banishment from the American team for "underage" drinking. One might also think that sex would be another thing to make him lose focus. It is apparent that Julian attempts to have it with Clare, though his also having it with Anna is more aligned with her as a destructive force.

The power going off and no one being at the rung door when Julian and Clare are kissing suggest Anna's supernatural influence. Julian's dreams of kissing Anna and kissing Clare suggest fantasy desires. Emma Lung may not be the gorgeous seductress that Anna is meant to be, but Brooke Harman as Clare adds a sensible attitude that undercuts her beauty and perhaps thereby makes Anna more of a temptation. The fact that Julian would have the footage of his Taekwondo fight playing while trying to seduce Clare suggests his egotism. The filmed moment of Julian's victory is repeated and then freeze-framed to suggest more of Anna's interest. Julian drawing Anna, as well as dreaming of having sex with her, continues his interest in her. It prefigures the scene where they have sex, although the act is not presented graphically. Rather the flesh of Chris Egan's Julian is exposed far more than Emma Lung's Anna, who is never seen naked or bare-breasted.

There is a prefiguring shot of Anna yelling at Julian, which is later revealed in the climax as her begging him, "Love me." The plot point of Julian breaking a vase isn't given a payoff apart from when he speaks to Harry on the phone and tells him nothing has been broken. Clare smoking in the toilet creates the expectation of an attack upon her, which is only partially met by the locked door and light going off. Anna's beseeching Julian to "tell me that you love me" is a sign of her neediness. It's a shame that we didn't hear Julian say it in the first sex scene — an utterance that can be acceptably made in the throes of lust — so that we only have Anna's word to go by. This would also help make Anna a less pathetic figure, although Julian's two sexual encounters with her attest to his complicity in the situation.

The vision of Julian hanging from a tree is presumably one of his dreams, although it prefigures his fate, if not his specific way of dying. There is a laugh from the way he cannot erase the lipsticked heart on the bathroom mirror. There is an unnecessary ambiguity attached to the issue of the "My Confession" e-mail since Anna denies sending. Of course she could be lying, but Julian is right when he asks, who else could have done it? Are we to think that it could have been Phil, who later jokes that he would be a better boyfriend for Clare? It is left unresolved.

In the finals fight Julian has flashbacks to Anna, including a shot of them having sex. In another she is strangling him, which is later shown in the climax, and her saying, "Tell me that you love me." The second round suggests that Julian's assumed inability to win the fight is misleading but the expectation that he will lose is eventually met. The idea that Anna is a ghost is suggested before the reveal of the Internet research scene, by Harry's telephone reaction to Julian's news that she has been in the house.

The screenplay overstates Anna's case she tells Julian three times, "It's over when I say it's over," even though Emma Lung makes it work. She also makes work the following scene where she repeats Julian's lines from their first scene together as black drops fall into the pool where she has retreated. The black drops don't suggest blood but rather death, and the treatment does not reveal where they are falling from.

The idea that Anna has taken Julian's assignment appears to be a small act of vindictiveness after his rejection of her. It helps that his failure to submit the assignment that puts his visa at risk is a sign of Julian's growing downfall, since he cannot fail his studies. The scene where he attempts to talk to Clare in front of the friends is presented as overplayed, particularly in the close-up used on Clare to show her refusal to speak to Julian.

Probably the most interesting thing to come out of the expository reveal of Anna's death is the idea that she is the only daughter of Harry's previous marriage. She had become a drug addict presumably as a result of her mother's absence and perceived rejection by her father. The idea of Anna as a drug addict makes her obsession with Julian more believable. She can be considered addicted to him, rather than just taken by his physical beauty and presumed superior sexual technique.

Anna confesses what she is to Julian —"My body's dead but not my spirit"— and she gets a bunch of horror movie conventional lines that Emma Lung sells. These include her correction that they have "made love" rather than had sex. "In dreams anything can happen" prefigures a montage of shots of Julian. "I'm yours forever," "I need you to cross over, to kill yourself to be with me," and "If you die in dreams, you die for real."

The scene has Anna's appearance change into her demon makeup with "This is my house. I set the rules here," and this is a look she maintains for the rest of the narrative. It is disappointing that Julian's change of mind, in agreeing to cut his wrist "to prove your love for me" with the knife she has provided, has Anna required to chase him in order to cut him. It reduces Anna to behaving like a human slasher rather than allowing her to demonstrate her supernatural powers, though perhaps they are limited. It also creates the expectation, not met, when he hides in the closet and we expect her to slash his face with the knife.

There is a shock image of Julian seeing himself in a vision in the bathroom mirror with a bloodied face. Him being locked inside the house recalls and pays off the scene where the front door was jammed. Clare and the friends coming to the house (because "I still love him") creates the expectation that they will save Julian from death. Wesley eventually hammers through the door after he fails to break it down when he throws himself against it. Julian is pushed down the staircase by Anna. The expectation that he is dead is initially not met by the hospital scene, where the nurse, whose face is masked by darkness, tells him he has been in a coma. Because the nurse's voice sounds like Anna, the reveal that she *is* Anna is not a surprise.

The idea that Julian has dreamed this moment as a dying fantasy is a meeting of the expectation that the fall down the staircase will kill him. A shot of Anna on the bed with Julian during the end credits is perhaps an unnecessary epilogue, showing what is assumed. Anna is with the dead Julian forever, although she does get a sequel-type comment with "Don't worry about Clare. I'll take good care of her too."

Directors John V. Soto and Jeff Gerritsen made their film debut with *Crush*, and they have not made another Australian horror movie to date. The film is also the only Australian horror title to date made by producer Deidre Kitcher, executive producers Ray Meadowcroll, Andrew Morgan, and Michael Favelle, and by the Nexus 6 Films production company.

Australian born Chris Egan began his career in television and made his film debut in a supporting role in the family action adventure *Eragon* (2006). Playing more supporting film parts and in television, he has not had another leading film role since *Crush*.

Born in the United States but raised in Australia, Brooke Harman also began in television and made her film debut in a supporting role in *Till Human Voices Wake Us* (2002). She has only appeared in more supporting roles and on television before and after *Crush*.

Emma Lung also began in television, making her film debut in a minor role in the musical comedy *Garage Days* (2002). After playing supporting roles and more television, she essayed the leads in *Stranded* (2005) and the thriller *Jammed* (2007); her prior role was a supporting one in *The Gates of Hell*. After *Crush* the actress appeared in a supporting role in the Australian horror title *Triangle*, more supporting parts and on television.

Release

Australia in April 2009 and the United States on DVD with the tagline "Attraction can be fatal."

Reviews

"Emma Lung delivers the film's most haunting performance.... Direction is confident, and the screenplay has enough texture to make it interesting as a story. Also in its favour is a naturalistic tone that many Hollywood films in this genre shy away from; the result is a fresh take and a clear Australian stamp."— Andrew L. Urban, *Urban Cinefile*, October 8, 2009

"A taut and eerie psychological thriller that makes a startling U-turn just when you think you know where it's heading. Soto's writing and directing is effective, delivering an assured and slick film filled with chills, scares and the alluring sense of the unexpected. Strong performances by Chris Egan and Emma Lung."— Louise Keller, *Urban Cinefile*, October 8, 2009

"Gerritsen and Soto set you up for what appears to be a standard fatal attraction film and then they pull the rug out from under you in the final act. A very solid young adult movie that has some disturbing concepts coming at you ... a solid dark genre experience."— Jeff Ritchie, *ScaryMinds*

"Despite troubling lapses of internal logic plus underwritten, poorly acted support, Crush delivers most of what it sets out to do. Egan and Lung [as] the film's biggest asset push proceedings a notch or two above similar movies. It's not like there's anything particularly new here, yet it's all handled with flair."— Colin Fraser, *Moviereview*

"*Crush* looks pretty, that's for sure, although a boring and repetitive soundtrack as well as a flat and uninspiring direction make it a major disappointment.... Egan's American accent is poor and the big misfire is Emma Lung, who here is nothing more than a .5-dimensional babe-in-a-bikini."— Glenn Dunks, *Stale Popcorn*, October 20, 2009

"What might seem like a standard film premise is given a nice horror twist. The first half is a little bit slow at times; however, once the plot develops, Crush comes alive with energy and momentum. This rollercoaster ride of suspense has Lung and Egan generate some fireworks with dynamic confrontational scenes."— Brandon Sites, *Big Daddy Horror Reviews*, June 27, 2011

DVD

Released by Phase 4 Films on July 23, 2010, and Paramount Home Entertainment (Australia) on October 8, 2009.

Damned by Dawn

Odin's Eye Entertainment/AKB (Amazing Krypto Bros), 2009 [aka *The Banshee*]

CREDITS: *Director:* Brett Anstey; *Producers:* Brett Anstey, Luke Gibson; *Associate Producer/Editor:* Dave Redman; *Screenplay:* Brett Anstey based on a story by Brett Anstey, Russell Friedrich and Rob Townshend; *Photography:* Reg Spoon; *Music:* Phil Lambert, Scott McIntyre; *Special Makeup Effects:* Justin Dix; *Production Design:* David Jackson; *Sound Design:* Tristan Meredith; *Costumes:* Georgiana Russell-Head; *Sound:* Chris Bullock, Ben Hardiman, Michael Olsen, Charlie Sarroff. Color, 84 minutes. Filmed in Ballarat and Dandenong, Victoria, from August 22 to October 29, 2006.

SONG: "Bones of a Rabbit" (K. Hart, M. Wright), Young Heretics.

CAST: Renee Willner (Claire O'Neil); Bridget Neval (The Banshee); Dawn Klingberg (Nana O'Neill); Taryn Eva (Jennifer O'Neill); Danny Alder (Paul); Mark Taylor (Simmo); Peter Stratford (Bill O'Neill); Nina Nicols, Trent Schwarz (Ghosts).

Synopsis

Claire O'Neil and her boyfriend, Paul, visit the country home of her father, Bill. They learn that her grandmother, "Nana" Dawn, is dying. Dawn warns Claire not to interfere with the "Lady of Sorrows" when she comes for her. Paul's sighting of a banshee prefigures the death of Nana, as does the screams in the night that are heard by all the household. Bill, Paul and the neighbor Simmo go into the woods to investigate the screams. The banshee appears back at the house and is seen by Claire and her younger sister, Jen. Claire pushes the screaming banshee off the balcony outside Nana's room. This leads to the dead awakening and rising from their burial in the woods, and "Damned by Dawn" to be written on the bedroom wall.

Paul is killed. Bill and Simmo follow the sound of crying into a mine shaft, where they see a skeleton with a scythe. Bill runs back to the house but Simmo is caught by a flying skeleton. Paul returns as a zombie and wounds Bill, though Claire manages to overpower him. Jen goes to Simmo and is attacked by another skeleton. Jen is whisked away after the banshee cries to signal her death before Claire can save her. Claire and Bill drive away from the house, pursued by skeletons. The car crashes, and Bill is taken. Claire finds her way to the mineshaft. Nana tells her that by interfering, Claire is responsible for what has happened. Nana, now a demon, chases Claire and realizes that she is pregnant, but when the banshee appears, Claire releases the spirits of the O'Neil family from the urn Nana had given her which destroys the banshee. Claire then sets the body of Nana alight so that she can be cremated as she had wished.

Notes

This title shot on digital video features the malevolent supernatural being in the form of a banshee and the dead who appear as various skeletons, one in particular who brandishes a scythe. Director Brett Anstey employs the postmodern techniques of expressionist camera angles, blackouts, fast and slow motion, point of view, and CGI and blue screen effects. The treatment's pleasing use of silence to create suspense is soon overwhelmed by optical effects and silliness.

The film opens with the sound of breathing and a title card which reads, "Oh she mournfully wails/ In the midst of the silent, lonely, lonely, night/ Lamenting, she sings the song of death." Fog around the farmhouse and rolling clouds are presented for atmosphere, although the banshee will later be shown to exhale her own form of mist. The bloody corpses of dead chickens said to have been killed by a fox prefigure the bloody deaths to come. The fox trap set by Bill also prefigures the one in which Claire gets her foot caught at the climax. Nana's aging makeup reads as extreme and because of this, it makes her seem hardly different in the climax when she is meant to be a damned soul.

Anstey will make a lot of use of the shock effect in the film. This begins with the appearance of the banshee that Paul's car nearly hits at night when his attention is distracted by his eating pizza. The banshee flying behind him, unseen by him, creates the expectation of a strike that is not met. The conventional storm with thunder and lightning is again used as a premonition of trouble ahead. The sight of the banshee in the period photograph of Nana as a child with her older relatives is rationalized by the information that her mother died the day after it was taken, although the banshee appears more out of place than necessary in it.

When the banshee's screams wake up everyone in the household, Bill, Paul and Simmo going into the woods to investigate makes them Men in Peril. However, the narrative inverts the expectation by having the banshee appear back at the house instead. Anstey uses the conventional shot of the banshee twisting a door knob for suspense when she enters the house. She can fly but she can't seem to move through doors. The expectation of her going to Jen is created but not met when she only looks in her room then goes to Nana's room after Claire hears knocking against the door. Claire's hiding in the closet and leaving Nana in her bed suggests that Nana is dead. When the banshee goes out onto the balcony to scream, the expectation is created that Claire will push her off it. This is met and the banshee being impaled is what sets off the dead rising, although the return of the banshee shows that the impaling has not done her much harm.

When Paul trips over a disturbed grave which separates him from Bill and Simmo, this and his looking into the hole in the ground and the skeleton that appears behind him all create the expectation of a strike against him, which is met. Anstey has blood splash onto the camera lens for the suggestion of the death of Paul, a self-conscious device that is not used anywhere else in the treatment. The shock appearance of a skeleton to Claire is followed by Bill appearing to her, although no connection is made between the two. Nana being dragged away is what sets the family to search for her, rather than letting her go as she had requested, although Claire's mistreatment of the banshee had already begun the trouble.

Bill and Simmo go back into the woods, and they don't immediately see the body of Paul hanging from a tree apparently by his own intestines. Neither do they see the blood on the ground that is also presumably Paul's. It takes the clichéd action of Bill walking backwards to find Paul and his apparent disembowelment. This will get a later payoff when more of his intestines fall from him when he returns as a zombie.

Bill and Simmo hear crying in the mineshaft, which leads them to go inside, again becoming Men in Peril investigating a noise. The bugs on the mineshaft floor seem to prefigure the presence of demons. This is because they will be seen again for Paul's attack, his return to the house and when Claire goes into the mineshaft in the climax. The crying is ambiguous since it may be that of Nana, or it may be the skeletons luring the two men. The former is confirmed when Nana is shown to Claire later in the mineshaft.

When the men get to the center, we aren't shown their point of view. Rather, Anstey goes to a blackout. The men are then seen running outside the mineshaft and being followed by the scythe-wielding skeleton. Bill shoots the skeleton in the head, causing it to explode, a human disposal of a supernatural being.

Bill, Claire and Jen watch Simmo being attacked by another skeleton with scythe but do nothing to help him. When Jen later goes to him to retrieve the gun ammunition he had obtained, she does attempt to keep him away from the approaching skeleton when she finds that Simmo is not dead. Claire reading from Nana's diary explains the banshee waking the dead and how "they are coming for us." Her dream of the returning Paul and Jen being attacked by the zombie will both get payoffs when both occur. Paul's real return is heralded by a funny moment where Bill opens a door and has his throat grabbed by Paul. Paul's zombified reality is evident from the bugs that come out of his mouth and his stomach wound. His accusation to Bill, "You left me to die," has some merit, although his human strategies of punching Bill and slapping and then strangling Claire seem disappointing for a supernatural being.

When Claire tries to save Jen with the rifle she has the potential to be a female warrior, although she will not get to fire it. She faces the darkened doorway of the shearing shed where it appears that the banshee teases her by throwing out bullets and then Jen's tongue. This is before the wounded Jen is found to be outside with the banshee behind her and the flying skeletons behind them. The banshee's scream pre-empts Jen being taken, just as she had attempted to pre-empt the death of Nana. Claire driving away from the farmhouse with Bill has him reading more of the diary to supply the prophecy, "This nightmare will only end once the banshee tastes the poor blood of the last surviving O'Neil." The flying skeletons act like kamikazes as they fly into the car's windshield and disintegrate, leaving grey soot. Claire finding Nana's St. Christopher medallion seems to be a token of luck that will save her.

The issue of Claire being pregnant, which there have been subtle references to previously, would seem to be the plot point that spares her from the banshee. This follows the idea that Claire is the last surviving O'Neil. It would seem that baby crying had been heard in the mineshaft and Nana's observation of it precedes the banshee's insight. It is the banshee's licking of Claire's head wound blood that chokes the creature from screaming much like the way the *Queen of the Damned* was made vulnerable to an opportunistic attack before her defeat in that story. The opening of the urn then is paid off to release the spirits who defeat her. A prologue where Claire screams at something unseen suggests that perhaps she is not saved or that Anstey wanted the possibility of a sequel.

In the DVD audio commentary Anstey says the skeletal ghosts were inspired by the harpies in the action fantasy *Jason and the Argonauts* (1963). The film is the feature debut for Anstey, who has not made another Australian horror title to date. It is also the only Australian horror movie for producer Luke Gibson, associate producer Dave Redman and the production company the Amazing Krypto Bros.

Renee Willner made her feature debut in the film and it is her last title to date. Indian born Bridget Neval began her career in television and made her film debut in *Damned by Dawn*, her last film to date. Dawn Klingberg appeared in the Australian horror title *Prey* and continued in film shorts and television. Taryn Eva also made her film debut in *Damned by Dawn*, her only title to date. Danny Alder made his film debut in a minor role in the comedy *Blurred* (2002), and after appearing in film shorts and television, *Damned by Dawn* is his last movie role to date. Mark Taylor also began his career in television and made his film debut here, after which he appeared in more television. Peter Stratford had previously appeared in *Snapshot*.

RELEASE

Screened in the United States on October 19, 2009, at the Screamfest Horror Film Festival and released in Australia on April 15, 2010. The taglines are "When the banshee cries ... the dead will rise" and "The dead will rise." The DVD audio commentaries make mention of scenes that were deleted and the "Making of *The Damned* Film" featurette shows footage from some. The deleted scenes include Nana writing in her diary, a family dinner scene, a subplot that featured romance between Simmo and Jen, Bill vomiting after he leaves the mineshaft, Bill being covered in bugs, Simmo volunteering to get ammunition although Bill doesn't want them to separate, and more of Claire running in the woods.

REVIEWS

"Low-budget B-movie throwback that delivers pretty much what you'd expect. The script and plot are second-rate, the acting ropey and the CGI amateurish, but horror fans may still find the odd piece of enjoyment from a handful of suspenseful moments, a couple of gory death sequences and some decent make-up work."— Gary Collinson, *Flickering Myth*, March 8, 2011

"It has some great ideas and it has some grand ambitions, but it just never quite gets it right. It's a film that is difficult to dislike but even with the best intentions many viewers will be, despite their wishes, underwhelmed."— Matt Compton, *Nefarious Films*, September 12, 2010

"With its Hammer Horror ambiance and Evil Dead appreciation of blood-and-guts hauntings, the film is one of the best of its kind, with a hybrid old-fashioned/modern sensibility and the sort of well-paced narrative movement that too many Hollywood films forgo in order to numb the audience with rapid-cut hysteria."— Robert Hood, *Undead Backbrain*, February 27, 2010

"The acting quality's not too bad for a B-movie. The general premise of the story is solid also, nicely written and paced. [But] the special effects are woeful, truly bad. It's creepy and tense in parts but on the scare-o-meter scale it ranks down pretty low."— Ramius Scythe, *Horror Chronicles*

"The banshee looks like a Halloween costume, and the flying evil spirits are well-rendered but unoriginal. Performances are at the mercy of flat characterization. [It's] no *Evil Dead 4* with Anstey merely distilling elements of the Raimi film into a proficient low-budget film that is on-par visually with some studio direct-to-DVD horror sequels."— Eric Cotenas, *DVDBeaver*

"Flawed, and the possessor of a particularly lackluster second act, [it] deserves kudos for its interesting premise that isn't quite enough to save the entire production.... It looks no better than most any other trashy DTV horror, and that's a shame, as clearly Anstey is aiming higher."— Paul Pritchard, *DVD Verdict*, October 29 2010

DVD

Released in the United States by Imagine Entertainment on November 9, 2010, but no release in Australia to date.

Daybreakers
Lionsgate and Paradise Production/
Screen Australia/Furst Films, 2009

CREDITS: *Screenplay/Director:* The Spierig Brothers; *Producers:* Chris Brown, Sean Furst, Bryan Furst; *Co-Producer:* Todd Fellman; *Executive Producers:* Jason Constantine, Peter Block; *Photography:* Ben Nott; *Editor:* Matt Villa; *Music:* Christopher Gordon; *Production/Costume Design:* George Liddle; *Special Makeup Effects:* Steve Boyle. Sound: Wayne Pashley Mpse; *Art Directors:* Bill Booth, Eugene Intas; *Set Designers:* Klaus Kastberg, Jacinta Leong, Paula Whiteway; *Ethan Hawke's Makeup:* Carla Vicenzino; *Willem Dafoe's Makeup:* Samantha Lyttle. Color, 94 minutes. Filmed at Riparian Plaza, Brisbane; Robina Train Station, Robina; Brisbane, Queensland; and at the Warner Roadshow Studios, Gold Coast and Warner Bros. Movieworld, Oxenford, Queensland, from July 16 to September 10, 2007.

SONG: "Burning Love" (Dennis Linde); "Running Up That Hill" (Kate Bush), Placebo, heard in closing credits.

CAST: Ethan Hawke (Edward Dalton); Willem Dafoe (Lionel "Elvis" Cormac); Claudia Karvan (Audrey Bennett); Michael Dorman (Frankie Dalton); Isabel Lukas (Alison Bromley); Vince Colosimo (Christopher Caruso); Sam Neill (Charles Bromley). Harriet Minto-Day (Lisa Barrett); Jay Laga'aia (Senator Wes Turner); Damien Garvey (Senator Westlake); Sahaj Dumpleton (Homeless Vampire); Allan Todd, Des Coroy (Businessmen); Gabriella Di Labio (Businesswoman); Ben Siemer, Peter Welman (Police Officers); Callum McLean, Jarrad Pon, Victoria Williams, Zoe White, Aolani Roy (Vampire School Kids); Tiffany Lamb (News Reader); Renai Caruso (Coffee Shop Attendant); Chris Brown, Kirsten Cameron (Subway Commuters); Carl Rush (Al Walker); Paul Sonkkila (General Williams); Todd Levi (Commissioner Turnbull); Wayne Smith (Inmate 4075B); Berni Chin, Kevin Zwierzchaczewski (Lab Technicians); Joel Spreadborough (Vampire Subject); Lisa Cunningham, Amanda Buchanan (Nurses); Jane Wallace (Bromley's Assistant); Mungo McKay (Colin Briggs); Emma Randall (Ellie Landon); Charlotte Wilson (Joy Watkins); Rowan Smith (Police Officer in Car); Bryan Probets (Subsider in Kitchen); John Gibson (Detective Cosgrove); Robyn Moore (Forensic Investigator Simms); Troy MacKinder (Officer Hobbs); Christopher Kirby (Jarvis Bayom); Glen Martin (Coffee Buyer); Michelle Atkinson (Mother); David Vallon (Janitor);

Candice Storey, Simon Burvill-Holmes, Anne Bennetts (Onlookers); Kellie Vella (Subsider in Garage); Scot McQade (Security Desk Officer); Jack Bradford (Security Guard 1); Jason Chin (Medic); Konrad Whitten (Weathered Human); Mark Finden (Young Vampire Cadet); Anthony Cogin (Loop Group Captain); Lisa Adam, Amanda Bishop, Nick Christo, Anthony Cogin, Beth Daley, Keiran Darcy-Smith, James Evans, Elizabeth Friels, Anita Heigh, Bartholomew John, Andy McDonell, Brian Meeghan, Tiriel Mora, Julie O'Reilly, Keith Scott, John Xintavelonis (Loop Group). Uncredited: Tyson Bradly, Byron J. Brochman, Michael Browning, Matthew Wollaston (Vampire Soldiers); Joel Amos Byrnes (Security Guard); Eddie L. Fauria (Street Cop); Mirrah Foulkes; Michael Ienna (Louis); Selina Kadell (Debate News Anchorwoman); David Knijinenburg (Vampire Commuter); Alex Revan (Rygar).

Synopsis

In 2019 America is inhabited by vampires who feed off the dwindling blood supply of humans. At Bromley Marks Pharmaceuticals humans are used as blood cows. Hematologist Edward Dalton works on a blood substitute but a test on a vampire results in death. With the vampire population being allowed less and less blood, the ones deprived of it turn into feral "subsiders." Driving home from work Edward's car collides with a group of humans, led by Audrey Bennett. Sensing that Edward can help her, she takes him to meet her leader. Lionel Cormac is a mechanic and former vampire who has become human after being burned by the sun. Lionel takes Edward to a country vineyard, where Edward uses the airtight wine fermentation tank to burn himself from the sun. He is "cured" of his vampirism and transforms back into a human.

Charles Bromley sends Edward's brother Frankie to find him. Frankie fails but agrees to "turn" Bromley's human daughter, Alison, into a vampire. With no more humans to provide blood, the supply is stopped. Martial law is introduced to cleanse the city of subsiders, which includes Alison. Edward contacts his fellow Bromley researcher, Christopher, who has discovered his own form of blood substitute. Christopher betrays Edward, and Audrey is taken. Edward and Lionel are found by Frankie, who bites Lionel. Edward realizes that the cure is treated vampire blood. He goes to Bromley to exchange the cure for Audrey. Bromley tells him he has Christopher's substitute and bites Edward, turning back into a human. Bromley is left by Edward to be devoured by the army that has swarmed into the building. Frankie offers himself to the hoard to help Edward and Audrey escape. Christopher appears to kill them so that his cure can never be discovered. Lionel appears and kills Christopher. The three survivors drive away into the daylight sun.

Notes

This meld of science fiction and horror features vampires for the theme of the malevolent supernatural being. The main character starts off as an antagonist and, by transforming into a human, becomes the protagonist. The Spierig Brothers follow up their previous Australian horror title, *Undead*, with a far less quirky and more conventional treatment. They use the postmodern techniques of expressionist camera angles, jump cuts, fast edits, zooms, point of view and slow motion. With another obtrusive score, they rely upon shock effects. The narrative meets most expectations created and has a climax mired with successive antagonists and contrivances. However, the Spierigs do create an atmospheric world of casual cruelty. They provide the occasional striking visual image to support some of the Gothicism attempted, some humor, and an interesting subplot which explores vampire incest.

A flying bat is seen as a shock effect under the opening credits. This will be repeated before the end credits, and suggests the tale of vampires to come. The girl vampire we see who allows herself to be burned by the rising sun is the first of other vampires who will be burned in this way, with the idea that she should commit suicide like this attesting to desperate times. On the DVD commentary, the Spierigs state that the intention of this prologue was to set up the dilemma of immortal children who will never grow up as the downside of being vampires.

Edward's vampirism is introduced visually by the funny shot of his bodiless clothes seen in a car mirror reflection before his person is revealed. The blood selling stand in subway is a witty variation on a coffee stand, which gets a later payoff when a customer revolts against the blood rationing. The vampire soldiers' neck clamp and electroshock treatment of the homeless vampire prefigure their cruelty in the climax when they will attack their own. The humans we see being bled at the Bromley Marks Pharmaceutical blood farm recalls the blood cows from *Thirst*.

The testing of Edward's blood substitute on a vampire involves the use of shock for the vomit he spews and his head bursting as well as gore from the diseased reaction. The issue of the day the nar-

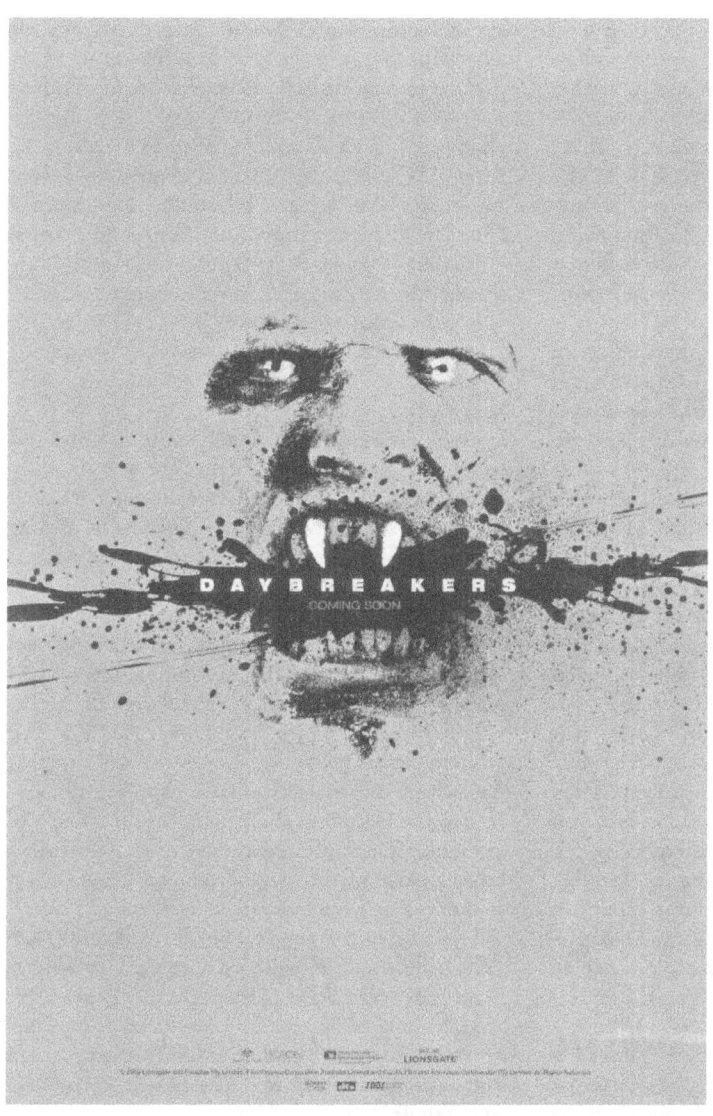

Poster for *Daybreakers* (2009).

rative begins being Edward's birthday isn't given any plot payoff, apart from the fact that birthdays are meaningless to vampires. The home invasion by the subsider seems to exist so that we can see easily it is for Audrey to also invade Edward's home.

The Spierigs use the first of their flashbacks for Lionel's memory of his becoming human after being burned by the sun when he is thrown from a crashed car. Audrey's trust in Edward is demonstrated by her willingness to cut her herself in order to feed him her blood. When the humans move to the vineyard, Edward asks if it is safe. This is a reasonable question since Frankie and soldiers will soon descend upon it. Lionel replies, "Being human in a world full of vampires is about as safe as bare backing a five dollar whore." When the car that Jarvis drives to collect Alison and other renegade humans blows a tire, the expectation is created for an attack by Frankie and the vampires once he sees how the tire was shot out deliberately. There is an impressive aerial view of the vampires advancing on either side of Jarvis and his convoy.

Edward, Audrey and Lionel stay behind at the vineyard for Edward's experiment when the others flee to Senator Turner's cabin, sparing them from the massacre that occurs there. The Spierigs inter-cut between the experiment and Alison as a prisoner of Charles Bromley, who is revealed to be her father. Her stabbing of him during a hug is prefigured by the blood drops on his shoes. Just as Edward succeeds in repeatedly burning himself in the wine fermentation tank to turn back into a human, Frankie turns Alison into a vampire by biting her. The DVD commentary points out that Edward was to have originally undergone the same attack of boils that the vampire subject had in the earlier failed experiment, and that Frankie's apparent easy retreat from the vineyard was to allow him to return to attack Alison.

When Charles visits Alison there is a marvelous moment when she smears her blood over his mouth, thinking he wants to drink her blood. Although Charles doesn't do so, the suggestion of incest is created. Another strong image is Charles seeing the milking room empty of humans left to bleed. The sign we had previously seen in the subway that said "Capture Humans" with the Uncle Sam Needs You image is now shown to have been vandalized with the words "Now what?" written over it.

Edward, Audrey and Lionel drive to the Senator's cabin in Lionel's car that has "From the ashes spring new life" written on its side. Ethan Hawke is lit to look much healthier here as a sign that he is now human. The scene where subsiders are dragged in chains behind a tank into the sun to burn is marred by obvious use of CGI for the burn, as was the girl vampire, and Lionel's and Edward's burns. There is a heavenly choir on the soundtrack, with the sight of the chains dragging nothing after the burning redeeming it. There is a cut from Alison being recognized by Frankie as one of the subsiders to a photograph of her former self that Charles looks at.

Edward, Audrey and Lionel wait to surprise Christopher in his house, and his bad decorating is meant to clue us to the fact that he should not be trusted. The expectation that he will betray them is met when he disappears behind a screen and Audrey is shot and taken away when she goes after him. When Frankie turns up at Lionel's Cormac Custom Restorations Garage, the expectation is created that he too will betray Edward and Lionel. This he does by biting Lionel. The DVD commentary remarks that Frankie's sickly appearance is to suggest that he, like Alison before him, had been feeding off himself.

The Spierigs have Edward pause to look at Frankie's reaction to the biting and save what Edward sees for his later flashback in confrontation with Charles. The camera pans up blood drops on a sofa to reveal Audrey cut and bleeding in Charles' office, and the comical sight of Charles drinking her blood from a brandy glass. The flashback of Edward with Frankie is first seemingly used for Edward to tell Charles how Frankie has told him how he "turned" Alison. After Charles bites Edward, it is used again for Edward's reveal that the cure is treated vampire blood and that since Charles has bitten Edward, Charles now "turns" back into a human. This helps to give an explanation to the moment where Charles bites Edward, because although it is expected, we don't understand why he does it.

Charles tied to a chair in the opened elevator and facing the vampire soldiers is an appropriately Gothic end for him. The Spierigs use an overhead camera shot for the attack, with Charles' head being ripped off in the fury a gruesome capper. When Edward and Audrey appear to be entrapped by the soldiers, a succession of surprise appearances adds unintentional comedy as deus ex machina. First Frankie appears smashing through the lobby in a car and offers himself to the soldiers to save Edward and Audrey. The frenzied attack upon him this time is shot from above but with a zoom in and held as poetic gruesomeness.

Then, the second flank of soldiers attacks the first flank because the first flank has now transformed into humans. The camera observes the carnage as if it is a battle scene. Then Christopher arrives to kill Edward and Audrey, but he is shot by Lionel. When Edward goes to Frankie's the expectation that he will come back alive to do something is not met. It is not immediately apparent that the golden light that appears is not is the sun; the surviving humans escape and drive off into the sunrise. Edward's voiceover tells us, "We have a cure. We can change you back. It's not too late." The vampire bat from the opening credits reappears as a final shock effect.

In the DVD commentary the Spierig Brothers state that scenes showing more of the love affair between Edward and Audrey were deleted because it was felt they fell in love too quickly. The ending was also re-shot after a test screening to make it more upbeat. They also say that their interest in horror is more in fantasy rather than realism, which explains the tone of their film, which features grand guignol gore without the accompanying tone of suspense or fear. Although the Spierigs claim that the narrative is original, the horror title *The Last Man on Earth* (1964) used the idea of a plague that has turned the world population into vampires.

Born in Germany, the Spierig Brothers first and prior film was *Undead*; they have not made another to date since *Daybreakers*. Producers Chris Brown had previously made *Komodo*, *Hellion: The Devil's Playground*, and *Triangle*. The film is the only Australian horror title made by Lionsgate, producers Sean and Bryan Furst of Furst Films, co-producer Todd Fellman, and executive producers Jason Constantine and Peter Block. Paradise Productions had previously made *Hellion: The Devil's Playground* and *Triangle*.

American Ethan Hawke made his film debut as a child star in the lead in the family adventure *Explorers* (1985) and after playing supporting roles, was the lead in the comedy *Mystery Date* (1991). He transitioned to adult roles with leads in the action adventure *Alive* (1993), the romance *Before Sunrise* (1995), the science fiction romance *Gattaca* (1997), the romance *Great Expectations* (1998), and the mystery *Snow Falling on Cedars* (1999). In the 2000s, the actor continued in leading roles as the title character of *Hamlet* (2000), *Tape* (2001), the romance *Before Sunset* (2004), for which he also co-wrote the screenplay and was nominated for the Best Writing Adapted Screenplay Academy Award, the crime drama *Assault on Precinct 13* (2005), and the crime drama *Staten Island* (2009), his prior title. Hawke was nominated for the Best Supporting Actor Academy Award for the crime drama *Training Day* (2001), and has not had a leading film role since *Daybreakers*. He has also directed two features: *Chelsea Walls* (2001) and *The Hottest State* (2006), which was based on his own novel and for which he also wrote the screenplay.

American Willem Dafoe made his film debut in an uncredited minor role in the western *Heaven's Gate* (1980), and scored the lead in *The Loveless* (1982). After playing more supporting roles the actor played the lead in the action comedy *Roadhouse 66* (1984), the war actioner *Off Limits* (1988), the title character in *The Last Temptation of Christ* (1988), and the historical biography *Triumph of the Spirit* (1989). In the 1990s Dafoe essayed the leads in the crime dramas *Light Sleeper* (1992) and *White Sands* (1992), the biographical romance *Tom and Viv* (1994), the romance *Victory* (1995), and the crime drama *The Boondock Saints* (1999). In the 2000s the actor was the lead in the crime drama *Animal Factory* (2000), the romances *Pavilion of Women* (2001) and *Before It Had a Name* (2005), the comedy *Go Go Tales* (2007), the horror thriller *Anamorph* (2007), *The Dust of Time* (2008), and *Antichrist* (2009). After *Daybreakers* he played supporting roles and the lead in *A Woman* (2010).

Claudia Karvan appeared in *Nature's Grave*, and after her supporting role in *Daybreakers* worked on television. Michael Dorman appeared in *Acolytes* and went on to the Australian horror films *Triangle* and the lead in *Needle*. Isabel Lukas began her career in television and made her film debut in a supporting role in science fiction action adventure *Transformer: Revenge of the Fallen* (2009). Since *Daybreakers* she has done more supporting roles and more television.

Vince Colosimo made his film debut as the lead in *Moving Out* (1983) and followed this with lead in *Street Hero* (1984) and work in television. In the 2000s the actor played more supporting film roles as well as the lead in *Walking on Water* (2002) and the comedy *Take Away* (2003), and more television. After his supporting role in *Daybreakers*, he continued with more of the same and has not played another leading film role to date.

Sam Neill was also born in New Zealand and made his film debut in a supporting role in that country's *Landfall* (1975) following this with leads in *Ashes* (1975) and the action thriller *Sleeping Dogs* (1977). In the 1980s Neill essayed leads in the horror mystery *The Final Conflict* (1981), the biography *From a Far Country* (1981), and the crime adventure *Robbery Under Arms* (1985), as well playing supporting roles and working in television. In the 1990s the actor had the leading role in the comic crime thriller *Death in Brunswick* (1991) and the action thriller *Hostage* (1992), and was top-billed in the family adventure *Jurassic Park* (1993), the romance *Country Life* (1994), the horror fantasy *In the Mouth of Madness* (1995), and the comedy *The Revengers' Comedies* (1998). In the 2000s Neill was the lead in the comedy *The Dish* (2000), was top-billed in *Jurassic Park III* (2001), the war drama *The Zookeeper* (2001), and played the title character but was not top-billed in the comedy *Dean Spanley* (2008), his last lead to date. After *Daybreakers* the actor continued in supporting film roles and on television, and has also directed seven documentaries.

Release

United States on January 8, 2010, and February 4, 2010, in Australia, with the taglines "In 2019, the most precious natural resource ... is us," "The battle between immortality and humanity is on," and "The battle for blood begins."

Reviews

"[An] impressively styled thriller.... The narrative may flag, but the doomsday atmosphere and George Liddle's production design remain vivid until the final, blood-splattered reel."—Jeanette Catsoulis, *The New York Times*, January 8, 2010

"What's most striking about this sophomore effort by the Spierigs is their visual flair. Even if this won't go down as one of the best horror flicks of the year, it's sure to be one of the best looking of the bunch."—Chris Hartley, *The Video Graveyard*, January 10, 2010

"The premise may not be entirely original, but the treatment is — the combination of very bloody vampire effects and a grisly sense of humor works well and should guarantee the film a cult following.... Though *Daybreakers* has some illogicalities, it's basically a lot of gory fun — for those who like this sort of thing."—David Stratton, *At the Movies*, December 6, 2009

"I think these two guys are so talented. I absolutely hooted when the experiment with substitute blood went wrong in that. It's a judgment of excess and I just think it works really, really well in this. I think it's a good story and it looks great. Performances are terrific and they're clever."—Margaret Pomeranz, *At the Movies*, December 6 2009

"A nifty genre piece from Aussie twins Michael and Peter Spierig who put some oomph into an overworked theme. Despite the star presence of Ethan Hawke and Willem Dafoe, [it] is a B movie, with all the disreputable low rent, lowbrow pleasures that implies, [but] it brims over with fierce retro fun."—Peter Travers, *Rolling Stone*, January 7, 2010

"There are pleasures here: The 'Subsiders,' degenerate, starving, cannibal Nosferatu, are effectively awful; Sam Neill is hambone-wicked as a vulpine CEO. But wearisome 'Ain't it cool?' video-game splatter-violence is all that's memorable of the action, while a (mixed) metaphorical subtext of conservationism can't save a text that squanders its actors." — Nick Pinkerton, *The Village Voice*, January 5 2010

DVD
Lionsgate on May 11, 2010.

Family Demons
Peacock Films/Saylavee Productions, 2009

CREDITS: *Screenplay/Director:* Ursula Dabrowsky; *Producer:* Sue Brown; *Executive Producers:* Stuart Sturgess, Bruce Crompton; *Associate Producer:* Sharoy Pancione; *Photography:* Hugh Freytag; *Editor:* Chop Suzee; *Music:* Michael Taylor; *Art Director:* Colin Moore; *Special FX Makeup:* Vanessa Di Palma; *Sound Design:* J.B. Williams; *Sound:* Eli Flugelman. Color, 79 minutes. Filmed on location in Adelaide, South Australia, in January, 2006.

CAST: Cassandra Kane (Billie); Kerry Reid (Annalis Marcel, aka Mother); Alex Rafalowicz (Sean); Tommy Darwin (Mother's Boyfriend); Chrissie Page (Grandmother Ghost); Nathan O'Keefe (Hoon Kevin); Joe Rafalowicz (Hoon Wayne); Jet Freytag-McElwee (Granddaughter); Anthony "Grizz" Saska (Angry Neighbor); Arthur Stefanopoulos (Gas Station Attendant); Stacey Littler (Mother as a Teenager); Gabriel Partington (Patrick); Damien Woddards (Stalker); Eliza Lovell (Nurse).

Synopsis

Billie lives with her alcoholic mother who keeps her prisoner in their Brompton home, often choosing to buy liquor rather than food. Sean comes looking for someone at the house and finds Billie. He tells her he recognizes her as a former school mate, although Billie refuses to let him into the house. When Billie finds her mother drunk one morning she takes money and goes to buy food. On the way back Billie is chased by two men. She is saved by Sean, who is traveling with them. Billie's mother learns Billie had left the house and chains her in the laundry. In an argument Billie pushes her mother, who hits her head and is taken to the hospital.

Sean returns and frees Billie. They spend the day at the beach. She agrees to go away with Sean. Her drunken mother appears back in the house and slashes Billie's arm with broken glass. Billie kills her with a hammer and buries her in the back yard. Billie has visions of her bloodied mother in the house. Billie learns that her mother has died in the hospital and digs up the grave. She finds Sean's body, since it appears that Billie had actually hammered Sean to death. Nine months later, Billie gives birth after having been raped by her mother's boyfriend. Billie is now an alcoholic and keeps her daughter chained in the laundry.

Notes

This title appears to mix the themes of the horror of personality with the malevolent supernatural being in its cyclic tale of an alcoholic mother and her enchained daughter. Director Ursula Dabrowsky uses the postmodern techniques of jump cuts, superimposed dissolves, point of view, slow motion, blackouts, and hand-held camerawork, with an obtrusive score as well as unnecessary extreme close-ups and echoed voices. Clearly working on a low budget, Dabrowsky's treatment is also compromised by some poor lighting and one disappointing performance. However the narrative takes an interesting turn halfway through to redeem it.

An opening title card reads: "It's been said that sinister things happen in sleepy, conservative towns. The city of Adelaide is no exception. One summer night, a bizarre crime took place in the suburbs. It involved a teenage girl who lived with her alcoholic mother. For years, the events of that night were kept a secret. Now they are part of Adelaide's long, disturbing history of abductions and murders."

A prologue will feature a flash forward and shows shots of the house with care given to sound effects of a clock ticking and a faucet dripping. A bloodied Billie is seen next to the leg of her presumed victim. We see Billie dig a hole, bury the body, clean away the blood from where it had been dragged, and deposit a necklace she had taken from the corpse into a kitchen cupboard jar. Dabrowsky then goes to what we will learn later is Mother as a Teenager receiving the same necklace from a schoolboy. The use of slow motion photography acts to both add sentiment and foreboding to the scene, since in the later return to it we will see how the girl was grabbed and presumably raped in the same location after leaving the boy.

The introduction of Billie with her mother suggests that perhaps Billie is the same girl in the prologue and that she has been abducted. This idea is eventually dismissed. The fact that Sean says he recognizes Billie from school implies that she was not always kept a prisoner in the house. We wonder why this treatment has begun, and this plot point is never explained. The mother being a mean alcoholic is demonstrated in her slapping Billie when she asks her, "Haven't you had enough?" The meanness is also apparent from the mother chaining up her daughter. When Billie is followed by the hooligans, the expectation is created that she will be attacked. This is particularly when she becomes cornered by one of them. Sean as her rescuer is delayed when he is struck in revenge for hitting one of the hooligans. However, the expectation is not met when Sean does manage to get to Billie in time.

The mother has the flashback to getting her necklace, as a replay of the earlier scene, and it is followed by her additional vision of a long-haired female demon who is presumably Grandmother Ghost. We aren't given any backstory for Billie or her mother, but the cyclic pattern of the narrative also suggests that perhaps the Grandmother had incurred the same abuse upon her daughter as the mother does upon Billie. Another reading of the Grandmother is that she wasn't abusive in life but appears now as the mother's alcoholic vision of guilt. When the mother hits her head after being pushed by Billie, the expectation is created that she is dead. This is something the narrative will surround with ambiguity when the mother is seen in hospital.

Sean's return to Billie is convenient to aid her being unchained, but it can be accepted as more than contrivance, given his earlier helping her with the chasing men. The hospital scene suggests that the mother is not dead, because we imagine the nurse who lets her visit would speak to Billie differently if that were the case. The mother's second vision of the Grandmother Ghost would not seem necessary if the mother was dead.

Sean's car breaking down when he is on the way to take Billie away with him is a conventional contrivance to delay his further helping her. However, it allows for the scene where Billie appears to have her arm slashed by her mother with broken glass. The fact that the mother still wears her hospital gown at home perhaps suggests that what we see is not real. This is something we will later assume is the case when Billie sees that she does not have a cut on her arm after all, although the moment is initially presented as real. Billie waiting in the laundry holding a hammer while her mother attempts to break the door down is another conventional horror movie moment, although at least Billie is armed.

Billie's maniacal repeated blows upon her mother suggest an explosion of revenge for the abuse she has endured, with the only blood shown as that spattered on Billie. Dabrowsky repeats the opening shots of the house interior and the bloodied Billie next to her mother's leg. However, the burial scene is given more detail, on top of the previous coverage we have seen. The burial site being disturbed from below and the subjective camera as point of view both suggest the mother has risen from the dead. This is also suggested by a quick shot of what appears to be the mother's hospital gown unseen by Billie as she has a bath.

Dabrowsky uses other conventional shots like a door slowly opening unseen behind Billie as she looks out the window. There is later an empty liquor bottle rolling into the kitchen and a slowly opening cupboard door. Billie's sight of the mother is also delayed while we see her walking behind Billie in the house. The kitchen cupboard jar into which Billie had put her mother's necklace is now paid off with the sight of the jar now missing the necklace. This could be interpreted as the mother taking it back, or as later shown, that Billie never put the necklace in the jar in the first place.

When Billie investigates a noise that sounds like scissors cutting in the bedroom, she is the conventional Woman in Peril. Although she doesn't find her clothes cut, there are scissors on the bed. We again see the vision of the mother behind her before Billie does. The phenomenon of her being locked in the house would seem to be another malevolent and supernatural act. The doorknob moving is another conventional horror scare device and Billie getting a kitchen knife is her armed reaction. The front door being open and then closing before she can get to it is a funny tease. When her name is spoken leading her to the living room, she is again the Woman in Peril.

Billie seeing Mother in the living room is the

final reveal. It is introduced by a gust of wind that blows Billie's hair as she enters. Mother's boyfriend at the door is perhaps the payoff to the earlier doorknob turning. Billie being able to open the door to see him may be an indication that it was never locked and that she was not locked in, since it being locked may be part of her delusion about her mother being alive. Billie running is understandable but her return is not. Her being knocked unconscious by the boyfriend is a shock. Dabrowsky supplies the suggestion of his rape of her by showing him undo his trousers and then going to blackout, with her pregnancy presumably the result.

When Billie returns to consciousness, there is no direct evidence of her rape. Her vision of her mother drinking in the living room is then replaced by a brightly lit vision of a healthier and happier looking mother in her bedroom. She tells her, "You stay with me. You'll always be safe." This secondary vision is clearly fictional, but it is unknown as to what has caused this change in Billie's visions and her view of her mother. She awakens with no cut on her arm, and a flashback to remind us of how we thought the mother had cut Billie's arm. After the telephone rings, we get the visual information that her mother has died in the hospital.

Billie checking the burial site of her mother coincides with Sean finally returning to the house. The repeat of Billie in the laundry with the hammer scene shows that it was Sean who came in the door, and Sean who is buried. This twist may have some timing problems, but it is still a satisfying one. Thunder and rain are shown as the conventional storm of foreboding before we see that Sean's car keys and not the mother's necklace are in the kitchen cupboard jar.

A title card reads "9 months later." Billie's scream of pain is clearly labor, with the knife seen used to cut the umbilical cord and the requisite blood of home childbirth shown. This bloodied Billie naturally recalls the earlier bloodied Billie after we thought she had killed her mother, although this time the birth is real since a child is seen for the narrative epilogue. Billie is now shown as a drinker like her mother. She sits in the same living room chair, and keeps her daughter chained in the laundry. The child holding a doll shows that she is not perhaps as victimized as Billie herself was.

The film marked the debut of Ursula Dabrowsky and is the only one she has made to date. It is also the only Australian horror movie made by Producer Sue Brown and production company Saylavee Productions.

Cassandra Kane began her career in television, made her film debut with *Family Demons* and has not made another title since. Kerry Reid made her film debut in a minor role in the family drama *Opal Dream* (2006) and worked in television. After *Family Demons* she appeared in other supporting film roles. Alex Rafalowicz made his film debut in a supporting role in the musical biography *Shine* (1996), and has been seen on television and in other supporting film roles.

Release

Australia screening on March 25, 2009, at the A Night of International Horror Film Festival. No Australian wide release apparent, and no American wide release or DVD release to date. The tagline is "They never let you go."

Reviews

"Ursula Dabrowksy weaved her magic and went buck naked wild on the mind pieces.... One of the best haunted house yarns to come across my screen in quite some time, with added psychological twists to have us arguing about what was real and what wasn't. I simply loved it." — Jeff Ritchie, *ScaryMinds*

"This film may not be the best horror of the year, but it is a fair effort and definitely a commendable first attempt.... While I found the direction to be for the most part ordinary, there were one or two exceptional moments. The acting carried the film; in fact Reid's portrayal of Billie's hideous mother was nothing short of brilliant." —Deborah Louise Robinson, *Stalk 'n' Slash*

"An Australian indie that combines atmosphere and storyline for one hell of a mindfuck.... The cycle of child abuse has rarely been dealt with in horror so deftly." — Superheidi, *Fangirltastic*, November 7, 2009

"A true horror film with a message about inter-family relationships, yet, the film is also a scary ride through one family's closet, which is full of bloody and ghoulish looking skeletons. Thrilling, tense, and taut, *Family Demons* is an enjoyable tale that capitalizes on the horror, but delivers a commentary on abuse and alcoholism as well."—*28 Days Later Analysis*

DVD

Released in Australia by Peacock Films on June 23, 2010.

The Horseman
Kastle Films, 2009

CREDITS: *Screenplay/Producer/Director/Editor:* Steven Kastrissios; *Producer:* Rebecca Dakin; *Photography:* Mark Broadbent; *Music:* Ryan Potter; *Production Design:* Amanda Broomhall; *Sound:* Andrew Lovrin; *Makeup:* Dallas Ashton; *Special Effects Makeup:* Veronique Keys, Daniel Haig; *Set Dresser:* Emma Hodgson. Color, 98 minutes. Filmed in Brisbane, Queensland, from November 20 to December 16, 2006.

SONGS: "Click" and "Output," Ryan Potter, "Zar Bar Budim," Ryan Potter and Steven Silk.

CAST: Peter Marshall (Christian Forteski); Brad McMurray (Derek); Jack Henry (Finn); Christopher Sommers (Pauly); Evert McQueen (Jim); Steven Tandy (Devlin); Bryan Probets (Walters); Chris Betts (Constable Hilton); Damon Gibson (Chuck); Ron Kelly (Detective Adams); Robyn Moore (Irene); Caroline Marohasy (Alice); Hannah Levien (Jesse); Greg Jones (Warren); Mick Glancy (Bernie); Rhye Copeman (Eddy); Cameron McKay (Beefy); Warren Meacham (Richards).

Synopsis

Forty-four-year-old Christian Forteski is a professional pest controller. His teenage daughter, Jessica, has been found dead from a drug overdose. He receives a videotape in the mail entitled *Young City Sluts 2* in which Jessica stars. Christian sets about to wreak revenge upon those responsible. He tortures and kills the cameraman Walters, the distributor Devlin, the director Finn and his bodyguard Jim and his brother Eddy, who had sex with Jessica in the video. Christian also befriends Alice, an eighteen-year-old hitchhiker who asks for a lift in his car to get to Rockhampton. He picks her up again after learning she is pregnant. They are stopped by Constable Hilton, who takes them to the house of Derek. It appears he is a drug dealer who was also involved in the video. Christian manages to overpower and kill all of Derek's henchmen and Derek. He also rescues Alice, whom Derek had tried to kill.

Notes

This exceedingly brutal and unpleasant title shot on digital video features the theme of the horror of personality in the form of a father killing for revenge over the death of his teenage daughter, who appears to have died of a drug overdose. Director Steven Katrissios employs the postmodern techniques of slow and fast motion, expressionist camera angles, hand-held camerawork, blackouts, and point of view. His treatment indulges in torture porn as the basest form of suspense. While the series of graphic sequences presents how ugly male to male fighting is, the expectation of the protagonist defeating whoever he is challenging is always met. Equally the protagonist acting as a vigilante creates a lead character of moral ambiguity. This makes for a troubling lack of empathy given the torture he applies, which the narrative subplot concerning his aiding another teenage girl does not help to balance. The level of testosteroned hysteria occasionally threatens to make performances comic, although one is more likely to find the scenes of violence unwatchably repellant. The alternate scenes between the protagonist and his traveling companion read as bland and flat in counterpoint.

The narrative begins with footage of Jessica still alive. Her death will be presented to us via a flashback of Christian at the morgue, although we don't see Jessica die. Additionally we don't see her willingness to participate in the video making even if her mental state is affected by her being on drugs. This plot point creates a layer of complicity that Christian denies. The beating of Walters by Christian is presented as a shock effect, and the blood from Walters' broken nose prefigures the excessive bloodletting to come from Christian's future victims. Kastrissios spares us the sight of Walters being burned alive, which is suggested by Christian leaving the smoking house. When Christian visits Devlin at the warehouse the expectation is created of his strike, which is met. Devlin's throat-cutting is also only suggested, as is the attack of Finn's penis and later Jim's penis.

There is irony when Christian turns off the television porn channel in the Motel Inn room that he shares with Alice. His sight of the results of her cutting herself leads to her acknowledgment of the signs of his own behavior. Jim self-cuts with a pen knife given to him by Jessica, he says, to help him feel emotion rather than the numbness he otherwise endures. This character trait may be also designed to create empathy for Jim as a tortured soul, but it fails to do so. Alice is also presumably meant to represent Jessica re-born, and the denouement allows Christian to rescue her in a way that he could not rescue his own daughter.

The appearance of Irene at the scene of Jim's torture is a surprise. It allows for the exposition of how it was she who mailed Christian the video after she read about Jessica's death in the newspaper. Irene is also a surprise as the wife of Jim, who does not attempt to help him. Her double betrayal is contextualized by her disapproval of what was done to Jessica and her perception of Jim's involvement. One expectation that is not met is Irene's fear of Christian attacking her.

This scene also features the fortuitous arrival of Eddy to the house in light of Christian's torture of Jim to find out the brother's whereabouts. There is an amusing irony in Christian's anger at Pauly for leaving the video-making scene since Christian considers that this allowed the others to do what the man would not. Pauly is spared from murder because he begs for his life as a family man and is a payoff to his first being seen by Christian with a woman and child.

Christian giving Alice his cell number after he drops her off is paid off when she soon calls him to get her, although there is no reason for her change of heart that necessitates Christian to avenge her. Her being pregnant serves to make him even more protective and perhaps sets up her narrative moral survival. Christian finally scattering Jessica's ashes in the sea is a payoff to his having the ashes, and in one scene, impulsively throwing them in a trash can to be later retrieved after food scraps have been removed from them.

His having taken Finn's cell phone after Finn had told him that is where to find the names of the others involved in the video is used for Christian to see a text Derek sends to Finn, presumably unaware of Christian having killed Finn. Although he has been told by Pauly that Derek was the one to have left the scene of the shoot with Jessica, Christian decides that he has finished the pursuit. It is odd how Constable Hilton identifying Christian from his car and driver's license should lead him to Derek's house. This suggests more information known by criminals rather than by the police. This is perhaps because Christian had paid for the two hundred and thirty-one copies of the video from Devlin with his credit card.

The idea that Hilton has a criminal agenda for Alice

Poster for *The Horseman* (2009).

when he takes her away from Derek is ambiguous, given that he does not hurt her, although Christian kills him based on the assumption that he intends to. After Christian defeats two of Derek's men it's a relief to see Derek momentarily defeat Christian and have him tied up. His receiving torture from Chuck is satisfying as poetic justice, given the moral ambiguity and lack of empathy established for the protagonist. His previous victories over the other men creates the expectation that he will also overpower Chuck and eventually Derek. Derek stabbing Christian is not a mortal blow, and Chuck receiving a text message is a suspense device to stop him from burning Christian's eye. It also gives Christian time to use the key to the handcuffs he wears that he has conveniently found on the floor.

When Christian sees that Derek has Alice in a shed with another man we cannot tell what, if anything, has been done to her. We will later see she has a head injury, and it appears that the man that we had seen who now exits the shed is carrying videotapes. Christian's approach to him is signaled by the reflection of him in the man's car window that the man does not see. This man appears to be more a meek suburban consumer than a fighter, which prefigures his easy murder. In another suspense device, Derek's attempt to smother the tied up Alice with a pillow is interrupted by him hearing a noise, presumably Christian. Derek's investigation of the noise is him as the Man in Peril. Regrettably, Derek's prior supremacy over Christian is not repeated. Kastrissios adds rain to the climactic fight and Christian's delay in comforting the apparently alive Alice is contextualized by the fact that he has killed all the potential antagonists.

In the DVD director's audio commentary, Kastrissios explains that the character of Christian as an ordinary man was influenced by the crime drama *The Limey* (1999). In that title an ordinary man seeks revenge upon the man he believes to be responsible for the death of his daughter. Neither DVD audio commentaries nor the making-of featurette explains the title of the film, which is the feature debut for Kastrissios. He has not made another Australia horror to date, nor has producer Rebecca Dakin or the production company Kastle Films.

Peter Marshall made his film debut in a minor role in the crime drama *Stormy Monday* (1988) and appeared in more film supporting roles and on television prior to and after *The Horseman*. It is his only leading film role to date. Brad McMurray began his career in television and made his film debut in a supporting role in the action fantasy *Godzilla: Final Wars* (2004). He would continue in television and film supporting roles prior to and after *The Horseman*. Jack Henry also began his career in television, then made his film debut in a minor role in the thriller *Naked Betrayal* (2002). He was seen in film shorts prior to *The Horseman* and later appeared in more shorts and film supporting roles.

Christopher Sommers also began his career making film shorts and made his movie debut in a supporting role in the romance *Unfinished Sky* (2007). He was in more shorts, on television and more film supporting roles prior to and after *The Horseman*. Evert McQueen made his film debut in a minor role in the family comedy *Inspector Gadget 2* (2003). Before and after *The Horseman*, he worked in film shorts, television and more film supporting roles. Steven Tandy started in television and made his movie debut in a minor role in the comedy *Coming of Age* (1986). He continued in television and film supporting roles prior to and after *The Horseman*.

Bryan Probets made his film debut in a minor role in the family adventure *Hildegarde* (2001). He continued in television and film supporting roles before and after *The Horseman*, including the Australian horror movies *Triangle* and *Daybreakers*. Chris Betts made his film debut in a supporting role in the crime drama *Bootleg* (1985) and appeared in television and film supporting roles prior to and after *The Horseman*, including *Contagion*.

Damon Gibson made his film debut in a supporting role in the thriller *Marine* (2006). *The Horseman* is his last title to date. Robyn Moore began her career in film shorts and made her feature debut in a minor role in *Undead*. She would continue in television and go on to appear in a supporting role in *Daybreakers*. Caroline Marohasy made her film debut in *The Horseman*, her only film to date.

Release

Screened in Australia on August 3, 2008, at the Melbourne International Film Festival, in the United States in April 2009 at the Newport Beach International Film Festival, and in November 2009 at the American Film Market. No apparent wide release in the United States, going straight to DVD, but an apparent wide release in Australia on July 8, 2010. The taglines include "He has some questions," "An act unforgiven. A father lost in grief" and "He can't bring his daughter back, but he can send her killers to hell." The Australian DVD has deleted scenes that include Christian's ex-wife

Helen with him in Jessica's bedroom after the funeral, Christian having a conversation with Jessica when she comes home at 7 o'clock one morning where he expresses his disapproval of her lifestyle, and Christian and Finn first outside the gym and then in the office to show how Christian gets access and how Finn asks to see Christian's penis after offering him a part in his next porno film.

REVIEWS

"The scenes of violence, though they're gruesome, are well staged. There is a reluctant sense of being mesmerized by what approaches torture-porn, but ultimately that sense of not being able to stand another violent scene is overwhelming.... Certainly a calling card for Kastrissios' skills as a filmmaker."—Margaret Pomeranz, *At the Movies*, July 7, 2010

"I found the film incredibly nasty and repetitive. It's got a plot that is minuscule and it's mostly a series of encounters which always end in some kind of violence. I think that at least the two leading actors are fine, [but] it is just so dispiritingly sadistic [that it's] horrible."—David Stratton, *At the Movies*, July 7, 2010

"A riveting revenge thriller.... It's a high impact, well crafted film that pushes the boundaries in every direction. Notable for its intensity, the screenplay stays simple—and brutal. The fight scenes are among the most realistic and harrowing fight scenes I've seen.... All the performances are outstanding."—Andrew L. Urban, *Urban Cinefile*

"Raw, bleak and confronting, *The Horseman* presents a tale of vengeance far removed from the typical by refusing to merely play out the payback for cheap thrills. Rather, it explores the circumstances' emotional and visceral horror. It's a refreshing approach and an impressive film."—James Gillett, *Digital Retribution*, May 18, 2010

"An excellent piece of filmmaking that is unapologetic in its approach to the source material. Kastrissos has delivered a classic of modern Australian filmmaking and an exuberance that will stick with the audience. This is a multi layered cinematic masterpiece.... Go saddle up for *The Horseman*, the ride is irresistible."—Jeff Ritchie, *ScaryMinds*

"A gripping revenge film with an incredible kinetic energy. The fight scenes are brutal, raw and don't look choreographed. Most of the more extreme acts of violence occur off-screen, making their impact far more disturbing.... Peter Marshall [has] an astonishing nervous energy ... an excellent début film by writer/director Steven Kastrissios."—Thomas Caldwell, *Cinema Autopsy*

DVD

Released in the United States by Screen Media on June 15, 2010, and in Australia by Umbrella Entertainment on December 6, 2010.

The Loved Ones
Omnilab Media/Ambience Entertainment, 2009
[aka *The Loved Ones—Pretty in Blood*]

CREDITS: *Screenplay/Director:* Sean Byrne; *Producers:* Mark Lazarus, Michael Boughen; *Executive Producers:* Christopher Mapp, Matthew Street, David Whealy, Bryce Menzies; *Photography:* Simon Chapman; *Production Design:* Robert Webb; *Editor:* Andy Canny; *Music:* Ollie Olsen; *Costumes:* Xanthe Heubel; *Sound:* John McKerrow; *Art Director:* Robert Webb; *Set Dressers:* Victoria McKenzie, Harvey Mawson; *Makeup/Hair:* Zeljka Seanin. Color, 81 minutes. Filmed in Melbourne, Victoria.

SONGS: "Superstar" (Sophie Koh, T. Reid), Sophie Koh; "Dirty Thoughts" (C. Whitty, T. Kommedal), C.C. Martini; "Idols and Anchors" (I. Kilpatrick, W. McCall, B. Gordon, J. Ling), Parkway Drive; "Hell Hole" (Blachford, Buscomi, Barry), Witch Hats; "Lonesome Loser" (D. Briggs), Little River Band; "Lay Me Down" (Abbe May), Abbe May; "God's Dead (Meet the Kids)" (British India), British India; "Typhon" (Ollie Olsen), Ollie Olsen; "Menoetius" (Ollie Olsen), Ollie Olsen; "Simulated 01" (Ollie Olsen), Ollie Olsen; "Simulated 02" (Ollie Olsen), Ollie Olsen; "Simulated 03" (Ollie Olsen), Ollie Olsen; "Simulated 04" (Ollie Olsen), Ollie Olsen; "Simulated 07" (Ollie Olsen), Ollie Olsen; "The Long Drive Home" (Sarah-Jane Wentzki), Princess One Point Five; "The Sharpest Claws" (M. Collins), The Dirtbombs; "Princess Crowning" (Geoffrey Russell), Geoffrey Russell; "Solid Gold" (Black Diamond Heavy), Black Diamond Heavy; "Agile, Mobile and Hostile" (M. Collins, D. Kroma, Andre Williams), Andre Williams; "Not Pretty Enough" (Kasey Chambers), Kasey Chambers; "She's Not the Only One" (Dinh, Hartney, Byrne, Beltrame, Honda), Little Red; "Snuff is

My Business" (Black Lake Vengeance), Black Lake Vengeance; "Let's Roll" (Mammoth Mammoth), Mammoth Mammoth; "Fool" (Dinh, Hartney, Byrne, Beltrame, Honda), Little Red; "Gimme the Awesome" (Endles Boogie), Endless Boogie; "Lost Cause" (W. Walsh, R, Knight), Cosmic Psychos; "Oh So Lonesome For You" (Pete Molinari), Peter Molinari; "Not Pretty Enough" (Kasey Chambers), Robin McLean; "Mirrorball of Death" (The Loved One Remix) (Ollie Olsen), Shaolin Wounded Men; "Homecoming" (Robert McKenzie), Robert McKenzie.

CAST: Xavier Samuel (Brent); Robin McLeavy (Lola Stone, aka Princess); Victoria Thaine (Holly); Jessica McNamee (Mia Valentine); Richard Wilson (Jamie, aka Sac); John Brumpton (Daddy); Andrew S. Gilbert (Paul Valentine); Suzi Dougherty (Carla); Victoria Eagger (Judith Valentine); Anne Scott-Pendlebury (Bright Eyes); Fred Whitlock (Dan); Leo Taylor (Teacher); Brandon Burns (Take Away Shop Attendant); Stephen Walden (Timmy Valentine); Igor Savin (Rhys Agnew); Eden Porter (Keir Willis); Tom Mahoney (Duncan Fletcher); Gully McGrath (Keir Willis 8-year-old); Stevie-Lou Answerth (Princess 8-year-old); Liam Duxbury (Duncan Fletcher 11-year-old); Jessa (Dog).

Synopsis

Teenager Brent is driving the car with his father, Dan, as a passenger when he swerves to avoid hitting a bloodied boy on the road. The car crashes into a tree and Dan is killed. Six months later Brent is haunted by guilt and self-mutilates with a razor blade. Schoolgirl Lola Stone asks him to go to the prom but he declines since his date is his girlfriend, Holly. Lola and her father kidnap Brent and keep him prisoner as her latest fallen Romeo. Brent's best friend, Jamie, takes Mia Valentine to the prom. The Stones torture Brent, drilling a hole in his forehead in an attempt to turn him into a lobotomized zombie. Brent fights back and pushes Daddy into a basement pit where Lola's other fallen Romeos are kept and who devour him.

Lola pushes Brent into the pit. She also overpowers Police Officer Dan Valentine, who has come to rescue Brent. Dan is the father of Timmy, who was the boy that Brent's car had avoided running down. After killing her lobotomized mother, Bright Eyes, Lola tells Brent how she intends to kill his mother and Holly. Brent climbs out of the pit and pursues her in Dan's police car. He finds Holly, who is being chased by Lola. Brent runs Lola down.

Notes

This story features the theme of the horror of personality in the form of a psychotic girl and her father who victimize boys she fantasizes as potential boyfriends and describes as "fallen Romeos." Director Sean Byrne employs the postmodern techniques of expressionist camera angles, slow and fast motion, jump cuts, fractured editing and point of view. His treatment presents sadism and cruelty as torture porn. The narrative concludes with a happy ending, although the protagonist incurs major physical damage, but it also includes a subplot that doesn't receive any significant payoff. There is plenty of bloodletting and gore, with razor blade cutting, the use of a hammer and electric drill, a fork for skin carving and a car running over a person.

A prologue presents the car accident that resulted in the death of Brent's father. Brent is driving and hits a tree after swerving to avoid hitting the bloodied boy, Timmy Valentine, who had escaped from the Stone house. Presumably Timmy has died, and the scenario gets a climactic repeat in Brent driving and swerving to avoid Holly on the road. The bloodied Lola on the road is paralleled with Timmy, although she is more antagonist than victim and gets deliberately hit by Brent's car as payback. A title card reads: "Six months later." Brent's changed appearance hints at his trauma, and his guilt is expressed via the razor blade he wears around his neck to cut himself. The narrative will provide a perverse play off on Brent's cutting by the cutting he will receive from Lola.

Byrne presents Lola as more pathetic than vulnerable and this lack of empathy for her will make her seem more psychotic than understandable. This is a disappointment since she then is a monster without dimension, although her asking Brent to the school dance shows she has some courage. Byrne shows a little of Holly's breast in the sex scene in her car with Brent, though not enough to consider this exploitative. The cuts we see on Brent's body are ambiguous since they may either be from the car accident or from Brent's self-cutting. Lola is revealed watching the couple have sex after Brent moves his hand from the window that he has held there in the act, with the fact of Lola watching an early sign of her desperation for Brent. The scene where Brent climbs the rock face as a potential means of suicide is said by Byrne in the DVD director's audio commentary to prefigure his ease in climbing the tree on the Stone estate and scale the human steps he makes to get himself out of the pit.

The long sequence of Lola and Daddy torturing Brent is nearly unwatchable, despite the progression of activities that occur, and Byrne wisely inter-cuts to the date between Mia and Jamie. This date has no real plot payoff and perhaps can be read as comic relief in light of Jamie being clownish and hardly the type one would expect Mia to go for. However, Mia as a Goth creates the false expectation that perhaps she has a relationship with Lola. Mia's depression may be due to the loss of her brother, but it may equally be the result of her being a teenager who does not conform to the conventional school population, since there are no other Goths seen to be friends with her. She can also be interpreted as another alternative to Holly and Lola. Mia is not as psychotic as Lola, who does not present at school as looking radical, and is not as popular as Holly is, the good girl who is slightly bad in having sex with Brent.

The interior of the Stone dining room has a mirror ball and balloons as an imitation of the school dance décor. Bright Eyes is presumably the Stone mother who appears to be lobotomized, and she prefigures the fate of Brent. Byrne adds suspense for the moments where Lola gives Brent ten seconds to urinate into a glass before Daddy nails his penis to the chair, and her making him suck her finger is a perverse twist on the gender opposite often used to suggest fellatio. Brent's getting out of his hand restraints creates the expectation of his escape, which is met but later foiled when he is caught in the tree outside the house. The expectation of his not being able to escape again is created after his feet are nailed to the floor. However this expectation too will be foiled when he does free himself, with his sitting back down after the standing form of slow dance he has with Lola stopping the kiss that she and Daddy attempt to have. The suggestion of incest between father and daughter is also apparent from Daddy's point of view of her bottom when she changes into the pink party dress he has gotten her, and from her telling him before the kiss how he is the prince she has been waiting for.

The possum road kill that Daddy and Lola pick up on the way back to their house after kidnapping Brent will help to introduce the cement pit underneath the room's floor, where possum screams suggest the lobotomized three fallen Romeos held captive there. Their animalistic noises are presumably due to the same treatment we see Brent receive when he is injected in the neck with blue Drano to rob him of his speaking voice. The resultant noise also adds a primal reaction to the further torture of having his feet nailed to the floor by knives, his chest carved with a fork and salt thrown on the wound, and having his forehead drilled. Byrne supplies what he calls in the audio commentary a switcheroo when we see Daddy approach a car, then Mia and Jamie having sex in a car. The switcheroo is that the person who knocks on the car window is the teacher who had thrown them out of the dance hall and not Daddy as expected, although it would seem inconceivable that Jamie would have parked on the Stone estate.

Brent using his razor blade also creates the expectation that he will be able to avoid the electric lobotomy. Byrne toys with this expectation as the drill stops just as Lola is about to touch Brent's forehead. However, she does drill into him on the second attempt. It seems that them not being able to successfully finish their process by pouring hot water into the hole is what spares Brent from becoming as disabled as the other victims. Before Brent is able to fight off the final stage of the lobotomy, his idea that he is defeated is represented by Byrne with shots of his father, his mother, and Holly as farewell edits.

When Brent finally uses the razor to cut Daddy's face the expectation is again created for his escape. The repeated slashing of Daddy is Brent's emotional catharsis for the torture. His pushing Daddy into the pit to become a road kill meal for the three loved ones is a deserved payoff for Daddy. Lola returning after Brent has punched her in the face is a shock effect and foils of the expectation of Brent's escape. Byrne uses the black screen for the closed trap doors of the pit as Brent's point of view.

There is an initial ambiguity about the three fallen Romeos attacking Brent, since the darkness creates the suggestion that they have defeated him. This is another expectation not met; they are not seen again, suggesting it is they who have been defeated. Lola smothering Bright Eyes with a pillow would seem to be the payoff to her implied jealousy of her mother. Dan not calling for police backup when he gets to the Stone house may be considered foolish and predetermining his demise, but perhaps in a small country town, there is no backup to be called. The expectation is again created, when Brent hears the car drive up, for his escape and that Dan would rescue him. Brent does use the police car to eventually escape. Brent climbs out of the pit when he makes a stairway out of the corpses of Dan and the other fallen Romeos. It is convenient that Lola is not there to stop him, since she has told him of her intention to leave to kill his mother and Holly.

The climactic battle on the road includes the expectation of Lola killing Holly. It is not met when Holly fights her off. While Brent's car running into Lola is presented as fortuitous accident, the impact does not kill her. Byrne uses a zoom to end on an extreme close-up of Lola's eyes to suggest Brent's oncoming car and a shock effect for the impact of her head being struck by the car.

In the director's audio commentary on the DVD, Byrne advises that the film was influenced by *The War Zone* (1999) and the crime action thriller series *Kill Bill*. Lola is said to have a five-year-old girl's interest in princesses and fairy wings combined with the body and mind of a teenager with raging hormones. The director also says that the form of lobotomy presented in the treatment was copied from the actions of the serial killer Jeffrey Dahmer, who used the same drilling into the frontal lobe and boiling water technique. Byrne also comments about the torture porn element of the treatment, in opposition to the attitude that torture is the basest form of suspense. He claims that he deliberately chose to prolong the moments of torture to make them supposedly more dramatically intense, and to give them what he misguidedly sees as an additional comic touch.

The film was the feature debut of Byrne, who has not made another Australian horror title to date. It is the only Australian horror movie to be invested in by OmniLab Media, which distributed *Dying Breed*, also made by the production company Ambience Entertainment and the producer Michael Boughen and executive producers Christopher Mapp, Matthew Street and David Whealy. The film was the only Australian horror title to be made by producer Mark Lazarus and executive producer Bryce Menzies.

Xavier Samuel started his career in television and made his film debut in a supporting role in *2:37* (2006). He continued in film supporting roles and on television, and after *The Loved Ones* had the lead in the Australian horror title *Road Train* and other supporting film roles.

Robin McLeavy also began her career in television and made her film debut in a supporting role in the comedy *48 Shades* (2006). After *The Loved Ones* she continued in television roles. Victoria Thaine made her film debut in a supporting role in the biographical comedy *The Night We Called It a Day* (2003). Besides working in television and other supporting film roles, she essayed the leads in *Floodhouse* (2004) and *Caterpillar Wish* (2006). After *The Loved Ones* the actress worked in television.

Jessica McNamee started her career in television and made her debut in the film, working only in television afterward. Richard Wilson was born in England and began in television, making his film debut in a supporting role in *Deck Dogz* (2005). He continued in television and film supporting roles prior to and after *The Loved Ones*, though he essayed the lead in the comedy *48 Shades*.

John Brumpton previously appeared in *Storm Warning* and *Nature's Grave* and appeared in television and other film supporting roles prior to and after *The Loved Ones*. Andrew S. Gilbert made his film debut in a supporting role in *Mortgage* (1989), and has appeared in other film supporting roles and on television before and after *The Loved Ones*. Suzi Dougherty is another actor to have begun her career in television and made her film debut in a supporting role in *Body Melt*. She has appeared in more television and other film supporting roles prior to and after *The Loved Ones*, including a minor one in *Queen of the Damned*.

Release

Screened in the United States on October 31, 2009, at the AFI Film Festival, in November 2009 at the American Film Market, and on May 2, 2010, at the San Francisco International Film Festival. While there has been no wide release for the film in the United States to date, the film received one in Australia on November 4, 2010. The taglines include "You don't have to die to go to hell," "Don't break her heart," and "Prom night can be torture."

Reviews

"Slipping into the torture porn genre with ease, [it] has been stripped down to its bare essentials, with no plot elements to stumble on.... It's pointless complaining about some of the sillier moments because it's their silliness that adds the fun to this genre. But beware; the silliness gives way to scenes that may send you to counseling."—Andrew L. Urban, *Urban Cinefile*

"Seemingly inspired by Brian de Palma's *Carrie*, this horror comedy is given no holds barred treatment. The morbid jokes and the shocking moments of horror, all played straight by an excellent cast, plus some moments of grisly originality, combine in a film that's better than the average for this sort of admittedly dodgy exploitation piece."— David Stratton, *At the Movies*, November 3, 2010

"This was an ordeal [and] I wonder what sort of twisted mind can create this scenario, but I think there's a lot of talent in the film. It's not [one] that you actually can enjoy, but I imagine a genre audience is going to laugh their way through this and really enjoy it." — Margaret Pomeranz, *At the Movies*, November 3, 2010

"It works on every level: the comedy, the performances, the effects, and the visceral terror that Byrne evokes with ease." — Julian, *Digital Retribution*, April 2, 2011

"It does have a degree of similarity to torture porn films but it isn't as depressingly bleak or cruel. Exploitive, gut-churning and nasty, but it delivers the shocks and scares in a way that is inventive enough to make the experience of seeing the film a lot of fun rather than an ordeal." — Thomas Caldwell, *Cinema Autopsy*

"A rollercoaster screwball horror fest that will leave you breathless and quote possibly disturbed. Just be careful the next time somebody asks you out — saying 'no' could be murder.... [It] takes a claw hammer to your frontal lobe and beats you until you're dazed, confused and totally thrilled!" — Matt Adcock, *Darkmatters*, September 27 2010

DVD

Released in Australia by Madman Entertainment on March 16, 2011.

Prey
Top Cat Films/Bad Cat Films, 2009
[aka *The Outback*; *Dreamtime's Over*]

CREDITS: *Director:* Oscar D'Roccster; *Producers:* Robert Lewis Galinksy, Elizabeth Howatt-Jackman; *Executive Producers:* George Adams, Mark Pennell; *Co-Executive Producers:* Chris Unuduwara, Michael Canty; *Associate Producer:* Lyndi Adler, David Allan-Jones, Yod Sukwiwst, Brett Davies, Rod Birch; *Screenplay:* John V. Soto; *Photography:* Andy Topp; *Editor:* Geoff Hitchens; *Music:* Dave Cornelius; *Costumes:* Paul Warren; *Sound Design:* Tristan Meredith; *Production Design/Art Directors:* Lance Whitehouse, Harvey Mawson; *Special Effects Makeup:* SharpFX; *Sound:* Paul (Clackers) Clark; *Hair/Makeup:* Zolka Stanin. Color, 76 minutes. Filmed at the Campbellfield Studios in Melbourne, Victoria, in Perth, Western Australia; and Alice Springs, Northern Territory.

SONGS: "Don't Wanna Do This," "Particles," "What You're On," "Judging the Fall," "Black Lotus," "60 Days of Night," "I See in You," "Where the City Meets the Sea," "Destroy Everything You Touch."

CAST: Jesse Johnson (Gus Lawton); Natalie Bassingthwaighte (Kate); Christian Clark (Jason Albert Sneaver); Natalie Walker (Ling); Ben Kermode (Matt); Kristin Sargent (Annika); Nicholas Bell (Bill, The Rifleman); Dawn Klingberg (Kora); Pamela Shaw (Morgan Weissmann); Jennifer Hanson (Waitress); Joe Hasham (Motel Clerk); Gigi Kami (Cupping Patient); Naomi Kimany (Little Girl Kate); Bruce Hughes (Judge); Robert Lewis Galinksy (Barrister); Elizabeth Howatt-Jackman (Instructing Solicitor); Suharb Ladho (Gus' Mentor); Felix Branden Marshall Galinksy (Oscar); Oscar Tamsim Sherazada Galinsky (Felix); Rocco Howatt-Jackman (Rocco); Louie Howatt-Jackman (Louie); Leon Stripp (Sean); Brett Sheerin (Paul).

SYNOPSIS

A group of friends decide to drive into the outback on the way to a surfing trip. They are led astray by a map given to Kate along the way by Bill, a mysterious stranger. Unknown to the group, Bill has deliberately mislead them in his plan of revenge upon Kate. Her brother had twenty years previously run down his mother, Kora, in a road accident. Bill had killed Kate's brother and his male traveling companion, but she had escaped. Bill again summons the Aboriginal power of Kadaicha and uses snakes to get Kate. She is a doctor and learns that she is also pregnant, which surprises her boyfriend, Gus, who has also come for the trip. Gus has a vision of Kora on the road and stops his car, finding a snake that his friend Jason kills. Further along the way, Jason's car gets stuck in dirt and when he tries to dig it out a snake appears. The car falls on him, and he is thought to be dead. The group tries to drive away but only drive around in a circle. They decide to stay where they are for the night.

Matt is attacked by Jason, who now appears as a zombie and throws him into a pit of snakes. Kate attempts to help him. Having an allergic reaction to the snake bites, Matt's head explodes and he dies. Gus is also attacked and is killed. Annika dies when the crystal she carries is lodged in her chest after a snake causes one of the cars to hit her. Matt takes Ling and Kate to a pit of snakes. Bill appears and paints Aboriginal images on Kate's torso. She manages to free herself. Advised by a vision of Kora that

Bill must be killed to end the curse, Kate kills Bill by beating him to death with his own rifle. Kate frees Ling, who had been buried up to her neck. Together they drive away and find the highway back to civilization.

NOTES

This title combines the themes of the horror of personality with the malevolent supernatural being in its tale of a man who uses Aboriginal powers to seek revenge upon specific American tourists in the outback. Director Oscar D'Roccster uses the postmodern techniques of point of view, expressionist camera angles, jump cuts, freeze frames, zooms, blackouts, CGI, rear projection, and grainy black and white footage with light flashes and quick cuts for flashbacks. The narrative's use of Aboriginal powers as malevolent recalls the Aboriginal concerns of *The Last Wave, Dark Age, The Dreaming*, and *Kadaicha*. The female protagonist who becomes a warrior recalls *Lady, Stay Dead, Fair Game, Contagion, Out of the Body, The 13th Floor, Komodo, Ghost Ship, Undead, See No Evil, Black Water, Storm Warning, Slaughtered, Triangle, The Clinic* and *Road Train*. The narrative uses the same Aboriginal legend of Kadaicha here as a dreamtime creature who takes the form of a snake.

The narrative also includes zombies as the victims reborn and snakes as the tools of the main antagonist. D'Roccster supplies plenty of bloodletting, shocks and gore. There are snake bites, an exploding head, a forcibly inserted crystal, the use of a chainsaw, someone buried up to their head in the ground, needles thrust into eyes, and beatings to death. The treatment of this simple narrative is minimalist and occasionally cheesy, but there are redemptive beautiful shots of scenery and a use of genre conventions that don't always meet expectations. The protagonists are American, another example of producers thinking that American accents will make the film more appealing to an international market, although here the narrative provides no context for the characters to be American other than presenting them in a fish-out-of-water story.

Storm clouds under the opening credits suggest trouble, although only a brief dust storm will appear in the treatment. The DVD audio commentary tells us that there are also images of snakes and that the titles have cinders to prefigure the fire effect presented when Jason and Matt become zombies. The prologue shows Kate's brother being killed by Bill's rifle, in the same manner that Kate will later kill Bill. It also shows the brother as a seeming willing victim to Bill's strike as he stands in front of a full moon. This idea of the brother being under some sort of control is also suggested by him dragging the body of his unnamed companion — who we only later learn is dead from being shot by Bill — so that he will also fall into the snake pit. It is also suggested that the companion becomes a zombie when he reappears from the ground after having been shot by Bill and before the brother is struck by Bill.

A title card reads "20 Years Later." D'Roccster uses freeze frames to identify each of the people except Matt, who arrives later and who will be in the traveling group, and split screen and jump cuts for the presentation. Matt's entrance as a gay man is noticed by the women. The repeated implication of Ling's bisexuality — since we see her having sex with Jason but later touching and kissing Kate — is an added touch of homosexual interest. When the group poses for a photograph, we see in the resultant shot that their eyes are all red. This is something that they do not comment on but which prefigures the zombies to come.

In the car that Gus drives, Kate has a nightmare vision of Gus as a zombie. This prefigures her fate, although he claims not to hear her awakening scream. His vision of Kora is not validated; he stops the car to look for her but doesn't find her. Rather it seems that Kora's spirit cannot rest because she disapproves of Bill's plan for vengeance. This is something she vocalizes in the climax when she encourages Kate to kill him.

Kora's appearance and the snake under the car that Gus sees are both shock effects. An exchange between Jason and Matt provides a mild joke. Jason scolds Gus for his sudden stop after seeing the vision of Kora. Since Jason was following in his car, he tells him, "I almost rear ended you." Matt's response, "You should be so lucky," is a not too subtle reference to anal sex. It is also a follow up to his sexual interest in Gus, when he was introduced to him earlier. Matt with Annika will also provide another moment of humor when they mimic the "Yes" of Ling that they hear in the next room of the motel when she has sex with Jason. The fact that Ling is on top of Jason for the sex rather than in the submissive position underneath him, and him being tied to the bed, are perhaps also signs of her sexual freedom.

Kate dreaming of herself running in a black and white flashback is not a presentation of herself in a memory, although she will do this later. The idea that she is pregnant gets paid off in the climax since Kora knows it and uses it as part of the reason to kill Bill. It also adds a physical vulnerability to Kate, who will be presented as the strongest of the three women both as a doctor and as a warrior. The appearance of Bill to Kate at the car while Gus is away has the suggestion of a dream since he disappears so quickly, although he does supply the map and the bead necklace she buys as real things. Bill paints his face and body as an Aboriginal warrior, but oddly the narrative removes him until the climax. Perhaps it is enough that he summons the spirit and sends the snakes to attack the group members, but the expectation of his strike is not immediately met.

Like the full moon that appeared the night Kate's brother was killed, the full moon in the present is equally foreboding. We don't know if the snake that approaches Jason under the car kills him, or the car falling on him. When his car is moved to gain access to the body, Gus unintentionally drives over Jason's hat. His body being rolled over reveals a shock effect of his bloodied face. When Matt hears what appears to the sound of an animal in distress, his investigating presents him as the Man in Peril, the equivalent of the conventional female in peril.

Jason is shown to be reborn as a zombie with his wounds lit by fire; however, the expectation of a strike is not met. D'Roccster delays showing what Jason does to Matt. Instead we see Kate's dream of herself running as a little girl, although the girl is not yet identified as herself. Kate hearing and investigating the noise of Matt's screaming has her as the Woman in Peril, although she will not get to Matt before he is thrown into the snake pit by Jason.

The expectation of Matt being killed by the snakes is also not immediately met when he is brought back, though we aren't shown how. The display of his disfigured face begins the treatment's most gruesome special effect. His allergic reaction to the bites and to the adrenaline Kate gives him results in his face pulsating, bloating and eventually exploding. The resultant blood is shown to land on the faces of the attending group.

The banging of the back door of the car where the bodies of Jason and Matt are left now presents Gus as the Man in Peril when he leaves the girls to stop it. However, his fate is another narrative point that is delayed. The idea of the three girls in the car is a conventional horror representation of vulnerability. It allows Kate to speak of the loss of her brother to pay off the prologue and to link Kate to the man killed by Bill. D'Roccster even repeats some shots of the prologue, and now Kate also makes the connection between the little girl she has dreamt of and herself.

Kate is again the Woman in Peril when she goes looking for Gus. A leg sticking out of the ground is revealed to be a buried doll, with the black and white memory sequence shows the doll to belongs to Kate. When all three women look for Gus separately, they are all Women in Peril. Annika finding a shoe that will be identified as belonging to him creates the expectation of her being attacked, which her heard scream also suggests. This expectation is not met, although it is revealed that the shoe has led Annika to find Gus dead. We don't ever learn what killed Gus, although the injury shown later to the back of his head may either be a result of the snake bite or attack by Jason or Matt. D'Roccster repeats an aerial view of the three girls around Gus' corpse.

When the girls try to take Gus' body back to the car that holds the corpses of Jason and Matt, it stands by itself, as if he has been empowered as a zombie. The girls try to flee by driving away but the car quickly becomes stuck in the dirt again. An attempt to use another car is stopped by Annika's desire to go back for her crystal. The expectation of her being the next victim is created. While the fact of snakes helping the stuck car to be dislodged is perhaps a contrivance, it is a surprise that it is the car that strikes her. D'Roccster goes all out with bloodletting with the crystal in Annika's chest. The expectation that Kate will be able to remove it to save her is not met when the crystal breaks, leaving some inside her. Unlike the boys, however, Annika will not be seen to rise again as a zombie.

The narrative furthers the presentation of the remaining girls as Woman in Peril, with the observation that Matt is missing from the back of the car. This may suggest that perhaps he was responsible for the attack upon Gus. The arm of Jason, who is in the back of the car grabbing Kate, is another shock effect. Ling cutting off the arm with a conveniently found chainsaw is perhaps too much, although it presents her as a warrior. There is a laugh from how Ling has to break the hand's fingers to release them from the grip of Kate's neck, with Kate decapitating Jason in his second advance. The girls going to get car keys from Gus creates the expectation of his attacking, but this is not met. Ling cutting off his legs with the chainsaw as a precautionary move pays off when he awakens and Ling also cuts his throat, although no blood appears.

Kate taking a clothed shower at this point seems another plot contrivance; we expect her to leave the location. The shower seems to exist solely for Ling to watch her, so it's rather funny that it should be the zombie Matt who is revealed to be behind her in the car as a shock moment. What happens to Ling is left untold. The same device is used for Kate after the shock of her being attacked by Matt behind her in the car as well. Her being strangled and the blackout create the expectation that both girls have been killed. However, this expectation is not met, after more black and white flashback, as presumably the unconscious memory of Kate, shows her the little girl in a car with her brother and his companion.

A scream that is eventually revealed to be that of Ling returns us to the present, as we see the awakened Kate tied to the ground and Ling buried up to her head and surrounded by stones that are circled by snakes. This entrapment and torture recalls the same in *Wolf Creek*, with a parallel made between the travelers used as prey by a mad resident. What is interesting here is how the zombie Matt with the fired head is used to entrap the girls and then falls dead. Ling's predicament is classic Gothic horror, with the expectation created that she will be attacked, which ironically never happens.

Bill's return to the narrative allows for more exposition. His rationale is that Kate is "guilty." More black and white memory shows that Kora was accidentally run over by the car containing her brother and that she is his mother. We see how Bill shot the companion. Although the prologue showed how the brother got to the snake pit, we are never told how the little girl Kate got back to civilization, although she has seemed to overcome her trauma spectacularly well by having become a doctor.

Bill painting the Aboriginal artwork on her torso may be part of his ritual for killing, although she is the only one seen to be painted in this way. Or perhaps this is simply a plot device to distract Bill from seeing Kate freeing herself? Bill painting Kate's torso is also significant since we know her to be pregnant. The expectation of him murdering her is created, as is one of Ling being done in by the snakes, but the expectation of Kate's escape from him is also created when we see her get the first hand free. With the fact of Bill being focused on making more paint and not looking at Kate comes the further contrivance of her having syringes in her pocket. The expectation of her strike is met when she plunges them into his eyes for more Gothic excess.

The spirit of Kora gives a rather remarkable speech to Kate whereby she recommends the murder of her son: "End it. End it now. Only you can stop this. He killed your brother and vengeance has awakened Kadaicha's dark side. He will bring hell to the earth. It is the only way to put things back and protect your child. He will be his presence here on earth if you don't end it now."

This speech indicates that Kora is spirit enough to be aware of Kate's pregnancy; however, the film's epilogue suggests that perhaps Kora is not being totally truthful since the narrative concludes with the suggestion that Kate carries a snake inside her.

Kate's repeated striking of Bill, rather than shooting him with the rifle, is an emotional and physical catharsis for her anger over the murder of her brother and her friends. We don't see Kate freeing Ling from her trap but as dawn breaks the girls escape by finding the connection of the dirt road to the highway and their freedom. Ling kissing Kate on the mouth may be more than just friendly gratitude. Their comment "We survived" is juxtaposed with the shot of Kate's painted torso; the image suggests her womb and the snake inside it. This image also opens the way for a film sequel, not been made to date.

The DVD commentary says the cars halted in the same spot where Kora was killed, an Aboriginal burial site, and that Kate was age six when the original event occurred. The two men traveling with her were both her brothers, although this is never made apparent in the narrative. Kadaicha is a dreamtime creature of protection whose powers are misused by Bill, which explains Kora's rejection of him and willingness for him to be killed by Kate. The necklace that Bill gives Kate is said lead to Kadaicha to her, that the blood wounds on Jason and Gus are from the snake, and that the power of Kadaicha is what supposedly overrides the car's compasses and GPS. To further exploit the lesbian subtext, it is also remarked that the scene of Kate having a clothed shower was edited to remove the participation of Ling in the shower, although these cut scenes do not appear on the DVD.

The commentary and the making-of featurette, *Sacred Sites*, both advise that D'Roccster was a replacement director and the original was fired in post production. Although the name of the original director is not given, it is believed to have been Scottish born George Miller. *Sacred Sites* states that the narrative was inspired by the real life story of two American backpackers who disappeared in the Western Australian outback in 1987 and whose car was found in an Aboriginal sacred site. Apparently Natalie Bassingthwaighte was originally cast as Annika. The producers wanted to get Don Johnson, the father of Jesse, to play Gus. The characters of Bill and Kora were said to have been written as Aboriginals, but the producers could not cast Aboriginal actors in the roles since they did not like the idea of them playing antagonists.

Prey is the only Australian horror movie to date by director Oscar D'Roccster, who is rumored to actually be a cat. It is also the only Australian horror title by producers Robert Lewis Galinsky and Elizabeth Howatt-Jackman, associate producer Lyndi Adler, co-executive producers Chris Udunuwara and Michael Canty, and the production company Top Cat Films. Executive producer George Adams previously made *Wolf Creek* and executive producers Mark Pennell and Pete Ford made *Storm Warning*.

American Jesse Johnson began his career in television and made his film debut in a supporting role in the actioner *Redline* (2007). After *Prey* he appeared in film supporting roles. Natalie Bassingthwaighte also began her career in television and made her film debut in a supporting role in *When Darkness Falls* (2006). After *Prey* she has worked in television.

Natalie Walker launched her career in television and made her film debut in a supporting role in *Beef Palace* (2007). She has appeared in more television and film shorts before and after *Prey* to date. Ben Kermode is another actor who began his career in television and made his film debut in an uncredited part in the mystery *The Nines* (2007). He played in supporting film roles and more television prior to and after *Prey*. Christian Clark began his career in television and made his film debut in a supporting role in the action fantasy *Gabriel* (2007). He also appeared in *The Gates of Hell* and *Crush*; after *Prey* appeared in more television and film supporting roles. Also started in television, Kristin Sargent made her film debut in *Prey* and continued in television afterward.

British born Nicholas Bell began his career in British television and made his film debut in a supporting role in the Australian war drama *Father* (1990). He would be seen in Australian television and film supporting roles prior to and after *Prey*. Dawn Klingberg also began her career in television and made her film debut in a supporting role in the romance *Kostas* (1979). She appeared in more television and film supporting roles before and after *Prey*, including *Damned by Dawn* (2009).

Release

Australia on May 12, 2009, and the United States on June 23, 2009, with the taglines are "Some places should be left sacred...," "Dreamtime's Over," "When the hunter becomes the hunted," and "Vacation's over...."

Reviews

"A hybrid that doesn't have enough juice in any of the genres in which it plays to be effective, despite some promise in its conception. Without enough characterisation to get us involved and lacking in storytelling strength, *Prey* lets our attention wander, instead of gripping it."—Andrew L. Urban, *Urban Cinefile*

"The movie has atrocious dialogue, acting that your local community drama group wouldn't accept, an altogether ridiculous plot that can't be taken seriously, topped off by more plot holes than you would want to poke a stick at."—Jeff Ritchie, *ScaryMinds*

"The script could be re-worked to make me care about the characters. The effects could be a lot better. The story could be changed to provide an actual plot. It could also do away with the trappings of the modern day horror film with the scratchy quick takes like in *The Ring*."—James Ferguson, *HorrorTalk*, February 4, 2011

"Abysmal.... Conceptually muddled and visually dreary, *Prey* makes the recent *Friday the 13th* remake look like a triumph of imagination and skill. A film that aims so low and fails so miserably deserves nothing but contempt."—Jake Wilson, *The Age*, May 14, 2009

"Standard genre fare. Nothing about it is really bad (aside from a few bad moments of compositing), but none of it is really good either. Fans of Australian horror or backwoods slashers might find something redeeming in the film, but pretty much everyone else should give the flick a pass."—Gordon Sullivan, *DVD Verdict*, July 30 2010

"You know that you are in bad company, when the main actress cannot come up with any acting talents and the director uses a fictional name—D'Roccster. The execution of this God awful film is comparable to a six-year-old sitting behind the camera."—Michael Allen, *28 Days Later Analysis*, December 21, 2010

DVD

Released by Xenon on July 13, 2010. Released in Australia by Paramount on March 3, 2011.

The 7th Hunt

CineGear Productions/Coherent Productions, 2009 [aka *The Hunt*]

CREDITS: *Screenplay/Director/Editor:* J.D. Cohen; *Co-Director:* Darren K. Hawkins; *Producers:* Romy Teperson, J.D. Cohen, Marilyn Somella; *Associate Producers:* Gina Stojanovski, Branko

Stojanovski, Helen Trajcevski; *Executive Producers:* James Larkin, Philip Feinstein, Kris Allen; *Photography:* Christopher J. McHardy; *Music:* Samantha Fonti; *Production Design:* Hannah York; *Sound Design:* Villain; *Makeup/SFX:* Lauren Clarke; *Costumes:* Elizabeth Hamilton; *Ms. Bailey's Clothes:* Lorna Jane; *Sound:* Nathaniel Watkins; *Visual Effects:* Lee Launay. Color, 99 minutes. Filmed in Sydney, New South Wales, from August 6 to 31, 2007.

SONGS: "Never Help Anyone" (Cassady Maddox), The Charles Manson Experiment; "Eliot" (Yaniv Finkelstein, Tanith Sherman), Centipede; "Icarus" (Yaniv Finkelstein, Tanith Sherman), Centipede; "Killing Flaw" (C. Lum, J. St. Clair, M. Howell, P. Howell, R. Marsh, T. Marsh), Vers; "Renunciation" (Hellett, Tabacchi, Paul Rodwell, David Lawford), Sub Lucis Ortum.

CAST: Imogen Bailey (Ariel Clarke); Jason Stojanovski (The Sniper); Matt Charleston (Ricky Walker); Tasneem Roc (The Hand); Cassady Maddox (Callie Clarke); Sarah Mawbey (The Inquisitor, aka Catherine); Kain O'Keefe (Chris Roberts); Darren K. Hawkins (The Hacker); Olivia Solomons (Sarah Fairmont); Malcolm Frawley (The Knife); Christopher Galletti (The Mastermind, aka The Captain); Nicole Sero (Anna); Paul Ayre (Coach); Louis Hunter (Tom); Erin Connors (Andrew); Josh Picker (Nyteblayde); Chloe Traicos (Laura); Tanya (Ariel's Friend); Jaclyn Albergoni (Pool Player); Samantha Sheridan (Barmaid); Katie Timpano (X Girl); Romy Teperson (Fetish Girl 1); Katya Uzzell (Fetish Girl 2); Johnny Lahoud (Dominant Man); Miles Holt (Caleb); Philippe Moon (Matthews); Philip Feinstein (Disgruntled Man).

Synopsis

A group of militant vigilantes kidnap, torture and kill twentysomethings they profile as targets. The latest victims are rich girl Sarah Fairmont, deaf athlete Ariel Clarke and her Goth sister Callie, computer nerd Chris Roberts, and womanizer Ricky Walker. They are all held captive in different rooms at the same location. Their individual torture is watched on a multiple video screens by The Mastermind, who also monitors the blood pressure and pulse of the targets. Sarah is killed by The Knife. Ricky is made to jump off a ledge as suicide by The Hand. Ariel is kept captive by The Sniper while The Hacker toys with Chris. The Inquisitor drugs and plays with Callie. The Inquisitor turns off the video camera that observes her action with Callie. The Mastermind is angered and orders The Hand to investigate.

The Hacker kills Chris after cutting off his fingers one by one after promising that all the captives will be released if Chris can disable the computer system's firewall protection. The Inquisitor stabs The Hand before she can attack her with her martial arts moves. The Mastermind then orders The Sniper to kill The Inquisitor as a revenge for her killing of The Hand, who was The Mastermind's daughter. The Sniper releases Ariel, telling her that he was once a target who has vowed revenge upon the group. Ariel uses The Knife's own weapon to kill him. Callie manages to free herself from her bonds and overpowers The Inquisitor, hog-tying her. Ariel finds Callie, and their attempt to escape the house is stopped by The Mastermind, who is shot by The Sniper. However, The Sniper then shoots Ariel and Callie, admitting that he had lied to them.

Notes

This title features the theme of the horror of personality in the form of military vigilantes as the antagonists of a group of five twentysomethings. Director J.D. Cohen employs the postmodern techniques of expressionist camera angles and hand-held camerawork, jump cuts, whiteouts and blackouts. He fails to enliven the narrative, which reads as postmodern torture porn. There is an attempt to provide empathy for some of the victims and even some gallows humor. However, the tiresome treatment and the problematic performances of the antagonists, which range from arch to poor, ultimately provide more boredom than excitement. Horror cinephiles may appreciate the bloodletting and the various forms of torture. These include stabbing, shooting, cut fingers, beatings, electrocution and tasering, and suffocation with a plastic bag over the head. The fact that this stuff is hard to watch is also due to the dramatic principle that torture of an immobilized person is the basest form of suspense.

A prologue presents as a victim of the antagonists an unnamed and bloodied girl, who is chased then cornered by the group, who amusingly display a variety of methods of attack. Her pursuit is intercut with newspaper articles that single out words to tell of missing people but deny any real context. The narrative then presents the five new targets, with profiles appearing on screen of their names and their alleged crimes. The nature of the crimes implies that the targets have done things personally to members of the group. This is a plot point that will be furthered when The Hand states that she had known a girl whom Ricky had slept with and dumped, and the issue arises of whether The Inquisitor actually knows Callie since such an acquaintance is against the rules of the group.

Cohen uses a shock effect when The Knife appears to strike Tom, who is with Sarah. His neck being snapped suggests a murder, unlike the neck snapping of Ricky performed by The Hand that does not kill him. Blood from the gunshot of Ariel by The Sniper is the treatment's first bloodletting. This will be continued with the torture of Sarah, Chris' fingers being cut off, and The Knife's digging out the tracking device from Ariel's leg. Sarah's vocal empathy for The Knife's facial scar may be a strategy to make him stop, which works momentarily. It also plays off The Hacker's comment about how The Knife hates Sarah because she is young and beautiful, "something he never was." The torture of Callie as a Goth also has a sly humor in view of art that The Inquisitor interprets to mean that Callie enjoys pain, although later Callie will reveal that it is actually the opposite since she is a "dominant."

The title of the film suggests a seemingly fairer game than that in *Turkey Shoot*, but the reality is that only The Hand gives her targets a reasonable opportunity to defend themselves. All the others are bound and Ariel has her own disadvantage in being deaf. Ariel makes an interesting beseech to The Sniper: "Why are you doing this to me? Not that your excuse is worth hearing. Not that I can." The expectation of her being shot is created but not met when she is later shown to still be alive. In one scene The Hand's beating of Ricky is presented with them both in shadow. Cohen uses fast motion footage for Callie's drugged hallucinations of her torture by The Inquisitor. Before Ricky jumps off the ledge we hear echoed repeats of some of The Hand's lines and his jumping image is repeated.

The issue of whether The Inquisitor knows Callie is proposed by her having Callie's art book and her story of Simon, whom The Inquisitor says was her boyfriend. She later advises that this is a lie, perhaps confirmed by the fact of her also presumably being the partner of The Mastermind. Callie having posed naked for Simon's cam is said to be Callie's crime. Cohen uses a circling camera around The Inquisitor and Callie when she asks for a confession. He plays The Inquisitor's dialogue over The Hand looking at the corpse of Ricky to suggest that their earlier antagonism will be paid off. He cross-cuts between The Inquisitor's chamber, and The Hand's approach, to further the idea of an oncoming fight. The expectation of the fight is not met when The Inquisitor disposes of The Hand quickly by stabbing her.

The cross-cuts to Ariel and The Sniper have an eventual payoff which is not immediately apparent, when it appears that The Knife strikes Ariel. A flashback is used to explain that The Knife was actually removing the tracking device from her leg. Although the flashback is said to be that of Ariel to cover exposition as told to Callie, we get the standard convention of Ariel seeing herself in her own memory. Cohen uses a different lighting state for the scenes we have seen that he repeats for the setup for Ariel to stab The Knife. Cohen will use the same lighting state for The Sniper's later flashback, though again he will see himself in what is said to be his memory.

The idea of The Sniper releasing Ariel is presumably motivated by the empathy provided for her condition, although he will kill her eventually anyway. He tells of having once been a target who survived. This is something he also claims The Inquisitor was, but it is actually unbelievable given that none of the other vigilantes are seen to spare their victims. Therefore his murder of The Mastermind would seem to a political move to make him the new leader with his ally, The Inquisitor. The Inquisitor being hog-tied is never given a payoff other than The Mastermind hanging her while still tied from the same crucifix that Callie was.

The expectation of Callie falling down the staircase when she backs away from The Mastermind is one cliché not met, and The Sniper's shooting of Ariel after The Mastermind is one of the few genuine surprises in the narrative. There is also ambiguity attached to Callie's fate, since Cohen goes to a blackout after The Sniper's shot is heard, but we don't see if Callie is shot or not. The assumption is that she has been shot, and this provides a bleak downbeat ending to the narrative where it appears that evil triumphs and the protagonists do not.

This is the only Australian horror film made to date by director J.D. Cohen, co-director Darren K. Hawkins, producers Marilyn Somella and Romy Teperson, executive producers Kris Allen and James Larkin, and the production companies CineGear Productions and Coherent Productions.

Imogen Bailey began her career in television and made her film debut in a supporting role in *Man-Thing*. She has appeared in more television and supporting roles prior to and after *The 7th Hunt*. Jason Stojanovski also began his career in television and made his film debut in a supporting role in *Subterano*. He has appeared in other film supporting roles prior to and after *The 7th Hunt*. Matthew Charleston also launched his career in television, made his film debut in *Two Door Mansion* (2007), and appeared in television and supporting film roles prior to *The 7th Hunt*, his last title to date.

Tasneem Roc is another actor who started in television and made her feature film debut in *The 7th Hunt*, after which she worked in more television. Kain O'Keefe also started his career in television and made his film debut in a supporting role in the sports biography *Swimming Upstream* (2003). He went on to appear in more television and film supporting roles. Darren K. Hawkins made his film debut in a supporting role in *Something About A.J.* (2002), and continued to appear in television and more film supporting roles prior to *The 7th Hunt*, his last title to date. The actor also wrote the screenplay for and directed the thriller *Next Door to the Velinskys* (2010).

Cassady Maddox made her film debut in a supporting role in the thriller *Sum of Existence* (2005); *The 7th Hunt* has been her last title to date. Sarah Mawbey debuted in this film; it is her only title to date. Olivia Solomons made her feature film debut in a minor role in *Sum of Existence* and has appeared in film supporting roles and television prior to *The 7th Hunt*, her last title to date. Malcolm Frawley also made his film debut in a supporting role in *Sum of Existence*, and has continued to be seen in film supporting roles prior to and after *The 7th Hunt*. Chris Galletti is another actor to have begun his career in television and made his film debut in a minor role in the crime drama *BMX Bandits* (1983). He continued in television and film supporting roles prior to and after *The 7th Hunt*.

Release

In Australia in 2009, date unknown. Screened in the United States at the New York City Horror Film Festival and on August 15, 2010, at the Atlanta Horror Film Festival, then released straight to DVD with the tagline "Five Victims, Five Killers. One Aim ... To Survive."

Reviews

"Remarkably intense and viscerally graphic at times ... the acting and filming was professionally done with a story that keeps interest and provides a few thrills. The acts of torture vary in intensity but do the trick when they need to."—*Horror News*, February 26, 2011

DVD

Released by Vanguard Cinema on February 22, 2011. No DVD release in Australia.

Storage
Rich Vein, 2009

CREDITS: *Screenplay/Director:* Michael Craft; *Producers:* Michael Craft, Gregor Drugowitsch, Elizabeth Symes; *Executive Producer:* David Lightfoot; *Associate Producers:* Tom McSweeney, Julie Forster, Stuart Freeman; *Photography:* Tony Luu; *Editor:* Geoff Lamb; *Music:* Gary McDonald, Lawrence Stone; *Costumes:* Vanessa Loh; *Production Design:* Michelle Sotheren; *Sound Design:* Vic Kaspar; *Sound:* John Schlefelbein; *Makeup:* Veronique Keys; *Art Director:* Christopher Cox; *Special Effects:* Clint Ingram, Dan Houwelling, Jeremy "J.J." Piggott. Color, 90 minutes. Filmed in Brisbane, Queensland.

SONGS: "Mistakes" (Carlyoni, Cran, Stadish), The Devastations; "No Vibe No Sirobe" (Utomo, Falkland), Young and Restless; "Fuji" (Beehre, Carr, Dodge), Minuit; "March of Clouds" (Joel Byrne, Wolf and Cub), Wolf and Cub; "Persist" (M. Kennedy, L. Prue), All India Radio; "Gonna Make You Happy Tonight" (Edgar, Hall, Gates), Tripod; "The Hill Song" (Kate Miller Heldeke, Yanto Browning), Dovetail; "Black and Blue," DisInfektor; "She's a Liar" (Pete Cullen, Brian L'Hullier, Mick and Aaron Lucioux), Daybridges; "Smoke and Mirrors" (Hermannlusson, Diblassio, Citawarman, McKee), Snowman; "You are a Casino" (Hermannlusson, Diblassio, Citawarman, McKee), Snowman.

CAST: Damien Garvey (Leonard Walker); Matt Scully (Jimmy); Saskia Burmeister (Zia); Robert Price (Malcolm); Sally McKenzie (Carol); Elise Greig (Marla); Robert Mammone (Francis Piasecki); Mark Bullus (Jobbo); Rizzo, Ginger, and Flower (Rats). Uncredited: Craig Ingham (Storage Unit Holder); Shevaun Lee Steffens (Prostitute).

Synopsis

Malcolm is the father of the seventeen-year-old Jimmy. He takes his son to a cinema screening of *Death Wish 2*, and afterwards a man in the street tries to rob them. Malcolm is accidentally stabbed in the struggle. Jimmy's single Uncle Leonard takes him in and gives him a job at his City Storage facility. Leonard tells Jimmy about the strange customers he rents storage units to. One day Jimmy hears the renter of unit 830, Francis Piasecki, moaning inside the unit and sees him holding a gun. Jimmy confronts Francis, who is angered by Jimmy's invasion of privacy. Leonard smooths over the conflict and Jimmy seeks the help of the facility's receptionist, Zia. They use lock picks to open unit 830. However they get caught by Leonard, who fires Zia, and then goes into the unit.

Inside is one of the sealed barrels that Leonard provides for long term storage, where Francis keeps women's dirty clothes and the gun. Leonard refuses to contact the police since he has little faith in them. Jimmy visits Zia in her motel room and gives her his paycheck to cover money Leonard should have given her. They make love and she asks him to go away up north with her. Leonard takes Jimmy with him to Francis' house, after Francis has demanded a refund for the six months' rental he has paid for the unit. Believing Francis has killed his wife, Leonard kills him and returns the body to the storage basement. Leonard tells Jimmy how he has killed other men he has learned have committed crimes and uses storage units to hide the evidence. Jimmy does not believe that Francis killed his wife and refuses Leonard's offer to join him in his killings. Leonard locks him in a caged room. Zia comes looking for Jimmy. Leonard demands that Jimmy kill her to save his own life. After agreeing to do it, Jimmy and Zia get away from Leonard in a fight. Leonard finds them and kills Zia, but Jimmy manages to kill Leonard with a nail gun.

Notes

This crime thriller shot on digital camera features the theme of the horror of personality in the form of an opportunistic serial killer who finds his victims in the workplace. The narrative is interesting in that the killer's practice is revealed late in the proceedings and that it involves changing a protagonistic character into an antagonistic one. Director Michael Craft uses the postmodern techniques of slow motion, point of view, and expressionist camera angles. Apart from a conventional climactic chase, his treatment is compelling and performances are impressive. Bloodletting is sparse but when used is effectively gruesome, and rats are used for the storage facility location to add atmosphere.

A prologue begins with Malcolm and Jimmy watching *Death Wish 2* (1982) and Jimmy laughing at Charles Bronson's killings, since he later tells he thinks the film is silly. This seeming callow insensitivity to violence will not be repeated in his later responses to the strikes against his father, Francis and Zia. It is noteworthy that the killing of Malcolm is shown to be accidental and due to his attempt to fight back against the robber. Malcolm's blood is the first real bloodletting in the film, after that shown in *Death Wish 2*. The rats we had seen in the location for the death scene in the film also prefigure the rats in the storage facility. This adds atmosphere and later gets a payoff in the rat that is killed as a trap for Leonard. In the making-of featurette on the DVD, Craft advises that the images under the opening credits show the possessions of different unit clients. They are the Doll Collector, The Adventurer, and the Survivalist, who are not seen otherwise.

The grainy black and white CCTV (closed circuit television) footage in the facility is used to provide an alternate point of view. It also operates for plot points given the view of what is assumed to be Francis' wife's leg in the trunk of his car, Jimmy in the caged cell, and the final shot of Jimmy in Leonard's office. The plot point of the barrels Leonard shows to Jimmy will get a later payoff in Leonard's use of them to dispose of bodies with sulphuric acid and Jimmy's use of one for Leonard's body. Jimmy's nightmare of Francis dressed as the robber who was responsible for killing Malcolm slashing his throat is the subconscious continuation of his concern over what he has seen.

The throat slashing provides more narrative gore, and Craft uses Leonard's hand on Jimmy's shoulder when he and Zia open Francis' unit with the lock picks as a shock device. Leonard is prepared to humor Jimmy by looking in the box within the barrel in the unit. It is the bloodstained clothes that begin Leonard's belief that Francis has killed his wife rather than just keeping her dirty clothes as mementoes to revisit.

The sex scene between Jimmy and Zia is interesting in her being the presumably older and more aggressive partner. Zia's removal from the narrative for a stretch of time makes her return pleasing, even though her fate is an unhappy one. The skeleton masks that Jimmy and Leonard wear when they break into Francis' house add ghoulishness to the action. The sadism of Leonard's water board torture of Francis suggests the revelation to come about his identity as much as it also shows Leonard's training as an ex Special Air Service soldier. The treatment Francis receives reverses our feeling toward a character that has seemed previously unlikeable, so that now we empathize with his plight.

Craft presents Francis' aural and visual point of view when he is tied and hanged upside down and being hosed with the shower faucet. Jimmy makes the rational observation that he admits to having killed his wife only because that's what Leonard wants to hear. Leonard also making Francis record a goodbye message into a tape recorder gets a payoff when we see Leonard later transfer the recording to Francis' cell phone.

The plastic bag that Leonard puts on Francis' head suggests that he is going to be killed by being suffocated, but the bag is actually used to contain the resultant blood from Leonard's strike with a hammer. The mannequins that Leonard and Jimmy find in the trunk of Francis' car explain the arm that they had seen on the CCTV footage. The slow motion used for Leonard's burning of the car recalls the slow motion burning of the unit effects of Stuart, who was thought to be a child abuser and whom Leonard will later admit to have killed. The rats in the boiler room basement when Leonard takes Francis' body to be destroyed with acid in a barrel again highlight the Gothic atmosphere of the storage facility. Leonard breaking Francis' bones so that his body can fit in the barrel is more aural gruesomeness.

Leonard's confession to Jimmy for having killed Stuart four months previously and being a serial killer — although he doesn't use that phrase — is a surprise. The emotionalism that Damien Garvey brings to the admission is another surprise. Although it comes from his anger over the killing of Malcolm, we assume that he has been killing before his brother's death. The emotionalism eases the transition of character from someone we assumed to be protagonist to antagonist. It also aids his rationale for not trusting the police, who did not find Malcolm's killer, did not stop Stuart, and have not stopped Leonard.

Leonard's rationale is, "I do what must be done because no one else will do it. No one except me." It is the mindset of the trained soldier we know him to be from the photograph of Leonard in uniform, with Malcolm, that Jimmy looked at when he first arrived. The idea of Leonard as a soldier is continued in the way he will stalk Jimmy and Zia in the climax. His argument is also said to convince Jimmy to join him in the quest, although the idea that they only find perpetrators who use the facility would seem to severely limit their hunting territory. Jimmy's refusal to join Leonard comes from the belief that Francis did not kill his wife, to which Leonard replies, "Even if he didn't do it, he would have done it sooner or later. You could see it in him." This interpretation of Francis' previously demonstrated hostility seems a convenient denial of the possibility of his grief over the wife who left him by suicide.

After Leonard knocks Jimmy unconscious, Craft uses a blackout for the transition to Leonard seeing him on the CCTV screen in the caged cell with a rat near him. The silent scenes of Leonard's now solitary existence make his loneliness evident. Craft uses a superimposed shot of his car arriving at the facility over one of Leonard sitting on his bed. Zia's return and confrontation with Leonard makes us fear for her, since even though we see him behaving in a benign manner, we know what he is capable of. His telling her about a letter he has for her from Jimmy downstairs and the gun he holds on her creates the expectation of her being his next victim.

Leonard has no real reason to kill her since she is unaware of his actions, and it seems he has decided to use her as bait to test Jimmy's loyalty. However, as with Leonard's murder of Francis, Jimmy's agreement to kill her rather than be killed is only said to momentarily appease the maniac. The expectation of Jimmy to attempt to fool Leonard is met after Leonard opens the cell door as Zia's scream makes Leonard drop the gun and Jimmy attacks him.

Zia's running and leaving Jimmy rather than getting the gun may indicate her moral fate, although she does stop in the corridor. Her indecision about going back is solved by Jimmy's appearance. Jimmy's inability to lock the door behind them to keep Leonard out allows Leonard to pursue them, although Leonard seen retrieving the gun suggests that he could have blown through a locked door anyway. The three characters knowing the layout of the facility informs their chase. It doesn't stop Leonard from easily finding Jimmy and Zia, which Craft presents in another shock effect with him behind the fire exit door that Jimmy opens.

Leonard shooting Zia in the forehead is another shock, immediately dashing our expectation that she will escape, and prefiguring the way Leonard will also be killed. In spite of Leonard's army skills presumably aiding his tracking of Jimmy, Leonard's yelling for him is an expression of his anger and frustration that does not make him concerned about revealing his location. It appears that Jimmy makes a deliberate noise from a loose door to make Leonard investigate it and entrap him. This presents Leonard as a conventional Man in Peril, given a twist since it has the antagonist investigating a noise.

The rat that Leonard finds dead in the rat trap, which may also explain the noise he has heard, signals his own entrapment by Jimmy when Jimmy is revealed behind Leonard holding the nail gun to the back of his head. The expectation that Jimmy cannot kill Leonard is momentarily met, acknowledged by Leonard's taunt. However, the strike and the resultant blood pouring from the hole in Leonard's forehead is perhaps the treatment's most gruesome display of bloodletting.

Craft uses the CCTV footage to show Jimmy putting Leonard's body in a barrel, an ironic fate for him. Jimmy puts Zia in the back of her car but we don't see what happens to her body after that. A CCTV shot of Jimmy in Leonard's office suggests that perhaps he will become what Leonard wanted him to be after all. After a zoom in, he turns off the CCTV camera. This is a clever ending to the narrative. The turning off of the camera also perhaps suggests that Jimmy will not pursue Leonard's quest. However, the use of the CCTV cameras does pose one problematic question. Whose point of view are we seeing?

In the making-of featurette on the DVD, Craft discusses the parallel between the narrative and the real life story of John Bunting and his teenage accomplice, James Vlassakis. The case was known as the "Snowtown Murders" and "Bodies in Barrels Murders." These men were serial killers who acted as vigilantes in the 1990s in South Australia. They killed twelve people they thought were bad, disposing of their bodies in barrels of acid, and using their credit cards. The case is said to be the biggest serial killer rampage in Australian history to date. The older professional and the younger novice is also a dynamic portrayed in the movie *Acolytes*. Craft also says that he wanted the narrative to provide a twist on the conventional revenge story. Jimmy does not avenge the death of his father by searching for the culprit but rather is faced with Leonard, who is seeking his own form of abstract revenge. The featurette has a funny edit from the prosthetic used for the hammer killing of Francis to actor Robert Mammone sitting on the set reading a book. It also shows how Craft played the victim of the water boarding torture to experience what he would be asking Mammone to do for the scene.

Michael Craft made his feature film debut with *Storage* and has not made another Australian horror title to date. It is also the only Australian horror title made thus far by producers Gregor Drugowitsch and Elizabeth Symes, and the Rich Vein production company. Executive producer David Lightfoot had previously made *Wolf Creek* and *Rogue* and went on to produce *Coffin Rock*.

Damien Garvey began his career in short films and after working in television made his movie debut in a supporting role in the comedy *Spudmonkey* (2001). After doing more television and supporting film roles, he essayed the lead in *Storage*. He went on to appear in a supporting role in *Daybreakers*, but has not had another leading film role to date.

Matt Scully began his career in television and *Storage* has been his only feature film role to date. Saskia Burmeister also began her career in television and made her film debut in a supporting role in the biographical adventure *Ned Kelly* (2003). After appearing in more television and film supporting roles, she essayed the lead in the comedy *Hating Alison Ashley* (2005). After *Storage*, played the lead in the thriller *Rampage* (2010). Robert Mammone was previously seen in *Man-Thing*, and appeared in more television and film supporting roles.

Release

Australia on August 13, 2009, but no release in the United States. The taglines are "The deeper you go the darker it gets" and "Nothing gets out."

Reviews

"A little gem of a horror thriller, unpredictable and intense."— Andrew L. Urban, *Urban Cinefile*

"Craft delivered up the shocks, the rats, the plot twists, and a good dollop of tension to top it off with. I was held pretty spellbound through the course of the film."— Jeff Ritchie, *ScaryMinds*

"A sleeper hit ... an incredibly tight and well-paced piece of work and makes writer/director Michael Craft a name to watch out for."— Julian, *Digital Retribution*, January 24, 2010

"The director manages a strong visual appeal, and effectively portrays the menace [and] eeriness of the locations. What really gives the film that extra something is its unpredictable story that goes off in unexpected directions, but yet manages to retain a realistic quality. An underrated, under appreciated, under seen gem."— Brandon Sites, *Big Daddy Horror Guide*

"A fantastically taut, nerve-shredding Australian horror with more twists and turns than a particularly elaborate rollercoaster ride. The set-up is brief and to the point, but paves the way for a slow-burning psychological thriller that may just have you on the edge of your seat." — Sara Law, *Gorepress*

"[An] Australian jewel. What really makes *Storage* stand out are the diabolical twists and turns in the screenplay [and] Craft is smart enough to keep things simple although the ending was a bit of a disappointment.... I will never drive by a storage facility again without wondering what might be going on inside." — Greg Roberts, *KillerReviews*

DVD

No American DVD release to date. Released in Australia by Anchor Bay Entertainment on February 10, 2010.

Triangle

Framestore/Dan Films and Pictures in Paradise, 2009

CREDITS: *Screenplay/ Director:* Christopher Smith; *Producers:* Jason Newmark, Julie Baines, Chris Brown; *Executive Producers:* Steve Norris, Mark Gooder, Stefanie Huie; *Associate Producer:* Jonathan Taylor; *Photography:* Robert Humphreys; *Editor:* Stuart Gazzard; *Music:* Christian Henson; *Production Design:* Melinda Doring; *Costumes:* Steven Noble; *Makeup and Hair:* Shane Thomas; *Sound:* Craig Walmsley; *Art Director:* Bill Booth; *Set Designers:* Eugene Intas, Klaus Kastberg; *Set Decorator:* Glen W. Johnson. Color, 95 minutes. Filmed at Warner Roadshow Studios, Queensland, and on location in Brisbane and the Gold Coast, Queensland, and Sydney, New South Wales, in June 2008.

SONG: "Anchors Aweigh," Glenn Miller and his Orchestra, the Band of John Paul College.

CAST: Melissa George (Jess); Michael Dorman (Greg); Rachael Carpani (Sally); Henry Nixon (Downey); Emma Lung (Heather); Liam Hemsworth (Victor); Joshua McIvor (Tommy); Jack Taylor (Jack); Bryan Probets (Driver).

SYNOPSIS

Jess is a waitress and the young mother of an autistic son, Tommy. She agrees to join her customer, Greg, on his yacht, *The Triangle*, to go sailing with his friends. At sea the yacht faces an electrical storm. One of the passengers, Heather, is washed away and the boat is capsized. The group comes across the ocean liner, the *Aeolus Miami*, at sea. They board it, although they can find no one else on it. Jess has a sense of having been on the liner before. Greg, Downey and Sally are shot by an assailant with sacks over their heads. Jess is chased by a woman. She fights her off and before the woman falls overboard she tells Jess, "If they board, kill them all."

Jess observes the group re-boarding the liner. Seeing herself, she learns that a pattern emerges. She attempts to save the others by killing them over again to stop them from re-boarding after she learns that the assailant is herself. Jess escapes from the repeating scenario by washing up on an island after the last time she falls overboard. Jess gets back to her home and observes herself as an abusive mother. She kills her double and hides the body in her car. The corpse is thrown from the trunk when the car hits a truck and Tommy is killed. The Jess that was driving the car survives the crash. A taxi driver takes her to the harbor where Greg and his friends await her to set sail again on the fateful trip, which it seems Jess is fated to relive for ever.

NOTES

This psychological thriller features a mix of the theme of the horror of personality and the malevolent supernatural being. It has a *Twilight Zone*–style narrative that uses doppelgangers, repetition of scenes and alternate point of view. Although this approach hovers between contrivance and silliness, what makes it ultimately perhaps too clever for itself is its ambiguity and lack of resolution.

Director Christopher Smith uses the postmodern techniques of blackouts, point of view, slow and fast motion, jump cuts, hand-held camerawork and CGI effects. He also creates a treatment as a star vehicle for his leading actress to play multiple parts. Although her performance is effective and appropriately strange, and Smith seems to enjoy having her turn around slowly, since she does it multiple times; Melissa George, however, lacks the emotional range to incur audience empathy for what appears to be a psychological breakdown. The treatment also has plenty of bloodletting, and a few resonant horror images.

The American accents of the Australian cast reads as a marketing choice for the film's international sale, although there is no specific American location given in the narrative apart from the *Aeolus* being named *Miami*. In the making-of featurette on the DVD, Smith comments that the Miami link is because the location is meant to be off the coast of Miami, which also supplies the "hook" of the Bermuda Triangle. Additionally, the protagonist's use of weaponry initially seems to present her as another female warrior. This seemingly aligns her to the ones in *Lady, Stay Dead, Fair Game, Contagion, Out of the Body, The 13th Floor, Komodo, Ghost Ship, Undead, See No Evil, Black Water, Storm Warning, Slaughtered, Prey, The Clinic* and *Road Train*. However, this is revealed to be misleading.

The film's opening image of Jess holding Tommy will be repeated later in the narrative with Jess's return and after she has killed her double. Her telling him that he has had "bad dreams" would seem to prefigure her forthcoming experience, as does Jess's dream of herself being washed up on the beach as she sleeps on the yacht. The distress call that Greg overhears is more prefiguring; we will later see Sally make the call from the liner and hear Greg's same replies. The electrical storm with its thunder, lightning and dark clouds seen in daytime operates as the horror movie conventional storm that sets a stage of dread.

British poster for *Triangle* (2009).

The storm sequence has Smith's first use of fast motion photography to heighten the action to an almost cartoonish pitch. It's a shame that the narrative disposes of Heather so quickly when she is washed away in the storm and never recovered, presumed drowned. Sally's hopes that Heather will be on the liner offers the promise of a payoff that is not met, including the initial possibility that perhaps Heather is the masked assailant.

The fact that a 1932 ocean liner is floating in the sea suggests that it is not real, something reinforced by the obvious use of CGI. It also recalls the similarly haunted liner of *Ghost Ship*. The fresh fruit that the group finds to eat will be exposed as an illusion in the second loop when the fruit is seen to be decomposed, although the apple eaten by Victor and the banana eaten by Downey seem real. A plaque on the liner allows for the legend of

Aeolus. He is said to have been the "Greek God of the winds and the father of Sisyphus, who was condemned by the gods to the task of pushing a rock up a mountain only to see it roll down again ... as punishment for making a promise to death that he did not keep." A parallel is presumably to be made between the tale of Sisyphus and the fate of Jess. She must keep repeating the same scenario perhaps because she has killed Tommy, though that is presented as an accident.

The message "Go to Theater," said to be written in blood on the bathroom mirror, is the narrative's first display of blood. This moment will be paid off when we see Jess write it in Downey's blood. The blood drops on the floor that Downey and Sally see are presumably those of Victor, although later this is ambiguous. The bloody Victor is the first person to have been wounded; he presumably dies from the injury we later see was accidentally inflicted by Jess. That Victor should blame Jess and try to strangle her prefigures us seeing her cause the accident, but is the first suggestion that Jess's odd behavior on the liner makes her seem the prime suspect.

We don't see Greg having been shot until later in the narrative, but his dead body is shown with Downey and Sally, and again them blaming Jess for shooting him prefigures a later scene when she appears with a gun. The others being fired at when Jess is with them shows that she cannot be the shooter. Since she *is* later shown to be the shooter in the form of one of her doubles, realistic explanations are not something the narrative seems to rely upon.

The shooter is a figure wearing a sack over her head, although the fact of the person being a woman is only revealed when she speaks to Jess in the confrontation to come. When Jess takes a kitchen knife and then an axe to go after the shooter, she is shown to be the conventional Woman in Peril, though here armed and not powerless. Jess' resourcefulness will be especially highlighted in her ability to fight off the shooter's shotgun when it is fired at her and her physical dexterity apparent from her ability to run and climb between ship levels. This sequence also has Smith using the same fast motion action as in the storm sequence, and he uses a shock effect for the shooter's appearance behind Jess before Jess sees the shooter. The shooter is only revealed to be a woman after rather pathetically throwing the gun at Jess and retreating from Jess' swinging axe. Her identity as a Jess double is not displayed until later.

The jazz music that Jess hears leads to her finding a record player. It plays Glenn Miller and his Orchestra's version of "Anchors Aweigh," although we don't know who started the player. The song will get a payoff when Jess sees a band playing it in a park. She sees the yacht passengers signaling to the liner as they had been seen to do previously when Jess was with them. Jess sees herself as one of the yacht's group, and the narrative loses its hold on reality. How can Jess see herself in the past when it's not apparent that she is dreaming? And how can we now be back in time?

Smith's audio commentary points out how Jess walks through a mirror and how it is her mirrored reflection that leads her into the second loop, as a sign of the loss of reality. Scenes of the group's entrance to the liner are now repeated but from Jess' point of view. The group's Jess now finding her own dropped keys makes sense in hindsight because we have seen the double Jess drop them.

Jess sees the vision of Downey in the sea and being eaten by seagulls. This is despite the fact that seagulls aren't known to eat human flesh. The image is still gruesome. The figure is later identified by Jess as being Downey when she tries to show the living Victor the sight. Given that it appears that Jess' visions and her predicament make her the victimized protagonist, it's not a surprise that Victor doesn't see what she sees. However, his response to her telling him what she believes—that there are now two of her—is appropriately funny in his skepticism. His line about "Watch the grabbing" in the way she implores him gets a payoff in her accidentally pushing him against a wall spike that causes the hole in his head.

When Jess confronts her own doppelganger and aims a rifle at her, it raises a laugh in the face of the victim's raised hands. The expectation is created that she will not be able to kill her own double, which is met by her firing but missing. The confrontation also changes the previously seen scene with Jess and Victor where he strangles her for pushing him into the spike. Now he doesn't do this, although presumably he still dies, as Jess follows her double into the theater to find Greg, Downey and Sally.

Downey and Sally are not shot this time, a variation of the previous scene. This time Jess is revealed to be the shooter of Greg when we see her remove the mask that we have seen the shooter wear, and she takes Downey and Sally to a cabin to kill them. The throat slashing and repeated stabbing of Downey is perhaps the film's most savage directly presented killing. Sally's escape from being stabbed allows for the alternate Jess to pursue her to help rather than harm her.

When this Jess finds Sally on the upper deck, there is the shock effect of gulls flying at her. Smith provides a multitude of images of Sally being dead near the dying Sally. As with the image of Downey in the sea being fed upon by gulls, here gulls feed off the corpses. The latest Sally dying in front of Jess is a surprise, given that she has survived the stabbing by running around the liner. A third Jess then watches one double of herself attacking another double with the axe on a lower deck, in an extreme long shot presumably to mask the axe strikes, and the attacked Jess is thrown overboard. In the DVD audio commentary Smith says that this axed and thrown overboard Jess was the Jess that had killed Downey and attacked Sally. The Jess that axed and threw overboard this Jess is observed by the third Jess on the upper deck to see the yacht arriving again.

The idea is proposed that the yacht returns with its passengers to start the pattern over again when all the group has been killed onboard — "It returns when they're dead." Jess's advice to Victor that she "knows how to save you" is based on her idea of stopping the passengers from initially boarding the liner. However, as Jess has always previously hidden from view when the yacht approaches, this seems a radical departure from the pattern. One might think that another way to save them would be not to kill them, but this doesn't seem to occur to Jess. We also see her attempt to stop the ship in the engine room unsuccessfully, before she accepts the idea that she must kill the others and dons the sack hood to go about it.

Jess finds Downey dead in the bathroom, presumably having written "Jes" on the mirror in his blood to identify his killer. This leads her to write the "Go to Theater" message also in his blood. Her throwing Downey's body overboard is presumably what leads to him being food for the gulls. After Jess is seen dressing as the shooter with the sack over her head and confronting Greg with the rifle, he recognizes her shoes and identifies Jess as the shooter. She hesitates, creating the expectation that she will not be able to shoot him. But she does shoot Greg, and Downey and Sally in the theater. After she chases another Jess double, we get a repeat of the initial deck confrontation with Jess again falling into the sea. However, this time she awakens, with the pattern seemingly broken.

Jess' hitchhiking a ride back to her home is covered in the shorthand of seeing her arm stuck out as a signal. But once she is home, what are we to make of her seeing herself as an abusive mother to Tommy? The doorbell we had heard in the film's opening scene is repeated to show it as a decoy for the second Jess to get from the back yard the weapon used to kill the bad Jess. The killing is obscured by having the struck Jess hidden behind a bed. The fury of her repeated strikes recalls the savagery of the cabin killing of Downey. The opening shot of Jess cradling Tommy is now repeated with a context provided for Tommy's anguish apart from him being autistic. A gull flying into the windshield of Jess' car is a shock effect and funny after she has told Tommy, "Mommy's nice," as opposed to being the bad Mommy.

Smith repeats the idea of the multiple dead images in the sight of multiple dead gulls on the riverbank where Jess throws the gull she has struck. She is distracted by Tommy's anguish over the gull blood on the windshield and doesn't see the oncoming truck her car drives into. Smith uses a pan across onlookers. This reveals the dead Jess that the second Jess had put in the car trunk and has presumably been released via the smash, Tommy, and then a doppelganger Jess watching, with this Jess being the driver of the car who has survived the crash.

The taxi driver who offers her a ride initially suggests another dead soul but is then revealed to be perhaps real. He drives her to the harbor to meet Greg for the yacht's sailing. Smith elaborates in the audio commentary that her decision to go with the driver is her deliberate choice to go back into the loop to attempt to save Tommy or at least spend time with him again when she gets out of the loop. Jess' apology to Greg is now presumably contextualized by her having killed Tommy. Perhaps it can also be read as an apology in advance for her forthcoming killings of him and Victor, Downey and Sally. The narrative therefore seems to conclude with Jess as a tormented soul who cannot rest. She must board the yacht to board the liner for the repeat of the pattern of her Sisyphus-like eternal purgatorial punishment.

In the making-of documentary on the DVD Smith speaks of the narrative's three time loops as having been inspired by the mystery *Last Year at Marienbad* (1961). The liner was built on the jetty outreach of Southport Spit, so that ocean views could be supplied for three sides. The corridors of the liner are said to recall *The Shining* with the bathroom used for the blood mirror message, also shown to be in room 237. In his audio commentary Smith also mentions how he wrote twenty-five drafts of the screenplay and in an earlier one how Tommy was aged twenty years when Jess returned home, a plot point that was abandoned.

Smith says his intention with the film was to make a "satisfying riddle" that was inspired by *The Shining* and the 1919 Sigmund Freud essay "The Uncanny," which supposedly Stanley Kubrick also used for *The Shining*. Smith claims that the narrative has three readings. They are: 1. a realistic Bermuda Triangle mystery, 2. that what happens is all a dream, and 3. that what happens is due to Jess having a psychological breakdown. He also says that originally the ocean liner was to have appeared out of fog at night. The sack mask that Jess wears was an idea copied from the sack mask of the killer Jason Voorhees in the horror title *Friday the 13th Part 2* (1981). Also Jess' t-shirt and hot pants outfit, that recalls the outfit of Jodie Foster's child prostitute in the thriller *Taxi Driver* (1976), had been suggested by Melissa George.

Although known as the director of other horror titles like *Creep* (2004), *Severance* (2006) and *Black Death* (2010), *Triangle* is the only Australian horror title to have been made to date by Christopher Smith, producers Jason Newmark and Julie Baines, executive producers Steve Norris, Mark Gooder and Stefanie Huie, and associate producer Jonathan Taylor. Producer Chris Brown had previously made *Komodo*, *Hellion: The Devil's Playground* and *Daybreakers*. *Triangle* is the only Australian horror title for the Framestore production companies and Dan Films. The production company Pictures in Paradise had previously made *Hellion: The Devil's Playground* and *Daybreakers*.

Melissa George began her career in television and made her film debut in a supporting role in the science fiction thriller *Dark City* (1998). After playing more supporting film roles and television, she essayed the lead in the crime drama *The Betrayed* (2008) prior to *Triangle*. She has not played another leading film role to date. Michael Dorman was previously seen in *Acolytes* and *Daybreakers* and later played the lead in the Australian horror title *Needle*. Rachael Carpani also began her career in television and made her film debut in a supporting role in the comedy *Hating Alison Ashley* (2005). *Triangle* is her only other film credit to date.

Henry Nixon previously appeared in *Safety in Numbers*. After *Triangle* he worked in film supporting roles and on television. Emma Lung was previously seen in *Crush*, and after *Triangle* had more supporting film and television roles. Liam Hemsworth began his career in television and made his film debut in a supporting role in the science fiction mystery *Knowing* (2009). After *Triangle* he was in more supporting film roles. Joshua McIvor made his film debut in *Triangle*, his only screen appearance to date.

Release

Screenings on October 24, 2009, at the Scream-Fest Film Festival and November 9, 2009, at the American Film Market but no wide release, as the film went straight to DVD in the United States. Released in Australia on April 29, 2010. The taglines include "The Forecast is Evil," "A Passage to Hell," "Save Our Souls," and "Fear Comes in Waves."

The DVD has two deleted scenes. They are Heather telling Sally how she thinks she is still in love with Greg when they are talking about Jess being his new love interest, and Jess abandoning steering the yacht as Greg's instructs to pull Victor up back onto the yacht after he was washed overboard during the electrical storm, which results in the yacht capsizing. Smith also mentions moments that were removed that include Jess in the armory holding a gun to her mouth to consider suicide before she finds the necklaces under the grate, and how the shot of Jess seeing the pile of dead seagulls on the riverbank was originally to have also appeared in the earlier scene when she arrives at the yacht.

Reviews

"Too loose and too contrived, the plot is left with lots of gaps, and there is insufficient stuffing in the characters to make us care much about them.... With more work, the script could have finished up as a creepy entry in the ghost ship sub-genre, but as it stands it is less than satisfying."—Andrew L. Urban, *Urban Cinefile*

"The film is masterfully directed by Smith, and he gleans some wonderful performances from his Australian cast. Admittedly Melissa George seems somewhat flat at first, but as her character is forced to deal with the various positions she's put in, she gets an opportunity to shine."—J.R. McNamara, *Digital Retribution*, December 15, 2010

"Director/Writer Smith has made an intricate house of cards masterpiece ... a stunning performance in the lead from Melissa George ... with the cinematography being absolutely brilliant. Christian Henson's haunting score adds to the whole atmosphere that Smith creates, giving the audience a chilling experience in the macabre."—Jeff Ritchie, *ScaryMinds*

"It starts strongly, [but] wears thin as the story continues — when you're seeing the exact same actions occur on screen for the third or fourth time it begins to feel like padding. The violence is sporadic and extremely well done but those looking for a gorefest should head elsewhere."—Gareth Jones, *Dread Central*, September 3, 2009

"Triangle isn't a perfect film, but it will certainly stay with you after you watch it. I enjoy a good mindf&*k

movie and Triangle certainly fits the bill.... [It] gets a lot of mileage out of its relatively low budget [and] the acting is solid [with] kudos to Melissa George." — Mike Long, *DVD Sleuth*, January 27, 2010

"One of those films that did not seem terribly promising at first glance but proved to be a case of one taking a punt on a title at random and being immensely rewarded as a result.... The bulk of the show rests on the shoulders of the fine and underrated Melissa George." — Richard Scheib, *Moria — science fiction, horror and fantasy film review site*

DVD

Released by First Look Studios on February 2, 2010. Icon Home Entertainment (Australia) on October 5, 2010.

The Clinic

Great Southern Land Entertainment/RMB Productions, 2010

CREDITS: *Screenplay/Director:* James Rabbitts; *Producer:* Samuel Pinczewski; *Executive Producers:* Bob Marcs, Jonathan Shteinman; *Co-Producer:* Dennis Kiely; *Photography:* Brad Shield; *Editor:* Ryan Boucher; *Production Design:* Nicholas McCallum; *Costumes:* Catherine Wallace; *Music:* Kirke Godfrey, Jason Fernandez, Angela Little; *Sound:* Tim Lloyd; *Art Director:* Sam Lukins; *Makeup/Hair:* Suzy Kelly. Color, 90 minutes. Filmed on location in Deniliquin and Sydney, New South Wales.

SONG: "Silent Night" (Franz Xaver Gruber/Joseph Mohr), Tony King.

CAST: Tabrett Bethell (Beth Church); Freya Stafford (Veronica); Andy Whitfield (Cameron); Clare Bowen (Ivy); Marshall Napier (Officer Marvin Underwood); Liz Alexander (Ms. Shepard); Sophie Lowe (Allison); Boris Brkic (Hank); Marcel Bracks (Duncan); Adrienne Pickering (Jane Doe); Slava Orel (Russian Man, aka Boris); Inga Romantsoya (Russian Woman, aka Svetlana); Harold Hopkins (Grave Digger); Anni Finsterer (Locker Room Woman); Bob Marcs (Police Officer 1); Laurence Fleming (Beth's Father); Kelsey McKenzie (Paramedic); Cecily Polson (Woman on Porch); Chris Holloway (Police Officer 2); Zac Wise (Beth as Baby); Damenica Brain, Mya Crampton (Beth's Newborn Daughter); Evie Isabella Green, Lexi Willow MacMaster (Beth's Graveyard Daughter); Tilly Rose Faure-Brac, Ella Ruby Reeson (Babies in Cage).

Synopsis

In 1979 pregnant Beth Church and her fiancé, Cameron, are driving in the Australian outback. Their car is run off the road by an ambulance. They decide to stay the night at a motel near the town of Montgomery. Cameron is unable to sleep and goes in search of food. Not finding anything open, he returns to his room but discovers Beth is missing. Cameron calls in the police. He accuses the motel manager, Hank, of showing an inappropriate interest in Beth and punches him. Officer Marvin arrests Cameron. Cameron manages to get the policeman's gun, and after handcuffing him to a post, drives off with his car. He returns to Hank, who tells him that Beth is at the local abandoned abattoir.

At the abattoir Beth awakens to find that her baby has been removed from her. She tries to leave the compound but cannot since it is surrounded by wire fencing. She meets three other women in the same situation. Together they search for their babies. They find the Locker Room Woman. From a pregnant woman whose stitches have been deliberately cut open, they learn that another woman is attacking the women. She is trying to find the colored tag that will match that on the babies found in cages in the nursery.

This woman methodically attacks and kills Allison, Ivy, and Veronica. She is defeated by Beth, whom she asks to save her baby with Beth's. Beth goes back to the nursery and finds the cages empty. She is taken by Hank and Marvin to the office of Dr. Shepard. The doctor gives Beth's baby to a Russian couple that had been at the same motel as Beth. The Russian man goes to shoot Beth and the cleaner, Duncan, appears. In a shoot-out the Russian kills Duncan and Duncan kills the Russian woman. Dr. Shepard tells Beth that she is the child of the same adoption service. Beth stabs the doctor to death. The police arrive. Beth is now rejoined with her baby, although she learns that Cameron has been killed in a car accident when he was on the way to the abattoir. Beth visits the grave of her birth mother. She sees a man that the Grave Digger implies is her father and she walks after him.

Notes

This well-directed title features the horror of personality with two antagonists. One is the manager of an adoption business which has pregnant women murdered for their babies. The other is a mother who has lost her child and attempts to murder the others in her group to help her identify which baby is hers. Director James Rabbitts employs the postmodern techniques of expressionist camera angles, point of view, hand-held camerawork, jump cuts, blackouts, and slow and stop motion. He uses relatively restrained bloodletting in the stabbings and shootings. The narrative is unusual in presenting a scenario with mostly female characters. The lead has moments as a warrior which recalls the same in *Lady, Stay Dead, Fair Game, Contagion, Out of the Body, The 13th Floor, Komodo, Ghost Ship, Undead, See No Evil, Black Water, Storm Warning, Slaughtered, Prey, Triangle,* and *Road Train*. The narrative also has the early removal of the male protagonist as a potential savior for the female one.

An opening title tells us that 1979 was six years prior to the advent of DNA testing. This will prove to be pertinent to the climactic reveal of Beth's birth situation, when she learns that she herself was a child adopted through Dr. Shepard's barbaric agency. The ambulance that runs Beth and Cameron's car off the road will be later seen as belonging to the agency. No rationale is given for it to run the car off the road other than to recall other hostile road vehicles seen in *Roadgames* and *Road Train*. The fact of the time being Christmas also plays into the theme of birth, since Christmas is the time of the celebration of the birth of Christ. Although Hank will be presented as opportunistic and sexist, he is not quite the rural cliché of the inbred lowlife that has been seen in other Australian horror titles. The doll's head in the swimming pool is a nice reverberant touch to the idea of dislocated children.

Beth's nightmare will be repeated in the narrative and shown to be properly understood at the climax. It uses a storm as a sign of impending danger, with a baby crying and a river of blood surrounding it, filling up a carving of roman numerals. Initially the nightmare is thought by the couple to express Beth's fear for her new baby based on a former miscarriage, although it will be interpreted to mean other things later. Marvin's duplicity and alliance with Hank is suggested by his excessive force in handling Cameron, and later by his carelessly eating noodles as he drives the police car. Rabbitts has Marvin's speech slowed when he speaks to Cameron after knocking him unconscious to perhaps suggest Cameron's audio point of view.

Beth awakens in the ice bath water no longer pregnant and with a bloodied scar. Her nudity is perhaps exploitative since we wonder why she needed to be topless to be operated on. Why the clothes she dresses in feature the Roman numeral DCVIII is unclear, although we recall the Roman numerals in her nightmare. The expectation of her being stopped is not met when she leaves the room and wanders around the abattoir and then the property. Her failed effort to dig a hole under the perimeter fence is presumably because she is too weak after the operation. Her visions of the other women with the same clothes and surgical scars will be revealed to be real after the blackout that suggests her loss of consciousness. The fact of Veronica being a doctor is both a convenience for the medical problems to come but also part of the professional profile that Dr. Shepard's agency is interested in. When the women hear screams and all investigate, they are the conventional Woman in Peril.

The discovery of the Locker Room Woman is prefigured by the pool of blood they find on the floor and the trail that leads to the locker room. The bloodied woman they find is still alive with her operation stitches having been re-opened, demonstrating that there is a second antagonist, apart from the general one of the abattoir, who kidnapped them and took their babies. Rabbitts intercuts to Cameron and his being hand-cuffed in Marvin's car. Marvin's gun seen from Cameron's point of view creates the expectation, which is met, of him grabbing it to turn the tables on Marvin.

One might think that Marvin would have the training to disarm Cameron, although this is not evident, since he allows Cameron to make him uncuff him and then let himself be handcuffed around a pole. We eventually see that Marvin has been released, though not how. Cameron leaving Marvin in this state does make him a vulnerable figure in the outback, even just from dehydration, although we don't have much empathy for him.

The decision for the four women to split into two pairs would seem to dilute their group power, even though it allows for them to cover more territory in their search of the abattoir. They have an awareness of an antagonist in the location, and the expectation is created for a strike against one of them. The video monitors we see show that the women are being watched by what appears to be the Russian couple from the motel. The video maintenance recalls the same behavior in *Innocent Prey, Razor Eaters* and *Storage*. When Ivy and Allison get separated, Ivy breaks into a refrigerator so she can eat. This is a plot point that is later paid off when Beth gives Duncan candy, but it also leaves Allison alone. This is important since Allison, by not speaking, has presented as the most vulnerable of the four women. It makes her the easiest target and thus the first to be attacked. Allison as a Woman in Peril is further represented by her holding a lamp as she enters a darkened room.

Although we don't learn what this room is, the flies, cockroaches, flickering light and electrified bug catcher are foreboding. It is a bug that gets in her spectacled face that causes her to drop the lamp and the figure of another woman to be seen behind her. The expectation that the woman is Ivy is not met, particularly as this woman holds a knife. Ivy and the two others hearing Allison's scream suggests the strike. Allison also having the Polaroid camera that Ivy has found gets a payoff twice. First, from when Ivy goes to Allison, trips and a photograph is taken. This creates the expectation, not met, of it having been taken by the killer — though who has taken it is never explained. Secondly, supposedly Allison has taken a photograph of the killer before she is killed. We are not shown this, but the photograph presents the killer as having long blonde hair.

We also learn from Veronica that the killer has re-opened Allison's stitches, as was the case with the Locker Room Woman. This is to remove something which we will later learn is the colored baby tag implanted by Shepard. The photograph will also allow Veronica to see that the killer, aka Jane Doe, wears the same Roman numeral tops that the other women wear, and that the sequence of numbers places her one before the others. This means that she is one of the group who appears to have turned against them, for reasons to be explained later.

The narrative returns to Cameron, and we think him silly for returning to the motel. His confrontation with Hank results in blood from Hank's broken nose and his confession of the abattoir location where Beth has been taken. This information confirms Hank's alliance with Shepard's agency, as will be also later be demonstrated when he and Marvin return Beth to Shepard's office. The babies shown in the nursery in cages with colored foot tags makes the connection to the tags being removed from the stitched wounds.

Cages as holding pens for babies is a seemingly further example of Shepard's cruelty. Veronica's offer to perform the operation to remove the women's tags is a reminder of the plot convenience of her being a doctor. Although the only person she will do this for is herself, it is a great plot point to avoid the threat that Jane Doe holds over them.

The two dogs that the women find on their way to the veterinary laboratory where Veronica plans to operate are first seen fighting over what could be food, and the dogs' chase of the women again separates them. The expectation of Ivy to be an easy dog victim is not met; she hides effectively under a metal plate. Rather it is Veronica and Beth who are the easier victims. They fall into a pit, although their pursuing dog does not follow them in. This fall will conveniently make the women lose consciousness.

The narrative returns to Cameron for the last time, as his car hits road spikes and the expectation of his death from the crash is met. What is fascinating about this plot outcome is that Cameron, representing Beth's conventional savior, has been eliminated. The expectation is created that she will not be saved.

Beth's nightmare is repeated when she is unconscious. We can now read the Roman numerals as those she wears. The dream prefigures her current situation with the baby considered to be who she seeks. Veronica awakens her out of the dream, but now she is a weakened figure in light of the fall having dislocated her knee. The expectation is created that the dog is waiting at the top when Beth gets out, which is not met, but also that after Beth leaves Veronica will be vulnerable to the returning dog's attack. That the dogs never return to the narrative is disappointing, although the killer is still present as an antagonist.

When Ivy emerges from her hiding place the expectation is also created that her dog is waiting, but this is not met, and the moo of the cows in pens nearby create a false aural scare. The counter for the turnstile she walks though suggests that the path she has taken is the way to a slaughtering machine. This is another expectation not met, although when the counter shows that something else has passed through the turnstile, the expectation is again created for it to be the dog. The cows mooing also suggest that there is something disturbing around, apart from Ivy, who does not seem to disturb them. Rabbitts uses a shock effect for the reveal of the thing to be the killer when she grabs Ivy and cuts her throat, although the strike features a restrained presentation of the wound.

A return to the video room shows the observers with files on the women and drawing a red line over that of Ivy to show her elimination. "Silent Night" is heard when Beth approaches Duncan's room. The song is shown to come from a record player, apropos for 1979. When she hides and sees Duncan approaching with the body of Ivy, it both tells her of the death and creates the expectation of Duncan as a threat, although we know him not to be the female killer. Duncan discovers Beth in his room by seeing her reflection in a mirror as she sees his reflection in the same mirror. The expectation of his strike against her is not met. We see that he is afraid, perhaps because of his apparent retardation.

Beth becomes the aggressor and is trying to get Duncan's keys off him as her character begins to become a warrior, after she attempts to pacify him with some of the candy Ivy had stolen. The resultant chase and Beth's success in taking Duncan's keys creates the expectation of her escape. Her return to Veronica in the pit also shows Beth's moral strength in spite of her presumed awareness of Veronica being an injured liability.

Beth makes the splint for Veronica, and the expectation is created of the killer being in another car in the junkyard and attacking. Veronica's door being momentarily jammed before she can get out in time is a conventional suspense device. As Veronica attempts to operate on herself in the veterinary laboratory, Rabbitts adds the stress-inducing obstacles of the killer at the door and the lights turned off to make it hardly the ideal surgical environment. When Beth goes to find a light, Veronica's vulnerability is finally paid off. She sees the killer in the reflection of the mirror she uses to see her own stitched area. This is presented as a shock effect and meets the expectation of the killer getting into the laboratory. The killer has time to cut Veronica's throat before Beth returns to attack her. Beth's momentary defeat is enabled by a conveniently placed protruding wall spike on which the killer is impaled, but only after the killer uses the opportunity to attempt to also open Beth's stitches.

The death of Veronica is perhaps the treatment's most empathetic. It raises the question of whether Beth will now attempt to cut open the killer's stitches to see the color of her tag, the same action that the killer has being doing to the other women. It certainly raises the expectation that the killer will strike again to get at Beth, and it is unclear whether Beth sees that the killer has freed herself from the impalement. When Beth sees legs on a floor ahead of her in the bathroom, it is a surprise that they belong to the killer, who is wounded and digs into her own stitches to find the colored tag.

Seemingly too injured to attack Beth, the woman asks her to promise to take her baby with her if she finds it alive. This is a promise we believe that Beth will keep, since she can hardly hold the child responsible for the killer's actions, but one that she does not since she will only later find her own baby. The killer also tries to rationalize her behavior by saying that she was told by Shepard that it was the only way for her to be able to identify her own baby. She shows Beth a photograph of herself with Shepard.

Although the killer woman will die, there is a lack of empathy for her in the face of her having murdered the Locker Room Woman, Allison, Ivy, and Veronica, despite her rationale. Her holding her baby tag in a closed fist creates the expectation that perhaps Beth will have to break her fingers to see the color of the tag. This expectation is not met. The issue of the colored tags is dismissed when we see Beth drop them on the floor when she goes to the nursery and the expectation of the babies no longer being there is met.

We are not shown who approaches Beth since their identity is concealed behind a flashlight that is shined on her. The reappearance of the ambulance from the opening scene creates a bad expectation, as does us seeing Hank and Marvin carrying the unconscious Beth into Shepard's office. The Russian couple in the office aligns them with Shepard as we see Beth chained to the floor. Her having to witness her baby given to the Russians is more of Shepard's cruelty. Shepard's personality is also suggested by the playing of classical music which implies both refinement and perversion. Although the adopting couple is Russian and not German, there is also a Nazi association made with Shepard, Aryan children, and the Lebensborn program.

Beth's triumph as the surviving woman ironically seems to doom her baby to be taken away from her, since Shepard's agency prioritizes the physically strongest. Like all conventional villains, Shepard gets to explain her actions to the protagonist before planning to kill her. The fact that Beth may be shot by the Russian man who is taking her baby is further insult to her humiliation. "This is the only place on earth where adopting parents can evaluate the mother of a prospective child before purchasing it," Shepard tells Beth.

The expectation of her being saved is created when someone appears in the background holding a rifle. The idea that it is Cameron is dismissed when the person is surprisingly revealed to be Duncan. His apparent simpleness allows for both Beth and Shepard to attempt to manipulate him to their advantage. Duncan's seeming mental impairment is an odd component of Shepard's agency, although we never learn where he originated. His repeated false bang of the rifle at the Russian man suggests that perhaps he will not be the problem to Shepard imagined. However, her frustration when he does not obey her command to shoot Beth leads her to say lines that cause him to rebel. She says, "You stupid retard. Do as you're fucking told."

The resultant shooting is full of surprises. Duncan is shot by the Russian man and accidentally shoots the Russian woman. Shepard's anger subverts her desire for Beth to be killed. When Beth uses the keys she had earlier taken from Duncan we wonder why she hadn't used them earlier to free herself. Beth with Duncan's rifle is again a presentation of the mythology of Beth as a female warrior.

Finding the video room, the expectation of Beth's shooting the screens is not met. This is perhaps because she is aware of wasting bullets. Her finding her crying baby alone is a surprise and thought to be perhaps a trap. However, Shepard appears without apparent physical weaponry, although she presumably thinks that telling Beth of her origin is psychological weaponry. When Shepard tells Beth that she was a child adopted through the agency, Beth's nightmare is seen for the third and last time. It is now read as Beth's memory of herself, although with the convention of being able to see her own self in memory.

The expectation of Beth shooting Shepard is not met; the gun is out of bullets, a conventional suspense use. Beth's attack of Shepard results in her stabbing her with the keys. This recalls the stitched wounds of the other pregnant women. Rabbitts' use of an angelic choir for Shepard's demise is perhaps a bit much. During Beth's attack she has flashback memories of the dead women presumably to remind us of her and our loss. When we see Beth with her baby we wonder how safe she is when we assume that Hank and Marvin are still around as threats. However, the sight of another ambulance and police car confirm that she is safe. A police officer gives her Cameron's wallet to verify his death. Beth's victory is therefore clouded with the sadness of having lost her fiancé.

An epilogue shows Beth now with darker and shorter hair, presumably to convey the passage of time, at a cemetery. The headstone of Lydia Hayes she attends is presumably that of her biological mother. The man she passes before she reaches the headstone is given a payoff when the Grave Digger tells her that he has a missing wife. Beth's intention to follow him as her biological father happens after she rejects the offer of the Grave Digger for a ride, presumably now gunshy of accepting any offers from strangers.

James Rabbitts made his feature film debut with *The Clinic* and has not made another Australian horror title to date. Neither has producer Samuel Pinczewski, co-producer Dennis Kiely, or executive producer Bob Marcs. It is the only Australian horror title to be made by the production companies Accelerator Films, Great Southern Land Entertainment, and RMB Productions. Executive producer Jonathan Shteinman previously produced *Like Minds* and the documentary *Not Quite Hollywood*.

Tabrett Bethell made her film debut in *The Clinic* and went on to the film supporting role and television. Freya Stafford began her career in television and made her film debut in a supporting role in the comic crime thriller *Gettin' Square* (2003). She would do more television and film supporting roles and after *The Clinic*.

British born Andy Whitfield also began his career in television and made his film debut as the title character in action fantasy *Gabriel* (2007). He would appear in more television prior to and after *The Clinic*. Clare Bowen also began in television and made her film debut in a supporting part in *The Combination* (2009). She would appear in more television, and after *The Clinic* essayed the lead in the thriller *10 Days to Die* (2010).

Marshall Napier was born in New Zealand and began his career in New Zealand television. He made his film debut in a minor role in action comedy *Goodbye Pork Pie* (1981) and appeared in film supporting roles and television prior to and after *The Clinic*. He essayed the rare film lead in *Lie of the Land* (1985). Liz Alexander is another actor to have started her career in television; her film debut was a minor role in the family adventure *Ride a Wild Pony* (1975). She appeared in more television and film supporting roles prior to *The Clinic*, essaying the lead in the thriller *The Killing of Angel Street* (1981). *The Clinic* is the actress' last title to date.

Sophie Lowe also began her career in television and made her feature film debut in a supporting role in the mystery *Beautiful Kate* (2009). She continued in television and supporting film roles. After *The Clinic* she appeared in the Australian horror movie *Road Train*. Boris Brkic started acting in television and made his film debut in a supporting role in the comic crime thriller *Death in Brunswick*

(1991). He would continued in television and film supporting roles, including *Ghost Ship* and *Dying Breed*. *The Clinic* is his last title to date.

Marcel Bracks made his film debut in a minor role in the comedy *Doing Time for Patsy Cline* (1997), and has appeared in television and film shorts prior to *The Clinic*, his last title to date. Adrienne Pickering also began her career in television and made her film debut in a minor role in the romance *Candy* (2006). She appeared in more television and film supporting parts, and after *The Clinic* was seen in the Australian horror title *The Reef*.

RELEASE

Screened in the United States on November 4, 2009, at the American Film Market and on October 10, 2010, at the ScreamFest Horror Film Festival; no wide feature release apparent. Screened in Australia on July 25, 2010, at the Melbourne International Festival, with the wide release date unknown. The DVD tagline is "The truth lies within."

REVIEWS

"Doesn't rely on gore or torture, but manages to present a movie simply brimming with intent and intelligence.... Ozploitation is alive and well in this excellent thriller by James Rabbits."—Jeff Ritchie, *ScaryMinds*

"A hackneyed, sub-par genre exercise, painfully stuck in the rut of its slowly capitulating narrative.... Everything that emanates from these characters' mouths is compromised by the exasperating familiarity of it all. I have to admit, however, that [it's] a devilishly clever and twisted, if ludicrous, idea at heart."—David O'Connell, *Screen Fanatic*, August 19, 2010

"Just when I thought I'd had enough of 'let's tie a woman up and do stuff to her' movies, along comes *The Clinic*, which gives the sub-genre a breath of fresh air, thanks to a unique scenario, a decent twist, and way above average technical and acting qualities."—*Horror Movie a Day*, October 10, 2010

"A better than average thriller that works on more levels than it fails. There is enough tone and competent work behind the camera to suggest that Rabbitts has some real talent for the genre.... [It] might not scare the hell out of anyone but it makes for some interesting entertainment."—Greg Roberts, *KillerReviews*

"A blatant steal of so many that have gone before it. Tosh and nonsense, and poorly presented to boot."—Colin Harris, *Pick 'n' Mix Flix*

"[It] isn't a bad watch at all. It's a bit out there concept wise and it does tend to stretch the levels of believability to near breaking points on occasion ... if not on all occasions, but ultimately we found it to be a pretty decent thriller."—Christopher Armstead, *Film Critics United*

DVD

Released in Australia by Paramount Pictures on February 17, 2011.

Needle

Lightning Entertainment/ Filmscope Entertainment, 2010

CREDITS: *Director:* John V. Soto; *Screenplay:* John V. Soto, Anthony Egan; *Producer:* Deirdre Kitcher; *Associate Producers:* Kane Manera, Steve Padbury, Ron Walter; *Executive Producers:* Sean Baguley, Ray Meadowcroft, John Lee; *Photography:* Stephen Windon; *Editor:* Jason Ballantine; *Music:* Jamie Blanks; *Production Design:* Nigel Devenport; *Costumes:* Susi Rigg; *Sound:* Glen Dillon; *Makeup/Hair:* Peta Hastings. Color, 85 minutes. Filmed in Swanbourne, South Perth, and the University of Western Australia in Crawley, Perth, Western Australia.

SONGS: "Long Strong Diamond" (Buchen, Fraser, Braha, Stone), Baggsmen; "Reaction" (Bonzio, Mario Williams, Savell), Dead Letter Circus; "Try It" (Sharred, Stevens, Xavier), Infusion; "Sunshine City" (Kurjakovich, Harrison), The Larys.

CAST: Michael Dorman (Ben Rutherford); Travis Fimmel (Marcus Rutherford); Jessica Marais (Kandi Shaw); Tahyna Tozzi (Mary Matthews); Trilby Glover (Isabel Du Pont); Khan Chittenden (Jed); Luke Carroll (Nelson); Nathaniel Buzolic (Ryan Simmons); John Jarratt (Paul the Coroner); Jane Badler (Professor Banyon); Ben Mendelsohn (Detective Meares); Michael Loney (Robert Shaw); James Hagan (Samuel Rutherford); Malcolm Kennard (Detective Roddick); Murray Bartlett (Tony Martin); Quinton George (Mr. Joshua); Caroline McKenzie (Eliza Louise Shaw); Sam Longley (Basketball Coach); Igor Sas (Dr. Halmany); Samantha Murray (Nurse); Louise Baguley (Nurse Assistant); Olivia Ledger (Young Kandi); Rhian Glossop, Kylie Jones, Mathew Kuhn (Paramedics); Jon Doust (Priest); Vivienne Garrett (Mrs.

Symonds); Simon Dagnall (Mr. Symonds); Charlotte Devenport (Killer's Hands); Sean Baguley, Dave Woolfden, Eric Charles, Dominik Pestkowski, Damien Hicks, Ryan Marriott, Scott Bruce, Shane Parsons, Glen Spark, Rob Towner, Sally Towner, Tni Lena, John Warr, Sybil Culloton, Rick Rowley (Police Officers); Jason Peterson, Simon Winter, Troy York, Lachlan Lewis, Marc Sputore, Ashleigh Sarris (Forensic Officers); Simon Baguley (Store Attendant).

Synopsis

Ten years ago art dealer Robert Shaw is telephoned by his business partner, Samuel Rutherford, and accused of stealing from him. Shaw is mysteriously punctured and killed by the 18th century voodoo machine that is held by Rutherford and later known as "Le vaudou mort." In the present day, Rutherford has recently died. He has bequeathed the machine to his son. Ben is an archeology student at St. Mary's College in Brisbane, Australia. A photograph is taken of Ben with his friends and the machine. Images from the photograph, wax and the blood of the unidentified person who has stolen the machine from Ben is used to create victims of the thief.

Ryan, Nelson, and Isabel are burned by lightning and cut from the needle that cuts into the voodoo doll, and die. Ben's estranged half-brother Marcus has sailed into town. He has taken a job as a police forensic photographer and together the brothers attempt to solve the murders. Marcus takes Ben to the house where Shaw had lived and died. He and Ben learn that Ben's supposed friend Kandi is actually the daughter of Shaw and the person who has been conducting the voodoo killings. She overpowers Marcus and attempts to make his girlfriend, Mary, the next victim. She is stopped from killing Mary and Ben when Mary and Marcus use the machine against Kandi, who dies. One month later Marcus and Ben throw the machine into the sea when they are out sailing Marcus's boat.

Notes

This title uses a mix of the themes of the horror of personality and the malevolent supernatural being, since the antagonist here uses the supernatural powers of voodoo to indirectly kill her victims. Director John V. Soto employs the postmodern techniques of expressionist camera angles, blackouts, point of view and slow motion. There is bloodletting for the attacks which combine skin cutting via the needle used by the killer on a voodoo wax doll and lightning strikes which are said to burn the body from within. Soto supplies suspense with the created expectations of the strikes as well as two other scenes where locations are investigated. The constant score has enough variations to not make it obtrusive. However, Soto is more successful with the action scenes than with those of exposition, which read as dull and enervated. No plot rationale is provided for why the leading character is an American, which suggests a commercial consideration made for the international marketing of the film. Additionally, the performance of Travis Fimmel is troublesome, given his mannered methodisms.

The prologue of the death of Shaw lets us hear the American accent of Rutherford, which will translate to Ben and Marcus. We also see the lightning and inexplicable voodoo cut into Shaw's torso that will kill him, with the excess of blood from the strike an indication of the excess Soto will use in the future strikes. While he only suggests the machine via shots of the turning interior gears, this will allow for a progressive demonstration of the killer's technique since more is revealed in each strike as to how the machine works. The fact that it conveys the power to kill is perhaps a contrivance aligned to the assumption in the belief in voodoo that the narrative assumes, although how the lightning fits in with the transposed cuts by the needle onto the body of the victim is not explained.

The plot point of Isabel being French gets a joke in the fact that she is unable to translate "Le vaudou mort." Her lesbianism and relationship with Kandi seems to have been added for heterosexual titillation since we see how the sight of the women kissing pleases the three male friends and later Marcus. Kandi's implied role as the more passive lesbian, who doesn't want her parents to meet her lover, also prefigures Kandi's murder of Isabel as someone she describes as more Ben's friend than hers in the climax. The identity of Kandi as the killer is prefigured by her asking Nelson, the one who takes the photograph of the group, for a copy.

The killings of Ryan, Nelson and Isabel are all prefigured by the feeding of the machine their heads from the photograph and blood from the killer, as well the melting of candle wax to make a new doll. The hands of the person performing these acts are gloved, so as not to reveal the person's identity. The expectation of the strikes are all created by this device, with the first one on Ryan also featuring his running on a football field. A series of lights he passes explodes by the lightning hits, and his death is suggested by the killer's candle being blown out. When Marcus arrives to photograph Ryan's corpse, the flash cuts suggest both the lightning strikes and the flash of his camera, and provide shock displays of Ryan's bloodied state.

The idea that Nelson, as the person who took the photograph, was the killer is nullified when he is the next victim. The expectation that he will fall from the interior climbing-wall he scales is an expectation not met. Nelson claims that he can hear the sounds of the machine's gears. These cannot be heard by Tony Martin, who is the trainer with him, and it suggests that Nelson has more awareness than Ryan had, although this awareness will still not save him. The voodoo doll's arms and legs being broken off is a variation of the cuts made on Ryan, although Nelson also gets cut. Soto shows one arm of Nelson's becoming detached but spares us the sight of his second arm and his legs being detached.

While Ben has no apparent motive to be the killer, despite his claims that the machine has been stolen from him, the practical joke he played on Professor Banyon in her class does seem to present him as a duplicitous character. Marcus has been estranged from Ben because he blames him for the unexplained death of their father after Marcus and Samuel had supposedly argued. This presents him as another possible suspect, although the fact of him being the forensic photographer makes it seem less likely. The fact of Marcus being Ben's half-brother and thereby looking nothing like him can also be seen to present Marcus as suspicious. The already mentioned performance of Fimmel as Marcus unintentionally adds to the character's shiftiness. Professor Banyon and Mary are also proffered as potential suspects. Both of them are given reasons to dislike Ben in light of the practical joke against the professor and his rejection of Mary's romantic interest. While all these theories will prove to be unfounded when the true killer is revealed, the fact that more than person could be considered as the killer is perhaps a sign of the narrative having some density.

When Professor Banyon brings in Dr. Halmany to speak to Ben about the machine's origins, he supplies some Gothic resonance to the narrative. What was previously considered a stage prop is now the vehicle for supernatural power as a "tool for revenge." As Halmany, Igor Sas is one of a number of the supporting actors, like Jane Badler's Banyon and

Poster for *Needle* (2010).

John Jarratt's Paul the Coroner, who is clearly superior in screen charisma than the actors playing the younger protagonists. An exception is Jessica Marais as Kandi, who will have her moment in the film's climax.

The murder of Isabel is prefigured by the footage of her as she swims in her pool and the voodoo machine's action. Soto does not make the choice of exploiting the actress's nudity in the context as others may have done. Isabel being blinded by the killer's voodoo is another variation on her previous modus operandi. One has to wonder whether the fact of her being a lesbian and perhaps the too-insistent lover of Kandi allows for the narrative's most cruel attack.

Marcus and Ben go to visit Eliza Shaw at the Waterford Mental Institution, and all the trouble they have taken in getting in to see her and the gothic potential of the situation is wasted when they leave after speaking to her so briefly. There is a presumably unintentional laugh in Ben's turning away to retch when he sees Isabel's wounded face. The visit to Professor Banyon's office comes with the created expectation of her death from the askew wall hanging and blood seen before her body is discovered. This is an expectation met, despite the death not being prefigured by the killer's voodoo technique. Although no one admits to killing the Professor, and she isn't included in Kandi's death montage of victims, it is still assumed that Kandi is her killer. Soto supplies a fake scare in Marcus turning around a chair that wears a hooded jacket as if it is the Professor, and her body is revealed from the inadvertent light of Marcus' flashlight that he puts down to sit at her desk.

For the climax, Soto separates Marcus and Bill so that they can have different discoveries. Ben's behavior of not going with Marcus into Shaw's house is judged as cowardly by him. Marcus will find the voodoo machine but be knocked unconscious by Kandi. Ben discovers Jed's bloodied corpse in a shock effect. Jed's killing is, like that of Banyon, not prefigured by the voodoo machine and lightning. Jed being in the car with Kandi prior is enough of a link to suggest that she has killed him. Ben enters the house after being scared by the discovery and wanting to find Marcus. He becomes the Man in Peril by investigating the sound of a closing door. The reveal of the blonde Kandi as the killer comes with a flashback with her as a brunette child. Her attempt to kill Mary with the machine's technique while the bound Mary is in the same room allows for more reveal of how the machine works.

Kandi's line to Ben, "Your pain is like sweet nectar to me," is a classic protagonist taunt. Regrettably, she is also saddled with the howler, "The sins of the father are visited on the son." Her physical attacks on Marcus and Ben present her as the perverse kind of female warrior. Her willingness to let Mary untie Marcus and her not cutting Ben's throat when she has the chance are plot contrivances. This is made worse by the fact that she doesn't take him outside the house for any specific reason. It is also aligned to the timing that is needed for Mary and Marcus to use the machine against Kandi — in a great narrative twist — while she delays killing Ben.

Soto inter-cuts between the two situations to up the tension, and then gives Kandi a moment of vulnerability when she is struck. The black-and-white flashbacks that serve as reminders of the victims are not presented with any point of view. The ongoing plot point of Mary's rejection by Ben is finally paid off when he accepts a kiss from her after Kandi is killed and Mary has effectively saved his life.

This plot point is continued, albeit less directly. We hear Ben telling her on his cell phone that he is headed back to her after he and Marcus dispose of the machine by throwing it into the sea. They do not destroy it, to spare themselves the curse that would be set on them, but rather put it somewhere safe, creating the potential for a film sequel. Ben says, "I never want to see that thing again."

John V. Soto had previously made *Crush*, and *Needle* is his last title to date. Producer Deidre Kitcher previously produced *Crush*. The film is the only one to be produced by associate producer Kane Manera, who had acted in *Crush*, executive producer Sean Baguley, and the production company Filmscope Entertainment. Michael Dorman had previously appeared in *Acolytes*, *Triangle*, and *Daybreakers*, and he later worked in film supporting roles and on television. Travis Fimmel began his career in television and made his film debut in the lead role in the thriller *Restraint* (2008), his only leading film role to date. He has otherwise appeared in film supporting roles and been seen on television. Jessica Marais was born in South Africa and made her film debut in a supporting role in the sports drama *Two Fists, One Heart* (2008). She otherwise has been seen in television.

Tahyna Tozzi is another actor to have started her career in television; she made her film debut in a supporting role in the thriller *Beautiful* (2009). She has been otherwise seen in film supporting roles and on television. Trilby Glover made her film debut in a minor role in the family adventure *Son of the Mask* (2005) and has been seen in other film supporting roles and television. Khan Chittenden also began his career in television and made his film debut in a supporting role in *Caterpillar Wish* (2006).

As well as appearing in television and more film supporting parts, he essayed the lead in *West* (2007) which has been his only leading film role to date.

Luke Carroll also began in television and made his film debut in a minor role in the comedy *Dallas Doll* (1994). He followed this with more television and film supporting roles, essaying the lead in the comedy *Stone Bros.* (2009). *Needle* is his last title to date. Nathaniel Buzolic is another actor to have started in television and made his film debut as the title character but not top-billed in the crime mystery *Offing David* (2008). After *Needle* he would be seen in more television. John Jarratt had previously appeared in *Rogue*.

Release

The taglines include "Ten Suspects. Six Clues. One Killer," "Someone is killing the students at Saint Mary's College," "Your fate has been chosen" and "Will make your skin crawl." Screened at the Oz Film Festival in Australia on August 27, 2010, and the ScreamFest Horror Film Festival in the United States on October 9, 2010. No apparent wide release in either country.

Reviews

"A reasonably slick looking low budget horror that manages to hold the interest and tease the brain a little as you bounce from suspect to suspect.... The finale lets it down a little, generic is its style, but manages to entertain thanks to a couple of good performances and an attention grabbing plot."—Kyle Scott, *The Horror Hotel*, June 15, 2011

"An interesting well executed thriller, with plenty of twists and turns to entertain horror fans. Mystery is an element which seems almost inherent to the film and while the killer can be identified about halfway through the film; the questioning and double guessing of the killer's identity is what is important."—Michael Allen, *Associated Content*, December 6, 2010

"It's fairly light on gore and at times it evokes comparisons to the much maligned 90s era of serial killer flicks. If you're willing to look past these elements, however, you'll find an above average slasher with a refreshingly original plot device."—Alex Scott-Webster, *KillerFilm*, October 20, 2010

"Soto squanders any promise the film might have had with some leaden handling and a plot which is nowhere near as clever or fiendish as it seems to think it is.... Simply lifeless throughout, with very little to offer even the least demanding of genre fans."—James Mudge, *Beyond Hollywood*, May 31, 2011

"Starts strongly with the first few deaths being satisfyingly brutal and gruesome, but loses its way towards the second half. When the killer is finally revealed, and the reasons for the revenge, you probably won't care particularly. And neither did I, but then I also didn't feel too short-changed as, despite its flaws."—Daniel Benson, *Horror Talk*, June 24 2011

"Very much an old-school slasher movie, but by using the element of voodoo it somehow revitalises the much-maligned genre, making it feel fresh and new at the same time. And like all good slasher should, the end of the film leaves it wide open for a sequel, which I'd definitely see."—Phil Wheat, *Blogomatic3000*

DVD

Released by High Fliers on June 11, 2011, in Britain but not available in the United States or Australia.

The Reef

Prodigy Movies, 2010 [aka *Shark Attack*]

CREDITS: *Screenplay/Producer/Director:* Michael Traucki; *Producer:* Michael Robertson; *Co-Producer:* Tiare Tomaszewski; *Associate Producer:* Dean Toovey; *Executive Producers:* Michael Baskin, Janine Pierce; *Co-Executive Producers:* Richard S. Guardian, Rich Goldberg; *Photography:* Daniel Ardilley; *Editor:* Peter Crombie; *Music:* Rafael May; *Production Design:* Adam Head; *Sound:* John O'Connell; *Costumes:* Jenni Sant; *Makeup/Hair:* Sheldon Wade. Color, 84 minutes. Filmed on location at Port Lincoln, South Australia and Bowen, Hervey Bay and Lady Elliot Island, Queensland.

CAST: Damian Walshe-Howling (Luke); Zoe Naylor (Kate); Adrienne Pickering (Suzie); Gyton Grantley (Matt); Kieran Darcy-Smith (Wazza, aka Warren); Mark Simpson (Shane).

Synopsis

Queensland international boat deliverer Luke goes on a yachting trip from Fisherman's Wharf to the Signet Reef. He is accompanied by his Sydney friend Matt, Matt's girlfriend Suzie and sister, Kate, who is also Luke's ex-girlfriend. Leaving the island, the yacht scrapes against a reef and capsizes. Since there is a hole in the bottom of the yacht, Luke decides the best strategy is to swim for land. Matt and Suzie agree to go with him. Crew member Warren and Kate decide to stay with the upturned yacht. When she sees the three swimming away, Kate changes her mind and joins them.

The group finds in the water a large dead turtle that apparently was attacked by a shark. A shark appears and attacks Matt, who separates from the others to retrieve his floating board. The three watch Matt die from a bitten off leg and leave his corpse behind. Although it seems that the shark returns that night, it does not attack until the next day after the group has spotted a large reef ahead of them. Suzie is taken by the shark. After Kate and Luke reach the reef, he is taken when Kate is unable to lift him out of the water in time. A title card reports that Kate was rescued the next day by a passing fishing boat. No remains of Warren and the yacht were ever found.

NOTES

This low-budget title features the theme of the horror of personality in the form of a great white shark. It is not considered a malevolent supernatural being since its killings are simply the feeding of a natural sea creature. Director Michael Traucki employs the postmodern techniques of point of view, jump cuts, hand-held camerawork and slow motion, and he uses shock effects. He creates suspense even if his score is obtrusive. The narrative is simple with a boat trip that goes askew, recalling *Triangle*. While not all created expectations are met, the succession of victims follows a logical and sometimes moral order.

The narrative's presentation of the soap opera of the reunion of Luke and Kate is redeemed by the yacht hitting the reef after fifteen minutes as the first obstacle. The Luke-Kate coupling is given a shock effect when he appears behind her under water and because it prefigures them as the last survivors. The raft that hits the bottom of the sea is another shock effect that prefigures the yacht doing the same. It also provides a reason why the raft cannot be an alternate vessel once the yacht is no longer seaworthy. After the capsizing, Matt's seeming disappearance and then his apparent entrapment in a cabin are both created expectations of his demise that are not met. However, they do prefigure Matt as the shark's first victim.

The decision to leave the boat is pitted against the idea that the current will make it drift out to sea. This is even if it stays afloat, which Luke says is unlikely. The risk of dying of dehydration accompanies his suggestion of swimming for land. When Luke and Matt go underwater to search for items in the boat, the expectation is again created of a strike. The thumping heard from the others by Luke and their calls of "Get out" and "Shark" add to this. However, the expectation is not met, and this expectation dismissed is also met when Luke goes down again to recover the distress signal EPIRB and the thumping he hears is revealed to be the container knocking against a door. Another shock effect is used when a shark is expected but Luke finds a small fish instead.

Another expectation not met occurs with Kate's change of mind about staying with the yacht. This one is perhaps less a surprise, given the romantic scenario established between her and Luke. Since Warren has warned that the suits that the others wear make them resemble seals and his fear of joining the others is based on a fear of sharks, the narrative then allows Traucki to create suspense from the idea that a shark will eventually appear to strike. This expectation is played by movement in the water and then the appearance of the dead turtle which Matt finds has been attacked, in another shock reveal. The fact that Matt goes ahead of the others to look at the turtle also prefigures his death, which is enabled by his leaving the others to retrieve his float board.

The narrative's return to Warren is a surprise. It is the only time it does so, to present the splashing around the yacht caused by a shark whose fin we see above the water line. This seems enough to suggest that his fate is sealed because the yacht will sink. It is also possible, given the speed at which the others travel, that the shark that would kill Warren would also be the same one to menace them. Luke uses goggles to look under water for any sharks; this repeated device and shots of the swimmers can be read as the shark's point of view. However, Traucki does not use a subjective camera for the shark's advance.

Luke's view of the shark underwater and then our view of the fin above water are paid off by a shock moment when the shark emerges next to the four and passes them. Matt's strike results in the first bloodletting. His death oddly evokes empathy more for Kate's distress than Matt himself. When Suzie yells at Luke, blaming him for the predicament, it signals her as the next victim as a moral stance. The splashing around the three at night creates an expectation of a strike that is not met. Traucki uses a blackout after the splashing for ambiguity, although the next morning will show that the three have survived.

The large protruding reef seen ahead creates the expectation of their escape from the shark. We only see one shark, so we presume that it has a private agenda or is very, very hungry. The three small reefs that the swimmers will rest on out of the water operate as little sanctuaries. An argument could be made that the time spent on them, despite it providing physical rest, delays the three getting to the safer larger reef and ultimately costs two lives.

The three stopping when they see a fin which Luke wrongly thinks to be that of a dolphin also evokes the same feeling that they are wasting time. Suzie's resultant strike by the shark is presented by suggestion rather than with literal visualization. However, the shark returning to take Suzie, now in a pool of blood, gets a visual payoff when she disappears under water as if she has been pulled under by the shark. The fact that the same shark takes Suzie after having eaten Matt the day before is a time line that is perhaps more believable than it's later taking Luke, although this last strike has a perversity attached to it.

When Luke goes to retrieve his float board, the same expectation of a strike that was made against Matt is created but not met. Katie's bloodied foot, presumably from the climbing on the small reefs, is only paid off by the bandage applied by Luke later being shown to drop off in the climactic swim to the big reef. Their mutual declarations of "I love you" are the resolution of the doubt over the issue raised in the early scene on Signet Reef. This is surely a case of adversity clarifying one's emotions, and they have a funny exchange over the issue of swimming beyond the third small reef to get to the big one:

LUKE: You ready?
KATE: No.
LUKE: Me neither. Let's go.

This exchange also loads the anticipation of both of them surviving the swim, which the narrative will not provide a happy answer to. The shark shown under water creates the expectation of its third strike. Luke uses generosity to help Kate climb up the slippery large reef first, but she is not physically strong enough to help him out of the water in time before the shark arrives to take him.

Although a title card tells us that Kate is to be rescued the next day, the narrative's tone is affected by the death of Luke, who is presented as the protagonist. Perhaps we are to agree with Suzie after all in thinking that the predicament is to be blamed on him and therefore he deserves to die as a consequence. In spite of Kate's

Poster for *The Reef* (2010).

survival, the death of the narrative protagonist gives the film a downbeat denouement.

In the DVD making-of featurette "Shooting with Sharks," Traucki tells how the real shark footage demanded a change in narrative to accommodate what had been captured. He had discovered what is said to be a true story of three people in the sea who had been stalked by a shark for the basis of his screenplay in a book about sharks.

Director Andrew Traucki previously made *Black Water* and has not made another Australian horror title to date. Producer Michael Robertson and the production company Prodigy Movies made *Black Water* and later the Australian horror movie *Road Train*. *The Reef* is the only Australian horror film made to date by associate producer Dean Toovey.

Damian Walshe-Howling began his career in television and made his film debut in a supporting role in *A Wreck, a Tangle* (2000). He appeared in more television and film supporting roles prior to and after *The Reef*, his only lead film role to date. Zoe Naylor also began her career in television and made her film debut in a supporting role in the thriller *The Book of Revelation* (2006). She has been seen in more television; *The Reef* is her last title to date.

Adrienne Pickering previously appeared in *The Clinic* and after *The Reef* was seen in television. Gyton Grantley made his feature film debut in a supporting role in the comedy *Blurred* (2002) and followed up with television and film supporting roles.

RELEASE

Screened at the Cannes Film Festival on May 17, 2010, and wide release in Australia on March 17, 2011. No release in the United States to date. The DVD tagline was "Pray you drown first."

REVIEWS

"The characters aren't all that interesting or well developed. Fortunately, the lengthy scenes in which the four frightened swimmers are menaced by a white pointer are chillingly well handled. The film scores high marks on the suspense meter, but flounders in the human relationship department despite perfectly good performances from all concerned."— David Stratton, *At the Movies*, March 16, 2011

"The early scenes hamper the film a little bit because the characters are not well established. If more time had been spent building those up there would have been more investment in the survival of them once they get in the water. But once that journey happens it is tremendously effective."— Margaret Pomeranz, *At the Movies*, March 16, 2011

"Traucki's cast excels at various aspects of fear, and the editing is seamlessly done. Traucki has kept it simple. It's short, sharp and to the point, and the careful, measured use of shark footage is exemplary."— Andrew L. Urban, *Urban Cinefile*

"An engaging thriller where the viewer can't help but sympathise with the protagonists. The performances are all very solid. Undeniably the best shark movie since Jaws."— Devon Bertsch, *Digital Retribution*, March 21, 2011

"The characters are convincingly developed, likeable and well acted so that we genuinely feel concern for them. The Australian tourist industry will hate it but *The Reef* is an extremely effective watery horror/thriller."— Thomas Caldwell, *Cinema Autopsy*

"If anything in particular actually lets *The Reef* down, it would have to be the rather abrupt and unsatisfying ending, and the way in which it completely abandons the one character that chooses to stay with the boat. [But] foibles aside, it is ultimately a successful survival tale."— Gareth Jones, *Dread Central*, January 18, 2011

DVD

Released in the United Kingdom by Momentum Pictures on January 24, 2011. No DVD release in the United States or Australia to date.

Road Train

Prodigy Movies, 2010 [aka *Road Kill*]

CREDITS: *Director:* Dean Francis; *Producer:* Michael Robertson; *Executive Producers:* Michael Baskin, Janine Pearce; *Screenplay:* Clive Hopkins; *Photography:* Carl Robertson; *Editor:* Rodrigo Balart; *Music and Electronic Tonalities:* Rafael May; *Production Design:* Ian Jobson; *Makeup/Hair/Special Effects:* Tracy Phillpot; *Costumes:* Heather Wallace; *Visual Effects:* David Nerlich; *Sound:* Will Sheridan. Color, 87 minutes. Filmed on location in the Hawker District of the Flinders Ranges, South Australia, April to June 2009.

SONGS: "Kiss You Till You Die" (Xebedie, Rafael May); Xebedie "Whipping Horse" (Dominic McDonald, Rafael May), Dominic McDonald; "A Runner" (Sophie Lowe), Sophie Lowe.

CAST: Xavier Samuel (Marcus); Bob Morley (Craig); Georgina Haig (Liz); Sophie Lowe (Nina); David Argue (Psycho, aka Frank).

Synopsis

Four friends are on an outback camping holiday. They decide to race their car with a road train — a haul truck — on the highway. The truck runs them off the road and the driver, Craig, is the only one of the four to be seriously injured. The truck is parked close to the accident. The four go to it and find it abandoned. When Psycho, the presumed driver, returns firing a gun at them, they take the truck from him. Sleep overwhelms the four in the truck's cabin, including Marcus, who is driving. They awaken to see that the truck has strayed off the highway onto a dirt road embankment. Thinking they are unable to turn the truck around, Marcus and his girlfriend, Liz, go for a walk. The estranged couple argues over the fact that Liz had slept with Craig, who is Marcus' best friend. She leaves Marcus to look for help. Liz finds a rundown shack while Psycho finds Marcus. Liz returns to the truck. She attempts to turn it around with Nina, after she fails to find the missing Craig, who has ventured into the back of one of the haul trailers.

Marcus returns, having shot Psycho with his own gun, and attacks the girls, who overpower him and tie him to the truck. Craig appears rejuvenated and unties Marcus, but only so that he can overpower him. Craig makes Marcus' head get crushed under the oncoming wheel of the truck. Craig tells Liz that he wants to be with her and takes her to the back of the trailer. He also lures Nina there, where she sees a machine that breaks down bodies so that blood can run the truck. She locks Craig in the trailer. He escapes and together he and Liz attempt to overpower Nina in the cabin as she is driving. She is unable to stop the truck from crashing into a car with a caravan (travel trailer), but pushes out Liz, who dies on the road. Craig takes Liz's body into the trailer to be processed, as has Marcus'. He also tries to push Nina into the machine but she escapes. He chases her in woods. She shoots him with the Psycho's gun she has kept in her bag. Nina sees people drive the truck away. She is left among the ruins of the smashed caravan car, as the truck drives on with its new victims.

Notes

This title shot on digital camera features the theme of the malevolent supernatural being in the form of a haul truck that is supposedly possessed by evil spirits and possesses nearly all those that drive it. Director Dean Francis employs the postmodern techniques of point of view, slow and fast motion, jump cuts, expressionist camera angles and hand-held camerawork, blackouts, CGI and optical effects, and an obtrusive score. His treatment cannot save a narrative that overwhelms us with contrivance so that the audience loses interest in the protagonists. There is some bloodletting and gore. A head is crushed under the truck's wheel, and a machine processes body parts for blood to empower the truck. A surprisingly graphic sex scene opens the film. However, while this is some initial suspense, created expectations are met and the pleasingly swift entry into conflict soon gives way to disbelief and boredom.

The film is unusual in its saving the credits until the end. The opening sex scene between Craig and Nina is more graphic than the conventional Australian horror sex scene. The narrative provides a parallel between Liz hearing the sex and making an advance to Marcus, which is rejected presumably in favor of sleep. It is only a third way into the narrative that we learn of Liz's indiscretion with Craig as perhaps the real reason for Marcus' rejection. The car of the protagonists being rammed by the truck is introduced. It creates the narrative expectation of a conflict similar to the made-for-television mystery thriller *Duel* (1971). Here, too, the driver of the truck is not seen, at least not driving the truck. This makes the plot being about the truck and not the driver as the antagonist a surprise. It perhaps rationalizes why Psycho as the driver is left behind in the narrative so quickly for the time being.

Craig being the one who is hurt the worst from the car crash seems appropriate, given that he was driving the car and had provoked the truck against the wishes of the others after they are first rammed. The severity of Craig's injuries will become a plot point. There is the assumption that they will kill him, and the fact that he is cured by the truck alludes to its supernatural powers. The blood from Craig's wound is the first blood in the treatment, although the others seem to have bruises and scratches as well. The truck having stopped near the car crash creates the expectation that perhaps the driver has not finished with them. Although we hear Psycho shooting his gun in the distance, we never learn specifically why he has stopped the truck.

When Marcus and Liz investigate the truck there is suspense from the expectation of the driver being close. Francis uses a shock effect for Liz seeing boots which are revealed to belong to Marcus, although we think surely she has seen them before. There is another shock effect, though less successful, when the camera advances on Liz, who has her back to us, and a hand touches her shoulder. This is revealed to be that of either Craig or Nina. The fact that neither speak in their approach is following genre conventions.

The truck's hood ornament of three dogs barking is a symbol that will be repeated as a vision of three live dogs with red eyes barking. Craig's studying it is shown to be so intense, with extreme close-ups of his eyes and mouth, that Nina's saying his name is muted. It follows that Craig's fascination with the ornament, and his wound, should make him the most possessed of the group and the narrative's main antagonist as the tool of the evil truck. In the director's commentary on the DVD, Francis says that the ornament is meant to reference Cerberus, the mythical three-headed dog that guards the gates of hell.

Francis uses superimpositions for Marcus's drowsiness in driving the truck, with a shot of him over the point of view of the road. The vision also includes the three red-eyed dogs. Francis supplies a beautiful scenic shot after the truck stops of a daytime rainbow and clouds over hills. This adds to the opening panoramic opening shot of the desert at dawn and a later shot of scenery that resembles a painting in its beauty.

Craig's illness creates visions of the three red-eyed dogs, maggots and red storm clouds juxtaposed with Nina's attempts to create a fire to signal an overhead plane. The narrative also separating Marcus and Liz from these two requires Francis to cross-cut between their fates. Even though they each have their dramas, it tends to dilute the overall tension. Craig reaching into the red truck cabin — the red color design recalls that in *Roadgames*— to find a key is a contrivance. This is particularly as the gore apparent from the interior suggests the blood machine; it's hard to see where a key could be easily stored.

However, the expectation of his arm being pulled into the trailer is not met. Francis delays showing us what Craig sees in the trailer, although his repeat of the three dogs vision clues us that whatever is inside ain't gonna be pretty. The expectation of Craig being entrapped in the trailer is partially met; the door closes behind him, although it does not appear locked, and we hear his scream.

The expectation of Marcus drinking his own urine from the water container is met, as is the expectation of him spitting it out. The expectation of Liz finding help at the house she comes across is not met. The house's interior suggests it has some connection with the road train, as does her drinking a red substance from a closed can which gives her the same vision of the red-eyed dogs, although neither of these plot points will be explained. When Psycho appears and chases Marcus, the expectation is created that Marcus will be shot. Thankfully Marcus does not lead Psycho to the truck where Craig and Nina wait, as Liz had warned him not to. Francis creates ambiguity in the sound of a gunshot after Psycho finds Marcus' hiding place.

When Craig emerges from the back of the trailer he vomits, which may be due to his injury or the fact that he has drunk blood from the machine. The return of Marcus shows that he somehow defeated Psycho, as he also wears Psycho's jacket. However, his threatening Liz and Nina with the gun is inexplicable. We wonder if he has somehow inherited Psycho's assumed road train madness, although the girls' ability to overpower him shows the waning of the psychosis. The disappearance of Craig's wound suggests the rejuvenating powers of the blood he may have drunk. His freeing of Marcus from being tied up by the girls leads to the shocking moment of Craig holding Marcus down in the path of the truck's wheel so that his head is run over. The impact is suggested by the blood spurt on Craig, although later it appears that Marcus has also been decapitated. This blood is the only the second presented in the treatment and the first as a result of a deliberate act of face-to-face antagonism.

Craig takes Liz to the trailer, and it also has ambiguity. We don't know whether he intends to feed her into the machine as he has presumably done with Marcus or have her join him by drinking the blood. Nina hearing Liz calling her name also has ambiguity, since Craig has told Liz that Nina is going to be a victim. Nina hence locking Craig in the trailer is not a surprise. It suggests that her character has the potential to be a survivor and a female warrior, which will both prove to be correct. Nina as a warrior is also reflected in her shoes with their leg straps. She recalls the female warriors seen in *Lady, Stay Dead, Fair Game, Contagion, Out of the Body, The 13th Floor, Komodo, Ghost Ship, Undead, See No Evil, Black Water, Storm Warning, Slaugh-*

tered, *Prey*, *Triangle*, and *The Clinic*. Tellingly, it is Nina who is finally able to turn the truck around when Marcus and Liz failed to do so. This alters the previous dismissive view they had of her. The fact that she seems to have never become possessed by the spirit of the road train suggests she has a superior morality, which prefigures her eventual escape. Regrettably, however, her stopping to go to the trailer and the blackout that follows seems a reductive and more conventional act.

The body parts on the conveyer belt, the flowing blood, and Marcus' body in the machine are perhaps the treatment's most gruesome display. Marcus' legs sticking up score a perverse laugh. After Nina escapes, the appearance of Craig in the truck's cabin is not a surprise. Liz's appearance clarifies the previous ambiguity over her. The expectation of Nina being unable to stop Craig from taking control of the truck, so it will crash into the car trailing the caravan, is met. We never see the victims of the collision, but a teddy bear on the road suggests a child was involved. Our feelings about Liz's death, after Nina pushes her out of the cabin, are mixed. It does seem that she had been allied with Craig, and the expectation that she has not died from the fall is not met.

When Craig tries to lure Nina back into the trailer after he deposits Liz's body inside, the expectation of Nina trying to lock him in again is met. Her attempt being unsuccessful allows for his superior masculine strength to force her in. When he pushes her toward the machine to be killed the moment of horror redeems the film's prior contrivances. It provides empathy for Nina as the protagonist, and her ability to escape from him does not meet the expectation created of her death.

Francis plays with Craig's chase of her in the woods. When he catches her, Nina's hesitation in shooting him suggests that she will not. This expectation is not met, since she and we know how duplicitous Craig is. The shot has the bullet going through his back. We don't know who the people are that take the truck away from Nina. Perhaps they are survivors from the collision? Her being left among the collision's debris still suggests a victory for her since she has escaped Craig and the truck. This is even if we don't know that she will be able to get back to the safety of civilization. However, since the narrative had begun with the protagonists already in the outback, it seems fitting that it should also end with the remaining one still there.

In the DVD audio commentary and the making-of documentary, Francis advises that originally two children had been cast to appear as passengers of the caravan car. It was decided not to use them since the collision showed that they would not have survived. The teddy bear we see is a remnant of the idea. Because of excessive rain occurring on location, several pages of the screenplay had to be dropped. The film is the first and only Australian horror title made to date by director Dean Francis, executive producers Michael Baskin and Janine Pearce, producer Michael Robertson and the production company Prodigy Films previously made *Black Water* and *The Reef*.

Xavier Samuel played the lead in *The Loved Ones* and later appeared in film supporting roles. Bob Morley began his career in television and made his film debut in *Road Train*. He has not appeared in any titles since. Georgina Haig began her career making short films, and after some television appearances also made her film debut in *Road Train*. She followed up with more television and film supporting roles. Sophie Lowe had an earlier appearance in *The Clinic*, and after *Road Train* would essay the lead in the thriller *Blame* (2010). David Argue appeared in *Razorback*; *Road Train* is his last title to date.

Release

Screened in Australia on May 28, 2010, at the Dugong Film Festival and received a release on October 21, 2010. Released straight to DVD in the United States with the tagline was "Driven to hell." The DVD shows moments and scenes as deleted scenes. They are Marcus and Liz talking in their tent, Craig masturbating, a snake seen at the campsite by Nina and Marcus, Nina and Liz looking for the truck keys that Marcus had thrown away as Craig watches them, and Nina attempting to disconnect the trailers from the truck's cabin. The making-of featurette also shows outtakes that include Nina making coffee and talking to Liz at the campsite, and Psycho saying more to Marcus when he catches him.

Reviews

"Nothing too original in the concept, but Francis adds a mystical element, and while that's a good creative idea, it isn't carried off with enough assurance to satisfy and ends up mystifying us instead ... a strong story and offers plenty of visually exciting imagery, which are well exploited."—Andrew L. Urban, *Urban Cinefile*

"A supernatural horror yarn that's surprisingly effective, at least for a while. It helps that Francis obviously knows how to direct, and that his actors rise to the occasion—

there are good performances here. The film looks great and, although the plot gets a bit out of control before the end, it delivers." — David Stratton, *At the Movies*, October 20, 2010

"It's got tension galore. But, this film is tremendously derivative. There is only a certain number of ways you can create that phony sort of tension in film. And he uses just about every single one but, at the same time, I think it is impressive as a first feature." — Margaret Pomeranz, *At the Movies*, October 20 2010

"I absolutely detested the movie from first scene to last, it underlines all that is wrong with modern Boredwood driven horror, and makes a mockery of the gains made by independent fill makers in Australia.... [It] fails on all levels ... one of the worse horror flicks ever made." — Jeff Ritchie, *ScaryMinds*

"Gorgeously shot, which just adds to the surprisingly compelling peril-em-up plot.... A fun thrill ride that will please horror fans and road movie lovers with strong stomachs alike. It might make you look twice in your rear view mirror next time a huge HGV pulls up behind you too!!" — Matt Adcock, *Dark Matters*, September 27, 2010

"For about half of its running time, it is an intriguing film; however, as it progresses the narrative starts to become confused and muddy.... Well made, well acted but the potential of the material is never fully realized because *Road Kill* doesn't know how to resolve its own ideology in a coherent manner." — Brandon Sites, *Big Daddy Horror Reviews*

DVD

Released in the United States by Phase 4 Films on September 28, 2010, and in Australia by Pinnacle Films on March 11, 2011.

Slaughtered

Red Sparrow Films, 2010 [aka *Schooner of Blood*]

CREDITS: *Screenplay/Producer/Director:* Kate Glover; *Co-Producers:* Ben C. Lucas, James Harris; *Executive Producers:* Phillip Waeland, Patrick Fischer; *Photography:* Nathan Martin; *Editors:* Richard Bruce, John Palmer; *Music:* Hook; *Production Design:* Maddie Stewart; *Special Effects Makeup Design:* Aline Joyce; *Makeup:* Michelle Arkwright, Leanne Bailey; *Sound Design:* Alex Joseph. Color, 75 minutes.

CAST: Chloe Boreham (Jamie); Christopher Tomkinson (Ryan Lacey); Cassandra Angelia Swaby (Sarah); Steven O'Donnell (Jack); James Kerley (Ash); Erica Baron (Kirsty); Michael Lewis (Jasper); Tudor Vasile (Luke); Roger Adam Smith (Crazy Ralph); Curtis Oakes (Tim); Robin Royce Queree (Stan, the Pig Trucker); Marc Kay (Simon); Jeremy Gordon (Policeman). Uncredited: Adam Gelin (Vinnie).

Synopsis

Jamie and Sarah are barmaids at a country pub. Jamie is dating the manager, Ryan Lacey. Sarah is trying to break up with her boyfriend, Luke, because she is more interested in co-worker Ash. A new worker, Jasper, joins the pub, whose staff also includes barmaid Kirsty and deputy manager Jack. Jack and Ryan find the dead body of a local drunk, Simon, that has been left in the pub's billiard room. The police are summoned. Ryan locks down the pub, not letting anyone leave, and plenty of customers are still drinking there. The body of another local, Vinnie, is found. The staff waits for the police, and they are picked off one by one by a person with a hacksaw who wears a glass-encrusted mask and a trench coat. He kills Sarah, Kirsty, the Pig Trucker, Luke, Tim, and Jack. Jasper survives since a policeman arrives to see Jamie killing Ralph, who it appears is the killer. After Jamie leaves the pub with plans to meet Ryan later, we see him hiding the bloodied hacksaw in the pub's safe.

Notes

This low budget effort features the theme of the horror of personality in the form of the manager of a country pub who murders his group of friends and a few customers for reasons undisclosed. Director Kate Glover employs the postmodern techniques of point of view, blackouts, slow motion, flash and jump cuts, and expressionist camera angles. Her framing is occasionally weak but she has a greater problem in presenting reality in her treatment, since the killings take place in a working pub with oblivious if inebriated customers. Performances are also troubling; however, the narrative provides false shocks as well as real ones. There is some humor and plenty of bloodletting.

The narrative begins with a full moon, never a

good sign in a horror movie. A subjective camera is used to create the expectation of the strike upon Simon, whose throat is cut. Flash-cuts are provided to suggest his being repeatedly struck and bled. The subjective camera will be a device initially repeated, but after some false expectations are created with it, it is soon abandoned.

A title card reads "24 hours later." Glover uses false expectations for the disappearance of Luke from the car after he has offered to drive Sarah and Jamie to work. Luke's anger with Sarah over his awareness of her lack of interest in him, as presented in the opening group scene in the pub, suggests that perhaps he will be the killer. This turns out to be misleading. Equally misleading is the suggested threat of the Pig Trucker, who gives the girls a lift to the pub and comes on to Sarah.

The first sign that an attack has taken place is the discovery of the body of Simon. It is prefigured by blood drops from a pool of blood on the floor of the level above on the faces of Ryan and Jack. Simon's body having been left on the billiard table is surely a message left by the killer. It is ironic that Ryan should allow Simon's blood to drop onto his face, although in doing so, he creates an alibi. Glover creates a false shock when Jasper enters the cellar to scare Sarah. There is another in the subjective camera point of view that leads to Ash approaching her.

The idea that the killer has connected the beer tap to the chest of the dead Vinnie so that blood is poured into a glass by Jamie gets a laugh. Another subjective camera point of view watching Sarah and Ash kiss will prove to be creating an expectation being met. Ash leaves Sarah alone when he hears a noise which turns out be a fight in the pub, the opposite of the conventional use of investigating a noise, since it leaves Sarah alone to be the Woman in Peril.

The attack upon Sarah is the first reveal of the killer and his mask having pieces of glass on it, adding to the suggestion of disfigurement to his face. The glass also alludes with hindsight to the killer being Ryan since glass is part of his stock in trade as a barman. When we finally see Ryan he has a cut on his face which may have been caused by a blow from Ralph. Or perhaps it came about during the struggles of his attacks upon the victims, particularly when he fell down the staircase with Jack.

The killer is first seen behind Sarah by us but unseen by her, and after he cuts her arm she hides in the lift that operates between the bar and the cellar like a dumbwaiter. Although she is seen in the bar by Kirsty, the killer still manages to get Sarah out of the lift and tie her to a wall so that she is stabbed and her arms are tied up above her. Found to be still alive by Ash, Glover drains color from the moment when Ash is struck by the killer as a shock effect. His putting broken glass in a glass and then feeding it to Sarah so that we see the glass making holes into her throat continues the glass motif of the killer. Presumably thinking this is not enough to kill her, the killer then breaks her neck.

When Jamie follows Kirsty into the ladies' room, another shock effect is used for the reveal of the killer in the toilet stall next to Kirsty. Jamie's staying in the stall on the other side of Kirsty rather than leaving her stall and opening Kirsty's stall door reads as utter stupidity. So does Kirsty not leaving her stall, which the killer then climbs into. His touching her face results in a cut from a glass piece, and the stabbing of Kirsty with his hacksaw results in blood flowing onto the floor of Jamie's stall.

The scene gets what is perhaps the narrative's biggest laugh when Jamie hits her head on the sink after she leaves her stall and sees Kirsty's bloodied body, with the strike making Jamie unconscious. The killer's hesitance in attacking Jamie may be understood later when we learn that he is Ryan, although it seems that his decided intention to hurt her is interrupted by him hearing a noise and being scared away.

Ryan's attempt to move the drinkers to a different area of the pub is done half-heartedly, which makes the issue of the drinkers still being there during the murders unbelievable. The plot point of the pub's telephone being dead is confusing, since Jasper says it is, but later it rings. Even if the telephone is dead, we assume that modern teenagers all have cell phones, even in the country. Another shock effect is Luke appearing outside the pub glass door wanting to come in but being locked out. His doing so would not seem to align with him being the killer. He disappears as quickly as he has been seen, only later to appear dead in the men's room, though we don't see how he got into what is presumed to be an interior convenience.

Jack going into the games room to pay the Pig Trucker shows the Trucker presumably dead, seen by Jack but not us. Jamie watching Jack on the video monitor results in her seeing the killer with his hacksaw behind him but unseen by Jack. Jamie's initial yelling to Jack at the video monitor seems as dumb as her previous behavior in the bathroom. It's a relief then to see her go into the games room after Jack, but not to find a pool of blood and for her to see the bloodied and dead Pig Trucker with his eyes removed. Jamie with a shovel in the courtyard gets no payoff since she follows the trail of blood from the courtyard, back into the pub and into the men's toilet. The shock effect of her finding Tim smoking in the stall with Luke's body gets a perverse laugh. This is a payoff to the earlier scene where the underage Tim had attempted to buy cigarettes from Sarah. Now Tim tells Jamie that he took Luke's ID since he figured the dead Luke no longer needed it, although one would think that whoever sold him the cigarettes would also know Luke.

When Jamie hears cries for help, she investigates as a Woman in Peril given the assumed proximity of the killer. Her tripping over Jack's legs as she enters the kitchen also gets a laugh. Glover uses another conventional shock effect for the reveal of the killer behind the refrigerator door that Tim opens and closes. When Jamie knocks the killer unconscious with a fire extinguisher, she doesn't think to remove his mask or to hit him a second time as Jack recommends. This hesitation leads to the killer regaining consciousness and grabbing Jack as he runs past after Jamie. But again, after the killer is unconscious after the grapple with Jack down two flights of stairs, Jamie does not take the opportunity to remove his mask. When Jamie manages to climb out the cellar grated window, the expectation is created and met that Jack will not be as fortunate. Jasper finding the dead Sarah and Ash is a surprise since the idea of Jasper being the killer had been a strong possibility, since he is the new person in town.

Jamie has a schizophrenic attitude about running from the pub or coming back, where she knocks on the glass door but isn't allowed in by Ralph. This suggests that perhaps he is the killer, and she gets the conventional scene of finding a car that is missing its keys. When Jamie returns inside the pub with a hockey stick there is the suggestion of her as a female warrior. She recalls the warriors in *Lady, Stay Dead, Fair Game, Contagion, Out of the Body, The 13th Floor, Komodo, Ghost Ship, Undead, See No Evil, Black Water, Storm Warning, Triangle, The Clinic* and *Road Train*.

Her following a cord revealed to be that of the one used by Jasper continues the confusion over whether the phone works or not. He is hiding in the same lift that held Sarah and, refusing to be with Jamie, leaves her alone. When she finds the dead Jack and the killer's mask next to his body, it is an obvious ruse since we know Jack not to have been the killer. Ralph standing over Ryan with an axe is read by Jamie to mean to her that Ralph is the killer, thus justifying her striking him repeatedly with the stick. The fortuitous arrival of one policeman suggests that Jamie is now safe, although Ryan putting the hacksaw into the safe in the epilogue also suggests that he has been the killer. Glover uses a post-credit shot of the bloodied Tim crawling and reaching for the camera as an odd self-conscious touch.

The film is the only Australian horror title to date made by director Kate Glover, co-producers James Harris and Alastair Kirton and Ben C. Lucas, executive producer Patrick Fischer and Phillip Waeland, and by the production company Red Sparrow.

Chloe Boreham made her debut in *Slaughtered*, and it is her last film to date. Christopher Tomkinson began his career in television and made his feature debut in the film, also his last title to date. Cassandra Angelia Swaby made her film debut in a minor role in animated comedy *Happy Feet* (2006); *Slaughtered* is her last title to date.

Steven O'Donnell made his film debut in a minor role in *Undead* and has appeared in other film supporting roles and on television prior to *Slaughtered*; his last title to date. Erica Baron made her feature film debut in a supporting role in *Academy* (2007) and has not appeared in a film since *Slaughtered*. Marc Kay previously appeared as the body double for Jack Thompson in *Man-Thing*.

Release

Screened on February 27, 2010, at the Australian Film Festival but no wide release apparent in Australia or the United States. Released straight to DVD in the United States. The taglines include "You'll be legless ... Armless ... Headless...." and "Everyone's getting slaughtered in the pub tonight!"

Reviews

"Glover keeps her pace up fairly effectively during the course of the movie, stages her death scenes well, and feeds out enough information to keep patrons coming back for another round.... Recommended to slasher fans."—Jeff Ritchie, *ScaryMinds*

"Has more than its share of plot holes and character defects but it wins out by sheer persistence. Three cheers, or should that be three beers, for *Slaughtered*, a little murder movie that you should definitely tap into whenever and wherever you can."—Michael Helms, *Fangoria*, May 8, 2010

"A completely unpretentious slasher that probably would've been much more engaging with better production values. The film's intentions are good, and it feels very much like an 80s slasher that just happened to be made in the wrong decade." — Devon Berstch, *Digital Retribution*, October 25, 2010

"An impressive first effort from Kate Glover, who should be proud of herself and her cast and crew for creating this film. Despite its flaws, it was still an entertaining slasher to watch and makes me look forward to what Glover does next." — *Fatally Yours*

"The plot is threadbare and the resolution is lacking, but the low-budget urgency to capitalize on a nifty location is milked for all it is worth.... While this is a fun ride on the whole, the ending has a sour after-taste that will leave audiences disappointed and scratching their heads." — Zig Zag, *Horrortalk*, October 22, 2009

"If it was intended to be a parody, it doesn't work. It suffers from a major case of predictablosis with a second string of budgets disease. Although it must be said the gore jobs aren't bad at all.... Silly but inoffensive stuff, notable only for being one of the few slasher films directed by a Sheila." — Hud, *Vegan Voorhees*, July 2, 2010

DVD

Released by Scanbox Entertainment on May 31, 2010, in the United Kingdom. No DVD release in the United States or Australia currently available.

Bibliography

Andreacchi, Mario, and Rob George. Audio commentary for *Fair Game*. Beyond Home Entertainment, 2008.

Anstey, Brett, et al. Cast audio commentary on DVD of *Damned by Dawn*. Imagine Entertainment, 2010.

_____. Crew audio commentary on DVD of *Damned by Dawn*. Imagine Entertainment, 2010.

Bertrand, Ina. *Cinema in Australia: A Documentary History*. Kensington: New South Wales University Press, 1989.

Blanks, Jamie, et al. Audio commentary on DVD of *Storm Warning*. Reel DVD, 2008.

Boland, Michaela, and Michael Bodey. *Aussiewood: Australia's Leading Actors and Directors Tell How They Conquered Hollywood*. Crows Nest: Allen and Unwin, 2004.

Brand, Simon. *The Australian Film Book 1930–Today*. Sydney: Dreamweaver Books, 1985.

Brennan, Richard, and Vincent Monton. Audio commentary on DVD of *Long Weekend*. Umbrella Entertainment, 2004.

Brown, David Michael, Stacey Edmonds, and Doug Turner. Audio commentary on DVD of *I Know How Many Runs You Scored Last Summer*. Anchor Bay Entertainment, 2009.

Buckley, Anthony. "You Know Where We've Been, But...." *Cinema Papers*, March–April, 1975: 31–33.

Burnett, Ron. "Ann Turner Interview: Take the Bunny and Run." *Cinema Papers*, March 1989: 6–11.

Byrne, Sean. Director's audio commentary on DVD of *The Loved Ones*. Madman, 2009.

Chaleyer, Rani. "The Making of *Coffin Rock*." Featurette on DVD of *Coffin Rock*. Ultrafilms, 2009.

Collins, Diana. *Hollywood Down Under: Australians at the Movies, 1896 to the Present Day*. North Ryde: Angus and Robertson, 1987.

Corliss, Richard. "Cinema: Up Under." *Time*, September 8, 1980: 80.

Craven, Ian. *Australian Cinema in the 1990s*. London, Portland, OR: Frank Cass, 2001.

Crumplin, Kelvin. "The Making of *Safety in Numbers*." Featurette on DVD of *Safety in Numbers*. SafetyinNumbers Film, 2005.

Dark, Gregory, and Dan Madigan. Audio commentary on DVD of *See No Evil*. Sony, 2008.

De Roche, Everett, and Richard Franklin. Audio commentary for *Patrick*. Umbrella Entertainment, 2009.

Dixon, Wheeler Winston. *A History of Horror*. Rutgers University Press, 2010.

Dolen, Kelly. Audio commentary on DVD of *The Gates of Hell*. Rapidfire Distribution, 2010.

Dwyer, Jody, Rod Morris, and Michael Boughen. Audio commentary for *Dying Breed*. Ambience Entertainment, 2009.

Fasano, Jon, and Joe Harris. Writers' commentary on DVD of *Darkness Falls*. Sony Pictures, 2003.

Fitzgerald, Michael. "A Killer on the Road" (review of *Wolf Creek*). *Time*, October 31, 2005: about 60.

Flowers, Joshua. "The Making of *Black Water*." Featurette on DVD. Sony Pictures, 2008.

Francis, Dean. Director's commentary on DVD of *Road Train*. Prodigy Films/Pinnacle Films, 2009.

_____. "The Making of *Road Train*." Featurette on DVD of *Road Train*. Prodigy Films/Pinnacle Films, 2009.

Galinsky, Robert Lewis, and Elizabeth Howatt-Jackman. Audio commentary on DVD of *Prey*. Paramount, 2009.

Galinsky, Stephen R. *Sacred Sites: The Making of Prey*. Featurette on DVD of *Prey*. Paramount, 2009.

Gilligan, Sean. "The Making of *Storage*." Featurette on DVD of *Storage*. Anchor Bay Entertainment, 2009.

Ginnane, Antony I. Introduction to DVD of *The Survivor*. Umbrella Entertainment, 2008.

Ginnane, Antony I., and Rod Hardy. Audio commentary for *Thirst*. Synapse Films, 2008.

Glenn, Gordon, and Scott Murray. "*The Cars That Ate Paris*: Production Report." *Cinema Papers*, January 1974: 18–26.

Going to Pieces: The Rise and Fall of the Slasher Film. Think Film/Starz Entertainment/Candy Heart Productions, 2006.

Hall, Sandra. *Critical Business: The New Australian Cinema in Review*. Adelaide: Rigby Publishers, 1985.

Halliwell, William K. *The Filmgoers' Guide to Australian Films*. North Ryde, London: Angus and Robertson, 1985.

Harrison, Gregory. Audio interview on DVD of *Razorback*. Umbrella Entertainment, 2005.

Hartley, Mark. *A Coffee Break with Antony I. Ginnane*. Feature on the DVD of *Patrick*. Umbrella Entertainment, 2009.

_____. "A Good Soldier." Director featurette on DVD of *Turkey Shoot*. Umbrella Entertainment, 2003.

_____. *Jaws on Trotters: The Making of Razorback*. Documentary on DVD of *Razorback*. Umbrella Entertainment, 2005.

_____. *Not Quite Hollywood: The Wild, Untold Story of Ozploitation!* City Films Worldwide/Madman Films/Magnolia Pictures, 2008.

_____. *Turkey Shoot: Blood and Thunder Memories.* Featurette on DVD of *Turkey Shoot*. Umbrella Entertainment, 2003.

Hartley, Mark, and Rod Hay, and Carla Hoogeveen. Audio commentary for *Night of Fear*. Umbrella Entertainment DVD, 2005.

Hay, Rod, and Tony Bonner. Audio commentary for *Inn of the Damned*. Umbrella Entertainment DVD, 2005.

Heagreaves, John. Interview, 1995, with Tony Walls on DVD of *Long Weekend*. Umbrella Entertainment, 2004.

Hegeman, John. *The Legend of Matilda Dixon*. Featurette on DVD of *Darkness Falls*. Sony Pictures, 2003.

Helms, Michael. "*Cthulthu*: The Return of H.P. Lovecraft." *Cinema Papers*, February 1996: 14–16.

Hewitt, Jon, et al. Audio commentary on DVD of *Acolytes*. Madman/Palace Films, 2009.

Jarratt, John. *Meet Mick Taylor*. An interview with John Jarratt on the DVD of *Wolf Creek*. Optimum Releasing, 2005.

Jones, Alan. *The Rough Guide to Horror Movies*. Rough Guides, 2005.

Kael, Pauline. *Taking It All In*. New York: Holt, Rinehart and Winston, 1984.

_____. *When the Lights Go Down*. New York: Holt, Rinehart and Winston, 1980.

"Kane," and Jed Blaugrund. Audio commentary on DVD of *See No Evil*. Sony, 2008.

Katrissios, Steven. Director's audio commentary on DVD of *The Horseman*. Screen Media, 2010

_____, Peter Marshall, and Rebecca Dakin. Crew and cast audio commentary on DVD of *The Horseman*. Screen Media, 2010.

Kay, Glenn, and Stuart Gordon. *Zombie Movies: The Ultimate Guide*. Chicago Review Press, 2008.

Kumon, Terry. *Dissecting Watch Me*. Featurette on DVD of *Watch Me*. Scopofile, 2006.

Lamond, John D. "Confessions of an R-rated Movie Maker." Interview on DVD of *Nightmares*. Umbrella Entertainment, 2004.

Lantieri, Michael. Director's commentary on DVD of *Komodo*. Sterling Home Entertainment Millennium Series/Lions Gate, 2000.

Liebeseman, Jonathan, et al. Filmmakers' commentary on DVD of *Darkness Falls*. Sony Pictures, 2003.

Lomar, Danielle. The Making of *Triangle*. Featurette on DVD of *Triangle*, Dan Films and Pictures in Paradise, 2009.

Long, Chris. "Australia's First Films 1894–96: Facts and Fables. Part One." *Cinema Papers*, January 1993: 36–43.

_____. "Australia's First Films 1893–96: Facts and Fables. Part Two." *Cinema Papers*, April 1993: 36–43, 62–63.

_____. "Australia's First Films 1894–96: Facts and Fables. Part Three." *Cinema Papers*, May 1993: 34–41, 60–61.

_____. "Australia's First Films 1894–96: Facts and Fables. Part Four." *Cinema Papers*, August 1993: 34–39, 62–63.

_____. "Australia's First Films 1894–96: Facts and Fables. Part Five." *Cinema Papers*, October 1993: 38–43, 59–61.

_____. "Australia's First Films. Part Seven: Screening the Salvation Army." *Cinema Papers*, April 1994: 34–41, 64–66.

_____. "Australia's First Films: Part Ten. Federation Film." *Cinema Papers*, October 1994: 56–61, 82–83.

_____. "Australia's First Films: Part 11. Aborigines and Actors." *Cinema Papers*, December 1994: 57, 80–81.

_____. "Australia's First Films: Part Fifteen. Under Southern Skies (1902)." *Cinema Papers*, October 1995: 38–41, 54–55.

_____. "Australia's First Films: Part Sixteen. New Light on the Limelight Department." *Cinema Papers*, December 1995: 34–37, 56–57.

_____. "Australia's First Films: Part Seventeen. First Producers in Europe—1904." *Cinema Papers*, February 1996: 34–37, 54–55.

_____. "Australian Cinema 1894–1904: Part Nineteen." *Cinema Papers*, June 1996: 42–45, 61.

Long, Chris, and Bob Klepner. "Australia's First Films: Part Eighteen. Morals and the Mutoscope." *Cinema Papers*, April 1996: 34–37, 54–55.

Long, Chris, and Pat Loughren. "Australia's First Films 1894–96. Part Six: Surprising Survivals from Colonial Queensland." *Cinema Papers*, December 1993: 32–37, 59–61.

Long, Chris, and Pat Loughren. "Australia's First Films: Part Eight. Soldiers of the Cross." *Cinema Papers*, June 1994: 60–65, 84–85.

Long, Chris, and Clive Sowry. "Australia's First Films. Part Nine: Soldiers of the Cross." *Cinema Papers*, August 1994: 60–67, 82–83.

Long, Chris, and Clive Sowry. "Australia's First Films. Part Twelve. The Royal Visit Films of 1901." *Cinema Papers*, March 1995: 40–43, 56–57.

Long, Chris, and Clive Sowry. "Australia's First Films. Part Thirteen. Foreign Producers in Australia, 1901." *Cinema Papers*, June 1995: 40–43, 55.

Long, Chris, and Clive Sowry. "Australia's First Films. Part Fourteen. Our First Producers Abroad." *Cinema Papers*, August 1995: 36–39, 57–58.

Long, Joan, and Martin Long. *The Pictures That Moved: A Picture History of the Australian Cinema 1896–1929*. Melbourne: Hutchinson Group, 1982.

McFarlane, Brian. *Australian Cinema 1970–1985*. Richmond: William Heinemann Australia, 1987.

_____. Book review of The Avocado Plantation: Boom and Bust in the Australian Film Industry by David Stratton. *Cinema Papers*, March 1991: 64.

McFarlane, Brian, and Tom Ryan. "Peter Weir: Towards the Centre." *Cinema Papers*, September–October 1981: 322–329.

McFarlane, Brian, Geoff Mayer, and Ina Bertrand. *The Oxford Companion to Australian Film*. South Melbourne: Oxford University Press, 1999.

McKay, Mungo, and Dirk Hunter, and Emma Randall. Audio commentary on DVD of *Undead*. Lionsgate, 2005.

McLean, Greg. The Making of *Rogue*. Featurette on DVD. Genius Products/Weinstein Company, 2008.

_____. Audio commentary on DVD of *Rogue*. Genius Products/Weinstein Company, 2008

McLean, Greg, et al. Audio commentary for *Wolf Creek*. Dimension/Genius Products, 2006.

Martin, Perry. *Kangaroo Hitchcock: The Making of Roadgames*. Featurette on the DVD of *Roadgames*. Anchor Bay Entertainment, 2003.

Martin, Perry, and Richard Franklin. Audio commentary on DVD of *Roadgames*. Umbrella Entertainment, 2008.

Mathews, Sue. *35mm Dreams: Conversations with Five Directors about the Australian Film Revival*. Ringwood, Victoria: Penguin Books, 1984.

Moran, Albert, and Tom O'Regan. *An Australian Film Reader*. Sydney: Currency Press, 1985.

Moran, Albert, and Errol Veith. *Films in Australia: An Introduction*. Port Melbourne: Cambridge University Press, 2006.

Moran, Albert, and Errol Veith. *Historical Dictionary of Australian and New Zealand Cinema*. Maryland: Scarecrow Press, 2005.

Murphy, Martin, and Ian Iveson. Audio commentary on DVD of *Lost Things*.

Murray, Scott. *Australian Cinema*. St. Leonards: Allen and Unwin, 1994.

_____. "The Last Wave: Production Report." *Cinema Papers*, October, 1977: 147–153, 183.

_____. *The New Australian Cinema*. Melbourne: Nelson, 1980.

_____. *Oxford Australian Film 1978–1994*. Melbourne: Oxford University Press, 1995.

_____. "Tony Williams Talks about *Next of Kin*." *Cinema Papers*, June, 1982: 242–245, 291.

Oreck, John. *Max on Set: Ghost Ship*. Featurette on the DVD of *Ghost Ship*. Warner Bros. Pictures, 2002.

Pike, Andrew, and Ross Cooper. *Oxford Australian Film 1900–1977*. Melbourne, Oxford, Auckland, New York: Oxford University Press, 1980.

Read, Eric. *The Australian Screen*. Melbourne: Lansdowne Press, 1975.

_____. *The Talkies Era: A Pictorial History of Australian Sound Filmmaking 1930–1960*. Melbourne: Lansdowne Press, 1972.

Read, Gregory J., and Carlo Giacco. Audio commentary on DVD of *Like Minds*. Magna Pacific, 2007.

Roddick, Nick, and Hector Crawford. "The Rules of the Game." *Cinema Papers*, September 1985: 20–22.

Rosas, John Paul. "The Making of *Darkness Falls*." Featurette on DVD of *Darkness Falls*. Revolution Studios, 2003.

Rymer, Michael, et al. Audio commentary on DVD of *Queen of the Damned*. Warner Home Video, 2002.

Sabine, James. *A Century of Australian Cinema*. Port Melbourne: Mandarin Australia, 1995.

Schickel, Richard. "Cinema: Up from Down Under." *Time*, December 4, 1978: 69.

Shirley, Graham, and Brian Adams. *Australian Cinema: The First Eighty Years*. Hong Kong: Currency Press, 1983.

Smith, Carter, and Jeff Betahcourt. Audio commentary on DVD of *The Ruins*.

Smith, Christopher. Audio commentary on DVD of *Triangle*. Icon Home Entertainment, 2010.

Spierig Brothers. "Behind the Scenes: The Making of *Undead*." Featurette on DVD of *Undead*. Lionsgate, 2005.

Spierig, Michael, et al. Audio commentary on DVD of *Undead*. Lionsgate, 2005.

Spierig, Peter, Steve Boyle, and Michael Spierig. DVD commentary for *Daybreakers*. Lionsgate, 2010.

Stanley, John. *Creature Features: The Science Fiction, Fantasy, and Horror Movie Guide*. New York: Boulevard Books, 1997.

Stewart, John. *An Encyclopedia of Australian Film*. Frenchs Forest: Reed Books, 1984.

Stratton, David. *The Avocado Plantation: Bloom and Bust in the Australian Film Industry*. Sydney: Macmillan, 1990.

_____. *The Last New Wave: The Australian Film Revival*. London, Sydney, Melbourne, Singapore, Manila: Angus and Robertson, 1980.

Sumner, Bob. *Horror Movie Freak*. Krause, 2010.

Traucki, Andrew, and Nerlich, David. Audio commentary on DVD of *Black Water*. Sony Pictures, 2008.

Tulloch, John. *Legends on the Screen: The Narrative Film in Australia 1919–1929*. Sydney: Currency Press, 1981.

Turner, Ann, Peter Thompson, and David Stratton. Interviews on DVD of *Celia*. Umbrella Entertainment, 2009.

Verhoeven, Deb. *Twin Peeks: Australian and New Zealand Feature Films*. Melbourne: Damned Publishing, 1999.

Index

Numbers in **_bold italics_** indicate pages with photographs.

Acolytes 110, 166, 230, 231–234, 236, 249, 267, 288, 293, 302
Alison's Birthday 57–60, 67, 78, 129, 149, 165, 166
Andreacchio, Mario 99, 100, 101, 101, 102, 118, 119, 120, 121

Black Water 99, 103, 132, 134, 147, 158, 191, 212, 220–223, ***221***, 227, 279, 290, 295, 306, 308, 309, 312
Blanks, Jamie 228, 229, 230, 247, 248, 249
Bloodmoon 136–139, 170
Body Melt 106, 110, 139–142, 213, 277
Bourke, Terry 13, 14, 15, 16, 19, 20, 21, 22, 23, 24, 60, 61, 62, 63

The Cars That Ate Paris 9, 17–19, ***17***, 28, 84, 88, 99, 228, 257
Cassandra 37, 54, 82, 83, 89–95, ***90***, 110, 132, 133, 136, 155, 166
Celia 114–117, ***115***, 196
The Clinic 99, 103, 132, 134, 147, 158, 191, 212, 222, 227, 279, 290, 294–299, 306, 308, 309, 312
Coffin Rock 208, 226, 231, 254–257, 288
Contagion 99, 102–106, 110, 132, 134, 147, 158, 191, 212, 222, 227, 273, 279, 290, 295, 308
Crush 230, 241, 257–260, 282, 293, 302
Cut 94, 149–155, ***151***, 166, 199, 204, 226

Damned by Dawn 241, 260–263, 282
Dark Age 28, 51, 74, 78, 95–98, ***96***, 127, 204, 238, 279
Darkness Falls 162, 170, 171–176, ***174***
Daybreakers 166, 191, 213, 234, 249, 263–268, ***265***, 273, 288, 293, 302
The Dreaming 28, 56, 102, 111, 118–122, ***119***, 127, 128, 216, 279
Dying Breed 204, 227, 235–239, 255, 277, 299

Eggleston, Colin 32, 33, 34, 35, 36, 37, 80, 81, 82, 89, 90, 91, 92, 93, 94, 106, 107, 108, 109, 110, 246, 247, 249
End Play 24–27, 37

Fahey, Murray 147, 148, 149, 158, 159, 160, 161
Fair Game 84, 99–102, 103, 121, 132, 134, 147, 158, 191, 198, 212, 222, 227, 279, 290, 295, 308, 312
Family Demons 268–270
Franklin, Richard 38, 39, 40, 41, 42, 43, ***43***, 44, 64, 65, 66, 67
Friday the 13th 11, 126, 151, 213, 282

The Gates of Hell 213, 239–242, 259, 282
Ghost Ship 99, 103, 132, 134, 147, 157–162, ***159***, 170, 191, 212, 222, 227, 279, 290, 295, 299, 308, 312
Ginnane, Antony I. 43, 47, 51, 71, 98, 121

Halloween 11, 56, 67, 151
Hellion: The Devil's Playground 59, 132, 144, 148, 155, 162–166, ***164***, 194, 204, 234, 266, 293
Hemmings, David 52, 69, 70, 71, 72, 78
Hitchcock, Alfred 23, 31, 37, 38, 43, 44, 65, 67, 68, 206, 257
The Horseman 271–274, ***272***
Houseboat Horror 56, 122–126
H.P. Lovecraft's Cthulhu 155–157

I Know How Many Runs You Scored Last Summer 242–246, ***243***
Inn of the Damned 9, 16, 19–24, ***21***, 45, 61, 63, 79
Innocent Prey 37, 56, 80–83, 104, 110, 296

Jaws 40, 85, 87, 98, 306

Kadaicha 28, 59, 105, 111, 126–129, 135, 166, 279
Komodo 56, 99, 103, 132, 134, 145–149, ***146***, 158, 166, 191, 212, 222, 227, 266, 279, 290, 293, 295, 308, 312

Lady, Stay Dead 23, 60–63, 79, 99, 103, 132, 134, 147, 158, 191, 212, 222, 227, 279, 290, 295, 308, 312
The Last Wave 10, 19, 27–31, ***28***, 87, 98, 111, 118, 119, 127, 279
Like Minds 205–209, ***206***, 256, 298
Long Weekend (1979) 32–37, ***33***, 43, 54, 56, 65, 82, 89, 91, 94, 95, 107, 110, 123, 177, 246, 247
Long Weekend (2008) see *Nature's Grave*
Lost Things 176–179
The Loved Ones 117, 231, 238, 274–278, 309

Man-Thing 146, 192–196, ***193***, 213, 284, 288, 312
McLean, Greg 67, 200, 201, 202, 203, 224, 225, 226

Nature's Grave 37, 166, 177, 226, 230, 233, 246–250, ***248***, 267, 277
Needle 226, 234, 267, 293, 299–303, ***301***
Next of Kin 72–74, 117, 204
Night of Fear 9, 13–16, 20, 22, 23, 37
Nightmare on Elm Street 9, 11, 243
Nightmares 37, 52–56, 82, 98, 140
Not Quite Hollywood 19, 51, 56, 59, 63, 67, 74, 78, 87, 98, 100, 102, 139, 208, 298

Out of the Body 78, 99, 103, 105, 130–133, 134, 135, 147, 158, 166, 191, 212, 222, 227, 279, 290, 295, 308, 312
Outback Vampires 82, 83, 94, 105, 106–110, ***107***, 141

Patrick 10, 38–44, ***39***, 46, 64
Picnic at Hanging Rock 1, 10, 31
Prey 99, 103, 134, 147, 158, 191, 204, 212, 222, 227, 230, 241, 262, 278–282, 290, 295, 308, 312
Psycho 13, 22, 26, 43, 61, 80, 107, 108, 125

Queen of the Damned 166–171, ***169***, 277

Razor Eaters 145, 179–183, 238, 296
Razorback 31, 83–89, ***85***, ***86***, ***87***, 96, 98, 144, 228, 309

Index

recurring motifs: aboriginal issues 28, 96, 97, 98, 111, 112, 118, 127, 193, 279, 280, 281; female nudity as sexist exploitation 20, 21, 22, 60, 73, 91, 103, 123, 124, 125, 130, 141, 164, 177, 194, 214, 215, 243, 244, 295; female warrior 61, 62, 99, 101, 103, 105, 132, 134, 137, 138, 139, 162, 191, 210, 212, 220, 222, 227, 229, 279, 280, 290, 295, 297, 298, 308, 312; foreigner in a strange land 18, 29, 39, 200, 227, 228, 279; international casting 21, 53, 64, 71, 75, 80, 87, 158, 214, 224, 240, 246, 279, 290, 300; rural ocker 18, 21, 84, 85, 86, 103, 144, 188, 193, 200, 202, 227, 228, 236
The Reef 222, 299, 303–306, **305**, 309
The Ring 217, 219, 282
Road Train 88, 99, 103, 132, 134, 147, 158, 191, 212, 222, 227, 277, 279, 290, 295, 298, 306–310, 312
Roadgames 26, 43, 47, 51, 63–68, **66**, 84, 158, 295, 308
Rogue 204, 222, 223–227, **225**, 231, 256, 257, 288, 303
The Ruins 163, 194, 250–254

Safety in Numbers 196–199
Scream 11, 150, 155

See No Evil 99, 103, 132, 134, 147, 162, 191, 195, 209–214, 222, 227, 241, 279, 290, 295, 308, 312
The 7th Hunt 196, 282–285
The Shining 74, 292, 293
Slaughtered 99, 103, 132, 134, 147, 158, 166, 191, 212, 222, 227, 279, 290, 295, 308, 310–313
Snapshot 37, 43, 44–48, 51, 90, 143, 145, 262
Soto, John V. 258, 259, 300, 301, 302
The Spierig Brothers 188, 189, 190, 191, 264, 265, 266
Storage 226, 256, 285–289, 296
Storm Warning 99, 103, 132, 134, 147, 158, 166, 191, 204, 212, 222, 226, 227–231, 233, 249, 255, 277, 279, 282, 290, 295, 308, 312
Subterano 67, 88, 94, 132, 183–187, 199, 285
The Survivor 51, 52, 68–72, **70**, 78

The Texas Chain Saw Massacre 16, 239
Thirst 48–52, **49**, 71, 98, 101, 264
The 13th Floor 99, 103, 105, 129, 132, 133–136, 147, 158, 166, 191, 212, 222, 227, 279, 290, 295, 308, 312

Trauki, Andrew 220, 304, 306
Trenchard-Smith, Brian 75, 77, 78, 79, 130, 131, 132, 230
Triangle 99, 103, 132, 134, 147, 158, 166, 191, 199, 212, 222, 227, 234, 259, 266, 267, 273, 279, 289–294, **290**, 295, 302, 304, 308, 312
Turkey Shoot 63, 71, 75–79, **76**, 98, 132, 133, 198, 233, 284

Undead 99, 103, 132, 134, 147, 158, 187–192, **190**, 212, 222, 227, 264, 266, 273, 279, 290, 295, 308, 312

Voodoo Lagoon 213, 214–216
Voyage into Fear 66, 141, 142–145, 166

Watch Me 216–219
Weir, Peter 11, 17, 18, 19, 27, 28, 29, 30, 31
The Wicked see *Outback Vampires*
Wolf Creek 12, 67, 98, 154, 155, 159, 166, 178, 199–205, **201**, **202**, **203**, 226, 228, 230, 232, 236, 238, 281, 282, 288

Zombie Brigade 110–114

www.ingramcontent.com/pod-product-compliance
Lightning Source LLC
Chambersburg PA
CBHW081539300426
44116CB00015B/2682